Adult Development and Learning

A Handbook on Individual Growth
and Competence in the Adult Years
for Education and the Helping Professions

Alan B. Knox

Adult Development
and Learning

Jossey-Bass Publishers
San Francisco · Washington · London · 1977

ADULT DEVELOPMENT AND LEARNING
*A Handbook on Individual Growth and Competence in the Adult Years
for Education and the Helping Professions*
    by Alan B. Knox

Copyright © 1977 by: Jossey-Bass, Inc., Publishers
                     615 Montgomery Street
                     San Francisco, California 94111

&

Jossey-Bass Limited
44 Hatton Garden
London EC1N 8ER

Library of Congress Catalogue Card Number LC 76-50719

International Standard Book Number ISBN 0-87589-319-8

Manufactured in the United States of America

JACKET DESIGN BY WILLI BAUM

FIRST EDITION

Code 7718

A joint publication in
The Jossey-Bass
Higher Education & Behavioral Science Series

Special Advisor,
Adult and Continuing Education

CYRIL O. HOULE

University of Chicago & W. K. Kellogg Foundation

Preface

This handbook provides a selective but comprehensive overview of tested knowledge about adult development and learning, in a form useful to people who help adults adapt, learn, and grow. These professional practitioners include teachers, social workers, ministers, nurses, supervisors, counselors, librarians, psychotherapists, psychiatrists, college and university administrators, continuing education administrators, and group workers.

During the past two decades, much of my research has been on aspects of adult development and learning. Reviewing the research literature for these studies and preparing the syllabus and materials for my courses on adult development and learning (which I have taught each year) have indicated how scattered the relevant research literature is and how much it has increased every year. In the meetings and workshops that I conduct yearly for practitioners in various fields who work with adults, requests have been frequent for a comprehensive overview of empirical knowledge about adult development and learning. The small but increasing number of books on adult development deals mainly with aging and gerontology, with little attention to young adulthood. The outpouring of popular articles and books on the transitions of adulthood focuses primarily on the problems of women and of the middle aged. Further, most research about adult learning has been reported in the scholarly literature intended only for other researchers. In contrast, in this handbook I seek to consolidate our current understanding of adult development and learning at large—young adult as well as old, working men as well as women, unschooled as well as learned—and point to the implications of this tested knowledge for action by practitioners in various professional fields.

Practitioners may use this volume in various ways, including the following: (1) To help adults identify and cope with the problems and opportunities they are likely to confront by knowing when and under what circumstances change events are likely to occur during adulthood. (2) To estimate the duration and intensity of major adjustments that a particular adult may face and recognize the options available to the individual at these choice points. (3) To understand effective and ineffective patterns of personal coping or adjustment and recognize when special services, assistance, or intervention is needed. (4) To obtain a general overview of trends regarding stability and change during adulthood and understand the dynamics that produce these changes. Or (5), simply to check what we currently know about specific characteristics of adulthood and where more information can be found about them.

Because I try to illuminate general adult functioning in the following pages, rather than focusing narrowly on specific programs or services for adult development, I have organized the book around six major topics: the *context* for development; *performance* of adults in family, education, work, and community roles; the physical *condition* of adults; their *personality;* their *learning* of new competencies; and, finally, *interrelationships* among these several factors that affect adult functioning. Each of these topics, together with implications of research on the issue for professional practice, forms the basis for one or more of the ten chapters.

Chapter One deals with the types of practitioners who typically facilitate adult development and learning, along with concepts of stability, change, development, and interrelationships that can enhance their efforts. Chapter Two deals with ways in which the societal context of family, community, and nation influences the process of adult development and learning. Chapter Three deals with adult life cycle trends in performance in the family. Chapter Four is a parallel presentation of generalizations about age-related trends regarding performance in education, occupation, and community. Chapter Five deals with physical condition and health and also presents developmental trends for sensory functioning and mental health. Chapter Six deals with stability and change in personality characteristics, including self-concept, adjustment, and morale. Chapter Seven deals with age trends in learning abilities and strategies, including memory and problem solving. Chapters Eight and Nine examine interrelationships among the major variables from the preceding chapters. Chapter Eight focuses on women's roles in family and work, and Chapter Nine on change events. Chapter Ten is a summary of major generalizations from throughout the book, along with implications for action by practitioners and for social policy.

Some readers may find the book of interest in gaining broader perspective on their own personal development. It may also appeal to graduate students who are preparing themselves for careers in education and other helping professions. An increasing number of university courses are devoted entirely or in part to adult development and learning in fields as diverse as developmental psychology, continuing education, family life, educational psychology, social work, clinical psychology, anthropology, and recreation.

The extent and rigor of the studies upon which the generalizations in these chapters are based vary greatly from topic to topic. As a result, the extent of confidence that practitioners can place in these generalizations also varies. For example, many generalizations reflect the experience primarily of white middle-class Americans. Because adult life tends to reflect the societal context in which it occurs, and because—unfortunately

—only a few studies report findings that show detailed similarities and differences among adults from various social class levels, from various minority group backgrounds, and from various countries, further research is needed to validate these generalizations across a wider range of adults. However, even partial explanations of human behavior can contribute to sound decisions if they are applied wisely; and I have sought to point out the major limitations of our knowledge about various groups whenever essential in the text.

In sum, I hope my book can provide a comprehensive developmental perspective on adulthood for practitioners in helping their adult clients learn and adapt. I have used a preliminary draft as a text for several recent courses, and the reactions of students, colleagues, family, and friends have been most helpful.

Urbana, Illinois   ALAN B. KNOX
March 1977

Contents

The Author

Alan B. Knox, professor of education at the University of Illinois at Urbana-Champaign, is primarily concerned with continuing education of adults. His current research and writing focuses on adult learning and development, administration of educational programs for undereducated adults, continuing professional education, and the public service and continuing education function of institutions of higher education.

From August 1973 to August 1977, Knox served as associate vice chancellor for academic affairs and director of continuing education and public service at the University of Illinois at Urbana-Champaign. In that role, he had overall responsibility for continuing education, public service, and extension activities of all colleges and institutes at the Urbana-Champaign campus.

Knox was chairman of the Commission of Professors of Adult Education during 1975–1977. He has been a speaker or consultant in most professional fields and frequently conducts workshops on helping adults to learn.

Knox received his bachelor's degree, two master's degrees, and his doctorate from Syracuse University. His Ed.D. was awarded in 1958. He has published over thirty articles, chapters, and books, ranging across many aspects of adulthood (including learning, personality, and participation), as well as many aspects of continuing education of adults.

During the 1950s Knox held a variety of adult education teaching, research, and administrative positions with public schools, industry, and university sponsors in upstate New York, and had two short assignments at Chautauqua and at the Center for the Study of Liberal Education for Adults at the University of Chicago. His major position during this period was as administrator of the Adirondack Conference Centers of Syracuse University, which were part of the adult education division.

Between 1960 and 1965 Knox was an associate professor of adult education, chairman of the Department of Adult Education, and director of the Office of Adult Education Research at the University of Nebraska, Lincoln. As department chairman, he established a new department and supervised graduate programs for students pursuing master's degrees or doctorates. As institute director, he initiated and conducted dozens of research and evaluation projects, including one of the most comprehensive studies of adult learning to date (*The Influence of Speed, Set and Prior Knowledge on Adult Learning*, with Douglas D. Sjogren, 1965).

Between 1965 and 1971 Knox was a professor at Teachers College, Columbia University. He was director of the Center for Adult Education, a research institute engaged in a variety of research and evaluation projects on adult and continuing education. He was also the principal advisor for graduate students majoring in the development and administration of adult education in the Department of Higher and Adult Education. His major research projects during these years focused on education for less-advantaged adults, such as noncollege-bound adults and participants in adult basic education. Other research activities included organization analysis; adult development during young adulthood; appraisal of the needs of professionals for continuing education; and the stability, effectiveness, and modifiability of learning strategies of adults. Each year he served as a consultant or speaker to dozens of organizations and groups.

Knox is married and the father of five children. He is active in a variety of recreational activities, including painting and sculpture, listening to classical music, skiing, tennis, swimming, and sailing.

Figures

Adult Development and Learning

A Handbook on Individual Growth
and Competence in the Adult Years
for Education and the Helping Professions

Development During Adulthood

The realization of adult potential has become the sign of our times. In earlier eras, attention to human growth and development was focused on childhood and adolescence, and adulthood was considered a period of stability. Rapid social change, pluralistic and equalitarian values, and an aging population have shifted our attention to the dynamics of the processes by which adult life unfolds.

For those who view the life cycle in the most stereotyped terms, preadulthood is characterized by growth and change. Family, school, and community foster growth and development as personality and abilities are formed so that the person can function as a mature adult. Having prepared for life, adults perform established roles in family, work, and community until forced to slow down by the infirmities of old age.

In fact, adulthood is composed of ample portions of outward adaptation and internal change, along with the established patterns of interests and activities that appear to be so stable over the years. We can gain useful insights into adult

1

functioning by considering the mix of stability and change that occurs during adulthood. Some changes, such as increased confidence or decreased speed, occur gradually. Others, such as marriage or retirement, occur more abruptly. As a result of changes in physical condition, personality, and environmental conditions, adult performance is continually modified as the individual interacts with his or her social and physical environment.

Consider Jan, a young woman who worked as a real estate agent for four years. Her decision to enter the real estate field and her satisfaction with it were influenced by her family circumstances and the local real estate market. As she gained experience with clients, houses, and other agents, Jan doubled and redoubled the competence she acquired while studying for the real estate license examination. After the first few years, many tasks became routine—obtaining listings of houses to be sold, arranging for appraisals, helping a client to decide which houses to visit, finalizing a sale, and preparing for a closing. Having become a competent real estate agent, Jan now can enter either an extended period of stable performance or a period of change by specializing, by qualifying for a broker's license, or even by leaving the real estate field altogether.

The choice of stability or change, and even the deliberateness of the choice, is influenced by both personal and situational considerations. Personal considerations might include satisfaction with the activities and rewards of a real estate agent in relation to alternative careers, desire to become a broker with its greater prestige and burdens, and desire for more income. Situational considerations might include accommodation between work and family roles, activity in the local real estate market as reflected in her income, and interactions with others in the real estate agency. If Jan is satisfied with her work, income, and associates, and if her work supervisor and her husband and children are supportive, it is likely that her work role will be quite stable for some years. However, if she becomes either bored or overwhelmed with her work, if she wants the challenge of starting her own agency, if the bottom falls out of the local real estate market, if she suddenly becomes the head of her household, if a new but inept supervisor makes her life unbearable, or especially if several of the foregoing changes occur together, it is likely that a job change will occur.

A desirable change, such as qualifying for a broker's license, typically depends on a period of stable performance that demonstrates satisfactory competence and results in sufficient self-confidence to undertake the change. Personality characteristics such as self-esteem, willingness to take risks, and decisiveness affect when and how a decision is made to move toward a career change. The decision to prepare for a broker's license entails a commitment to engage in systematic learning to pass the exam and acquire the competence to be successful in the new role as a broker. The availability of study materials, association meetings, a real estate course, and experienced brokers to consult, affects the ease and effectiveness of the educational effort.

Another example of the interaction of stability and change to produce adult development is provided by the experience of Paul, a middle-aged man interested in gourmet cooking. After years of enjoying other people's cooking, Paul decided several years ago to take up cooking as a hobby. Especially on the weekend after a busy week as an administrator, Paul enjoys the solitary time spent in the kitchen with ingredients and utensils preparing an unusual and delicious meal. However, he also enjoys sharing the meal with others who appreciate gourmet cooking. A review of his menus over the years reveals a pattern of stability and change. A new type of dish such as the souffle is added to his repertoire. The addition may reflect his own interests alone or those of his gourmet friends. The initial dish of this type tends to be among the easier ones to prepare, but with growing experience and confidence, the more unusual recipes are attempted. After many successful souffles, they tend to drop out of the menus to be replaced by a new type of dish. The pattern over the years is an alternation between stable periods, during which competence is consolidated and its fruits are enjoyed, and change periods, during which new challenges are confronted and new directions are pursued.

The pattern of Paul's progress is influenced both by his approach to cooking and by his circle of friends who appreciate gourmet cooking. His approach may mainly reflect the attractiveness of a few hours of solitary activity in the kitchen, in contrast with working with people all week. Or the attractive part may be sharing the meal with discerning and appreciative friends. Paul may be driven by a competitive pursuit of excellence, or he may relish the social experience of the meal and introduce unusual and well-prepared dishes only to the extent necessary to remain an accepted member of the gourmet group. His gourmet friends may also influence the development of Paul's hobby in various ways. If they place extreme emphasis on excellence and novelty, while Paul mainly enjoys the social experience, he may conclude that he is not in their league and either drop gourmet cooking altogether or reserve it for less discerning friends.

The interactions of stability and change over time and the transactions of the individual with the social and physical context that are illustrated by Jan and Paul tend to occur in most instances when an adult does anything well. Excellence in most fields entails periods of stable performance, interspersed with periods of change. Actors, musicians, and dancers concentrate on the presentation of a high-quality performance for the audience but explore various approaches and interpretations during rehearsals. Athletes use practice and training sessions to increase competence and to try new strokes or plays, but during competition the emphasis is on performance. The manufacturer emphasizes efficient production until a research and development breakthrough or a style change results in product modification. In each instance, the period concerned with reflection or improvement makes possible the high level of performance, which in turn contributes to further progress. Systematic learning by adults accompanies many transitions. The individual's abilities and commitments interact with people and things. The individual's outlook helps determine whether a problem is perceived as a threatening obstacle that produces frustration and disillusionment or as a challenging opportunity that produces growth and renewal.

Facilitating Adult Development

Helping adults learn, adapt, grow, and change in various ways has become an increasingly widespread and familiar activity in our society. The United States and many other technologically developed nations have evolved institutions and methods to assist adults of all ages in dealing effectively with the problems and opportunities of rapid social change. Many of the developing nations are creating programs to help adults become competent in a modern society as part of human resource development efforts. Programs to facilitate adult learning set, as well as echo, the tempo of the times.

Those who facilitate adult learning typically do so as a small part of one or more of their major life roles, although those in the helping professions may devote most of their time to this task. Most of adult learning occurs outside educational institutions. Practitioners who help adults change in purposeful, systematic, and sustained ways include a college professor who teaches an evening or off-campus course for adults who attend the institution part time; a nurse or other health professional who conducts patient education sessions for patients who need to adapt to newly diagnosed health problems; a social worker who helps unwed mothers cope with social, financial, and emotional adjustments during the months surrounding the birth of their babies; a person who leads a discussion group for adults sponsored by a church or a library; a counselor or therapist who works with adults coping with major emotional problems; a recreation specialist who helps older adults acquire proficiency in leisure time activities; a work supervisor who organizes staff development sessions in which employees acquire new competencies for a change in work activities; a clergyman who counsels a bereaved member of the congregation or who conducts an adult discussion group; a teacher who devotes two evenings a week to a basic education course for undereducated adults; and a member of a professional association who plans a two-day workshop on new developments in the field, preceding the regular association meeting.

A basic knowledge of adult development and learning has several uses for such practitioners who work with adults. One use is for a better understanding of the holistic or comprehensive character and coherence of an individual's adult life. Knowledge of adult life comes, however, from many fields of research and scholarship—the biological sciences, the social and behavioral sciences, the humanities, and various professional fields, such as education and social work—each of which focuses on selected aspects of adulthood. The overview of adult development presented in this book is intended to help practitioners synthesize and apply relevant knowledge from these fields.

A second use of an overview of adult development is for a better understanding of interrelationships among the successive phases of the adult life cycle. As the average life span is extended, each young adult can expect to proceed not only to middle age but also to old age. A few generations ago in many families at least one parent did not live to see the youngest child reach adulthood. Today many people live to see their great-grandchildren. The overview of adult development provided here should help practitioners assist adults in planning for and achieving a full life and to help communities create opportunity systems for all members of a four-generation society.

A third use of adult development concepts is for a better understanding of developmental processes that typically occur during the months or years in which adults make transitions from one role or pattern of activity to another. Some transitions are relatively abrupt, such as starting the first full-time job, getting married, having the first child, moving to a new community, experiencing the death of a spouse, and retiring. Such role change events present adults with both problems and opportunities. Adults are likely to be successful in coping with these transitions if they both recognize that such transitions typically occur during adulthood and are aware of the alternative ways of making them and of the approaches that tend to be especially effective. Practitioners who work with adults can help them gain this perspective and make the transitions satisfactorily.

A fourth application of generalizations about adult development is to enable adults to gain greater insight and perspective on their lives. Some stereotypes of adulthood emphasize an almost automatic set of adult activities and outlooks. In actuality, rapid social change, a pluralistic society, and alternative life-styles present adults with many choices and opportunities for growth. Practitioners can help adults combine contemplation and action. Contemplative knowledge comes both from perspective on the experience of others and from introspection regarding one's own experience. Generalizations regarding adult development reflect the great range of individual differences that increase throughout most of adulthood. Practitioners can help adults understand that their trends and transitions are similar to some people like themselves but contrast with some others. Practitioners can also indicate that knowledge, including self-knowledge, results from active participation in the known reinforced by contemplative knowledge.

In general, an overview of adult development can help practitioners use organized knowledge about adulthood more effectively as they deal with action decisions in helping adults learn and change. A developmental perspective can enable practitioners to emphasize continuing education as well as remedial education, community psychology as well as clinical psychology, preventative health as well as remedial health, and the opportunities created in adulthood as well as the problems created in childhood.

Practitioners can apply generalizations about adult development and learning: (1) to understand age-related characteristics of adults in a community or in a classroom at one point in time and (2) to understand the trends and processes of change in individual adults over time. Each of these two kinds of information serves some purposes well and others poorly. For example, findings about the characteristics of adults of various ages who are most likely to participate part time in educational programs, along with cross-sectional distributions of learning ability test scores, would be useful in the orientation of those about to teach adults for the first time. However, because of major increases during the past three or four generations in the average number of years of formal education, such information is inadequate and misleading for predicting changes in a specific individual over time. My grandmother completed eight years of formal education as a youngster, and I completed twenty. Few would conclude that when I am eighty-five, my level of formal education will have declined from twenty to eight. It is only slightly more reasonable to assume that her vocabulary level or ability to solve computer-programming problems at age eighty-five is a useful estimate of what my ability level will be at that age. This book reviews generalizations about age-related characteristics of adults and explores implications regarding both the age structure of society, which reflects generational changes, and age changes of individuals, which reflect developmental processes, but the emphasis is on the developmental process.

The organization of the chapters of this book reflects a rationale about adult development and learning. The essence of the rationale is that practitioners who help adults adapt and change deal with the functioning person whose performance reflects his or her aspirations and limitations, as well as the demands and constraints of his or her societal context. Thus those who facilitate adult learning and change can use tested knowledge not only on the orderly and sequential changes that all adults experience over time, but also on the developmental changes that individual adults are likely to experience. This rationale constitutes a naturalistic model of adult functioning that can help practitioners use tested knowledge about adult development and learning as they assist adults with various characteristics (including age) to learn, adapt, grow, and change.

Practitioners typically deal with the whole functioning person, unlike some scholars who conduct research on narrow aspects of behavior, such as memory, reaction time, or self-concept. Although knowledge about the societal context provides useful background, the practitioner typically wants to apply generalizations about adult development and learning to decisions related to performance, including occupational tasks, recreational activities, and health practices. Although behavioral scientists distinguish between knowledge, skills, and attitudes, performance usually entails all three domains. Even changes in coping that involve no physical skill almost always entail a combination of knowing and feeling. Therefore, practitioners seek to comprehend the mix of knowledge, skills, and attitudes that constitute both current and desired performance, as well as the developmental trends and processes related to selected areas of performance.

Thus the nurse who conducts a series of sessions for prospective parents is likely to be effective if she understands both their facility in handling their firstborn and their concern about ways in which the addition of children often affects relationships between husband and wife. The clergyman who helps a middle-aged widow through a period of bereavement is likely to be effective if he understands both the typical stages of grieving and that the process includes the widow's understanding of new realities and her ability to deal with her feelings about those realities. The social worker who works with older adults in a comprehensive senior citizens' center is more likely to be effective if she understands typical major adjustments, such as loss of work satisfactions, emergence of chronic health problems, and reorientation of relations with spouse. In each instance, the practitioner uses an understanding of relatively predictable developmental processes or mechanisms to facilitate performance.

Concept of Development

The term *development* refers to the orderly and sequential changes in characteristics and attitudes that adults experience over time. Earlier, or antecedent, characteristics help shape subsequent, or consequent, characteristics. An understanding of these antecedent-consequent relations in the lives of adults can increase the ability of practitioners to predict trends and to assist adults in their efforts to learn and change. Developmental changes occur over time, but few occur as a result of time. A change in activity or outlook typically evolves from gradual alterations of physical condition, societal expectations, and personal values. Personality changes in particular tend to be gradual modifications of basic ways of functioning, not abrupt changes in the kind of person an individual is.

This use of the term *development* is intended to minimize the imposition of value judgments on the changes: such value judgments occur easily in child-development research, which emphasizes growth and improvement. The complex and subtle changes that occur during adulthood, however, do not lend themselves to the easy characterization that "more is better." Each stage of life tends to have its own values that are used to judge which combinations of changes are most desirable and constitute progress. A venturesome and incautious approach to learning may be most desirable for the youngster; the reverse may be most desirable for the oldster. The shift from adult leadership of neighborhood youth groups in middle age to equally enthusiastic reading about and discussion of social issues in old age can be viewed as a contraction of life space from the activist orientation of youth, but it can also be viewed as an expansion and extended engagement with mankind. In this book the term *adult development* even covers changes that most people consider deterioration, partly because development includes not only the physical changes within individuals but also the changing relationships to the societal setting within which they function and the ways in which adults accommodate their physiological and the societal domains.

Developmental changes are sequential in the sense that earlier characteristics help shape subsequent characteristics. Each person continues to evolve and change throughout life. Some of the changes constitute deterioration, especially for older adults. Changes reflect both choice and necessity. The changes are orderly to the extent that an understanding of the characteristics, experiences, and events of adults during earlier periods provides a useful basis for predicting and understanding subsequent behavior. This predictability applies to the individual adult as well as the practitioner who tries to be of assistance.

An adult's prior relevant experience is a major reference point for judging and handling new experiences. However, during adulthood the meanings of past experiences and the influence they have on the way a person perceives and responds to new events continually change. Parent-child relations have different meanings for the mother of adolescent children than they had for her when she was their age, especially if she did not resolve her own conflicted feelings about adolescence by the time she reached young adulthood. Working relationships and production quotas have different meanings for the new foreman than they had for him as a worker a few years before. In each instance, changes in role relationships bring about changes in perspective that encourage the individual to reinterpret previous experiences and feelings.

In addition to the evolving trends for the individual adult, two major results of these developmental changes are reflected in the characteristics of the adult population. One result is the increased range of individual differences that occurs in the general population from adolescence to young adulthood and middle age. Substantial evidence indicates that, at least through the first six decades of life, as people grow older they become increasingly different from each other. Specialized interests and talents develop, and the range of abilities widens. For this reason, developmental trends should be charted separately for men and women with varying characteristics such as verbal ability, health, and formal education.

The second result is the differences that occur from generation to generation. The development of adult abilities, interests, activity patterns, and coping mechanisms reflects in part the societal context in which the individual lives as a child and as an adult. Because the past century has witnessed rapid social change in nutrition, formal education, occupations, geographic mobility, and general use of technology, characteristics of the older generation today do not provide an accurate estimate of what the characteristics of the younger generation will be when they get to be the same age. Practitioners who work with adults need to be able to use information about age-related population characteristics, but they should avoid confusing such information with knowledge of developmental trends for individual adults.

The great variability among adults, both within each generation and from generation to generation, makes it difficult for individual adults to grasp essential current and unfolding features of their own lives and to recognize similarities and differences between their lives and those of others. One helpful way to do so is to understand the developmental processes that occur when adults experience change events, such as the birth of the first child, selection for a major leadership role in a community organization, or an extended period of unemployment. Some ways of approaching change events are reactive and defensive, with much attention to the problems and little attention to the opportunities. Other approaches emphasize opportunities, potential, and growth. Practitioners can help adults use systematic learning activities to stimulate and guide the growth process so that their individual and collective past can help shape the future.

Developmental concepts are useful because they contribute to the enhancement of individual lives. Both desirable and undesirable developmental changes occur gradually throughout adulthood. If the individual can understand and anticipate these changes as normal, there are several benefits. One benefit is that many of the changes can be approached, not as isolated problems, but as part of the total life cycle, affected by changes that preceded them and affecting changes yet to come. This perspective contributes to a realistic view of each stage and sometimes provides a touch of humor. Another benefit is that the individual recognizes more options in the process of coping with adjustments. These insights can also be shared with others.

When few people lived beyond young adulthood, it seemed reasonable to conceptualize childhood as preparation for adulthood and to assume that the goals of young adulthood applied to the remainder. As more adults reached old age, we have discovered that development continues throughout life and that many adults now reach levels of understanding and achievement that only a fortunate few attained in the past. A life-span view of development includes attention to openness, flexibility, creativity, and choice at each stage of the adult life cycle.

Adult development is affected by the outlook of the individual adult, including the sense of current self and ideal self. The ideal self includes attention to competencies and priorities for responsible action, openness to feelings and creative efforts, and concern for others. The humanities have much to contribute to adults who seek a fuller and more enduring sense of their ideal self, along with enriched aspirations. The self is in turn authenticated through involvement.

Adult development tends to be concentrated especially around periods of change, such as role changes in family, work, and community. Many people fear and resist changes, reacting to them with regret about what might have been and using their regret as an excuse for inaction. As a result, they become more vulnerable and less open, and their restriction of experience leads to narrowness. However, change events can also heighten an individual's potential, increase susceptibility to influence, and provide an impetus and an opportunity to grow. Adults who are more open but have a sense of direction are able to reconcile contradictions between the old and the new and achieve growth through action and contemplation. Developmental concepts should assist adults to manage life's major decisions in positive ways that enable them to learn more about the problems and about themselves in the process. An understanding of adult development can enable practitioners to help adults become more open to opportunities for growth and more effective in their learning activities.

Interrelationships

Generalizations about the societal setting or context of the adult at various stages of the adult life cycle include attention to the socioeconomic and political demands and constraints that influence adult performance, along with social norms and expectations regarding adults of various ages. The societal context is especially influential on adult performance as it occurs in the household (family home, boarding house, nursing home) and in the family as a social institution. The societal context is also influential through other social institutions in which adults function (economic, religious, educational, cultural, political).

The ways in which a society regards young adulthood, middle age, and old age are also reflected at community and national levels in the priorities given to services and programs for each age group. Varying priorities are indicated by public statements about needs and by actual appropriations for health, education, welfare, housing, and transportation programs that serve adults of various ages. Differential societal demands and constraints on adult development occur within subcultures related to socioeconomic status and ethnic origin. Societal concern for people of various ages is also related to the national age distribution, which influences personal as well as occupational, social, and political decisions. In addition to generational differences and social change, the societal context reflects the national setting and historical era. Their combined influence on adult development can be illustrated by the careers of Mozart and Napoleon. A prolific composer during a transition period between one style of music and another, Mozart died at age thirty-five from kidney disease. Napoleon's exile and death from a gastric ulcer at age fifty-two followed a rise to power partly caused by unsettled political conditions in France and a fall from power partly caused by changing international relations. Aside from their prospects for greater longevity as a result of contemporary medical care, the careers of each would probably have been markedly different if they had lived in the United States during the twentieth century.

Social, cultural, and religious traditions vary in the ways in which they interact with adult development. For example, although there is some variability, the major organized religions have emphasized adult capacity for growth. Most religions encourage adult members to resist their lesser selves and strive for their greater selves as a continuous process of becoming. The belief system in many religions, especially those that emphasize growth by adult members, tends to encourage members to achieve moral and ethical growth, to establish greater solidarity with mankind, and in general to increase their courage to be and to become. For adults who are strongly committed to such a religious tradition, their societal context can have a powerful influence on personality and performance.

Many research findings related to context come from the fields of sociology and gerontology, along with anthropology, economics, political science, education, recreation, and social work. Understanding the impact of societal contexts on adult development can help practitioners comprehend the stimuli that adults of various ages perceive, just as understanding the physiological trends of adulthood can help them comprehend adult responses.

Developmental generalizations about performance lie between generalizations about the societal setting and the physical self. Generalizations about performance include the major life roles of adulthood. They are usually grouped around occupational, family, and community life cycles. The occupational life cycle includes getting established in a lifework, career changes, and retirement. It also includes shifts in prestige level and transitions from specialist to administrative roles. The family life cycle includes leaving one's parents' home, performing the roles of spouse, parent, aunt or uncle, and changing relations with siblings and aging parents. The community life cycle includes social participation as citizen, organization member, church member, and user of leisure. Participation in purposeful, systematic, and sustained learning activities, which for pre-adults is termed the *student role,* occurs for an increasing portion of United States adults as an adjunct to various other roles.

In each of these major life roles, adults confront a shifting pattern of developmental tasks or role changes as they progress from young adulthood to middle and old age. The relative attention to each role and the performance of it reflects personal interests and abilities as well as societal expectations and opportunities. The aggregate pattern of role performance forms the individual's life-style. Many of the research findings on role performance come from sociology, social psychology, and gerontology. Understanding changing role expectations and role performance during adulthood can help practitioners comprehend the ways in which adults shift their patterns of participation.

Developmental generalizations about the adult's body include attention to general physical condition, the senses (such as vision and hearing), and physical and mental health. Biological changes, such as the onset of reproductive capacity, help define the transition to adulthood. Other biological changes, such as menopause, deterioration of vision, and general slowing down in old age, interact with personality to shape major transition periods during adulthood. Heredity and health are major influences on life-span. Some influences on condition, such as nutrition and physical activity, are largely under the individual's control. Other influences, such as accidents and stress, reflect both situational conditions and personal efforts, such as accident prevention and stress avoidance. Many of these research findings come from the fields of biology, physiology, physiological psychology, clinical psychology, psychiatry, and geriatrics. In addition to the contribution these findings make to a general understanding of the adult life cycle, they are useful in assisting adults of various ages to learn new skills.

Developmental generalizations about stability and change in personality include attention to self-concept, motivation, values, attitudes, and interests as they are reflected in choices made, ways of coping, and adjustment. Personality consists of tendencies that influence adult functioning, have continuity over time, and go beyond immediate biological or societal influences. These tendencies include ways of dealing with strong and conflicting feelings, ways of relating to other people, ways of dealing with major role changes, orientation toward personal growth and actualization of potential, sense of self and relation to others, extent of complexity and integration of the self, ways of maintaining a margin of energy beyond that consumed in coping, use of defense mechanisms, and ways of narrowing gaps between desirable and current circumstances.

Knowledge of an adult's personality patterns allows accurate predictions of future behavior. Of particular interest to practitioners who work with adults is the evidence of relative stability in adult personality from year to year but of great change from decade to decade. Understanding the process by which adult personality patterns change can help practitioners comprehend ways in which adults can become more effective in their efforts to learn and change. In addition, developmental generalizations about adult personality are useful in helping adults change attitudes and achieve greater adjustment and happiness. For some adults personality development includes an increasingly mature capacity for growth. The innocence of childhood yields a natural curiosity and growth. For many people adolescence and young adulthood brings a false maturity in which surety is more important than wonder and answers are more important than questions. For those who achieve a mature capacity for growth, the wisdom of age born of experience is not innocence but simplicity.

Developmental generalizations about learning abilities and strategies during adulthood include attention to age-related trends in various learning abilities and in the dynamics of learning that occur during a learning episode. Understanding such trends can help practitioners comprehend ways in which adults with various characteristics, including age, can learn most effectively. Adulthood is replete with problems and opportunities and requirements for adjustment and response. Many adults respond by becoming more rigid and closed. Some seize on growthful and mind-stretching experiences. Practitioners who understand adult development can help their clients gain understanding from their experience, use reason to control chaotic forces within and without, and attend to their feelings. Because most of the developmental generalizations about adult learning deal with the cognitive domain, they are especially useful in assisting adults of various ages to acquire knowledge. In addition, there are substantial individual differences among adults in patterns of mental development. These differences reflect heredity, health, schooling, and personality.

The foregoing generalizations about the adult's societal setting, role performance, physical condition, personality, and learning can be used to comprehend the current functioning of any individual. For this to occur, it is important to view performance as a result of the transaction between the individual and his or her environment. Many generalizations from the social and behavioral sciences can contribute to a better comprehension of adult development if they are collected and analyzed to reveal developmental processes and trends over the months, years, and decades. The unique contribution of the literature on adult development is a set of organized generalizations that emphasize the holistic, or comprehensive, character of an adult's life and the developmental processes with which it unfolds.

This transactional approach to understanding adult development and learning in naturalistic settings is the main reason this book deals mainly with research conducted in the United States. The small but growing body of research findings about development and learning by United States adults is very limited on most topics, but the findings were obtained and can be interpreted within a similar set of societal settings. Although there is also a growing literature on adult development and learning in other countries, there is still too little cross-national research to allow a satisfactory synthesis of findings from various countries on topics that deal in part with the varying characteristics of national settings. Therefore, the chapters of this book are based mainly on United States research, with very selective use of findings from other countries, such as British research on physiology or skill acquisition.

Although there is great variability among adults, much of the tested knowledge about adult development and learning is summary information about middle-class whites. Available generalizations about social class differences are typically reported in this book as two broad categories: blue collar and white collar. The white collar category includes adults who have higher levels of formal education, occupational prestige, and income. Finer distinctions are reported where they are available regarding social class, ethnic or minority group, and men and women.

As a way of illustrating some of the basic concepts and relationships in the foregoing rationale for adult development, the following case example was prepared. The case presents a fictionalized account of Fred, who was born in 1883 and who died in 1970 at the age of eighty-seven. The brief biography outlines some of the major transactions between Fred and the society in which he lived; indicates the intertwining of family, occupational, and community activities; and suggests relationships between performance, physical condition and health, personality, and learning style. Brief references to some of his children and grandchildren indicate similarities and differences in patterns of adult development in successive generations. This brief biography gives more attention to activities and events than to thoughts and feelings. However, it does portray an unfolding life to which generalizations on personality and learning apply.

Fred's Life

Fred was born in 1883 in the capital of a northeastern state. Chester Arthur was president then, and the times were prosperous after the depression that followed the Civil War. Fred's father was an engineer for the railroad. When he was a child, Fred's family had no electricity, telephone, or car. Fred was the fourth of six children, with two sisters and three brothers. Most of the family's friends and neighbors had similar religious and ethnic backgrounds. Fred was an average student in school; was short, wiry, and energetic; and enjoyed active sports. He graduated from eighth grade before the turn of the century. Fred's adolescent daydreams focused more on athletic accomplishments than on occupational success. Few of the boys he knew went on to high school, and those who did wanted to prepare for college. Formal education was not an important part of Fred's plans. He did not seriously consider going to high school and was never an active reader. He entered the new century with his formal education behind him, but with a lifetime of learning ahead of him.

The next twenty years of Fred's life were characterized by much interweaving of societal and personality stability and change. The Teddy Roosevelt of San Juan Hill had become President Roosevelt for two terms. This was a period of high immigration, which continued through Taft's term, and one of general political stability but steady economic growth for the country. Fred and his peers formed basic attitudes toward diversity and change during this period. For Fred, they were years of activity and exploration, the transition from adolescence, and the fullness of young adulthood.

The athletic activities that had been satisfying during school years continued to consume much time and energy and to provide a sense of accomplishment and fellowship. It was baseball in the spring and summer, football in the fall, and ice skating and bobsledding in the winter. His active leisure life reflected access to opportunities, high energy level, and lack of strong competing interests. Sixty years later Fred still glowed when he told of being the small but tough member of the football team who was catapulted over the line with the football in his arms as his team's secret weapon against an especially tough goal line stand. Although he started to fish and hunt more in the nearby lakes and fields during his late twenties and thirties, Fred's leisure activities during his late teens and early twenties were vigorous outdoor sports.

This high level of physical activity was paralleled in his work. Fred's early work experience entailed heavy labor as he acquired experience and competence in various forms of construction, repair, and mechanical work. For a major portion of this period, he worked for a roofing company and served an extended apprenticeship to learn the trade of tinsmith.

Once he was working steadily and had saved some money, Fred could think seriously of getting married. Fred was married when he was twenty-two years old, and he and his bride lived in the home of her parents for a few years until they could afford to set up housekeeping. His father-in-law was a successful cattle buyer who traveled widely and was away for extended periods. His mother-in-law was born in Europe and learned to read English by translating the letters her husband sent while away on business trips. After she received her new husband's first letter and had her pastor read it to her, she decided that having anyone else read them was unsatisfactory, and she proceeded to learn to read English in record time. In contrast to her own adjustments to a new language and country, her husband's family had lived in the area for ten generations and had been among the early settlers. Fred's wife was one of twelve children, eight of whom survived to adulthood. In contrast with Fred's relatively short height, his new brothers-in-law were all over six feet tall. Fred's height began to influence his sense of self.

In 1906 when he was twenty-three years old, Fred and his wife had their first child, a daughter. The subsequent decade was a period of great change and adjustment for Fred and his family. During that time, the country moved from the relative stability of the Taft presidency through the tumultuous times of the Wilson era and World War I. The decade brought a rapid succession of changes to Fred, but some aspects of work and family life became more stable. For most of the decade he worked for a local roofing company. Three additional children, all daughters, were born during this period, the youngest during several years when his work took the family to live in a town about sixty miles to the west. The family was pleased to move back to the city in 1920 and to be close to relatives and friends again. Work considerations were influential in the decision to move away, but family considerations were influential in the decision to return. Also during this fifteen-year period, basic marital relationships evolved. Fred's sense of adult identity stabilized. Some influences on his sense of self were the residue of past experience in his family growing up, in school, in sports, and in work. Included were a self-concept as a friendly hard-working person who trusted others and could be trusted by them. Other influences were situational, such as being the father of daughters and the husband of a strong-willed wife. His wife had the main responsibility for family finances, including savings. Financial security was a continuing concern, and at the time of retirement both of them expressed regret that reluctance to go into debt had prevented them from ever buying a house; instead they rented throughout the years. By the start of the 1920s, when Fred was in his late thirties, the basic patterns of his family, occupational, and community life were well established. Community activities consisted mainly of church, a fraternal organization, and bowling. Unlike some of his family and friends who were ten years younger, the war had not greatly disrupted his personal life.

The 1920s and 1930s were stable and active years for Fred. Soon after his move back to the city, Fred went to work with the railroad as a sheet metal worker, using the skills he had acquired with the roofing company. He was now working for a large national corporation instead of a small local company, and the railroad job provided greater security and a pension during retirement. Having little seniority, however, he was paid low wages during a period when family expenses were increasing. To help with family finances, Fred's oldest daughter left high school after her junior year and took an office job with the state government for a year or two; she then returned to high school to graduate. Most of her friends completed high school.

During the late 1920s and early 1930s, Fred's three oldest daughters were married, and his first few grandchildren were born. At family picnics and at holiday get-togethers, such as Thanksgiving, it was apparent how much the family was growing with the additions of sons-in-law and grandchildren.

Fred's oldest daughter married a young attorney whom she had dated since high school. His decision to study law was influenced by an older brother and a family friend who were attorneys. The Great Depression started during their first year of marriage. Although the Depression kept many young couples from buying their own homes, they did buy an old farmhouse near the outskirts of the city, where they raised three boys. Fred's lawyer son-in-law had grown up in the city, and because his blacksmith father believed that his sons should work with their heads instead of their hands, he found himself with an old house to be remodeled but without the know-how to do so. Fred spent many days working with his son-in-law and teaching him about the tools and procedures of repair and construction. Fred's daughter and son-in-law continued to live in this house throughout their lives. Having a legal practice in the area was a strong inducement to stay.

Fred's recreational activities shifted during middle age; the football and bobsledding of young adulthood were replaced by softball and horseshoes. He continued to hunt and fish, and in the early 1930s he began to bowl, a recreational activity that continued throughout his life. For several decades he bowled regularly in three leagues and even rolled a 300 game. The extent and proficiency of Fred's bowling reflected both his physical condition and the opportunities provided by bowling alleys connected with the church and the fraternal organization to which he belonged. The excellent physical condition and coordination he developed in his youth served him well in later life. His only major health problem during this period was an operation for a hernia condition that was partly hereditary and also occurred to other family members over the generations. His weight gradually increased, and during his fifties he developed something of a paunch. During the 1930s and 1940s, Fred's use of leisure time was also affected by the advent of radio and movies. Fred's mother died before the start of World War II at the age of eighty-four. Because many family members lived in good health until their eighties, long life was taken for granted.

Coolidge, and Hoover, and Roosevelt's New Deal during the Depression seemed like a long time ago to Fred and his family during the early 1940s when the United States was in the midst of World War II. This era brought rationing at home and concern for happenings in other parts of the world. Women were employed in jobs formerly held by men. Fred became a foreman with all the paper work, supervisory responsibilities, and relations with management that the foreman role entailed. Although Fred had not done much recreational reading over the years, he was now having to do more and more work-related reading. His memory was excellent, especially for the large volume of detailed specifications and dimensions he worked with every day, but he depended mostly on oral communications. He once decided not to hire an eager young man who took notes on everything Fred explained to him during an orientation tour because "what would he do if he lost that notebook?" As a foreman, Fred enjoyed the planning and interpersonal relations but not the paper work. During the postwar years, under Truman and during Eisenhower's first term, Fred continued to work for the railroad, experienced growing responsibility and regard from his coworkers, and was encouraged to continue as general foreman until past age seventy. After thirty-five years with the railroad, he received a large retirement dinner and a small pension, and he retired.

The 1940s and 1950s brought some changes in family and community life for Fred. Television and air travel became commonplace. Fred was in his mid-fifties when his youngest daughter was married, and Fred and his wife moved to the suburbs near the homes of two of his daughters. Another of his daughters had lived with them occasionally for periods when her husband was away. One of these periods was during the war. Her husband and son were in military service, and the son was wounded in action. Soon after the war, Fred's oldest daughter's eldest son graduated from high school and went to college; he never seriously considered any other course of action; and most of his high school classmates also went to college. Many college classmates received support from the G.I. Bill. When Fred and his wife celebrated their fiftieth wedding anniversary in 1955, all his children were still alive, as were one of his brothers and one of his sisters.

Bowling continued to be Fred's most physically active recreation; he bowled once or twice a week. By the time of his retirement, however, most of his contact with active sports was as an avid viewer of television. Family visiting and card playing now constituted a larger portion of recreational time than did active sports, which was facilitated by having the families of all four daughters and hundreds of relatives and old friends residing in the metropolitan area. During this period, Fred also went through the chairs in his fraternal organization, which entailed much memorization of ritual. His lawyer son-in-law, who had also done so some years before, helped him learn the material. Fred began to wear glasses as he approached retirement.

Fred and his wife lived together in retirement during the late 1950s and the 1960s. With the small pension from the railroad, social security benefits, frugal ways, lack of major illnesses, and family assistance with housing expenses, they got by and even left some savings when they died within a year of each other.

Soon after Fred's retirement, his oldest daughter's eldest son completed his doctorate and moved to teach at a university in the Midwest. The grandson sold his house in the East and purchased a house in the Midwest for his wife and three children.

In comparing and contrasting the broad patterns of young adulthood for grandson and grandfather, we find both similarities and differences. In each instance a man went West with his wife and three young children to settle in a new community where there was work he wanted to do. In each instance a fourth child was born after the move, and the family subsequently moved back to the East. Each move entailed a change of employer but constituted a consolidation of career since it involved the same basic type of work. In each instance, during the young adult period, there were shifts in occupational, family, and community activities, and both husband and wife made adjustments and changes in attitudes toward self and others. However, the differences associated with level of formal education, reading orientation, extent of geographic mobility, occupational prestige, and approach to real estate transactions were substantial. In trying to understand these two lives, it is important to recognize the influences of social change, social class, and personal change or development.

Fred's grandchildren and great-grandchildren grew up in an era of greater security and affluence than the one that Fred's children knew. In contrast with a modest standard of living, two world wars, and a major depression, Fred's grandchildren became adults during the postwar economic and baby boom. Earlier marriages, larger families, suburban living, more education, and varied job opportunities characterized the postwar period. However, the period was also characterized by constant minor anxieties such as regional conflicts in Korea, the Middle East, and Vietnam and rising rates of violence, drug abuse, and inflation. As reflected in homes, cars, and appliances, most of Fred's grandchildren enjoyed a higher standard of living than he did at their age. Their occupational and family outlooks contrasted markedly with Fred's, especially for the grandson who became a university professor during a period when higher education was expanding rapidly. Teaching and research included the types of activities that Fred liked least. His grandson was able to select career tasks that interested him most, was optimistic and confident about the future, and easily moved from one region of the country to another. However, he did not have Fred's sense of local roots.

As Fred's night vision, reaction time, and stamina diminished, he redefined what he could or should do, and these shifts in self-concept influenced his activities. For example, he began to drive more slowly and carefully. Soon after Fred's sixtieth wedding anniversary, he decided to stop driving his car at night because of increasing difficulty seeing after the brightness from headlights of oncoming cars. A few years after he gave up night driving, he sold his car because he was concerned about his ability to drive safely in case of an emergency. Family members and friends provided transportation after that.

Fred continued to mow his lawn until the end, and he also continued to bowl, finally with a senior citizens' league. His weight declined, and he lost the paunch he had developed in his fifties. He began to do volunteer work a day a week in a hospital in the city. His decision to embark on this new venture reflected his long-standing tendency to keep active; the encouragement of his oldest daughter, who had been a hospital director of volunteers; and an effort by the hospital volunteer program to encourage older adults to do volunteer work. In the final years, Fred's hearing continued to be satisfactory, but his wife's declined, and she began to use a hearing aid. She began to sleep less, and he began to sleep more.

Fred's life illustrates many of the generalizations about adult development that are contained in this book. The course of his life was the result of many influences. The person he was during late adolescence reflected not only heredity and childhood experience in family, school, and neighborhood, but also the community and era in which he grew up. His enjoyment of sports and his disinterest in further education were influenced by the talents and encouragement he received and in turn influenced his educational level and type of occupation. Local employment opportunities and the timing of wars and depressions affected his career. His wife, children, and relatives influenced his family life. Excellent physical condition was an asset.

However, Fred's personality characteristics and approaches to learning also influenced the course of his life. The security and satisfaction he derived from being a competent and valued member of the team and his reluctance to take risks influenced his decisions to live almost all his life in the same county. These same personality characteristics also affected many career and family decisions. Family relationships provided direction and satisfaction to Fred's life. His friendly and energetic nature enhanced his interpersonal relations in work and leisure. His ability to learn from experience, especially from observation and conversation, compensated for his lack of reading.

Fred's talents and interests influenced his participation, which in turn influenced his competence and commitments. Change events and choice points, such as marriage, job changes, community moves, and the decision not to buy a house, reflected who he was as a person but also helped form who he became as a person. In later life Fred became even more like himself as subtle features of his role performance in family, work, and community were stripped away, and his essential self was revealed more clearly. Good health, good friends, and good fortune contributed to a satisfying and giving life. However, the coherence and integrity of his life mainly reflected his choices and efforts.

The purpose of this book is to provide an overview of developmental processes that affect the ways in which adult life unfolds. Developmental generalizations include a comprehensive concern for the functioning adult. Societal opportunities and expectations influence adult performance in family, work, and community. Performance is also influenced by the individual's physical condition and personality. Learning and adaptation occurs constantly during adulthood, and practitioners in many fields help adults learn systematically. Lifelong learning, as illustrated by Fred's life, is indeed a reality.

Use of Generalizations

A comprehensive and developmental perspective on adulthood can enable practitioners in education and the other helping professions to help their adult clients acquire such a perspective for themselves. This is important because by definition the clients' active participation is essential for effective practice in the helping professions. Adult life is complex, with many interweaving trends of stability and change in family, work, and community that are punctuated by major change events and affected by the individual's goals and aspirations. A holistic and developmental perspective can reduce the tendency toward either oversimplification or inaction because of the overwhelming complexity of reality.

Practitioners can use generalizations about adult development and learning in many ways. Included are facilitation of client self-directedness, linking of client needs with relevant resources, and articulation of services with those from other specialists. Such efforts are enhanced by an appreciation of the interrelatedness of developmental trends. Some aspects of adult functioning, such as values and learning ability, are quite stable during most of adulthood. Some changes, such as in self-confidence or reaction time, take place gradually. Other changes, such as marriage or retirement, occur more abruptly. During most of adulthood, social participation is quite stable, but there is a gradual developmental shift in orientation from action in young adulthood, to understanding in middle age, to introspection in old age. Short-term developmental trends occur that reflect changing role relationships and personality development, such as sense of personal identity in early young adulthood and concern about productivity in middle age. Practitioners can help adults recognize such likely trends and adjustments. Some developmental shifts are subtle. The character of an activity tends to change from one stage of adulthood to another. Similar attitudes have somewhat different meanings at various ages.

However, each stage of life tends to have its own values for judging the desirability of behavior. Such insights can enable practitioners to approach the specific and immediate concerns of adult clients in holistic and developmental ways. Adults who recognize developmental changes as normal can approach many changes not as isolated problems but as part of the total life cycle, affected by experiences that preceded them and affecting experiences yet to come. Such a perspective helps the individual to recognize more options.

Practitioners can assist adults to realize their potential more fully through personal assertiveness and growthful relationships with others. An optimistic approach to life is associated with sense of direction and assertiveness. The aspirations and attitudes formed as a result of individuals' transactions with their societal context are also modified by such transactions. Learning occurs throughout life, incidentally as well as deliberately. One way adults can increase the likelihood of change is to place themselves in situations that encourage what they want to become. This occurs in college, in work settings, in family situations, and in living arrangements for older adults. Practitioners can help adults recognize some of the major forces that affect their lives, capitalize on those that are desirable, and try to deflect those that are undesirable. Adults can be encouraged to revise old dreams and create new ones to provide a sense of direction. Practitioners can encourage adults to associate with role models whose approach to life is growthful and to be alert to societal expectations and opportunities that foster continued growth.

Major change events tend to have great influence on adult development. Practitioners can help adults understand how change events disrupt the stability that is usually maintained by personality, habit, and the expectations of others. Change events may be met with apprehension, regret, and inaction, but they can also present opportunities for growth. The need for adaptation associated with most change events tends to produce heightened readiness to learn. Practitioners can help adults resist the tendency to panic and become more proactive through combining action and contemplation. Activities such as assertiveness training, values clarification, and priority setting can help. Many other resources and opportunities for growth exist in every community. Practitioners in many fields can help create circumstances under which adults with various characteristics including age learn effectively. Fortunately there has been an increase in educational opportunities for adults provided by almost every type of organization and institution in our society. A critical contribution of practitioners in education and the other helping professions is to help adult clients effectively relate such knowledge resources to their action problems and opportunities.

🌿 2 🌿

The Context
for Development

🌿🌿🌿🌿🌿🌿🌿

Adults function within a social environment of family, community, and nation that influences their development and learning. They are embedded in an interpersonal network that shapes their lives and that can be used to promote their development (Sarason, 1976). This chapter describes some of the influences of the societal context at various stages of the adult life cycle. It contains implications for action by practitioners regarding community differences, social change, age-related stereotypes and attitudes, intergenerational relations, social class, living arrangements, and opportunities for social participation. Because these societal characteristics vary substantially from nation to nation, because much of the tested knowledge related to adult development and learning is from studies conducted in the United States, and because most of the readers of this book are likely to be working with adults in the United States, this chapter is focused on the current societal context of the United States.

A primary influential feature of the social environment is the community setting. While many small United States

31

communities remain rural and preindustrial, most communities of any size are characterized by urban, industrial values and practices. Urbanization has brought about some new relationships between the individual and the community, including loss of a sense of continuity and community. This trend has special implications both for the middle generation of adults in the United States, and for the dependent young and old.

In recent generations, the rapid rate of social change has been a second major contextual influence on adult development. The impact of rapid social change has been reflected in age distributions, educational levels, work patterns, and, most recently, changes in the job market for college graduates.

A third pervasive and powerful societal influence consists of the value society places on young adulthood, middle age, and old age, as reflected in the judgments implicit in such policies and practices as job seniority, mandatory retirement, senior citizen housing, minimum ages for public office, and restriction of scholarship aid to full-time college students (Goldberg, 1973).

There is some evidence that adult development does not occur uniformly across all strata of society, and thus social class is another influence on human development and learning. Typical indices of social class in this country are levels of income, formal education, and occupational prestige.

Institutional and family living arrangements provide both physical and social environments that influence adult development. The impact of the college setting on full-time students provides one example; another is the increasing variety of living arrangements for older adults.

Finally, the broader community opportunity system influences adult development through the accessibility of programs and services and the availability of friends and acquaintances who affect personal choices of interests and who provide useful information and advice.

Community Differences

I shall illustrate the variability among community settings by contrasting two prototypes that indicate the differential demands and constraints on adults at various ages (Burgess, 1960). These prototypes focus on extremes that are somewhat nonrepresentative of contemporary United States society. Variations do exist, however—even though the mass media such as television and the mobility provided by cars and airplanes, along with an expanding middle class, have homogenized popular culture and values and minimized differences related to neighborhood, community, and region.

One prototype community setting is called manual, or folk, or preindustrial. The manual community setting is characterized by primary reliance on human and animal power and low energy consumption as reflected in the use of electricity and machines. Adult roles are determined by the family and small groups. Only a few really remote communities or neighborhoods in the United States can still be characterized as manual, although some big city neighborhoods have some characteristics of the manual prototype setting, such as low educational and income levels. Until the past two or three generations, most Americans lived in such communities. In the technologically underdeveloped countries, most people still do.

The other prototype community setting is called machine, or industrial, or postindustrial. The machine community setting is characterized by extensive use of electricity and power-driven machinery, by high energy consumption, and by great reliance on impersonal knowledge sources, along with higher levels of income and formal education than in the manual prototype setting. The machine community setting is not primarily a function of community size. Some small cities afford striking examples of machine communities, as do some well-to-do farming or ranching communities.

Most people in the United States live in neighborhoods or communities that would be classified as machine. The following paragraphs discuss some characteristics of communities that are relevant to adult development and indicate the different effects of those typical features in manual and machine settings.

The rate of social change is an influential community characteristic, and it affects role expectations. In the manual setting the rate of social change is slow, and most adults can anticipate what the patterns of their lives will be like. In the machine setting the rate of social change is rapid, and few people are sure how their roles will change during the coming decades.

People depend on various knowledge resources for a sense of direction and for dealing with the practical problems. In the manual setting there are few written sources of knowledge, and people rely heavily on word of mouth to obtain important information. Older adults are thus an important knowledge resource in the manual community. They have "know-how" that is valued in family, work, and community. In the machine setting knowledge comes from impersonal, written sources. Trial attorneys and auto mechanics consult books to keep up to date on new developments. Moreover, because of social change and reliance on formal education, younger adults are often a knowledge resource for older adults.

The basis for personal status or prestige varies in the two settings. In the manual setting status is ascribed by role, age, and property. Members of the family and the community exercise a high degree of control of status, and it is difficult for an individual to change from one status level to another through achievement. In the machine setting greater emphasis is placed on achievement of status or prestige through personal achievement, and achievement is defined in primarily economic terms. There tends to be less recognition for community service than for economic success. Ambitious younger people tend to be relatively optimistic regarding their upward mobility. In the past minority groups have been less optimistic, but their pessimism seems to be slowly changing.

The prototype community settings differ in the predictability of role expectations. In the manual setting expectations regarding marriage and occupation are based on tradition, predictable, and reinforced by knowing the same persons in various role relationships. This predictability creates high social cohesion, but it can be oppressive for the individual. In the machine setting expectations regarding marriage and occupation are ever changing and unpredictable. Because there are alternative forms of role performance, the range of options is increased;

but the individual also experiences greater cross-pressures. Social roles tend to be so splintered that most acquaintances are known in only one role, which can lead to greater freedom but also to greater insecurity and loneliness.

Another characteristic that affects adult development is the proportion of people who survive to old age. In the manual setting fewer of those who are born survive to old age than in the machine setting but those who do tend to be hardy and valued as exceptional. On the other hand, more people in the machine setting live to old age, especially women. Although medicine keeps more old people alive, it has not been able to eliminate the chronic diseases that afflict the aged. Thus some people perceive old age as a social problem rather than an accomplishment.

In manual settings the holders of economic power tend to be older men who are often the property owners. In machine settings more of the economic power is exerted by younger men, who are part of the new middle class of managers.

Regarding job demands, in manual settings most of the farming, business, or cottage industry is located in or near home, which tends to emphasize collective productivity. This creates interdependence between the older workers, who generally own and best understand their particular business, and the dependent younger workers. In machine settings work most often occurs in locations away from home, such as a factory or an office or even a large corporate farm. Younger workers tend to hold more social and economic power in this setting. Industrial workers, for example, use speed, strength, and flexibility, which tend to decline with age. Postindustrial workers rely on mental flexibility to keep up with rapid innovation, and acceptance of innovation tends to decline with age.

In the manual setting the process of job entry is usually personalized and ritualized on the basis of family and friendship relations. In the machine setting job entry tends to be impersonal and competitive; formal education serves a screening function for the meritocracy. In the manual setting job exit also tends to be personalized. Often it includes a gradual transfer from active to more passive duties, except in instances of incapacity or death. The machine setting has given rise to impersonal rules for mandatory retirement.

The meanings of leisure differ in the two prototype settings. With the broad definition of work and necessary activities for family and community life that characterizes the manual setting, leisure time is indistinct and emphasizes social events. The boundaries of working hours and days in the machine setting are more distinct, and leisure can mean any enjoyable activities, such as leisure reading and taking vacations. By contrast, during periods of unemployment or retirement, leisure can mean unproductiveness, loneliness, and escape. Like work, leisure in the machine setting is becoming organized through an age-graded leisure industry, which includes travel and entertainment.

Family relationships contrast somewhat in the two settings. The manual setting is characterized by relatively high intergenerational interdependence and frequent interaction among family members; physical and social provision for the three-generation family when it occurs; clear distinctions between men's and women's work; and a typically subservient status for women in patriarchal settings, along with interdependence and partnerships by husbands and wives in some farm and small business settings. Young people are viewed as assets, sources of increased manpower, and a basis for security in old age. Older adults help out with chores, mind children, provide oral information for rituals and entertainment, and help resolve family disputes. In the machine setting there is often intergenerational insulation and only occasional contact; more widespread dwellings and differing norms for the two-generation nuclear family; and a shift of economic, health, education, and welfare functions from the extended family to large community organizations. Young people are relatively independent and are often considered a liability, and an increased expense. Older adults are sometimes dependents and perform few important roles.

Geographic mobility is greater in machine settings. In manual settings there is little mobility because most family members remain in their home town, except for some young people, men especially, who move to larger communities to seek work. In the machine settings there is much mobility among members of all generations, including young adults and, increasingly, retirees.

Community services are provided quite differently in the two settings. Housing, recreation, health, education, and welfare for adults are mainly provided by family and friends in the manual setting. In the machine setting most of the housing, recreation, health, education, and welfare needs of adults are provided through organized community auspices, with the support of government or community agencies.

Regarding the power of older adults, individual older adults tend to have substantial family and economic power in the manual setting. In the machine setting the power of individual older adults is less and is based on the collective use of political power, as reflected in such legislation as Social Security, Medicare, and the Older Americans Act.

A much more detailed diagnosis of specific community settings can be made by using demographic information, such as U.S. Census Bureau reports and National Assessment of Educational Progress (NAEP) findings. NAEP findings indicate that among adults between the ages of twenty-six and thirty-five knowledge levels vary little with community size and type, with the exception of the major metropolitan areas. Young adults from well-to-do neighborhoods score well above average and young adults from poor neighborhoods score well below average. These differences in knowledge level mainly reflect level of education and social class. However, for all other types and sizes of communities, the average knowledge level for young adults is very similar (U.S., DHEW, 1975).

Once the adult's community context is better understood, practitioners can formulate questions from the foregoing distinctions regarding the two prototype settings to help adults identify the aspects of their neighborhoods and communities that constitute demands and constraints to be taken into account in efforts to learn, adapt, grow, and change. Knowledge of the differences between machine and manual settings can be useful, for example, when young people who have never been away from their remote rural communities leave stable and predictable role expectations in family, work, and community; go away to school in a rapidly changing, impersonal, and pluralistic urban area; and confront alternative life styles. Both ghetto dwellers who move to the suburbs and lifelong urbanites who retire to the country experience an adjustment in addition to the contrast in community size. A practitioner can facilitate the transition by helping adults recognize distinctive features of both the communities they are moving from and the ones they are moving to. If individuals are leaving friends and relations on whom they are very dependent, recognizing the dependency can help them establish satisfactory social relationships after the move.

Social Change

For three centuries, Americans have experienced one of the most rapid rates of social change on earth, and the rate has been accelerating. During our first two centuries, the societal changes reflected the pioneering effort to establish a new nation by adapting Old World traditions to a new environment. During the past hundred years, technological change has been the engine that has powered social change. In recent decades the rate has become so furious that some observers have expressed increasing concern about "future shock" and whether people can adapt to such a rapid rate of change (Toffler, 1970, 1972, 1974; DeMott, 1971).

Change rates have differed greatly for various aspects of U.S. society. The rates have been fastest for those aspects of life most closely related to science and technology, such as pharmaceuticals or electronics. The rates have been slowest for those aspects of life most closely related to personal values, such as provision of equal opportunity regarding employment and housing. Economic change has typically been faster than political and social change. Given the benefit of hindsight we can say that not all change has constituted progress, as illustrated by practices related to conservation and pollution of the environment.

In a slowly changing, homogeneous society, children and adolescents can learn much about what future patterns of adolescent and adult development will be like from their observation of the adolescents and adults of various ages with whom they interact daily. New practices and values can be introduced to younger generations, and the older generation experiences a minimum of dislocation and obsolescence. However, in a rapidly changing, pluralistic society, adolescents become young adults in a world that is substantially different from the world that confronted their parents and grandparents. Also the characteristics and activities of grandparents provide an inadequate prediction of the lives that grandchildren will lead when they become grandparents (M. Mead, 1970).

Some contrasts between young adults and older adults, such as educational level, type of occupation, and attitudes toward social issues, mainly reflect social change and the differing experiences of the generations when they were young. Other contrasts, however, such as stage of family life cycle and physical activity level, mainly reflect changes that the individual adult experiences over the years. This distinction between personal change and social change should help adults interpret generational differences and guide their own efforts to adapt and change systematically.

Social change and its relevance to adult development is well illustrated by work patterns and the practices of economic institutions. Most workers in the United States are engaged in specialized jobs that did not exist a generation or two ago. In addition, the proportion of people who work in professional specialties, technical fields, and clerical and service occupations has increased greatly, and the proportion of people who are engaged in farming, produce raw materials and goods with their hands, or are laborers has decreased greatly. For a representation of the decade-by-decade trend since 1900 in the percent of workers in each major occupational category, see Figure 1.

Young people who enter the work force tend to fill newly created jobs. Sometimes the phasing out of unneeded jobs occurs faster than normal attrition due to retirements, which results in either occupational retraining of unemployed adults

Figure 1. Occupational Distribution: Trend Between 1900 and 1970 in
the Percent of the Labor Force Within Each Major Occupational Category

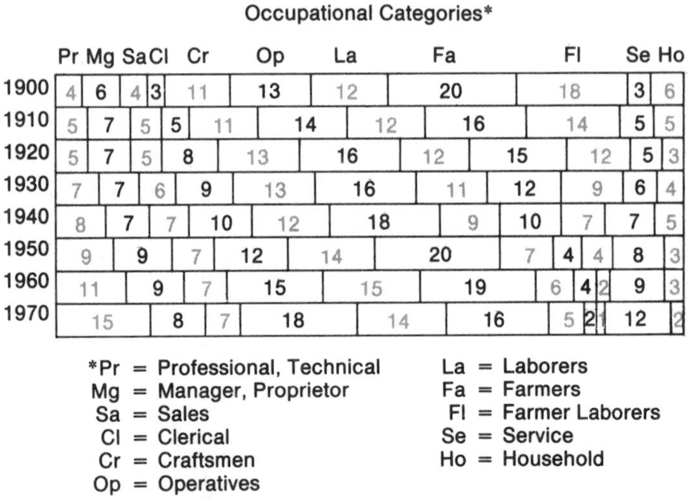

Occupational Categories*

	Pr	Mg	Sa	Cl	Cr	Op	La	Fa	Fl	Se	Ho
1900	4	6	4	3	11	13	12	20	18	3	6
1910	5	7	5	5	11	14	12	16	14	5	5
1920	5	7	5	8	13	16	12	15	12	5	3
1930	7	7	6	9	13	16	11	12	9	6	4
1940	8	7	7	10	12	18	9	10	7	7	5
1950	9	9	7	12	14	20	7	4	4	8	3
1960	11	9	7	15	15	19	6	4	2	9	3
1970	15	8	7	18	14	16	5	2	1	12	2

*Pr = Professional, Technical   La = Laborers
Mg = Manager, Proprietor   Fa = Farmers
Sa = Sales   Fl = Farmer Laborers
Cl = Clerical   Se = Service
Cr = Craftsmen   Ho = Household
Op = Operatives

Source: U.S. Census (1960, 1973b).

for available jobs or unemployment for the displaced workers. Such trends increase the proportions of older workers in occupations that have been in existence for several generations and the proportions of young workers in the newly created occupations. For example, farmers tend to be concentrated in the older categories, and those in clerical, operative, and service occupations tend to be concentrated in the younger categories (U.S. Census, 1973b). For a general indication of the current age distribution for broad categories of occupations, see Figures 2 and 3.

Age-related work rules further affect the relation between age and type of work. Restrictions on minimum age for employment and prerequisite formal education requirements establish lower age limits. Cooperative work-study programs by schools and colleges tend to lower these age limits, while high unemployment rates tend to raise them. Unwritten rules set upper age limits beyond which adults do not receive serious consideration for certain positions or for entry into full-time formal education to prepare for those positions. Seniority rules provide some protection for older workers, but they may in-

Figure 2. Current Age Distribution for Broad Occupational Categories: Men (in Percent)

	under 25	25–34	35–44	45–54	55–64	65 +
Professional, Technical	11	34	25	19	10	3
Managers	5	20	27	26	18	4
Sales	16	22	21	21	14	6
Clerical	24	22	19	19	13	3
Craftsmen	12	24	23	23	16	2
Operatives	22	24	20	19	13	2
Transport	16	24	23	21	14	2
Laborers	34	18	16	16	13	3
Farmers	4	12	18	26	26	14
Farm Laborers	32	17	15	15	14	7
Service	25	17	17	17	17	7
Household	22	11	13	16	22	16

Source: U.S. Census (1973b).

Figure 3. Current Age Distribution for Broad Occupational Categories: Women (in Percent)

	Under 25	25–34	35–44	45–54	55–64	65 +
Professional, Technical	18	26	21	19	13	3
Managers	7	14	22	20	21	6
Sales	23	13	18	24	17	5
Clerical	31	19	19	19	10	2
Craftsmen	14	18	23	25	16	4
Operatives	16	20	23	25	14	2
Transport	11	26	30	21	9	3
Laborers	24	18	21	21	13	3
Farmers	7	12	20	25	23	12
Farm Laborers	21	19	22	21	14	3
Service	24	17	20	21	14	4
Household	13	11	15	23	25	13

Source: U.S. Census (1973b).

crease the difficulty with which younger workers enter many occupations, especially during periods of high unemployment. Mandatory retirement rules restrict the proportion of older adults who are working.

In addition to affecting the age distributions in various occupations, social change influences work satisfaction. Such trends can combine in paradoxical ways. For example, work is

becoming more agreeable during a period in which it is becoming less central as a life interest. However, for the person
who wants to work but is unable to do so, unemployment creates many problems. During periods of high unemployment,
the unemployed twenty-year-old confronts financial, social, and
personal problems, for the lack of a job blocks the development
of an adult identity and the establishment of a career. The
sixty-six-year-old who was forced to retire typically experiences
a decline in satisfaction as well as in income. Average family
income when the head of household is over sixty-five is about
half that of younger families. However, the proportion of older
persons below the poverty line has declined in recent decades.

   Another influence on many aspects of adult development
is the change in levels of formal preparatory education. Figure
4 shows the trend since 1900 in the proportion of high school
graduates each year as a percent of the seventeen-year-old population. The period of rapid increase in high school completion
rates was between the 1920s and the 1940s. By 1970, the number of persons who graduated that year was 75 percent of all
seventeen-year-olds (U.S. Census, 1960; U.S. Census, 1975). The
trends for high school and college attendance during the past
two generations are reflected in Figure 5. In Figure 5 the number of young people who graduate from high school each year
and the number who enter college that fall are computed as a

Figure 4. High School Graduates as a Percent of Seventeen-Year-Olds: 1900–1970

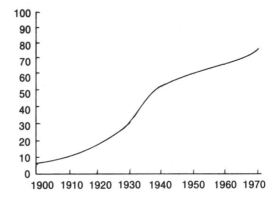

Source: U.S. Census (1960, 1975).

Figure 5. High School Graduation and College Entrance: Percent of Pupils
Who Entered Fifth Grade Eight Years Earlier: 1930–1975

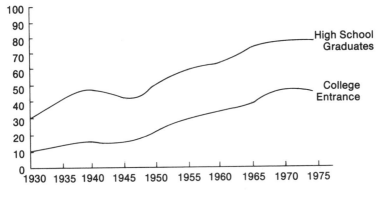

Source: U.S. Census (1975).

percentage of pupils who entered fifth grade eight years earlier.
The figure shows a decline in both high school graduation and
college entrance during World War II and a drop in college
entry rates in the early 1970s (U.S. Census, 1975). However,
the first-time degree-credit enrollment in institutions of higher
education each fall increased from 50 percent of the number of
high school graduates the previous spring in 1958 to 60 percent
in 1974 (U.S., DHEW, 1976). For a representation of the trend
between 1900 and 1970 in the percentage of persons aged
eighteen through twenty-four who were enrolled in college,
see Figure 6. The fact that, for all students, the number of
college seniors in 1974 was about 56 percent of what the number of college freshmen had been in 1971 indicates the general
higher education persistence and attrition rates (U.S., DHEW,
1976).

　　Many forms of participation in work, family, community,
and part-time educational activities are associated with an
adult's level of formal education. Therefore, trends toward
higher educational levels in the adult population must be considered in efforts to understand many aspects of adult development, especially in an interpretation of findings from
cross-sectional studies. As young people have entered adulthood
with higher levels of formal education, as immigration rates

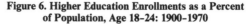

**Figure 6. Higher Education Enrollments as a Percent
of Population, Age 18-24: 1900-1970**

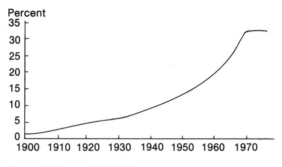

Source: U.S. Census (1960, 1975).

have declined, and as the older people with less formal education have died, the average level of formal education in the
adult population has risen rapidly. From 1940, when the
median number of years of formal education was 8.6 for adults
generally, to 1970, the median has risen to 12.1 years for adults
generally and 12.6 years for young adults. This trend has continued into the early 1970s (U.S., DHEW, 1976). In addition,
increasing proportions of the adult population—in recent years
more than thirty million a year—have been participating in
part-time programs of adult and continuing education with
each passing decade. Although participation rates decline with
age, the effect is to increase the educational level of the general
adult population. Participation rates in adult education are
higher for adults with more formal education. As the level
of formal education rises for older adults, so does the demand
for adult education (Johnstone and Rivera, 1965).

The impact of changing national economic and social
conditions on adult development is dramatically illustrated by
the trend reversal in the job market for college graduates. After
decades of expansion in the demand for college and advanced
degree graduates, in 1970 the job market began deteriorating
rapidly as reflected in unemployment, underemployment, and
salary levels for recent college graduates as compared with recent high school graduates. Because this trend reversal results
from a deceleration of growth in job demand for college graduates, in combination with a massive increase in supply in the

1970s, it appears that the somewhat depressed job market for college graduates is likely to persist through the 1970s. In contrast with the 1960s, the rate of growth in college manpower intensive sectors of the economy slowed more during the early 1970s than in the remainder of the economy. Although this trend applies to the aggregate of all college graduates, there is great variability among occupational fields. Fields such as business, health, and engineering continue to experience a demand for graduates while fields that have mainly prepared teachers and college professors have experienced a decline in demand.

This decline in the college job market partly accounts for the general decline in the demand for higher education. However, the impact has not been the same for all categories of young adults. The proportion of eighteen- and nineteen-year-old males in relation to all college students declined from 44 to 33 percent between 1969 and 1974, and the decrease was greatest for young men from lower-middle-class families. The percentage for young women has stabilized but not declined. Between the mid-1960s and the mid-1970s, black males experienced increases in college enrollments, managerial jobs, and starting salaries. College enrollment rates by adults in their thirties and beyond have also been increasing. In contrast with the 1960s, during the early 1970s male college graduates have on the average experienced declines in starting income, along with increases in underemployment and unemployment (Freeman, 1971; Freeman, 1975; Freeman and Hollomon, 1975; Taubman and Wales, 1974; McMahon, Hoang, Wagner, 1976). The career prospects for a high school graduate during the early 1970s were less encouraging in many fields than they were a decade or two earlier.

Social change relevant to adult development is also reflected in trends since 1900 in the age distribution (see Figure 7). The trend of a decreasing proportion of children continued until the 1940s but has since been reversed. With a declining birth rate in the late 1960s and early 1970s, the proportion is likely to decline again in the late 1970s and 1980s. There has been an increasing proportion of United States adults who are beyond age sixty-five, currently about one out of ten (more

Figure 7. Age Distribution: 1900-1970 (in Percent)

	under 14	14-24	25-34	35-44	45-54	55-64	65+
1900	33	23	16	12	8	5	3
1910	31	22	16	13	9	5	4
1920	30	20	16	13	10	6	5
1930	28	20	16	13	11	7	5
1940	24	20	15	14	12	8	7
1950	26	16	15	14	12	9	8
1960	29	15	13	13	12	9	9
1970	30	16	13	12	11	9	9

Source: U.S. Census (1975).

than twenty-one million). As the proportion increases, so do the general public awareness of the problems and opportunities of later life and the pressure by older adults for programs and services. During the past few decades, this trend has been reflected in health and housing programs for older adults and reduced fares for movies and public transportation. One result is a shift in the proportions of public and private funds devoted to programs and services for various age groups.

There are, of course, many other aspects of social change that affect adult development. From decade to decade, general social and economic conditions change. A western frontier, a gold rush, an economic depression, a major war, an inflationary period, or a period of extended peace and prosperity—each condition presents to adults of all ages a differing mix of problems and opportunities (Erikson, 1975). As shifts occur from one set of social conditions to another, in addition to uncertainty and adjustments for individuals, generation gaps are widened. For example, many of the parents who started their families during the depression in the early 1930s had difficulty understanding and accepting their offspring's use of credit when they started their families during the prosperity of the 1950s and 1960s (Elder, 1974). The distinctive mix of problems and opportunities that are evident during each period of history, influence adult decisions regarding education, occupation, family, and community. In addition to the distinctive features of current social conditions, the rate of change affects people's expectations. During the nineteenth century, many adults thought in terms of lifelong commitments to place of residence, spouse, and occupation. In recent generations, rapid rates of social change have contributed to a recognition by many adults that they are likely to be faced with major adjustments regarding community, family, and occupation. These shifting expectations vary with social class level. For example, especially during the 1950s and 1960s, a move to a new community for college-educated young adults typically reflected an upward career spiral, while those who had not completed high school typically moved to find a job. During the early 1970s young college graduates often confronted unattractive job-related moves. Improved retirement incomes and increased availability of retirement communities have altered many retirees' expectations regarding living arrangements.

One aspect of social change is geographic mobility. Geographic mobility is more widespread than most people realize. Half the family heads in the United States live at least one hundred miles from their birthplaces, and one out of five lives more than a thousand miles away. Frequent and long-distance moves contribute to a loss of the traditional sense of the home town and interfere with the establishment of roots in any community. The average United States citizen moves more than a dozen times during his or her lifetime, and one out of five moves at least once a year. Eventually this nationwide mobility may contribute to a greater sense of national unity, but in the short term many individuals spend long periods of their lives feeling like strangers instead of neighbors.

Increased geographic mobility has reduced the sense of community that traditionally came from the continuity of contact with home town, family, and friends. Reduction of the sense of community tends to weaken the feelings of security with which people confront changing circumstances and conflicting choices. Many adults experience difficulty distinguishing change from progress and become unable to make decisions. When confronted with a welter of conflicting choices and no clear sense of direction, the safest course of action seems to be no action at all. When there are so many pressures to respond, people may fail to notice that they are no longer initiating but only reacting.

Creativity and growth call for thoughtful involvement and a sense of direction. A personal sense of self and priorities enables a person to interpret social trends and pressures in relation to personal growth and development. Practitioners can help adults understand the wellsprings of their security and self-esteem, which provide them with the basis for responsible involvement. Typical sources of security are beliefs, family, friends, and achievement. Adults can also come to understand the societal influences that discourage responsiveness and frustrate growth. Recognition of dehumanizing influences in one's life better prepares the individual to counteract or at least deflect them. Small adjustments in work, associates, or leisure activities can help one become the sort of person one wants to become. A sense of self and direction can enable an adult of any age and walk of life to interpret new developments as desirable or undesirable. Desirable adjustments can be approached as a challenge and stimulus for continued development. Undesirable fads can be recognized as such.

Rapid rates of social change make it more difficult to obtain from the older generation useful precepts and examples for role changes and other adjustments that they never experienced. Practitioners can help adults anticipate and understand the transitions that they confront and learn from others who have had relevant experiences. Many people who successfully achieve some role changes, such as a divorce or a major job change, experience a process similar to a rite of passage (Van Gennep, 1960). The social processes of separation, transition, and incorporation of the new role relationships typically occur in sequence. A personal transformation of feelings about self and others tends to occur as well. An adult who understands how this adjustment process works is more likely to complete the journey and avoid the frustration and confusion of disengaging from the old role relationships without becoming engaged in the new.

One result of these types of societal changes is that contemporary adults of all ages are frequently expected to make major adjustments in their lives. Changed problems and opportunities bring pressure on the adult to adapt and learn. Some of the resulting growth activities are informal and gradual, but some are major and entail systematic educational efforts (*Saturday Review*, 1975). Another result of rapid social change is that the experience of previous generations provides an inadequate guide to how the individual should grow and change. This uncertainty for the individual adult is further heightened by changes in general societal attitudes toward adulthood itself.

Attitudes Toward Adulthood

The foregoing discussion of influences of the community and national setting on adult development and learning has emphasized structural factors such as social change and work rules. In addition to these structural factors, norms and expectations are communicated in more diffuse but nonetheless powerful forms, such as societal attitudes toward adults of various ages. Widespread attitudes toward men and women, old and young, and people with varying backgrounds contribute to stereotypes that shape individual aspirations and performance. Although most of the studies on this topic have focused on attitudes toward the aged, they allow some generalizations about attitudes by adults of various ages toward successive stages of adulthood.

There is some agreement among a representative sample of United States citizens regarding stages of adulthood (Cameron, 1969b). Young adulthood is considered to have an early stage between eighteen and twenty-five and a late stage between twenty-six and thirty-nine. Middle age is considered to have an early stage between forty and fifty-five and a late stage between fifty-six and sixty-four. Old age is perceived as an early stage between sixty-five and eighty and a late stage between eighty-one and death when people are considered aged. The stereotypes that people hold of adults at various ages reflect a shift from perceiving late adolescents and early young adults as active, energetic, and outgoing; to perceiving middle-aged adults as understanding, mature, restrained, and controlled; to perceiving the old and the aged as energyless, inactive, socially inefficient, and mystical (Aaronson, 1966; Neugarten and others, 1964; L. Harris and others, 1975).

People in the United States perceive adults of all ages in a generally favorable way, but young and old alike typically perceive older adults less favorably and as less desirable to be around than younger adults or people in general (Tuckman and Lorge, 1952, 1953, 1954, 1956; Axelrod and Eisdorfer, 1961; Kogan, 1961; Kogan and Shelton, 1962a, 1962b). Throughout childhood and adolescence, attitudes toward older adults become progressively more negative (Hickey and Kalish, 1968; Kastenbaum and Durkee, 1964). We might expect an even greater contrast. During the past century, children's books have reflected slightly less positive stereotypes of older adults than of younger adults, but the stereotypes of older adults have not been as negative or sharply delineated as has been assumed (Seltzer and Atchley, 1971). The stereotypes of the elderly on contemporary television programs are more negative. Older adults are underrepresented in noncartoon television programs. With increasing age of male characters, the proportion of "bad guys" increases. The proportion of characters that experience success declines with age and the proportion that experience failure increases (Aronoff, 1974). (Future longitudinal studies may well reveal that as adults proceed through adulthood, the stage they are in rises and then falls in perceived attractiveness as they pass through it.)

There is evidence that a person's attitudes toward older adults are related to the person's experience with older adults and the person's personality characteristics. It appears that adults with more formal education and more experience with a range of older adults have more positive attitudes toward the elderly. Adults who encounter burdens or conflicts associated with older adults have more negative attitudes toward the elderly (Mc-Tavish, 1971; Kalish and Johnson, 1972). College students with living great-grandparents perceived fewer "elderly" characteristics in their grandparents than did similar students without living great-grandparents. The grandparents were of the same age for the two groups of students (Bekker and Taylor, 1966). Because dependency is a salient quality attributed to old people by the younger generation, people with strong nurturance needs have more positive attitudes toward old people (Golde and Kogan, 1959). Attitudes toward aging also vary with social class level. White collar adults use a higher age limit for middle age and also have more positive and less restrictive attitudes toward the aged (Thorson, 1975; Thorson, Hancock, and Whatley, 1973, 1974).

There is also evidence of some cross-generational conflict between young adults and old adults that is related to perceived characteristics of old people. The young assume that assistance is a major need of old people; older adults themselves want a positive response from others. The young assume that death and dying are major fears of old people; older adults themselves fear financial insecurity most. The young emphasize interest in the family as a major pleasure of old people; older people emphasize their desire for companionship and love. Both young and old adults perceived that old people resent younger people, although older adults themselves were more specific in their references to rejection and lack of concern by young people. The elderly see themselves as more autonomous and less nurturing than younger adults see them, and many report high satisfaction and morale in spite of the problems and resentments associated with growing old. In general, many older adults are concerned about being set apart or rejected, are aware of some of the negative attitudes of young adults, and try to cope with this situation to achieve acceptance and minimize rejection (Kogan and Shelton, 1962a, b).

In addition to stereotypes of the elderly by younger persons, adults of all ages have images of adults in other age categories. These images reflect the individual's beliefs about the values and personality characteristics of adults in other age categories. When values or personality characteristics have been objectively compared, the generational differences are very small, especially when based on intrafamily comparisons. For example, the reported desire for affiliation is somewhat higher for adolescents and the elderly than for middle-aged adults, and these differences were accurately perceived by all age groups. The reported desire for achievement is somewhat lower for adolescents than for adults of all ages, and this difference, too, was accurately perceived by all age groups. By contrast, for autonomy and nurturance no actual age differences occurred, but some age groups were misperceived. Adolescents were misperceived by middle-aged adults as being more autonomy oriented than they actually were, and the elderly were misperceived by younger people as being less autonomy oriented than they actually were. In addition, the elderly were misperceived by younger people as being more nurturance oriented than they actually were. The misperceptions occurred in relation to personality characteristics for which no actual age differences occurred, and not in relation to characteristics for which there were actual age differences in self-descriptions. Middle-aged adults were never misperceived, in contrast with the elderly who were included in the misperceptions that did occur (Ahammer and Baltes, 1972).

The attitudes of the aged toward young adults reflect both young adult roles and the adjustment of the elderly. Older adults tend to have more positive attitudes toward military personnel than toward young people in general, but less positive attitudes toward college students. Older adults with high life satisfaction and close relationships with their own offspring perceive the young as better adjusted, more autonomous, and more acceptable to them than older adults with low satisfaction and poor filial relationships. It appears that satisfied older adults accept young adults and have little need to project their own dissatisfactions and aggressions on others (Cryns and Monk, 1972).

Attitudes based on misperception and projection can be dysfunctional. Erroneous attitudes can interfere with constructive and satisfying interpersonal relations and can help isolate the victims of false stereotypes, be they of youth or the aged. Practitioners can help adults of all ages to recognize how they and the victims of false stereotypes are imprisoned by such attitudes.

Other people's attitudes toward a category of people influence our own attitudes toward them. Generalized societal attitudes and the attitudes of other people who are significant in our lives can be especially influential if we lack firsthand experience. Inaccurate stereotypes are more likely to develop and persist in ignorance. When stereotypes, such as those about the typical college student, politician, or senior citizen, are reinforced by mass media and self-serving motives, they can become firmly entrenched. This can be especially dysfunctional when the stereotype is of a category of people with which one must sometimes interact and which one is likely to become, such as an older adult. Such false stereotypes damage oneself as well as the person who is treated as a stereotype rather than an individual human being.

Realistic attitudes toward aging are more likely to develop when people of all ages interact with older adults, especially those who typify the elderly person the individual is likely to become. Social change has altered societal expectations of age appropriate behavior during adulthood. As middle-aged adults interact with older adults, they can learn ways to predict and guide their adaptation to old age (*Counseling Psychologist*, 1976). Practitioners can foster realistic attitudes toward the elderly, or any category of people, by providing an overview of individual differences within a category and by encouraging firsthand contact. This can be especially effective when young and old join forces in a common cause.

Intergenerational Relations and Political Power

We have reviewed three aspects of the national setting that influence the process of adult development and learning: community variations, social change, and attitudes toward various adult age groups. Together they indicate differences among the generations and some of the differential societal demands and constraints that affect adults of various ages. Rapid social change has widened the disparity between generations, and decreasing contact between the generations has increased misunderstandings. When young adults hold unrealistically negative stereotypes of older adults, one unfortunate result is that when they themselves grow old the negative stereotype can affect their image of themselves. Quite aside from stereotypes, advancing age increases the extent to which adults ascribe importance to age norms and place constraints on adult behavior in terms of age appropriateness. In the young, especially young

men, there is some denial of age as a valid dimension by which
to judge behavior (Neugarten, Moore, and Lowe, 1965). Many
want to be considered as adults, not young adults. It is likely
that younger adults are restive with the restrictions of age
norms, while older adults perceive some of the advantages of
age norms such as predictability.

Intergenerational relations and differential societal influences are also illustrated by the use of political power to
obtain redress of grievances. During the late 1960s and early
1970s, some young adults on college campuses engaged in
crowd action and civil disobedience to protest social ills that
affected them. In many instances, confrontation and violence
ensued, which in part reflected student perceptions that they
had little power through established channels and that the
possibility of gains was worth the risks. Although some younger
faculty members joined forces with them, few older adults
did so. A few years later, Maggie Kuhn convened the Gray
Panthers, a group organized to protest social ills affecting older
adults and obtain redress of grievances. Although also marked
by determination and high purpose, the Gray Panthers and
other militant groups of older adults have differed greatly in
style from that of the students who were involved in the
college disorders. The "man bites dog" angle of press coverage
reflects the incongruity many people see in a relationship between militant action and old folks. Another feature of the
Gray Panthers is their success in attracting college students and
other young adults. This joining of forces by very young adults
and very old adults reflects recognition of their shared status
as dependent adults.

The middle generation of adults between their thirties
and their sixties tends to carry the burden of concern for programs, pennies, and progress. As members of the middle generation, they usually hold positions of power and responsibility
in which they are expected to deal with public problems. The
typical viewpoints of the young, middle, and old generations
toward the current transition to postindustrialism illustrate
a shifting perspective during the adult life cycle. During the
past hundred years an emphasis on production has been accompanied by such values as achievement, competition, self-

control, and endurance of distress. The current shift in emphasis toward services and consumption has been accompanied by such values as self-actualization, collaboration, self-expression, and capacity for joy. The recent upsurge of concern about physical and social ecology dramatizes this shift of emphasis and reflects a reaction against the consequences of technology such as pollution. People in responsible positions are urged to use planning and administrative strategies that include more people. The young and the old tend to take a moralistic and antibureaucratic stance, partly because the establishment is largely composed of the middle generation. In every generation there are doomwatchers, futurists, and pollyannas. However, there is a tendency for the middle generation's energy and thoughts to be consumed with present-oriented tasks and responsibilities. During late adolescence and early young adulthood, people without an investment in the current procedures who want a piece of the action can provide fresh viewpoints and sometimes launch a crusade. Older adults, who may never have accepted some technological developments, can become willing allies of the young as they become more concerned about the human element. There has always been a special affinity between the young and the old that has often been aided by the insulation provided by the middle generation. There are indications that this coalition of young and old may be shifting from the family to the community setting. The likely impact of this pincers movement on the middle generation is unclear. Increased attention to quality of life and self-fulfillment seems probable. It is also likely that current shifts in intergenerational relationships will affect the image of adulthood that young people form. It seems unlikely that a college student who has participated in Gray Panther projects will form popular stereotypes of the aged. However, the tendency for young radicals to become middle-aged members of the establishment is all too familiar (Rapoport and Rapoport, 1975).

Social Class

Both problems and opportunities are associated with the social class level of the individual adult. For example, when facing a period of transition or presented with a choice such as further education or a job change, adults characterized by high income, formal education, and occupational prestige are likely to have more options from which to choose and greater resources to implement their choice than those from less-advantaged backgrounds. On the other hand, their sense of social class may constrain them from making certain choices just as effectively as lack of resources or options constrains the less-advantaged.

The social class level of the young is established by parental status: parents' level of education, cultural interests, and encouragement regarding educational activities influence the interests, aspirations, and activities of their offspring, as do those of parents' friends, neighbors, and older siblings. Studies of college attendance indicate that the association between parents' social class and children's college enrollment is far closer than that between the children's academic aptitude and college enrollment (Feldman and Newcomb, 1969; Trent and Medsker, 1968). The proportion of college students from families in the range from $4–$15 thousand of annual income has decreased from about 70 percent a decade ago to about 50 percent today (U.S., DHEW, 1976). With formal education level having become a major meritocratic criterion for personnel selection in many companies, parental social class has a powerful and far-reaching influence on a major aspect of adult development.

Few studies of adult development have classified developmental trends by detailed social class level. Therefore, except for those studies, two broad levels of social class will be used throughout this book: white collar and blue collar. The white collar level of social class includes adults with at least two years of college, or adults in the top three of seven levels of occupational prestige. Most of the adults in the white collar level are in the upper income range. The blue collar level of social class includes the remaining adults with lower levels of income, education, and occupational prestige.

This use of two broad social class levels for the analysis of settings and trends for adult development is necessitated by the current lack of tested knowledge on which to base more precise distinctions. There is, for example, a category of low income office workers who don't fit the usual pattern of either white collar or blue collar and have been referred to as grey collar. In spite of this lack of precision, indices of social class, such as level of income, education, or occupational prestige, are so highly associated with work, leisure, and education that social class level cannot be ignored.

Education, geographic mobility, and the mass media have contributed to a great overlap in the values and practices of adults classified as white collar and blue collar. However, the distinctions between blue and white collar adults help us recognize important social class influences on adult development and discourage a thoughtless imposition of middle-class values. Practitioners can use their knowledge of class distinctions to improve their understanding of relationships between social class and adult development and thereby appreciate the influences of the client's background and setting in an effort to facilitate the individual's growth.

Social class comparisons across generations pose several problems of interpretation that should be noted. Given the rapidly rising average levels of formal education for successive generations, older adults who may have achieved more than average levels of formal education in their day may be less than average in comparison with younger adults several generations later. For retired adults, useful comparisons related to social class are more difficult, because they are no longer active in their occupations, and their income levels have typically declined. In practice, former occupation is typically used for comparison purposes.

Members of minority groups are differentially reflected in analyses of social class across generations. In general, adults in minority groups, such as blacks, chicanos, and American Indians, have been subject to discrimination by majority groups and have confronted various barriers to equal opportunity and upward mobility. As a result, minority group adults have been concentrated in the lower levels of social class indices. During the past decade or two, there has been increasing access for minority groups to education, occupations, and housing, and

age group comparisons for members of minority groups partially reflect this aspect of social change. Unfortunately, few
studies related to adult development and learning contain data
on minority group adults, and when they do, the data are
sometimes not reported separately. Recent improvements in
employment and income of black workers, especially college
graduates, reflect rapid social change. As a result, cross-sectional
data provide a very inaccurate estimate of developmental comparison between black and white workers.

Most adults in the United States associate mainly with
family, friends, and coworkers who are similar to themselves
in social class level and interests. This reflects social stratification by neighborhoods and work settings and influences adult
development and learning in various ways (Fried, 1973). As
adults confront problems, choices, and decisions, they usually
seek information and advice from people they know (Katz and
Lazarsfeld, 1955). The specific people to whom they turn for
advice varies from topic to topic, as they seek information
or reassurance from someone they trust who can add new or
valuable information. These friends and associates serve as
opinion leaders, and their influential function has been well
documented.

The characteristics and specific functions served by opinion leaders varies substantially between white collar and blue
collar adults. When a white collar adult confronts a major role
change or personal problem, such as a job change or mental
difficulty, he or she is likely to seek information from three
types of sources: media, such as books; experts, such as counselors; and associates, such as friends. By contrast, the blue
collar adult typically seeks instrumental information only from
associates, such as friends or local clergymen, but their associates are usually less aware of relevant opportunities and
resources than the associates of white collar adults (London,
Wenkert, and Hagstrom, 1963). Reliance on personalized and
familiar information sources by blue collar adults reflects lack
of trust of impersonal sources, avoidance of reading generally,
insufficient familiarity with many relevant programs and ser-

vices, and inadequate financial resources to pay the costs of experts and media.

When a white collar adult decides to buy a car, he or she is likely to read a consumer magazine review of the several makes being considered and to talk with an automobile mechanic about relative servicing problems. Blue collar adults are more likely to tell their friends they are thinking of buying a car and to consider mainly the leads the friends supply. Although in this example the associates of blue collar adults may be more familiar with cars and their maintenance than the white collar adult's impersonal expert, in most cases their infrequent use of impersonal information sources for instrumental purposes may insulate them from useful resources and reinforce the cycle of poverty that binds them. There is little evidence to date about the extent to which the social services created or expanded during the past decade have altered the pattern of information seeking by blue collar adults.

The concepts of life-space and life-style help distinguish between the typical experiences of blue and white collar adults. *Life-space* refers to the scope and complexity of the social environment with which the individual deals at all times. It includes the network of friends and acquaintances with whom the individual interacts by personal contact, telephone, and correspondence. *Life-style* refers to the quality of those interactions as reflected in the individual's specific interests, activities, and commitments.

The contrasting life space of blue collar adults and white collar adults affects opportunities as well as problems. The life-style of the blue collar adult generally revolves around work, home, and informal activities with family and friends; it tends to be neighborhood oriented. Blue collar adults pay little attention to any but the most major national and international issues. The life-style of the typical white collar adult is oriented more toward events, activities, and ideas in the larger community and beyond. Some white collar adults are actively involved in a variety of formal organizations. Others frequently attend cultural events. Participation in either type of broader community activity extending beyond the local neighborhood, is highly associated with social class level (London, Wenkert, and Hagstrom, 1963). This is especially so for instrumental organizations, such as service clubs and community agency boards, in contrast with expressive organizations, such as bowling leagues and card clubs (Babchuck, 1965).

It should be recognized that the extent of an adult's participation in community organizations and events is not entirely a matter of personal choice. Family tradition and occupational aspirations encourage white collar adults to run for elective offices and to participate in service clubs and fraternal organizations. Most of the participants in community organizations are from white collar occupations. They are active in the Parent-Teachers Association, the League of Women Voters, the American Association of University Women, and so forth. Thus the ways in which community organizations function reflect the white collar orientation toward formal procedures, written communications, and implicit conventions in the ways in which people relate to each other in large, impersonal associations. The formal characteristics of community organizations tend to discourage blue collar adults from participating, quite aside from any constraints that arise from the time, place, and cost of participation. Moreover, the formality is sometimes reinforced by the expectations of upwardly mobile blue collar adults.

Participation in community organizations and events influences adult development and learning in various ways. Entering a new activity or assuming a new leadership responsibility often places great pressure on an adult to acquire new competencies. Other participants, such as more-experienced committee members, are usually willing to show a new member the ropes. In some organizations, formal orientation activities are provided. The combination of expectations and resources for change provides powerful encouragement for most adults. Contact with a variety of other people and activities also alerts a member to new opportunities. For some white collar homemakers, community volunteer activities not only facilitate a transition from an earlier period when the demands of young children consumed most of the homemaker's time, but also provide a way of exploring interests, skills, and opportunities for part-time or full-time employment.

In addition to the socialization that occurs after an adult assumes a new responsibility or enters a new role, some adults acquire new knowledge and skill and experience a shift in attitudes in anticipation of a desired future change. Examples of this type of anticipatory socialization include learning to play bridge and golf in hopes of being invited to join the country club, learning bookkeeping and accounting procedures to prepare for promotion from a clerical position, or learning discussion leadership techniques in anticipation of selection as leader in a community organization.

Participation in community organizations also provides contact with other like-minded people who serve as role models and provide encouragement. Community involvement can be especially valuable when an adult confronts a major and unfamiliar adjustment, such as the loss of a spouse through death or divorce. For example, in an adjustment like a move to a new community, participation in community organizations provides an orientation to the community and an introduction to new acquaintances and friends during a period when the adult typically misses the security and predictability of his or her established pattern of participation in the former community.

The blue collar adult does not participate in voluntary associations but relies mainly on family and friends for many of the functions served by the white collar adult's participation in community organizations. Although the extent and variety of the blue collar adult's life space may be more restricted, experiences with family and friends can be rich and satisfying. For many blue collar adults, informal activities with family and friends provide satisfactory sources of new experiences and support and encouragement when needed.

The foregoing comparison of participation in community organizations by white collar and blue collar adults has emphasized the contrasts. In actuality, although the extent of organizational participation is highly associated with social class level, most blue collar adults participate in some organization such as in a church or union. Indeed, they share with most white collar adults certain attitudes about the desirability of a lifestyle that is more characteristic of white collar adults: a higher standard of living, quality education for their children, eating well, good health, responsible citizenship, and self-expression. At the same time, some people question the desirability of some of the accepted white collar values, such as extreme competitiveness and privatism. In examining relationships between social class and adult development, practitioners are challenged to develop ways of making needed opportunities and services available to blue collar adults in a form that fits their life-style.

Living Arrangements

The societal context is influential on adult development mainly through social institutions such as family, work, and community organizations in which adults interact most intensively with others. This section gives special attention to family relationships and other forms of living arrangements—in particular, the college campus as an institutional setting that has an impact on young adult students, the household of middle-aged couples and members of their family, and the various settings in which older adults live.

The College Campus. Before presenting a review of the impact of college on students, let us take time for an overview of the college as an institution. The college campus as a setting for learning, growth, and change has a long history. The popular image of college is "a place where bright young people go when they complete high school, stay four years, and get an education." In actuality, higher education in the United States contains substantial diversity and has experienced major changes in recent decades. Although many of the oldest and best-known American universities are privately endowed, in recent years most college students attend tax-supported institutions of higher education. More than seven out of ten enrollments currently go to public institutions, and while total enrollments in all private institutions have changed little during the past two decades, public college and university enrollments have nearly tripled, and community college enrollments have increased about fourfold (U.S., DHEW, 1975, 1976). Of course the number of college age youths has also increased greatly during this period. Diversity is also reflected in size, prestige, and levels of degrees granted. Enrollment of full-time students ranges from a few hundred to tens of thousands on a single campus, and some institutions have multiple campuses. Prestige ranges from major universities with distinguished faculties that attract students from throughout the world to institutions that are virtually unknown outside a section of a state. The range includes community colleges that offer two-year associate degrees, four-year colleges, and universities that provide doctoral and advanced professional study. For the following summary of tested knowledge about the impact of college on students, attention is focused on young adults who attend an undergraduate degree program full time at any type of college and university.

It is difficult to analyze the impact of college on students because there are so few studies of non-college-bound young adults or of what happens to them during the same time the students are in college. The social class differences between college-bound and non-college-bound young adults compound the problem. In addition, there is evidence that intellectual and personality change occurs for all people during adolescence and young adulthood and that the rate of change is greatest for the intellectually most able, who, of course, are somewhat more likely to attend college.

The college experience affects students in various ways. Knowledge is acquired and demonstrated on examinations. When employers use the college degree as a criterion for selecting employees, sometimes regardless of major, the degree serves both as a personnel selector for employers and as a way of increasing life chance for students. The term *life chance* refers to the richness of available opportunities. College also has an impact on the personality, often changing values and attitudes. Many studies of the impact of college on students have focused on personality change (Feldman and Newcomb, 1969; Heath, 1965, 1968).

In general, there is substantial evidence that college does

have an impact on students. The impact is greatest on those students who are ready to change, either because they are psychologically open to new experiences, or because they are open to the influence of others. There are many studies indicating that changes in several personality characteristics have been occurring between the freshman and senior years in most United States colleges and universities in recent decades. Students become less authoritarian, dogmatic, prejudiced, and conservative toward public issues and more sensitive to aesthetic experiences. They generally become more open to multiple aspects of the contemporary world. Intellectual interests and capacities increase, but commitment to religion decreases. Students also become more self-confident, independent, and ready to express impulses. It should be noted, however, that similar young adults who do not attend college also show increasing openness to new experience and growing tolerance, but perhaps not to the same extent.

Institutions of higher education vary in the extent and type of impacts they have on students, and these variations are associated with the characteristics of the students that institutions attract. Colleges have images that attract students who want to have the characteristics that the colleges want to help them acquire. Academic capacity and family social class level are associated with various intellectual dispositions and political liberalism and tend to characterize students who enter (in decreasing order) private universities, public universities, private colleges, public colleges, and two-year community colleges. The more prestigious institutions are more likely to attract and admit students who have already most nearly attained the characteristics of an educated man or woman. The distinctive influence of various colleges reflects the impact of both attracting distinctive student bodies and then accentuating those distinctive characteristics.

Within an institution, different experiences associated with various academic majors typically have effects beyond those attributable to initial selection into those major fields. The greatest impact most often occurs when institutional, faculty, and student characteristics complement and reinforce one another. For example, reinforcing conditions tend to occur in small, residential, four-year colleges in which similarly oriented faculty members and students have ample opportunities for formal and informal interaction. There is some indication that personality changes revert somewhat after college unless supported by postcollege environments.

The context of college also influences the lives of the somewhat older adults who attend. The thirty-year-old who decides to attend college part time typically confronts both barriers and facilitators. Examples include scheduling of courses, regulations regarding financial assistance to part-time students, encouragement from friends, general economic conditions, and guidance with the decision-making process in which the advisor relates information about educational and occupational opportunities to personal abilities and goals. Practitioners who assist adults with such transitions typically help them increase the facilitators and reduce the barriers to their own development.

The impact of the college experience on learning and development of both young and older adults is associated with the characteristics of the people who enter the experience, with their formal and informal activities while there, and with the supportiveness of subsequent experiences. Similar relationships occur for adults in settings other than college. One major study followed up high school graduates four years later regardless of whether they attended college. Those who attended two years of college increased several characteristics related to maturity less than those who attended for four years; those who were working during the four years increased even less than the two-year students. The scores of young women who became homemakers and were neither working nor in college during the four years beyond high school actually declined on selected personality measures such as flexibility, autonomy, intellectual curiosity, and tolerance for ambiguity (Trent and Medsker, 1968).

The Middle-Aged Household. Middle-aged couples who live in relatively standard households also interact with their physical and social settings. The character of their home setting is affected by the backgrounds and choices of the couple. Home

characteristics include size, expense, attractiveness, and neighborhood, but they also include number of children, other persons living in the household, types of family activities, and the
general spirit or social atmosphere in the home.

A crucial factor in the influence of home and family
setting on adult development and learning is the extent to
which it encourages change and growth and self-actualization.
Down through the centuries it has been assumed that the home
should facilitate child development. There is striking evidence
about the extent to which the home environment is associated
with the intellectual development of the child (Bloom, 1964).
There is also some evidence that a reading orientation in the
adolescent's home environment is associated with the extent
of subsequent part-time educative activity by non-college-bound
young adults (Knox, 1970). One of the main influences, at
least in rural areas and small towns, on participation by homemakers in occasional educational activities, such as home extension clubs, is their perception of the spouse's attitude toward
doing so.

Listed below are some of the major characteristics of
home and family settings that seem to be positively associated
with adult development and learning.

1. General acceptance by family members that adult life
   entails growth and change: for example, a woman
   might receive encouragement from her husband and
   children to obtain more education or accept major
   community responsibilities.
2. Familiarity with other adults as role models engaged
   in systematic learning and adaptation.
3. Availability of learning resources for adults in the
   home, such as books, recordings, and study guides.
4. Awareness of opportunities for organized learning for
   adults outside the home.
5. Opportunities for adults to engage in activities that
   help clarify needs to grow and change.
6. Willingness for adult members to spend time and

money on continuing their education, along with encouragement and recognition when they do.

7. Willingness of other family members to adapt to changes that result when an adult member does learn and grow and change.

8. Experience by children with their parents' learning so that they enter adulthood assuming that learning is a lifelong process.

Changes in a home and family setting tend to be cumulative and to interact and reinforce each other. The interaction occurs among family members and between attitudes and performance. Practitioners can help adults understand that these interactions may have a spiral effect. A familiar downward spiral often occurs when there is marital discord and the marriage seems to be heading for divorce. An uncaring attitude or a thoughtless act can lead to resentment by the spouse, which is acted out in critical comments or annoying behavior that seems unrelated to the actual cause of the resentment. Once the downward spiral is begun, various family members often become involved to some degree, and, unless some constructive effort is made to gain some perspective on what is happening and break the cycle, negative attitude begets destructive action and the marital relationship steadily deteriorates. Practitioners are often consulted at this stage, and sometimes it is too late. Although it is more difficult, especially in a home not characterized by love and respect, an upward spiral can also be achieved.

Functioning families maintain their equilibrium and viability because in the complex and often delicate balance of interpersonal relationships, the constructive and cohesive forces are greater than the destructive and divisive forces. The achievement of an upward spiral in desirable relationships among family members has a similar dynamic. If a middle-aged couple with adolescent children disagree about the amount of entertaining they should do, one approach that might lead to an upward spiral would be to diagnose the forces that press for more entertaining and the forces that resist the current amount (Lewin, 1948, 1958). The level of an activity of this type tends to be in quasi-stable equilibrium between such opposing forces. Examples of forces that urge more entertaining include enjoyment that one or both partners may gain from the social activities, benefits related to either partner's work life, feelings of accomplishment at being an effective host or hostess, and acceptance of obligations that entail entertaining. Examples of forces that may resist even the current amount of entertaining include pressure to spend family funds for purposes that one or both partners may value more, preference for other types of social activities, competition with children for use of the living room, and feelings of inadequacy in the host or hostess role. Many couples would be aware of some of these dynamics. An advantage of explicitly discussing them is that both partners are likely to gain a greater understanding of and commitment to the adjustments that could be made so that this aspect of their relationship could become more mutually satisfactory.

Our discussion of middle-aged couples as they interact with their home and family settings in ways that influence adult development and learning has been restricted to relatively standard middle-class households and living arrangements. In actuality, great variability exists in the contemporary United States. The variations related to community size or section of the country are more apparent than the variations related to social class, composition of the household group, family life-style, and social atmosphere in the household as reflected in the members' attitudes toward each other. In some households, especially those that do not contain young children, the activities of family members are focused elsewhere, and the home is like an airline terminal with members passing each other coming and going but sharing few important activities or events. In some households, especially those of some elderly couples, almost all the activities of family members occur within the home. Some households include only one adult, while others include four or five. Some households seldom include anyone unrelated by blood or marriage, while in others those with kinship relations are outnumbered by nonrelated members.

Variety of Life-Styles. It appears that during the past three generations there has been some increase in the variety of family living arrangements and life-styles in the United States. Contrasting arrangements are illustrated by the suburban father who spends four hours a day commuting to and from work and rarely sees his younger children except on weekends, and by the ghetto mother who is the head of the household because employment opportunities are greater for minority women than for minority men. The impact of family living arrangements on adult development and learning, which is similar to the impact of college on students, results from the match between the characteristics and aspirations of the couple who establish the home and the character of the home environment that they help create. The extent to which that home environment will influence adult development is also related to the reinforcement that occurs between formal and informal activities and attitudes and actions.

Housing for the Elderly. At the turn of the century, when fewer people reached old age, there were three typical living arrangements for the aged: maintaining one's own home, moving in with family, or going to the old folks' home. In the past generation there has been a sharp increase in other living arrangements for the elderly. Examples include retirement hotels, nursing homes, public housing for the elderly, and retirement communities.

Practitioners can help adults identify and plan for the retirement living arrangements they find desirable and feasible, which may entail helping middle-aged adults understand the actual living arrangements of older adults. More than half of the heads of households over sixty-five own their own homes, although some do not live in them (Brotman, 1972). Most older adults are satisfied with their housing and resist attempts to make them move (Lawton and Nahemow, 1972). Most elderly adults are reluctant to live with their grown children unless it is necessitated by financial or health conditions. About one third of the adults over age sixty-five who have living children do live with them (Troll, 1971). Retirement communities provide another option for those who can afford them. Only a small percentage of adults over age sixty-five are institutionalized, and only a small percentage of them are in nursing homes and other long-term care facilities. However, because of terminal declines, a relatively high percentage of deaths occur in long-term care facilities (Kastenbaum and Candy, 1973).

Each of these alternatives has its costs and benefits. For example, when elderly adults live with their grown children, low expense and high family interaction are benefits, but there may be high costs in the form of care provided by family members, along with friction and resentment. A downtown retirement hotel may have relatively low rent, maid service, a dining room, and easy access to activities, but the neighborhood crime rate is often high. Living in a low income housing project may cost little and provide contact with younger families, but tolerance by the elderly for the activity and noise of unrelated children tends to be low, and crime rates against the elderly in such settings tend to be quite high. Remaining in the same community after retirement does allow continued contact with old friends. In one city, older residents of apartment buildings in which at least half the households contained at least one person over age sixty-five had more friends than those in buildings with fewer residents over sixty-five. This is especially important for blue collar adults who typically depend more on friends from the neighborhood (I. Rosow, 1967). Residents of retirement communities, who typically have higher incomes, health, and morale, report less interaction with family but more with friends (Bultena and Wood, 1969). Primary contact with other older people who are in the same boat provides retirees with a supportive reference group. Each living arrangement has a distinctive mix of interaction and solitude.

The accessibility and satisfactoriness of these alternative living arrangements vary substantially with the health and wealth of the older adult. As is typically the case, the poor have fewer and less-attractive options than the well-to-do. Few blue collar adults can afford the well-known and attractive retirement communities. A retirement trailer park is more likely. As in the case of students and colleges, the matching that occurs between the elderly and their living arrangements reflects both preferences and capability. White collar adults who can afford to buy a home and pay for the health and recreational services in a retirement community are likely to have the interests and abilities to make these living arrangements satisfactory for themselves and their new neighbors. Blue collar adults who are in poor health, lack financial resources, and go to the least expensive custodial facility available are unlikely to arrive with high expectations about specific features of a stimulating and supportive environment. Under these circumstances, unless leadership is provided by a practitioner concerned with facilitation of adaptation and change, the living arrangements are not likely to rise much above a minimal custodial level.

There is evidence that alternative living arrangements for the elderly vary in their influence on role performance (I. Rosow, 1967; Carp, 1969; Gelwicks, 1970). For example, those who live in urban apartment buildings and hotels for the elderly interact more with others their age, and this enhances their performance as friends and neighbors but somewhat reduces their activities in family roles. Retirement communities have a unique pattern of role performance in which some activities are encouraged and others discouraged. For example, group recreations such as entertaining and shuffleboard are encouraged, and babysitting with grandchildren and visiting former work associates are discouraged. In general, however, older adults are not as isolated and have more contact with the younger generations than is typically assumed.

One feature of living environments for the elderly is the extent to which they encourage docility. There is a tendency as individual vigor and competence decrease to shift control over personal decisions from the older individual to others, thus forcing the older person to become more dependent. Some homes for the aged discourage independence even to the extent of using drugs to enforce docility, and even expensive retirement communities tend to be highly programmed. In addition, dependency is associated with social class level (I. Rosow, 1967). The white collar older adult tends to be less dependent than similar blue collar older adults under comparable circumstances.

Adults can be helped to gain increased identification and satisfaction from most living arrangements. Familiar possessions help most people feel at home. Being able to bring one's own pictures and furniture or to arrange the existing furniture enables most adults to identify more with a living space as theirs. This applies to a college dormitory, a family living room, or a room in an old folks' home. Similar flexibility and planning can encourage social interaction. For example, informal social contact can be increased by locating a well-lighted lounge area with chairs, tables, and magazines adjacent to a central location where the incoming mail is picked up. Practitioners who are aware of the ways in which living arrangements frustrate or facilitate adult development can help establish social policies that provide adults with attractive alternatives from which to choose and can help adults choose among the alternatives wisely. As with the range of family arrangements, educational institutions, and community organizations, housing arrangements vary in the types of pressures the individual experiences. Some encourage social interaction and some encourage solitude. Some emphasize autonomy and some emphasize dependence. Practitioners who understand the typical pressures toward conformity and change in various settings can help adults make satisfactory selections (Wohlwill, 1966; Sherman, 1974; Labouvie-Vief and Baltes, 1975). In general, for adults of any age or walk of life, it seems desirable for each person, when a choice is possible among alternative settings, to select a setting that encourages what the adult wants to become. The process of becoming is reflected in both activities and satisfactions (Butler, 1975).

There are many paths through adulthood. From the beginning of young adulthood until the beginning of old age, adults become more different from one another, in part because of the different paths they take and the different experiences they have. However, experience and outlook are also associated with whether the individual is a man or a woman; whether he or she lives in a small town or a big city, is poor or well-to-do, has little or much education, and is black or white; and whether English is his or her native language.

An unemployed young black man who lives in a poor section of a large city with high unemployment rates experiences a combination of societal characteristics and trends that influence his experience and outlook. His interest in further career education is influenced by his perception of how likely he is to be able to use his increased competence in light of probable employment opportunities and practices. A practitioner might help him to take both past experience and future prospects into account by considering employment rates for black men in various categories of age and educational level, for several communities and time periods that vary regarding the unemployment rate. Adding information about relevant educational opportunities and financial assistance might enable the young man to diagnose more accurately the societal influences on his life and cope more effectively as a result. Assistance from a practitioner is especially important because most of the generalizations about adult development are based on studies that describe the general population but fail to reflect the unique circumstances of minority groups. In addition to providing relevant information, the practitioner can help the adult relate the information to his own background and interests.

Many older adults are poor. The median income for families in which the head of the household is over sixty-five is about half that of younger families. There have been improvements in recent decades, however. About 1970, approximately two out of ten older adults were classified as poor compared with three out of ten a decade earlier. The parallel trend for older black people from seven out of ten classified as poor about 1960, to four out of ten about 1970, also indicates the much higher proportions of blacks who have lived below the poverty line. With increasing numbers of adults living beyond age sixty-five, it has become clear that more programs and services are needed by older adults, many of whom are unable to pay for them. Such generalizations about the societal context of aging are useful for those who set social policy.

However, an increasing proportion of adults enter old age with relatively high levels of education, health, and income.

Such adults need generalizations about societal influences and adult development that apply to them (Rose, 1966). Those with higher levels of formal education tend to cope more effectively with tasks and adjustments. Higher levels of income can widen the range of opportunities for living arrangements and social activities. An understanding of typical patterns of adult development for people such as themselves, along with the societal facilitators and barriers they are likely to confront, can enable many people to deal more effectively with their problems and their opportunities (Bennett, 1968). Practitioners who understand these various paths through adulthood, along with typical societal influences on them, can assist the adults they serve to increase their own performance and satisfaction.

Contextual Opportunities

For adults of all ages, there is substantial evidence that the opportunity system in a community affects adult participation. An adult is more likely to engage in an activity that is readily accessible than one that is preferred but less accessible. This applies to such activities as book reading (Ennis, 1965), organizational participation (Wright and Hymen, 1958), and educational programs for adults (Johnstone and Rivera, 1965). There is also evidence that the same basic generalization applies to church participation and use of health services.

Most practitioners who provide services for adults—especially blue collar adults—have discovered that accessibility, like beauty, is in the eye of the beholder. Many of the programs and services that adults have said they would use if they were only available already existed. One of the continuing tasks of practitioners who work with adults is to interpret programs or services so that the adults concerned are familiar with the programs and feel that if they decided to participate they would feel accepted. The concern about being rejected in unfamiliar settings is very widespread.

Awareness of opportunities also helps clarify needs related to the program or service. Adults tend to be aware of the needs and interests that they or friends or acquaintances have had satisfied before by participation in a program or service. When they respond to general questions about their needs or interests, adults are likely to respond by reference to the familiar. However, when examples of programs or services are presented, many adults are able to compare a tangible program with their own interests and, in the process of doing so, increase their awareness of their own needs. In some instances, this results in a shifting of priorities, and an adult may eventually select a program suggested by a practitioner as more relevant than others the adult considered before becoming aware of a wider range of alternatives (James and Montross, 1956).

Awareness of available opportunities is not the only influence on adult participation, however. Interests and costs also impinge on decisions to participate. Interests evolve from earlier experiences in family and community. Ability to pay depends on both income level and competing demands for funds. For example, when young adults move from a small community where they grew up to a large city, they confront many opportunities. Some opportunities present them with stimulating entertainment, anonymity, and expanded social space in which to experiment and crystallize their sense of occupational and social identity. The same city setting also presents young adults with uncaring exploitation, exclusion, loneliness, and boredom. The opportunities that are seized and resulting satisfaction depend in part on the individual's prerequisite experience, resources, and priorities.

Participation in organizations benefits the individual as well as the community. In addition to satisfaction and enjoyment, such participation enables an adult to explore new interests and acquire new competencies. This can be especially important in the process of role changes such as a youngest child's starting school, a move to a new community, loss of a spouse, and retirement.

If the individual understands what he or she wants from organizational participation, need satisfaction is more likely. This applies to the selection of an organization to join, as well as the selection of activities to undertake as a member. The person who seeks friendly and like-minded companions might select a recreational group, such as a bowling league, and emphasize good conversation, while the person who seeks to exercise leadership might select a service-oriented group, such as a United Way committee, and emphasize helping members achieve organizational goals. Practitioners can be especially helpful by assisting adults to locate organizations that fit their life-styles and aspirations. A particularly valuable ingredient in the matching process is the availability of role models who can provide encouragement.

Although many organizations welcome new members, some adults are discouraged by subtle barriers. The person with a Spanish accent or dark skin may feel like an outsider, the young adult may feel that the organization is run by and for older people, the mother of young children may experience difficulty because of a lack of child care arrangements, a middle-aged adult from a blue collar family may be unfamiliar with formal organizational procedures, the older adult may experience barriers in the form of evening meetings or stairs to climb. In some instances, such barriers reflect discrimination by the members, which practitioners can sometimes help to reduce. In many instances, however, barriers to participation are inadvertent, and if the adults who confront them are aware of the barriers and of ways to overcome them, changes can be readily made.

Some barriers to participation extend beyond organizational practices. Transportation for older adults is an example. There is no car in almost half of the households in which the head is over sixty-five. This is about three times the rate for younger families (Revis, 1971). Many areas lack low-cost public transportation, and, without a car or money for public transportation and physically unable to walk long distances, many older adults are barred from organizational participation, necessary services, and people who are important to them. Increased service and reduced fares for public transportation have increased use by the elderly. Some organizations provide their own transportation, such as a bus or a car pool. Careful scheduling of the time and location of organizational activities can also reduce transportation barriers.

Case Example: Lois

There is little tested knowledge about the contexts that young adults confront or about the influences of these contexts on the paths through life that they take. The following example of a middle-aged white collar homemaker suggests some of the alternatives and influences.

Lois, a middle-aged white collar homemaker, who met her husband in college, was married, and bore and raised three children, might confront any one of the following home situations at age forty-five:

1. Lois might be living in a large, attractive suburban home, with a successful husband and three teen-age children, and she might devote a substantial amount of her time to volunteer and recreational activities.
2. Following ten unhappy years that culminated in a divorce, Lois might now be living with her three children, her second husband, and his two children in an apartment building, and she might have a part-time job.
3. After her husband died ten years ago, Lois might have gone back to school in a small city. Her widowed mother might have lived with them during the past six years and helped with the home and children.
4. Lois might have left college before she graduated and then worked to help her husband through graduate school. Her husband might have had great financial success and about five years later requested and received a divorce to marry another woman. Large alimony and support payments might have enabled her to remain home and raise the children. Lois might not remarry but might move to a small town in a region in which some of her relatives live.
5. Lois might now be living in a nice neighborhood of

a large city in a big old house, where she has been
working with her husband in their family business for
most of their married life. Her mother-in-law might
have died ten years ago. As a result her household
might include her father-in-law, the three children, a
live-in housekeeper, one or two other relatives, and in
most recent years an exchange student.

6. Lois might have lived in five similar suburban areas
over the years, in increasingly larger homes, to accom-
pany her husband who was frequently transferred.
Their oldest child might have been killed in an accident five years ago, and Lois might have been ill frequently over the years. It is likely that she would have
discovered several families in their present suburb
whom they had known in the suburbs of other cities
years before.

Some of the factors that determined Lois' actual path
through life existed more than twenty years before when she
first married. They include her intelligence, physical and mental health, the satisfactoriness of her parents' marriage, similar
characteristics for her husband, and the mix of similarity and
complementariness in Lois' relationship with her husband. The
characteristics that Lois and her husband brought to the marriage reflected what they had each received from their parents
in various ways and had developed from other experiences during childhood and adolescence. At marriage the bride and
groom probably had some understanding of what each found
especially attractive and, to a lesser extent, unattractive about
the other, but these perceptions changed and became more detailed within a few years. The likelihood of a satisfactory marriage would be greater if they shared similar backgrounds, had
complementary needs, got to know each other well by going together for a year or more, and both really wanted to get married.

Other influences on the path Lois actually took were the
decisions and efforts she and her husband made when they were
married. They include his job choices and performance, decisions to move, relations with in-laws, basic approach to child

rearing, Lois' work and volunteer activities, and the extent to which each of them actively worked at creating a successful marriage.

Still other influences are accidental and unpredictable. They include the factors in occupational success that are beyond the control of the individual worker, such as swings in the general economy or in the growth or decline of a specific industry. They also include the unpredictable and largely unpreventable illnesses and accidents that can so greatly affect the course of people's lives.

All of these influences were cumulative and helped shape subsequent events and decisions. Some, such as job choice and performance, influenced income level and the type of housing they could afford. Some, such as shared values regarding the relative priorities of various categories of expenditures (housing, insurance, clothing, food, entertaining, and family activities), influenced the type of housing they selected and what they did in the household. Some attitudes and role models influenced the extent to which they had shared values and communicated effectively with each other.

Relations with family and friends were likely to be related to geographic mobility. If both Lois and her husband had grown up in the same geographic area and settled there when they married (unless there was some unusual problem regarding in-law relations), a substantial portion of their social life would be likely to entail association with relatives and old friends. Such family closeness can provide a sense of security and support in times of stress. It can also result in family disputes, interference, demands, and in-law problems. If, however, Lois and her husband moved far away from their families, although there would be correspondence and phone calls and occasional visits, the contact between Lois' children and their grandparents and other relatives would typically be marginal. For the geographically mobile family, unusual circumstances can produce a form of family closeness. Examples include moving to a suburban community where a favorite sister or cousin already resides, or a divorced wife being joined by her widowed mother to help manage the household, or the retired grandparents deciding to move to the community where their children and grandchildren now live.

Conclusions

One of the main challenges to practitioners concerned with adult development is to understand the major influences that the societal context has on adult development, to help clarify public policy issues, and to propose changes in programs and services that are likely to improve adult productivity and satisfaction. This is no easy task. People concerned with all aspects of society (including economic, religious, family, political, and recreational institutions) have important contributions to make. A distinctive contribution can and should be made by scholars and practitioners who are concerned developmentally and holistically with adulthood.

The increasing rate of change, complexity, and geographic mobility that characterizes our society is undermining our sense of security and community and is increasing the importance of adult capacity for adaptation and learning for an uncertain tomorrow (Toffler, 1970, 1974; Sarason, 1974). Clear understandings and sound proposals regarding adult performance entail attention to individual, societal, and transactional aspects of adulthood. Such transactions occur in relation to primary groups, formal organizations, communities, and the larger society. A dynamic tension between individual and societal concerns is probably inevitable as adults interact in all societal contexts. A better understanding of the processes and outcomes of such transactions can contribute to an enhanced quality of personal and community life (Argyris, 1964; Barker, 1968; Turney-High, 1968; Proshansky, Ittelson, and Rivlin, 1970; Klausner, 1971; Sarason, 1976).

Practitioners who work with adults are continually challenged to match client needs with the programs and services that are provided. This is illustrated by the field of leisure and recreation services. As adults have attained more leisure time, public and private providers of recreational facilities and services have expanded, and the leisure field has become more complex, formalized, and institutionalized. Practitioners in leisure services for adults confront such policy issues as the specification of target markets, differentiation and competition among providers, services to the less advantaged, multiple use of facilities, identification of needed services, mix of financial support, and marketing of services. Each of these issues entails attention to the individual adult, the opportunity system, and transactional patterns between adults and their societal context (Rapoport and Rapoport, 1975).

In many fields, concern about policy issues, future directions, and planning has led to a consideration of alternative futures. Although past attempts to predict the future have usually been inaccurate owing to unforeseen circumstances, there is growing expertise in the identification of alternative futures and the analysis of probabilities and influences. This provides the basis for identifying social and economic indicators of change, initiating public discussion of the relative desirability of the alternative futures, and building public support for policies likely to increase the probability of more desirable alternative futures (Kahn and Weiner, 1967; Toffler, 1972). Applying this process to a consideration of the societal context of adult development would be an enormous task. However, on a more modest scale, it would be possible to analyze the settings of one segment of the adult population (for example, college students, middle-aged blue collar women, or retired white collar adults) in relation to one role domain at a time (such as work, family, or leisure). The analysis might focus on feasible as well as desirable changes that could be made to create settings that encourage adults to become more productive, happy, and fulfilled human beings (Sarason, 1972).

Summary

Adult development reflects the individual's ongoing flow of transactions with his or her societal context, which includes people, groups, and organizations related to adult roles in family, work, and community. Personal characteristics, such as alertness, accumulated experience, and personality, influence the extent to which adults reach out to use resources and confront problems in the context of family, community, and world. Such personal characteristics also affect how an adult responds to the problems and opportunities that are encountered.

In the United States, rapid social change, widespread mobility, loss of a sense of community, and societal attitudes toward various age groups combine to affect the process of adult development. In a slowly changing society, adolescents and young adults can see in their older relatives and friends the sorts of people they themselves are likely to become. Values and practices are introduced to the young, and the older generations experience little obsolescence. By contrast, in our rapidly changing pluralistic society, young adults confront a world that is different in many ways from the one their grandparents knew as young adults.

Occupational change is reflected in the high proportion of older workers in longstanding occupations and in the high proportion of young workers in newly created occupations. Age-related work rules, such as minimum age and education requirements and mandatory retirement age, further affect the relation between age and type of work. Poor economic conditions increase unemployment, which adversely affects the self-concept of those who are most likely to be unemployed, such as young men from minority groups, older workers, and women who work part time.

Trends regarding extent and types of educational preparation affect adult role performance in work, family, and community. During this century, the gradual increase in the proportion of seventeen-year-olds who have graduated from high school was interrupted by a rapid increase in completion rates between the 1920s and the 1940s. By 1970, three quarters of the age group graduated from high school. The proportion of the eighteen-to-twenty-four age group enrolled in college increased rapidly during the 1950s and 1960s and leveled off in the early 1970s. In recent years, the first-time degree-credit enrollment in institutions of higher education each fall has been about 60 percent of the high school graduates the previous spring, and more than half the entering freshmen are graduating seniors four years later. As young people enter adulthood with more formal education and older people with less formal education die, the average level of formal education of adults has risen rapidly.

Beginning in 1970 the job market for college graduates began to deteriorate as the long-term growth in job demand for college graduates slowed and supply increased, reflecting earlier increases in birth rates and more recent increases in rates of college attendance. The impact on attendance rates and job prospects has varied with student characteristics. For example, the rates have been stable for young women, have increased for black males, and have decreased for white males from lower-middle-class families.

Social change has also been reflected in the age distribution. The proportion beyond age sixty-five, currently about one out of ten, has been increasing and, with recent declines in the birth rate and rising average longevity, is likely to continue to increase. This has increased the pressure for programs and services for older adults. Shifting social conditions, such as depression, war, inflation, urbanization, and unemployment, contribute to uncertainty, adjustments, and in some instances a widening of the generation gap. Increased geographic mobility has weakened the individual's sense of security and community. It is unclear whether this loss of a sense of local roots is leading to a greater sense of national unity.

Practitioners can assist adults to gain a broader perspective that includes the distinction between social change and personal change as a basis for interpreting generational differences and guiding adults' own efforts to adapt and change systematically. A proactive stance toward life and society is enhanced by a sense of security, self-esteem and direction as the basis for responsible involvement. A recognition of dehumanizing societal influences that discourage responsiveness and frustrate growth helps the individual counteract or at least deflect them. Desirable adjustments can serve as a stimulus for continued development. Small adjustments, such as decisions regarding educational, family, work, and community settings, can increase the likelihood that adults will become the sorts of people they want to become.

Variations in community settings also influence adult development. In manual community or neighborhood settings, characterized by low energy consumption and slow technological change, communication tends to be oral and personalized, and older adults typically serve as role models and as important sources of community experience. By contrast, most United States communities are characterized by the technological impact of the machine, high energy consumption, rapid social change, reliance on written communication, and transfer of many services from family to community agencies. As a result adults confront uncertainty and cross pressures regarding role performance and expectations in family, work, and community. This contributes to both great freedom of choice and uncertainty of direction. With the exception of inner city neighborhoods, metropolitan suburbs, and some remote rural areas, where population characteristics largely reflect social class differences, knowledge and attitudes have become quite similar across community settings.

Societal attitudes toward various stages of adulthood affect adult development. In actuality, many values and personality characteristics, such as autonomy and nurturance, tend to be quite stable from generation to generation in a family. However, middle-aged adults tend to misperceive adolescents as more autonomy oriented than they are, and young and middle-aged adults tend to misperceive older adults as less autonomy oriented than they are. People's stereotypes of age trends shift from active and outgoing in young adulthood to understanding and restraint in middle age, to constricted activity and increased introspection in old age. Such stereotypes partly reflect personal experience as a counterbalance to attitudes acquired from the media and other people. For example, those with more positive attitudes toward the elderly tend to be white collar, to have older living relatives, to have avoided major burdens or conflicts with older adults, and to have strong nurturance needs.

Such attitudes toward various age groups, when combined

with social change and community variations, influence inter-generational relations as well as adult development. For example, an unrealistically negative stereotype of older adults can affect the self-image of the young adults when they grow old. The middle generation tends to occupy positions of power and responsibility: to be the establishment. Increasingly, the very young adults and the very old adults who share a status on the dependent fringes of adulthood take a moralistic and antiestablishment stance. It seems that a special affinity between the young and the old is aided by the insulation provided by the middle generation.

Both problems and opportunities of adulthood are affected by the social class level of the individual adult, including the life-style and social space associated with white collar or blue collar status. For example, in recent generations level of formal education has become a major criterion for personnel selection, and going to college is more related to parental social class than to student academic aptitude. During the past decade, the proportion of college students whose parental income is above average has increased and the proportion from families with below average incomes has decreased.

Although social class values and practices have become more intermixed, practitioners can use distinctions between white collar and blue collar adults to recognize differences related to participation and information seeking and to minimize thoughtless imposition of middle class values. Community participation helps illustrate how social class influences adult development. The blue collar life-style tends to be neighborhood oriented and instrumental information is sought mainly through oral communication with family and friends. The white collar life-style tends to be somewhat more oriented toward activities and ideas in the larger community and beyond, and instrumental information seeking tends to include more use of media and experts. In each stratum, friends and associates serve as opinion leaders and influence choices. Community organizations tend to reflect white collar orientations toward formal procedures and written communications, which discourages participation by many blue collar adults. The benefits

of community participation include acquisition of new competencies, exploration of interests, and encouragement by role
models. Practitioners can assist blue collar adults to enter and
benefit from community groups and can assist white collar
adults to gain greater satisfaction and encouragement from informal activities with family and friends.

Living arrangements in households and institutions influence adult performance and personality. The demands and
constraints of the immediate context have a similar influence
on adult development for young college students, for middle-
aged couples in their households, and for older adults in the
various settings in which they live.

During the past generation, a much higher proportion of
young people have attended college full time than ever before.
They have done so in a wide variety of institutions, and there
has been a major increase in enrollments in public institutions.
This college experience does have an impact on intellectual and
personality change, although those who attend college are most
likely to change anyway, and personality changes tend to revert
unless supported by the postcollege environment. Colleges that
are most influential on personality development have images
that attract students who are open to the types of changes that
the colleges want them to acquire, and then accentuate those
distinctive characteristics. During the college years students tend
to become less authoritarian, dogmatic, prejudiced, conservative
toward public issues, and committed to religion. However,
intellectual interests and capability increase, and students become more sensitive to aesthetic experiences and open to multiple aspects of the contemporary world. Similar young adults
who do not attend college also show increasing openness to new
experience and growing tolerance, but perhaps not to the same
extent. Practitioners can help people achieve a useful match
between personal and institutional characteristics and to continue personality and intellectual development beyond college.

The household setting can influence the attitudes and
performance of family members in ways that are similar to the
impact of college on students. Functioning families maintain
their equilibrium and viability, because, in the complex and

often delicate balance of interpersonal relationships, the constructive and cohesive forces are greater than the destructive and divisive forces. When a marital relationship begins to deteriorate, a practitioner can sometimes help both partners gain a greater understanding of the situation and a commitment that each could make so that their relationship could become more mutually satisfactory. A home and family setting is more likely to facilitate adult development when it is characterized by family acceptance of change during adulthood, familiarity with adult role models who adapt, availability of learning resources for adults in the home, awareness of educational opportunities for adults, allocation of family resources for adult learning, willingness of other family members to adapt to change by an adult member, and experience by children with their parents' learning activities so that the children enter adulthood with positive attitudes about lifelong learning.

Living arrangements for older adults that used to consist mainly of maintaining one's own home, moving in with family, or going to the old folks' home, now also include retirement hotels, nursing homes, public housing for the elderly, and retirement communities. The accessibility and satisfactoriness of these alternative living arrangements vary substantially with the health and wealth of the older adult. Although many older adults live on very limited incomes, most are satisfied with their housing and resist moves. Most older adults prefer not to live with their grown children unless it is necessitated by financial or health conditions. Each alternative living arrangement for the elderly has its costs and benefits. Residents of retirement communities report less interaction with family but more with friends. Some environments, such as homes for the aged or retirement hotels, encourage dependency more than others. Practitioners can help adults recognize the distinctive features of alternative settings and select a setting that encourages what the adult wants to become.

Community opportunities also affect adult participation and development. Participation is more likely when the activity is visible, attractive, accessible, and affordable and fits the individual's experience and priorities. Practitioners can help adults locate organizations and activities that fit their life-styles and personal aspirations regarding recreation, service, or learning.

Most of all, practitioners can help adults acquire a more proactive or initiatory stance regarding their transactions with individuals, groups, and the larger society. A better understanding of how the societal context influences adult development contributes to a broader perspective that adults can use to guide their own activities and aspirations. Generalizations about shifting educational levels, occupational trends, and the advancing age distribution are manifestations of social change that adults can usefully differentiate from personal change during the adult life cycle. A better understanding of the influence of social class levels, community settings, and intergenerational relations on adult development also contributes to a perspective that enables adults to recognize some of the major forces that affect their lives, capitalize on those that are desirable, and try to deflect those that are undesirable. A sense of personal direction can help adults deal with societal attitudes toward various stages of adulthood as well. A more proactive approach to adult life can also enable men and women to select and shape living arrangements and community activities so that these interpersonal relationships encourage what the individual wants to become.

❧ 3 ❧

Family Role
Performance

❧❧ ❧❧ ❧❧ ❧❧ ❧❧ ❧❧ ❧❧ ❧❧

This chapter describes age-related trends in family role performance for United States adults. Practitioners who work with adults regarding aspects of family life find that developmental trends in physiology, health, personality, and learning are most useful when related to specific aspects of role performance. For example, a marriage counselor who understands developmental trends in self-concept by young adults wants to apply the generalizations to helping husbands and wives function more satisfactorily in family roles. Family life counselors or educators who conduct discussion groups for middle-aged adults with aging parents may be interested in generalizations about personality, physical condition, and learning in old age, but they are primarily concerned with using those generalizations to help discussion group members work out realistic and satisfactory relationships with their parents.

Practitioners who better understand the trends in role performance can help adults with whom they work gain greater insight into their own evolving life experiences and options because shifts in family performance affect other aspects of adult development. The ways in which adults understand and deal with major family role changes such as marriage, parenthood, and widowhood influence happiness, self-concept, and other types of performance in job and community (Lansing and Kish, 1957).

The Family Life Cycle

The family life cycle is the most familiar and studied domain of adult performance. Almost everyone grows up in a family. About 90 percent of United States adults get married, and most of them proceed at the same general pace through a similar series of family life transitions and role changes.

The continuity of the family life cycle is hinged by critical periods of transition, which are typically related to role changes. In addition to creating shifts in performance and participation during adulthood, role changes are associated with changes in such personality factors as self-concept and attitudes toward others. Transitions during role changes entail learning and adjustment as the adult alters role performance in relation to changes in role expectations. The early period of young adulthood, from eighteen through twenty-five, typically includes two of the critical role changes of adulthood: marriage and the onset of parenthood. The youngest child usually starts school when the parents are in their thirties, thus beginning the transition to middle-aged family performance and participation. The early period of middle age, from forty through fifty-five, includes role changes related to the increasing independence of children as they leave the family for work, marriage, or college; the establishment of relations with in-laws; and adjustments in relationships with aged parents and between husband and wife after the children have left. The older couple confronts role changes associated with grandparenthood, and the retirement period includes changes related to transition from work, illness, death of spouse, and change of living arrangements. There are various ways of making each of these role changes and various influences on the satisfactoriness of the adjustment (Duvall, 1971). Practitioners can help adults understand and make decisions about these changes so that they are as satisfactory as possible.

The typical pattern of family life is so widespread among middle-class American families from almost all racial and ethnic backgrounds that it has become a stereotype. In this typical pattern, a husband and wife live with their children and divide responsibilities and power in generally equalitarian or somewhat patriarchal ways.

Contrary to false stereotypes, the typical family pattern characterizes most black families, especially white collar black families. Three quarters of all ever-married black men live with their wives. Exceptions to the typical pattern are the result of economics rather than ethnic factors. For blue collar families, especially those below the poverty line, family structure and socialization practices for white and black families are quite similar (Blood and Wolfe, 1960; Bernard, 1966; Parker and Keiner, 1966; Willie, 1970). Fatherless homes are widespread among families with the lowest levels of income and education. More than one third of all low income families are headed by women. Because a much higher proportion of black families than white families have low incomes, a larger proportion of black families deviate from the typical family pattern. For example, the husband is absent or separated in about one out of five black families, compared with about one out of twenty white families (U.S. Census, 1973b).

Most of the variability in patterns of family life is associated with level of income and education. The equalitarian pattern with two parents in distinctive but complementary and flexible roles is most typical of white collar families. The patriarchal pattern, in which the husband is dominant in family decision making, is also widespread (Goldberg, 1973). Among blue collar families at the lowest income levels, the matriarchal pattern (especially where heads of households are female) is fairly widespread, but at moderate income levels the patriarchal pattern is typical.

There are other variations in the family pattern associated with Oriental, American Indian, Jewish, and Spanish-speaking ethnic backgrounds. The two major categories of Spanish-speaking families, Puerto Rican and Mexican-American, each with distinctive traditions and family patterns, tend to emphasize contrasting roles for husbands and wives. (There are indications in recent decades, however, that equalitarian marriages are becoming more widespread among Spanish-speaking people, especially in white collar families.)

Many aspects of American life have changed markedly during the past generation, especially in family life (Clinebell and Clinebell, 1970; Norton, 1974; Eshleman, 1974). The roles of wife and mother are undergoing substantial transformation, especially in white collar families. The age at first marriage has risen during the past decade, and the birth rate has dropped sharply after more than a generation of baby boom. The employment rate for mothers of young children has increased, as has the divorce rate. The family is likely to continue as a social institution—more than nine out of ten American adults want to be married—but many women prefer equalitarian marriages in which both husband and wife work and share responsibilities for household and child care. A variety of alternative family forms and arrangements are emerging (Alpenfels, 1971; Cooper, 1970; Bernard, 1973). Little of the tested knowledge about family life is recent enough and focused enough on current trends to analyze the emerging forms, let alone evaluate their impact. I have included parenthetical comments in this chapter to identify features of family life that appear to be in transition.

Typical Marriage Patterns

One of the overriding tasks during the end of adolescence and start of young adulthood is mate selection. This process is influenced by the couples' values and attitudes (Winch, 1971; Eshleman, 1974).

During the past generation or two, there has been an increased tolerance of people with different backgrounds and greater independence in dating. As a result, the proportion of marriages between young people from different backgrounds has also increased. These "mixed" marriages entail more difficult adjustments than do marriages between people with more similar backgrounds, and a higher proportion result in separation and divorce (Coombes, 1966; Snyder, 1964).

Another trend during the past two generations has been toward younger first marriages. In the mid-1960s, the average age at first marriage for women was about twenty and for men about twenty-three, although some married in their teens (U.S. Census, 1973b, c; DeLissovoy, 1973). By contrast, between the turn of the century and 1940 the average age at first marriage was about twenty-two for women and about twenty-four for men. Although there has been substantial variation around this average, the trend toward earlier first marriages reflects the decline during the early decades of this century in young people's emphasis on the man's becoming established in his job before getting married. Those who attend college full time directly after high school tend to marry several years later than those who do not. The greatest decline in age at first marriage has occurred for white collar families (Moss, 1965). Since 1962 the average age at first marriage has been gradually rising (U.S. Census, 1973a).

Sometimes parents who were older and more established and had more similar backgrounds when they were married feel frustrated about the changing character of courtship and mate selection and their own limited influence on the process. When there is a very short or no engagement period, there is little time for parents either to influence the selection process or to get to know the prospective in-laws. Practitioners can help young people understand the choices they typically confront and the crucial function of adaptation and growth in successful marriages.

Most young Americans enter marriage with the hopeful and even romantic expectation that it will be successful and mutually satisfying (Pollis, 1969; Murstein, 1967, 1972; Blood and Wolfe, 1960; Farley and Hermalin, 1971; Moss and others, 1971). Actually, one of the two peak periods for marital unhappiness, desertion, threats of divorce, and divorce is between twenty-one and twenty-five years of age. Some influences on marital adjustment and happiness mainly reflect the experiences and attitudes that the couple bring with them to the marriage, and some influences reflect their interrelationships in the marriage (Paris and Luckey, 1966; Winch, 1967; Hurlock, 1968; Rosenberg and Sutton-Smith, 1968; Charney, 1972).

Listed are some of the main characteristics associated with successful marital adjustment that couples bring with them:

1. Similarity of backgrounds and values.
2. Effective interpersonal relationships. People with substantial earlier experience in social situations tend to acquire willingness to cooperate, ability to adjust to others, and the social insight to do so, which helps them adjust to marriage.
3. Satisfactory fit between actual mate and preference for ideal mate.
4. Complementarity of needs.
5. Compatibility of role expectations. By the time they are married, most people have formed expectations about the roles of husband and wife that reflect personality characteristics and experience with parents or other role models and with brothers and sisters. As more varied and equalitarian expectations evolve regarding the roles of husband and wife, compatibility is becoming a more complex but important objective.
6. Parents who are well adjusted to each other and have satisfactory relations with their children provide constructive role models and encourage their children to become well-adjusted adults.

Practitioners concerned with adult development can work with parents of adolescent children and others who have frequent contact with adolescents, such as people associated with educational, religious, and recreational programs, to help them understand influences on the success of mate selection.

There are few decisions more crucial to individual happiness and community well-being than the choice of a marriage partner and few for which there is less serious preparation. The reemergence of marriage brokers or heavy parental influence on mate selection seems unlikely. However, the long-standing but growing concern about the future of the family is increasing public discussion about the variety of ways in which young people can be helped to approach mate selection and marriage in more satisfactory ways. Such assistance is likely to include mass media awareness, peer group concern and individual conversations, and more formal family life education programs.

Listed are some of the factors associated with successful marital adjustment that entail evolving interrelationships between a husband and wife:

1. Satisfactory sexual adjustment. Influences on adjustment and satisfaction include experience and attitudes related to sex, and similarity of sexual desires.
2. Adequacy of family finances. People who marry young tend to have greater financial problems and insecurity than couples who marry when they are a few years older and are more established. Adequacy partly reflects the match between resources and aspirations.
3. Participation in family work and activities. This adjustment reflects the expectations and performance of the husband and the wife regarding homemaking tasks and their mutual satisfaction with the contribution of the other toward the running of the house.
4. Satisfactory relations with in-laws. In-law problems occur most often in the early years of marriage and are more common and troublesome in relations between the wife and her husband's mother and sisters because women devote more attention to family matters and the husband's family typically has less influence on mate selection. Satisfactory in-law adjustments are more likely when the two families have similar values, have happy homes and family lives, and get to know each other before the marriage and when the young husband and wife have their own house and are accepting of both sets of parents.

For most couples, the early years of marriage constitute one of the greatest transitions they will ever experience. A few years earlier as adolescents, their self-absorbed search for identity typically caused them to separate themselves from their families. Participation in education and work helped loosen associations with their childhood selves. Participation in courtship and peer group activities helped them acquire interests and norms that facilitate the transition to adulthood. Paradoxically, however, the responsibilities of late courtship and early marriage often displace some of the interests that brought the couple together. For example, the decision to be married tends to be accompanied by a reorientation from spending money on dating to saving money for married life.

As the couple interacts with peers, they take part in adult social institutions and become interested in a reintegration with their family in which they relate to their parents as other adults. Cohesion and help gradually replace criticism and rejection. The trend during the past generation or two toward more equalitarian relationships between men and women and among generations probably facilitates this transition (Miller, 1966; Rapoport and Rapoport, 1975).

It appears that adjustment in equalitarian marriages is aided by a mix of both complementary and similar personality traits such as temperament, needs, values, and interests (Winch, 1971). However, it also appears that some varied life-styles and marriage forms now exist during young adulthood and that marital and family relationships vary substantially from one to another. Although there is little tested knowledge regarding this variability, the proportion of conventional marriages during young adulthood has declined clearly during the past generation, and there has been an increase in student marriages, two-career marriages, and marriages characterized by involuntary unemployment and the counterculture. It is likely that most of these patterns allow for satisfying marriages and that much depends on the resourcefulness of the individual couple. Given the variety and uncertainty that many young people confront as they enter marriage, a crucial ingredient for success seems to be both partners' willingness and ability to learn and grow regarding important family goals and ways to achieve them.

Although marital stability and adjustment varies widely within each social class level, there is some association between adjustment and social class level. White collar families tend to have more satisfactory adjustment generally, partly because financial problems are not as severe. However, more blue collar families are cohesive, extended family systems, which reduces in-law problems and increases sources of companionship.

Marital relationships, of course, also reflect the attitudes and expectations of the partners. For example, among lower-middle-class newlyweds, descriptions of spouses tend to be mainly concerned with personality and responsiveness and little concerned with the roles and norms that are being clarified. Both men and women tend to express satisfaction at their increasing ability to express negative feelings; many refer to an increasing frequency of quarrels as promoting growth. At this early stage of marriage, growing dissatisfaction is usually attributed to external influences such as work or extended family conflicts (Lowenthal, Thurnher, and others, 1975).

In general, a happy adjustment to marriage is more likely to occur when: (1) the husband and wife individually have been happy people; (2) each partner gains satisfaction from role performance that fits the expectations of both; (3) each feels mature and stable love for the other; (4) there is satisfactory sexual adjustment; (5) there is sharing of interests and tasks related to recreation and care of the home.

The major sources of marital problems in the early years are sex, living conditions and finances, parental interference, and general incompatibility (Rollins and Feldman, 1970).

Marital adjustment is especially difficult for many blue collar families, owing to low levels of income, occupational instability, and lack of education, along with many problems that are especially severe for low income families within many minority groups. For example, three out of ten black families are classified in the low income category, and more than half of the black families with a female head are so classified. In addi-

tion, because black women have been more numerous and better
educated than black men, there is a tendency for them to marry
men with less formal education. Marital satisfaction tends to be
lower for black wives than for white wives, and marital satisfaction expressed by black husbands tends to be somewhat lower,
which probably reflects the broader occupational and social
problems they confront as much as their relations with their
wives.

Parenthood.   Many young women aspire to motherhood.
Fluctuations in birth rates have reflected numbers and timing
of children, not decisions to have no children. Even the high
birth rates during the 1950s and early 1960s were accomplished
mainly by closer spacing of births. The decline in birth rates
during the past decade has not greatly affected the proportion
of families with zero or one child; it has mainly resulted from
an increase in the two-child family and a decrease in the three-
and four-child family. During the past generation there has been
some increase in the proportion of babies born to teenage
mothers, which partly reflects an increase in the numbers of
persons in the adolescent and young adult age range. The decline in birth rate for females aged fourteen to seventeen since
the peak several years ago reflects an increase in the number of
abortions in that age group.

The birth of the first child is a crucial transition in adult
family responsibility and brings some difficult adjustments for
most couples (LeMasters, 1957; Rossi, 1968; Anthony and
Benedek, 1970). Young parents tend to take their new parental
responsibilities more lightly than do similar, but older, new
parents who tend to be more concerned and to defer some
personal interests in favor of parental responsibilities (Bossard
and Boll, 1966). Listed are some of the main contributors to
unsatisfactory adjustment to parenthood:

1. Negative attitudes toward parenthood during the first
pregnancy. Pregnancy often involves mixed feelings and shifts
in expectations and relationships between husband and wife.
Premarital pregnancy brings additional strains, especially if it
precipitated an unlikely marriage (Dame and others, 1965).
Estimates of the proportion of women who are pregnant when

they are first married run as high as one of five. Positive attitudes toward parenthood are associated with fewer psychosomatic complaints, especially for women from blue collar families (Rosengren, 1961).

2. Feelings of parental inadequacy. When the first child is born or adopted, most parents lack preparation and experience for their new roles, especially those who must cope with an atypical child. For many mothers, the first year of motherhood entails substantial feelings of inadequacy that are reflected in depression, friction with family, and the fervent desire to flee from motherhood. For parents who were already unhappy and discontented, parenthood can bring further unhappiness and maladjustment (Loesch and Greenberg, 1962). However, successful experiences with parenthood can bring greater happiness and gratification, and most parents who have a second and third child feel increasingly adequate in the role as parent.

3. Unwillingness to accept role changes. Societal expectations and inescapable tasks precipitate abrupt role changes and related adjustments for new parents (Hobbs, 1965). If parents accept these changes as part of a desirable transition, parenthood can be a period of growth and fulfillment. However, if they are not prepared to change, the crisis of parenthood can lead to maladjustment and deterioration of family relationships. Differential readiness for parenthood can cause considerable marital strain, even before conception. To the wife who leaves a career for childrearing, motherhood may seem an unfair replacement of a familiar, satisfying role with one that is unfamiliar. Some husbands resent their displacement by the baby as the wife's center of attention and they have difficulty coping with concerns about increased expenses, decreased sexual responsiveness, and restrictions on activity. A successful transition to parenthood can be facilitated by helping couples develop more realistic and compatible expectations about parenthood during the year or two before and after the birth of the first child. In past years, white collar couples tended to regard parenthood as the fulfillment of marriage and children as a source of pride and hope, and blue collar couples tended to regard parenthood as the inevitable payment for sex relations

(Bossard and Boll, 1966), but this distinction is probably disappearing, because of the increasingly widespread use of contraceptives in recent years.

The onset of parenthood tends to produce a period of great information seeking and learning, especially for the mother. Reading, classes for expectant parents, and informal conversations with those who have experienced the process of birth and care of a young baby increase greatly, especially in white collar families. One of the practitioner's greatest challenges is to facilitate the blue collar couple's search for useful information about parenthood. It is essential for all parents to understand the importance of the first few years of life to the development of an individual. For example, babies who never develop a sense of trust in parents or other important adults in their lives, or young children who are never taught to share toys, can suffer from the resulting handicaps for many years in school, work, and family settings. Children do not require constant supervision from parents or day-care workers, but they do require love, understanding, and accessibility when brief and unanticipated teachable moments occur.

The success with which husbands and wives respond to the problems and opportunities of parenthood is reflected in the feelings and relationships of family members. High family solidarity includes sharing love, interests, viewpoints, and activities. If parents get satisfaction from accomplishment and awareness of personal growth, it is more likely that they will become increasingly satisfied and confident in their parent role. When parents are able to create and maintain family solidarity or togetherness while respecting the individuality of each family member, the benefits are both immediate and long term. The immediate benefits include the sense of nurturance that parents receive which helps to compensate them for the inevitable disruption and conflict that children cause periodically, especially during adolescence, and the support and encouragement that parents provide to the children as they strive to achieve a sense of selfhood. The long-term benefits include the good role models the parents provide, which profoundly influence their children's choices of career, recreation, and family life (Stone, 1962).

Marital dissatisfaction tends to reach a peak during the years when children are growing up and leaving, but their departure is only part of the reason for the dissatisfaction (Blood and Wolfe, 1960; Burr, 1970; Crosby, 1973; Rollins and Feldman, 1970). For example, the attitudes of lower-middle-class parents, especially wives, toward their marriage are more negative at this stage than in earlier or later years. Although there is evidence of general disillusionment and conflict with children, wives tend to express most dissatisfaction regarding relationships with their husbands. Their dissatisfaction partly reflects discrepancies in role expectations. Husbands tend to emphasize wives' performance and tasks as wives and mothers, and wives tend to emphasize husbands' performance as provider and idiosyncrasies such as wasteful hobbies.

Many middle-aged, lower-middle-class men emphasize their wives' virtues, and acknowledge that they do not meet their wives' expectations. The husbands also express regret that they did not spend more time with their children. It appears that early in marriage attention is focused on basic economic and family requisites and that after they are somewhat assured, there is an increase in attention to values such as companionship and expressiveness. Paradoxically, during a period when some husbands shift from instrumental achievement toward more expressive concerns, their wives (whose recent life has been dominated by expressive concerns as a wife and mother) shift toward more instrumental activities such as work outside the home. Although beliefs in support of traditional sex-role differentiation seem to be waning, emotional allegiance to traditional patterns remains strong among lower middle class couples (Lowenthal, Thurnher, and others, 1975; Blanck and Blanck, 1968).

For many mothers the end of childbearing occurs around age thirty and for most well before age forty. As a result, the youngest child entering school signifies a major transition period, especially for the mother who is not employed outside the home. After years of virtually full-time responsibility for the care of young children, the availability of a large amount of time each week when all the children are in school forces most nonworking mothers to rethink their interests, activity patterns, and roles. As the mother's age when the youngest child enters school has declined and as life expectancy has increased, many women can anticipate about half their lives remaining after their youngest child has entered school. In recent decades, an increasing proportion of mothers have obtained employment outside the home.

The proportion of mothers of school age children who combine homemaker and worker roles has increased relatively recently. However, there has been sufficient tested knowledge to indicate that under favorable conditions maternal employment need not have any major adverse effects on the children. Early studies found that maternal employment was associated with family friction, child neglect and maladjustment, delinquent behavior, and less time devoted to homemaking tasks and family social life (Blood, 1958). These early studies, however, disregarded social class differences, maternal dissatisfaction, and provision for child care. In more recent studies, where these characteristics have been similar for working and nonworking mothers, findings indicate that maternal employment itself does not adversely affect children (Orden and Bradburn, 1969; Wallston, 1973; Hoffman and Nye, 1974). Practitioners can help working mothers approach their dual roles in ways that minimize adverse effects on the children.

The large number of United States working wives with grown children is associated with varied but still discriminatory employment opportunities and with differentiated patterns of accommodation between worker and homemaker roles. These patterns of accommodation are in turn associated with social class level, the numbers and ages of children, paid household help, and employment opportunities for women, all of which are associated with community size and economic base. Perhaps the most influential factor in the satisfactoriness of wives working outside the home is the attitude of family members, especially the husband's.

There has been some shift during recent decades in societal acceptance of working wives, especially in white collar families, and this trend is likely to continue. In families in which the wife has strong career interests, the husband has sincere equalitarian attitudes, and all family members are willing to devote family time and money to achieve tasks traditionally performed by the homemaker, the woman's dual roles as worker and homemaker can be exceedingly satisfactory. For some women, the high level of satisfaction and fulfillment that is derived from outside work contributes to a more desirable quality of relationship with other family members that more than compensates for any reduction in quantity of contact and shift in family responsibilities that may result. The likelihood of this happy result is increased if the homemaker is able to handle the inescapable complexity and balancing of priorities, especially during this era in which well-established and generally accepted role expectations for this dual role are just evolving (Rapoport and Rapoport, 1965, 1971b). More and more women are learning how to do so and are sharing their conclusions with others.

In past generations the mother of young children who was employed outside the home typically had to achieve the transition to this dual role with little assistance. Currently it is becoming easier to make the transition to a dual role because of greater societal acceptance of such arrangements, more community and employer facilities such as day-care centers, and increased willingness by young couples to evolve appropriate family role relationships. As with many other developmental mechanisms, a transition period related to role changes entails adjustment and learning for the homemaker and for other family members, and the transition is more likely to be successful if the people associated with the transition learn and adapt in the process.

Conflict between Parents and Adolescents. If the youngest child's starting school marks the beginning of the transition between the young adulthood and middle-aged periods of the family life cycle, then the launching of children as they leave the family for work, marriage, or college completes the transition to middle age. The adjustment of each adolescent to young adulthood is unique. However, the first one or two children to do so present a special challenge because the parents lack experience.

Most adolescents strive to achieve a greater sense of
identity as mature self-reliant adults, to become productive
persons, and to be able to enter into intimate relationships with
others. Their assertiveness contributes to intergenerational conflict, which is reflected in the second peak for marital instability
between forty-one and forty-five years of age (F. B. Turner, 1954;
Paris and Luckey, 1966; Carter and Glick, 1970) and the rise
in adolescent suicides during the late teens (Jacobziner, 1965;
Dublin, 1963). The typical pattern is for an increase in intergenerational conflict from the early to the late teens, followed
by a lessening of conflicts between late adolescence and young
adulthood. There are of course many and varied exceptions,
such as early and easy adjustments for some families and explo-
sive breaches that are never resolved for others.

Relationships between adolescents and their parents tend
to be especially difficult around the time they leave school. When
adolescents graduate or drop out of high school, they confront
critical decisions regarding education, family relations, and
work. Decisions about further education include considerations
of academic ability and entrance requirements, personal interest
and program quality, costs and ability to pay. Decisions about
whether to continue to live at home include both considerations
of convenience and expense and desire to leave the setting associated with childhood. Decisions about work include considerations of type of job and of how to obtain a specific job.

During this period, the adolescents give up their sense
of secure dependence and idealized conception of their parents,
and their parents learn to accept their independent offspring,
sometimes with a touch of envy. A wide range of issues can
produce intergenerational conflict during this period, and there
are an infinite number of specific manifestations (Laing, 1971;
Bengston, 1970; R. Hill, 1965). One of the issues that cause
clashes between parents and adolescents is the issue of limits.
From the parents' viewpoint, the issue of limits includes when
to be firm and how to be permissive without implying lack of
concern. From the adolescent's viewpoint, the issue of limits
includes what to accept as a legitimate boundary and how to

pursue without too much guilt activities of which parents probably disapprove but that adolescents view as within their personal province. Another issue is participation in family activities.
From the parents' viewpoint the issue includes how much part
adolescents should take in family outings and chores and how
much they should participate in the decision making. From the
adolescent's viewpoint the issue includes how much to participate and how to deal with the almost inevitable discrepancy in
expectations. A third issue is communications. From the parents'
viewpoint the issue includes how much to ask about the adolescent's personal life, how much to reveal of one's own, and how
to keep the lines of communication open, especially during
stressful periods. From the adolescent's viewpoint the issue
includes how much to reveal, especially regarding controversial
matters. Although various and useful procedures are advocated
to deal with these types of issues, perhaps the essential ingredients are love and the patience that comes from an understanding of the transition that is occurring. Loving and accepting
parents encourage their offspring to become happy and extro-
verted people; rejecting parents help produce anxious and
introverted people (Siegelman, 1965).

   Little is known about how adolescents and their parents
share and mesh their interests during the transition from
adolescence to adulthood. It seems desirable for parents to
maintain a balance between control and permissiveness. They
must accept some assertiveness as an important way in which
adolescents establish an adult identity. If a satisfactory sense of
adult identity is not achieved at this stage, the individual is
likely to experience difficulty with subsequent stages of development until a sense of selfhood does develop.

   In addition to the personal experience, there is a societal
side of the transition to adulthood. Adolescents acquire the
values of the family and community while they are growing up.
When they have children of their own, almost all will reflect
the same values in their adult lives. During the transition,
however, many adolescents assert values that adult society believes in but does not always act on. In addition, because young

people may not know how to accomplish their objectives and have little power to do so, their attitudes and behavior can be quite negative. However, if middle-aged adults can tolerate adolescent challenges to their assumptions and authority and to those instances in which they do not practice what they preach, they can come to appreciate that the reassertion of values by the young makes an important contribution to cultural continuity and societal renewal (Ginott, 1969; Troll, Neugarten, and Kraines, 1969; P. Cameron, 1971; Boshier, 1973; Boshier and Thom, 1973; Rapoport and Rapoport, 1975).

Usually both parents and their children contribute to intergenerational conflict. Although all family members are typically involved, friction seems to occur most often between mothers and daughters (Bath and Lewis, 1962). Fathers' relationships with adolescent children have been studied far less often than relations between mothers and children. Contributions to conflict by parents and their adolescent children occur on both sides and interact. Adolescents contribute to friction with parents by behavior that conflicts with parental preferences, such as avoidance of responsibility, inconsiderate treatment of parents, and relations with peers or use of money that conflicts with parental admonitions. Parents contribute to friction with adolescents by having unclear or conflicting expectations, by being overly protective and restrictive, or by expecting adolescents to assume responsibilities that are too great or which they believe belong to the parents (McCord, McCord, and others, 1963; Whitmarch, 1965). If parents can combine increased independence and privileges for their adolescents with increased work and responsibilities, at a rate that adolescents want and can handle, their offspring may accept the change as evidence of a shift of emphasis from childhood to young adulthood, which facilitates their own transition. Adjustments by parents and adolescents help reduce the earlier parent-child tensions and improve interpersonal relationships generally (Powell, 1955). The emancipation process tends to be more effective for the mother with interests of her own than for the mother who views the impending empty nest as an unwanted and early retirement. Practitioners can help parents and adolescents understand this transition period so that both can contribute to solutions, not just to problems.

Marriage of Offspring. When a son or daughter is married, the parents acquire a daughter- or son-in-law and other in-laws. This tends to compound the parents' adjustment to the marriage of their offspring. In getting married their son or daughter commences the family life cycle as the parents did a generation earlier. However, the parents are now at the other end of the transaction as the ones left instead of the ones leaving. In addition, social change and a generation of living and personal change contribute to disparities between their outlook and that of the young couple. As was the case a generation earlier, a longer courtship and engagement period enables the parents to get to know the future in-law and his or her family. When this occurs the in-law relations are usually better than when there is little or no contact before the wedding.

Adjustments to in-laws are especially difficult for the wife who becomes a mother-in-law because she must make greater changes for the new mother-in-law role. Various factors tend to make the adjustment to children's spouses more difficult (Bossard and Boll, 1966). Among the sources of friction are: (1) a history of severe conflict with the offspring; (2) parents giving too much advice; (3) expecting to continue the type of relationship that existed before the son or daughter was married; (4) expecting the in-laws to have the same type of relationship as exists for the offspring; and (5) living together in the same household. Successful adjustment is aided by similarity in family economic, religious, and ethnic backgrounds; constructive helping patterns; and efforts by members of both generations to establish interpersonal relationships that facilitate need fulfillment and personal growth. Practitioners can also facilitate the adjustment by helping parents understand this transition.

Relations between Parents and Grandparents. The middle-aged couple with children entering adulthood also typically have parents entering old age. The members of the middle generation tend to become increasingly aware of their multi-generation family, especially when a wedding and a funeral occur close together or when heavy expenses for college for the

younger generation and for a serious illness for the older generation coincide. A member of the middle generation may decline
a job promotion that entails a distant move in deference to
children in high school or aging parents. On the other hand, a
major wedding anniversary for the grandparents can be a special
occasion for the extended family to assemble. In addition to
the memories, upset, and satisfactions that such events bring,
they highlight family continuity and tradition. Even though
geographic mobility has separated many families, there is still
much contact and assistance within families. Correspondence,
telephone calls, and sending tape recordings through the mail
help maintain contact. Visiting and vacation trips may be
initiated by each of the three generations. Such happy shared
experiences help offset resentful feelings by the oldest generation
that they are forgotten, by the middle generation that they are
overburdened, and by the younger generation that they are not
appreciated (Streib, 1965; Sussman, 1965; Vedder, 1965; Benaim
and Allen, 1967; Beresford and Rivlin, 1969; R. Hill and others,
1970; Franzblau, 1971; Kalish and Johnson, 1972).

In spite of the decline in recent generations in the proportion of living grandparents who live with their grown children or grandchildren, there is widespread evidence of modified
extended families that entail intergenerational contacts and
exchanges of help (Hill and others, 1970). The middle generation tends to influence the extent of family solidarity and contact
maintained by members of the extended family. Efforts to
achieve and preserve a desirable life-style are reflected in decisions about status changes related to marriage, work, education,
and allocation of resources. Recent generations have been increasingly responsive to planning and management of the family
life cycle. Extended family members, such as nephews, cousins,
aunts, and grandparents, more often live in Spanish-speaking,
American Indian, and black nuclear family households than
in white middle-class households. This partly reflects a low income level that precludes other living arrangements.

The stereotype of the white collar family is of the nuclear
family with little extended family contact, but the reality is of

modified extended families. Practitioners with an understanding of adult development can help members of all generations understand typical patterns of relationship among three- and four-generation families and explore ways in which their own extended family network can become more satisfactory for all concerned. Currently, special attention is being given to the middle generation.

The ten to twenty years between the time the youngest child leaves home and the onset of retirement typically entail fewer role changes and adjustments than occur during the earlier stage of middle age and young adulthood. Because of the trends toward younger parental age when the youngest child leaves home and longer life expectancy, most couples spend about one third of their married life without dependent children in their household (Glick, 1955; Hurlock, 1968). During the decade or two after these couples become a family of two again, they typically face adjustments to each other and to their aged parents. Some adults confront additional changes and adjustments during the decade or two before retirement, such as a major career change, a move to a new community, or singleness due to divorce or death of the spouse.

Many couples whose children leave home before the parents reach retirement must adjust to the loss of an active parent role, which was a major aspect of life for several decades, especially for the wife. Although the transition is gradual and can be anticipated as it approaches, adjustment can be difficult. However, for some couples with a satisfactory relationship, where the wife has career or other interests that compensate for reduced time devoted to motherhood, and where the husband is reducing his emphasis on career, the period before retirement can provide the time and resources for companionship and shared activities that may have been difficult to achieve in earlier years. Many other couples feel a growing disenchantment during the later years of marriage. This trend reflects a general drop in intimacy, marital satisfaction, and adjustment. Extent of sharing and sexual intercourse tends to reflect general adjustment regarding other forms of companionship and interaction (Pineo, 1961).

Quite aside from couples who experience separation, desertion, and divorce, there is considerable marital unhappiness during the decade or two before retirement, with the late forties and early fifties constituting a crisis period for married women and the fifties a crisis period for married men (Bossard and Boll, 1966; Hurlock, 1968).

Many couples must adjust to becoming grandparents at about the same time as they are adjusting to their aged parents. This can intensify feelings of being the generation in the middle. The younger generation of grown children, especially those who settle in distant communities, may become so absorbed in their welter of new tasks that there is a major decline in contact with their parents. This period of disengagement is sometimes punctuated by requests for assistance by the young couple. The aged generation has typically entered retirement and in some instances has become more dependent because of economic or health reverses. The prospect and the actuality of the death of one's parents present a dual dilemma for many middle-aged couples, a concern about imminent loss and a revival of mixed feelings about relations with parents that often have lain dormant since adolescence.

The adjustment of the middle-aged person to the elderly parent is affected by the social class levels of the two nuclear families, the condition of the elderly parent, the parent's living arrangements, and the history of intergenerational relationships. In families where both the middle-aged and the aged generations are blue collar, there is greater continuity of values and practices and more frequent contact, sometimes even a shared household, than is the case for white collar families (Sussman, 1960). Some middle-aged white collar persons who experienced upward social mobility from the blue collar family in which they grew up try to bury their past and thus have little contact with their aged parents. Aged parents with adequate finances and satisfactory health are more likely to experience a happy relationship with their middle-aged children than aged parents who constitute an actual or potential burden.

Most adults want to have contact with members of their extended family, including parents, grown children, and other relatives. However, most United States adults prefer to maintain separate households if possible. The three-generation household presents potential difficulties for all concerned. To function satisfactorily, members of each of the generations must usually make some adjustments. The members of the oldest generation confront adjustments from the responsibility and authority of being the head of a household to the secondary position of living in someone else's household. The members of the youngest generation confront adjustments to the sometimes differing values and expectations of two older generations. The members of the middle generation confront multiple adjustments related to increased burdens from and consideration for the older generation, intensification of in-law problems, the shift toward a more feminine household in many instances because of the greater longevity of women, greater interference in relations between middle and younger generations, and increased stress between husband and wife. When aged parents have severe financial and/or health limitations, the alternative to living in the household of a middle-aged offspring is often institutionalization. In making this choice, a trade-off must often be made between the financial burden and the burden of interpersonal relationships. Some middle-aged persons who place an aged parent in a nursing home have mixed feelings related to concern for their welfare, resentment of the financial burden, and guilt about not caring for the parent in the household.

The adjustment of the middle-aged adult to the elderly parent is influenced by their relationships in earlier years. Included are such factors as a loving and affectionate relationship generally, lack of feelings of rejection by parents during adolescence, parental approval of the marriage, and favorable attitudes toward in-laws (Cavan, 1965).

Grandparenting. As middle-aged adults become grandparents they typically add a new role relationship that can at least partly compensate for a diminished role relationship as parent. In recent generations of white collar families in the United States, grandparents tend to relate to their grandchildren in one of the following five ways (Neugarten and Weinstein, 1964):

1. *Fun-seeking.* Most grandparents prefer a "pleasure without responsibility" relationship with their grandchildren. It allows them to have fun with their grandchildren and avoid resistance to their advice as old-fashioned and unwanted interference. Instead they emphasize playful informality and restrain their impulses to give advice. This fun-seeking relationship is especially widespread for grandparents under the age of sixty-five.

2. *Formal.* Grandparents who have little significant interaction with grandchildren except special treats for special occasions have a similar but more restrained relationship than the fun-seeking grandparents.

3. *Parent substitute.* Grandmothers and sometimes grandfathers may assume responsibility for the care of grandchildren because of the absence of a parent due to death, divorce, or the necessity of working.

4. *Family wisdom.* Grandfathers and sometimes grandmothers may develop a relationship that emphasizes the provision of special knowledge, skills, or resources to grandchildren.

5. *Distant figure.* Especially when there is substantial geographic or social distance, some grandparents appear infrequently from afar for brief contact on special occasions with their grandchildren.

There are of course other less common relationships in white collar families. In blue collar families, for which there is less detailed tested knowledge and in which the grandparent more often lives in the household, grandparents may be transients, periodically visiting for months at a time; sick and cared for in the home; or hosts, offering their homes to the younger generations. Each kind of grandparent establishes differing relations with grandchildren. Many grandparents with two or more sets of grandchildren may have one relationship with a set of grandchildren who are geographically and socially close and another relationship with other sets of grandchildren. Relations with grandchildren also tend to change over the years as the grandchildren grow older and as the grandparents find the encounter less satisfying and come to prefer less contact and responsibility.

Encounters with grandchildren partly reflect the benefits that the grandparents receive. Especially for younger grandparents, satisfactions are associated with interest in and understanding of the activities and interests of the younger generation, stimulation from seeing old experiences reflected in young eyes, and active creation of a relaxed and mutual relationship between generations that is often more readily achieved by grandparents, who do not have to deal with the intensity of the parent-child relationship (Bossard and Boll, 1966). Some grandparents find their lives greatly enriched as a result of satisfactory relations with grandchildren. When it is not possible for grandparents and grandchildren to interact, foster grandparent arrangements allow both generations to gain some of the benefits (Saltz, 1971). Practitioners can help members of all generations understand grandparent relationships and ways in which they might become more satisfactory for those concerned.

In contrast with the early stages of marriage, which are characterized by many change events, there are few adjustments during the extended post-parental period, which averages about sixteen years. The nuclear family consists of only husband and wife, and the emphasis in family life shifts from coping with external changes to interpersonal relationships between the husband and wife. For example, lower-middle-class couples, particularly the husbands, who are still married just before retirement tend to experience an improvement in marital relationships after the departure of children. Companionship, emotional ties, and personal qualities receive more attention than role performance when spouses describe each other. Although preretirement couples anticipate increased sharing of activities, both recognize the potential for increased friction after retirement (Lowenthal, Thurnher, and others, 1975).

Retirement. Retirement presents another period of transition, change, and adjustment for most older adults. Although retirement and disengagement are also related to the occupational and community life cycles, there are some unique influences on family performance (McKain, 1968). Most American husbands confront the transition from worker to retiree during their sixties because the typical mandatory retirement age set by employers is about sixty-five. However, health problems may lower the retirement age for some workers, and special and scarce abilities may raise it for others. Most wives confront a form of retirement between five and twenty years before their husbands do, when the youngest child leaves home, and many obtain outside employment. In most instances the reduction in time devoted to the mother role is gradual and is replaced by time devoted to new or expanded activities such as employment, community organizations, and informal activities with family and friends. For many homemakers the transition entails feelings both of having lost satisfactions associated with care of dependent children, and of having gained freedom to pursue personal interests without the restrictions imposed by dependent children. Wives are often younger than their husbands; but because they tend to retire at an earlier age, their retirement from work typically occurs before that of their husbands. Thus the husband's retirement entails adjustments for the wife as well as the husband.

The male retiree typically spends more time around the house than he ever did before, except perhaps during periods of illness. If the retired husband is not prepared with new or expanded activities to replace the time devoted to employment until the abrupt start of retirement, the impact on the wife is like the addition of a dependent. One way a wife can help with this transition is assisting her husband to find attractive tasks that will provide him with a greater sense of usefulness and participation (Kerckhoff, 1964). This adjustment is somewhat easier in white collar families than in blue collar families because white collar husbands are more likely to accept home-related tasks as consistent with their self-concept as a man, and are more likely to have a history of shared leisure and recreational interests and activities with their wives (Kent, 1966). In general, if the retired couple's relationship has been mutually satisfactory over the years, then the great increase in the time the husband is in the home is likely to contribute to the happiness of both (Peterson and Payne, 1975). However, the onset of retirement is likely to increase the unhappiness of a long-standing frictional relationship (Lopata, 1966). If the wife has been employed before the husband's retirement, the pattern of adjustment will be affected, especially if the wife continues to work for some years. The relation between retirement and family life is also associated with the relative longevity of husband and wife. Because women live much longer than men, for couples over sixty-five about two thirds of the husbands are living with their wives compared with about one third of the wives who are living with their husbands. For those whose spouse dies around the time of retirement, the adjustment problems are typically multiplied.

Adjustment to retirement is associated with relationships with offspring. When contemporary retirees were young people, fewer people survived to old age and the family had the main responsibility for their care and support. Most of the elderly who were in old folks' homes or other institutions were there because they lacked offspring or were neglected by them. During the past three generations the burden of meeting elderly people's financial, health, nutritional, recreational, and companionship needs has shifted from the family to the government and organizations that provide assistance to the aged (Vedder and Lefkowitz, 1965).

Aging trends are reflected in living arrangements. Nearly 90 percent of those over sixty-four, whether married or widowed, maintain independent households. Living entirely alone is becoming increasingly widespread, especially for older women, over one fourth of whom (mostly widows) live alone. Many older people resent the decline in feelings of obligation toward parents and the little family contact and support that occurs.

Living in independent households or in institutional settings does not result in complete isolation from offspring. About 84 percent of the older people who have living children live less than an hour away from the nearest child, and a similar proportion see one of their children at least once a week. Many maintain some contact through phone calls and correspondence. The elderly from white collar families have greater contact with relatives, mostly their children, than do those from blue collar families. This reflects more equalitarian relations between generations and adequate resources to maintain contact from a distance.

The adjustment to retirement can be very difficult for older people who become dependent, such as husbands who retire from the role of family provider and assume a subordinate role in their wives' domains, and older adults who move into the households of their offspring and become dependent on them for financial support and companionship (Swenson, 1962). Institutionalization often entails similar adjustments to dependency (Kalish, 1971). Practitioners can help adults better understand and deal with retirement.

Relocation. A transition that can occur at any age is a community move. As with retirement, a move to a new community is related to occupational and community participation as well as to family activity, but there are some unique interactions with family life for married couples during the adult life cycle. At any stage of adulthood, the effectiveness of the adjustment to a new community is associated with: (1) previous experience with similar moves, (2) the attractiveness of the move, (3) the distance moved, (4) the similarity of the new community, and (5) the availability of people and organizations in the new community to help the couple establish a social life.

The general task that confronts a couple of any age when they move to a new community is to become established, to put down roots, to feel at home there. Except for retirees, having a satisfactory job and acceptable housing in the new community are necessary but not sufficient conditions for making the transition. Some of the additional adjustments relate to withdrawal from the old community, such as ending a lease or selling a house and phasing out responsibilities and relationships with organizations, family, and friends that cannot be maintained after the move. Other adjustments relate to the new set of interpersonal relationships that adults establish in a new community. When a couple moves, they at least have each other for companionship when they first settle in the new community. As each partner meets new people through work, neighborhood, and organizations, a selection process occurs as the couple and others take the initiative to become better acquainted. The new couple in town develops their circle of friends out of this pool of acquaintances. The process is compounded when each partner finds different people congenial in making new friends.

The process of transition to a new community differs somewhat between blue collar and white collar families. More blue collar families move because of a problem in the old community—such as a reduction in work opportunities—reluctantly leaving family, friends, and familiar surroundings. During the past two generations, this displacement has been dramatically illustrated during the 1930s depression and during the postwar migration from rural to urban areas caused by automation in farm and factory. The choice of the community to move to is influenced by the places where the blue collar family already has family and friends who tell them about opportunities and help them get established. The people the couple gets to know in the new community are typically associated with neighborhood, work, and perhaps church. Adjustment can be especially difficult, for example, for families that move from rural Puerto Rico to New York City, when they have been very dependent on the extended family at home.

White collar families are more likely to move because of an attractive opportunity in the new community, the experiences of aeronautical engineers, middle-aged executives, and history professors in the early 1970s notwithstanding. Many white collar families accept a move more easily because of their satisfactory experience with earlier family moves and a cosmopolitan interest related to reading, travel, and college experience. The move is often facilitated by: (1) their own financial resources, (2) help with moving expenses by employers, (3) use of community services to help make the transition, and (4) the greater likelihood that they will know some people in a new community because of varied social contacts during the years. In addition, white collar families typically join community organizations, which helps them become oriented to the new community and make new friends.

The transition process varies somewhat from stage to stage in the community life cycle. For young couples with no children, no home to sell, and little furniture to move, the move to a new community may seem like an adventure, with homesickness occurring only if there were very close family ties. In a family with only preschool children, the mother may get to know the neighborhood but experience difficulty adjusting to the larger community. Elementary school children help expand the family acquaintances through their friends and youth groups. Adolescents tend to resist a move, especially during their last few years of high school when relations with peers and the culmination of high school activities are so important to them. Especially for couples who have not moved before, a move after the children have left home may seem undesirable because of the departure from old friends whose companionships may be even more important after the offspring are grown. Couples who can afford to move to a retirement community weigh the gain of services and fellowship with older adults against the loss of old friendships and familiar surroundings.

For families at any stage of the life cycle, communities provide assistance to newcomers through such groups as the Chamber of Commerce, religious groups, and employers. Forms of assistance include local directories, invitations to join social groups, help with housing or other arrangements, and just friendly efforts to help newcomers to feel welcome. Practitioners can recognize instances when such assistance is inadequate and take the initiative to expand services to facilitate the transition for newcomers.

Other Family Patterns

The foregoing descriptions of developmental processes related to family performance during adulthood were confined to adults who marry, have children, and live together until retirement. There are, however, many other patterns of the family life cycle. Included are couples who never have children, adults who marry for the first time in middle age and then have children, marriages that end in separation, divorce, or early death of the spouse, new family arrangements that result from remarriage, and adults who never marry. During the past two generations, as there has been an increase in divorce and in employment of women, there has also been an increase in alternative living arrangements that adults can consider. Because this differentiation is more recent, there is far less tested knowledge about these family life cycle patterns than there is about the more typical pattern in which a couple has children in young adulthood, launches them in middle age, and then becomes a family of two again. However, because a variety of life-styles and family patterns are emerging and because family role performance varies accordingly, it is important at least briefly to describe other major family patterns. During the past decade there has been increasing attention to emerging forms and future directions for family life (Bernard, 1966; Otto, 1970; Alpenfels, 1971; Nye and Berardo, 1973; Bowman, 1974; Eshleman, 1974). Because these new family patterns are less usual than the typical pattern, those who follow them tend to receive less assistance from mass media and shared experience from others who have followed the same pattern. Therefore, practitioners can be especially helpful by assisting those who follow the new patterns to understand the particular pattern they are pursuing and ways to make it as satisfactory as possible, in some instances by changing to another family pattern and in other instances by making the selected pattern function more satisfactorily.

Childless Couples. Couples who never have children of their own and do not adopt them remain childless because of either inability or choice. Some couples fail in their attempts to have children but do not obtain medical help to find out why and overcome the obstacle, perhaps by using fertility medication. The resulting frustration can lead to marital conflict. Similar conflict can result when the couple want children and are unable to have them, but one or both of them are unwilling or unable to adopt children. Couples who choose not to have children do so for various reasons; for example, both husband and wife have careers they do not want to affect by having children, they are unwilling to assume the responsibility for rearing children, or they want to avoid transmitting a congenital defect to offspring.

Some childless marriages are very full and satisfying. A childless marriage is more likely to be satisfactory if both partners prefer not to have children, and if the wife has some major interests to give her life meaning and direction. During young adulthood when other young wives are heavily involved in motherhood and ambitious young husbands are heavily engaged in work, a childless wife is likely to have a special need for companionship from her husband. As with single adults, childless couples may gain satisfaction from relations with nieces and nephews. In middle age, contemporary childless couples usually realize that the lack of children does not threaten the security of their old age. They may even conclude that the lack of child-rearing expenses allows them to accumulate increased retirement income. Any regrets about not having children are likely to center on loss of richness of experience in the present and lack of connection with the future (Veevers, 1973).

Late Marriages. Those who marry for the first time during their thirties or beyond delay marriage for various reasons, such as (1) to complete extensive formal education and become established in a career, (2) to care for an ill or aged parent, (3) to complete a prison sentence, (4) to resolve emotional problems, (5) to enjoy independence before settling down to marriage, (6) to locate a mutually satisfactory marriage partner, or (7) to pursue undistracted an all-consuming career interest.

Unlike those people who marry after forty, those who do so for the first time during their thirties usually marry someone similar in age. It appears that those who marry for the first time during their thirties experience as much marital adjustment and happiness as those who do so during their twenties and substantially more than those who marry in their teens.

Most of the couples who marry for the first time during their thirties have children. There are few generalizations about how they approach marriage and parenthood in contrast with those who marry between eighteen and twenty-five. The somewhat older parent tends to be less casual and more concerned about parenthood, an approach that can have benefits (such as serious attention to the child's needs) and liabilities (such as overprotectiveness). In general, few people who marry for the first time during their thirties attempt to remake their partners, there is an emphasis on companionship, and their prospects for marital happiness are excellent.

Atypical Patterns. Some family patterns lack some of the ingredients typically associated with family life. Examples include common-law marriages, unmarried parents, and older orphans.

The common-law marriage, in which a man and woman live together without any legal-religious marriage ceremony and usually have children, has occurred for many generations and has accumulated much social and legal precedent. Such arrangements have often been casual in urban areas, but they can be very durable, especially in rural areas. In some low-income Spanish-speaking families, the practice has been termed consensual union.

During the past decade, instances of the consensual union, often without children, appear to be increasing among white collar, as well as blue collar, young adults. Unmarried parents are those who were never married but have and care for children. Most of them are unwed mothers. There appears to be an increase in the proportion of unwed mothers who keep their babies. This reflects a decrease in social stigma and an increase in family acceptance compared with a few generations ago. Changing adoption practices and life-styles also appear to be widening the range of people who are unmarried parents or guardians. In some instances, families contain no parents, such as when children are orphaned and one of the oldest siblings is old enough to become the head of the household. Each of these atypical family patterns presents some unique problems for all concerned, but there is too little tested knowledge available to describe typical functioning or identify influences on effective functioning under the circumstances.

Divorce. Some marriages end in divorce. Such marriages share many characteristics with all other marriages, but have some characteristics that are related to their termination in divorce and to adjustments by the couple to divorce. The general trend for most United States couples during the first two decades of marriage is toward increasing disenchantment and a decline in marital adjustment and satisfaction (Pineo, 1961; Rollins and Feldman, 1970). Although there is an increase in marital satisfaction in the postparental period, about one out of five married couples living together state that they are actively unhappy or dissatisfied with their life (Jacobson, 1959; Campbell and Converse, 1975). Many divorces end a relationship characterized by marital maladjustment and conflict that many married couples continue to endure. In addition to marriages that terminate in divorce, there are many not included in divorce statistics that in effect terminate through annulment, legal or informal separation, or desertion.

Divorce has become increasingly widespread in the past fifty years (Carter and Glick, 1970). In 1920 the annual divorce rate was 8 per 1,000 married women. There was a decline during the 1930s Depression and a sharp rise to 17 per 1,000 married women following World War II. The divorce rate declined to about 10 per 1,000 married women during the 1950s and early 1960s and then began to rise sharply to its present unprecedented high. Because the total population has been expanding, the number of divorce decrees in 1969 exceeded the former peak in 1946, even though the rate in 1969 was only 13 per 1,000 married women. At that time about 15 percent of the men and 17 percent of the women under seventy years of age who had ever been married had been divorced. Current best estimates are that about one third of United States marriages end in divorce.

Divorce, as well as desertion, is more common in urban and suburban areas than in rural areas. Divorce and separation rates are higher for blue collar families than for white collar families (Udry, 1966; U.S. Census, 1973b). The divorce rate among men declines with level of education and income. Women with four years of college have the lowest divorce rates, and those with five or more years of college have the highest divorce rates. The rates are higher for nonwhites than for whites, and for nonwhites the divorce rate increases with the level of formal education, but the separation rate decreases.

The ages with the highest divorce rates are understandably related to the periods of greatest marital conflict and unhappiness in the early twenties and early forties. The peak year for separations is the first year of marriage and for divorces, the third (Paris and Luckey, 1966). Two fifths of all divorce decrees are granted to couples married less than five years (U.S. Census, 1975). There are more divorces among childless couples than among couples with children, partly because childless couples do not have to deal with the problems of child care and support after the divorce (Goode, 1964). When divorced couples do have children, they tend to be young. In over half of all divorces, the children were under seven years of age when their parents were divorced.

Although the peak age at divorce is in the early twenties, and the rate gradually declines until a secondary peak in the forties, divorce occurs throughout adulthood, and half of all divorces occur when the couples are between their mid-thirties and their mid-fifties. The median number of years of marriage at the time of divorce is more than seven, compared with a median duration of about five years in 1950, but in many of these instances the number of years of functioning marriages is about four years less because of extended periods of separation or desertion before the official divorce decree. Because the peak number of years of marriage at the time of divorce is three, followed by a gradual decline with the exception of a secondary peak after about twenty years, the median of more than seven years of marriage at the time of divorce is an average that applies to very few who are divorced. Very few divorces occur after age fifty-five. When they do they typically reflect long-standing problems and resentments combined with the removal of constraints related to children or finances.

The experiences and influences associated with a divorce are typically complex. People who are divorced vary greatly in the main factors that are associated with the divorce. A divorce is usually the result of multiple causes even though one may seem dominant.

Some causes of divorce are related to courtship and marriage. Compared with marriages that do not end in divorce, a higher proportion of divorced couples entered marriage under the following circumstances: (1) a very brief period of courtship or engagement that provided too little opportunity to get to know each other and prospective in-laws; (2) major differences in religious or ethnic backgrounds of the two families; (3) marriage at a very young age (teenage marriages have twice the divorce rate that marriages during the twenties have); (4) forced marriage as a result of pregnancy; (5) overly romantic and unrealistic expectations about marriage; and (6) unsatisfactory marital role models, usually because either or both of the parental couples had unhappy marriages (Levinger, 1966; L. G. Burchinal, 1965; Prince, 1962; Hauser and Hobart, 1964; Lowrie, 1965; J. T. Landis, 1963).

A major cause of unhappy marriages is unhappy people. Poorly adjusted, unhappy people with emotional problems often get married with the hope that marriage will solve their problems and make them happy. The result is usually the reverse. The responsibilities and tensions associated with marriage generally contribute to personal and marital maladjustment that increase the likelihood of divorce. In comparison with couples who are reasonably happily married, a much higher proportion of divorced people are characterized as tense, hypercritical, or depressed. Some divorced adults are poorly adjusted generally (Pinard, 1966).

The experience that the partners had with their siblings during childhood is also associated with extent of divorce and separation. Men who were only children have the highest divorce rate, which may reflect pampering; women who were only children have the lowest divorce rate, which may reflect close association with homemaking. Men who were the oldest of their siblings have lower divorce rates than women who were the oldest. In traditional marriage patterns, the early assumption of responsibilities of an oldest boy helps him become an effective father and husband; being an oldest girl helps with parenthood but contributes to marital friction (E. Hall, 1965), probably because being an oldest child makes it more difficult to accept a subservient relationship.

Other influences on divorce are associated with family functioning. Early parenthood reduces the time available for marital adjustment before having to deal also with parenthood, and it is associated with higher divorce rates (Christensen, 1963). When marital disagreements result in withdrawal of affection by either or both partners, the progressive decline in understanding and cooperation that typically ensues contributes to the deterioration of the relationship and sometimes divorce. Additional influences on divorce that are associated with interpersonal relations include extreme striving for success, differential type or rate of change by either or both partners, and inadequate emphasis on family activities.

The level of the divorce rate reflects these personal and interpersonal characteristics of couples, but it also reflects societal factors that either encourage or discourage partners in an unhappy marriage to seek to end it by divorce. These societal factors include the extent of religious and societal acceptance of divorce, the availability of employment opportunities for women that provide a viable alternative to an unhappy marriage, and the existence of various life-styles that provide a contrast to a specific marital situation.

The reasons given by wives who apply for divorce vary between white collar and blue collar families. White collar wives refer mainly to psychological and emotional reasons, such as excessive demands, lack of love, and infidelity. Blue collar wives refer mainly to physical and economic reasons, such as drink, abuse, and financial problems. Other reasons given by wives include mental cruelty and neglect of home and children. Husbands refer to sexual incompatibility and difficulties with in-laws as reasons for divorce (Levinger, 1966). The personality characteristics of men who divorce are similar to the personality characteristics of men who remain married, but this is not the case for women, who in the past have been expected to make more personal adjustments on behalf of the marriage than men. Women who are divorced in middle age tend to have had personality characteristics in adolescence that contrast markedly with the adolescent personality characteristics of women who remained married. Those who remained married had been characterized during adolescence as both submissive and productive, both conventional and prone to intellectual pursuits. Those who were most happily married had been characterized as low in independence and self-indulgence and high in conventionality. By contrast, those who were divorced had been characterized in adolescence as self-indulgent, nonconforming, negativistic, and rebellious.

There are also shifts in reasons for divorce at various stages of the family life cycle. For example, divorce is associated with premarital pregnancy in the twenties, adultery in the thirties, and drink in the forties. (There are undoubtedly instances in which the reasons for divorce are positive and promote growth for both parties, and the dissolution of the marriage is amicable, but these instances are seldom reflected in the records of marriage counselors and divorce courts.)

Divorce is usually traumatic for all concerned. For many people, it is even more upsetting than the death of a spouse because of the social attitudes toward divorce and the tension and bitterness that typically precede it. General life satisfaction is typically lower for divorced and separated adults than for any other category (Campbell and Converse, 1975). This difficult adjustment is reflected in the high rates of admissions to mental hospitals for adults during the postdivorce period (Pinard, 1966). For younger adults, the end of a long marriage is more traumatic than the end of a short one, for older adults the pattern is reversed (Goode, 1956). For younger adults a divorce following a short marriage can be viewed as correcting a mistake, and a divorce following a longer marriage is more likely to involve children and major adjustments. For older adults a divorce following a long marriage tends to resolve a long-standing conflict, and a divorce following a short marriage tends to entail dashed hopes. There are many specific adjustments that affect most people associated with a divorce, including (1) apprehension about a forthcoming divorce, (2) the divorce itself, (3) the use of the child as a weapon by one parent against the other, (4) changed feelings, (5) implications of personal and family failure, (6) children living with one parent, (7) attitudes by peers, and (8) remarriage (J. T. Landis, 1963).

Concern about the welfare of the children is a major consideration when couples consider divorce. This is understandable because marital conflict is upsetting to children, and divorce can be damaging to the self-concept of the child, especially when it entails great uncertainty and divided loyalties. However, when the husband and wife are emotionally divorced but continue to reside together amid great conflict, the damage to the child can be even greater (Despert, 1953; Goode, 1964; J. T. Landis, 1963). Adolescents from broken homes tend to be better adjusted than those from unbroken, unhappy families (Perry and Pfuhl, 1963).

A divorce typically produces major adjustments for all affected. Various types of practitioners are usually associated with the process, from fields such as law, social work, education, employment, finance, and mental health. As in several other major adult role changes such as retirement, practitioners who deal with divorce-related matters must recognize that fragmentation of advice and assistance can easily occur. Practitioners with an understanding of adult development can try to keep in mind that each person affected by a divorce must somehow accommodate the multiple adjustments and pressures. Several types of practitioners who share a developmental approach can more readily cooperate and help family members learn, adapt, and grow so that the divorce process is as little destructive and as much constructive as possible (J. Epstein, 1974).

Widowhood. Most marriages end because of the death of a spouse. Becoming a widow or a widower can occur at any stage of the family life cycle. However, the proportion of marriages that end because of the death of a spouse is very small during the first year of marriage, increases gradually through middle age, and accelerates through old age (see Figure 8). The trends for men and women differ, as do the adjustment problems at various stages of the adult life cycle.

Although Figure 8 is cross-sectional, showing the proportion of all adults who are currently widows or widowers, it provides an estimate of the increasing likelihood with each passing year that a marriage will be ended by the death of a spouse. To describe this age trend more accurately for individuals, it would be necessary to remove the influence of the societal trend for more people to survive until old age. At the turn of the century, widowhood for men in young adulthood

Figure 8. Widowhood: Percent by Age Category

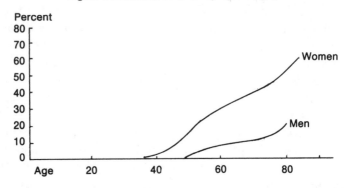

Source: U.S. Census (1973a).

was more common than now because wives often died in child-birth, and more common for both husband and wife in middle age. Today there is a higher proportion and a much higher number of adults who experience the death of a spouse for the first time in old age.

The death rates for successive age categories of husbands are higher than those for wives, reflecting the impact of military service, fatal accidents driving and at work, and higher death rates from causes such as circulatory illness and alcoholism, especially in the older years. As a result, with each passing year of age, an increasingly higher proportion of married women lose their husbands due to death. For the older population, there are more than 130 wives who have been widowed for every 100 husbands who have become widowers, not taking into account remarriages. The death rates are higher for blue collar families and for nonwhites, in part reflecting poorer nutrition and health and more hazardous conditions at home and work. Because the death of a spouse is a more widespread occurrence for older couples than for younger couples, there are differences as well as similarities in the way in which survivors cope with the adjustment at various stages of the family life cycle.

In contrast with other adult role change adjustments, the death of a spouse typically occurs abruptly. There is usually little time between finding out the likely time and cause of death of a spouse and its actual occurrence. This is especially so during young adulthood when the proportion of deaths from fatal accidents is higher than it is from chronic illnesses.

There are many and severe adjustment problems that confront a husband or wife who experiences the death of a spouse at any age (Cavan, 1963; Berardo, 1970; Lopata, 1973). The period just before the death of a spouse and the grieving afterward are very difficult. In addition, the survivor typically confronts problems related to economic security, loneliness, and social relationships. Widowhood usually worsens the family financial situation, whether the survivor is the husband or the wife. Medical and funeral expenses reduce savings or increase debt. If the husband or a working wife dies, family income is reduced. When the wife dies, there is increased expense to replace some of the services she provided. Preparation in the form of social security benefits, insurance policies, and savings can substantially reduce the financial adjustment problem of widowhood. The problem of loneliness is more difficult to plan for and cope with. Except when marital love and affection has been entirely replaced by bitterness and resentment, the death of a spouse is accompanied by a great feeling of loss and a void related to formerly shared activities. This loneliness is intensified when the survivor depended heavily on the departed partner and is somewhat alleviated if the surviving partner has close and satisfying social relationships with friends and relatives (Adams, 1971). However, social relations with in-laws and with friends who were closer to the departed partner tend to be reduced with widowhood, especially for activities with couples. Survivors of happy marriages tend to idealize the departed spouse, miss them, preserve their memories, and reduce the resulting loneliness through social participation or remarriage. Survivors of unhappy marriages tend to find relief and liberation with the death of the resented spouse, and although there may be some guilt associated with these feelings, widowhood seems relatively attractive by contrast with the unhappy marriage.

For the white collar widow, adjustment problems vary somewhat depending on whether the husband died during young adulthood, middle age, or old age. The young widow from a white collar family typically has insurance benefits or other financial resources to use during the transition and at least some post-high school education that helps her obtain a satisfactory job. Especially when there are several young children to raise, less expensive housing and a reduced standard of living are likely. The transition from full-time homemaker to working mother may require difficult adjustments. Adjustment problems and loneliness are usually further intensified by unfulfilled sexual desires. For widows under thirty-five who want to remarry, the prospects are relatively good, but prospects decline thereafter. Wives who become widows in middle age typically have fewer child-care problems than young adult widows, but they have similar problems with employment, reduced standard of living, and sexual fulfillment. Widowhood in old age is widespread and expected by most white collar wives. Neither child care nor employment are major aspects of the transition. The period after the death of the spouse is a likely time for a change in housing arrangements, such as moving to a smaller house or apartment, moving in with relatives, institutionalization, or moving to a retirement community. Sexual fulfillment may decline as a problem, but physical attention, affection, and concern remain.

The blue collar widow confronts similar adjustment problems, depending on her age when her husband died, but she typically has fewer resources available. Her extended family usually provides a larger proportion of support and assistance than white collar families. Because of her more limited resources, the financial crisis occurs soon after the death of her husband. Her limited formal education places most well-paying jobs beyond reach, unless she acquires further education as an adult. She may already have experience as a working mother, or she may know about the experience of acquaintances who are raising children without a husband due to widowhood, desertion, separation, or divorce. The trends for blue collar wives who become widows during middle and old age are similar to those for white collar wives, although financial and social resources are more limited, except for support provided by the extended family with whom the older widow is likely to share a household.

The white collar widower with young children confronts a major disruption to family life. Unless there is an older daughter who can perform part of the homemaker role, the options include a housekeeper, boarding house, or remarriage. Although there is typically no decline in income, expenses often rise somewhat. Loneliness is a major problem, but sexual desires are more readily fulfilled for the widower than for the widow. It is the psychological and social adjustments that are most important and difficult for men whose wives die during middle and old age.

The blue collar widower confronts similar problems to those of the white collar widower, but his options are limited by his resources. If he has young children and does not remarry soon, it is likely that they will be raised by relatives who are willing to take them into their homes. Other options include a substitute homemaker in the form of an older daughter, or the widower's mother or aunt. Isolation is a major problem for many aged widowers (Berardo, 1970).

More than half of those who are widowed do not remarry during the subsequent five years. Many never do. If they had no children, the remainder of their lives tends to be similar to what it would have been if they had remained single, except for memories, in-laws, and other legacies from their departed spouse. If they are widowed with young children, they confront problems of raising them alone. Many widowed parents find it helpful to meet with other parents without partners, to benefit from discussion of shared problems. Aside from useful ideas and social support, such groups sometimes result in friendships that lead to remarriage. Most of those who remain widowed for more than ten years have satisfactorily adjusted to singleness. Those who are widowed in old age may confront severe adjustment problems because the loss is so great, and adaptability is more restricted than in earlier years.

As with divorce and retirement, widowhood affects many domains of life and entails contact with various practitioners whose efforts should be as well coordinated as possible (Hunt,

1966). Because widowhood is so widespread, it seems desirable for practitioners to emphasize planning for widowhood in the contact they have with clients during adulthood. Such planning can include not only matters related to funeral arrangements and financial provision, but also matters related to social and leisure activities in family and community (Silverman, 1973). Educational and counseling services can assist adults at both the planning stage before widowhood and the adjustment stage afterward.

Remarriage. Remarriage by adults who were widowed or divorced is fairly widespread. In more than one out of five marriages each year, it is a remarriage for one or both of the new partners. In recent years, most of those who were divorced were married only once, almost one out of five had married twice, and a small proportion had married three times or more. The pattern of remarriage varies between the widowed and the divorced. As with single adults, after about thirty years of age there is a decline for each successive age group in the proportion of divorced and widowed adults who remarry. There are peaks around twenty, thirty, and forty-five years of age (Goode, 1964; Udry, 1966). The remarriage rates decline faster for women than for men (Jacobson, 1959). Men are about four times more likely to remarry. The remarriage rates are highest for the divorced, somewhat lower for the never married at comparable ages. During the past forty years, there has been a gradual increase in the remarriage rate. For example, for women who were widowed or divorced between thirty and thirty-four years of age, 4 percent remarried within a few years in 1940, compared with 11 percent in 1970.

A higher proportion of divorced adults remarry within five years than is the case for those who are widowed. Half of the men and one quarter of the women who are widowed are remarried within five years of the death of the spouse (Goode, 1956; P. H. Landis, 1950). By contrast, about three quarters of divorced adults remarry within five years after the divorce (Jacobson, 1959; Udry, 1966). In recent years it appears that about four out of five of those who divorce eventually remarry. This sooner remarriage for divorced adults reflects "triangles" in which one partner seeks the divorce in order to remarry, the period of separation or desertion that often precedes the divorce, the somewhat younger average age for divorce, and the tendency of some divorced adults to try to solve their adjustment problems by remarrying. Divorced men tend to remarry several years sooner than divorced women, partly because fewer of the men have custody of children who can be an impediment to remarriage (Bernard, 1956). Divorced adults are more likely to marry a divorced adult than one who is widowed or single (Goode, 1964).

When adults remarry during their forties, they typically marry someone about their own age. However, when they remarry during their fifties, they often marry someone substantially younger. Three quarters of the men in their fifties marry younger women; almost one out of twenty of the new wives are more than thirty years younger. Many of those who remarry in middle age seek to regain youth through their young spouse. The rate of remarriage, as well as divorce, is higher for blue collar than for white collar families.

The process of remarriage typically differs in several ways from the original marriages. When a woman remarries, the courtship period is shorter and the wedding is usually less elaborate, with fewer people, less expense, and a shorter wedding trip. When a single woman marries a man who was previously married, the courtship and wedding are more similar to that for two previously unmarried adults.

A crucial question regarding remarriage is, how successful is it? The answer depends on whether the remarriage is compared with a seldom-achieved ideal, the earlier marriage, or living without a spouse. One indicator of failure is the divorce rate for those who remarry. The divorce rate is half again as high for remarriages as for first marriages, and the divorce rate for remarried women is somewhat higher than for remarried men. The average length of marriage for divorcees decreases with each marriage. Remarriage for widows is more stable than for women who are divorced. Financial problems tend to be greater for remarriages, especially between divorced persons (P. H. Landis, 1950; Jacobson, 1959; Eshleman, 1974).

In most remarriages there are children involved. Three quarters of the women who remarry have custody of their children by a previous marriage, as do one third of the men who remarry. About one quarter of remarried couples have children from that marriage. There are often major problems of adjustment between stepchildren and stepparents, which can be especially difficult if the stepparent was never a parent. These adjustments tend to be more effective when the children are young.

Some of the major influences on the success of remarriages are: (1) fairly realistic expectations about what is important in marriage, based on experience from the earlier marriages, along with strong motivation to succeed; (2) adequate financial resources; (3) moderate societal acceptance of remarriage, especially in urban areas; (4) lack of many dependent children; and (5) emphasis on companionship and meeting the needs of both partners.

There are some aspects of remarriage that are associated with the stage of the adult life cycle at which it occurs. Remarriage during young adulthood typically entails problems related to the preceding divorce, such as finances and acceptance of stepparents by their school-aged stepchildren. However, the divorce rate is lower for young adults than for middle-aged remarriages. Middle-aged remarriages typically entail problems related to adjustments to each other and to altered living patterns. For older adults, remarriage provides the prospect of companionship. However, the major problem is that there are millions more older women than older men. For the older widow or divorcee who wants to remarry, the problem is compounded by the tendency for older men to become remarried to women who are much younger than they are (P.H. Landis, 1950; Bossard, 1951; Eshleman, 1974).

Concern about remarriage, especially in connection with divorce, tends to center on its impact on the children and the person who remarries. In most instances, remarriage is not harmful to the children; their adjustment to stepfathers tends to be somewhat better than their adjustment to stepmothers. More than nine out of ten remarried mothers report that the lives of their children are the same or improved following the remarriage (Perry and Pfuhl, 1963).

Most remarriages are satisfactory, even though personality problems are somewhat more prevalent among divorcees than among those who do not divorce, and divorce rates for remarriages are somewhat higher. For most divorced adults who remarry, the major problems with the first marriage concerned interaction with the first mate. Many people whose interaction with their first mate led to frustration and divorce achieve fulfillment and a successful marriage with another mate. Most people learn something from an unsuccessful marriage that they can apply if they remarry. Furthermore, a second marriage of a divorcee is usually compared with a first one that was dissolved in conflict. About nine out of ten remarried divorced mothers report that their present married life is much better than the former marriage (Goode, 1956; Eshleman, 1974). Practitioners can be especially helpful in helping those who remarry better understand their earlier marital experience so that it contributes to the success of the subsequent marriage.

Single Adulthood. About one out of twelve United States adults have never been married. The majority of single adults are men, mainly because young men marry later than young women. Because of women's greater longevity, a majority of older unmarried adults are women. Because of population growth, the number of single adults has been increasing, even though up until a decade ago the proportion was decreasing (Reiss, 1966). In recent years there has been an increase in persons between twenty-five and thirty-four years of age who have never married. Some single adults marry during middle age and beyond. Most adults who never marry remain single by choice. The paths that single adults follow through life contrast in various respects with those of adults who marry and have children.

During adolescence, boys assume that they will marry but are typically more concerned about deciding on and preparing for an occupation. By contrast, adolescent girls place far more emphasis on marriage in their plans and self-concept. Some girls marry while in high school or college or immediately after graduation, but many prefer to work a year or two and look around before getting married (Christensen and Swihart, 1956). When single adults leave their parents' homes, they seldom return to live there. Those women who do not marry by their late twenties confront some unfavorable stereotypes, although this is less so today than it was a generation or two ago. Most single women in their twenties state that they want to marry, whether they are working or not (Chilman and Meyer, 1966). The recent trend toward later first marriages appears to be a delay of marriage, not a commitment to remain single. At about thirty many single women become less optimistic that they will become married and shift their goals and interests to work and a pattern of life that does not include marriage (Doty and Hoeflin, 1964). As thirty approaches many women feel an increase in anxiety, which then decreases as there is an adjustment to new life patterns and goals. Some do not resign themselves to remaining single and join groups and organizations where they are likely to meet eligible bachelors. The attractiveness of marriage is especially high for lonely young adults with low self-esteem or other maladjustments who hope that marriage will help them solve their psychological problems. It often has the opposite effect.

It is likely that there is a parallel explanation for men who remain bachelors; however, there have been few studies of unmarried men, so most of the literature reflects speculation and stereotypes. The family background and several personality traits of married and never-married males tend to be very similar (Rallings, 1966). However, situational factors seem less influential on extended bachelorhood than for women during recent generations, and it seems likely that personality characteristics and personal preferences mainly account for those men who remain single. Although the personality characteristics of single women tend to be similar to those who marry, this is not the case for men. As adolescents, men who remain single tend to be characterized as less conventional and compliant and more independent and negativistic than those who subsequently marry. Those who marry tend to have been more liked and liking and more gregarious, warm, and giving than men who remain single.

There are various reasons why some men and women remain single; some reasons are related to adolescent experiences, and some are related to adult options. There have been very few studies of single men. However, among college graduates, when married women were compared with unmarried women, more of the single women had the following characteristics: (1) grew up in blue collar families so that upward social mobility interfered with marriage; (2) had major family obligations before twenty-five; (3) rebelled against strong family pressure to become married; (4) had less culturally approved heterosexual activity between sixteen and twenty-five years of age; (5) were more variable in self-esteem, with some very high and some very low; and (6) were academically competitive as a means of upward mobility (Klemer, 1954).

Some of the reasons men and women remain single reflect the options and choices they confront as adults. Included are feelings of self-sufficiency, disillusionment, family responsibilities, unwillingness to divide time between family and career, and inadequate access to eligible and attractive prospects for marriage (Chilman and Meyer, 1966; Doty and Hoeflin, 1964; Rallings, 1966). The greater tendency for white collar men to marry blue collar women than for blue collar men to marry white collar women increases the proportions of white collar women and blue collar men who remain single.

In middle age, the circumstances and prospects associated with singleness differ for men and women. Single men can devote the time, effort, and money that might otherwise have been spent on family life on occupational activities that are likely to provide both satisfaction and reward in middle age. Responsibility for aging parents is more likely to be financial than direct care. If the single man decides to marry in middle age, the prospects are much greater than for the single woman of the same age. Some single women also strive for occupational achievement, many for the same reasons as single men, but some to compensate for lack of acceptance and satisfaction in family roles. Single women with intense upward mobility strivings and high occupational achievement can become frustrated when they receive lower occupational rewards than men in comparable positions. Job discrimination lowers prospects for promotion or reemployment, which heightens feelings of inferiority, and the lower prospect of marriage removes that alternative. The greater likelihood that a single woman will agree to care for elderly parents can further compound the problem.

Many single adults are able to adjust to aging and retirement more effectively than married adults because of earlier life experiences associated with singleness. Most single adults establish living arrangements, activity patterns, and interests that transfer quite well into old age and are less likely to confront the major adjustment of the widow or widower whose entire life was the family or the job (Lowenthal, 1964a).

As with all other categories of adults, there is great variability among those who remain single. On the average, general life satisfaction is lower than for any category of married adults (Campbell and Converse, 1975). However, remaining single has both advantages and disadvantages. Remaining single can be very satisfactory for the adult who is unmarried by choice and has companionship. There are, however, strong societal pressures on single adults to become married. Increasing tolerance of alternative life-styles will benefit those who prefer to remain single and will reduce the pressure that sometimes precipitates unsatisfactory marriages. Practitioners can help increase understanding of singleness as an acceptable alternative.

Single men and women who want to marry but are thwarted by personal or societal barriers typically become frustrated when their normal desires for marriage, family life, companionship, affection, sexual expression, and parenthood are blocked. Although most single adults satisfactorily adjust to this frustration, the proportion of single adults admitted to mental hospitals is higher than for married adults. It is, however, lower than the proportion of those who are widowed or divorced (Klemer, 1954; Knupfer, Clark and Room, 1966). One of the most difficult adjustments for many single young adults relates to sexual satisfaction. The opportunities for nonmarital sex are greater in recent decades, but the constraints are still high, especially for women (Clifford, 1962; Goldstein and Mayer, 1965; Rubin, 1965).

Single Parents. Some single adults become parents. The extent and trends for illegitimate births are reflected in the records of live births by unwed mothers by age and race of the mother. During the past decade about 9 percent of all live births have been illegitimate, compared with about 4 percent during the two preceding decades. In 1976 the rate of illegitimate births reached a record high and the increase was highest for white women. The rate of legitimate births by married women increased during the 1940s, was high during the 1950s and early 1960s, and has since dropped sharply. By contrast the rate of illegitimate births by unmarried women has risen steadily during the past three decades. The proportion of illegitimate births to all live births has been more than 25 percent for nonwhites during the past decade or two, compared with about 4 percent for whites. By 1969 the percentage of illegitimate first births had risen to more than 10 percent for white mothers and to more than 50 percent for black mothers. In about three quarters of the illegitimate births each year, the mothers range from fifteen to twenty-four. In a small percentage the mothers are under age fifteen.

The percentage of single women in their late twenties dropped to about 10 percent; in their early thirties, to about 6 percent; and in their late thirties, to about 5 percent. There are now fewer women in their thirties because of low birth rates in the late 1930s and early 1940s, than there are in the age range from fifteen to twenty-four. One out of five illegitimate births are produced by mothers between twenty-five and thirty-nine, a relatively high illegitimacy rate for women in this age range given their numbers.

The unwed parent, especially the unwed mother, has some distinctive characteristics and problems in comparison with the vast majority of single adults who do not have offspring. The illegitimacy rate is much higher for blacks than for whites, and there tends to be greater acceptance of children born out of wedlock in black than in white families. Almost

all black unwed mothers retain their children, compared with
less than two thirds of the white unwed mothers. This acceptance of illegitimacy reflects many influences including income
level, family and neighborhood attitudes toward unwed mothers,
opportunities for adoption, and personality traits of the
mothers. Unwed mothers who retain their children tend to feel
less concern about social acceptance than those who put their
children up for adoption, and their need for a mother-child
relationship tends to be relatively strong. Although acceptance
of unwed mothers, as well as parents without partners generally,
has increased in the past decade or two, both mother and child
confront major financial and social problems (Vincent, 1961).
For example, for the immature unwed mother with unrealistic
expectations, there is a higher incidence of child neglect and
abuse than for comparable persons who are married. This is
another area where practitioners tend to consider both prevention and remediation.

Professional Assistance

The process by which practitioners come to understand
clients and help them establish linkage with relevant services
and resources varies with client characteristics, the type of practice to be modified, and the background of the practitioner.
A marriage counselor working with a potential divorce by the
white collar parents of three young children confronts different
interrelationships from those confronted by the nutrition specialist helping an older blue collar homemaker provide more
nutritious meals for less money. However, in addition to the
variability in the process by which practitioners help adults
modify practices, there are commonalities that are illustrated
by the following examples from various areas of family
life. The illustrations include family relationships, adolescent assertiveness, loss of family roles, divorce, and grandparenting.
  Family Relationships. Today's parents of young children are aware of more patterns of relationships among
husband, wife, and children than were young couples several

generations ago. Although basic values regarding marriage and the family have changed little over the years, there has been increased acceptance of various forms of marriage and parenting. A mother of two young children might turn to a clergyman for help in dealing with her feelings of being overwhelmed by the responsibilities of motherhood. Having the main and constant care for young children can lead to feelings of imprisonment, especially if other young mothers are not available with whom to share experiences and feelings. The sense of being incarcerated can be especially intense if the onset of motherhood terminated an active occupational and social life and if both the husband and wife come from family traditions in which the father performs a minimal role in the parenting of young children.

The clergyman might encourage the young woman to broaden her perspective on parenthood. He could do so by talking to her, suggesting reading materials, and encouraging her to talk with her husband and with other mothers who currently share or recently shared her experience with the onset of motherhood. Other young mothers can help her realize that her experience and feelings are widespread. Readings and conversation can indicate various ways in which parents deal with responsibilities for young children and the process by which the current stage shifts to the next when the youngest child enters school. She and her husband can discuss various patterns of fathering along with ways in which equalitarian marriages contribute to mutual development. Women who recently moved to the next stage of the family cycle, along with social agency personnel, can help the young mother recognize the contributions of small friendship groups, day-care facilities, and social activities through which she can get away from the constant care of children for periods of time.

Adolescent Assertiveness. The transition from adolescence to young adulthood tends to be stressful for parents as well as for the person making the transition. For the adolescent, a degree of assertiveness is a necessary part of the process of establishing an adult sense of identity. If a parent understands this, it is somewhat easier to accept and deal with such assertiveness. Other sources of conflict are also usual during this stage. If both the adolescent and the parents recognize that they each contribute some of the conflict, and if both strive to resolve it, satisfactory conflict resolution is more likely. In the same way in which a sense of trust developed in the family setting helps the individual to be trusting in other social relationships, assertiveness and conflict resolution procedures learned in the family can assist young people to function generally. A practitioner, such as a counselor or educator, might talk with family members who are experiencing a stressful adolescent transition and help them understand reasons for differing viewpoints and ways to resolve or accept them. Doing so with several families is sometimes very helpful because they learn much from each other.

Loss of Family Role. Family role relationships are sometimes diminished or lost. For example, as the youngest child starts school or leaves home for college, work, or marriage, the time and attention devoted to the parent role are reduced. Parents' reactions to this "empty nest" experience range from relief to regret. For women who think of themselves mainly as mothers, it constitutes a severe loss of identity as well as of a role relationship. The loss of a spouse through death or divorce typically also entails major adjustments. Practitioners can help adults deal with such losses of family roles by showing them that their extended family and close friends contain people with whom replacement role relationships can be established. Throughout history and in all types of societies, when important family relationships are lost, substitutions are made from more distant relationships. Interaction with nieces and nephews can increase after the death of one's own child. Similar shifts in visiting patterns, exchanging gifts, and confidant relationships can occur following the loss of a parent, spouse, or sibling. Adoption of a child is a familiar way of dealing with the loss of one's child. Another way to help someone adjust to a family loss is through mutual assistance groups such as Parents Without Partners or Widow to Widow (Silverman, 1973). Members of such groups can sometimes help adults broaden their understanding and feelings about the adjustment process and recognize available sources of assistance and alternative courses of action.

Divorce. Those who divorce while children remain in the household face the prospect of single parenting. Mothers usually obtain custody of the children, so most divorced single parents are women. Because four out of five persons who divorce eventually remarry, most of them within four or five years, single parenting tends to be a transition category. Practitioners can help those who divorce to understand the nature of the transition and identify supportive services related to child care, education, employment, and self-help groups that can help them perform better as a single parent.

Grandparenting. Increased geographic mobility, modern means of transportation and communication, and various living arrangements for older adults have increased the ways in which grandparents relate to their grandchildren. In many families there are extensive and varied interactions among three generations and across the extended family (Hill and others, 1970). However, grandparenting may become a problem for quite different reasons, such as when an older adult is prevented from interacting with grandchildren, or is forced to live with children and grandchildren. Practitioners can help grandparents understand the various forms grandparenting can take with, for example, grandchildren who live in the household or those who visit less than once a year. Foster grandparent arrangements are available in many communities for those without sufficient access to their own grandchildren. Contact with other grandparents can help an older adult concerned about grandparenting to recognize some of the affinity and special relationships that can be established with adolescent grandchildren and to understand ways to help grandchildren adjust to the remarriage of a grandparent after the loss of a spouse.

Case Example: Joyce Kingsley

During the period spanning late adolescence and early young adulthood many people develop a clearer sense of separate identity. For those who attend college and get married, performance in the roles of student and spouse contributes to and is affected by personality development.

The following case example illustrates evolving family role performance during late adolescence and young adulthood for a middle-class girl who completes college. This example deals with only one of many family role transitions, stages of adulthood, and strata of society. It does, however, indicate developmental relationships among societal context, family role performance, and personality. Performance in college and additional learning activities are also considered. These interrelationships are well illustrated by the case of Joyce Kingsley (R. W. White, 1961).

Joyce's high school years were characterized by accomplishment and satisfaction. From her minister father and school teacher mother, she internalized a code that emphasized religious values, social duty, and personal excellence. In her small high school, she was an excellent student and held such leadership positions as president of the student government. Joyce enjoyed being in the middle of things and having people look up to her, both in school and as a member of a minister's family. As a result, she entered college with gilded optimism, unaware of the extent to which her adolescent context sustained the satisfying interpersonal social relations but retarded the development of closer friendships.

Joyce attended a large and prestigious eastern private college. She studied hard but continued to live and help out at home, so she was less active in college-related groups than she wanted to be. She did not know any other students at the college before she entered, which interfered with making friends, as did her timidity in talking to professors and her tendency from high school to stand against the mores of the crowd. She was also unaware of the extent of her dependence on her mother and on her boyfriend Renn, with whom she had an idealistic romance during high school but who entered a university some distance away. She readily accepted her mother's expectations as her own code in matters such as the centrality of religion in her life, inhibition of her impulses, and a somewhat bleak duty to serve others that contrasted with her general lively enthusiasm.

Having lost the exalted position that she enjoyed during high school but still wanting the approval and respect of her peers in college, Joyce responded by turning to the sources of esteem and support she had previously drawn on. One of them was Renn. Her first visit to his university for a weekend was very unsatisfactory. Renn and his roommate wanted very much to be one of the gang, but Joyce, who was depressed by her college adjustment problems, seemed unresponsive to a fun-filled weekend. Joyce did not hear from Renn for three months after the weekend, which added to her bewilderment.

By spring Joyce was becoming more outgoing and worrying less about her grades. She became active in organizations, made many friends, and began dating two or three times a week. She sought out friends with serious interests, was reassured that she need not be without partners, and became less confident of her future with Renn. However, her feelings remained attached to him, and they were again reciprocated so that during the fall of her sophomore year they were engaged.

The strong feelings of separation during her freshman year were replaced by a sense of belonging. During her last two years of college there was never enough time to satisfy her wide range of interests. She took part in student organizations; creative endeavors such as music, cooking, and pottery; and social activities. Joyce increasingly enjoyed meeting people and sharing their interests, but felt that her relationships lacked intimacy and depth. Her best friends tended to be older or younger, she tended to be somewhat distant, and she was uncertain how to deepen a friendship. Privacy, independence, and pursuit of her own desires had suffered from too great an acceptance of her mother's domination and both her parents' ideas of good conduct. Her outlook was enthusiastic, her approach was rewarded, and her resentment and rebellious impulses were well controlled. However, one result was a lack of humility and tolerance that would have facilitated intimate friendships.

After graduation, Renn was assigned to a military research unit on the West Coast. Joyce also obtained a job there, and they planned to be married the following spring. She was amazed but pleased that she readily relaxed the strict, almost prudish, standards she acquired from her parents and accepted the fact that other people on the West Coast held different standards, even though she did not accept them for herself. Joyce was still concerned about having so few close friends and so much uncertainty about how to make new friends. She expressed the sense of being different from everybody. As she became better able to understand other standards, her social development progressed.

Joyce's job was in a youth recreation center. She found herself at variance with some policies and personnel, especially regarding insufficient opportunities for the development of serious interests by the young people. When several orders were issued that she believed adversely affected some of the few serious programs, she wrote a letter of protest and then a second letter to higher authorities and parents when she got the official runaround. She even resigned from her job in the process, but she did achieve some results. Joyce made much progress during her year on the West Coast in freeing herself from unquestioned parental influences and in acquiring greater independence and confidence to feel and act in her own right.

In the spring, Joyce and Renn were married, and when he completed his military service they returned East and lived for a while in an apartment in Joyce's parents' home. This experience increased Joyce's awareness of the issue of dependence in her relations with her mother and her husband. Joyce's mother did not try to dominate Joyce, but her strong personality and Joyce's long-standing deference to her made it difficult for Joyce to be independent. Renn noted that she was a different person around her mother. He helped her through this period while they lived in Joyce's parents' home, but he also resisted Joyce's attempts to dominate him.

In addition to her pressure for Renn to conform to her expectations, Joyce experienced difficulty in becoming freer and warmer and in achieving a satisfactory sexual adjustment. At the outset, her sexual relationship with Renn was an irksome obligation, but after a frustrating year, a satisfactory adjustment was achieved. In contrast with Joyce's idealized view of her family life at the time of her college graduation in which she repressed disagreeable features, five years later she was able to make a more frank and objective appraisal. Her growing sense of independence and her sense of support and security from Renn and her friends allowed her to depend less on an unrealistically rosy picture of her family.

Renn accepted an attractive new position, and he and Joyce moved to the Midwest. Although things went well for them, Joyce became increasingly distressed by her inability to conceive. Her physician gave them both a clean bill of health, but counting days and using temperature charts did not result in conception. As her tension level rose, her physician suggested that Joyce take up some work that would occupy her interest. With her heart still set on having children, she enrolled in school to study social work, a decision influenced by her experience in the military youth center on the West Coast during the year after her college graduation. This occupational choice sharpened her conflict between fighting for one's standards and the tolerant acceptance of others that characterizes social group work.

Joyce began to realize how much she had depended on her mother and Renn for support; her selfish demandingness and anxiety prompted constant proofs of closeness. Her romanticized expectations became too much for Renn, and he began to consider divorce. His rebellion was influenced by the near collapse of the marriage of some good friends, during which Renn concluded that he was more interested in the wife, Sandra, than in Joyce. During this period, Joyce experienced the unhappiest and loneliest time of her life. She was sometimes so upset that she could not force herself to go to class, and at one point she sought counseling. Renn's rebellion was a blow to her sense of pride, morality, and self-confidence. A ten-day trip to a conference with some classmates helped Joyce rediscover her confidence in herself and recognize that some part of her life did not depend on Renn. When she returned, Renn and Sandra had stopped seeing each other, and the long slow process of rebuilding their marriage began for Joyce and Renn.

Joyce came to realize how central Renn had been to her development, security, and happiness, and how devastating his loss would have been. Their new relationship encouraged their individual development, which meant greater freedom, self-respect, and maturity. In the process, Joyce was able to reduce the inhibition of feeling that blocked warm friendships and ease of human relations. During the decade after her graduation from high school, Joyce's personality and interpersonal relations interacted and developed greatly as reflected in her acceptance of independence and in her ability to give and receive love.

The specific pattern of developmental changes that Joyce experienced during this decade was unique to herself. However, most young people evolve and change during late adolescence and young adulthood as they interact with larger social systems, such as family, school, and work setting, and community groups, such as church and recreational organizations. Specific interpersonal relationships with mother or father, husband or wife, siblings or close friends, change over the years in ways that reflect the personality of the individual, the attitudes and activities of the other people, and changing contextual circumstances. Practitioners can help clients understand this developmental process, including the alternative courses of action from which they can choose. Joyce considered whether to work full time when she and Renn were unable to have children, and she considered several types of work. Her choice reflected both her personal preferences and abilities and the available job opportunities. She decided to obtain further education as part of her career development. Finally, she and Renn adopted several children. Practitioners can help adults recognize such choice points, weigh the advantages and disadvantages of each major alternative, and assume some responsibility for systematic adaptation through contemplation about the choices, educative activity to increase competence, and action to follow through on choices.

Sexual Activity

Although this section on sexual activity is included in the chapter on family role performance, it is related to many aspects of adult development and learning. There are many forms of sexual activity. Most of the research on sex and age during adulthood deals with sexual intercourse, but there are other forms of sensual expression, including casual and public physical contact, such as an affectionate embrace between two old friends, as well as more intimate activities such as kissing or masturbation.

There are many dimensions of sexual and sensual activity in addition to performance. Sexual activity is somewhat related to physiological condition and is affected by illness, fatigue, and general aging. However, it is also greatly influenced by personality characteristics, such as attitudes toward oneself and others. It is shaped by the demands and constraints of both primary groups and community characteristics (Katchadourian and Katchadourian, 1972).

There are some trends in the extent and type of sexual activity during adulthood, but there is great variability within each age group. This variability reflects earlier life experiences, personal characteristics and values, and societal context. Even more than for most other forms of activity, it is difficult to analyze and explain the variability among adults in extent and type of sexual activity.

For most late adolescents and young adults in the United States, sexual activity is a major influence on daily life. This influence is heightened by the somewhat different patterns in strength and expression of the sex drive for men and women at various ages, the societal emphasis on sex and romantic love, and the relatively long span between puberty and marriage.

Sexual activity and attitudes toward sex during young adulthood are affected by previous sexual experience and attitudes formed during childhood and adolescence. Excessive emphasis on information about the evils or hazards of sex, such as disease or pregnancy, or aggressive or offensive sexual encounters can foster negative attitudes toward sex and reduced sexual activity, such as female frigidity or male impotence (Ehrmann, 1959; Kirkendall, 1965; Vincent, 1956). There are studies that show both positive and negative influences of petting and premarital intercourse during adolescence on sexual adjustment during young adulthood (Reiss, 1966; Kinsey and others, 1948; Bell and Blumberg, 1960; Lowrie, 1965). For both

men and women, the influence on subsequent sexual adjustment seems to depend heavily on attitudes toward self, partner,
and activity. Favorable adjustment is more likely to result from
premarital sexual activity characterized by affection, respect,
and love for the other person. Unfavorable adjustment is more
likely to result from premarital sexual activity characterized by
aggression, guilt, and exploitation of the other as an object.

For many young couples, there is an improvement in the
quality and satisfaction of sexual experiences during the first
year or two of marriage. For example, among lower-middle-
class newlyweds, husbands report that in contrast with premarital sex or the early months of marriage, when sex was
viewed as athletics or entertainment with attendant anxiety,
sex had become more all-encompassing and characterized by
mutual love. Many newlywed women also described sex as more
emotionally satisfying, although about one quarter report ambivalence or declining satisfaction (Lowenthal, Thurnher, and
others, 1975).

Extent of sexual activity follows a somewhat different
pattern for men and women during the adult life cycle. The
typical index of activity is number of sexual outlets per week
including intercourse and masturbation. For males, the rate of
outlets peaks in the late teens or early twenties and gradually
declines throughout adulthood. Boys who reach sexual maturity
earlier in adolescence typically have higher rates of sexual outlets throughout adulthood. Those with above-average rates compared with other young men in later years have above-average
rates compared with other older men (Kinsey and others, 1948;
Kirkendall, 1958; Masters and Johnson, 1965; Shuttleworth,
1959; Whalen, 1966). The general trend of declining sexual
activity during middle and old age is of particular concern to
many men, who tend to assume the main responsibility for the
change. Wives also tend to attribute a decline in sexual activity
to their husbands. It appears that more men than women associate a sense of self-worth with sexual activity (Pfeiffer, Verwoerdt, and Davis, 1972).

For females, the rate of sexual outlets is more constant
during adulthood but typically peaks in the late twenties. As

for males, the extent of sexual activity for females reflects both physical drive and other factors, such as inhibitions and inter-personal relations (Kinsey, 1953). In addition, most women experience a bimodal monthly fluctuation in sexual desire that peaks about the time of ovulation and again just before men-struation. During middle age, many women experience in-creased interest in sexual activity, which partly reflects a reduction in earlier inhibitions.

During adulthood the rate of marital intercourse averages about two and a half times a week in the early twenties, to slightly less than two times a week in the late thirties, to slightly less than once a week at age sixty. The interest in and enjoyment from sexual activity tends to be somewhat higher for white collar than blue collar couples, in large part reflecting the greater emphasis on togetherness and interaction in and out of the home for white collar couples in contrast with the greater separateness for blue collar couples (Rainwater, 1966).

Against the backdrop of such trends and averages, the individual adult strives for happiness, deals with disappoint-ment, endures frustration, and experiences joy related to sexual activity. At each stage of the adult life cycle there are somewhat differing influences on the adult's efforts to deal with sexual activity and its relation with other aspects of life.

For the single young adult, more widespread use of con-traceptives and greater societal acceptance of premarital inter-course contribute to less frustration and guilt than was typical a generation or two ago. This trend has resulted in greater ac-ceptance of various life-styles for young adults, in which in-creased freedom of choice is accompanied by greater pressure on the individual to assume personal responsibility for the chosen course of action. Abortion has become a widespread way of dealing with unwanted pregnancies and is now the second most frequent operation, following tonsillectomies.

The disparity between the values of premarital virginity and the actual incidence of premarital sexual intercourse is large and has increased substantially during the past decade. The average proportion of adults who ever experienced pre-marital intercourse is higher for males than for females and increases with the amount of formal education. During much of this century, about two thirds of all males had experienced premarital intercourse (Ehrmann, 1959). However, the rate for blue collar males is much higher, about nine out of ten (Kinsey and others, 1948). The rate for females has not varied as greatly between blue collar and white collar families. Around World War I, there was an increase in the incidence of premarital intercourse by females. Between the mid 1920s and the mid 1960s the rates were quite stable at about one out of five for females who attended college and about one out of three of those who did not. For about half the women, premarital intercourse was limited to their fiancés. During the 1960s contraception and sexual candor increased, and there was a corresponding increase in premarital sexual intercourse by female college students, along with decreasing guilt feelings about it. Most of the increase was among couples who were not engaged, from about one out of ten in the late 1950s to about one out of four in the late 1960s (Bell and Chaskes, 1970). (Recent estimates are that as many as three quarters of all college men and women have had premarital intercourse at the time of graduation. This would constitute little change for men but a large increase for women since 1970.) Among young white collar married working women, it appears that the proportion that had engaged in premarital sexual intercourse is even higher than had been the case for female college students before the 1970s. Recent estimates are that about half of all women aged fifteen through nineteen have had premarital sexual intercourse.

Sexual satisfaction is a major factor in marital adjustment. Among the main factors associated with sexual dissatisfaction are disillusionment because the actuality falls short of a highly romanticized expectation, fear of pregnancy, disagreement about use of contraceptives, and low orgasm rate for the wife (Rapoport and Rapoport, 1964; Gebhard, 1966; Freedman and Combs, 1966).

The term climacteric refers to the end of fertility. For women it includes but extends beyond the transition period of menopause, which typically occurs between forty-five and fifty, and which has occurred when there has been no monthly menstrual period for a year (Parker, 1960). There are various normal patterns for the cessation of the menstrual flow. Menopause results from a temporary disequilibrium of the endocrine system. In the early stage, although the production of pituitary hormone continues normally, there is a failure of the ovarian function, which interferes with the typical pattern of menstruation. This stage is sometimes accompanied by emotional upset. In the latter stage, pituitary hyperactivity affects metabolic and vasomotor functioning as the body seeks a new endocrine balance. This transition typically entails three physiological symptoms: flushes, sweats, and hot flashes. Additional symptoms may include fatigue, headaches, insomnia, dizziness, frigidity, and general nervousness, which may reflect psychological reactions to environmental stress as well as endocrine changes (Neugarten and Kraines, 1965). In more extreme instances, some women experience emotional disturbances during this transition, such as intense feelings of depression, hostility, and guilt, that typically reflect both physiological and environmental influences. However, most women accept menopause as a natural and inevitable process, a temporary "pause that depresses." The women for whom the menopause is most disturbing tend to be those whose earlier psychosexual attitudes were quite negative.

The ease with which the individual makes the transition and achieves a new balance in the endocrine system depends partly on the rapidity of the decline in ovarian functioning. The use of estrogen and other medications under medical supervision soon after menopausal symptoms begin to occur can slow the hormonal changes and ease the transition. As the ovarian hormones decline, the relative influence of the woman's male hormones increases. At the end of the transition period there is a new plateau of constancy. The adjustments associated with a hysterectomy are similar. Frigidity seldom results from either menopause or a hysterectomy, and when it does, the cause is typically not physiological.

In middle age, both men and women experience some changes in sexual activity. There is a gradual decline in average rates of marital intercourse that parallels the decline in many physiological functions between the thirties and the fifties.

Some influences on the decline are physiological, such as a general decrease in physical condition and vigor, overweight, menopause or a hysterectomy, and health problems, especially those affecting the urethra or prostate gland. Gradual declines in the male sex drive are similar for most middle-aged men but continue to reflect wide differences in level at the onset of young adulthood.

Most changes in sexual activity during middle age reflect both psychological and situational influences. For instance, females acquire more inhibitions regarding sex in our society than do males. For some middle-aged women these inhibitions decline and their interest in sex increases. During this period their husband's interest in sex is declining, especially if he is somewhat older. As a result of this disparity, many wives are sexually unsatisfied (Bossard and Boll, 1955; Masters and Johnson, 1965). Even without this disparity, some middle-aged adults acquire a value system that glorifies youth and places extreme emphasis on physical appearance and activity. Such people often fear a physical and sexual decline.

Sexual performance is interrelated with self-concept and marital adjustment, especially for men. Even though sexual changes occur very slowly for men, and reproductive powers extend into the sixties and seventies, gradual changes in hormone balance and in physical appearance and vitality cause some men to become anxious about their virility. Some women experience similar concerns. Marital relationships during this period can affect this anxiety in various ways. If the partner is understanding and supportive and encourages self-confidence and growth, a husband or wife can emerge from the transition with a greater sense of self and direction. The adjustment is likely to be even better if the middle-aged adult is experiencing satisfaction and accomplishment in other roles. However, anxiety about virility and sexual attractiveness can affect sexual performance. If the partner reacts to reduced sexual responsiveness with derision or withdrawal, the result is often marital conflict as reflected in further reduced sexual compatibility, extramarital sex, or divorce. This contributes to the second peak in marital discord and divorce in the early forties (Wallin and Clark, 1964; Clark and Wallin, 1965).

Some middle-aged men and women revolt against the loss of youth and engage in a "second adolescence." Because of this the period around age forty is sometimes referred to as the "dangerous age." Men in particular tend to seek a younger woman as a lover or second wife (Vincent, 1968). The results can be ironic if he is unable to meet her physical demands, and, instead of reducing his virility anxiety, the situation increases it (Cuber and Harroff, 1965; Wolfe, 1975).

Some of the same interrelations between aging and sexual activity in middle age become intensified in old age. With the exception of the small proportion of older adults who have a physical incapacity, marital intercourse can be continued through the sixties and seventies. The main influences are psychological and environmental, not physical. Compatible and affectionate relations with the spouse are a major influence. As in middle age, mutual interests, respect, and love are far more likely to sustain marital sex in old age than estrangement and conflict. Other influences include marital status and the prevailing societal attitude that sex is inappropriate for older adults (J. T. Freeman, 1961).

Especially for the older woman, the capacity for sexual performance is typical as long as there is regular sexual stimulation. Once an older adult ceases sexual intercourse for an extended period, it is seldom resumed. There is an increase in male impotence beyond age fifty that affects about one out of five by sixty-five years of age and one out of two by age seventy-five (Kinsey and others, 1948). The male climacteric occurs later than the female and occurs more gradually. The decline in gonadal functioning produces many of the same changes as menopause and is often accompanied by symptoms such as headaches, insomnia, and emotional instability (Ruebsaat and Hull, 1975). With advancing age the male's preliminary orgastic phase is longer and erection occurs closer to ejaculation (Masters and Johnson, 1965).

Sexual activity seems to be an important factor in the

physical and psychological well being of many older adults (Christenson and Gagnon, 1965; Pfeiffer, 1969). A major disparity in sexual desire between older husbands and wives can add another source of conflict during a period beset by major and difficult adjustments. For older adults who are single or widowed, or whose spouses' interests create restrictions on sexual intercourse, masturbation and erotic dreams and daydreams provide compensation for lack of sexual activities (Christensen and Gagnon, 1965; J. T. Freeman, 1961). It seems that greater societal and personal acceptance of sexual activity as a natural and constructive part of life for older adults would help many men and women maintain and enhance a positive self-concept during a period of life when they are forced to deal with major losses.

For many generations, sexual activities and feelings have been very important and sometimes very troublesome in people's lives, but they have not been as well understood or candidly discussed as many less important aspects of life. Sex shares this distinction with death. During the past generation, however, there has been a striking increase in candor regarding both topics. Because of the importance of sex and the current transition in practices and attitudes related to sex, practitioners in various fields (such as law, education, social work, recreation, and physical and mental health) often confront issues related to sex (Masters and Johnson, 1970).

Delivery of Family Services

Generalizations about shifts in family performance during the adult life cycle are useful to practitioners who help adults to learn, change, and adapt. Practitioners working in various fields, such as education, counseling, social work, recreation, and health, often can facilitate the adult's efforts to modify practices. Examples include learning child-care practices before the birth of the first child, changing food preparation practices after the children leave and there is a family of two again, and modifying financial practices after the loss of a spouse. To facilitate the change process related to practice adoption by adults, the practitioner will find three types of understanding helpful: (1) understanding of the adult client system, (2) familiarity with the capability and services related to the resource system that are relevant to the client system, and (3) recognition of ways to establish effective linkage between the resource system and the client system that will encourage adoption of useful practices by the adult clients.

Developmental generalizations about family performance can help the practitioner better understand the adult client system in several ways. One way is to anticipate the likely extent and types of performance and participation by white collar and blue collar men and women of various ages. The following are some examples of performance-related characteristics of subpopulations of adults, along with ways in which practitioners might use an understanding of adult development to assist a client: (1) helping young couples with very different backgrounds to recognize the special adjustment problems they are likely to confront; (2) helping young couples deal effectively with parenthood and child rearing; (3) exploring with working mothers of young children ways to perform their dual roles satisfactorily; (4) helping members of the middle generation relate more satisfactorily with their extended family network; and (5) alerting newcomers and community agencies to the adjustments that typically occur in a move to a new community and to the ways in which practitioners can help. Practitioners can use developmental generalizations about adult performance to anticipate both the likely adult life cycle changes in participation and the typical needs for learning and adaptation associated with these change events. Some examples of typical changes in the family life cycle are: (1) marriage, (2) birth of first child, (3) youngest child starting school, (4) move to a new community, (5) last child leaving home, (6) divorce, and (7) death of spouse. In such instances, practitioners can help adults anticipate the types of changes that are likely to happen, recognize the alternative ways in which to deal with such changes, and prepare for and cope with the change as satisfactorily as possible.

A better understanding of adult development can help

the practitioner identify services and resources that are relevant to a client system and develop and interpret the resource system so that it is really accessible to a target population of adults. For example, information seeking by blue collar adults is typically oriented toward informal interpersonal contact with family and friends in the neighborhood. Use of impersonal information sources such as mass media and experts for instrumental purposes is unusual for blue collar adults. Therefore, practitioners who seek to serve blue collar adults with educational or social service programs related to family problems are more likely to reach them with programs that fit their life-style and that minimize the barriers imposed by white collar approaches to participation and information seeking.

There are various ways in which practitioners can help establish linkage between the resource system, such as an educational institution or a social agency, and the client system of adults in a target population. Effective linkage is more likely if the practitioner understands the dynamics of change processes and linkage mechanisms. The literature on diffusion and adoption of practices provides many generalizations about stages of adoption, about characteristics of those adults who are most likely to be at each stage of the adoption process, and about typical information sources at each stage (Rogers and Shoemaker, 1971). The process by which adults typically become aware of and adopt a new practice or decide to engage in a new activity includes a movement through stages such as apathy, awareness, interest (commitment), trial, and adoption (action). The innovators who are first to adopt a new practice tend to be more highly educated and more oriented to outside information sources but less a part of the client system than the early adopters who are next to adopt the practice (Menzel and Katz, 1955; Coleman, Katz, and Menzel, 1957; Katz, 1957). As adults move from apathy to interest to action, there tends to be an increase in the importance of personal information sources (Rogers and Beal, 1957; Rogers, 1957; Beal and Rogers, 1960).

As practitioners plan for innovation through the dissemination and use of knowledge, there are seven factors that contribute to the effectiveness of the linkage process (Havelock, 1969): (1) the number and variety of collaborative relationships between the client system and the resource system, (2) the extent of systematic coordination of the dissemination strategy and the extent of coherence of the messages, (3) the favorableness of the social climate and the openness of the client system to change, (4) the capacity of the resource system to provide new ideas and useful assistance, (5) extent of regard and reinforcement received by the clients for adoption, (6) the familiarity and proximity of resource system and client system, and (7) the variety and extent of the facilitating forces that encourage practice adoption.

Practitioners associated with all types of resource systems, such as educational institutions, social agencies, and health-related institutions, seek to facilitate the process by which desirable practices are diffused and adopted by adults. This is sometimes referred to as social intervention (Hornstein and others, 1971). This adoption process occurs in relation to many domains, such as work, recreation, shopping, and community activities. The foregoing overview of practice adoption and ways to facilitate linkage with resource systems also applies to practices related to marriage and family life, even though research on this process has been somewhat limited.

Practices related to family life may be internal to the family—such as a family council in which parents and children periodically discuss rules, plans, and adjustment problems—or external to the family, such as use of financial planning services or marital counseling. The practitioner may understand general dynamics of marital relationships, family life cycle trends regarding marital satisfaction, or community services available to family members (Babchuck and Bates, 1963; Lederer and Jackson, 1968; Burr, 1970; Blenker, Bloom, and Nielson, 1971; Mace and Mace, 1974). However, provision of such information tends to have far less impact on performance than experience and discussion. Experiential education programs for adults have become more widespread in recent years, especially for the better educated. In addition to programs and services designed to help resolve severe family problems, there has been a growth of marriage enrichment programs sponsored by social agencies and religious groups.

The main purpose of marriage enrichment programs is to make good marriages better. Impetus for such programs has come mainly from the marriage and family counselors who have experience with many couples who made a mess of a first marriage but learned about marital relationships and themselves in the process and applied their hard-won insights in a second marriage. More than a million adults have participated in such programs during the past decade. A typical program occurs in a residential conference or retreat setting for a weekend. Thirty or forty couples attend a program led by three or four couples, sometimes with the assistance of a clergyman or a counselor.

The emphasis is on experience and changed practices. Participants discover that all couples experience dissatisfaction and conflict, fear and loneliness. Group discussion sessions are interspersed with written statements about marital concerns and expectations that couples prepare separately and discuss in the privacy of their own rooms. Couples tend to focus on problem areas such as work, money, health, and relatives, but the emphasis throughout is on candor, nonverbal communication, and affection. The weekend enables many couples to discover and practice ways to deal with disagreements and feelings of estrangement that they can continue to use when partners feel hostile, inadequate, rejected, or tense. The program helps them adopt practices that facilitate openness and sharing.

Religious institutions have been especially effective sponsors because of the reliance on informal and personal information sources that encourage members to become aware of acquaintances' participation and to decide to participate themselves. The voluntariness of participation contributes to initial openness, and the association with members in other activities helps reinforce changes. However, trying new practices and discovering that they work tends to be most influential.

Experienced practitioners recognize that each human being is unique and that throughout most of life the range of individual differences increases. Generalizations about adult development are most useful when they alert practitioners to variations and trends that otherwise might not be noted. An understanding of the various ways in which families deal with the transition when adolescents become young adults and leave home, along with the critical ingredients that affect the satisfactoriness of the process, can be very valuable, for practitioners who work with such families. Such insights do not provide a standard procedure that all families should follow. Instead, they yield an appreciation of variability among people as well as usual and unusual developmental trends. This can enable the practitioner to help specific clients gain greater insight into their own situations and values and greater perspective on the experiences of others. Perhaps most importantly, they can be helped to understand the evolving and changing nature of human lives and to recognize how they can use choice and learning to help direct their own lives.

Summary

Although almost everyone has some family experience, the patterns of family life are quite varied. There is a widespread pattern in which a young couple is married, has children, and remains married until death. Other patterns include childless couples, unmarried parents; couples who marry late and have children late; divorced, widowed, and single adults; and remarried adults. Within each of these patterns, part of the variability is associated with level of income and education. Among white collar families that follow the widespread pattern, the husband and wife typically divide responsibilities and power either in generally equalitarian or in somewhat patriarchal ways. This occurs for the majority of both white and black middle-class families.

There has been a gradual decline in age at first marriage during the past two generations (especially for white collar families) followed by a rise during the past decade. For those who follow the widespread pattern, early marital adjustment is associated both with characteristics that the partners bring with them and with evolving interrelationships between them. Personal characteristics associated with marital happiness include personal adjustment, similarity of backgrounds and values, effective interpersonal relationships, complementarity of needs, compatibility of role expectations, and well-adjusted parents. Interpersonal relationships associated with marital happiness include mature and stable love for each other, satisfactory sexual adjustment, adequacy of family finances, participation in family work and activities, and satisfactory relations with in-laws. Blue collar families tend to experience less marital adjustment, which reflects low levels of income, occupational stability, and education. However, more blue collar families have cohesive extended family systems, which can reduce some in-law problems and increase sources of companionship.

Parenthood has been fairly stable during the past generation or so, during which time there was little change in the proportion of families with zero or one child. There was, however, an increase after World War II in the proportion of families with three or more children, followed by a decline in larger families during the past decade. Many young women say they aspire to motherhood. The onset of parenthood can be a difficult adjustment, especially when parents approach it with feelings of parental inadequacy, negative attitudes toward parenthood, and unwillingness to accept role changes. The prospect and first year or so of parenthood tends to produce much information seeking, especially for mothers, a process that practitioners can usefully facilitate, especially for blue collar families. If new parents are able to achieve family solidarity while encouraging the individuality and growth of each family member, the prospects for satisfying family life are enhanced.

There is some evidence of more equalitarian marriages and a decrease in sex-role differentiation among young white collar couples, but among blue collar couples the emotional allegiance to traditional patterns remains strong. When the youngest child enters school, a major transition typically occurs, especially for the mother who is not employed outside the home. Many nonworking mothers rethink their interest and activity patterns at this time, and the proportion of employed mothers of young children has been rising rapidly in recent years. Under favorable conditions, maternal employment need not have any major adverse effects on the children. Perhaps the greatest influence on the satisfactoriness of wives' working outside the home is the husbands' attitudes. Societal acceptance of working wives has increased in recent decades. For some women, work satisfaction contributes to an improved quality of family life that compensates for reduced contact and shifts in family responsibilities. Practitioners can help working mothers balance the complex dual roles of work and motherhood in ways that minimize adverse effects on the children.

The launching of adolescent children as they leave the family for work, marriage, or college constitutes a challenge and transition for the parents as well as the adolescents. Most adolescents strive to achieve a sense of adult identity, to become productive persons, and to enter into intimate relationships with others. During this period adolescents give up their sense of secure dependence and idealized conceptions of their parents and become more independent and assertive. Although it may be difficult, it is important that parents accept some assertiveness as part of the process of establishing adult identity, which is vital to subsequent development. Practitioners can help parents and adolescents understand this transition period so that both can contribute to solutions and not just to problems. Adolescent assertiveness contributes to intergenerational conflict. It sometimes helps middle-aged adults to tolerate this challenge to assumptions, authority, and instances in which they do not practice what they preach, if they appreciate that the reassertion of values by the young makes an important contribution to cultural continuity and societal renewal. As parents are able to extend increased independence and responsibilities at a rate that adolescents can handle, the offspring often perceive this shift in parental expectations as evidence of the shift from childhood to young adulthood, and this facilitates their transition.

When offspring are married, the parents acquire in-laws. Successful adjustment is aided by an understanding of the transition, similarity of family backgrounds, constructive helping patterns, and interpersonal relationships that facilitate need fulfillment and personal growth.

Middle-aged couples with children entering adulthood typically also have parents entering old age. The middle generation tends to be influential on the extent of family solidarity and contact with members of the modified extended family network that occurs. Such extended networks are fairly widespread, especially for blue collar families, and are reflected in the composition of the household for some ethnic groups. The adjustment of the middle-aged adult to the elderly parent is influenced by their relationships in earlier years. The postparental but preretirement couple typically confronts fewer role changes than during earlier stages of adulthood.

The loss of active parent roles tends to be followed by the gain of new roles as grandparents. Especially in white collar families, grandparents tend to relate to their grandchildren in ways that have been referred to as fun seeking, formal, parent substitute, family wisdom, or distant figure. During the postparental period, there is usually a shift from coping with external changes to interpersonal relationships between the husband and wife. Retirement brings other adjustments. For many homemakers, an early retirement adjustment occurs when the last child leaves home. This often entails mixed feelings including lost satisfactions from active parenthood and gained freedom to pursue personal interests. When the husband retires from his job, he usually shifts from the role of family provider to a subordinate role in his wife's domain. This role reversal also occurs when aging parents move into the households of their offspring and become dependent on them for financial support and companionship. In general, a mutually satisfactory relationship over the years contributes to a satisfactory relationship in retirement with the great increase in time together. However, a long-standing frictional relationship is likely to contribute to increased friction and unhappiness with the onset of retirement.

With increased geographic mobility, many families experience a move to a new community. The effectiveness of this adjustment is associated with having satisfactory work and housing in the new community, previous experience with similar moves, the attractiveness of the move, the distance of the move, the similarity of the new community, and the availability of people and organizations in the new community to help establish a social life there. The transition to a new community varies with the stage of adulthood. For a young couple with no children and little furniture, the move may be relatively easy, compared with that of an older couple with a house full of belongings and adolescent children, who often resist a move during the high school years. Older couples may weigh the gain of services and companionship with other oldsters against the loss of old friendships and familiar surroundings.

In addition to the foregoing widespread pattern, there are other patterns of the family life cycle. Some couples choose not to have children because of concern about unwanted responsibilities, conflict with careers, or congenital defects. Childless couples realize that today this does not threaten the security of their old age. Those who marry for the first time and have children during their thirties experience about as much marital adjustment and happiness as those who do so during their twenties and more than those who marry in their teens. The somewhat older parent tends to be more concerned about the child's needs and can become overprotective. Some atypical family patterns include common-law marriage, unmarried parents, and older orphans living together.

Divorce has become more widespread. A few years ago, about one out of six adults who had ever been married had been divorced. Current estimates are that about one out of three current marriages will end in divorce. Divorce and separation rates are higher for blue collar families than for white collar families. The divorce rate for men declines with level of education and income. Women with four years of college have the lowest divorce rates, and those with five or more years of college have the highest divorce rates. The two ages with the highest divorce rates are in the early twenties and the early forties. General life satisfaction is typically lower for divorced and separated adults than for any other category. A major cause of unhappy marriages is unhappy people. When a poorly adjusted, unhappy person with emotional problems marries, it is often with the hope that marriage will solve the problems and bring happiness. The result is usually the reverse. Although personality characteristics of divorced men are similar to those of men who remain married, divorced women were characterized in adolescence as more self-indulgent and nonconforming, and women who remained married were characterized as more submissive and productive. This in part reflects societal expectations that women would make more personal adjustments on behalf of the marriage. Some of the causes of divorce are related to circumstances related to courtship and marriage, such as very brief courtship, major differences in backgrounds, very young age at marriage, forced marriage due to pregnancy, overly romantic expectations about marriage, and unsatisfactory marital role models. Many of those who divorce subsequently remarry or in other ways proceed to very satisfactory lives. The difficult experience can produce insights into one's self and the marital relationship that can provide the basis for future growth. Practitioners can help adults proceed through the adjustment process as constructively as possible.

Widowhood is one of the most abrupt and difficult adjustments that most people experience. More than half the men and women who are widowed do not marry during the subsequent five years; many never do. Financial and other forms of preparation can reduce some of the problems of widowhood. The great feelings of loss and lack of affection typically constitute the main adjustment problems, which are somewhat reduced if the surviving partner has close and satisfying social relationships with family and friends. The death of a spouse is similar for blue collar adults, except that financial and social resources are more limited. However, the extended blue collar family often provides a larger proportion of support and assistance than is the case for white collar families.

More than one out of five marriages each year is a remarriage for one or both of the new partners. A higher proportion of divorced adults than widowed adults remarry within five years, and divorced men remarry sooner than divorced women. The success of remarriage depends on whether remarriage is compared with an ideal, the earlier marriage, or living without a spouse. The divorce rate is half again as high for remarriages as for first marriages. The divorce rate is lower for young remarriages than for those that occur in middle age, which seem to entail more difficult adjustments to each other and to altered living patterns. Some of the major influences on the success of remarriages include fairly realistic expectations, adequate finances, moderate societal acceptance, lack of dependent children, and emphasis on meeting the needs of both partners. About nine out of ten remarried mothers report that the life of their children is the same or improved following the remarriage and that their present married life is much better than the former marriage. Practitioners can help those who remarry better understand their earlier marital experience so that it contributes to the success of the subsequent marriage.

About one out of twelve adults have never been married. Some marry during middle age and beyond. Most adults who never marry remain single by choice. At about thirty many single women become less optimistic that they will get married, and their interests shift to work and a marriageless life pattern. Personality characteristics and personal preferences mainly account for men who remain single. Although personality characteristics of single women tend to be quite similar to those who marry, this is not the case for men. Those who remain single tend to have been characterized during adolescence as more unconventional and negative compared with those who subsequently married who were characterized as more liked and giving. As with all other categories of adults, there is great variability among those who remain single. Increasing tolerance of various life-styles would seem to contribute to singleness as an acceptable alternative.

Sexual activity is related to family performance, but it is also related to other aspects of adulthood, such as physical condition, health and personality characteristics including attitudes toward oneself and others. Sexual activity and attitudes toward sex during young adulthood are affected by previous experience. Favorable adjustment is more likely to result from premarital sexual activity characterized by affection, respect, and love for the other person. Unfavorable adjustment is more likely to result from premarital sexual activity characterized by aggression, guilt, and exploitation of the other as an object. For males the rate of sexual outlets peaks in the late teens or early twenties and then gradually declines throughout adulthood. The sense of self-worth of many men seems to be more associated with sexual activity than is the case for their wives. For females, the rate of sexual outlets is more constant during adulthood but typically peaks in the late twenties. As for males, extent of sexual activity for females reflects both physical drive and such other factors as inhibitions and interpersonal relations. During middle age, many women experience increased interest in sexual activity, which partly reflects a reduction in earlier inhibitions.

Widespread use of contraceptives and greater societal acceptance of premarital intercourse contribute to less frustration and guilt for the single young adult than was typical a generation or two ago. This has contributed to an increase during the 1960s and especially the 1970s in premarital sexual intercourse by female college students, and now the proportion who participate is about the same as the formerly higher rate for male college students.

The female menopause typically occurs during the late forties when the monthly menstrual period has ceased for a year. Most women accept menopause as a natural and inevitable process. Even though sexual changes occur very slowly for men and reproductive powers extend into the sixties and seventies for most, gradual changes in hormone balance and in physical appearance and vitality cause some men to become anxious about their virility. Some women experience similar concerns. If the partner is understanding and supportive, and encourages self-confidence and growth, a husband or wife can emerge from the transition with a greater sense of self and direction. Some middle-aged men and women revolt against the loss of youth and engage in a "second adolescence." It seems that greater societal and personal acceptance of sexual activity as a natural and constructive part of life for older adults would help many to maintain a positive self-concept. The capacity for sexual performance, especially for the older woman, is typical as long as there is regular sexual stimulation. However, once an older adult ceases sexual intercourse for an extended period, it is seldom resumed.

Practitioners from various fields assist adults with adjustments related to many aspects of family life. To do so effectively depends on an understanding of the clients to be served, the available resources and programs, and the ways to establish effective linkage between clients and resources to encourage adoption of useful practices by adult clients. This entails assistance not only in coping with adjustments, but also in anticipating the types of changes that are likely and recognizing alternatives to prepare for and deal with family transitions as satisfactorily as possible. Information seeking for instrumental purposes by blue collar adults tends to emphasize oral communications with family, friends, and acquaintances and not to include use of the mass media and experts. Therefore, practitioners who seek to serve blue collar adults with educational or social service programs related to family problems are more likely to reach them with programs that fit their life-style and information-seeking methods. Adults who are first to adopt an innovative practice tend to be more highly educated and more oriented to outside information sources, but less a part of the client system, than those who adopt the practice later. Practitioners can market their programs and services in ways that are likely to attract the types of adults they seek to serve. As adults move from apathy to interest to action, there tends to be an increase in the importance of personal information sources. In the actual programs related to family life, some types of activities tend to be especially effective in the modification of practices. For example, experiential education, such as occurs in marriage enrichment programs, is more effective than the mere presentation of information. Discussion in small groups and between partners enables couples to discover and practice ways to facilitate openness and sharing and deal with disagreements.

Practitioners can also help adults to understand the interweaving of developmental processes and goals that reflect both societal expectations and personal preferences. For example, increased societal acceptance and candor regarding alternative life-styles and patterns of family life allows single adults to give greater consideration to their personal goals and preferences than was the case in earlier generations.

As adults make personal and interpersonal adjustments during the family life cycle, they confront potential problems and opportunities. Practitioners can help them recognize and deal with both. For example, as the last children leave home for work, marriage, or college, a middle-aged homemaker may lose satisfaction from active parenting but may gain freedom to pursue personal interests. Similarly, an older couple that moves to a distant retirement community may lose contact with old friends and familiar surroundings but may gain supportive services and companionship with other older adults. A favorable balance between such problems and opportunities, and a developmental process that reflects personal goals and values, seems more likely if practitioners help adults understand likely transitions in family life and approach them proactively and planfully.

₩ 4 ₩

Education, Work, and Community Performance

Practitioners who work with adults in educational, occupational, and community settings tend to be most interested in generalizations about developmental trends regarding health, personality, and learning as they apply to adult performance in those settings. A work supervisor who better understands developmental trends in skill acquisition by middle-aged adults typically applies the generalizations to helping workers increase competence for improved work performance. A teacher of older adults who better understands developmental trends in memory and pacing typically applies the generalizations to help participants in a continuing education program learn more effectively.

Various forms of performance and participation serve as reference points against which practitioners decide on the rele-

171

vance of developmental generalizations and the significance of developmental changes. A nurse engaged in patient education sessions for older adults with recently diagnosed diabetes may be interested in generalizations about trends in sensory perception, learning ability, self-concept, and adjustment. She is likely to review these generalizations in an effort to understand her patients as learners who need to make some important adjustments. If she finds that between forty and sixty years of age, declines in learning ability are so variable and small that they have no practical effect on her adult patients' ability to learn, she is likely to give little further attention to that generalization as she plans educational sessions for older patients. If she finds that some illnesses that restrict cerebral blood circulation result in impaired memory, however, she can then provide such patients with written materials and other memory aids.

Shifts in performance and participation affect other aspects of adult development. The middle-aged adult whose earlier athletic prowess seems to be declining may experience some resultant alteration in self-concept and perhaps morale. The adult whose vision deteriorates abruptly around age fifty may erroneously conclude that his or her learning years are over.

The following review of stability and change in adult participation includes attention to three broad categories of activity: education and information seeking, occupation and work, and community activities (including participation in organizations, organized religion, and recreation). Attention is given to age trends for United States adults in general (and where research findings are available that separate data for white collar and blue collar men and women, they are included), along with brief descriptions of developmental mechanisms. Of particular interest is the changing fabric of participation from young adulthood through middle and old age.

Education

From adolescence through senescence adults engage in educative activity. Such activity forms a broad continuum that ranges from casual information seeking, such as reading a newspaper, watching television, or chatting with a friend, to intensive study, such as participating in an evening course, acquiring a new competency, attending a weekend workshop, or preparing a report based on library research. Adults vary greatly in the extent and types of educative activity in which they engage.

Some adults, especially those with higher levels of formal education, continually engage in educative activity. They read books and magazines, consult experts, and engage in part-time educational programs related to work, family, community, and leisure time. The new ideas and increased competencies they acquire enable them to adapt, grow, and change to solve the problems and grasp the opportunities that confront them. Educative activity is a central ingredient in a self-directed and evolving life-style.

At the other end of the continuum, some adults seldom engage in any activity for the main purpose of expanding what they know and are able to do. Their coping is characterized by habit, trial and error, and response to the expectations of others. Of course they continue to learn and change in slow and incidental ways, but this is a by-product of experience and not part of deliberate efforts to choose, and plan, and guide experience.

Most adults are between these extremes. They read newspapers and magazines but seldom books, they occasionally use radio and television deliberately to increase their competence, they set out to learn something new from time to time in informal ways, and they often seek the assistance of other people in doing so. Each year about one out of four adults engages in educational activities on a part-time basis, most of it provided by a wide variety of sponsors, such as schools, colleges, universities, libraries, churches, employers, associations, and community agencies. During a five-year period about one half of the adults in the United States participate in at least one externally sponsored adult and continuing education activity. However, extent and type of participation is distributed differently in relation to such personal characteristics as age and level of formal education.

Extent of information seeking and educative activity has been assessed in various ways. One way is whether the adult engaged in such activity during the previous day, month, year, or five years. Other indices of extent of participation include the number of activities engaged in, the amount of time devoted to the activities, the extent to which the adult learner gained knowledge and competence from the experience, and the extent to which he or she used or applied what was learned.

The broad range of educative activity by adults is typically categorized to reflect the channels and settings through which adults encounter information for the main purpose of increasing their understanding and competence. In all cases the current emphasis is on interaction with media and people for educative purposes, in contrast with entertainment and recreation, even though in most instances when an adult encounters media and other people there are elements of both learning something and gaining satisfaction from the experience. Information seeking outside any educational program is usually divided into use of impersonal media and interpersonal contact with others. Impersonal information seeking through the mass media is further divided into print media (newspapers, magazines, and books) and electronic media (films, radio, and television). Interpersonal information seeking is further divided into interaction with friends and with experts (counselors and specialists). More traditional forms of educational activity are divided into self-directed education (in which the adult learner assumes most of the teaching functions, such as deciding on objectives, selecting learning activities, and engaging in evaluation), and agency-sponsored continuing education programs for adults.

Information Seeking. The extent to which United States adults read newspapers, magazines, and books is highly associated with level of formal education but only slightly associated with age (Parker and Paisley, 1966). The association with educational level is especially high for reading for the purpose of obtaining information in contrast with entertainment and escape. Beyond age sixty, adults continue to read materials that are readily available, but there is a decline in use of print media that must be obtained outside the home, such as books from libraries and book stores.

Earlier studies based on selected populations found that about nine out of ten United States adults report reading a newspaper regularly (Link and Hopf, 1946; Knox and Anderson, 1964; Westley and Severin, 1964; Parker and Paisley, 1966; Rees and Paisley, 1967, 1968). However, in a recent national Gallup poll, two thirds of those questioned said that they read a newspaper daily. There is a slight association with level of education and age. There is a slight decline in middle age followed by a gradual increase, especially as reflected in time spent and number of newspapers read. During adulthood, time spent reading the comics declines and time spent reading news and editorials increases slowly. Men spend more time reading about news, business and financial topics, and, especially when they are younger, the sports section. Women spend more time reading about homemaking topics and the women's section, and this interest increases with age through the fifties. However, when newspaper reading is analyzed within educational levels, the differences between men and women largely disappear (Schramm and White, 1949; Parker and Paisley, 1966). About six out of ten report use of newspapers to meet specific information needs in a two-month period.

Earlier studies found that about eight out of ten United States adults reported reading magazines regularly (Knox and Anderson, 1964; Ennis, 1965; Parker and Paisley, 1966; Rees and Paisley, 1967, 1968). In a recent national Gallup poll, slightly more than half the respondents said that they read one or more magazines a week. Readership is highly associated with educational level but is unrelated to age except for a slight decline for older adults. Interest in magazine reading as a source of practical education declines slightly with age for adults with less formal education and increases slightly with age for the more highly educated. About four out of ten report use of magazines to meet specific information needs in a two-month period.

About four out of ten adults read hard-cover or paperback books regularly (Knox and Anderson, 1964; Ennis, 1965; Parker and Paisley, 1966; Rees and Paisley, 1967, 1968). In a recent national Gallup poll, more than one third of those questioned said that they read books to meet specific information needs in a two-month period. Level of formal education is highly associated with book reading; three out of five college graduates compared with one out of five adults who did not complete high school report reading one or more books during the previous month (Rees and Paisley, 1968; London, Wenkert and Hagstrom, 1963). More reading of nonfiction books is done by men and more of fiction and of books generally is done by women. However, when time available is held constant, such as in a comparison of employed men with employed women, the differences disappear (Parker and Paisley, 1966).

Book reading is little associated with age during adulthood. There is a slight decline with age (Ennis, 1965) which largely disappears when educational level is controlled (Rees and Paisley, 1967). Fiction reading is somewhat more frequent for young adults than for older adults. A decline in general book reading for adults over age sixty reflects barriers to access. For use of reference books and public libraries there are significant declines with age (Rees and Paisley, 1968). Public library use is much higher for adults with a higher level of formal education (Kronus, 1973). More than one third of the adult population used a library during the year, but one third has never done so.

For young adults, there are differences in reading habits between those who go to college and those who do not. Going to college entails substantial reading of text books and journals. In addition, more college students read news magazines than do those young adults who do not go to college (Trent and Medsker, 1968). Extent of newspaper and magazine reading for out-of-school youths is extensive and similar in amount to the general adult population. Although book reading for young adults who do not go on to college is less than for college students, it is greater than for the general adult population. About one third of non-college-bound young adults read no books during the year compared with about two thirds of the general adult population (Hendrickson and Foster, 1960; Knox, 1970).

Adult information seeking from print media varies greatly with level of formal education. Although there is substantial variability, many blue collar adults seldom read. Practitioners can be more effective if they accurately assess the extent to which their clients use print media and adapt efforts to facilitate learning and change accordingly.

Although radio and television are used mainly for entertainment, there is some informational use for the serious purpose of increasing understanding. When entertainment and informational use of electronic media are combined there are some adult life cycle trends. The proportion of adults who view television regularly increases from young adulthood to middle age and then declines into old age, but because the young and old adults who watch devote more time to doing so than the middle aged, the average amount of time spent on television is about the same from the early twenties until the late sixties. The proportion of adults who listen to radio regularly declines from young adulthood to middle age, then increases into old age, but because the young tend to listen for longer time periods and the old listen selectively, the average amount of time spent on radio declines during adulthood (Knox and Videbeck, 1964). Use of electronic media, especially television, is negatively associated with level of formal education. Those who view more television generally have less education (Steiner, 1963; Parker and Paisley, 1966). However, the age trend is even stronger for young adults. Non-college-bound youth view less television than the general adult population but listen to more radio (Knox, 1970). Adults who are active in cultural, educational, and professional activities, generally spend little time watching television (London, Wenkert and Hagstrom, 1963). However, when informational use of electronic media is analyzed separately, a different pattern emerges. Although general use of radio declines with age, informational use increases as adults become older (Parker and Paisley, 1966; Rees and Paisley, 1967, 1968). Although college-educated adults view less television than those with less formal education, a higher proportion of their viewing is for informational purposes. There is a general trend toward greater informational use of television for older adults, but there is actually a decline with age for adults with more education and an increase with age for adults with less education (Parker and Paisley, 1966). In a recent national Gallup poll, more than half the respondents said that they watched television to meet specific information needs in a two-month period. Radio and television appear to have potential for use by practitioners who seek to help adults increase their understanding and competence to deal with changes and adjustments during adulthood.

Interpersonal information seeking from friends and experts declines slightly during adulthood, but this reflects the lower average educational level of older adults (Troldahl and Van Dam, 1965; Troldahl, Van Dam, and Robeck, 1965; Rees and Paisley, 1967). Information seeking from friends tends to be on topics related to home and entertainment. Men typically consult experts about business and finance. Women typically consult experts about health and welfare concerns. The adult educational level is positively associated with extent of interpersonal information seeking related to business, health, and welfare. However, educational level is not associated with extent of information seeking regarding entertainment, and the solution of practical problems such as home maintenance. In a recent national Gallup poll, more than four out of ten respondents said that friends and relatives are an information source. Practitioners are sometimes sources of information and sometimes backstop other sources.

A better understanding of adult development can help the practitioner develop relevant services and interpret them to a target market of adults. For example, instrumental information seeking by blue collar adults is typically oriented toward informal interpersonal contact with family and friends. Use of impersonal information sources, such as mass media and experts, and participation in formal organizations are unusual for many blue collar adults. Therefore, practitioners who seek to serve blue collar adults with educational or social service programs related to occupational or community problems are more likely to reach them with programs that fit their life-style. For example, an adult basic education program for unemployed urban adults who read below the eighth grade level might encourage participation by locating outreach classes in local neighborhoods and by encouraging neighborhood opinion leaders and initial participants to tell potential participants about the program.

Educational Activity.   The participation rates that adults report for systematic self-directed learning projects depend on the interviewer's definition of self-directed or independent study and on the depth of probing used. Someone is likely to recall teaching himself or herself to play the piano a year ago, but that same person may not necessarily remember learning to assemble a bicycle that arrived in a carton with assembly instructions. A study that emphasized participation by adults in part-time educational programs sponsored by various organizations showed about half as many instances of self-directed or independent study as sponsored programs. It also showed that less than one out of ten adults had engaged in independent study during the previous year (Johnstone and Rivera, 1965). In a study that emphasized informal information seeking by adults, independent study was reported by more than half of the adults in the previous few years (Parker and Paisley, 1966). In a study that emphasized self-directed learning projects and probed deeply for instances, almost all adults reported at least one minor instance, and the average during the previous year was eight (Tough, 1971).

Especially for the more major instances of independent study, the participation rates were higher for adults with more formal education. One out of fifty adults who had not attended high school took part in independent study, compared with one out of ten of those who attended or completed high school, and one out of three of those who went on for a year or more of college (Johnstone and Rivera, 1965). Participation rates for major instances of independent study decline with age, from more than one out of ten for young adults, to one out of twelve for the middle-aged adults, and one out of twenty-five for older adults. Part of this decline reflects lower average levels of formal education for older adults.

There was a wide variety of reasons for undertaking learning projects, especially in the entire range of self-directed learning. The most common and important reason was the desire to use or apply the knowledge and skill, and the second most frequent reason was curiosity about a topic that was controversial or very important in the life of the learner. Other reasons that occurred in at least a third of the learning activities were pleasure in the learning activity, pleasure from the content, and a desire to possess or retain the knowledge and skill. Of lesser importance were enjoyment while practicing the resultant skill, impressing others, personal satisfaction from learning successfully, companionship, and personal commitment to complete a course once started (Tough, 1968a, b). Practitioners can find out the extent to which clients engage in self-directed learning, and can help them do so as a means of adaptation and change.

During late adolescence and early young adulthood, many men and women attend postsecondary educational programs full time for most of a year for some technical fields and for most of a decade for some professional fields. During the past generation an increasing number of adults in their thirties and forties are also doing so. In the past decade, about three quarters of the people in their late teens graduate from high school (U.S., DHEW, 1975). A higher proportion of those who do, come from white collar families, live in suburban neighborhoods, and have somewhat higher levels of verbal ability. About half the high school graduates continue for some form of full-time, postsecondary education. Except for the World War II period, there has been a steady increase in the proportion of pupils who entered fifth grade eight years earlier who graduated from high school and entered college. In 1972, 750 of each 1,000 students who had entered fifth grade in 1965 had graduated from high school, and 433 started college study. In the early 1970s there was a leveling off in the percentage who went on to college.

Entering and completing college is affected by many factors. Three major ones are the individual's intelligence, the social class level of his or her parents, and the individual's high school performance (Eckland, 1964a, b). College attendance is most highly associated with social class (Trent and Medsker, 1968). Role orientations of young women have some influence (Alper, 1973). The homes in which children and adolescents grow up vary in their abundance and encouragement of educative activity. White collar families tend to encourage educative activity somewhat more than blue collar families, although there is substantial overlap. Social class is associated somewhat with intelligence and is a strong source of encouragement and support regarding both high school performance and going on to college (Bloom, 1964). This is reflected in the college plans of high school seniors. One out of two seniors with family incomes over $25,000 plan to attend four-year colleges, compared with one out of eight seniors with family incomes under $5,000. However, there is relatively little relation to family income for those who plan to attend two-year colleges (U.S., DHEW, 1976). For those young adults who enroll in college, persistence and successful completion is heavily influenced by a combination of academic ability and motivation. Some of those who drop out of high school and of college subsequently graduate (Super and others, 1967; Trent and Medsker, 1968). In fact, those who withdraw before completion of a level of formal education (such as completion of three years of a four-year bachelor's degree program) tend to have higher rates of participation in subsequent part-time educational programs than do those who never begin that level of formal education (such as ending after completion of a two-year associate degree program).

The impact of college on students is varied. In addition to subject matter mastery and entry to occupations that require a college degree, there is evidence of a gradual increase during four years of undergraduate study in values such as open-mindedness, intellectuality, independence, confidence, and readiness to express impulses, along with a decrease in conservatism regarding public issues. Such attitude shifts tend to persist if the postcollege environment is supportive (Feldman and Newcomb, 1969). It is not clear how much change is attributable to personality change during late adolescence associated with the intelligence and openness to new experience of those who choose to attend college, and how much is attributable to the college environment (Trent and Medsker, 1968). Since 1955 increasingly larger proportions of college students are beyond the typical age range of seventeen to twenty-two. This is especially so for two-year community colleges. In 1974 one out of ten college students were over age thirty-five (U.S., DHEW, 1976). In recent years, about 6 percent of married women living with their spouses and between the ages of eighteen and twenty-four were enrolled in school. Middle-aged women who return to college typically achieve as well as or better in their courses than the younger students (Halfter, 1962).

Practitioners need to understand interactions between the institutional or organizational setting in which educational programs occur and the intellectual or emotional development of the learners. This applies to teachers and counselors working with people between the ages of seventeen and twenty-two who participate in continuing education programs on a part-time basis or return to college. Many generalizations about educational and career counseling have been focused on influences of the college environment on personal and career development, but some can be adapted for use by practitioners who work with adults.

The college setting is often characterized as one that fosters a prolonged period of psychological and intellectual development. Various vectors of student development have been identified, including achieving competence (understanding, interpersonal relations, physical skills), managing feelings (aggression, sex), establishing identity (coherence of beliefs and behavior), becoming autonomous (social interdependence based on personal independence), clarifying purposes and directions (work, family, leisure), freeing interpersonal relationships (spontaneity, intimacy, acceptance of differences), and developing integrity (beliefs that guide behavior) (Chickering, 1969).

Intellectual and ethical development of students has also been conceptualized as a sequence of stages in which the individual learner moves from simple and absolute ways of dealing with knowledge and values to more complex and pluralistic perspectives. The more simplistic learners assume that information is either right or wrong and that uncertainty is due to error. At more advanced stages of development, knowledge is understood as contextual and relative and finally there is student acceptance of the need for continual attention to identity and personal commitment within a relative context (Perry, 1970).

Practitioners can use such ways of conceptualizing student

development to help fit instructional or counseling approaches to learners' cognitive structures. For example, learners with more simplistic and absolute ways of dealing with knowledge and values may have difficulty in an educational setting characterized by diversity, uncertainty, and reliance on self-direction by learners. Practitioners can provide these learners with more structure and guidance for dealing with relative concepts and acquiring a greater sense of identity and commitment in dealing with knowledge and values. Learners who have achieved greater commitment to their own active role in learning and are able to deal with more relative knowledge can be encouraged in their freedom to learn in more self-directed and flexible ways (Perry, 1970; D. E. Hunt, 1970; Stern and Cope, 1956; R. J. Hill, 1960).

Each year during the mid-1970s, about one out of four United States adults engaged in at least one major continuing education activity on a part-time basis. In the early 1960s, one out of every five did so, which included about twenty-five million participants. During the subsequent decade the total number of adults in the population increased, and the level of formal education rose. As a result, during the mid-1970s the best estimate of the number of adults participating in major continuing education activities annually is between thirty and thirty-five million. Half of the adult population participates during a five-year period.

Two thirds of the part-time educational activities for adults are sponsored by a variety of institutions and organizations, such as colleges, churches, community organizations, employers, and schools (Johnstone and Rivera, 1965). Regarding topics studied, one third of participation is occupationally related, one fifth is related to use of leisure, and one eighth each are related to general education, religion and family.

As indicated in Figure 9, annual participation in continuing education declines with age. Among out-of-school youth under age twenty 16 percent participate in part-time continuing education programs. This somewhat low participation rate occurs in part because most college students, who subsequently account for high participation rates, are in school full time and thus seldom enroll in part-time continuing education programs.

The highest participation rate is 29 percent in the twenties, followed by 26 percent in the thirties, 21 percent in the forties, 16 percent in the fifties, 10 percent in the sixties, and 4 percent for persons aged seventy and older. The decline in educational participation with age results from many influences, some of which practitioners can do something about, such as location, topic, schedule, and cost.

Participation rates are comparable for men and women. Family life cycle shifts account for the major fluctuations during adulthood. In young adulthood, the participation rate of mothers is about two-thirds that of fathers, but the participation rate for young adults without children is the same for men and for women. The lower rate for young mothers reflects the restrictions of home and family responsibilities on activities away from home. Higher participation rates by fathers compared with similar men who do not have children seem to reflect the use of continuing education to increase occupational achievement to meet the greater economic demands of larger families (Johnstone and Rivera, 1965).

Level of formal education is more highly associated with extent of participation in continuing education activities than any other characteristic (Knox and Videbeck, 1963; London, Wenkert, and Hagstrom, 1963; Johnstone and Rivera, 1965; Parker and Paisley, 1966). The percentage of adults within each level of formal education who participate in continuing educa-

Figure 9. Part-Time Educational Participation: Percent in Each Age Group That Participated in Previous Year

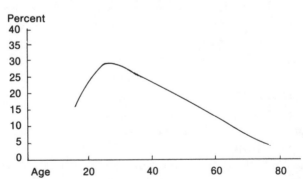

Source: Johnstone and Rivera (1965).

tion during a year is 6 percent for those with some grade school, 9 percent for those who complete eighth grade, 15 percent for those with some high school, 24 percent for high school graduates, 36 percent for those with some college, 39 percent for college graduates, and 47 percent for those who complete a year or more of graduate study. The relationship between level of formal education and part-time educational participation is presented in Figure 10. Educational level is one of the most important characteristics that practitioners can take into account in planning educational activities that will effectively reach and teach adults.

Income and occupational prestige are also associated with participation, but much less so than education, and education is about twice as influential as age. Although in the general population participation rates are somewhat higher for whites than for blacks, when they are compared within levels of formal education, participation rates are the same.

Initial exposure to continuing education tends to occur early in adulthood. Two thirds of all adults have participated in continuing education by the time they are thirty. Initial participation continues to occur throughout adulthood, however.

The reasons adults engage in continuing education activi-

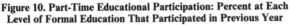

Figure 10. Part-Time Educational Participation: Percent at Each Level of Formal Education That Participated in Previous Year

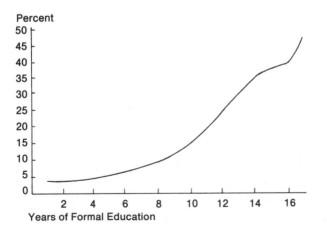

Source: Johnstone and Rivera (1965).

ties vary greatly and some of the shifts are associated with adult life cycle trends (Knox, 1968). Occupational considerations are influential for young adults with a shift from concern about job entry to interest in job advancement. Occupationally related continuing education is more widespread for men than for women. As men move from their thirties to their fifties they more often use continuing education for leisure interests. This shift does not occur for women because many younger women, especially those not employed outside the home, were already using continuing education for leisure interests. More older participants do so for general information and social contacts than is the case for younger participants (Johnstone and Rivera, 1965; Hendrickson and Barnes, 1967).

Reasons for participation in continuing education also vary with level of occupational prestige. At lower socioeconomic levels, the emphasis is mainly on coping with daily concerns. Blue collar men participate mainly for vocational reasons, especially preparation for a new job. Blue collar women participate mainly for vocational and homemaking reasons. For white collar adults, a small proportion of participation is for occupational reasons, mostly for advancement on the present job, and there is an increase in participation related to community and leisure concerns (Johnstone and Rivera, 1965). For participation in vocational education, the influence of occupation increases in relation to educational level, but age continues to be a major factor (Rees and Paisley, 1967). Especially in vocational programs, participation reflects directly felt needs and ability to benefit (Parker and Paisley, 1966; Dubin, 1972).

Although age and educational level are highly associated with rates of participation in continuing education, there are adults whose participation rates are much higher than would be anticipated on the basis of these characteristics alone. Examples of subpopulations for whom low participation rates would be anticipated on the basis of descriptive characteristics are out-of-school youths, middle-aged blue collar men, and older adults. One attitudinal characteristic that is associated with higher participation rates than anticipated is a sense of educational efficacy. A person with a high sense of educational efficacy believes that through further education the individual can gain greater mastery over his or her life and surroundings and that further education has practical consequences and utility. Among young people in their late teens and early twenties who do not go on to college and are dissatisfied with the type of work they do, a much higher proportion of those with a high sense of educational efficacy participate in continuing education than would be expected on the basis of age and educational level (Johnstone and Rivera, 1965). Almost half the recent high school graduates in middle-sized cities who do not go on to college participate in continuing education during a year's time and more than one out of ten participate in three or more years (Knox, 1970). Blue collar men with optimism about job advancement and a high sense of educational efficacy have much higher participation rates than similar adults without these attitudes (London, Wenkert, and Hagstrom, 1963; Knox, 1970). Older adults with a high sense of educational efficacy have higher rates of participation than young adults with a low sense of educational efficacy (Rees and Paisley, 1967). Achievement and persistence in some types of part-time educational programs are unrelated to age but mainly reflect educational experience and situational factors (Knox and Sjogren, 1964; Brown, Knox, and Grotelueschen, 1966).

Encouraging Participation. In general, although the types of continuing education and information-seeking activities in which adults engage vary substantially between men and women, the extent of participation is largely associated with level of formal education, age, and sense of educational efficacy. Practitioners can use information about these three characteristics for the clients with whom they work, along with information about their current patterns of educative activity and information seeking, in order to help the clients use educative activity to serve their purposes (M. L. Farmer, 1971).

There are various ways in which practitioners can market the services of an educational institution or a social agency. Findings from needs assessments and other forms of market research, along with generalizations about adult development, help practitioners understand the needs of adults in the target market. Such findings can also help identify the most likely channels of communications through which to reach the potential clients. When an adult becomes aware of and decides to engage in a new activity related to work, education, or community participation, he or she typically moves through stages of apathy, awareness, interest, trial, and adoption. Innovators and opinion leaders, who are among the first to engage in a new activity, tend to obtain information from the mass media to a greater extent than the early majority and late majority who may take up an activity later. Systematic efforts to encourage adults to use new knowledge typically entail a linkage process in which people who are familiar with both the resource system and the client system help clients alternate between their action problems and relevant knowledge resources (Rogers and Shoemaker, 1971; Havelock, 1969).

The process by which practitioners come to understand clients and help them establish linkage with relevant services and resources varies with client characteristics, the type of practice to be modified, and the background of the practitioner. A college professor who conducts a one-week seminar for physicians on new developments in the field confronts interrelationships that contrast with those confronted by a supervisor helping an able new manager from the blue collar ranks to be successful. An agricultural extension advisor assisting a young farmer to adopt a more satisfactory financial record system likewise confronts different client expectations and available services than a medical social worker helping a successful dancer adjust to the loss of both legs in an automobile accident. In addition to the variability in the process by which practitioners help adults to modify practices, there are some commonalities suggested in the foregoing review.

Occupation

A major task for most young men and an increasing proportion of young women is to establish themselves in an occupation. In our society, one's occupation is a major factor in shaping self-concept as well as in setting one's level of living and prestige. The occupational life cycle includes exploration of and establishment in some type of work during late adolescence and early young adulthood, a variety of mid-career adjustments, and termination of occupational activity through retirement or death. Although there are general occupational trends in productivity and satisfaction, there are variations for men and women and for blue collar and white collar workers.

Assessment. A variety of indices have been used to assess life cycle shifts in occupational performance. Most of the indices consist of relatively quantitative and objective evidence of performance such as pages published, inventions recorded, athletic records set, work-related accidents reported, and paintings produced. These indices emphasize some aspects of occupational performance and some types of occupations for which people bother to keep records. Type of work performed by successive age groups is an imperfect index of career development for individuals, because it mainly reflects rapid technological change during the past few generations. The jobs held by persons nearing retirement tend to be the types of jobs that were available two generations ago such as farming, business, and manufacturing, while more of the jobs held by young adults relate to service and technology.

Most of the evidence of occupational performance is based on indices of average performance that emphasize typical quantity of output. Little attention is given to variations in the quality of performance. Examples include the number of pages published per year by psychologists and the number of items produced per day by factory workers on a piece rate. There are wide individual differences among workers, but the more productive tend to remain productive with some decline in the later years. When peak performance in the form of a major contribution of highest quality is used as the index, the peak tends to occur earlier and to drop off sooner.

Extent of job change or turnover declines with age, and there is some increase in unemployment rates beyond middle age. Work-related accidents decline with age. The number of absences from work due to illness declines with age, but the length of the absence increases for older workers. The number of women in the labor force follows a different pattern from that of men, with a peak in early adulthood followed by a drop during the time when most are having and raising children and a second peak between age forty-five and fifty-four when more than half of all women in that age category are in the labor force. An effort to understand occupational life cycle trends in performance should take into account the indices that are germane to the specific purpose for which greater understanding is sought.

Occupational Choice and Establishment. Most adolescents realize that occupational choice affects both income level and life-style (Powell and Bloom, 1962; Holland, 1973). Young people confront a series of difficult occupational choices. Some of the choices are made deliberately and some of them are reactive and unintentional. The process of choosing and adjusting has become more difficult in recent generations as the variety of occupations has increased (Ehrle, 1970). This has encouraged unrealistic occupational goals and has made it more difficult for the individual to understand his or her interests and capabilities and their likely fit with potential occupations (Dansereau, 1961).

The process by which adults enter jobs varies greatly. Some people seem to drift into a job with little thought or planning. For some, the availability of a job when one is needed seems to be the critical ingredient. Some people agonize over a job choice with much introspection. Some take tests to predict job performance (Droege, 1967; Droege and others, 1963). Along with such personality characteristics as decisiveness, job choice tends to be influenced by the pattern of meanings or values that work has for the individual. In addition to receipt of income, work can enable the individual to meet a challenge, acquire and demonstrate competence, validate self-esteem, and engage in social interaction. Occupational decisions reflect both personal preferences and available opportunities. Early decisions regarding education, mate selection, and peer groups tend to influence career development. For example, a young woman who mainly wants to be a full-time homemaker may approach working as a short-term, fill-in activity until her first pregnancy and may have little interest in career advancement. A similar woman with career goals may be very ambitious and become frustrated by slow progress.

The success of the occupational choice and adjustment process is reflected in both productivity and satisfaction. These dual criteria are reflected in a widespread career expectation shift from freshman to senior year for college students. Both freshmen (Feldman and Newcomb, 1969).. (The increased comportunity to use their special abilities. However, over the years, seniors have also wanted to use their creative abilities and self-expression and have been less concerned about job security than freshman (Feldman and Newcomb, 1969). (The increased competition among college graduates for available positions that occurred in the early 1970s has no doubt increased the importance of job security.) During past generations, both college-bound and non-college-bound youths typically selected careers of the same general occupational prestige level as their parents', even when they selected occupations that were unrelated to those of their parents (Kinane and Pable, 1962; Simpson, 1962). (During the past decade, it appears that an increasing proportion of young people are experiencing downward mobility as they enter occupations that are lower in prestige than the entry occupations of their parents.)

Traditional views of occupational choice and establishment as a one-time process that occurs early in young adulthood are gradually giving way to a recognition that occupational development occurs during much of adulthood. Participation in family, work, and community interact during the adult life cycle, but for most men and many women occupational activity has a powerful influence on the structuring of family and community life (W. E. Henry, 1971).

In past generations, many people entered a field of work, or a major life role such as homemaker, with a sense of foreclosure. This included both a sense of lifetime commitment to a type of occupation, which foreclosed a major occupational change, and a sense of identity foreclosure as the individual accepted the security of role expectations instead of continued growth of self (Marcia, 1966). In recent years, however, an increasing proportion of men and women have recognized that occupational choice and adjustment entails major career changes at various points during the occupational life cycle. Some aspects of career development reflect personality and learning changes that are especially dramatic during late adolescence and young adulthood. Examples of such qualitative changes include analysis of the component parts and causal relationships of issues, synthesis of diverse elements into a more complex whole, and movement from absolute to relative semantic structures that include greater use of alternatives, qualifiers, and modifiers. Counselors who help high school and college students with career planning have noted that such changes contribute to career decision making. Other aspects of career development that tend to be influential on major occupational changes at any stage of adulthood include internal versus external locus of control, willingness to accept new roles and responsibilities, and risk taking (Heath, 1965, 1976; Perry, 1970).

Occupational preferences or interests are one outcome of educational activities. Such preferences are influenced by various factors including attractive role models and reinforcement of related attitudes and activities. Practitioners can assist adults of any age to recognize the various ways in which educative activity can facilitate the process of entering and becoming established in an occupation. In some instances, full-time preparatory education is a formal prerequisite for job entry. In addition, some part-time educational activities help adults explore occupational opportunities and personal preferences and increase the likelihood that the job choice will be satisfactory. Some educational activities, sponsored by employers, educational institutions, and associations, facilitate orientation and upgrading once on the job. Practitioners who are aware of such educational opportunities can better assist adults of any age with their career development. Practitioners can also help young workers understand the mentor-mentee relationship in which older, better-established members of the occupation work closely with beginners to help them "learn the ropes." This sometimes entails a formal apprenticeship but more often entails informal coaching and assistance. This may reflect the aspiration of the older worker to have "social heirs." The relationship tends to have a cycle that can be more satisfactory if both parties understand its probable course.

Because occupational satisfaction depends on the fit between job characteristics and individual interests and abilities, some of the factors associated with satisfactory occupational adjustment are specific to the person and the job (Healy, 1973; Quinn, Staines, and McCullough, 1974). Some of the factors that generally contribute to satisfactory choices are: (1) familiarity with the occupation based on relevant work experience (D. Harris, 1961; Rauner, 1962); (2) similarity between the occupation and personal interests as reflected in selection of and satisfaction from high school and college courses (H. M. Bell, 1960; Strong, 1958); (3) availability of occupational role models (A. B. Bell, 1970); (4) job requirements and expectations that are somewhat challenging but not threatening; (5) serious consideration of fit with personal interests and abilities without undue emphasis on prestige; (6) congruity with the individual's work values; and (7) socialization that occurs in educational and work settings and influences entry into an occupational field (Becker and Strauss, 1956; Becker and others, 1961; Henry, Sims, and Spray, 1971).

Productivity. A developmental understanding of occupational performance entails a definition of those activities classified as occupational; a recognition of the proportions of various segments of the adult population employed in the work force; an analysis of patterns of career stability and change; and an assessment of unsatisfactory, satisfactory, and outstanding levels of occupational performance. Available tested knowledge about occupational performance during adulthood is sufficient to provide a fragmentary overview of the occupational life cycle.

The terms *work, occupation,* and *career* can be defined broadly or narrowly. A broad societal definition includes any organized effort that produces goods or services that benefit society in some way, whether or not money or exchange is involved. Within this broad definition, occupational performance would include homemaking, home repairs, writing poetry, caring for grandchildren, and volunteer service on a community board. A narrow economic definition includes only those activities for which the individual is paid. The distinction between paid and unpaid effort has been doubly important. Money is the most widespread index of value, and in an urban society it is the only means for acquisition of needed goods and services. Partly as a result, people tend to equate personal productivity with work for pay. Although we appear to be in transition between a narrow and a broad definition of work, with the exception of some forms of scientific and artistic creativity, most indices of occupational performance from past generations are based on a narrow definition of occupation.

The composition of the United States work force has changed greatly during the past three generations. At the turn of the century most jobs were related to agriculture, business, and manufacturing. Most workers reported in labor or census occupational statistics were men. Although the work of many wives in the family farm or business contributed to family income, they were not included in statistics on the work force. Youth entered the world of work soon after leaving school and the average age at death was sufficiently low that the proportion of adults beyond working age was small. Only one in ten people lived through middle age. Today, higher rates of high school completion and postsecondary education delay entry into the work force. With the combination of an urban occupational structure, a younger age when families are grown, and a longer average life expectancy, more than half of all middle-aged women are now in the work force. With the combination of mandatory retirement and longer life expectancy, a large proportion of the adult population is no longer working. Although labor surpluses, unemployment and underemployment rates for various segments of the population fluctuate with the general condition of the economy and specific conditions related to agriculture or manufacturing, during the past generation the highest unemployment rates have occurred for urban minority youth, blue collar workers generally, and women (O'Toole,

1975). The high incidence of unemployment for the young is shown in Figure 11.

Life cycle trends in occupational performance for the adults in a community or region are greatly affected by societal trends such as change in the occupational structure. One result of the rapidly changing occupational structure is that many workers engage in several types of work in the course of their working lives. Practitioners can help adults understand and plan for multiple careers.

With the emergence of second and third careers, it has become more important to understand patterns of occupational stability and change as a basis for decisions that are likely to make careers more productive, orderly, and satisfying (Sheppard, 1971; Murray, Powers, and Havighurst, 1971; Wilensky, 1961; Parnes and others, 1972). In contrast with somewhat chaotic work patterns in which society loses efficient manpower and productivity and in which individual workers lose a sense of continuity and advancement, orderly careers are characterized by a coherent sense in individuals that there is a forward thrust and a purpose in their occupational activity. Career anchors contribute to occupational stability and coherence for some executives (Schein, 1975). This coherence may influence the individual's family and community activity as well. Although

Figure 11. Unemployment and Age: Percent of Labor Force in Each Age Category That Was Unemployed in 1970

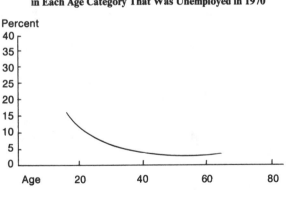

Source: BLS (1975).

a higher proportion of white collar than blue collar occupations are orderly and sequential, a better understanding of the dynamics of adult career development can so improve occupational decision making that any type of work becomes more productive and satisfying.

Some types of occupational decisions deal mainly with personal characteristics and concerns of the individual worker. Other decisions deal mainly with the ways in which jobs are defined and organized, such as the creation of sequential career ladders for blue collar workers. The career pattern of an adult results from the intersection of these personal and situational factors (Crites, 1969). For example, the combination of a personality factor, such as extent of self-direction, with situational pressures for stability or change in occupation helps explain many career patterns. When a person has low self-direction in a work situation and little pressure to change, the typical result is a predictable and routine career with advancement that follows seniority or other promotion rules. When a person has high self-direction in a work situation and little pressure to change, the typical result is a flexible career in which the initiative to change type and extent of work is taken by the individual. When a person has low self-direction in a work situation and much pressure to change, the typical result is a disjointed career, such as that of a blue collar worker who experiences technological unemployment or a young widow who must seek work. When a person has high self-direction in a work situation with much pressure to change, the typical result is a well-planned effort by the affected individual deliberately to select and prepare for work that constitutes a desirable next segment in the individual's career (Murray, Powers, and Havighurst, 1971).

Indices of Productivity. A developmental analysis of occupational performance might be based on various indices of productivity and quality of performance. One possible index is unsatisfactory performance, as illustrated by reject rate, accident rate, or substandard production rate in an industrial setting. Unemployment rates only partly reflect unsatisfactory performance; they also reflect supply and demand, seniority, and discrimination. Indices of unsatisfactory performance for various categories of adults can be used by practitioners for personnel selection, redesign of equipment or procedures, and planning of educative activities designed to reduce unsatisfactory performance.

Another index is typical, satisfactory performance as illustrated by annual output measures, such as salesmen's commissions and creative products by artists and scientists. Most indices of satisfactory performance are quantitative and assume only that the output is above a criterion of minimal satisfactoriness without much consideration of excellence or quality.

Indices of outstanding performance occur mainly for artistic, scientific, and athletic fields where there is a product or performance that can be judged for excellence and sufficient societal importance is attached to excellence that records are made and retained. Although we appreciate a taxi driver who is prompt, safe, and courteous and a mailman who is dependable regardless of weather conditions, workers in such fields are seldom recognized for outstanding performance in a way that allows an analysis of career trends in outstanding performance. However, various occupational fields are accumulating age-related data that could be analyzed to improve our understanding of developmental trends in outstanding occupational performance. Examples include the ages of winners of plowing contests for farmers, of entertainers who win awards, of typing contests for secretaries, and of persons in various professional fields who achieve the highest scores on examinations that are increasingly being used for relicensure and recertification.

During young adulthood occupational performance varies greatly among indices and subpopulations. Most of the tested knowledge is about men in white collar occupations, especially scientists and artists, and in athletics. However, there are some generalizations about blue collar men and about working women. The following subsections describe age trends in unsatisfactory, satisfactory, and outstanding occupational performance for adults with various characteristics.

Unsatisfactory Performance. On some indices of unsatisfactory performance, such as work-related accidents and ab-

senteeism by blue collar workers, the average record of young
adults is worse than that of middle-aged and older adults (Breen
and Spaeth, 1960; Chown and Heron, 1965; de la Mare and
Sergean, 1961; Featherstone and Cunningham, 1963). Regarding unsatisfactory performance by white collar workers, the
record books do not show how many aspiring scientists and
artists concluded that the results of their early efforts did not
warrant continuing and turned their attention to other fields.
In many instances, young adults are doing a type of work, acquiring increased competence for that type of work, and testing
whether they want to continue in that type of work or change
to another at the same time. Occupational stability is achieved
when the worker has sufficient long-term commitment to a job
that he or she begins to internalize the norms and practices,
and when the worker has sufficient familiarity to reduce many
of the instances of unsatisfactory performance such as errors and
accidents.

For most indices of satisfactory occupational performance, there are few important age-related differences between
twenty and sixty-five years of age but substantial variability
within age groups. There are some age trends in satisfactory
performance, however. Young adults perform somewhat better
in jobs that entail high-speed manual skills (King, 1955) or acceptance of new procedures. Air traffic specialists, whose jobs
are attention demanding and fast paced, tend to be more effective when they are under age forty. Older workers tend to perform better in terms of experience, steadiness, conscientiousness,
patience, and attendance (Rosenberg, 1970). There are also
some factors associated with age and satisfactory performance.
For example, many airline pilots pass rigorous medical exams
and perform well in middle age (McFarland, 1954; Spealman
and Bruyere, 1955). Middle-aged workers with children in high
school tend to be more affected by a job-related move to a new
community than young workers, and there is a steady decline
with age in job-related moves (Glick, 1955). Peak income occurs
on the average around age fifty.

For men and women alike, unsatisfactory occupational
performance trends during adulthood are difficult to identify.

This is partly because middle-aged adults typically set criteria that are used to judge unsatisfactory performance, and they apply the criteria mainly to middle-aged workers. The very young and the very old are underrepresented in the work force. For many indices of unsatisfactory performance, ability to perform is only one influence. Other influences on indices such as absenteeism or unemployment emanate from family life or from the employing organization. For example, over the years unemployment has been more widespread for blue collar than for white collar workers. In recent years, unemployment rates have been high for some categories of college graduates. However, these unemployment rates are influenced more by the economic system than by life cycle trends in occupational performance by individuals. The reaction to unemployment differs somewhat by social class, however. Blue collar workers tend to blame unemployment on society (such as economic conditions or the employer), while white collar workers tend to blame themselves for unemployment and think of themselves as failures (Goodchilds and Smith, 1963).

As indicated earlier, except in periods of full employment, unemployment is more a reflection of opportunity to work than satisfactoriness of performance. During the past decade there has been a gradual increase in the rate of unemployment. This in part reflects the high numbers of young people who have been entering the labor force each year. The unemployment rates have been generally higher for women than for men, and the disparity has typically widened as unemployment declined. For high school dropouts the unemployment rates have ranged from less than 5 percent for white men during the late 1960s to more than 20 percent for black men during the mid-1970s and have generally been highest for black men and women and lowest for white men. The unemployment rates during this period for college graduates have fluctuated between 1 and 4 percent for various subpopulations, but have typically been lowest for white men. Unemployment rates decline from more than 15 percent for those aged sixteen through nineteen to about 5 percent for those aged twenty-five to thirty-four and then remain fairly stable. The unemployment rates for women are consistently 1 or 2 percent higher than for men. The unemployment rates are much higher for minority groups than for whites, especially in the younger age groups (BLS, 1975; U.S., DHEW, 1976).

Satisfactory Performance. In almost all occupational fields there is a broad range of satisfactory performance, in which the variabilities within age groups are large and the trends across age groups are small. In practice, most jobs consist of a variety of tasks to be performed. Some tasks depend on physical speed, endurance, or coordinated skill. Other tasks depend on short-term memory, imaginative production of novel ideas, or diagnostic ability. In recent generations there has been a decrease in the proportion of tasks that depend on physical strength and an increase in the proportion of tasks that depend on application of a knowledge base (part of which must be acquired through actual work experience). In general, young adults are most likely to perform better than older adults in occupations that emphasize speed, strength, memory, and novel solutions.

There is a complex process by which young adults achieve a satisfactory or outstanding level of occupational performance. The process influences how many succeed and the age at which they reach a peak of productivity or achievement. A major ingredient is the work itself. Each type of job entails a unique set of demands, constraints, latitude, and critical tasks, so that successful performance is associated with some worker characteristics. Consider what is involved in being a successful welder, poet, nurse, carpenter, mathematician, secretary, athlete, or accountant. The way in which a job is defined or organized can therefore influence the extent to which it will be performed satisfactorily by workers with various characteristics, including level of age and experience.

In addition to the work itself, an occupation has incentives and rewards and a general public image. These characteristics influence the talent pool of other people with whom a young adult must compete to be successful. For most occupations there are educational and training programs to help prepare young people for successful job entry. Some are sponsored by schools and colleges and some by employers and labor unions. Their typical intent is to enable people to attain a satisfactory level of performance in less time than it would take with just work experience. In specific instances, formal educational requirements may facilitate and accelerate the process of becoming productive, or they may constitute irrelevant restrictions.

Another ingredient is the process of personality and vocational development that continues throughout late adolescence and young adulthood, somewhat independently of formal education experience. In addition to the extensive evidence that this maturing process occurs for college-bound youths, there is evidence that the process continues during young adulthood for those who do not go on to college and that work experience influences the process. There is also evidence that occupational development patterns for young working women who did not attend college differs from that of young men who did not (Feldman and Newcomb, 1969; Trent and Medsker, 1968; Knox, 1970; Mulvey, 1963). Also, non-college-bound young men become more reading-oriented over the years between their late teens and their mid-twenties.

Still another ingredient in the achievement of satisfactory occupational performance of young adults is access to opportunities. This includes exposure to people engaged in an occupational role, as well as the existence of job openings. All of these ingredients—work characteristics, education, personality development, and access—have an impact on average levels of occupational performance by young adults.

For some young adults there is an additional set of influences on occupational performance. Many women and members of blue collar families, especially members of disadvantaged and minority groups, internalize cultural stereotypes and develop more restrictive occupational aspirations than would be warranted by their abilities. Many have also confronted job discrimination over the years. A review of age trends in occupational performance should be interpreted in light of these realities.

Practitioners can assist adults with their career development by helping them understand typical patterns of satisfactory and unsatisfactory occupational performance for various categories of adults during the occupational life cycle, along with major influences on work performance. Adults with a more realistic understanding of career development should be better able to distinguish between the factors they can influence and those they are not likely to affect. They should also be better able to engage in self-directed and educative activities that can guide and enhance their careers (Crites, 1969; McClure and Buan, 1973).

Outstanding Performance. Outstanding occupational performance and achievement tends to occur somewhat younger in adulthood than satisfactory but less noteworthy achievement. For fields, such as sports, that depend heavily on physical capacities, peak performance tends to occur in the twenties and early thirties. In fields, such as the arts and sciences, that depend heavily on intellectual capacities, peak performance tends to occur in the thirties. For fields, such as administration, that depend heavily on social capacities, peak performance tends to occur even later in life (Lehman, 1953; Dennis, 1966). However, there is some variability for specific fields, the range of individual differences is great, and, especially in fields that depend heavily on intellectual and social capacities, productivity continues throughout the career.

There are variations among sports in the peak ages for outstanding athletic accomplishments. For sprinters in track and swimming, the peak occurs by the early twenties. For pugilists and baseball players, the peak is around age twenty-five with few records for a season set beyond age thirty-five. The peak for sports, such as billiards and golf, that emphasize skill and coordination occur in the late twenties and early thirties respectively, and outstanding performance has been recorded into the late forties for golf and into the late fifties for billiards. Outstanding performance in physical activities that emphasize endurance, such as the marathon or mountain climbing, tends to occur later than in activities that emphasize speed. Performance in sports, such as golf and billiards, that allow the person to use experience to plan a move changes more slowly over the years than performance in sports, such as tennis, boxing, and baseball, that require sudden response to unexpected moves.

Although peak performance for outstanding scientific performance is only a few years later than athletic performance, the decline is far more gradual for scientific performance. The point in the decline in peak performance that occurs around age forty-five for athletic activity, occurs around age seventy for scientific activity.

The peak age for outstanding discoveries in chemistry occurs in the late twenties, with a gradual decline through the fifties. The trend with age for contributions of lesser average merit is similar but occurs from five to ten years later. In fields such as chemistry and mathematics, young people of great capacity can begin early, concentrate on a narrow specialty, and achieve a high level of mastery and an original contribution at an early age. In a science-related field such as medicine, it requires some years for preparation and admission to practice before a physician is likely to make significant discoveries. The peak age for medical discoveries and inventions occurs in the late thirties followed by a gradual decline into the seventies. In the social sciences, the peak for original contributions occurs by the fifties.

The trend for outstanding works by philosophers is similar. However, when the larger volume of their writing is included there is a very even distribution during their careers from the mid-thirties through the mid-seventies. This reflects the tendency of philosophers to interrelate disparate aspects of experience.

Similarly, authors tend to reach their peak in their thirties and to remain productive throughout their careers. Many poets begin in adolescence, reach a peak around age thirty, and decline in productivity late in life by only about 50 percent. For writers generally, there is a plateau between the mid-thirties and the mid-forties, followed by only a gradual decline in productivity, which is still quite high after age sixty-five and even after eighty. For persons with ability, health, and motivation, adult life brings an expansion of vocabulary, experience, and literary skill.

In music somewhat different trends occur for performance and for composition. Musical talent and training tend to occur young, as do exceptional performances. Compositions for solo instrument or voice occur earlier than compositions for ensembles, such as symphonies and operas. For orchestral composition, the peak age for superior works is the thirties, but productivity remains substantial in the fifties. For the larger proportion of musical compositions the most prolific period is in the fifties.

Artists tend to produce their most widely acclaimed paintings when they are in their thirties. When three paintings are included, the peak occurs in the late forties. When fifty paintings are included, productivity is maintained at a high level throughout adulthood with high levels of performance in old age.

In fields such as administration, politics, and religion, outstanding performance typically occurs in the latter part of

Figure 12. Outstanding Achievement: Age of Major Accomplishment by Outstanding Authors, Philosophers, Painters, Scientists, and Athletes

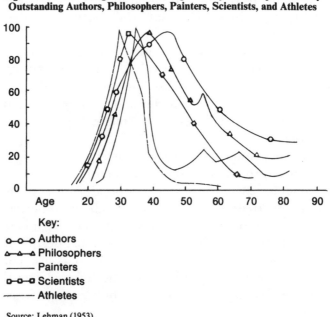

Key:

o—o—o Authors
▲—▲—▲ Philosophers
———— Painters
□—□—□ Scientists
- - - - Athletes

Source: Lehman (1953).

middle age and in old age with many instances in the sixties and seventies.

The relationship between outstanding achievement and age for five fields of endeavor is presented in Figure 12. Each is portrayed in relation to the age at which the highest proportion of outstanding accomplishments occurred. Athletic and scientific accomplishments peak at the youngest ages and decline relatively sharply. There tends to be a small secondary peak in old age for the visual arts. In philosophy and literature, the peak occurs later and a higher proportion of outstanding achievements occur after age fifty than in many other fields. These relationships between achievement and age are based on one or a few outstanding accomplishments by individuals. When a larger volume of outstanding achievements are included for each individual, creativity is maintained well into middle age and beyond for most scholarly fields (Dennis, 1966). Furthermore, some of the decline in creative output by older adults reflects the assumption of other responsibilities, such as administration (Zuckerman, 1957).

Variations Among Adults. Practitioners can use these generalizations to help adults better understand life cycle trends in outstanding achievement and to encourage any adult to engage in creative effort. The generalizations provide the basis for planning by adults of almost any age. Young adults can recognize how early in the career outstanding achievement tends to occur in some fields such as athletics and science. This understanding can enable those who are approaching outstanding achievement to focus their current efforts, but also to plan for subsequent stages of their careers. Although the one or two outstanding accomplishments may typically occur fairly early in a career, the quantity of valuable achievements continues throughout most of the career.

Most of the generalizations about achievement and age are based on data about performance by men in white collar occupations and in fields in which outstanding achievement receives public recognition. Although it is likely that there are similar relationships between outstanding performance and age for women and for adults in blue collar occupations, there is little evidence on which to base such generalizations. In addition to the scarcity of women entering scientific and artistic fields in past generations, in many instances age data were not recorded.

Creativity can occur in almost any type of endeavor. We think of it in relation to the arts and sciences, but it also occurs in management, child rearing, recreation, and community affairs. Many people who are creative in their own fields evolve very personal ways to nurture their creativity (MacKinnon, 1960). However, there are times when adults encounter blocks to their creativity that a practitioner can help remove. One way to do so is to review some of the activities that others have found to facilitate creativity. Listed below are five that might be considered.

1. Use periods of intermittent solitude to get away from distractions in order to concentrate on the exploration of creative solutions or directions.
2. Reflect on past obstacles or conflicts in order to gain understanding and help unblock thoughts and feelings and release new and effective approaches.
3. Allow fantasy to help open up new and unusual insights.
4. Accept one's individuality in order to discover new relationships and organization.
5. Persist so that action is added to idea to produce results.

Women in the Labor Force. The career cycle of women differs in several major ways from that of men, regarding the relation of satisfactory performance and age. Most of these differences are situationally induced and have little to do with physical and psychological characteristics of women as workers. There are some occupations characterized by precision, routine, or nurturance in which a high proportion of the workers are women, but it is unclear how much of the reason is natural talents and how much is restricted alternatives (Veroff and Feld, 1970; Kreps, 1976).

During the past generation, many young women have entered the work force. There tends to be some selectivity that differentiates those who do so from those who do not. For example, those with special talents and strong career interests tend to do so, and teen-aged mothers and the highly dependent tend not to. Age trends in productivity are affected by this baseline. During the late teens and early twenties there is an initial peak in employment rates for women, before many leave the work force to raise children. In recent years, fewer women leave the work force to raise children for more than short periods. For many young women in the work force during the past generation, the relation between worker and homemaker roles has been a source of ambivalence. These ambivalent feelings, along with occupational interests, affect aspirations, which are reflected in educational and occupational choice (Myrdal and Klein, 1956; H. Farmer and Bohn, 1970; H. Farmer, 1971). Some young women want to devote most of their adult life to being wives and mothers and prefer not to invest time and effort in education and work with anticipation of only short-term benefits. However, many young women have long-term career interests that they want to pursue without foregoing wife and mother roles. Some leave their occupation very reluctantly at the time of marriage or the birth of the first child.

During the past generation, working women have confronted discriminatory work rules and expectations that have restricted their mobility in most fields. As a result of such restrictions and discrimination, the combination of occupational and homemaker roles, and personal preferences and aspirations, the level of occupational prestige and income of working women has been below that of men. There is little tested knowledge about comparative performance of men and women in similar jobs. Because of sex discrimination, however, those women who move to higher level positions tend to do so on the basis of higher competence and superior performance compared to the men with whom they compete.

Some young women who continue in the work force do so out of choice. Some are single, some are married without children, and some take only brief maternity leaves. For a variety of reasons they decide that traditional homemaker roles as full-time wife and mother will be foregone or will take coordinate or secondary positions. Their long-term career commitments are typically strong, and their frustrations with obstacles to occupational progress and achievement are typically great.

Many young women continue in the work force out of necessity. Their preference may be to leave the work force and become full-time homemakers, but circumstances frustrate that preference. Some are single and unable to find a satisfactory mate. Some are married but work due to strong pressures to supplement family income. Some were married but work because widowhood, divorce, or desertion has made them the main means of support for themselves and sometimes their children. Some are unwed mothers. An estimated six-and-a-half million women are without a spouse in the household and serve as heads of households, and about two thirds have children under eighteen years of age (Kreps, 1971).

During the past generation there has been a great increase in the proportion of mothers of young children with husband present who are working outside the home. This increase reflects some general influences that affect employment trends, such as increased urbanization, shift in the occupational structure, and increased levels of formal education. It also reflects influences that are especially pertinent to working women, such as household technology; later marriages; declining birth rates; a sense of careerism, especially among college-educated women; and a level of aspiration about the desired standard of living that makes a second income seem necessary even for fairly well-to-do white collar families.

Compared with working women a generation or two ago, in recent years more young women are employed outside the home, fewer of them are out of the work force for very long when their children are young, and more women are employed during middle age. To illustrate the rapid increase in employment of mothers of young children, the percentage increased from three out of twenty in 1959 to three out of ten in 1974. The impact of family life cycle on women's occupational participation is still substantial, however. As of 1973, for women between the ages of twenty and twenty-four, more than seven out of ten of those never married, or married with spouse present but no children, were working. For those with the youngest child under three, one third were working, compared with almost one half of those with the youngest child between three and five. For women between the ages of twenty-five and thirty-four, almost nine out of ten of those never married and more than three quarters of those married with spouse present but no children were working. More than half of those with the youngest child between six and seventeen were working. For women between the ages of thirty-five and forty-four, almost eight out of ten who were never married and six out of ten married women with spouse present but no children were working. More than half of those with the youngest child between six and seventeen were working (Kreps, 1976). For many families, especially in the white collar category, both the preferences of the wife and the attitudes of the husband toward the wife working outside the home are influential (Arnott, 1972).

In middle age women who have been working right along are joined by women whose children are grown and who enter or reenter the work force. As a result, more than half of all women in their late forties and early fifties are in the work force. Many of those who join the work force in middle age, thus creating the second peak in the proportion of women employed, experience an adjustment to a full-time worker role. Part of the adjustment results from the lack of fit between their competencies and current job requirements. The widespread underemployment that is produced combines with unemployment due to low seniority to keep the productivity of middle-aged working women far below what would have been likely if they had been working steadily since young adulthood.

Many women in white collar and professional occupations work by choice and have maintained occupational continuity during adulthood. The proportion of women in professional occupations who are not currently married is far higher than for women in general. In recent years as there are more and more women in this category, new life-styles have been emerging that relate to both work and social life (Ginzberg and others, 1966; Bailyn, 1964; Kreps, 1976).

The employed mother has been of special interest as a category of working women. A majority have completed between ten and twelve years of formal education and have husbands whose annual income is below the national average. For all working women, about one out of three work in clerical occupations, one out of five in household and service occupations, and about three out of twenty in professional occupations. The distribution for working mothers tends to be similar. Their reasons for working are varied and fairly similar to those of men, with economic and mobility needs central, along with social contact with adults, independence, and achievement. Older wives tend to have less formal education than younger wives, and thus they hold jobs that have lower prestige and income (Nye and Hoffman, 1963; Hoffman and Nye, 1974).

Practitioners can be especially helpful regarding the career cycles of women, by helping both women and men to understand ways in which career development for women is both similar to and different from career development for men (Bailyn, 1970; Bardwick, 1974; Papanek, 1973). Included are interrelationships between work and family and sex discrimination in employment. (It appears that situational influences on career development are somewhat greater for women than for men.) During the past decade or so, there has been a great increase in educational and counseling programs aimed at career development of women.

Mid-Career Change. Shifts in economic conditions and mid-life reassessments of goals both contribute to mid-career occupational change (Hiestand, 1971; Clopton, 1973; Mills, 1966). For some blue collar workers, the dream of going into a more attractive type of work has a sustaining influence early in the career until it becomes clear that such a shift is not likely (Chinoy, 1955). Many middle-aged lower-middle-class men are preoccupied with their jobs and financial security, which results in more selective use of leisure (Lowenthal, Thurnher, and others, 1975). Some artists have undergone a major creative crisis during their late thirties or early forties. For some, this mid-life reassessment is reflected in the character of their work (Jaques, 1965). In recent years, especially for white collar adults, participation in education has become part of a mid-career change (Hiestand, 1971; Clopton, 1973; Schlossberg, 1970; LeFevre, 1972; Dalton and Thompson, 1971; Kaufman, 1974).

Practitioners can help adults better understand and deal with career changes. This often entails systematic efforts to increase competencies needed in the new role. However, it is also important for adults to understand the general process of occupational adjustment including the impact that it often has on other life roles.

Mid-career occupational changes can sometimes reach crisis proportions. An extended period of unemployment due to a recession, the closing of a plant in a one-company town, or massive layoffs of highly specialized personnel in the aerospace industry are dramatic examples. However, many workers experience undesirable occupational adjustments that constitute a personal crisis. Practitioners associated with the employer, union, professional association, employment agency, or community group can help the individual define and deal with the crisis. An increasing number of services for mid-career redirection are being established (Harrison, 1976; Pascal and others, 1975).

The problems associated with an undesirable occupational change are all too apparent. Loss of income, mounting debts, reduction of standard of living, damage to self-esteem and confidence, uncertainty about the future, are only a few of the burdens that result. Practitioners as well as friends can help adults experiencing such an adjustment both to deal with their feelings about the dislocation and to obtain satisfactory employment.

In addition to creating problems, major change events can present opportunities for growth. It is easier to consider moving to another part of the country, or changing to a different type of work, or readjusting the relative emphasis between work and family when some major occupational changes are required. Practitioners and people who have successfully accomplished a similar job change can also help the individual place his or her personal crisis in broader perspective. This perspective includes an understanding of the various ways in which others have successfully made the transition, such as a work or educational experience that constitutes a partial step toward a new career direction (Wirtz, 1975). A broader perspective also enables the individual to see beyond the personal loss and resentment related to the problem and keep in mind that the solution lies in relating personal and external resources to the opportunities that exist or can be created. Practitioners can help adults recognize the basic problems that may underlie the symptoms, locate relevant opportunities, and consider personal talents and priorities in the decision-making process (Schlossberg and Troll, 1976; Belbin and Belbin, 1968).

Mandatory Retirement. For older adults, trends in occupational productivity are associated with mandatory retirement. Older workers are concentrated in occupations that existed when they entered the work force and that have experienced the least growth and change. Many fields with high proportions of older workers are on the wane. Younger workers typically change jobs for the better, but older workers typically change jobs for the worse. Income levels decline with age beyond fifty (Schupack, 1962; Rosenberg, 1970). Workers' attitudes toward retirement generally become more negative as they approach retirement. This apprehension reflects concerns about both further reductions in income and the loss of the worker role with all its connotations of social engagement and personal productivity. The wide variations in acceptance of retirement are associated with economic condition, health, and personality. Some retired adults want to be occupied, not necessarily employed. However, large numbers of older workers resent mandatory retirement. Regardless of any benefits it may have for the economic system or younger workers, many older adults recognize that mandatory retirement cuts short their opportunities for occupational performance (Sheppard, 1970).

The process by which older workers terminate occupational activity varies greatly and, with the societal shift toward employment by large organizations, depends to a great extent on the personnel policies of employers. Many employers require that workers must sever employment at a specified age such as sixty-five. Some retirees who are able to do so locate another full-time or part-time job. Some employers have instituted a more flexible retirement policy that allows for changes in the type of work and reductions in work load and income so that the retirement process is more gradual. Although pension and retirement programs tend to reduce the average age at retirement, some are being used more flexibly. Women tend to retire somewhat younger than men, but when they retire in their early sixties on the average they have worked only a few years less than men who retire at the same age. Even though mandatory retirement forces many older workers to terminate employment, many continue with some forms of economically productive activity. A higher proportion of white collar workers than blue collar workers do so. Their satisfaction from work activity tends to be higher, which makes the loss of productive effort more difficult, but higher levels of postretirement income, health, social involvements, and varied abilities help with the transition and continued productivity (Simpson and McKinney, 1966).

Successful adaptation to retirement entails much learning and reorientation. Practitioners can help facilitate this transition in many ways, including preretirement counseling and preparation; retraining for postretirement careers; educational programs related to life roles, such as family, community, and use of leisure; and advocacy of policies and programs that help older adults adjust to retirement from work.

Satisfaction. People work for many reasons: money, status, satisfaction, recognition, service, companionship, and self-actualization (Terkel, 1972). Occupational satisfaction and dissatisfaction depends mainly on the fit between the characteristics of a work situation and the individual's important reasons for working. The variations in work values within each age group are substantial. The ways in which adults view work are affected by prior work experience and occupational aspirations. Attitudes toward work include some attention to the work itself as well as to associated benefits. In spite of job discrimination because of race, sex, and age, a gross matching process tends to occur in which employers seek to select employees who seem best for the jobs and in which workers seek jobs that seem best for them. As a result, jobs that provide high satisfaction from the work itself tend to be filled by people with much in their favor in terms of ability, preparation, aspiration, and lack of barriers due to discrimination.

This interaction helps produce two clusters of reasons for working. One cluster emphasizes benefits. For workers with a benefit orientation, little personal satisfaction is derived from the process or accomplishment of work. It is often viewed as a necessary evil, a heavy and unpleasant burden, an activity necessary only because of the need for societal maintenance and personal support and security. At the end of the work day, work concerns are readily forgotten. Satisfaction from leisure activities is fairly high in relation to satisfaction from occupational activities. The second cluster emphasizes work. For workers with a work orientation, the process and accomplishment of work is a major source of feelings of satisfaction, esteem, status, usefulness, companionship, and self-expression. Work concerns are pursued during evenings and weekends, and because satisfaction from work activities is high the relative satisfaction from leisure activities is lower (Friedmann and Havighurst, 1954; Herzberg, Mausner, and Snyderman, 1959; Havighurst, 1965; Meltzer, 1963, 1965).

Even though a higher proportion of white collar workers than blue collar workers are work oriented, both orientations occur in almost all fields of work. Blue collar workers generally feel more job dissatisfaction than white collar workers, partly because their limited satisfaction in the work itself makes dissatisfactions related to benefits and working conditions loom larger (Herzberg, 1966). Dissatisfaction tends to be especially high among workers who feel blocked by job discrimination related to race, sex, and age (Blood and Hulin, 1967). Working mothers tend to be frustrated trying to accommodate the roles of worker and homemaker while competing with men and single women who can concentrate more on their occupations. Many older women have less dissatisfaction about impending retirement, some because they experienced a similar adjustment when their children were grown and some because frustrated ambitions are not so difficult to set aside. Some workers deal with occupational dissatisfaction by compensation in which they invest time and effort in avocational or community interests (Falk, 1966; Friedlander, 1965).

The type of work done by individuals or heads of families typically influences their life-styles, including use of leisure. The impact of work on leisure depends on how remunerative, how satisfying, and how flexible the work is. An adult whose work and leisure interests reflect similar values, and whose income level and work flexibility are sufficiently high, is likely to experience many points at which work and leisure interpenetrate. By contrast, an adult whose work is very unsatisfying and who has minimal flexibility and income is likely to engage in leisure activities that are quite separate from work (Rapoport and Rapoport, 1975).

Work satisfaction during middle age is associated with life-style. For example, many lower-middle-class men believe that their work should be more important to them than it seems to be. Most have reached a plateau where they realize that major improvements are unlikely. Most of their wives who have worked have done so without a strong career commitment, have not sought occupational success, and so have not had to lower their sights. For most of the husbands, however, the mid-career discrepancy between aspiration and achievement affects satisfaction.

Some generalizations about career satisfaction emphasize shifts from younger to older workers. For example, there is a tendency for young adults to emphasize interesting jobs, income, and potential fame. Older adults tend to place more emphasis on independence from supervision and job security. Familiarity with such general career shifts can help adults understand and deal with specific career changes, such as job entry, change, reentry, and retirement.

Community

American adults engage in varied forms of social participation, but participation rates for specific types of activity vary substantially among men and women, among blue collar and white collar segments of the community, and among age groups. Shifting emphases on different types of activities during adulthood produce the changing fabric of participation that is the individual adult's community life cycle. Even though the activities included in the community life cycle are exceedingly varied, together they reflect the adult's choice to use discretionary time not required for occupation and family to engage in activities that in varying ways and degrees relate to the larger society, especially the local community. The location and diversity of the settings within which participation occurs do much to define the social space of the individual.

Community life cycle activities intersect with family, educational, and occupational life cycle activities even more than these three other clusters intersect. However, social participation does not include indices that are central to performance of occupational roles (such as productivity, interpersonal relations, or satisfaction), family roles (such as child-rearing practices, family income, or marital relations), or educational roles (such as objectives, activities, or achievement). Some social participation activities do intersect with occupational and family life cycle patterns, as is the case for participation in labor unions and recreational activities related to work and for entertaining, which can occur in the home as well as outside. Typical forms of social participation include involvement in organizations and voluntary associations, political participation, church and religious activities, attendance at public events, and participation in outdoor and indoor recreation including hobbies and informal activities with family and friends. These activities relate to the major adult life roles of organization member, citizen, church member, and user of leisure time.

Extent of participation in or association with these varied types of activities can be assessed in several ways. Typical indices include membership or contact, frequency of participation, amount of time devoted, extent of interest, and provision of leadership, initiative or control. Adult life cycle trends often differ for various indices. For example, the proportions of adults in successive age groups who participate may decline with age, but the average amount of time spent on the activity may increase. Or membership rates may be very stable with age, but frequency of attendance may decline.

Correlates of Participation. Type and extent of social participation are highly associated with socioeconomic status, especially level of education. White collar adults tend to be more active generally, to engage in more varied activities, and to engage in more complex activities than blue collar adults. This is especially so for participation in voluntary associations (Foskett, 1955; Freedman and Axelrod, 1952; J. C. Scott, 1957; Wright and Hymen, 1958). In the shift from school-centered activities in late adolescence to community- and family-centered activities in young adulthood, the backgrounds of the circle of friends become more similar and social-class-related preferences and practices become more influential. However, white collar adults typically have more mobility, freedom, and equality in moving up and down the social ladder for friendship (Dohrenwend and Chin-Shong, 1967). Throughout adulthood, white collar adults engage in more occupationally related social participation than do blue collar adults, such as work-related reading and entertaining. White collar adults also engage in more family-centered entertaining and visiting, although it is a smaller proportion of their total social participation than for blue collar adults. A higher proportion of white collar adults engage in tennis, golf, and games of strategy such as bridge. A higher proportion of blue collar adults engage in fishing and games of chance such as bingo (Cunningham and Johannis, 1960; Reissman, 1954; Sessoms, 1963; Sutton-Smith, Roberts, and others, 1963; R. C. White, 1955). More blue collar adults use taverns and places to dance for social participation. Unmarried blue collar adults have fewer options than their white collar counterparts, and being a good dancer is typically more important socially than it is for the white collar adult. White collar adults are more active in church-related activities and in church leadership positions. However, church participation typically constitutes a larger proportion of social participation for blue collar adults, and those who are members tend to attend services more regularly (L. M. Burchinal, 1959; Cline and Richards, 1965). In white collar families the wife role typically includes participation in community activities, while in blue collar families the wife role typically excludes such participation (Slater, 1960). A higher proportion of white collar adults are active in politics (Nie, Powell, and Prewitt, 1969a, 1969b). Many blue collar adults, especially when they are older, lack the money for proper clothes and related expenses for many forms of social participation.

Social participation tends to be similar in extent for men and women but different in type. Participation in community organizations tends to be somewhat higher for men in rural communities and for women in urban communities (Havighurst and Albrecht, 1953). More men join formal organizations, but attendance rates are higher for women (Freedman and Axelrod, 1952; J. C. Scott, 1957). White collar men tend to have a wider range of friendships than their wives (Babchuck, 1965). For lower-middle-class adults, men typically have a focused life-style in contrast with the fragmented life-style that is more typical of women. Leisure activities vary more between men and women than between age groups. Men tend to emphasize recreational activities while women emphasize sociability. Adolescent recreational activities influence leisure pursuits in young adulthood (Yoestring and Burkhead, 1973). During the courtship period and the early years of marriage, patterns of social participation by men and women become more similar and shift toward activities preferred by women (Cunningham and Johannis, 1960). Largely because of restrictions related to child care, young women have less varied recreation than young men, an especially difficult adjustment for women who were socially active during school years (Searls, 1966). Talking on the telephone helps reduce this restriction. The dual roles of working mothers also affect social participation. In middle age more of women's social participation is associated with family and community and more of men's social participation is somewhat work related. For white collar adults, both men and women report music and gardening as hobbies, but men report sports and women report domestic arts and handiwork (Terman and Oden, 1959). For older adults, the combination of work replacement and interest in physically active recreation tends to leave men with fewer leisure activities.

Marital and family status is associated with some types of social participation (Rapoport and Rapoport, 1975). For many women, having young children causes a shift from adult-oriented participation to participation in activities that are child oriented, or include children, such as leadership for youth groups or family outings. Especially for white collar families, marriage provides companionship and joint activities for husband and wife, such as couple's bridge or parties. For most parents of young children family responsibilities restrict time and money for outside social participation. Unmarried adults typically have more time and money for social participation. Especially in young adulthood, more of it is outside the home but with age becomes more home centered (Sessoms, 1963; R. C. White, 1955). Having a confidant is related to satisfaction regarding companionship by single adults (Lowenthal and Haven, 1968). Unmarried adults are less likely to interact with family friends out of a feeling of obligation. Widowed or divorced adults tend to withdraw and to be left out of social activities they formerly engaged in as couples. Some married adults are active in community activities because of a sense of investment and obligation related to the family life cycle. They are active in relation to church, school, youth groups, or political affairs, because doing so will benefit their children. Some single adults are active in community activities, because doing so meets some social needs that might be met by family life for married adults.

There are some relationships between extent and type of social participation and urbanness of place of residence. Rural and small town adults typically engage in more social participation than those in more urban communities, but less of it is in formal organizations (Wright and Hymen, 1958; Zimmer and Hawley, 1959a). Social participation by city adults differs greatly between those from blue collar and white collar backgrounds. Rural adults who move to the city typically experience a reduction in social participation. White collar city men in particular are relatively active in social participation with two distinct emphases, one on organizational participation and one on cultural activities (Axelrod, 1956; Bell and Force, 1956; London, Wenkert and Hagstrom, 1963; Windham, 1963; Wright and Hymen, 1958; Hearn, 1971). Suburban adults tend to be young or middle aged and white collar. Social participation is relatively high; emphasizes informal activities instead of formal organizations; and tends to be women oriented, partly because of the commuting patterns of men (Berger, 1961; Martin, 1956).

Social participation is somewhat associated with type and extent of occupational activity (Parker, 1971; Rapoport and Rapoport, 1965; Sussman and Cogswell, 1971; Heath, 1971). Working between forty and sixty hours a week reduces the time available for social participation but typically increases the income and contacts for social participation. Level of occupational prestige is associated with type of social participation, but level of formal education is even more highly associated.

Up until middle age, a portion of social participation tends to be related to work, but during middle age there is a shift from activities that reinforce work concerns to activities that contrast with work. Especially for older adults, the loss of the worker role greatly increases the time available for social participation, but the extent and type of impact on social participation is also associated with such factors as personality, health, and income (Goodman, Bley, and Dye, 1974; Nystrom, 1974). Poor health tends to reduce the extent of social activity and to shift the structure of participation toward more sedentary forms of participation in which the impact of the health problems is reduced. A higher proportion of older adults experience poor health (Havighurst, 1957a, b; Zborowski, 1962).

Role changes, such as the birth of the first child, the youngest child's leaving home, a major job change, a move to a new community, retirement, start of a major leadership role, or loss of a spouse affect the structure of social participation in some predictable ways. An increase in role responsibility, such as motherhood or a major promotion, tends to reduce social participation and increase participation related to the new responsibility. A reduction of role responsibility, such as loss of

a spouse or retirement, tends to increase time for social participation, and the expansions that occur tend to reflect personal
preferences.

In general, adults have a preferred level and type of social
participation. Above-average levels of unhappiness are typically
associated with participation below the preferred level (D. L.
Phillips, 1967).

Practitioners can use generalizations about correlates of
participation in order to plan and conduct programs and services that are likely to attract and serve the adults they seek to
reach. When the characteristics of adults in a target market in
a community match the characteristics that are highly associated with the type of participation the practitioner seeks to
provide, standard forms of publicity and delivery are likely to
be effective. However, when this is not the case, generalizations
about correlates of participation can suggest approaches to marketing and delivery of services that are likely to be more
effective.

Social Participation and Age. The shifts in social participation during adulthood are very complex as the following
review will indicate in some detail. The foregoing relationships
between participation and characteristics, such as blue or white
collar, men or women, marital and family status, urbanness of
residence, occupational status, health, and role changes, intersect with age because older adults differ from young adults in
each of these participation-related characteristics. More older
adults have blue collar backgrounds, are women, are no longer
married, live in rural areas or inner cities, have health problems, and are experiencing role losses. Comparisons between
adults at different ages provide a description of individual differences associated with age, but unless the association with
these participation-related characteristics is taken into account,
the age-related comparisons may obscure developmental shifts
during adulthood.

When only one form of participation, such as number of
organizational memberships, is analyzed, the trend during adulthood reflects an expansion and contraction. Other activities,
however, such as frequency of listening to the radio, contract

from young adulthood to middle age and then increase. As a result, there is a shift of time from one type of activity to another. When all activity during all of adulthood is considered, it can be characterized as a process that entails multiple shifts in the structure of participation. Every adult has twenty-four hours in each day and seven days in each week. Within broad limits, and in ways that combine choice and acquiescence, every adult allocates time to sleeping, eating, working, family-related responsibilities, systematic study, and social participation. The composite activities may be loosely or tightly packed, and on balance they may be satisfying or disagreeable. But an adult is always doing something, even if it is just sitting in the corner and staring at the wall.

Specific types of social participation follow quite different trends during adulthood. Some remain basically the same. Some decline and some expand with age. Some follow a cyclical pattern of expansion and contraction, and some alternate up and down periodically during adulthood. When analyzed together they reflect a changing mix from young adulthood, to middle age, and beyond. Just as an investor may periodically change and diversify his portfolio of stocks to meet his changing financial needs, circumstances, and purposes, so adults typically change the mix of their "portfolio of participation" during adulthood.

There are some general and widespread characteristics of the total structure of social participation during adulthood. One is that social participation is far more associated with social class characteristics, especially level of education, than it is with age. There is, however, a developmental shift in social participation, from activities that are physically vigorous and action oriented in late adolescence and young adulthood, to activities concerned with interpersonal relations and understanding in middle age, to activities that are cultural and private beyond middle age. This is especially so when age comparisons are made for persons in good health and within similar levels of education (Donald and Havighurst, 1959; M. Mead, 1957). This age trend in participation is similar to the trend in interests of men for a decline in active or competitive activities such as tennis and an increase in sedentary or noncompetitive activities such as gardening (Strong, 1951). It also parallels a shift during adulthood from community-centered participation to home-centered participation (Havighurst and Feigenbaum, 1959; Lopata, 1966). In addition to these shifts in participation, there are similar shifts in the meanings that social participation has for adults as they become older (Havighurst, 1957a).

The following analysis of stability and change during adulthood in nonsustenance participation is based mainly on the findings from a study that included data on fifty-two social participation variables from a large and representative sample of adults between twenty-one and sixty-nine years of age (Knox and Videbeck, 1964). Findings on age and social participation from other studies are cited where they are available. Twenty of the fifty-two variables were basic, with no significant differences among age groups. Twelve variables were declining, with significant decreases with age. Ten variables were expanding, with significant increases from young adulthood to old age. Four variables followed a cyclical pattern, with an expansion from young adulthood to middle age, followed by a decline. Six variables followed an alternating pattern, with significant fluctuations up and down during adulthood. The limitation of the study sample to noninstitutionalized adults under age seventy minimizes the impact of failing health in old age.

Almost half of the social participation variables followed the basic pattern with no significant changes between twenty-one and sixty-nine years of age. This finding was consistent with the findings of other studies that when the total fabric of participation is analyzed, much of it forms a highly stable plateau for most of adulthood with little evidence of major age-related change (R. W. White, 1963; Zborowski, 1962). Most of these stable variables are aspects of social relations and solitary activities that reflect such personality characteristics as activity level and values.

Six of the variables that follow the basic pattern of no significant change with age reflect the individual's general level of activity. Three relate to church participation. There is a gradual but nonsignificant increase in church membership and participation in church-related activities between the twenties and the sixties, and nonsignificant fluctuations in frequency of attendance at church services. This finding is consistent with the composite findings of other studies that when all five major dimensions of religious commitment are considered (experiential, ideological, ritualistic, intellectual, and consequential), the pattern is one of stability, with some increase during most of adulthood, the drop with advanced age reflecting the impact of declining health condition on ritualistic behavior outside the home. Religious participation is lowest in young adulthood and rises gradually in middle age. As church attendance drops in old age, activity related to home and personal concerns rises (Moberg, 1968; Vincent and Martin, 1961; Fichter, 1952; Zimmer and Hawley, 1959b; Glock and Stark, 1965). Although for specific congregations, communities, and segments of the population, there are major shifts in religiosity with age, in the general adult population the composite pattern is one of stability at least through the sixties. During the past decade, membership in churches and synagogues has been quite stable, including almost two thirds of the United States population. About four out of ten people attend services in a typical week.

The other three variables related to general level of activity that follow the basic pattern of no significant change with age are the proportion of the individual's six closest friends that he or she talks with about every day, whether there are two or more groups of friends that the individual meets with regularly for informal socializing, and the number of times during the year that the individual goes on trips or outings. There was a nonsignificant decline with age for the latter two variables. Even for older adults, although the number of activities declines, the extent of companionship and participation remains fairly constant beyond age sixty (Cavan and others, 1949; Goodman, Bley, and Dye, 1974).

Some of the basic variables reflect the total time commitments of the individual and his or her level of personal involvement. Included are the amount of time the individual devotes to projects and hobbies, to listening to music and viewing television, and to solitary activities generally, along with whether the individual reads newspapers and magazines and attends public meetings and the number of books read and public events attended in the previous year. It should be noted that for activities such as hobbies and reading, although the extent of activity may be stable, its meaning to the individual may change greatly during adulthood.

For two ratings of the individual's favorite leisure activity there was also no significant change with age between twenty-one and sixty-nine for the general adult population. The ratings characterize the activity along continua from creative to routine and from expansive to apathetic. A high degree of stability with age between age forty and seventy has also been found in other studies that have used these rating scales. Such characteristics of leisure reflect the complex dimension of personality rather than age, at least until age seventy and as long as good health continues.

A dozen of the social participation variables followed the declining pattern with steady decreases during adulthood. These variables reflect differentiation and variety in social relations. For half of these variables, there is a decline with age in the proportion of adults who read books, attend movies, listen to recorded music, attend athletic events, go on trips and outings, and belong to any informal friendship group. For the latter three variables, there is a nonsignificant increase during young adulthood followed by significant declines. The result is increasing numbers of adults who have dropped out of these types of activities with advancing age. Only part of the decline is accounted for by the association between level of education and participation. There is a similar trend for amount of time devoted to organizational participation, and the significant decline occurs following middle age. The age trends for ratings of favorite leisure activity are from gregarious to solitary and from active to passive. This reflects the decline from adolescence to young adulthood generally in strenuous activities (Searls, 1966; Havighurst, 1965). There is also a decline in amount of criminal activity with age and in the proportion of violent crimes (Keller and Vedder, 1968).

Ten social participation variables followed the expanding

pattern with steady increases during adulthood. These variables reflect informal intimate social relationships with members of primary groups. During adulthood, people spend more and more evenings and weekends with other members of the immediate family and are less frequently away from home. With increasing age, there is also an increase in the number of people individuals consider close friends and an increase in the proportion of the six closest friends with whom individuals agree and share interests, and in whom they feel they can confide. As they grow older, an increasingly higher proportion of adults have a favorite leisure activity that contrasts with work. There is also an increase from young adulthood to middle age in social competence and maturity.

Four of the social participation variables followed a cyclical pattern, expanding from young adulthood to middle age and then constricting. These variables reflect status-related active participation in formal types of interaction. The number of organizational memberships an individual holds increases from the low point in early young adulthood, reaches a plateau in the forties, and then slowly declines. In many organizations, there is some lag between becoming inactive and formally terminating membership. This age trend for organizational memberships is reported in many studies. The trend for political participation is similar, but the peak occurs about ten years later in life. Similar findings occur in other studies (Meyer, 1957; Trumbull, Pace, and Kuhlen, 1950). References to the cyclical pattern of participation tend to recur in the literature on the life cycle between late adolescence and the latter stage of old age. Examples include the general expansion and constriction of life space; the shift from adult-centered activities, to child-centered activities when there are young children in the home, and back to adult-centered activities when the children are grown; and the shift from self-centeredness by young people, to a greater concern for others in middle age, to increased self-centeredness in the latter part of old age.

Six participation variables followed an alternating pattern, with significant fluctuations up and down during adulthood. These variables reflect changes in roles and statuses during the adult life cycle. Some of these variables reflect the impact of shifting occupational and family responsibilities, such as frequency of attendance at meetings or at athletic events as a spectator and of gathering with informal friendship groups. Meeting attendance rises especially in early middle age in response to occupational and community pressures, and during these periods the other two types of activities decline. Fluctuations in the proportion of the week day spent with family members reflect shifting worker and family member roles. Participation in educational activities reflects both the decline in occupationally related participation and the increase in the proportion of educational participation related to other life roles, especially use of leisure. Rating of favorite leisure activity shifts from expressive to instrumental from the early twenties until the late thirties. This is followed by a return to more expressive concerns in the late forties, then to more instrumental concerns in the late fifties, and finally to more expressive concerns in later life.

Enjoyment. There are also life cycle shifts in the meanings and satisfactions that leisure activities have for adults. During adolescence, the leisure activities of many young people reflect their reactions against pressures that they perceive from family and school. There is a tendency at this stage to feel that the world is meaningless and that people do not understand. Leisure activities are sometimes used to explore possible plans for the future and develop inner resources. For young people who are alienated or bored, leisure activities may emphasize escape. Socializing with peers is especially important to many people during adolescence (Symonds, 1959; Keniston, 1965).

Young adult leisure interests tend to revolve around family, occupation, sex, and friendship, although not necessarily in that order of priority. Heterosexual relationships that typically developed during adolescence tend to settle into relatively enduring patterns during young adulthood. As young adults achieve a greater sense of identity, most of them are willing to enter into more intimate relationships in which they are expected to honor commitments to specific affiliations even though those commitments may call for compromises and sacrifices. Association with friends increasingly takes the place of family and community activities. Association with more experienced peers tends to influence the young adult's identification with and entry into adult social institutions. At this stage, the values and activities of peers can be quite influential in either desirable or undesirable directions. Contrasting trends regarding stability and change in leisure activities and enjoyments are especially apparent during this young adult period. For example, for women college graduates who are married and family oriented the decade after graduation tends to bring a decline in enjoyment of activities with male friends and of being alone listening to music, doing serious reading, walking, or daydreaming. There tends to be an increase in enjoyment of being alone with children and visiting relatives. Enjoyment of interacting with female friends and planning with others remains quite stable. For married men graduates, there tends to be a decline in enjoyment of activities with both female and male friends and of solitary activities such as listening to music or daydreaming. There tends to be some increase in enjoyment of serious reading and, for a small proportion, being alone with children. Enjoyment of planning with others, walking alone, and visiting relatives remain quite stable (Rapoport and Rapoport, 1975).

Friendship. A widespread and little understood but important type of social performance is friendship. For people who have lived their lives among extended family and friends and seldom encounter outsiders, making new friends is an infrequent occurrence. But for many mobile and rootless Americans the titles "nation of strangers" and the "lonely crowd" have a ring of truth. To be sure, some people so lack a sense of security and esteem that they remain friendless for fear of revealing themselves to others and being hurt. But most people who fail to establish desired friendships are barred by inadequate understanding of the important functions served by friendship and of effective procedures for making new friends (Lazarsfeld and Merton, 1954; Adams, 1971). The process of entering into friendship relationships is termed *friending.* Making an art of friendship has been identified as one of the developmental tasks of adulthood (Havighurst and Orr, 1956).

Practitioners can assist adults with friending by facilitating their entry into appropriate friendship groups and by helping them better understand the friending process. Many recreational, religious, educational, and community groups enable adults to make new friends as an important secondary function. A practitioner can sometimes accomplish much by merely helping a client select an appropriate group and take the initial step to enter it. Seemingly similar groups, such as church groups, bridge clubs, or regular customers at a tavern, can vary greatly in their attention to newcomers and friending. A practitioner who is familiar with a client and with various groups can help make an effective match. Practitioners can help interested adults understand friending through conversation, suggesting readings, and encouraging clients to reflect on their experience in friendship groups.

Some close friendships develop into a confidant relationship between two adults. Such close confidant relationships appear to be very important for most adults, especially during stressful periods. This type of sharing relationship entails trust and support that helps sustain hope. Various dimensions of friendship have been identified that describe aspects of close friendship that are important to adults. The most widespread dimension is similarity of experience, which includes shared experiences, activities, interests, and ease of communication. The second dimension is reciprocity, in which the relationship is characterized as supportive, dependable, accepting, trustworthy, and confidential. A third dimension is compatibility, which includes likeability and enjoyment. A fourth dimension is structural and includes geographic closeness, duration, and convenience. The fifth is the contributions that some friends make as role models because of the respect and admiration that they engender, the "ideal self" that they portray, the mentor relationship that they perform, or the help that they provide.

For lower-middle-class adults, the perceptions of qualities of friends remain very similar during adulthood. Men tend to emphasize similarity more than women do and women place greater emphasis on reciprocity. When descriptions of actual friends and ideal friends are compared, similarity receives more attention in descriptions of actual friends than ideal ones, while reciprocity is more often mentioned as desirable in an ideal friend. The discrepancy is greatest for this type of reciprocal confidant relationship, which is widely valued but not often realized. From late adolescence through middle age there tends to be a decrease in the discrepancy between descriptions of actual friends and ideal friends. This may reflect both greater selectivity in friends and an adjustment of aspirations. There is a tendency for the two or three closest friends to meet somewhat different needs for most adults. Women tend to report more complex dimensions of their friends than do men. From late adolescence to the onset of old age, perception of the qualities of friendship tends to become more complex. This seems to reflect the time that older adults have had to become aware of and appreciate the individuality of others (Lowenthal, Thurnher, and others, 1975). These findings substantiate the earlier conclusion that one of the developmental tasks of middle age is making an art of friendship (Havighurst and Orr, 1956).

Although some aspects of friendship are difficult to put into words, some insights can be expressed and shared. One starting point for many adults who desperately want to make new friends is to acknowledge that their needs for intimacy and relatedness are not being met. Another useful insight is that most enduring and mutually beneficial friendships entail an interdependency in which each member combines self-assertiveness and caring for others. Self-assertiveness includes recognizing one's own needs and expressing preferences and expectations. Caring includes respect for the integrity of others. The deepening of friendships is facilitated by relationships to which all members have a personal commitment (Morris, 1971; Lawton and Bader, 1970). Temporary relationships, such as encounter groups, can produce insights but typically lack the ongoing sense of community that is so important to the development of enduring friendships (Lieberman, Yalom, and Miles, 1972). In a setting characterized by interdependence, mutual commitment, assertiveness, and caring, it is possible for acquaintances to become friends. As a result of exchanges that are caring and growthful, friends become more willing to disclose themselves. Although similarities of backgrounds and interests are attractive, people develop through the exchange of differences. Honest but caring feedback is one form of exchange; but in the closest friendships, much communication occurs in the absence of words. One of the hallmarks of the finest friendships is mutual growth.

Interests and Opportunities. Active participation in community organizations is valuable to the individual and to the community. The community benefits consist of the programs and services received by the members or clients of the organization that enhance their education, health, leisure, or civic contribution. The personal benefits consist of the increased competence, satisfaction, accomplishment, or sense of service that the individual experiences. Often a practitioner can best help clients meet their needs by facilitating their participation in a community organization. The organization might be a community college, church, recreation agency, or voluntary association concerned with a community problem such as mental health or water pollution. For a practitioner to be effective in this helping relationship, it is useful to understand several aspects of the linkage process in addition to generalizations about adult needs and development.

An understanding of adult development should enable a practitioner to recognize salient needs and characteristics of the individual client. The needs may be deficiencies to correct or problems to solve. The needs may also be gaps to be closed between a generally satisfactory level of functioning and a high level of aspiration. In the latter instance, the client typically thinks of opportunities and enhancement more than of problems and deficiencies. For instance, if the clients are elderly black adults with very little formal education, many are likely to be reluctant to use community services or join community organizations. Gaining the clients' participation may take many months of the practitioner's time and the assistance of people who are very much like the clients but who have benefitted from contact with the resource organizations. However, if the clients are middle-aged, white collar adults, the mere mention by the practitioner of a relevant organization may be sufficient. If the clients are older adolescents or very young adults, interests may be so transient that the practitioner's function may be mainly to provide a varied range of opportunities for community participation. This allows peer groups of young people to introduce each other to attractive activities. For providers of leisure programs for young people, there is often an ebb and flow of participation by individuals but a sufficient market to sustain the program for an extended period. One benefit of leisure programs is that they help to keep recreational interests alive during the busy but private stage of young adulthood, so that the individual can resume activities in middle age that are of great value then and in later life (Rapoport and Rapoport, 1975).

Although there are strong associations between leisure activities and such characteristics as age and social class level of men and women, there is substantial variability within all categories of adults. Some people believe that enjoyment is possible only if such activities are separate from obligations such as work and family, while others find enjoyment in some aspects of all domains of life. Concerns that a heavy emphasis on home-centered activities would undermine creativity and community participation seem to be only partly confirmed. Some adults have a rich family life and are also active in external participation. Most adults, especially during middle age, perceive that they have little leisure time. They typically extend habit patterns from their work and family life into their "free time" with little imagination.

In old age, most people become freed from the clock. The types of leisure activities in which older adults engage largely reflect their past habits and experiences, but also reflect their levels of income, education, and health. There is some shift toward family and religious interests (Lehr and Rudinger, 1969).

During adulthood there are continuous shifts in social participation. These changing activity patterns in part reflect evolving needs and interests. They also reflect the opportunity system that helps create markets as well as serve them. Practitioners concerned with leisure and community participation can become more effective in their efforts to facilitate fulfillment and service by adults by better understanding the interplay between interests and opportunities.

Case Examples: Hal and Luke

The late teens and early twenties constitute a period during which there is typically much change in role performance (Ralston and Thomas, 1974). The transition from late adolescence to early young adulthood often entails floundering and trial in vocational development (Super and others, 1967), as well as exploration of adult roles related to family and community. Most of the research regarding this age group has been limited to the one quarter to one half who go on full time to college or other postsecondary education. Little tested knowledge is available about the substantial proportion of the age cohort who drop out of school before high school graduation or about the non-college-bound young adults who graduate from high school but do not proceed directly to full-time postsecondary education.

The following two case descriptions were drawn from a study of educative activity and occupational development by non-college-bound young adults (Knox, 1970). Both young men were in their mid-twenties and had grown up in the same metropolitan area. Their backgrounds were similar. Hal had not participated in any part-time educational programs in recent years, but Luke had. Following the brief case descriptions for each is a comment on developmental trends based on analysis of data from the entire sample of non-college-bound young adults between eighteen and twenty-six years of age.

At the time of the interview, Hal was twenty-three years old, married, but without children. He was one of ten children. Until retirement, his father was a construction laborer who never finished the eighth grade.

Hal himself almost did not finish high school. He had quit the vocational high school in the second half of eleventh grade. But he did return later and completed his diploma in night school. He had been a wood shop major, he said, because he had wanted to be a carpenter, but he did not care for high school.

As a full-time high school student, he was on the track team, and also managed several of the other teams, took care of the equipment, and helped the coach. He spent thirty-five to forty hours a week playing basketball, football, and baseball outside of high school.

His parents were somewhat concerned about Hal's progress in school. Reading material was scarce in his home, although they did have a dictionary. He said his parents had helped him with his homework from three to four hours a week and inquired about his progress at least twice a month. They wanted him to graduate, and wished him to get B's and C's, but they had been satisfied with C's. They also wanted him to go to college, but they did nothing to further this goal.

After high school, Hal took a full-time job as a shipping clerk. He worked at that job for a year and six months and then spent six months in the National Guard. Six letters of application and four months later, he landed his present job as a shipping clerk. Within the first year he advanced from packing to his current clerk's position, and he had been at this job for four years at the time of the interview. He was enthusiastic about his job, found the work lucrative, and believed that he had a good chance for advancement because the company was large. He also found plenty of variety on the job and complained only that he would like more freedom and that his supervisor was only sometimes satisfactory. He stressed independence and results as well as security and seniority as the characteristics most desirable to him.

Hal's wife was also a high school graduate. As indicated earlier, they had no children. He said his home was his greatest satisfaction, and his family was as important as other things in his life. Hal enjoyed being in the woods near animals and birds. Hunting was his favorite leisure time activity; otherwise, he liked to spend his spare time swimming or just being around the house. He was a bit of a loner, although he did mention belonging to a bowling league. Of the adults he considered most important in his life, all six felt education was very important, although only Hal's wife thought he ought to obtain more.

Luke's father, a high school graduate, worked as a foreman for a dry-cleaning equipment plant during Luke's adolescence. Luke's mother, who completed the eighth grade, worked full time as a waitress during Luke's high school years. Luke was the youngest of four children.

His major in high school was chosen because his brothers had done so before him, and although he liked wood shop, he did not think it was his line of work. He would have liked to have been a machine shop major instead, but the school had not offered many courses in this area while he was attending. Luke regretted the wood shop program he had taken and would have really preferred to have majored in business and prepared himself for college. While in high school he was on the track, football, and intramural badminton teams.

Luke's parents were interested in his education until he was about fifteen. Until then, Luke's father spent almost every night working with Luke on his homework. He described his father as a strong believer in education. Evidently, his father had been valedictorian of his class and was encouraged to go on to college.

When Luke first entered high school, he was told by his parents that if he wished to go to college, the money would be provided. But by the time he was fifteen both he and his parents assumed that he would go into steamfitting. Also, right around this time Luke's parents stopped taking an interest in his school work.

Luke was twenty-six when he was interviewed, and he had been employed full-time as a steamfitter and welder for the past seven years, with only one brief interruption about six months before. He had quit the job, because he disliked his supervisor; later he returned to the same job, because it was the only well-paying job for which he was qualified, and he had a wife and five children to support. He found little else attractive about his job except the pay. He was quite dissatisfied with his job. The two characteristics of a job that were most important to him, he said, were variety and the opportunity to use one's aptitudes.

Luke's wife was not a high school graduate although she did complete the tenth grade. All six of the most important adults in his life were really close friends and attended the same church. The only female was his wife. All six people felt that education was important, and three, including his wife, felt that Luke in particular should receive more education.

Luke's favorite leisure activities had remained the same since he was a teenager. He liked to hunt, fish, and box and belonged to a fish and game club. He had added photography to his earlier interests and hoped to join a photography club soon. The hunting and fishing were pleasurable because of the sense of freedom and independence being close to nature. He was also particularly fond of photographing nature subjects. He spent four or five hours a week reading five magazines: three sports magazines, one photography magazine, and *Reader's Digest*. When asked how he would rate his language facility, he rated himself as poor. His vocabulary test score was below the average of the other non-college-bound young adults in the study.

Luke participated in several adult education programs, including a job-sponsored apprenticeship program. He spent three hours one evening a week for five years taking courses in math and welding. He also spent sixty hours taking a high school evening course in photography.

Hal and Luke illustrate some of the trends that emerged from the total sample of non-college-bound young adults. During the seven or eight years after leaving high school, there were a number of developmental trends that reflected widespread shifts between late adolescence and early young adulthood for those who went to work instead of to college.

One trend was occupational development. The older young adults had progressed to somewhat higher status occupations, in contrast with those a few years out of high school. In addition, with age there was an increase in worker role performance ratings and in level of work satisfaction. Although there were exceptions, most of those who were working ex-

pressed the belief that they were making progress occupationally even though they hoped for greater improvements in the
future.

A second trend was increased participation in leisure and
community activities. The older young adults belonged to more
organizations, and the ratings regarding their leisure role performance and social adjustment were higher than for those a
few years out of high school. They were becoming more socially
engaged, a trend that is reversed for some elderly adults in a
process termed *disengagement.*

A related trend was toward an increased sense of mastery
over the social environment. This was reflected in higher levels
of planfulness and need for achievement for the older young
adults.

Another trend was toward more of a reading orientation.
The older young adults demonstrated greater verbal ability on
a vocabulary test, reported more time spent reading magazines,
and expressed more interest in work that requires reading.
However, the proportion of the significant others in the lives
of the older young adults who were perceived as encouraging
them to obtain more education, was smaller than the proportion
of significant others for those young adults who were a few
years out of high school.

Practitioners who understand these trends toward greater
social engagement by non-college-bound young adults, along
with shifting attitudes toward work, community, and information seeking, can help such young adults to gain perspective on
their unfolding lives. This developmental understanding can
also be shared with other people who are significant in the lives
of young adults.

People tend to take encouragement and assistance from
others for granted, except when it is much needed but not
available. Most adults have some other people in their lives
who are especially important or significant to them. These
significant others include not only a confidant but also the
people to whom the individual typically turns for reassurance,
advice, and encouragement. This occurs especially during periods of major change and adjustment. The contribution of

significant others in relation to change events contributes to adjustment to college by young adults as well as by men and women who return to college in mid-life. Significant others encourage some non-college-bound young adults to pursue their education, but are more likely to do so during the first few years after they leave high school than a few years later. Practitioners can help adults recognize the valuable contribution that significant others can make and if necessary suggest that adults seek out people who will encourage them to become what they want to become. This occurs for some support groups composed of people who are also dealing with a problem area such as alcohol, drug abuse, or being a single parent. Similar encouragement and assistance can occur for many transitions and with individuals as well as groups.

Summary

Along with the previous chapter on performance in family roles, this chapter on stability and change in performance in education, work, and community delineates the changing fabric of participation during adulthood.

Adults vary greatly in the extent and types of educative activity in which they engage from adolescence through senescence. This variability is greatly associated with social class level but only slightly associated with age. It is important that practitioners understand developmental aspects of educative activity by adults, because it is so central to a self-directed and evolving life-style.

Information seeking is positively associated with level of formal education, but little associated with age. There are small fluctuations. Newspaper reading dips slightly in middle- age, and there are small declines in magazine and book reading in old age. The proportion of adults who listen to the radio regularly dips slightly in middle age. While the average time spent listening declines, informational use increases with age. The proportion of all adults who view television regularly rises to middle age and then declines, but there is a decline with age for the more educated and an increase with age for the less educated.

Attending college full time following high school is highly associated with parental social class level and less so with the individual's intelligence and high school performance. During the past generation, increasingly larger proportions of college students are beyond the typical age range, especially in community colleges. Middle-aged adults who return to college typically achieve as well as or better than younger students. For all students, practitioners can increase educational achievement by fitting instructional and counseling approaches to the students' intellectual and ethical development.

The extent of adult participation in part-time or short-term continuing education activities is largely associated with level of formal education, age, and sense of educational efficacy. There is a similar decline with age for major instances of self-directed study and for participation in programs sponsored by educational institutions and other types of organizations, such as employers, churches, and professional associations. A better understanding of adults as learners can help practitioners establish more effective linkage between client systems and relevant resource systems and services.

One's occupation helps establish one's self-concept as well as one's level of living and prestige. Occupational decisions reflect both personal preferences and available opportunities, and the process of choosing has become more difficult as the variety of occupations has increased. Some of the influences on satisfactory occupational choice are: occupational information and experience, similarity between occupation and personal interests and values, availability of occupational role models and mentors, job requirements that are somewhat challenging but not threatening, and education and socialization to facilitate job entry. Career development often occurs throughout the work life, and it is influenced by attitudes such as assertiveness and willingness to accept new responsibilities. The rapidly changing occupational structure is resulting in multiple careers, which practitioners can help adults understand and plan for.

On some indices of unsatisfactory occupational performance, such as work-related accidents, absenteeism, and unemployment, the average record of young adults is worse than that of middle-aged and older adults. Unemployment rates are mainly affected by general economic conditions, and tend to be highest for urban minority youth, blue collar workers generally, and women.

Regarding satisfactory occupational performance, variabilities within age groups are large and trends across age groups are small. For example, although young adults are most likely to perform better than older adults in occupations that emphasize speed, strength, memory, and novel solutions, most of the variability in occupational performance by young adults reflects such ingredients as work characteristics, education, personality development, and access. Educational and training programs may accelerate the process of becoming productive or may constitute irrelevant restrictions. Furthermore, the maturing process that occurs for college students also occurs to some extent for those who do not attend college. Older workers tend to perform better in terms of experience, steadiness, conscientiousness, patience, and attendance. Practitioners can assist adults with their career development by helping them understand typical patterns of satisfactory and unsatisfactory occupational performance and the relative influence those patterns are likely to have on the major factors that affect work performance.

Outstanding occupational performance and achievement varies with the type of work. For example, in fields that depend heavily on physical capacities, peak performance tends to occur in the twenties and early thirties; in fields that depend heavily on intellectual capacities, peak performance tends to occur in the thirties; and in fields that depend heavily on social capacities, peak performance tends to occur even later. These relationships between achievement and age are based on the one or two most outstanding achievements by individuals. When a larger volume of outstanding achievements are included for each individual, creativity is maintained well into middle age and beyond for most fields.

People work for many reasons, including money, status, satisfaction, recognition, service, companionship, and self-actualization. More white collar workers emphasize work itself and deemphasize its benefits than is the case for most blue collar workers. This mainly reflects the type of work that each does. There are some shifts in expectations regarding jobs, from income, interesting work, and potential success for young workers, to independence from supervision and job security for older workers. Occupational adjustments also have an impact on other life roles. Mid-career occupational changes can reach crisis proportions and adversely affect family life, but they can also present new opportunities and directions. Even though mandatory retirement forces many older workers to terminate employment, this is especially difficult for many white collar workers whose work satisfaction tends to be high, and some continue with other forms of economically productive activity.

Practitioners can help adults who confront major adjustments related to productivity and creativity to recognize the basic problems that underlie the symptoms, locate relevant opportunities, and consider personal talents and priorities in the decision-making process. Activities that can be suggested to facilitate creativity include intermittent solitude, analyzing past obstacles, fantasizing to achieve new insights, accepting one's individuality, and following through.

Social participation, aside from performance in work and family, includes involvement in organizations, political activity, religious groups, public events, recreation, and informal activities with family and friends. During the courtship period and the early years of marriage, patterns of social participation by men and women become more similar, and the shift is toward activities preferred by women. During middle age more women's social participation is associated with family and community, and more men's social participation is somewhat work related. Parental responsibilities tend to restrict time and money for outside social participation and, for many women, shifts the emphasis to child-oriented activities. Up until middle age, a portion of social participation tends to be related to work, followed by a shift to activities that contrast with work. White collar adults engage in more occupationally related social participation than do blue collar adults.

Specific types of social participation follow quite different trends during adulthood, which produces a changing mix from young adulthood, to middle age, and beyond. In spite of the much greater association of social participation with social class level than with age, there is a developmental shift from activities that are physically vigorous and action oriented in late adolescence and young adulthood, to activities that are concerned with interpersonal relations and understanding in middle age, to activities that are cultural and introspective beyond middle age.

When the total fabric of participation is analyzed, much of it forms a highly stable plateau for most of adulthood. About half of social participation variables are quite stable during much of adulthood, and they mainly consist of social relations and solitary activities that reflect such personality character- istics as activity level and values. Examples include religious participation, which tends to be stable until declining health affects activity outside the home, and informal activities with close friends. Forms of participation that steadily decline dur- ing adulthood reflect differentiation and variety in social rela- tions, as illustrated by the proportion of adults who attend movies or athletic events, participate in outings, or read books. Forms of participation that steadily expand during adulthood reflect informal intimate social relationships with members of primary groups. Interaction with family and close friends tends to increase through middle age. Some forms of social participa- tion follow a cyclical pattern of expansion from young adult- hood to middle age followed by constriction, which reflects status-related active participation in formal types of interaction, such as the number of organizational memberships or extent of political participation. Participation variables that alternate up and down during adulthood reflect changes in roles and statuses in occupation and family, such as frequency of attendance at meetings. There are also life cycle shifts in the meanings and satisfactions that leisure activities have for adults, such as the tendency for leisure activities of adolescents to reflect their reactions against pressures that they perceive from family and school.

A little understood but important type of participation is friendship, and making an art of friendship has been identified as a developmental task of adulthood. Most people who fail to establish desired friendships are barred by inadequate understanding of the important functions served by friendship and of effective procedures for making new friends. Practitioners can help adults enter friendship groups and better understand the friend-making process. For example, aspects of close friendships include similarity, reciprocity, compatibility, closeness, and role models. Those who want to make new friends can be helped to acknowledge that their needs for intimacy and relatedness are not being met and to understand that the most enduring and mutually beneficial friendships entail an interdependency in which each member combines self-assertiveness and caring for others.

In general, practitioners can help adults of all ages gain a more comprehensive perspective on their participation in education, work, and community, with an emphasis on a more proactive stance toward life cycle shifts in the transactions between personal preferences and societal opportunities. Such transactions are illustrated by the way in which personal abilities and interests interact with opportunities and support to produce participation rates in full-time and part-time educational programs. In community settings shifting family responsibilities affect the extent to which recreational activities reflect personal preferences. In occupational settings personal values and willingness to take risks interact with changing occupational tasks to determine which activities the individual considers challenges but not threats. Practitioners concerned with supervision and education of adults can help workers anticipate likely short-term and long-term occupational changes related to job entry, mid-career changes, and retirement.

If adults understand likely long-term shifts in work values or social participation, they may be more able to be proactive in making decisions about short-term adjustments. White collar adults tend to be more proactive than blue collar adults in information seeking and educative activity. This is reflected in greater use of media and experts for instrumental information seeking. Practitioners seem to have a special obligation to assist blue collar adults to become more proactive and initiatory. A greater sense of self-direction can occur as workers recognize the relative influence that they are likely to have on factors associated with career development, as adult learners select educational activities that match their preferred learning styles, or as adults discover that they can take the initiative to increase creativity or enhance friendship. There are many ways in which practitioners can help adults gain a developmental perspective on their performance and on their own proactive role in the process.

❧ 5 ❧

Physical Condition

❧❧❧❧❧❧❧❧❧❧❧❧❧❧

Adult performance reflects both the physical condition and health of the individual and the demands and constraints of the societal contexts within which he or she functions. The individual's physical characteristics and condition include not only the presence or absence of illness and physical disability, but also the physique, strength, endurance, and vitality that contribute to the individual's energy level, pacing, and engagement.

Physical condition is affected by heredity, nutrition, exercise, previous illness and injury, and sensory functioning, as well as current state of physical and mental health. Furthermore, many aspects of physical condition consist of interrelated biological systems. Malfunctioning of some systems can adversely affect associated systems, such as the impact of sleep deprivation on physical coordination or the impact of inadequate blood circulation in the brain on memory. However, some systems can help compensate for reduced functioning of other

245

systems, such as increased acquisition of information from hearing and touch to compensate for blindness.

Some aspects of physical condition, such as height and appearance, are influenced by heredity. Appearance, especially weight, is influenced by nutrition. Cellular functioning, especially of the brain and nervous system, undergirds the functioning of organs, such as the eye or heart, and of entire systems, such as the circulatory or digestive systems. For many types of adult performance and participation, sensory functions, such as vision, hearing, and speech, are very important, and adult life trends in sensory functioning affect both performance and self-concept. Many skills entail reaction time and movement time, which are affected both by physical condition and by the way in which the individual processes information and makes decisions. The incidence of various types of physical and mental illness varies with the stages of the adult life cycle. Biological aging and deterioration affect both physical and mental health. In addition, some aspects of physical and mental health are interrelated. Although some older adults are greatly affected by ill health, many older adults are in good health.

Generalizations about adult life cycle trends in physical condition and health can help practitioners gain perspective on the specific people with whom they work (Long, 1972). This developmental perspective in part results from an understanding of typical characteristics of adults at a given stage of adulthood against which to compare a specific adult who is at that stage. The typical characteristics provide not a prescription for any individual, but a perspective from which the practitioner can identify and interpret aspects of physical condition and health that may be uniquely important to that individual. For most of adulthood, the range of individual differences increases, and there are many exceptions to each generalization. A developmental perspective also results from an understanding of elements of stability and change in physical condition and health during adulthood. In dealing with an individual adult client, it is helpful to understand the main trends that have led to his or her current condition and to recognize the likely future trends. A developmental perspective helps a practitioner pursue questions that are likely to yield insight into the functioning of a specific adult and suggest the types of assistance or intervention that will help the client achieve and maintain healthy and satisfying performance. It can also alert the practitioner to aspects of physical condition and health that can influence adult performance in family, work, education, and community and to ways of reducing barriers to performance and adaptation. The replacement of false stereotypes with accurate generalizations is most beneficial when applied to the facilitation of performance and adaptation by individual adults.

Practitioners who work with adults can minimize false stereotypes about older adults by making some distinctions between general trends in biological aging that affect everyone and specific forms of ill health that affect only some people. However, aging entails complex interrelationships among genetic and environmental factors that are little understood. *Biological aging* refers to the accumulated changes in people that lead to functional impairment and death. Beginning in middle age, the aging process is reflected in progressive declines in vigor and resistance to disease. It is currently not possible to separate age-related cellular changes from pathological cellular changes associated with diseases of old age. We do not understand many of the aging processes that affect the person at molecular, cellular, tissular, and organismic levels; which events indicate the cessation of cellular growth; or the bases for decremental changes that produce declines in functional competence (Timiras, 1972). The influence of biological aging on performance is reduced because the body contains cells and capacity that are not essential for normal operation. This excess capacity minimizes the impact of deterioration due to wear and tear, and of sudden strain (Milne and Milne, 1968). However, aging generally reduces adaptability.

Heredity and Environment

Physical condition is reflected in the individual's appearance, functioning, and longevity. One major influence on physical condition is heredity. At conception, some potential is established for longevity, and some individual differences in appearance and functioning are set. If everyone had the same environment and conditions of nutrition, exercise, stress, and assault, longevity would be similar for all, and individual differences in physical condition would mainly result from variations in genetic endowment. Short life spans seem to be genetically determined for individuals who have predispositions to fatal diseases, such as heart disease or cancer. Those who reach very old age tend to have long-lived parents (Smith and Bierman, 1973). However, there are large variations in living conditions and other environmental influences that also affect appearance, level of physical functioning, and longevity.

Heredity combines with environmental influences to produce physical condition. Some environmental influences, such as nutrition and activity, directly affect physical condition. Other environmental influences, such as the impact of disease or extended emotional stress on endocrine glands, affect physical condition both directly and indirectly through temperament. In addition to genetic endowment, parents influence the physical condition of their offspring in various ways. Included are parental age and health at conception; maternal nutrition and health during gestation; and the practices and conditions related to health, nutrition, and exercise that occur in the home environment during childhood and adolescence. As the adolescent becomes a young adult, in addition to environmental influences on physical condition, he or she has typically acquired habits and practices, such as those related to eating, drinking, smoking, health, and exercise, that have a continuing influence on physical condition.

Life Expectancy

The mixed influences of heredity and environmental circumstances are illustrated by generalizations about longevity (Pfeiffer, 1970). Although the average life span for people in the United States has increased dramatically in recent generations from less than fifty at the turn of the century to almost sixty about forty years ago and up to more than seventy today, most of the increase in life expectancy has resulted from reductions in death rates for infants and children. Most of the increase occurred before 1950. For adults at age sixty-five, the average number of remaining years of life has increased only two or three years since the turn of the century. The life expectancy for nonwhites is about seven years less than for whites (Milne and Milne, 1968).

The life expectancy is about seven years longer for women than for men: almost seventy-five compared with less than sixty-eight. Although more boy babies are born than girl babies, male death rates are higher beginning at birth, so that by age twenty, women increasingly outnumber men. For persons in the entire age range beyond sixty-five, there are more than 140 women for every 100 men. However, for those in the age range between sixty-five and seventy-four, there are about 130 women for every 100 men, and for those seventy-five and older, there are more than 165 women for every 100 men. Because most women marry older men, there are about four times as many widows as widowers.

Evidence of the genetic foundation of the natural life span is provided by the finding that for sets of twins who die after age sixty, the interpair life span difference is smaller for identical or one-egg twins than for two-egg twins. Also, persons with a smaller build tend to live somewhat longer than those with a larger build (Kallman and Sander, 1949). The age of parents at conception is also related to the condition and longevity of the offspring. Higher rates of birth defects occur for babies born of mothers who are substantially younger or older than the typical childbearing range of sixteen to forty, and some of the resultant abnormalities are associated with low life expectancy. If all babies were born of parents during the typical childbearing range, and if throughout life the offspring experienced similar environmental conditions, then the longevity of the parents would have a substantial influence on the longevity of the offspring. This influence includes a genetically determined biological aging process. The aging process consists of a progressive and irreversible reduction in the individual's ability to withstand stress and adapt, and it culminates in death.

In addition to a genetically determined aging process, longevity reflects the influence of differential environmental influences. Some people experience extended periods of malnutrition, inactivity, or overwork, and repeated illnesses and accidents. The result is an accumulation of impairments. It seems likely that the probability of incurring additional impairment at any time increases with the accumulation of previous impairments. The death rate would then reflect this accumulation of damage, along with a genetically determined aging process (H. B. Jones, 1956).

Some of the likely interrelations among heredity, environment, and longevity are illustrated by comparisons among countries or regions in the world with contrasting life expectancy rates. In some countries the death rate below age seventy is higher than the average. This reflects a harsher environment regarding nutrition, health conditions, and accidents in which those who survive beyond age seventy tend to be the hardier individuals. In these countries, the average death rate after age seventy is lower than for countries that have relatively low death rates before age seventy. In the Russian Caucasus region near the Black Sea, there is a small region with very high life expectancy. Many people live to be very old with lean, muscular, and healthy appearances. Some of the practices that seem to be associated with such unusual longevity are working hard physically, getting sufficient sleep, and seldom overeating (Milne and Milne, 1968; Leaf, 1973).

There are at least two processes associated with condition and longevity for which controlled stress seems to be associated with improved condition and longevity. They are immunity and exercise. Exposure to some infectious diseases typically experienced in childhood, such as mumps and measles, can lead to a "natural" immunity because as the body combats the disease, it develops a resistance that greatly reduces susceptibility to the disease in the future. Immunity can also be induced by a controlled exposure through vaccination or inoculation, such as occurs for diphtheria, typhoid fever, tetanus, and polio. There are many forms of immunity, and they vary in duration from much less than a year to many decades. During young adulthood and middle age especially, condition and longevity are partly associated with exposure to disease and immunity from it. With advanced old age, there appears to be a reduction in immunity.

Exercise is also a way of exposing the body to controlled stress. Some benefits of regular exercise, such as increased strength, endurance, and vitality, require that the individual physically overload the body in graduated increments.

The individual and society can pursue policies that will produce improved physical condition for people during a full natural life span. These policies include preventive and remedial practices related to public health, personal health, nutrition, exercise, and emotional stress. However, variations in the genetic endowment of longevity among people and genetic influences on longevity from generation to generation are more difficult to explain because the trait of longevity appears after the period of reproduction. This eliminates selective breeding for longevity. It therefore seems likely that hereditary influences on longevity occur through counterpart characteristics that are apparent during the reproduction period and are favorable to survival.

The probability that an individual will die within a year increases exponentially following maturity, especially after age thirty. Paradoxically, most indices of physical condition and functioning decline linearly. Functional capacities, such as muscle strength, vital capacity, basal metabolic rate, renal (kidney) clearance, and maximal breathing capacity decline about as much from age fifty to seventy as from age thirty to fifty. If the death rate was based only on decline in functional capacities, then it would also follow a linear decline. A likely explanation is that as functional capacities decline they interact with each other and with environmental hazards to produce an exponential doubling and redoubling of risk with increasing age. At younger ages, when functional capacity is higher, relatively few major hazards are sufficient to produce death. With increasing age, as functional capacity declines there is an exponential increase in the number of hazards sufficient to produce death. Falls and acute illnesses have more serious consequences as age advances. In addition, a malfunction can become cumulative and more readily produce a terminal decline in old age (Timiras, 1972). The individual can sometimes reduce the probability of death by changed practices (improved diet for obesity), by medication (insulin for diabetes), or by an operation (amputation for gangrene). Practitioners can help older adults recognize major hazards and take preventive measures.

Biological Relationships

The parts and functions of the human body are highly interrelated. Systems, such as circulation of blood and respiration, support other systems, such as the neurologic system, which includes the brain, the nervous system, and such sensory functions as seeing and hearing. Major reductions in oxygen supply result in irreversible damage to nerve cells. General physical condition reflects these interrelationships, as does the aging process. However, in reviewing developmental and aging trends, it is necessary to separate the various functions for analytic purposes. Following are the major biologic systems, along with some indications of measurements that have indicated changes associated with normal physiologic aging (Timiras, 1972; Barrows, 1971; Curtis, 1962; Kastenbaum, 1965):

1. *Cells.* Molecular and cellular functioning undergirds functioning at tissular and organismic levels. Cellular aging is affected by differential patterns of cell division for various types of cells and by change in cell composition with age.
2. *Support.* Measures of the skeletal support structure that vary with age include total height, length of the backbone (vertebral column), and thickness of cortical bone (from an X ray of the hand). The composition and brittleness of bones also changes with age, as do the condition of teeth and supporting bone and gums.
3. *Neurologic.* The functioning of the brain is assessed by an electroencephalogram. Both brain waves and the

results of standard neurologic examinations show age trends.

4. *Circulation and Respiration.* Aging trends for blood circulation are reflected in such measures as electrocardiograms or readings on systolic and diastolic blood pressure. Measures of respiratory functions include chest X ray of lungs, vital capacity, and diffusing capacity of the lungs. Several associated functions include renal (urinalysis, creatinine clearance), hematopoietic (hemoglobin, plasma volume), and immunologic (autoantibody titers).

5. *Nutrition.* Several processes and functions are loosely associated. Nutrition includes the amounts and types of food and fluid consumed (caloric intake, use of alcohol). The digestive system includes stomach and intestines. Age-related measures of the metabolic function include protein and cholesterol. These processes and functions are reflected in weight and appearance as measured by volume, mass, weight, circumferences, and skin fold thickness.

6. *Muscles.* Strength is measured by grip strength with right and left hands. Related measures of physiological strength and endurance include lifting, pull-ups, pushups, jumping, and running. Information about bodily repair of damaged tissue, such as a cut, which also varies with age, is included in this section.

7. *Endocrine.* Glucose tolerance is an age-related measure of one endocrine function. An associated process is bodily adjustment to changes in room temperature.

8. *Reproduction.* The functioning of the reproductive organs of men and women, such as prostate, ovaries, and uterus, changes with age.

9. *Senses.* Sensory functions for the reception of information include vision and hearing, which are measured regarding acuity, and taste, which is measured regarding threshold. The measurement is of the smallest amount of print, sound, and flavor that can be dis-

cerned. A related function is speech, for which measures relate to changes in voice quality with age.

Cells. The functioning of the human body and its organs and systems, such as circulation and digestion, that compose it is greatly affected by the cells of which the various parts of the body are constituted. Between birthdays, an adult's body remains fairly stable as a total organism and at the levels of organs, tissue, and even cells. However, the atoms and molecules that compose the cells are constantly changing. Cells constantly exchange molecules of many kinds as they obtain nutrients and energy from the environment and regenerate themselves. Although the process of renewal is not evident, only about 2 percent of the atoms that compose a human body on one birthday are still present on the next. Many of these remaining atoms are iron, an essential element in the hemoglobin of red blood cells that appears to be difficult to absorb from the environment. However, each week about half the water, potassium, sodium, and carbon molecules are replaced by fresh ones. Calcium stays longer before being discharged by the kidneys, but if its intake from food and hard water is insufficient, the bones become brittle (Milne and Milne, 1968).

The sweeping changes in the human body that are continually occurring at the atomic and molecular levels are balanced by stability at the cellular level. This stability is provided by an inherited guidance that is coded within the forty-six chromosomes in the nucleus of each body cell. At conception, the single cell of a fertilized egg divides in less than a day into a two-celled embryo. In doing so, each new cell receives a duplicate set of chromosomes. The second division takes about the same length of time to produce four cells with duplicate sets of chromosomes. The rate at which cell division occurs slowly declines. Nerve and muscle cells cease division around birth, whereas skin and blood cells continue to divide throughout life. Each division duplicates the individual's set of chromosomes, which maintains the stability and consistency of the unique human being (Milne and Milne, 1968).

A widely accepted feature of biological aging is a continuing reduction in the number and effectiveness of the types of cells that do not divide or that divide very slowly during adulthood (Timiras, 1972; Jarvik and Cohen, 1973). Several important types of cells that do not divide during adulthood are muscle cells and neurons of the central nervous system. As a result, the muscles of the body, including the heart, and the nervous system, including the brain, consist of fewer and fewer cells during adulthood, and those that remain are as old as the individual and in later years become less effective. For example, the softness and pliability of heart valves gradually reduces with age, and fibrous tissue increases. By contrast, some cells renew themselves. As they divide, they replace cells that died. In addition, as cells divide, they seem to discard some of the accumulated damage. Some blood cells live a few hours or a few days. Other cells that continue to divide and renew tissue are the epithelial cells of the skin and gastrointestinal mucosa, such as the lining of the stomach. However, the average number of consecutive doublings tends to be about forty, plus or minus ten (Timiras, 1972).

Cells engage in four basic functions: production of energy, synthesis of proteins, maintenance of cellular homeostasis, and reproduction. It is likely that cellular aging and death involves a derangement of these basic functions, but the mechanisms of cellular aging are little understood. Because of the essential role of nucleic acids in cellular functioning, it is likely that the progressive loss or dissipation of critical genetic material of the cell is a major mechanism of aging. However, tested knowledge from developmental physiology does not conclusively demonstrate causal relationships between changes in nucleic acids, cellular aging, and specific or generalized aging of the organism. Desoxyribonucleic acid (DNA) forms ribonucleic acids (RNA), which in turn synthesize the enzymes without which the cell could not survive. It appears that as DNA is dissipated over the years, the process that leads to cellular death begins (Timiras, 1972).

Cellular injury or aging appears to influence both cell degeneration, which is compatible with recovery, and more severe cellular damage, which is irreversible and leads to cellular death. Some cellular changes are associated with aging but are not necessarily a cause of aging. Included are an abnormal accumulation of cellular waste products and a marked decline after age forty in exchangeable potassium (Timiras, 1972; Jarvik and Cohen, 1973). As cells die there is a thickening of the connective collagen fibers that lie between the cells and a reduction of the elastic fibers of the blood vessels and skin. With advancing age, calcium nodules and fatty plaques accumulate between the cells. Although there is increased cross-linking and inelasticity at cellular and tissular levels with age, the influence on the functioning of organs and the total organism is only partially clear.

Some cellular changes reduce the adaptability of the organism to withstand disease and to repair accidental damage. However, the human body has an enormous reserve of cells in various organs. For example, an adult can survive with less than half of the liver, one kidney, one lung, and parts of the stomach and intestine (Timiras, 1972). Because the initial capacity of the nervous system to transmit information is over-determined, channel capacity can be substantially reduced by the death of nerve cells before the actual information load transmitted is reduced.

During the adult life cycle, the gradual reduction of ceiling capacity of the body to function and perform has relatively little impact on typical daily activities. For example, physiologic functions such as the regulation of blood glucose levels and acid-base balance remain relatively stable throughout adulthood under resting conditions. However, when physiologic functioning during adulthood is assessed under conditions of stress, there are major age decrements. When adults engage in heavy exercise, there is an age-related decline in the amount of blood pumped per minute by the heart (cardiac output). For older adults, this decline reduces the response to increased demand for blood circulation by contracting muscles that require increased oxygen and nutrients and elimination of metabolic waste products. Cardiac output for a young adult may increase eightfold as the body goes from a resting state to heavy exercise.

When an elderly adult engages in heavy exercise, although there is typically an even greater increase in heart rate and rise in blood pressure than for the young adult, cardiac output is less efficient and circulation is reduced, which restricts muscular performance. The progressive reduction in the amount of oxygen the blood takes up through the lung means that the older adult must breathe more heavily to move more air in and out of the lungs to respond to increased muscle demand for oxygen during heavy exercise. Under such conditions of physical stress, aged cells and tissues restrict physical performance (Timiras, 1972). This does not mean that older adults are unable to be physically active. Instead, practitioners can help older adults understand the reason for increasingly restricted physical performance and function well within those restrictions.

Support. An adult's height reflects heredity, childhood condition, age, and time of the day. Girls typically attain their maximum height by their mid-teens, and boys do so by their late teens. The pubescent growth spurt typically occurs around age twelve for girls and around age fourteen for boys and can add three or four inches to height in a single year. The height of most young adults mainly reflects their genetic endowment. Adults with tall parents are typically taller than adults with short parents. There is, however, a law of filial regression in which children of tall parents and of short parents tend to be closer to the average height of the total population. Nutrition, medical care, and activity during childhood and adolescence also influence height. Barring endocrine abnormalities, if environmental conditions were the same for all people, then height would be mainly inherited. However, nutrition and health conditions vary substantially between blue collar and white collar families and among nations. In this country, improved nutrition and health has contributed to increases during recent generations in the average height of young adults. Thus the main reason the average height of older adults is less than the average height of young adults is that several generations ago the average height for young adults was lower.

In addition, adult height declines gradually with age. In

addition to bone structure, height includes cartilage between bones, especially the discs between the bones in the vertebral column or backbone. Between twenty and sixty, adults typically shrink by more than half an inch as cartilage discs become thinner and the arches of the feet become flatter. A similar process occurs daily when the weight from sitting and walking in an erect position compresses the intervertebral discs. The cartilage discs expand during rest at night. As a result, erect height decreases up to an inch between morning and night. Changes in bone density occur with age. With the end of adolescence and skeletal growth, the production and accumulation of calcium declines. During adulthood some bones, such as the sternum, increase in density, but other bones, such as the ribs, long bones of the legs and arms, and vertebrae, decrease in density. This degeneration of the bones, called osteoporosis, occurs because the cells that produce new bone tissue die while the cells that cause bone degeneration continue to function. As a result, the bones typically become more brittle and take longer to knit if fractured. The onset of osteoporosis occurs in the late forties for men but rapidly increases after the menopause for women and is more severe. Sound nutrition in early life can reduce its severity.

Neurologic. Neurophysiologic aging affects the transmission of information between sense organs, the brain, and the periphery. In electrophysiologic terms, the central nervous system (CNS) can be thought of as a series of circuits. For example, an adult sees an object coming toward him or her through the air. Signals are transmitted along the optic nerve to the brain, then from one part of the brain to another, and then signals are transmitted along the central nervous system to activate the muscles of the arm and hand to reach up and catch or deflect the object. Similar to a telephone connection, the adequacy of signal transmission along the central nervous system (CNS) depends on more than the quality of the signal that enters the far end of the line. Some aspects of neurophysiologic aging appear to influence transmission.

The characteristics and condition of the human brain, along with the other parts of the nervous system, have an essential role to play in the regulation of vital physiologic functions (Blumenthal, 1970). Although there is substantial cell loss because neurons do not divide after birth, the reserve of nerve cells is so great that there is no direct impact on mental functioning. Brain weight increases until about age thirty, declines slightly for a few years, and then declines at an accelerating rate into old age (Himwich and Himwich, 1959). The average decline in total brain weight from the twenties to the eighties is about two hundred grams from an average maximum weight of more than thirteen hundred grams. There is also a parallel decline in the proportion of dry substance in relation to water; this decline is gradual in the thirties and forties but declines at a slightly accelerating rate in the fifties and sixties. A more rapid decrease in the proportion of dry substance in the seventies followed by an increase during the eighties seems to reflect the replacement of neurons with glial cells. In healthy adults, cerebral metabolic rate changes little with age. There tends to be a steady protein increase in both gray and white matter through young adulthood and middle age, but a regression after the mid-seventies. Because of the likely association between nucleic acids and memory, especially in relation to the characteristic memory decline with senescence, the adult life cycle trends in the content of RNA and DNA in the brain are of particular interest even though available generalizations are only suggestive. The amount of DNA increases steadily from the twenties until the nineties. The RNA content of the brain increases until about age forty, remains constant at that level through the forties and fifties, and then declines rapidly (Timiras, 1972). Cerebral blood flow, EEG alpha rhythms, and attentiveness tend to decline with age (Thompson and Marsh, 1973; Cameron, 1963).

The left and the right hemispheres of the brain control quite different aspects of perception, thinking, feeling, and physical movement. As a result, localized injury to a portion of the brain, such as from a head injury or a stroke, affects corresponding aspects of functioning. Patient education activities for adults who sustain brain injury can help them understand the connection between the damaged zone and the impaired functioning as part of the rehabilitation or compensation process. In some instances where portions of the brain are damaged or even destroyed, other portions of the brain can gradually take over much of the function in the process of relearning. Because of the different functions performed by the right and left hemispheres of the brain, some people experience ambivalence of thought and feeling. Practitioners can help adults learn with the whole brain.

There are several trends during adulthood in the functioning of the central nervous system (CNS) that appear to be related to a progressive slowing of reaction time and reduction in coordination. The general effect of these trends is a reduction in the efficacy of signal transmission, which progressively impairs "signal strength," and an increase in random background activity within the nervous system, which constitutes "neural noise." The aging trend is toward an impairment of the signal-to-noise ratio, which reflects various combinations of reduced signal strength and increased neural noise. Following are some of the main aging trends in the CNS:

1. *Cell Reduction.* Signals are transmitted along the nervous system by means of synapses between cells. A gradual reduction in the number of nondividing neurons over the years at some age begins to reduce the number of synapses so that there are too few to refine or smooth the signal which is transmitted. This would increase neural noise as well as decrease signal strength.

2. *Increased Random Activity.* Even for the neurons that remain, there appears to be some reduction in internal efficiency with age and an increase in associated glial cells. With age, reduced functional activity of the neuron-glia unit can account for increased random activity that produces neural noise.

3. *Increased Aftereffects.* For older adults, stimulation of the motor cortex tends to continue much longer after the stimulus stops. Such aftereffects blur subsequent signals. Long-lasting aftereffects for older adults

can slow simple tasks and interfere with short-term retention involved in complex tasks.

4. *Altered Arousal.* Some older adults require more stimulation for arousal. This decrease in activation may reflect reduced responsiveness with age. It may also reflect a compensatory response to prolonged overactivation of neurons due to stress and overwork, along with lowered synaptic resistance. With a reduced threshold, overstimulation can heighten tension, neural noise, and confusion. An older adult may screen signals because of a reduced tolerance for noise.

Part of the CNS effectiveness depends on the conduction velocity of peripheral motor nerves. Efferent pathways provide junctions between the nervous system and muscle systems. Maximum velocity of motor nerves decline only 5 to 10 percent in aged adults. Peripheral nerves contribute little to slowed reaction time in old age.

The autonomic nervous system (ANS) provides reflex regulation of organs and functional systems. With age there is some rise in the sensitivity of the autonomic ganglia, which reduces the ability to transmit signals to the periphery and reduces the adaptability of the ANS. Some of these changes benefit the older adult; for example, reduced transmission insulates the tissues regulated by the ANS from abrupt changes from nerve centers. In addition, hypothalamic control of the CNS over ANS functional systems declines with age. This reduces homeostasis and adaptability to environmental changes.

Circulation. Three highly interrelated functions are included within the circulatory system: the circulatory function, in which blood is circulated throughout the body to provide oxygen and nutrients for the cells and to remove waste, the respiratory function, in which inhaling allows oxygen to be transferred from the lung to the bloodstream and exhaling expels carbon dioxide, and the renal function, in which the blood is filtered by the kidneys to remove soluble wastes and water to produce urine. Between the twenties and the eighties there is a steady decline of about 1 percent per year in most of these integrated body functions. However, as with the neurologic functions, the body has excess capacity, and these declines cause few restrictions during most of adulthood for typical activity but do increasingly restrict performance during periods of maximum effort or stress (Spieth, 1964; Astrand, 1968; deVries, 1974).

The circulatory system includes the heart, which pumps the blood; the arteries, which transport the blood throughout the body and brain; and the veins, which return the blood from the tissues to be pumped again. The efficiency of the heart depends on the volume of blood propelled per beat (stroke volume), and it reaches its peak during adolescence and declines gradually during adulthood. As a result, for persons who are resting, the average quantity of blood pumped per beat by the heart at age ninety is about half of what it was at age twenty. As the adult becomes older, the heart must pump faster to maintain the volume of blood pumped per minute, and this increased heart rate is one cause of increased resting blood pressure. The maximal heart rate gradually declines from 195 in a twenty-five-year-old, to 175 in a fifty-year-old, to 165 in a sixty-five-year-old person. The reserve capacity of the young adult's heart is very great. Prolonged high heart rates or a lesion of a cardiac valve may be tolerated easily and cause no symptoms during the twenties but may cause disability or death in the sixties. With increased age there is a greater drop in blood pressure when suddenly rising from a prone to a standing position; this drop can reduce cerebral circulation and cause faintness.

Muscles besides the heart help to circulate blood. For instance, the contraction and relaxation of the leg muscles that occurs in walking yields more than 30 percent of the power needed for circulation. This facilitates the return of the blood to the heart against gravity and reduces the work of the heart. Although it is not clear whether high levels of physical activity reduce cardiovascular aging and disease, for adults of all ages physical fitness tends to improve stroke volume and circulation and reduce damage to the arteries. Blood flow varies among organs and with intensity of activity. There may be a thirtyfold increase in blood flow to an exercising muscle.

The elasticity and contractility of the circulatory or cardiovascular system, especially the larger arteries, is related both to functional effectiveness and degeneration. Elastic arteries, such as the aorta, stretch with the surge of blood during the cardiac systole and recoil during the diastole, which helps propel the blood. Other arteries contain more muscle fibers, and although they facilitate and regulate blood flow, they are also a major source of resistance to blood flow. The arteries are on the high-pressure side of the cardiovascular subsystem, and the life cycle thickening and loss of resiliency of the arterial wall is called arteriosclerosis. The major form is atherosclerosis, which includes the accumulation of plaques consisting of fatty accumulations and an increase in connective tissue. This process begins in early childhood and progressively interferes with the arteries' elasticity as well as their ability to exchange nutrients and gases necessary for the cells to function. Cholesterol accumulation increases throughout adulthood. Fatty streaks appear during the first decade, fibrous plaques appear from the second decade onward, and by the forties there is sufficient thickening and blocking of arteries so that clinical problems increasingly occur, such as bulges in artery walls (aneurysms), death of some heart tissue caused by insufficient blood supply (infarcts), moving blood clots (thromboses), death of peripheral tissues (gangrene), and hemorrhages of cerebral arteries (strokes). Atherosclerosis is the largest single contributor to death in the United States. Coronary heart disease is especially associated with hypertension, cigarette smoking, and high levels of cholesterol intake (Timiras, 1972; Smith and Bierman, 1973). Between young adulthood and middle age there is more than a one-quarter reduction in the cross section of the coronary artery that is open to blood flow in a normal heart. With increasing advanced age, chronic brain syndromes or cerebral arteriosclerosis restrict cerebral blood flow, which is associated with reduced oxygen concentration and cognitive impairment. This condition is increasingly widespread with age but is not an inevitable consequence of chronological age (Wang, 1969; Granick and Patterson, 1971).

The lungs effect the exchange of gases that is necessary for cellular functioning. As the blood flows through the small capillaries at the ends of the arterial tree, oxygen is transferred to the cells, and carbon dioxide is picked up and returned to the heart in the veins. In the circulation process, the blood passes by the thin membranes along the small air sacs in the lungs. When the person exhales, carbon dioxide is transferred from the blood to the lungs and is expelled. Inhaling adds fresh oxygen to the bloodstream. With increasing age there is an increase in unused air space in the lungs along with reduced elasticity. The amount of air that can be forcibly expelled from the lungs (vital capacity) thus declines with age. The amount of air an adult can move through the lungs in fifteen seconds (maximum breathing capacity) declines about 40 percent between age twenty and eighty. Restrictions on the maximum rate of breathing older adults can sustain limits the amount of oxygen supplied to the tissue cells. The ceiling of oxygen supply on muscle activity can be extended during extreme exercise. The muscles produce lactic acid and incur an oxygen debt. This mechanism improves until the thirties and then declines. When holding constant the amount of blood flow through the vessels of the lungs, the adult at eighty obtains about one third as much oxygen in the red blood cells as the adult at twenty. For comparable exercise, the older adult must breathe three times as hard. When combined with the greater restrictions on blood flow due to impairments of the circulatory system, such as atherosclerosis, the inadequate levels of oxygen supply result in tissue damage, which is especially serious in the brain.

Regular physical activity can help sustain physical performance for most older adults. For example, oxygen uptake is the highest the individual can attain during physical work, and it limits physical effort. The peak occurs in the early twenties, and the maximum oxygen uptake for the typical sixty-five-year-old man is about 70 percent of that for a twenty-five-year-old man. It tends to decline with inactivity; physically active men declined only 10 percent in oxygen uptake between their mid-forties and late fifties compared with more than 31 percent for similar men who were sedentary. Practitioners can help adults of all ages recognize the beneficial effects of regular and moderate exercise (Astrand, 1956, 1968; deVries, 1974).

The kidneys help remove soluble wastes and water from the blood, a function similar to the removal of gaseous wastes from the blood by the lungs. Before young adulthood about one quarter of the blood that leaves the heart goes directly to the kidneys to be filtered, compared with one eighth during old age, which extends by six times the number of hours required to clear the blood of wastes. After the thirties the number of functioning filtering units and the total weight of each kidney begin to decrease. However, because of the excess capacity of the kidneys, although the filtering process takes longer, the decline in capacity does not affect functioning. Degeneration of kidney arteries tends to increase blood pressure, which further restricts kidney blood flow and reduces kidney action, a cycle that results in progressive deterioration. Such degenerative difficulties are sufficiently rare so that kidney disease accounts for only 1 out of every 150 deaths in America and is the fifteenth ranking cause of death (Milne and Milne, 1968). However, kidney disease affects other functions that may result in death.

The human body develops immunities to many kinds of bacteria, viruses, and other parasites. Antibodies are formed in response to specific antigens. Immunities are maintained as a result of repeated exposures to the same infections. The susceptibility to infectious diseases is greater in childhood and in old age than in young adulthood and middle age. As children receive inoculations and are exposed naturally to infectious disease, immunologic competence develops as a defense mechanism against future exposure to such diseases. During preadulthood, the formation of antibodies and the resulting resistance to infection is part of the growth process. During much of adulthood, these cellular mechanisms typically provide protection against invasion by foreign substances. However, immunologic reactions are sometimes harmful to the immunized individual, as in the cases of hypersensitivity and allergy. Furthermore, immune mechanisms appear to deteriorate with age. A likely example of decline in immune mechanisms in late middle life is the reduced resistance to tubercular infection. It is not clear, however, whether an increase in immune deficiency in older adults is a cause or a consequence of aging (Timiras, 1972).

Nutrition. During the adult life cycle, some of the main changes that occur in weight and appearance result from nutritional practices and digestive functions. These changes also affect health, vitality, and self-concept. During adulthood the changes that typically occur in the digestive system tend to have little impact on performance. The major exceptions are cancers and stomach ulcers. Peptic ulcer, which is more common in men than in women, occurs in all ages, but symptoms typically develop between twenty and forty and reach a peak around age fifty. Peptic ulcer is associated with tension. There are some minor changes in the alimentary canal that typically occur during adulthood. The loss of teeth can affect chewing, which places greater demand on digestive juices for breaking down food. However, between the twenties and the sixties there is a reduction in the flow of digestive juices, which can contribute to digestive upset and weight gain. Thus, to maintain a satisfactory level of digestion, older adults can compensate for these changes by more attention to chewing food, careful selection of diet, and increased consumption of fluids. Many adults develop a condition in which pockets form in the walls of the intestines, and these pockets fill with food and other decaying materials (diverticulitis). This causes discomfort and the continuing feeling that a bowel movement is needed. This condition affects about 20 percent of forty-year-olds compared with 80 percent of eighty-year-olds (Timiras, 1972).

Throughout adulthood, a diet that is balanced in types of nutrients and moderate in caloric intake can contribute much to condition, health, and vitality. In general, a satisfactory diet applies to adults of all ages unless specific health conditions warrant restrictions. However, as adults grow older there are some shifts in typical nutritional patterns.

Nutritional adequacy depends on dietary intake, state of health, and activity level and differs somewhat with age for men and women. For example, the standard for iron and calcium intake for women between the ages of eighteen and forty-four is higher than for men because of menstruation and lactation. Regarding caloric intake, the percentage of people who are below the standard is much higher for women (17 percent) than for men (3 percent), somewhat higher for blacks than for whites, and somewhat higher for older adults than younger adults. For indices of malnutrition such as vitamins A and C, calcium, and serum protein and albumin, there is little change during adulthood. In fact, there is a trend toward improvement with age for vitamins A and C. There is little trend with age for iron intake or hemoglobin (related to anemia). For hemoglobin, there is little change between ages eighteen and sixty, but a somewhat higher proportion of older adults are below the standard. For iron intake, there are enormous differences between men and women. Between the ages of eighteen and forty-four all males are above the standard and all females are below their higher standard required to compensate for monthly menstruation. Otherwise, this index is little related to age but is somewhat worse for blacks and low income whites. For older adults, two thirds of those below the poverty threshold are below the standard compared with half of those with higher incomes. Obesity is slightly higher for women than for men but is little related to age (HRA, 1974; Howell and Loeb, 1969; Shanas, 1962).

Aside from desirable nutritional patterns at various stages of the adult life cycle, there are some trends in actual eating habits during adulthood. These trends partly reflect increasing incidence of health problems that affect diet, such as diabetes, stomach ulcers, or removal of the gall bladder. However, the trends mostly reflect shifts in personal outlook and the societal context. For example, some forms of malnutrition increase during old age. Some of the main contributing factors are: (1) low average income level so that many older adults cannot afford an adequate diet (can also restrict mobility needed to maintain a balanced food supply); (2) low familiarity with requirements for an adequate diet, especially in later life; (3) depression and lack of appetite; (4) loss of family or close friends to eat with, which removes some of the encouragement to eat regular meals at standard times. As a result, some older adults eat too little, eat irregularly, and eat an unbalanced diet. Some overeat, especially high-calorie foods, partly as a compensation for dissatisfaction in other domains. These forms of malnutrition are especially widespread for blue collar adults. A higher proportion of white collar older adults have a balanced diet and enjoy the benefits of adequate nutrition.

Practitioners can help adults of all ages understand the relation between nutrition and health. Some nutritional practices, such as excessive caloric intake or inadequate iron intake for young women, are preventive. Other practices, such as modification of diet for adults in their fifties who develop diabetes, are remedial.

A practice partly related to nutrition is alcohol consumption. In addition to the resulting damage to stomach, liver, pancreas, and nerve cells, high levels of alcohol consumption are often associated with the psychological and physiological dependency called alcoholism. The incidence of alcoholism is higher for men than for women, occurs in both white and blue collar families, and declines with age during adulthood. However, degenerative effects are cumulative, and mortality from alcoholic cirrhosis reaches a peak around age fifty and is higher for nonwhites below age forty-five.

During the past decade there has been a gradual increase in the proportion of adults who ever drink alcoholic beverages, from 53 to 57 percent. When combined with the temperance and prohibition eras during which today's elderly adults grew up, this historical trend toward more widespread use of alcohol accounts for a small portion of the decline in alcohol use with age. See Figure 13. At all ages, more men drink than women. The proportion of drinkers compared to nondrinkers increases sharply from adolescence to a peak in the early twenties. Although some drinking of alcoholic beverages by adolescents occurs in the homes of their parents, most of it occurs where no adults are present, mainly reflecting laws on minimum age for legal drinking. A year after leaving high school, about two thirds of all adolescents have a drink at least once a month. The conversion to drinking is higher for those who enter the mili-

Figure 13. Drinkers and Heavier Drinkers: Age Trends in Percent of Men and Women

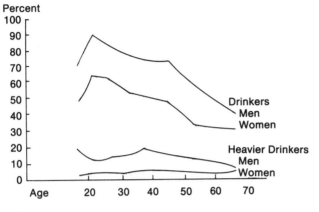

Source: NIAAA (1975).

tary service than for those who enter civilian employment and lower for those who enter college. This partly reflects social class differences.

The age trend for heavier drinkers and problem drinkers is different from the trend for the proportion of those who drink at all. For men, the proportion that consumes five or six drinks at an occasion is higher for those age eighteen through twenty than for those age twenty-one through twenty-four. There is a drop in the proportion of adults who are problem drinkers between twenty and thirty-five, followed by a rise around age forty and then a decline into old age. This temporary rise may partly reflect mid-life stress. For younger problem drinkers or alcoholics, a higher proportion are associated with mental health problems than is the case for older alcoholics. The incidence of problem drinkers is higher for men, blue collar, persons under age twenty-five, city dwellers, those who move from rural to urban areas, those from broken homes or other childhood disruptions, and single and divorced men. In recent years the proportion of problem drinkers for those who are separated has become larger than for those who are single or divorced. Especially for young adults, heavy drinkers have much higher mortality rates than those who do not drink heavily. Alcohol is associated with suicide and with motor vehicle deaths for both drivers and pedestrians. In addition to the evident problems associated with alcoholism, there may be an increase in caloric intake that increases weight and often a disruption of diet which contributes to malnutrition. Sometimes severe alcoholism is associated with weight loss because so little food is eaten.

For older adults, the incidence of problem drinkers is relatively low. Most of the older alcoholics were problem drinkers one to three decades earlier. More than half the older men drank when they were younger, and about half the former drinkers stopped drinking after their mid-forties. Most of them did so because drinking made them sick, or they felt that it was bad for their health. For those older adults who continue to drink, there is a gradual reduction in the quantity consumed on each occasion but little change in the frequency of occasions. For adults older than age sixty-five, the reduction that typically occurs is a decrease from a level of alcohol consumption which was fairly constant for about fifteen years. For blue collar adults, the proportions of heavy drinkers and of those who abstain are both higher than for white collar adults (NIAAA, 1975).

Practitioners can assist adults with alcohol problems by encouraging them to talk with others who are successfully controlling their alcoholism. The developmental process of recognizing the problem and accomplishing the mental, social, and physical adjustments is complex and typically requires much relearning and social support.

The typical weight peak occurs in the fifties. Most of the fluctuation in body weight during adulthood reflects increases and decreases in fat. During late adolescence about 10 percent of body weight is typically fat, compared with at least 20 percent in middle age. In the latter part of adulthood, there is a decrease in the weight of skeletal muscles, liver, kidneys, and adrenals, and an increase in the weight of the heart. The general result between twenty and sixty years of age is a decrease in muscle mass and an increase in fat tissue. There is also a shift of the fat from the surface of the body, where it helps give a rounded character to form and feature, to deeper parts of the body (Timiras, 1972). Of particular interest in relation to appearance is the adipose layer of subcutaneous fat between the muscles and the skin. In general, women carry proportionately more fat than men, and more of it is subcutaneous, between 40 and 90 percent more as measured by skin folds. However, the increase in relative skin fold thickness during much of adulthood is greater for men than for women. Most striking is the shift in the proportion of body fat from the arms and legs to the torso. There is also some shift with age from the upper trunk to the lower trunk. The result is the well-known "middle age spread" (Skerlj, 1954; Milne and Milne, 1968).

About middle age, most adults become more concerned about their physical appearance. In a society in which youth and youthful appearance has been highly valued, the onset of physical signs of aging tends to be viewed as evidence not of the approach of a venerable and revered stage of life characterized by wisdom and respect but of deterioration. "Crow's feet" wrinkles at the corners of the eyes and greying hair are typically unwelcome harbingers of widespread changes in appearance in old age (Plutchik, Weiner, and Conte, 1971). For example, with the wearing down and loss of teeth in old age, there is a shortening of the lower part of the face during a period when the length of the nose is increasing. Fingernails and toenails become thicker and somewhat more brittle. For elderly adults whose loss of suppleness prevents them from reaching their toes, this compounds their problems of personal care. By age forty, hair begins to thin and grey, and many men develop a bald spot or a receding forehead. The skin thins and becomes less elastic, with the result that it sags and wrinkles. In old age, the skin may remain flabby following a period of rapid weight loss. Women's skin is thinner than men's and thus reveals more of the bone and muscle structure beneath the surface unless it is cushioned by the adipose layer of fat. Whether these changes are viewed as signs of character and individuality or as signs of fading youth depends mainly on the values of the viewer.

Muscles. Skeletal muscles contract and relax to produce movement. For example, to open the hand, muscles along the back of the arm contract and pull the tendons connected with the tops of the fingers, while the sets of muscles along the underside of the arm relax. To close the hand, sets of muscles along the underside of the arm are activated to contract, and those along the back of the arm relax. A complex movement, such as a golf swing, reflects endurance, strength, timing, and coordination of many sets of muscles to produce a long, well-placed drive or to sink a long putt.

Especially after middle age, the loss of muscle cells has an impact on both strength and appearance. The development of sets of muscles through exercise has typically occurred by young adulthood. During adulthood, the level of endurance, strength, and coordination depends mainly on condition maintained by regular physical activity in work or recreation. After middle age, declines in circulation and respiration typically begin to restrict the level of activity that people had been able to sustain in young adulthood. In addition, cross-linking and the continuing loss of muscle cells produce a loss of contractibility. Those muscle cells that do remain are about as old as the individual and tend to become less effective. With age, contractile muscle fibers are gradually replaced by fibrous connective tissue that reduces suppleness. The age at which declines in muscle condition begin to restrict physical performance depends greatly on the types of physical activities that are desired and attempted. In old age especially the loss of muscle cells is reflected in the shape of the body. For example, for many old men, trousers hang straighter in the rear than they did in their youth.

During adolescence muscular development and strength is greater for boys than for girls. This partly reflects the boys' production of testosterone, which is a growth hormone as well as the male sex hormone. With comparable exercise, however, physical coordination develops similarly for boys and girls. Traditionally, sex-role stereotypes have encouraged boys to engage in activities that emphasize strength and endurance, such as football and track, and have encouraged girls to engage in activities that emphasize coordination, such as diving and dancing. Excellence of performance influences both popularity and self-concept (Coleman, 1961). During the late 1960s and early 1970s some of these stereotypes have been questioned. High school boys have enrolled in cooking classes in the home economics department, and high school girls have competed in formerly all-male athletic teams, such as track. It seems likely that shifting expectations and activities for young men and women during late adolescence and young adulthood will be reflected in future physical activity patterns of men and women during adulthood.

Physical strength reaches its peak during the twenties and then gradually declines (Espenschade and Meleney, 1961; Timiras, 1972). This is reflected in the ages of those who break records in athletic events that call for great strength and short bursts of energy. For many muscle groups, maximum strength in the sixties is about 80 percent of what it was in the twenties (D. Speakman, 1956; deVries, 1974).

Physical endurance to engage in extended work or exercise also declines with age, but the plateau extends further into middle age than for physical performance for short periods. This contrast is illustrated by the ages of outstanding performers in sprints compared with distance events in athletics. However, between thirty-five and eighty years of age there is about 60 percent decrease in maximum work rate without developing fatigue. By contrast there is only a small decline in the ability to perform moderate work. Many older adults are able to pace themselves in work and recreation so that they are able to maintain a consistent and high level of performance within the maximum level of capacity. The decline for physically active adults is substantially less than for sedentary adults (Milne and Milne, 1968; Astrand, 1968; Timiras, 1972; deVries, 1974). Practitioners can help adults gradually modify their physical activity to enhance their condition and vitality.

A process closely associated with muscle tissue is the repair of an injury, such as the healing of a wound. The healing process requires the disintegration of cells killed by the wound and the production of new living cells to match the old ones. When the skin is cut, substances from broken cells spread through live ones to stimulate nearby blood vessels to become engorged and to accelerate repair. White blood cells devour dead cells and invading bacteria. A scab of fibrin helps cover, protect, and close the wound, and then collagen fibers, capillaries, and newly divided skin cells complete the repair process. With advancing age, this repair process progresses more slowly, it is achieved less completely, and the scar is likely to be more evident (Milne and Milne, 1968).

Endocrine. Various glands in the body secrete hormones into the blood stream, many of which help regulate the body. Because they influence each other, it is helpful to view the endocrine system as an integral functional unit, even though each gland has a unique function. Often a malfunction by one gland is compensated for by other glands. Together they influence the general adaptation response of the individual. With increasing old age, there is a reduced output of anterior pituitary, adrenal cortical, and thyroid glands. Similarly, the incidence of diabetes doubles between the ages of fifty and seventy, and it is increasing in the general population of this country (Timiras, 1972; Smith and Bierman, 1973).

A typical function of the endocrine system is to help the body deal with stress situations. A familiar example is the flow of adrenalin that is activated by a frightening experience and produces a temporary increase in the energy and tension level of the body. However, extended anxiety states can bring about a chronic flow of adrenalin that maintains an undesirably high level of tension.

A different type of regulation is provided by the sex hormones as they influence the reproductive system. Both estrogen and testosterone are present in both sexes but differ in relative concentration. Estrogen levels for women are typically constant between twenty and forty years of age, followed by a decline and then stabilization at a lower level. The production of estrogen influences the functioning of the uterus, which reaches its growth peak at about age thirty and then experiences about a 50 percent weight loss by age fifty. During those twenty years collagen declines about 60 percent and elastin more than 40 percent. The weight of the ovaries decreases during the thirties. Men typically experience a gradual decline beyond the twenties in androgens. After age thirty there is a gradual decline in testosterone and cortisol. Each sex continually produces some of the opposite sex hormone. For example, males produce some estrogen, but the liver rids the body of excess. In later years, as the liver becomes less efficient, the balance of estrogen rises as the production of testosterone declines, which has a feminizing effect. The involution of the prostate begins in middle age. By the early forties, there is usually some irregularity in the thickness of the lining (epithelium). By the late forties some tubular atrophy has typically occurred. During the fifties there is usually some atrophy of muscles and fibrosis (Timiras, 1972).

A similar instance of body regulation is provided by temperature control. There are several related regulatory mechanisms that help maintain a balance between heat production and heat loss. Although there is a slight drop in skin temperature with age, under favorable conditions adults are able to maintain a satisfactory temperature control balance into old age. However, old people are less able to respond effectively to extremely high or low environmental temperatures. A major reason that older adults experience difficulty with high temperatures is their reduced rate of water loss from the skin through evaporation. Their increased difficulty with cold temperatures reflects reduced metabolic rate, decreased subcutaneous fat for insulation, and decreased thyroid reactivity to cold stress (Timiras, 1972).

In old age, therefore, the degeneration of the endocrine system reduces adaptability. Practitioners can help older adults recognize and compensate for this reduced ability to adapt to changes in physical conditions.

Senses

As the adult performs, interacts with others, and relates to the environment, functional effectiveness is affected by the ability to receive and transmit information. This especially includes vision and hearing, along with taste, smell, touch, and the related ability of speech. In general, there is reduced sensory input with age. This mainly results from lowered thresholds of excitation that make it increasingly difficult for progressively older adults to discriminate at lower levels of intensity. This means a loss of the softest sounds, the dimmest lights, and the faintest smells. The senses, such as vision and hearing, are neural structures and depend on the base functioning of the CNS. Sensory impairment further reduces the information-processing potential established by the CNS base. A way of compensating for impairment of one sense, such as hearing, is by greater reliance on other sensory input, perhaps in this case by lip reading (Corso, 1971). Both seeing and hearing new information may also help older adults remember the information better.

Vision. Sight is important for many activities. During adulthood, the aging eye and the related nervous system gradually reduce the quantity and quality of visual information that is received. However, with corrective lenses and satisfactory illumination, most adults can engage in almost any activity they want to throughout life without major restrictions caused by visual impairment. There are many age-related changes in the eye during adulthood that account for the subtle shifts in vision that typically occur. Most of the changes relate to the major structural characteristics of the eye.

An object to be seen can be characterized by size and contrast with surroundings. Perceived size is a function of both absolute size and distance from the viewer. Contrast includes both the comparison between the darkness of print and the lightness of paper and the effects of glare, which can greatly reduce the seeming contrast on shiny paper. In the assessment of the visual threshold, measurements indicate the smallest amount of light that can be seen in a darkened room or the smallest line of print that can be read on a reading chart.

The image of the object that is seen falls on the retina, which lines the back of the inside of the eyeball. This is similar to the recording of a scene on the film in a camera when the shutter is snapped. The retina includes both cone cells, which are concentrated in the center of the retina and function in bright light but in moderate light are more sensitive to long spectral light waves (yellowish-green), and rod cells, which are concentrated around the edges (periphery) of the retina and function in dim light such as moonlight but in moderate light are more sensitive to short spectral light waves (bluish green). The retina is connected with the optic nerve. The optic nerve relays the image from the retina to the brain.

The eyeball is filled with a fluid through which the light passes. The pupil is the small dark opening in the middle of the eye that dilates in the dark to admit more light and contracts in bright light. The blue or brown iris assists with the dilation and contraction of the pupil size. A lens (cornea) covers the pupil and front of the eyeball. As with the lens of a camera, the lens bends (refracts) the light rays from the object seen and focuses the image on the retina. The lens can become rounder or flatter in an effort to focus the image right on the retina instead of in front of or behind the retina. If an object is held too close to the eye, the lens is unable to accommodate sufficiently, and the image on the retina is blurred.

Vision and visual adaptation at age twenty partly reflects the condition of the eyes, including accumulated damage due to illness or damage and hereditary conditions, such as nearsightedness (myopia), farsightedness (hyperopia), and irregularity of the lens that typically blurs the image along an axis (astigmatism). In addition, there are typical life cycle trends in various aspects of the functioning of the eye. See Figure 14. Together they account for the extent and types of visual impairment at various stages of adulthood and indicate the types of compensations, such as corrective lenses, illumination level, or timing, that are likely to contribute most to optimum vision. To facilitate comparisons, each curve in Figure 14 is presented as a percentage of the maximum visual ability for each aspect. The base of the figure is divided to assist with comparisons at ages twenty, forty, sixty, and eighty. Listed are the main generalizations and explanatory notes on age trends for each of the selected aspects:

1. *Central Nervous System.* By late adolescence the CNS reaches a plateau in the speed and accuracy with which information is transmitted along the optic nerve and within the brain. There is a gradual decline

Figure 14. Vision and Age for Eight Indices of Visual Ability

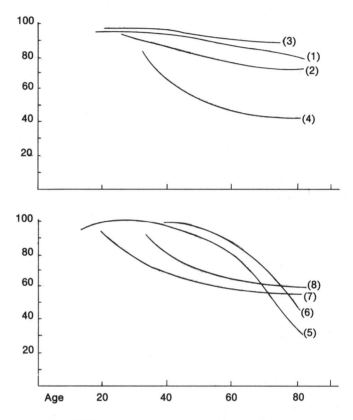

Source: Birren (1959).

in CNS capacity during adulthood. However, because CNS capacity so far exceeds the information load entailed in daily functioning, restrictions due to declines in CNS capacity are seldom apparent until old age.

2. *Pupil Size.* The average diameter of the pupil gradually declines with age during adulthood, under both light and dark conditions. As a result, less light enters the eye under comparable illumination for older adults, which is especially a problem under dark conditions (Birren, Casperson, and others, 1950).

3. *Pupil Change.* There is a ratio between pupil size in the dark and the difference between pupil size in the

dark and the smaller pupil size when exposed to the light. This ratio changes very little during adulthood, which indicates that when pupil size is held constant, the range within which the iris can dilate and contract the pupil changes little during adulthood.

4. *Adaptation Rate.* As the eye becomes accustomed to low levels of illumination, or "dark adapted," individuals are able to make out details in the darkened surroundings that they were not sensitive to before adaptation. The amount of time required for the eye to become fully dark adapted increases with age. The slower rate of visual adaptation for the older adult is apparent in such circumstances as going into a darkened theater and trying to find a seat or trying to see the road while driving at night after the brightness of oncoming headlights passes. Under these circumstances it takes substantially longer for the older adult to become dark adapted than it did during young adulthood.

5. *Light Threshold.* Once the eye becomes totally dark adapted, which takes longer for the older adult, there is a decline with age in the minimum intensity of light that can be seen. With age the cornea and the vitreous humor inside the eye become less transparent. The reduction in elasticity and transparency occurs because the lens continues to grow without shedding older cells. As the lens increases in weight and becomes yellowish, there is a decrease in the amount of light, especially violet light, that permeates the lens and reaches the retina. The minimum light threshold is relatively stable during young adulthood. However, after the fifties, there is a rapid acceleration in the intensity of the illumination required to be seen. It is estimated that the threshold intensity of illumination must be doubled every thirteen years beyond age twenty to be seen by the fully dark-adapted eye (McFarland and Fisher, 1955; Birren, Bick, and Fox, 1948). This can usually be compensated for by an increase in illumination (Guth and others, 1956). For

example, a 50 percent increase in illumination at age
fifty would match the minimum level of illumination
needed to achieve the threshold at age twenty.
6. *Visual Acuity.* Acuity is usually measured by using
an eye chart with lines of print that decrease in size.
The smallness of detail that can be discriminated is
expressed as a ratio between the distance between the
adult and the chart, over the distance at which the
presumably typical eye can discriminate the same detail. Thus, if an adult discriminated at twenty feet
the degree of detail discriminated by the typical eye
at thirty feet, the adult is said to have 20/30 vision.
Acuity increases during childhood and early adolescence and then remains quite stable between twenty
and forty years of age, and by about age fifty there is
typically a slow but accelerated decline (Slataper,
1950).
7. *Lens Accommodation.* The muscle action and elasticity of the lens enables it to alter its curvature or
flatness. This refractive power of the lens allows it to
make some accommodation, especially for close work,
so that the image falls distinctly on the retina. During
adolescence there is little change in lens accommodation. However, between twenty and fifty years of age
there is typically an appreciable loss of accommodation
power and elasticity of the lens, after which the decline is more gradual. A related trend, though not
included in the foregoing figure, is the relationship
between age and nearsightedness (myopia) and farsightedness (hyperopia). Between adolescence and the
start of middle age, myopes tend to become more my-
opic and hyperopes tend to become more hyperopic
(Morgan, 1958). In old age there is a trend toward
flattening of the lens, so that more adults become
farsighted and have difficulty accommodating for near
vision. For those who had been nearsighted, a reversal
of trend may occur. Likewise, swelling and sclerosis
of the lens increase myopia, which for farsighted
adults may also reduce hyperopia. In such cases, older

adults may find that their vision is improving and they can read without their glasses.

8. *Contrast.* The Weber Ratio is used to indicate the minimum visual contrast that can be discriminated when the illumination level of a spot and of the surrounding background are varied independently. With increasing age adults require more contrast.

In addition to the age trends for selected aspects of vision presented in Figure 14, there are some other generalizations about vision and age.

1. *Glare.* Because older adults are less able to see subtle visual contrasts, glare is an increasing problem in such activities as reading or driving. Too much illumination may reduce light threshold problems but increase glare problems. Tinted windshields may reduce glare problems in bright sunlight but may increase problems related to night vision.

2. *Peripheral Vision.* The progressive reduction with age in the number of rod cells in the retina tends to restrict peripheral vision. As a result, older adults are less likely to notice movement "out of the corner of their eyes."

3. *Color Vision.* There is little change during young adulthood and middle age in color vision. However, with the yellowing of the lens toward old age, less violet light is transmitted, and the older adult is progressively less able to match blues and greens (Gilbert, 1957).

4. *Disease.* With age there is a rising incidence of diseases that affect vision. Rates of blindness increase after age forty-five and sharply after age sixty-five. With advancing age during adulthood there is an increasing tendency for arteriosclerosis, glaucoma, cataracts, and tumors that affect vision.

5. *Depth Perception.* There is some decline in visual perceptual ability for older adults (Davies, 1965; Schwartz and Karp, 1967; Szafran and Birren, 1969; Bell, Wolf, and Bernholz, 1972).

The cumulative effect of these age-related changes in vision is that during young adulthood most adults notice few changes at all. About age forty many adults become aware of changes in vision, some of which occur somewhat abruptly in middle age. However, before age sixty-five less than half the adults in the United States wear corrective lenses. Beyond age sixty-five more than nine out of ten do so. Some of the ways in which adults of any age with visual impairment other than blindness can compensate for it so as to minimize restrictions on desired performance are (1) obtain and use corrective lenses if they are needed; (2) increase contrast by increasing illumination, reducing glare, sitting close, or using type that is larger and has greater contrast with the background; (3) allow longer time for exposure; (4) provide information in combined audio and visual form; (5) simplify sequences of information or exposure; (6) allow more time for adaptation between lighted and darkened surroundings and for recovery from stress.

Hearing. The ability to hear very soft sounds and very high frequency sounds starts to decline by adolescence, and the rate of hearing impairments increases gradually until the fifties when the rate increases abruptly and then climbs even more sharply beginning around age seventy. Progressive hearing loss (presbycusis) reflects many changes in the sensory, mechanical, and neural processes by which sound vibrations through the air are translated into information that is processed and stored in the brain.

Human speech, musical instruments, and rattling trash cans create vibrations that produce sound waves. Low, rumbly sound waves have a slow frequency, and high-pitched sound waves have a rapid or high frequency. The loudness of sound is measured in decibels. Some sound waves enter the ear and are transmitted through the auditory function to the brain. The likelihood that a sound will be heard is related to its loudness in decibels and, to some extent, its frequency in pitch.

The collection of sound waves by the outer ear and ear canal on their way to the eardrum is affected by the pliability of the epithelial lining of the canal and by any obstructions of the canal, such as accumulation of ear wax. As sound waves strike the eardrum (tympanic membrane), it vibrates and activates three small bones in the middle ear. Vibrations can also be transmitted to the eardrum and three small bones of the middle ear along the mastoid bone behind the ear. Hair cells along the shell-like inner ear translate vibrations into nerve messages that are transmitted to the brain (Milne and Milne, 1968).

Socially impaired hearing occurs when the hearing loss constitutes a reduction of about thirty decibels and other people become aware of the deficiency. The incidence of hearing loss of any kind and amount is less than 1 percent for persons under age twenty-five. Around age forty-five the rate begins to increase. For adults between sixty-five and seventy-four, the rate is more than 10 percent, and more than one out of four of those over seventy-five have a hearing loss. Most of the loss is at the high frequencies. For frequencies below high C, most older adults hear as well as they did when they were young adults. Men typically hear better than women at the lower frequencies, and women hear better at the higher frequencies. Some hearing loss at the high frequencies has occurred by adolescence and continues throughout life. Men experience greater hearing loss than women beyond their fifties, largely as a result of occupational exposure to noise. In addition, pitch discrimination gradually declines between the twenties and the fifties and then drops more abruptly. Furthermore, older adults experience greater difficulty with screening out interfering noises (Olsen, 1965; Corso, 1958; Lederer, 1961).

Progressive hearing loss (presbycusis) is caused by degeneration both of the conduction process and of the portions of the sense organ that are part of the nervous system. Conductive hearing loss has two causes: (1) atrophy or congestion of the exterior auditory canal, which reduces the size of the oriface, and (2) thickening of the eardrum and restrictions on the movement of the three small bones that transmit vibrations to the inner ear. The greater portion of presbycusis appears to be conductive, and much of it may be reversible. One form of neural presbycusis is the destruction of high pitch hair cells nearest the three small bones. As these cells die they reduce the ability to transmit high frequency sounds. This form of hearing loss especially reflects the impact of a lifetime of exposure to environmental noises (Timiras, 1972; Milne and Milne, 1968; Gloreig and Davis, 1961; Bergman, 1971).

As an adult of any age begins to experience socially impaired hearing, some adjustment is required. Listed are some of the main ways in which practitioners can help an adult with presbycusis compensate for the hearing loss:

1. Recognize that hearing loss is often accompanied by an increase in bewilderment and insecurity because of the loss of background sound and growing sense of deadness of the environment. Understanding and support are especially important during this transition period (Ramsdell, 1965).
2. Provide sound amplification at the source if feasible, such as an effective public address system for groups.
3. Encourage the use of a hearing aid if one seems needed. Fewer than 1 out of 200 persons under age sixty-five use a hearing aid, compared with more than 1 out of 20 over sixty-five.
4. Recognize that increased volume will help only for conduction deafness, and shouting will not help in cases of neural deafness.
5. Increase the signal-to-noise ratio by satisfactory acoustics and reduced background noise.
6. Enable the person to use facial and lip cues. This is easier in conversation and small groups than in large group settings.
7. Enunciate clearly, with special attention to difficulties related to consonants, mumbling, and dropping the voice at the end of a phrase.

Other Senses. There are also gradual changes in the other senses during adulthood. Most of the changes in taste sensitivity occur after age fifty. The taste buds atrophy first inside the cheeks, then on the tip of the tongue, then progressively toward the back of the tongue. The sweetness threshold in old age is about three times as great as that for a young adult. Sensitivity to smell begins to decline appreciably after age forty. Sixty-year-olds are able to detect and correctly identify faint odors less than half as well as twenty-year-olds. These changes in taste and smell can affect the interest of elderly adults in food. Tobacco smokers are much less able to detect odors than nonsmokers. The sense of touch increases until about age forty-five and then becomes less acute, and sensitivity to pain declines. The pain threshold increases somewhat at age forty-five and even more so after sixty (Woodruff, Friedman, and others, 1972). The sense of balance is at its best during the forties (Timiras, 1972).

The sound of one's voice provides a sense of individuality and a means of communication with others. There are some progressive changes in speech sound production during adulthood. Satisfactory speech sound production depends on breath support, vocal cord performance, and articulators, such as lips and tongue in the oral cavity. Especially in old age there are typically changes in these prerequisites of voice production. Reductions in strength and posture can restrict the amount and control of exhaled air, which reduces vocal intensity and duration. Atrophy of the larynx can reduce muscular elasticity, which changes vocal range and tone quality. Loss of teeth, atrophy of nasal tissues, and sluggishness of the tongue can produce nasal, breathy, or slurred speech (Timiras, 1972).

The frequency level of pitch declines during adolescence for boys and continues to drop slightly until middle age when pitch begins to rise gradually into old age (Mysak and Hanley, 1958; Mysak, 1959). By contrast, pitch changes little for women between middle age and old age (McGlone and Hollien, 1963). From middle age onward the rate of speech slows.

Movement

The general slowing of behavior from young adulthood to old age is widely recognized. Reaction time—the time lag between when the person sees, hears, or feels a stimulus and when he or she begins to respond—decreases rapidly during childhood, the rate of improvement slows progressively during adolescence, a plateau occurs during young adulthood, and there is a gradual increase in reaction time during middle and old age. The peak reaction time is typically reached just before age twenty, and by age fifty average reaction time has returned to about the average level of age fifteen. See Figure 15.

Many types of performance entail both reaction time and movement time. The reaction time or premotor phase entails perception of the stimulus by the sense organ, transmission of information to the brain, and selection of a response. The movement or motor phase entails carrying out the response or action. During adulthood the slowing or increase in reaction time is greater than the increase in movement time. Furthermore, the rate of increase in reaction and movement time is related to task complexity. The speed and accuracy with which adults perform simple tasks that entail both reaction and movement time changes very gradually with increasing age. However, especially for reaction time there is a more rapid increase with age in the time it takes to perform more complex tasks that entail a coordinated series of actions. Visual reaction time is slightly slower than auditory reaction time. The same gradual slowing process occurs for men and for women. However, progressively during adulthood the range of individual differences increases, and older adults become more variable in speed of behavior than young adults. Although there is some decline in manual

Figure 15. Reaction Time and Age

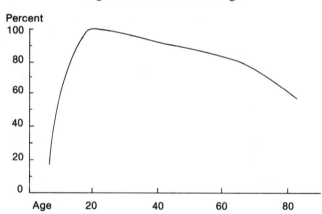

Source: Birren (1964a).

dexterity, after the thirties it is not reflected in occupational performance (Fozard, Nuttall, and others, 1972; Welford, 1959).

Some of the main influences on the progressive slowing of reaction and movement time during adulthood are: (1) reduced fidelity of CNS functioning resulting from loss of nerve cells, slowed peripheral nerve conduction, and changed synaptic conduction (Botwinick, 1965); (2) temporal disorganization resulting from a decline in the integrating function of the nervous system in combination with the endocrine system (Samis, 1968); (3) general condition reflected in the finding that the reaction time of older adults is more similar to nonathletic young adults than to athletic young adults (Botwinick and Thompson, 1968); (4) decisional ambivalence in which the older adult compensates for actual or assumed loss of capacity by taking more time to decide on a response that will be accurate and safe; (5) task complexity in which memory deficit, interference, and inflexibility in adapting to changes make it more difficult for increasingly older adults to engage in a continuous coordinated series of reactions and movements.

There are several ways in which practitioners who work with older adults can help them compensate for slower behavior. Many older adults typically compensate for reduced speed by increased accuracy, care, and attentiveness. Some slowness also reflects apprehension about making errors. Another form of compensation is to avoid situations that entail time pressures and potential surprises. In addition, clearer instructions can help reduce age decrements, and reinforcement procedures can increase speed and accuracy (Baltes and Goulet, 1970).

Sleep

Throughout adulthood, the daily cycle includes periods of activity and periods of inactivity and sleep. From young adulthood to old age, sleep becomes shorter, lighter, and increasingly intermittent. However, there are great individual differences in sleep patterns for adults at any age. Some people sleep only a few hours a night; others sleep at least eight hours. Some people awake refreshed and alert; others agonize through the first hour of the day. Sleep provides multiple benefits including rest, relaxation, escape, forgetfulness, and dreaming. However, the precise functions of sleep are not completely understood.

Typical sleep patterns include four stages that have been identified on the electroencephalogram (EEG) that records brain waves. Stage one sleep is relatively light and is distinguished by the rapid eye movement (REM) that occurs, often accompanied by dreaming. The other three slow-wave stages (NREM) constitute degrees of depth and increasing high-voltage–low-wave EEG activity. Stage four sleep is the deepest and occurs mainly during the first few hours of sleep. Usually when a person falls asleep he or she moves down to stage four sleep, remains there for an hour or two, and then progresses up through stage three and two to stage one REM sleep, during which dreaming usually occurs. The cycle is repeated during the sleep period with less time between REM sleep stages and less time in stage three or four deep sleep.

During adolescence, the total amount of sleeping time declines from childhood patterns, and the proportion of REM to NREM sleeps becomes stable at about 25 percent. Between the twenties and the sixties, total sleep time and the proportion of REM sleep remain the same, but the proportion of stage four sleep decreases steadily so that by age fifty stage four sleep is about half the proportion at age twenty. As stage four sleep declines during middle and old age it is replaced by stage three and two sleep. During adulthood there is a steady increase in the number of arousals during the night (Timiras, 1972).

With advancing age adults take longer to fall asleep; sleep less during the night but nap some during the day; and, after the sixties, spend less time in REM sleep. After the thirties an increasing proportion of time in bed is spent awake (Feinberg, 1969; E. Kahn, 1970). Aged adults compensate by spending more time in bed. Whereas sleeplessness can also result from unusual surroundings or pain, insomnia usually entails either temporary or persistent emotional upset. There is evidence that some brain processes during sleep, such as dreaming during the REM stage, are important for adequate cognitive functioning.

In addition to sleep, hundreds of biological and psychological functions follow daily circadian rhythms. These functions include body temperature, cell division, and metabolic processes. Jet lag has helped dramatize the importance of circadian rhythms and the upset that can occur if they are ignored. Practitioners can help adults understand sleep patterns and other circadian rhythms.

Physical Health

Some aspects of physical health reflect the aging trends noted in the section on biological relationships for the various systems, such as circulatory or neurologic. However, especially during young adulthood, many instances of restricted activity, disability, or death are due to accidents or acute illnesses caused by infectious diseases. In addition, although physical health and mental health are often considered separately, they are interrelated. In general there is an adult life cycle shift from illness that is acute or functional in young adulthood to irreversible or degenerative illness which is chronic or organic through middle and old age (U.S. NCHS, 1963). See Figure 16.

Most United States adults of any age carry out their major activities without significant limitations from physical illness (Wilkie and Eisdorfer, 1973). Although the rates of restricted activity and bed disability days per year increase with advanc-

Figure 16. Acute and Chronic Health Conditions That Restrict Activity: General Age Trends

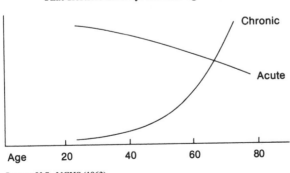

Source: U.S., NCHS (1963).

ing age, more than two thirds of older adults go about their daily activities without significant restrictions from physical illness. Bed disability occurs when an illness is sufficiently severe so that the patient is confined to bed. For adults over age sixty-five, 95 percent live in normal communities, and only 5 percent live in institutions. For those older adults outside institutions, only 5 percent are homebound due to disability, 6 percent require a mechanical aid or another person to get around, and 8 percent have some trouble getting around but do so without assistance. Thus, more than eight out of ten older adults in the community have no major limitations on their mobility.

Acute Conditions. Acute physical illnesses include infectious diseases (such as pneumonia and influenza), temporary digestive disorders, and accidents (such as lacerations, sprains, and fractures). In national health surveys, the impact of acute illnesses is reported as the number per one hundred persons per year for acute conditions, for restricted activity days, for bed disability days, and for conditions for persons currently employed. Especially for adults under age sixty, there is a slight decline with age in the number of acute conditions and a slight increase with age in the number of restricted activity days. For the number of bed disability days, there is an increase with age in some conditions, such as injuries and respiratory and digestive disorders, and a decrease with age in some conditions, such as allergic, infective, and parasitic diseases. For currently employed adults, there is a slight decline with age in the number of current acute conditions and accidents. For the total of acute conditions, there is a decline with age for various income groups, but the decline is greater for the higher income groups. Before age forty, adult deaths are caused mainly by infectious diseases and accidents. In young adulthood, more men than women die of accidents.

Chronic Conditions. Chronic physical illnesses include age-related conditions, such as arthritis, coronary heart disease, and arteriosclerosis. Orthopedic conditions are the only form of chronic illness with an appreciable incidence for young adults, but there are some incidents of digestive conditions.

Between age forty-five and sixty-four, the major chronic conditions include arthritis, rheumatism, and orthopedic and digestive conditions. For those sixty-five and older, the incidence of these chronic conditions increases, heart and circulatory conditions become a major health problem, and rates of hearing impairments increase. The incidence of dental and periodontal conditions rises steadily with age. Three quarters of adults over age forty-four have one or more chronic conditions. However, 14 percent of the noninstitutionalized adults over age sixty-four have no chronic conditions. As with acute illness, the incidence of chronic illness is consistently related to income level in that rates are lower for white collar than for blue collar adults. The three leading causes of death for adults are chronic conditions. Heart disease accounts for more than one out of three deaths, cancers for about one out of six, and strokes (or vascular lesions that affect the CNS) for more than one out of ten.

Relationships. The relation between three major causes of death throughout the life cycle is portrayed in Figure 17. The three major causes of death are accidents, cardiovascular diseases, and cancers. The accidents category includes all forms

Figure 17. Mortality Due to Neoplasms, Cardiovascular, Accidents, and Other Causes as a Percent of All Deaths at Each Age

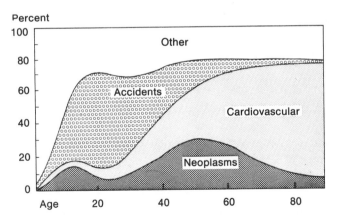

Source: Timiras (1972).

of accidental death of children and adults at home, work, and play and while traveling. Cardiovascular diseases include coronary heart attacks, strokes, and a variety of other conditions related to the circulatory system. The categories of cancers (neoplasms) include malignant tumors and other instances in which uncoordinated proliferations of new cells invade adjoining tissues. Within this broad category there are various forms of cancer that differ biologically, physically, and chemically. Cancer accounts for about one out of six deaths, second only to all forms of circulatory diseases for adults and to accidents for children. As indicated in Figure 17, during childhood and adolescence accidents constitute the main cause of deaths, especially for males. This continues to be the case into young adulthood, but during middle age cardiovascular diseases become the major cause for men as cancers do for women. In old age, cardiovascular diseases are the major cause of death. The peak for cancers occurs between forty and sixty years of age, during the forties for women and during the fifties for men. By contrast, cardiovascular diseases cause 50 percent of male deaths and 40 percent of female deaths. This is especially so for men in sedentary occupations. After eighty, however, cardiovascular diseases are responsible for more than 60 percent of mortality compared with less than 10 percent for cancers and less than 5 percent for accidents (Timiras, 1972).

The two major responses to illness are treatment and prevention. Medical and health treatment is unevenly distributed among United States adults. Some people are inordinately high consumers of health services, and some are hardly sick a day in their lives. Blue collar families obtain fewer medical and health services than white collar families for many reasons, including inability to pay, unawareness of their own health conditions, and lack of familiarity with health resources. Women avail themselves of health services more than men. The incidence of illnesses that require health services increases with age, and in general so does consumption of health services unless restricted by economic or other limitations. About one out of four older adults is hospitalized each year, compared with about one out of eight adults under sixty-five, and the older adults stay twice as long on the average. Older adults have half again as many physician visits but see a dentist less frequently than adults under sixty-five. For older adults, dental work usually relates to dentures.

Regarding prevention, the health, vitality, and longevity of most adults could be improved substantially through sound nutrition, exercise, and preventive health practices. However, most of the benefits of these practices would accrue during the current average life span; there would be no dramatic extension of the life span. For example, if all deaths from cardiovascular-renal diseases could be prevented, up to ten years might be added to the average life span, unless increased death rates for other diseases at higher age levels counteracted some of the increased longevity. Prevention of cancers might extend the average life span only two or three years, and prevention of fatal accidents only a year or two (Milne and Milne, 1968).

Stress. Systemic hypertension is a form of illness in which physical and emotional causes interact. The individual adapts to maintain a steady state (homeostasis) in response to external and internal challenges. Although these challenges may disturb well-being and endanger survival, the resulting stress can also test resiliency and strengthen adaptive capacity. Much depends on the way in which the individual deals with stress. The psychological mechanisms that are used can either reduce or increase the extent to which the physiological mechanisms increase hypertension. Adaptation to stress typically activates nervous, circulatory, and endocrine systems. As situational and physiological sources of stress make repeated demands on the general defense alarm system that prepares the individual for fight or flight, the continuous arousal can result in sustained hypertension (Henry and Cassel, 1969; Timiras, 1972). For example, the endocrine system can induce high blood levels of hormones (epinephrine, corticoids) that raise blood pressure. Dysfunction of the adrenal gland and the kidneys can combine as part of the aging process and lead to hypertension for older adults. Other factors that regulate blood pressure and can contribute to hypertension include cardiac output and arterial elasticity, blood volume and viscosity, and peripheral resistance.

The typical variability of normal blood pressure is between sixty-five and ninety-five millimeters of mercury (mm Hg) for diastolic pressure and between one hundred ten and one hundred sixty mm Hg for systolic pressure, but this varies with age and environmental and racial background. For example, the American Heart Association's suggested upper limits beyond which further diagnosis regarding hypertension is recommended are 140/90 for adults under forty and 160/95 for adults forty and over. The best source of evidence of the extent and duration of hypertensive disease is in the vessels of the retina as viewed with an ophthalmoscope. People also vary in their predisposition to hypertension even though there is a tendency for blood pressure to rise with age. Some achievement-oriented personality patterns appear to be associated with heart disease (Friedman and Rosenman, 1974). Conditions that arouse anxiety, frustration, anger, and pleasant anticipation can raise blood pressure for those who are predisposed to hypertension, whereas the same stressful conditions do not affect others. Hypertension is especially widespread for blacks.

For older adults especially, as the functioning of the several subsystems declines, the capacity of the individual to coordinate adaptive mechanisms is impaired. This affects both the stress reaction and the process of recovering from stress. There is even evidence that hypertension is associated with intellectual decline in older adults (Wilkie and Eisdorfer, 1971). However, a mild elevation in blood pressure may help maintain cerebral circulation in the aged.

Exercise. Many aspects of physical health are associated with regular exercise that is appropriate for the individual. In general, regular and moderate exercise related to work or recreation contributes to good posture, vitality, endurance, strength, circulation, and metabolism. In addition to emotional satisfaction and relaxation for sleep, exercise may develop collateral circulation that increases the capacity to respond to increased demand and helps prevent coronary heart disease.

The amount and type of exercise that is appropriate for an individual depends on his or her condition and interests. Especially for older adults, the individual's exercise history and physical limitations must be considered and an abrupt increase in exertion avoided. The maintenance of regular exercise throughout adulthood is most desirable, and increases in exertion level in later life should be gradual. Exercise activities that are interesting to the adult are most likely to be engaged in regularly (Smith and Bierman, 1973; Neale, 1969; Sonstroem, 1974). Practitioners can help adults of all ages understand the importance of regular exercise and forms of exercise that fit their interests and condition. For example, armchair exercises have been developed for use by older adults.

Relating Load and Capacity

For many indices of physical condition and health, the general trend during adulthood is for gradual declines in maximum or ceiling capacity. Adults vary greatly in their ceiling capacity related to physical condition and health, and the range of individual differences increases with age at least through the fifties and sixties. This variability reflects both hereditary endowment of physiological potential and accumulated experience related to nutrition, abuse, and exercise.

The meaning of changes in ceiling capacity to the individual depends on the interaction between capacity and load. The concept of load refers to the level of demand placed on the individual's capacities. This relation between capacity and load recurs in many spheres (McClusky, 1971). For active and energetic fifty-year-olds, shoveling snow typically places a load on their cardiovascular systems that is well within their capacities, and the result can be exhilarating. For sedentary and overweight fifty-year-olds, shoveling show may place a load on the system that exceeds the capacity and results in heart attack.

The main implications for action from generalizations about age trends in physical condition and health during adulthood have to do with the relation between capacity and load. Each adult, and each practitioner who works with adults, is more likely to make decisions that lead to productivity, satisfaction, service, and fulfillment if an optimum balance between capacity and load is achieved and maintained. When excessive load for the capacity creates a serious imbalance, attention can be given both to increasing the capacity and reducing the load. Serious imbalances are more likely to occur in old age. Many of the means of increasing the capacity are most effective before middle age. Planning and prevention are therefore crucial ingredients in efforts to improve condition and health for the latter part of life.

The human body has excess capacity that exceeds the limits reached by the performance and participation of most United States adults until about middle age. Then most adults become increasingly aware of signs of declining ceiling capacities. The main ways to achieve and maintain higher levels of physical condition during middle and old age entail undertaking sound nutrition, exercise, and health practices before middle age.

The population of older adults contains some who have severe health problems and many who are healthy and active. It is important to recognize that health is an intervening variable between age and performance. An unrealistic and negative stereotype of old age based mainly on the ill can discourage people of any age from engaging in the practices that increase the probability of a healthy and active old age. When older adults with all levels of health are included in age trends, the combined trend data can give a misleading indication of likely typical performance and encourage a lower than necessary level of expectation.

There are many ways in which adjustments can be made in physical load at those points during adulthood when the load does push the limits of capacity. Adults of any age can be helped to understand the actual limits of their own physical capacity and to pace themselves so that they can function within those limits. During late adolescence and young adulthood this may entail discovering that one's capacity far exceeds current performance and that by proper nutrition, rest, health care, training, and practice one's body is capable of great improvements in strength, endurance, and coordination in physical activities, such as swimming, track, skiing, and tennis. During old age, this may entail discovering that reaction time has slowed but that a satisfactory and satisfying type and level of performance can be maintained by simplifying behavioral sequences, slowing the pace, and emphasizing accuracy instead of strength and speed. For example, the aging tennis enthusiast shifts to doubles and emphasizes placement, or as the older adult's bodily capacity to adjust to extremes in room temperature declines, he or she can compensate by control of room temperature, selection and use of clothing, and use of baths.

In addition to efforts to increase physical capacity and to keep load within capacity, adults can engage in practices related to condition and health that are likely to reduce unnecessary impairments and risk of death. Some practices are most critical before adulthood. Examples include the benefits of nutrition and activity for mental growth during early childhood; the benefits of adequate nutrition, especially calcium for bone growth and condition; and the benefits of flossing teeth to prevent plaque and caries. Adults who understand how such practices can help prevent illness and impairment will reflect this understanding in their own behavior and use their roles as parents, grandparents, aunts, uncles, teachers, and health workers to help children and adolescents adopt practices that are likely to lead to sound health and condition during their adulthood.

During late adolescence and young adulthood, one of several ways to reduce unnecessary impairments and risks of death is accident prevention. Accident rates and rates of deaths due to accidents are highest during this period. A contributing factor is the venturesomeness that is especially prevalent during this age range. However, only a small portion of accidents occur when adults are deliberately courting danger. Most accidents are the result of carelessness, and high proportions occur at times and places where the hazards and likelihood of injury are predictably high. Each year, 7 percent of all United States adults injured in accidents were in moving motor vehicle accidents, compared with 14 percent in work accidents, 36 percent in home accidents, and 43 percent in accidents in all other settings, including recreation. However, motor vehicle accidents accounted for 13 percent of bed disabling accidents and 44 percent of all accidental deaths. The accidental death rate has declined in all categories during the past fifty years except for motor vehicle deaths, and even that has declined in recent years mainly because of the energy crisis and economic recession.

In contrast with the fires and drownings that predominate as causes of accidental death during childhood and adolescence, poisonings, drownings, shootings, and motor vehicle accidents predominate during young adulthood, and falls, fires, suffocation, and motor vehicle accidents predominate in old age. There are no types of fatal accidents for which the age range from twenty-five to sixty-four is relatively high (NSC, 1975; Rodstein, 1964).

In each setting, such as home, travel, work, and recreation, there are times and conditions when the incidence of accidents is especially high and where an awareness of high risk conditions and basic accident prevention practices can greatly reduce the accident rate. In some industrial work settings, much of the lost-time accident rate is associated with hazardous conditions. The consistent use of protective guards around moving machinery parts, warning lights and devices, safety shoes and hats, and standardized procedures can greatly reduce accident rates. In home settings, locations such as kitchens, hazards such as appliances and toys, and times such as late afternoon are associated with high accident rates. The benefits of accident prevention efforts tend to be greatest when concentrated on conditions associated with peak accident rates. In a sport such as skiing, high accident rates occur at the end of the afternoon when snow conditions are rough, lighting is poor, and skiers are fatigued. Accident rates can be reduced if the skier forgoes that last run before the ski lift closes or approaches it with increased caution. In driving, high accident rates are associated with holidays, speed, alcohol, and the onset of precipitation or near-freezing temperatures. Successful defensive driving results from anticipation of high-risk conditions and use of increased caution.

Another way to reduce the likelihood of impairment and death is to develop and maintain a level of physical condition exceeding that required for daily functioning. This excess capacity can constitute a reserve so that peak periods of load or stress do not exceed capacity and result in damage. The stress may take such forms as tension or exertion. Regular physical exercise can help reduce tension and increase strength, endurance, and recovery from fatigue. The increased participation rates by young women during high school and college in women's sports and coeducational active recreation should help increase their physical capacity. An increasing number of men and women engage in physical fitness programs designed to help them feel good and prevent damage to the cardiovascular system.

During young adulthood and middle age, regular physical exercise produces improvements in the functioning of the cardiovascular systems of sedentary people. In one study of the effects of eight weeks of physical training on sedentary males, there was little change in cardiac output, oxygen uptake during submaximal work, or mean arterial blood pressure, but there was an improvement in maximal oxygen uptake of about one third for young men and of about one fifth for middle-aged men. There was also an increase in stroke volume (Mitchell and Blomquist, 1972). Physical fitness specialists have demonstrated that adults in their sixties and seventies can also realize substantial improvements in physical condition from eight weeks of supervised exercises. Some of the pain that older people experience comes from insufficient movement. When older adults were physically active in their youth and have continued to walk a good deal, their earlier level of condition enables them to achieve substantial improvement in later life. Practitioners and friends can assist by providing encouragement and support.

By middle age most adults have established sleep patterns that either facilitate or interfere with adequate rest and relaxation during the remainder of adulthood. Practices that facilitate satisfactory sleep for adults include adequate health and nutrition; sufficient physical activity during the day to reduce tension; lack of sleep during the day; relaxing activity during the evening, including the relaxation that follows satisfactory sexual activity; insulation of the sleeping area from influences that typically interfere with sleep (such as light and noise); and psychological association of the sleeping area with feelings that encourage drowsiness rather than tension-producing thoughts and feelings about the conflicts and problems of the coming day.

Especially during the latter part of life, high levels of stress can contribute to impairments and even death. There are multiple causes of stress, some physiological and some situational. Some achievement-oriented personality patterns are associated with stress and hypertension. Major changes and adjustments for good or ill contribute to stress. In addition to the physical toll, high levels of stress and anxiety reduce awareness, learning, adaptability, flexibility, and growth. Such phenomena as tunnel vision under threatening conditions and memory impairment under conditions of high anxiety are familiar examples. Adults can become aware of their stress tolerances and try to avoid the piling up of stress-producing conditions that will exceed them. In old age, peak stress periods can precipitate a terminal decline. (Especially for younger and middle-aged adults with psychosomatic problems and difficulty handling stress, it appears that biofeedback techniques using electronic monitoring equipment can help the individual recognize and influence runaway emotional responses by intercepting the stress as it begins to rise.)

As maximum or ceiling physical capacity declines in old age to the point where it actually impinges on activity, one response is compensation. Some forms of compensation for physical decline are familiar, such as glasses and hearing aids. However, glasses do not compensate for a narrowed visual field or slowed dark adaptation. The individual must recognize the type of change that is occurring and practice scanning or allow more time to become accustomed to the dark. For example, in night driving the older driver can slow down when oncoming headlights are bright, look toward the side of the road, and close the eyes momentarily when the headlights are the brightest. Sometimes much of the compensation must be environmental, such as when there is low sound volume, poor acoustics, and much background noise that interferes with hearing by an adult with hearing impairment. Under such circumstances, a hearing aid may not help, and if the room is to be satisfactory for adults with hearing impairments, sound amplification at the source and improved acoustics can provide the needed compensation. Elevators and ramps are other modifications of the environment that enable adults with physical disabilities to minimize the limitations on their activities. An additional form of compensation is the adjustment of goals for performance so that they are feasible given the physical limitations.

Most of the ways in which a better understanding of developmental trends in physical condition and health during adulthood can be used to increase the quantity and quality of life entail efforts by both the individual adult and others, such as practitioners who work with adults. However, the mix varies between adjustments that require personal effort by the aging adult and societal adjustments that require efforts by practitioners and policymakers. Following are some typical problems related to condition and health during adulthood, along with examples of the types of efforts that can be made by adults themselves and by practitioners and others to help minimize each problem.

1. Inadequate Nutrition
    a. Adults can allocate sufficient resources for food to have an adequate diet as long as income level allows, can select a balanced diet, and can try to eat with others to encourage regular and balanced meals.
    b. Practitioners can help adults maintain at least minimum income levels, teach them the conditions of balanced nutrition, and help provide greater access to mealtime sociability.
2. Increasing Chronic Illness
    a. Adults can understand and use practices that are likely to sustain satisfactory health and condition and reduce the extent of chronic illness and can understand available health services that will minimize the problems associated with chronic illness.
    b. Practitioners can improve access to adequate health services and can educate adults about their role in reducing illness.
3. Increasing Social Isolation
    a. Adults can understand the typical influence of ac-

tivity and social interaction on performance and can exert themselves to maintain an optimum level of activity and social contact.

   b. Practitioners can help adults become aware of social and physical activities and can improve access to them.

4. Reduced Protection from Immunity

   a. Adults can understand that immunities tend to decline beyond middle age, that they are renewed by repeated exposure, and that traveling or moving to a new community often entails exposure to diseases for which they lack immunity.

   b. Practitioners can help adults acquire immunization where needed, recognize risks related to major shifts in exposure to disease, and learn how to compensate for reduced adaptability due to degeneration of the endocrine system in later life.

5. Increased Sensory Impairment

   a. Adults can recognize the available ways in which they can compensate for sensory impairment, and, unless income level prevents them from doing so, they can use them (glasses, hearing aids).

   b. Practitioners can help adults with sensory impairments by providing reinforcement through combined visual and auditory means, can maintain adequate levels of illumination and sound transmission, and can help adults obtain glasses or hearing aids.

6. Reduced Self-confidence

   a. Adults can emphasize goals and activities that are both desirable and feasible and are likely to lead to accomplishment, fulfillment, and feelings of self-worth.

   b. Practitioners can provide opportunities to engage in activities that fit adults' abilities instead of those that overemphasize their disabilities.

7. Poor Physical Condition

   a. Adults can realize that physical inactivity contributes to reduced vitality and endurance, can un-

derstand their physical limits, can recognize the importance of physical activity within those limits, and can engage in forms of exercise that fit their condition.
b. Practitioners can help adults recognize the importance of regular physical exercise and engage in exercise that will physically overload the body in gradual increments to increase strength, endurance, and vitality.

Practitioners who help adults learn in formal educational programs or in informal supervisory settings can use developmental generalizations about physical condition of adults in at least three ways: (1) as content for educational activities, (2) as guidelines to help adults learn skills, and (3) as considerations to facilitate any type of learning. Examples of topics related to physical condition and health that could be used as content for educational activities include safety education to prevent accidents, practices that promote sound physical condition and nutrition, and ways to intercept stress.

When a practitioner seeks to help groups of adults learn a skill, generalizations about condition and age can help the practitioner estimate each individual's physical potential and select instructional procedures that are appropriate for the individual's age and relevant experience. An example is gradually increasing exercise as part of a physical conditioning program for older adults. In general, practitioners are likely to be more successful in helping adults to learn if they engender positive attitudes toward the students' physical abilities in relation to learning activities. One of the best ways to increase self-confidence, especially in older adults, is to make sure the learner succeeds in initial learning tasks.

Mental Health

There are many characteristics of contemporary United States society that contribute to symptoms of mental or emotional illness. The societal characteristics include rapid social change, extensive geographic mobility, access to alternative life-styles, loss of a sense of community, discrimination barriers to equal opportunity, and conflicts among multiple roles. The symptoms of emotional illness include some that are personal, such as depression or anxiety, and some that have more apparent behavioral manifestations, which are reflected in rates of psychotherapy, psychiatric hospitalization, blatant drug abuse, aggressive crimes, and suicide. Many adults of all ages experience symptoms of emotional disturbance, especially during stress periods. In earlier years there was a tendency to categorize people regarding type of mental illness, such as neurotics, schizophrenics, and paranoids. In recent years many clinicians have found it more useful to categorize clusters of symptoms and to recognize that specific persons often have symptoms related to several clusters. One broad distinction between types of mental illness is between organic and functional. Organic mental illness includes symptoms that are chronic and degenerative and that tend to occur increasingly in old age. Functional or psychogenic mental illness includes symptoms that reflect developmental and situational influences.

Organic. Organic brain syndrome includes senile dementia, which is also referred to as senile brain disease or senile psychosis. Senile dementia is characterized by disorientation, confusion, and memory impairment. Although there is typically a mixed causality for senile dementia, it reflects impairment of brain tissue function, such as cerebral atrophy and plaque formation. Alzheimer's disease includes nerve degeneration. Reduced cerebral blood flow seems to be associated with damage to gray and white matter and to extent of dementia. The functional portion of the causality often reflects extreme social isolation in old age (Wang, 1969).

Functional. Some people enter adulthood with such severe emotional damage from childhood and so little self-esteem and personality integration that they are unable to function satisfactorily in any but the most sheltered circumstances. However, most adults who experience mental illness are viewed by themselves and by their associates as they enter adulthood as reasonably stable, normal, and well-adjusted people. The symptoms of emotional illness that they experience reflect not structural brain damage but functional problems as they deal with their own feelings and life situations. Some of these clusters of symptoms relate to life cycle changes.

Many people are familiar with the strong feelings of fear and anxiety that occur when they confront a threatening situation. Especially in childhood, some people are unable to deal with such circumstances and repress their feelings. The resulting anxiety is sometimes related to specific situations or physical problems. However, when there is a long-term core conflict with major life situations, a free-floating anxiety can develop. Psychoneurotic disorders tend to be reflected in shifting manifestations during the life cycle. Examples include phobias and tantrums during youth, hysterical reactions during young adulthood, obsessive-compulsive reactions during middle age, and hypochondriacal patterns during old age.

Sometimes a lack of personality integration, as reflected in oversensitivity, rigidity, and compulsiveness, is not sufficiently severe in relation to the life situations confronted to be diagnosed as psychoneurotic or schizophrenic. Then in middle age, as the demands of life overtax inadequate adaptive mechanisms, the individual may experience severe emotional disturbance. The basic problem existed for decades but emerged more clearly in response to situational stress.

Some forms of functional mental illness become more widespread with advancing age. Depressive reactions often reflect a turning inward of unconscious hostile impulses that are unacceptable to the self (introjection). Feelings of inferiority and guilt interfere with the adult's ability to test reality, and the individual tends to withdraw in periods of depression. Younger adults are more likely to become depressed as a result of introjection. This is less often the cause of depression for older adults. Depressive reactions become more widespread with advancing age, but for many there are more evident reasons for becoming depressed. In one study, one out of three older adults were depressed, and one out of five were disabled as a result. Twice as many blacks and blue collar adults were depressed as were white collar whites. The incidence of hypochondria also increases with age (Busse, 1954). In part, it may provide a way of shifting anxiety from psychic to physical concerns that may be less threatening. For some, sickness can provide a way of explaining failure. There is a tendency for psychosomatic symptoms to increase during adulthood. Such physical symptoms typically reflect psychological distress. In recent years, diffuse symptoms of lethargy and fatigue during middle age are being recognized as a reflection of concerns about personal fulfillment (U.S. Census, NCHS, 1970).

Older adults often experience repeated social and physical losses. Depression, sleeplessness, worry, and loss of self-esteem erode a strong sense of self. A loss of hearing may foster insecurity and fear. Reductions of outside contacts increase loneliness. Under these circumstances, delusions and feelings of persecution may seem well founded. It seems clear that the same cluster of symptoms would be interpreted differently if it occurred in someone in their twenties.

Suicide. In general, the suicide rate increases with age. However, the pattern varies greatly for men and for women. The rate increases steadily for men throughout adulthood and is highest in the postretirement period. By contrast, suicide rates for women are lower, increasing slightly from young adulthood to middle age and then declining after age sixty. The suicide rates are much lower for blacks than for whites. However, rates are high for some other minority groups.

It is estimated that there are seven to eight unsuccessful suicide attempts for each one that succeeds. The proportion of suicide attempts that succeed is lower for women than for men. Older men especially choose violent modes of suicide, such as shooting or jumping out of windows, that leave little doubt about their serious intent. The rising suicide rates for older adults reflect severe health problems, feelings of loss, depression, and access to lethal medications. Figure 18 presents age trends in the number of suicide deaths per hundred thousand persons in each age group for black and white men and women.

Suicides occur among adults with almost all characteristics, but there are some characteristics that seem to have an especially high relation to suicide. For example, some pro-

Figure 18. Suicide Death Rates by Age, Sex, and Race

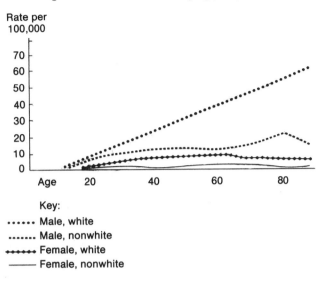

Rate per
100,000

Key:
...... Male, white
.... Male, nonwhite
♦♦♦♦♦♦ Female, white
——— Female, nonwhite

Source: Birren (1964a).

fessional occupations, such as physicians, dentists, and lawyers, have quite high suicide rates. Suicide rates also vary with marital status. The rates for single adults are almost double those of married adults, and the rates for widowed and divorced adults vary by age and for men and women but run from three to seven times as high as for married adults in the same age category. It appears that married life can provide a bulwark against some of the contingencies that lead to suicide.

The annual suicide death rate per hundred thousand United States adults has fluctuated substantially during this century. Since the end of World War II the rate has been fairly constant at between ten and eleven per hundred thousand, which was the rate at the turn of the century. The maximum rates of more than sixteen per hundred thousand have occurred during periods of economic depression, and the lowest rates have occurred during major wars. Over the years the suicide death rates for young men have been fairly constant, but those for young women have dropped. The rates for young women were substantially higher than for young men during the first two decades of this century, were the same during the 1920s, and have continued to drop, so that they are now less than one third those of young men.

Case Example: Driving

One familiar type of role performance that illustrates the interplay between condition, personality, and performance is driving an automobile. Competent driving requires physical coordination and skill, but it also requires judgment. Being able to drive a car is accompanied by actual and symbolic independence and status. The onset of driving is therefore understandably a significant and positive event for many young adults, and the termination of driving is similarly a significant but negative event for many elderly adults.

Although there is much variability in the effectiveness of drivers, accident rates serve as an index of unsatisfactory performance. During the late teens and early twenties, high auto insurance premiums, especially for young men, reflect the high accident rates. From the mid-twenties until the mid-sixties the auto accident rates are relatively constant, and there is an increase for older drivers. What accounts for this variability in role performance with age?

During the late teens and early twenties people are at or close to peak physical condition and health, as reflected in vision, hearing, and reaction time. Condition, therefore, seems to be unrelated to poor performance. Lower premiums for good students reflect differential accident rates in relation to high school achievement, which in turn may reflect factors associated with achievement, such as intelligence, social class, rule following, and risk taking. Lower accident rates for young people who are married and have children may reflect an increased sense of responsibility. Risk taking seems to be a significant influence on automobile accidents by young people. However, accumulated experience and judgment also seems to be influential. As more driving experience is accumulated, complex and uncertain driving problems become more routine. Furthermore, personal and secondhand experiences—including arrests for traffic violations, minor accidents, and near misses—dramatize for the new driver the seriousness of speeding, abrupt changes of direction, and hazardous road conditions and contribute to increased caution.

In this developmental process, many young drivers begin to drive in a carefree and venturesome mood, in which they confront routes, situations, and risks that are unfamiliar and unclear. As the young driver becomes more responsible generally and more aware of likely risks, and as newness is reduced and proficiency is increased, driving performance typically improves.

The steadily rising auto accident rate with increasing age partly reflects declining physical condition. In night driving (especially along unlighted streets), after the bright headlights of an oncoming car have just passed, it takes much longer for the older eye to accommodate to the dark than was the case in young adulthood. Reduced hearing can prevent the older driver from hearing horns and other important traffic sounds. Reaction time tends to increase, as does confusion from a jumble of partly irrelevant information. Based solely on trends regarding physical condition and health between middle and old age, auto accident rates might be expected to increase sharply during old age. However, the actual accident rates for older drivers depend on how the rates are computed. Accident rates per mile driven are relatively high; the rate for drivers in their seventies is similar to the rate for teenage drivers, and for drivers over eighty, the rate is even higher. But when the accident rate is based only on comparisons with other drivers in the same age group, the rate is moderate, and when it is based on all the people in the age group, the rate is low. This difference reflects the older adults who ceased driving, and the widespread reductions in their amount of driving (Case, Hulbert, and Beers, 1970; NSC, 1975; Planek and others, 1968).

However, experience and caution tend to increase with age and help compensate for some of the trends regarding condition and keep the accident rates down. Older drivers tend to drive more slowly, which allows them more time to react. The accident rates due to speeding by older drivers are relatively low. Auto accidents by older drivers are more often caused by turning problems, such as failure to yield and improper turning. Such accidents reflect condition-related restrictions such as reduced peripheral vision, lessened visual acuity, poor hearing, and even difficulty in turning the neck and torso to look back when changing lanes. Some older drivers learn to drive defensively and avoid situations where they may experience difficulty. They slow down and look away from oncoming headlights or give up night driving. They refrain from driving when weather or traffic conditions are most hazardous. In an effort to reduce risk, they develop routine ways of dealing with the condition of their cars, the length of time spent driving during a day, and their ways of approaching busy and confusing intersections. Such older drivers use aspects of learning and personality to compensate for aspects of condition in an effort to maintain satisfactory performance. Practitioners can help adults learn to drive defensively and to take aspects of condition and personality into account in order to have satisfactory performance.

The relationship between interests, condition, and performance that is illustrated by driving is also illustrated by other types of role performance. Effective role performance typically entails some matching of abilities and interests with expectations and opportunities. Each adult has some areas of ability and some areas of disability. Some low-ability adults do reliable and satisfactory work in jobs that many high-ability adults would find boring and perform poorly. Beginning drivers tend to lack judgment, and elderly drivers tend to lack fast reflexes. Practitioners can help adults enter into role relationships in family, work, and community that match their interests and abilities. Doing so may entail understanding one's abilities and role expectations, developing increased competence, and compensating for some areas of limited ability.

Summary

Generalizations about physical condition and health enable the practitioner to identify and interpret aspects of condition important to the individual. Such generalizations also suggest the types of assistance that will help the client achieve and maintain healthy and satisfying performance.

One major influence on physical condition is heredity. There are large variations in living conditions and other environmental influences that also affect appearance and level of physical functioning. Included are health conditions and practices before adulthood, adult nutrition and exercise, disease and emotional stress, and practices such as smoking and drinking.

Heredity and environmental circumstances also influence longevity. Most of the increase in average life expectancy occurred during the first half of this century. More people are living to become old, but maximum life expectancy has been fairly constant. As functional capacities decline, they interact with each other and with environmental hazards to increase sharply the risk of death with advancing age. Condition and longevity are especially associated with exposure and immunity to disease during middle age. The probability of incurring additional impairment at any time increases with the accumulation of previous impairments. With advanced old age, there appears to be a reduction in immunity. Throughout most of adulthood, regular exercise in which the body is overloaded in graduated increments contributes to strength, endurance, and vitality that add life to the years as well as years to the life.

The parts and functions of the human body are highly interrelated. Systems and functions that have particular pertinence for an understanding of adult performance include cells, support, neurologic, circulation, respiration, nutrition, muscles, endocrine, reproduction, and senses.

The atoms that compose the cells are constantly changing; only about 2 percent of the atoms that compose a human body on one birthday are still present on the next. This constant change is balanced by stability provided by the chromosomes in the nucleus of each body cell. Each new cell division creates a duplicate set of chromosomes. The rate of cell division slowly declines; nerve and muscle cells cease division around birth, and skin and blood cells continue to divide throughout life. Thus for parts of the body, such as the heart and the brain where cells do not divide, the number and effectiveness of cells decreases during adulthood. For parts in which cells divide, lost cells are replaced, and some accumulated damage is discarded. Because of the enormous reserve of cells in various organs, the gradual reduction of the body's ability to function at ceiling capacity has little impact on typical daily activities. Practitioners can use generalizations about cellular functioning to help older adults understand restricted performance and function well within the restrictions.

The height of most young adults in the United States mainly reflects their genetic endowment. Improved nutrition and health have contributed to increases during recent generations in the average height of young adults, which explains why the average height of older adults today is less than the average height of young adults. In addition, adult height declines gradually with age for the individual. Bones become more brittle and take longer to knit after middle age, but the severity of this condition can be reduced by sound nutrition in early life.

The condition of the brain and nervous system influences the regulation of vital functions. Brain weight increases until about age thirty, declines only slightly for a few years, and then declines at an accelerating rate into old age. In some instances when brain damage occurs, other portions of the brain can gradually take over much of the lost function. Practitioners can help the patient understand the connection between the damaged zone and the impaired function as part of the rehabilitation or compensation process. In the latter part of life, the progressive slowing of reaction time and coordination reflects reduced signal strength, which reduces responsiveness and adaptability.

The circulatory function is closely associated with the respiratory and renal functions. During most of adulthood these functions decline about 1 percent per year. Because of excess capacity, these declines cause few restrictions during most of adulthood for typical activity but increasingly restrict performance during periods of maximum effort or stress. Arteriosclerosis, reduced stroke volume, increased heart rate, and elevated blood pressure are widespread in later life. Gradual reductions in maximal breathing capacity limit the amount of oxygen supplied through the blood stream to the tissue cells.

The eighty-year-old obtains about one third as much oxygen in the red blood cells as the twenty-year-old; thus for comparable exercise the older person must breathe three times as hard. The decline in oxygen uptake is less for the physically active than for the sedentary. Practitioners can help adults of all ages recognize the beneficial effects of regular and moderate exercise. In old age it takes six times as long for the kidneys to clear the blood of wastes. Immunity mechanisms appear to deteriorate with age, and the susceptibility to infectious diseases is greater in childhood and in old age than in young adulthood and middle age.

Some adult life cycle changes in weight and appearance result from nutritional practices and digestive functions. Caloric intake is somewhat poorer for women than men and for older adults than younger. There is little change until old age for iron intake or hemoglobin (related to anemia) but a slight worsening in old age. For indices of malnutrition, such as vitamins A and C, there is little change during adulthood with a slight improvement in old age. The incidence of alcoholism is higher for men than for women, and it declines with age during adulthood.

During adulthood, the level of endurance, strength, and coordination depends mainly on condition maintained by regular physical activity. Physical strength reaches its peak during the twenties and then gradually declines, so that in the sixties it is about 80 percent of what it was in the twenties. Physical endurance to engage in extended activity also declines with age, but the plateau extends further into middle age than short-term physical performance. Many older adults are able to pace themselves in work and recreation so that they maintain a consistent and high level of performance within their ceiling capacity. Changes in the functioning of endocrine glands reduce old people's ability to respond effectively to extremely high or low environmental temperatures.

It becomes increasingly difficult for older adults to hear the softest sounds, smell the faintest aromas, and see the dimmest lights. The aging eye and related nervous system reduce the visual information that is received. However, with corrective lenses and satisfactory illumination, most adults experience few restrictions because of visual impairment. Few visual changes are noted until about age forty. In addition to lenses and illumination, visual impairments other than blindness can be compensated for by longer exposure time, combined audio and visual presentation, simplified sequences of information, and increased time for adaptation between lighted and darkened surroundings or recovery from stress.

Hearing impairments increase gradually until the fifties, and then the rate increases more rapidly. Pitch discrimination gradually declines between the twenties and the fifties and then drops more abruptly. Older adults also have more difficulty screening out interfering noises. Practitioners can help adults compensate for a hearing loss in several ways, such as providing sound amplification at the source, encouraging use of a hearing aid, recognizing that increased volume will not compensate for neural deafness and that a major hearing loss is usually upsetting, and providing clear enunciation and facial and lip cues.

The frequency level, or pitch, of speech declines until middle age and then rises gradually into old age for males but changes little for females. From middle age onward the rate of speech slows. Sensitivity to smell begins to decline after age forty, and most changes in taste sensitivity occur after age fifty. The sense of touch increases until the mid-forties and then becomes less acute, and sensitivity to pain declines.

General slowing during adulthood is widely recognized. The peak in reaction time is about age twenty, and by age fifty it has returned to about the average level of age fifteen. The slowing of reaction time is greater than for movement time. Older adults typically compensate for reduced speed by increased attentiveness and accuracy. Practitioners can use clear instructions and reinforcement procedures to help older adults improve speed and accuracy.

There are great individual differences in sleep patterns for adults at any age. The proportion of deep sleep declines during adulthood. Many older adults take longer to fall asleep and sleep less during the night but may nap during the day.

During adulthood there is a shift from illness that is acute or functional in young adulthood to irreversible or degenerative illness that is chronic or organic in middle and old age. There is a decline with age in total acute conditions for various income groups, but the decline is greater for the higher income groups. Accidents decline as a cause of death during much of adulthood, and in middle age cardiovascular diseases become a major cause of death for men as do cancers for women. In old age, cardiovascular diseases are the major cause of death for United States adults. However, most adults are without significant limitations from physical illness. For those over sixty-five, only 5 percent live in institutions.

There are many ways in which practitioners might assist adults in relation to physical condition and health. Regarding nutrition, these ways include income maintenance, understanding balanced nutrition, and access to mealtime sociability. Regarding illness, the ways include access to health services and health education regarding preventative care and use of health services. Regarding social isolation, they include increased awareness of and access to social and physical activities. Regarding sensory impairment, the ways include using adequate levels of illumination and sound transmission and combined visual and auditory methods of communication. Regarding poor physical condition, they include stressing the importance of exercise to increase vitality.

The physical health and condition of an adult reflects his or her transaction with the physical and social environment. This is even more true for mental health, as reflected in phobias and tantrums during youth and hysterical reactions during young adulthood. Obsessive-compulsive reactions are more typical of emotional problems during middle age, when the demands of life can overtax inadequate adaptive mechanisms. Depression for younger adults typically reflects introjection, whereas the more widespread incidence of depression for older adults reflects more evident current reasons. The incidence of hypochondria also increases with age. Although the suicide rate increases with age, it rises steadily for men after retirement but increases only slightly for women through middle age and declines after age sixty. Practices related to nutrition, exercise, and preventive health can help most adults add more life to their years.

6

Personality
During Adulthood

The image of adulthood is characterized by stability and pre-dictability. This is in contrast with the image of childhood and adolescence as the initial period of life characterized by growth and change. In actuality a person's performance throughout life is shaped by intertwining strands of stability and change. In a specific situation and time, the individual adult is subject to internal and social pressures. The internal pressures include drives and needs (such as hunger, sex, achievement, and affilia-tion) that vary in direction, strength, and level of conscious awareness. The social pressures include expectations and de-mands from other people who are significant in the life of the individual. Examples include a supervisor's urging of pro-ductivity, a spouse's need for affection, and a child's request for transportation. These significant others include those who are important to the individual and are influential on his or her life in both positive and negative ways, such as a beloved parent or a feared supervisor. The concept of personality refers to the characteristics and tendencies that provide continuity across specific times and situations and enable the individual and others to predict likely thoughts, feelings, and actions. The purpose of this chapter is to review major generalizations about adult personality, including aspects characterized by both continuity and predictable change during adulthood.

The literature on personality mainly concerns personality development during childhood and adolescence. Much of the personality literature that does deal with adulthood focuses on issues of concern to clinicians, such as psychologists, psychiatrists, and psychiatric social workers, who work with emotionally disturbed adults. However, there have been a modest number of reports on empirical research and a large number of efforts to synthesize generalizations from various sources about adult personality. Throughout life there is some tension between differentiation and integration of personality. Differentiation refers to complexity and specialization within the self and separation from the surrounding context. Integration refers to coherence and consistency across domains related to adjustment and effectiveness. Especially during late adolescence and young adulthood, this tension is reflected in the search for identity (Erikson, 1968). Too much differentiation and too little integration results in role diffusion. The tension partly derives from the extent of fit or consistency across the varied life roles that compose adulthood, such as the cluster of family member roles, and those related to work, community, education, and use of leisure. George Herbert Mead helped conceptualize this point by proposing that the individual typically strives to achieve a sense of self (or "I") that is consistent across the "me"s that interact with others in each of the multiple role relationships (1934). Adults tend to behave somewhat differently in their roles as supervisor, bowling team member, and parent. One central theme regarding adult personality is the shifting manner in which the person strives to maintain and enhance his or her sense of self from late adolescence and young adulthood through middle and old age.

Another theme that recurs in the literature on adult personality is the process of making choices or decisions. This executive function of the self or ego entails assertiveness, goal setting, and self-directedness. The choice-making process is especially critical when conflicts occur among loyalties, values, or interpersonal commitments. An example is the parent who has a chance to obtain money illegally during a period when family income is insufficient to buy enough food.

Feelings and attitudes receive major attention in the literature on personality (Rappoport, 1972). For example, conflict between personal and social goals produces tension and defensiveness. Personal goals reflect needs, values, and beliefs, such as a strong desire to help others. Social goals are reflected in interpersonal expectations, environmental press, and societal norms, such as strong incentives for competitiveness. Adult interests provide a manifest expression of preferences among alternative activities in terms of acceptance or rejection of person, place, thing, or activity. An example of an instrument that provides summary information about adult interests is the Strong-Campbell Interest Inventory (Campbell, 1971). One aspect of attitudes, values, and interests that is pertinent to those who help adults learn and change is the extent of rigidity or flexibility; another aspect is moral development.

Interpersonal relations typically entail some adaptation or adjustment. Early in adulthood, many of the adjustments are to the addition of new role relationships in family, work, and community. In later life there is typically increasing concern about loss of role relationships, life review, and anticipation of death. During adulthood there are shifts in contexts (such as community size) and goals (such as occupational goals) as the individual deals with aspirations, stress, and accomplishment. The satisfactoriness of this process of striving and adaptation is reflected in varying levels of morale and happiness.

A developmental understanding of adult personality includes a recognition of basic personality constructs, an understanding of the main trends regarding stability and change in personality during adulthood, and an appreciation of some of the major developmental mechanisms associated with changes in adult personality that occur during a few months or years. Longitudinal studies of the same people over the years have shown that there are various patterns of adult personality change (Haan, 1972; Haan and Day, 1974; Williams and Wirths, 1965). This contributes to the increased variability that occurs with age. Practitioners who work with adults can use a better developmental understanding of adult personality to plan and conduct educative and therapeutic activities to facilitate desirable changes in the affective domain. For example, a health practitioner engaged in patient education might use generalizations about self-concept, attitude change, and age to help a forty-year-old man with diabetes make the necessary adjustments in diet and medication.

The range of individual differences in most personality characteristics increases from the beginning of young adulthood until the beginning of old age. Even in some of the more stable aspects of personality, such as values and self-concept, gradual shifts are widespread, and substantial changes sometimes occur. One reason for this increased variability is that there are various patterns of adult personality change. One of the most stable characteristics is activity level. Although there is a general and gradual decline in quickness and level of activity during the latter part of life, the people who were most active among their age group during adolescence and young adulthood tend to be the most active among their age group during middle and old age. It is almost as though each person has a physical and mental "clock" that runs at a fast or a slow rate throughout life but that tends to run down gradually toward the end. The rate at which an individual's "clock" runs is reflected in various personality characteristics.

Most of the variability in adult interests is associated with social class background and reference groups. The differences in interests between men and women are moderate, and the differences associated with age are relatively small. Some of the differences in interests between younger and older adults today reflect differences in life-style orientation derived from the values and practices of the era in which each grew up (Woodruff and Birren, 1972). Continuity of values from generation to generation within a family is relatively great. The values of young adults are typically more similar to their parents' values than to those of other people in their own generation.

The balance between stability and change in personality for individual adults, in contrast with the great variability in personality patterns among adults generally, has several major implications for practitioners who work with adults. One is that individual clients can be helped to understand the extent to which personality change does occur during adulthood and can thus make realistic and optimistic efforts to achieve desired changes. With a better understanding of the great variability in adult personality patterns, practitioners should resist stereotypes about typical personality characteristics at any stage of the adult life cycle. For example, young adults who hold a stereotyped and inaccurate view of most elderly persons as rigid, negative, despondent, and dependent could be helped to discover that most older adults have contrasting and far more positive outlooks. This more accurate perception of aging will enable young adults to deal far more constructively with the elderly and with their own old age if and when it arrives. Moreover, when social policies regarding community programs and services for older adults are being reviewed, informed practitioners can urge that a range of opportunities be available for adults with widely varying outlooks, instead of a single approach, such as a downtown drop-in center, which assumes that all older adults are alike. The same basic point can be made about a range of opportunities to match great variability in outlook for adults of all ages. For example, there are many satisfactory patterns for women today that include just marriage and children, or just working, or many combinations of the two. Practitioners can help increase the viable alternatives and help clients recognize their options.

Personality Constructs

The concept of personality is global, dealing as it does with the interaction between individual and environment, commonality across role relationships, and continuity over time. Because the very definition of personality emphasizes predictability, the ways of conceptualizing personality (constructs) deal mainly with characteristics and tendencies that are widespread and stable over time, such as need achievement, need affiliation, cooperation, dominance, and gregariousness. These personality constructs are in contrast to universal characteristics, such as the biological endowments common to all human beings, and unique characteristics, such as detailed genetic composition and past experience. However, personality stability and change is influenced by characteristics that are universal, characteristics that are widespread, and characteristics that are unique (Kluckhohn and Murray, 1949; Baltes and Schaie, 1973; Mischel, 1969; Sanford, 1970).

Transaction. The transactional model is one way to conceptualize personality development that incorporates all the varied influences. This construct emphasizes interrelations among biological, experiential, societal, and historical systems as the individual interacts with his or her environment. As interaction occurs, a residue accumulates that takes various forms, such as physical condition, life experience, self-concept, attitudes, and morale. This accumulating residue produces personality. Early transactions, such as first impressions, are especially influential because they form a set or expectancy through which subsequent experience is filtered. For example, if an individual's early paintings turn out well and receive praise, interest and extent of painting is likely to increase along with some shift in self-concept.

As the individual interacts with the societal context, if there is a high degree of consistency among the biological and experiential aspects of self and with the demands and constraints of the societal context, then a high degree of personality stability and continuity would be expected. However, the societal context does not remain constant. During the contemporary period of rapid social change, the cohort of adults who are about the same age confront different demands and constraints from those faced by adults at the same stage of life (age cohort) one or two generations earlier (Woodruff and Birren, 1972). For example, the greater assertiveness of some young wives reflects greater societal acceptance and peer group encouragement, more equalitarian attitudes by some husbands, and more widespread employment of women. Historical change affects the physical and social characteristics of the societal context, as well as personal aspirations. If there is a low degree of consistency among the biological and experiential aspects of self and a changing pattern of demands and constraints of the societal context, less personality stability and more change would be expected (Lewin, 1935).

The transactional model of adult personality includes the influence of both maturational sequences and sociocultural forces on personality stability and change and several additional basic concepts (Maddi, 1972; Neugarten and Datan, 1973; Looft, 1973):

1. Anxiety and defensiveness-producing conflict between personal and societal goals is widespread but neither universal nor inescapable, and it can be dealt with through a degree of transcendence of society instead of mere conformity to it. A person with a transcendent approach to life would emphasize individuality, assertiveness, imaginativeness, reflectiveness, and openness to experience.

2. There is a great force toward human fulfillment through the enhancement of life beyond survival, in which a varied and satisfying life results from striving to achieve the twin goals of (a) actualization of inherent personal potential for successful individual living and (b) striving toward ideals for successful group living and improvement of the quality of life in the society.

3. Personality development occurs throughout life as a result of the person's experiential transactions in society (Corah, 1965; Elder, 1971). The individual makes efforts to reduce tension that results from large incompatibilities. For example, personality change reflects learning as a result of major gains and losses of role relationships in family, occupation, and community. The individual also seeks small increases in tension by creating gaps between current and desired circumstances. The individual's customary level of

excitation is used to interpret the desirability of a current tension level as one that is neither too meager nor too intense.

The transactional model of adult personality development does not synthesize but does accommodate some of the main concepts of the three most familiar general models of personality. Following are brief overviews of the way in which personality is conceptualized in each of these three models, along with an indication of some of the persons whose writings have helped develop them (Maddi, 1972; Hall and Lindzey, 1970). There has been very little empirical research to test these theoretical formulations as they apply to adults.

Conflict. The most familiar model of personality is based on the writings of Sigmund Freud. Freud assumed that the individual is in conflict with society. As the individual's impulses, id, or striving for gratification collides with societal forces as reflected in the superego, or conscience, an uncomfortable level of tension and anxiety is produced. Unrestricted expression of impulses leads to destruction of the self and others (psychosis). Unrestricted imposition by the society leads to excessive guilt and defensiveness (neurosis). Emotional illness results when only personal urges or only societal restraints are acknowledged. The aim of life is therefore to compromise and reduce conflict, tension, and anxiety. The result is good citizenship, defined in terms of responsibility, conformity, morality, dependability, consideration, and generosity. The conflict is greatest between the young child and adult society, and Freud concluded that the basic patterns of personality are set for good or ill during childhood. Because personality develops in response to similar societal pressures, the processes and stages of personality development are seen as basically the same. He believed that stability of personality is common but not universal during adulthood and that dependability and predictability vary with the extent to which the individual child or adolescent acquired satisfactory methods of tension reduction and effective defense mechanisms. Attention to personality development during adulthood consists mainly of remedial efforts to minimize the unfortunate effects of inadequate development during three stages of childhood and one stage of adolescence. Such theorists as Murray, Sullivan, Jung, and Erikson provide greater attention to adult development within this conflict model. Rank and Angyal deal with an intrapsychic version of the conflict model in contrast with the psychosocial version of Freud. Dollard and Miller provide a stimulus-response explanation of parent-child conflict, and Cummings and Henry provide a social deterministic explanation of disengagement in old age, both of which share major elements of the conflict model of personality development.

Fulfillment. Growth, change, actualization, and striving toward ideals characterize the fulfillment model. In contrast with the conflict model, the fulfillment model conceptualizes one great force of striving to improve life for the individual and society. Theorists such as Maslow and Rogers emphasize self-actualization, and theorists such as Adler and Allport emphasize striving toward ideals for successful group living. In contrast with the conformity and compromise proposed in the conflict model, the fulfillment model assumes that much of the conflict occurs because the society has become inhuman and punitive in some ways, and this affects the individual through uncaring significant others. However, defensiveness is seen as an unfortunate necessity under adverse circumstances instead of a sign of successful living and mental health. Thus the fulfillment model sets transcendence of current society as the highest form of living. Continuing personality change throughout life is the central concept of the fulfillment model with its emphasis on actualization and striving.

Consistency. In the consistency model, personality change results from encounters between the individual and the world of experience as the person deals with discrepancies between expectations and current circumstances. One side of a gap is defined by the current circumstances of actual experience in the entirety or in selected domains of an individual's life as perceived by the individual. The other side of the gap is defined by the individual's expectations. The sources of expectations may include typical past experience, self-concept, level of personal aspiration, or expectations about what the world should be like. Theorists such as Kelly and Festinger state that very large gaps or discrepancies produce intensely uncomfortable dissonance, tension, and anxiety that the individual seeks to reduce by narrowing the gap or discrepancy. Efforts to reduce the discrepancy may include a change in current circumstances, a change in expectations, or perceptual distortion and denial of actual circumstances as a form of defense. McClelland indicates, however, that people typically enjoy small incompatibilities, such as recreational diversions and occupational challenges, and even seek them out. Fiske and Maddi emphasize that the person's customary discrepancies or gaps serve as a baseline against which to assess current gaps to decide whether the discrepancy is excessive and tension reduction efforts are needed, or the discrepancy is in an acceptable range, or there is too little discrepancy and some increase in tension is warranted to reduce boredom or provide greater challenge. Theorists who use a consistency model do not restrict the content of personality concerns to sexual or interpersonal discrepancies; instead they include all major instances of cognitive dissonance and affective discrepancy. Because the consistency model is not oriented toward a dominant psychosocial conflict or unfolding life force, there is little emphasis on developmental crises, stages, or themes that are universal. It is assumed that there are great individual differences and variability in the extent to which people seek or avoid variety and tension and in the domains or aspects of life that are important to a person. For the consistency theorist, more of the salient aspects relate to the periphery of personality than to a core of personality that is common to all mankind.

Stability and Change. The several personality models vary regarding the relative influence that impulses, society, conflict, striving, and discrepancies have on the ways in which the individual deals with strong feelings, interpersonal relations, discrepancies, and decisions. Personality constructs focus on tendencies that influence functioning and have continuity in time beyond immediate biological or societal influences. The constructs are typically used to understand and predict current performance. However, an interest in adult learning and development includes attention to the extent of stability and change in personality during adulthood. Are there predictable trends in general personality patterns from late adolescence through young adulthood to middle and old age? Theorists who follow the psychosocial conflict model typically assume that most of personality development occurs before adulthood and that stability characterizes personality during adulthood, except for people who experience abnormal psychological problems. Fulfillment and consistency theorists assume that there is significant personality change during adulthood, although they vary in their explanations of why and how major personality changes occur. In the transactional model, it is assumed that the main impetus for personality change during adulthood may come from either the individual or society, that personality change in a given direction is more likely when facilitated both by personal impulse or striving and by societal encouragement, and that personality stability occurs during adulthood when there is great consistency in both personal characteristics and societal circumstances. Both longitudinal and cross-sectional studies indicate that during adulthood there is more change than stability and that for some adults and periods of time, the changes are major.

Some of the main generalizations about extent and type of personality change during various phases of adulthood are:

1. The typical rate of personality change between late adolescence and middle age is great enough to enable growth and adaptation but not so rapid as to threaten personal security (E. L. Kelly, 1955; Tuddenham, 1959; Roher and Edmonson, 1960; MacFarlane, 1964).

2. The extent of change varies across aspects of personality. For example, values, vocational interests, aggressiveness, and general adjustment tend to be more stable than other personality variables and self-ratings (E. L. Kelly, 1955; Symonds, 1961; Edwards and Wine, 1963).

3. Between adolescence and young adulthood, early intelligence measures are more predictive of later ad-

justment than early personality measures (Anderson, 1960a, b).

4. Between childhood and young adulthood, stability of such personality characteristics as passivity, anger arousal, and dependence tends to be associated with the influence of societal expectations regarding roles of males and females (Kagan and Moss, 1962).

5. During late adolescence and young adulthood, extent of personality change is greater for persons with higher levels of intellectual ability (Plant and Minium, 1967; Trent and Medsker, 1968).

6. During young adulthood, extent of change varies among people with differing personality characteristics. For example, compulsive and rigid young adults changed little between age eighteen and thirty, compared with other types of young adults, some of whom changed dramatically during this period (H. E. Jones, 1960).

7. Some personality shifts from late adolescence into young adulthood are reversed after age twenty-five or thirty into middle age. This trend reversal occurs for various traits and subpopulations. For both men and women, masculinity increased until age thirty and then decreased (Terman and Miles, 1936). Neuroticism increased for women teachers until age thirty and then declined (Phillips and Greene, 1939). Vocational interests of men, especially those related to skill, daring, and change, become more positive until the mid-twenties but then slowly become more negative through the fifties (Strong, 1943). Similar trend reversal has occurred for women college students for whom there was a shift from freshman to senior year toward greater independence and expression of impulses and less authoritarianism and ethnocentrism, followed by a reversal of trend toward conventional adjustment four years after graduation (Freedman and Bereiter, 1963). A similar reversal occurred for maturity scores for women who neither went to col-

lege nor went to work after high school graduation
(Trent and Medsker, 1968).

8. There are increases in both differentiation and integration of the self between young adulthood and
middle age (Corah, 1965). Differentiation includes
body concept, sense of separate identity, and complexity of personality. Integration includes binding
together and organizing parts of the personality (Witkin and others, 1962). Beyond young adulthood there
is some increase in introspection and concern for the
meaning of life (Kuhlen, 1945).

9. A variety of contrasting personality patterns occur
for older adults, and they are associated with differing rates of personality change and adaptation (Williams and Wirths, 1965; Reichard and others, 1962;
Britton and Britton, 1972; Haan and Day, 1974;
Neugarten, 1972; Simon, 1971).

10. From middle to old age there is often a gradual shift
from active to passive mastery that accompanies a
shift toward reduced life space, conservation of energy, increased interiority, and flattened affect. However, adaptational patterns that are stable with age
enable the aging adult to cope with the environment
in habitual ways (Neugarten and others, 1964).

In general, there is substantial evidence of personality
change throughout life (Honzik and MacFarlane, 1973). Before
adulthood the annual rate of personality change is greater and
the stages and processes of change more similar, mainly reflecting biological maturation. During adulthood periods and domains of stability are interspersed with major personality
changes, and the patterns of personality stability and change
vary greatly among adults with contrasting personality characteristics. Practitioners can use these models and generalizations about adult personality to interpret to adult clients likely
elements of stability and change during adulthood. Practitioners
can also use these generalizations to help plan effective assistance efforts.

Two personality theories—Jungian and organismic—

have been fairly influential on practitioners because of the attention given to continued personality development throughout adulthood. Jung characterized adolescence and early young adulthood in terms of sexual values, ascendent vital processes, physical energy, extraversion, impulse, vigor, and passion, along with a degree of dependence as the self is established in family and community. By contrast, around age 40 people are characterized as less biological, vigorous, and impulsive and more cultural and introverted. Self-actualization occurs as values are reevaluated, physical energy is displaced by psychic energy, vigor is replaced by wisdom, and the individual is transformed into spiritual man. At this stage, the equilibrium of the psyche can be upset if there are insufficient satisfactory outlets for excess energy. Old age is characterized by increasing rigidity, dependence, and loss of self confidence (Jung, 1957). However, with the exception of mid-life reevaluation and the distinction between introversion and extraversion, Jungian personality theory has received little attention or confirmation by empirical research on adult development. Angyal (1941) and others who espoused an organismic personality theory emphasized the interconnectedness among the physical and psychological parts of the individual and between the individual and his or her social environment. A search for meaning and relatively enduring personality processes provide continuity. However, the influence of the past on the present is continually changing, and the contemporary psychological environment is seen as very influential. Early attempts to influence the environment shift to efforts to accommodate to the environment. During adulthood symbolic functions develop, there is more emphasis on thinking and less on acting, behavior is easier to foretell, and the individual becomes more rigid and less open to influence. Such general formulations contribute to a holistic conception of personality development.

Self-Concept

A critical aspect of personality is the sense of self or identity. Although late adolescence and young adulthood tends to be the familiar period during which young men and women experience identity crises and strive to stabilize ego identity, the sense of self actually evolves throughout life. The term *identity* refers to the self one feels oneself to be. An identity evolves as a person contrasts what is "me" with what is "not me." This sense of self is greatly influenced by role models and expectations but is partly constructed from within by the person. Especially during childhood and adolescence, as the person is exposed to the social judgments of others and accumulates preferences and feelings of competence, the sense of self or identity becomes richer, fuller, and more stable. In addition to the distinction between the "me" and the "not me," the growing sense of self includes a recognition of the "I" that is common to the multiple "me"s of various major life roles, such as child, sibling, peer, student, and worker (G. H. Mead, 1934). The executive function of the ego or self that is reflected in goal-setting, planning, and accommodation of contending forces is characteristic of adulthood.

The individual's perception and feelings about self influence many aspects of functioning. The positiveness of self-concept and level of self-esteem tends to increase until middle age and then to stabilize or gradually decline (Lehner and Gunderson, 1953; Veroff and others, 1962; Lowenthal and Chiriboga, 1972). Part of the increased positiveness of self-description reflects a rational self-limitation and reduction of aspiration. For older adults, a decline in self-esteem is influenced by recent disruptive life experiences, such as loss of spouse or job, and by a lower standard of living than anticipated (Kaplan and Pokorny, 1970). In general, when compared with younger people, the outlook of older adults is characterized as more likely to feel that they have positive moral values; somewhat more likely to feel adequate as spouse and parent; equally likely to feel adequate in job performance (if still working); almost as likely to view their intelligence as being as good as others'; less likely to feel that they are in good health; less concerned about their weight; and less likely to admit shortcomings (Riley and others, 1968).

The developing sense of self reflects many influences. During childhood, such significant others as parents and teachers (and, increasingly, close friends) have a major impact on self-concept. During adulthood, experiences with friends and work interact with individual aspirations to modify the individual's sense of self. Friendship patterns differ substantially for men and women, in contrast with the relative similarity for each over the years from the onset of marriage to the onset of retirement. However, changes in many indices of self-concept during adulthood are greater than changes in friendship patterns. A major activity such as work also has a major influence on self-concept and self-esteem. For many adults, work provides a vehicle for striving for a sense of personal worth; recognition by others who matter; a sense of influence on one's life course; and a sense of individuality, growth, and achievement. In addition, from time to time, many adolescents and adults become concerned about overdependence on others to define who they are (Marcia, 1966; Organ, 1973; Blanck and Blanck, 1974; Lowenthal, Thurnher, and others, 1975; *Counseling Psychologist*, 1976).

Ego Development. Identity is only one crisis or theme associated with the development of the ego or self during life, as conceptualized by Erikson (1950, 1956, 1968, 1974). Although people may confront ego crises at various stages of life and may return to a type of ego crisis several times during a lifetime, Erikson asserts that failure to resolve an ego crisis at one stage makes it more difficult for the individual to resolve subsequent ego crises.

Five of the eight epigenetic developmental stages, or ego crises, are described by Erikson as occurring during childhood and adolescence. They entail developing trust, autonomy, initiative, industry, and identity. Infants acquire a sense of basic trust rather than a sense of basic mistrust as a result of interaction with the persons who are most central in their care and who have a positive approach to giving and trusting. For example, if early mutual exchanges between mother and child create a cradle of faith in which the mother meets the infant daughter's physical and psychological needs and gains satisfaction in doing so, it is more likely that the daughter will develop a sense of trust in her mother and in herself, and a sense of hopefulness about her world.

Young children acquire a sense of autonomy while com-

bating a sense of doubt and shame as a result of the exercise
of self-control without loss of self-esteem. Parental provision of
a combination of freedom and limits allows children to explore
and expand with the secure feeling that they do not have a
burden of responsibility that exceeds their feelings of capacity.
Children acquire a sense of initiative and overcome a sense of
guilt as a result of the mastery of new tasks that increasingly
occur in widening settings of school and neighborhood.

During late childhood and early adolescence, youngsters
acquire a sense of industry and fend off a sense of inferiority.
Peers become an increasingly important reference group. Efforts
to improve and succeed occur within an awareness of the threat
of failure, which can serve as a counterbalance to half-hearted
efforts. Freedom from marital and occupational commitments
allows adolescents to shift attention to personal qualities and
roles that seem attractive without having to deal with all the
interrelationships and implications that are actually entailed.

During late adolescence and early young adulthood, a
typical concern is to acquire a sense of identity and to overcome a sense of identity diffusion. The youth searches for a
sense of self in which the process of becoming shifts from identification with ideals to an integration of such identifications into
an ego identity that has fidelity and a feeling of personal au-
thenticity. Many young people want to become their own persons, not just the persons others want them to be. During this
period, delinquency may reflect a negative identity in an effort
to regain mastery in a situation in which positive identity elements seem to be inaccessible. A moratorium period between
youth and adulthood allows the individual to explore patterns
of identity before more binding commitments are made. Such
exploration can entail personal extremes and societal disap-
proval, which can be threatening. Some low income, minority
group parents, in encouraging their children to achieve upward
social mobility, discourage their children from identifying with
themselves as parents. This can place an additional burden on
the young person who is striving to establish a sense of identity.
The persistence to start and complete tasks contributes to
planfulness and a sense of identity. This often relates to the

youth's appraisal of the dynamics of leadership and follower-ship. Many adolescents seem to have a great need to polarize as a way of dealing with many alternative ideals. By strong and rigid commitment to their own group's values and rejection of opposing groups, they focus their sense of themselves.

As the adolescent or young adult becomes an interde-pendent member of society, peers replace parents as sources of support and values and serve as intermediaries in the search for a stable sense of self in family, occupational, and community roles. Many youth are also attracted to one or two adults who have significant past associations or who are attractive in rela-tion to emerging concerns as significant others. These significant other adults can be very influential on adolescent development. Extensive conversation with someone of the same age and sex is also a means of identity searching.

Erikson sees the identity crisis of late adolescence as especially critical. The promise of finding oneself and the threat of losing oneself are closely connected at this stage. The indi-vidual faces the crisis of making a choice that fits personal preferences and societal opportunities. The society faces the difficulty of extending to the adolescent sufficient latitude with-out denying societal responsibility. The moratorium can fail for several reasons. Either the individual or society may settle on a choice of identity and adult commitment that is premature and partial. Examples include early marriage, forced and un-satisfactory occupational choice, and permanent stigma for minor delinquent behavior. The individual may also be so threatened by the choices and commitments of adulthood that he or she feels inadequate as a person and refrains from the assumption of adult responsibilities. If the moratorium is suc-cessful, the youth blends from adolescence into adulthood as a fit is achieved between past potential and experience, current sense of identity and aspirations, and societal expectations and opportunities for the future. Similar transitions seem desirable at every stage of adulthood.

The three developmental stages or ego crises that Erikson describes as occurring during adulthood entail developing a sense of intimacy, of generativity, and of integrity. If the individual has developed a strong sense of identity, he or she is more likely to enter into the life of the community with a mix of adult freedom and responsibility.

During young adulthood, the individual acquires a sense of intimacy and solidarity and avoids a sense of isolation as a result of the achievement of a personalized pattern of living in which joint intimacy in love or work or both deepens individual identity. In marriage and in work, collaborative and career efforts include friendships, mutual trust, and dealing with elements of cooperation and competition. In marriage, intimacy and solidarity provides a healthy setting for potential offspring. A person can fail to resolve this developmental crisis by unwillingness or inability to become involved and find a sense of shared identity. The result is a sense of distance and isolation, which sometimes results from an idealized image of collaborative relationships.

In the second developmental stage of adulthood the individual acquires a sense of generativity and avoids a sense of self-absorption. This concern for the next generation varies with the work and family status of the individual. For the married adult, a sense of generativity results from building on accumulated experience and wisdom to create a family setting that will nurture the next generation. For adults without children this may be reflected in concern about the next generation as manifested in nieces and nephews, students, friends' children, and in support for community services, such as education and child care. For any adult, personal and creative efforts that contribute to subsequent generations counteract the extent of self-absorption that estranges the individual from the community.

In Erikson's final developmental stage the individual acquires a sense of integrity and avoids despair by accepting the societal and personal life cycle as it is, with few major regrets. This often entails a new, different love of one's parents. Failure to resolve this crisis results in a sense of despair and fear of death as the conclusion of an unfulfilled life.

Some of the more detailed developmental mechanisms by which a sense of identity is stabilized during young adulthood are illustrated in the case study of "Joseph Kidd," in

R. W. White's longitudinal study of personality development (1961). Joseph Kidd attended a major university to study pre-medicine, at the strong urging of his blue collar parents. In doing so, he felt caught in the cross pressures of strong maternal dominance and expectations regarding his upward mobility; his internalization of the dominant values of his childhood neighborhood, which included little press toward upward mobility and a college education, but instead emphasized ethnic solidarity, easy money, and exploitation; and his own lack of strong commitment to a college education or becoming a doctor.

As a college student, Kidd was uncertain of himself, erratic, unable to study effectively, fearful of others, and driven by his emotions. He frequently observed other people and then tried to act out their personalities. He often acted childishly to attract attention. He said that he could not make a decision on his own and follow through on it, for his activities were guided by external forces. He had an idealized and nonphysical orientation toward girls. During his college years, Kidd's relationships with family and friends deteriorated, and his self-esteem declined. Finally he flunked out of college and went to work.

In the stable conditions of a well-defined job in a hierarchical business organization, Kidd's self-doubts began to recede, he selectively accumulated experience, and his sense of himself become stronger and more stable through performance of a consistently defined role. He began to assert his autonomy by supporting himself and by making occupational decisions, and his parents reduced their control and became more accepting of his efforts. He learned to resist the ambitious pressure that had made his home life so unhappy, and his resentment decreased. His sex life, which had gone from idealistic abstinence to frequent intercourse without emotional attachment, was beginning to incorporate affection. This contributed to a more positive self-image. He returned to school to complete a degree, but with reduced occupational aspirations. His job met his expectations without the imposition of excessive demands, and, especially after a promotion, he began to realize that he was competent. Unlike his experience as a premed student when his life was disorganized by his rebellion against parental pressure, his life was now organized by his occupation.

After graduation, Kidd entered the military service as a private during World War II, and he was able to drop many goals and pretensions. He was satisfied and even carefree with his role. During his first year in the service, there were numerous escapades, but during the second year his performance was satisfactory and several senior officers took an interest in him. One appointed him to supervise eighty men. Kidd was miserable. He had gotten along with the junior officers and he liked to be "with" the other fellows, not "over" them. He disliked administering discipline and issuing commands. His interests were moving him toward a different sense of identity. A well-defined and attractive position seemed to deflect his developing sense of self, so it failed to stabilize his self-concept and instead had a transient negative effect.

After four years in the service, Joseph Kidd returned home, enrolled in a summer session chemistry course, which he found painfully difficult, helped around his father's flower shop, applied to some medical schools, and waited. He was not very happy and his life threatened to resume its former disorganized pattern. Then in competition with more up-to-date competitors, his father's once prosperous flower shop began to decline. With the encouragement of his mother and the acquiescence of his father, Kidd took on the project of rescuing the family business. The effort was successful, and it represented the greatest attempt he had ever made to exert an influence on his environment. The results stood as a monument to his ideas and labors, and the process helped clarify his image of himself as a friendly fellow and a businessman. This major incident helped stabilize and transform Kidd's identity through the expectations, privileges, and opportunities associated with his occupational role and status.

Between the ages of nineteen and twenty-nine, although there were many vicissitudes in the development of Kidd's sense of self, the overall trend was toward increased stability. He began to recognize his own intentions and purposes and to discover that he could be effective, somewhat self-directing, and respected, which brought him satisfaction. After the flower shop was again flourishing, Kidd became bored with the comfortable life he had as a business assistant to his father, which only required working a dozen hours a week. He began to develop interests that he found pleasurable, such as music and golf, and to become more interested in achievement. He left his father's business and eventually progressed well in a large industrial organization in another city, in part through hard evening study. He married and had four children, became sought after by family and work associates as someone they could depend on, and made a place for himself in community life. Once erratic and with strong feelings of inferiority, Joseph Kidd made intelligent use of his capabilities, gained self-confidence and effectiveness; used his personal experience with insecurity to understand and deal effectively with others who were insecure; and increasingly became able to work with people, to persist, and to accomplish. He enjoyed public speaking and was elected for three terms on the city council. His involvement and emotional investment in family life tended to be slight because even though his roles as husband and parent were largely acquired from social expectations, it was his own preference in occupational and political roles that strengthened and stabilized his identity.

For most people, as the sense of self becomes more stabilized, it becomes more distinct, coherent, and free from transient influences. Identity becomes stabilized by repeated successes, but with age a single failure has less power to greatly increase or decrease self-esteem. The adult with a strong sense of identity can use accumulated experience to make a self-judgment. From adolescence throughout young adulthood there is typically a trend toward self-consistency or self-objectivity in which the developing sense of self results in sufficient maturity to compare pretensions with abilities and opinions of self with the opinions of others. This degree of maturity may occur by age twenty or it may not occur until the thirties, but when it occurs a firm sense of identity has become stabilized.

Empirical Findings. Most of the generalizations regarding self-concept during young adulthood are based on studies of college students. However, there have been some studies of self-concept in which the sample has consisted of young adults who graduated from high school but did not go on to college full time (Trent and Medsker, 1968; Knox, 1970). In one study of non-college-bound men and women between the ages of eighteen and twenty-five who were working or seeking work (Knox, 1970), two instruments were administered that deal with self-concept. One was the set of six FIRO-B scales that provide a profile of self-concept related to interpersonal behavior, such as inclusion, control, and affection (Schutz, 1958). The second was the twenty-eight scales extracted from the Tennessee Department of Mental Health Self-Concept Scale (TSCS) that provide a more complex profile of self-concept (Fitts, 1965).

On the FIRO-B scales, the profiles for the non-college-bound young adults were similar to those for a norm group composed mainly of college students. The one difference was that the non-college-bound young adults typically viewed themselves as having less control or influence over others in interpersonal relations than their peers who were in college (Knox, 1970).

On the TSCS the profiles for the non-college-bound young adults were generally similar to norm groups from the general population of adults who were judged average or better on level of adjustment or degree of personality integration. The profiles did not vary substantially with sex, race, education, or intelligence but did differentiate groups of psychiatric patients. There were several ways in which the self-concept profiles of non-college-bound young adults differed from the profiles for the general population of adults with satisfactory adjustment. These differences seem to reflect the period of family and occupational adjustment that typically occurs during the late adolescent and young adult years, especially for those who attend a high school with a strong college entry orientation but do not go to college. The non-college-bound young adults tended to have relatively positive self-concepts; however, their view of self as reflected in performance, behavior, and action, was less positive than their view of self as reflected in identity or in satisfaction or acceptance of self. They also tended toward more extreme positive or negative views of self than occurs for the general adult population, such as greater defensiveness regarding self-criticism.

The profile is based on a conceptualization of self-concept that underlies a fifteen-cell matrix with five columns on aspects of self and three rows on identity (who I am), satisfaction (acceptance of self), and behavior (how I act). The aspects of self are physical, moral, personal, family, and social. Half the items related to each cell are worded positively and half negatively (Fitts, 1965; Knox, 1970).

The TSCS has been used for many studies of adults. The norm group for the TSCS was composed mainly of adults and college students who were functioning satisfactorily. There are few age-related trends in self-concept within the age span between twenty and sixty years of age, except that the variability scores are below average (W. Thompson, 1972). Moderately low variability scores indicate high consistency from one area of perception to another and satisfactory personality integration. Within the general adult population, TSCS profiles have been obtained for varied samples of adults judged to be well integrated and unusually effective in their occupational and personal performance. Their profiles are very similar and reflect an optimal self-concept characterized by high self-esteem, good personality integration, moderate defensiveness and self-differentiation, low conflict and variability, and low indication of pathology. College students typically have low variability scores, which is characteristic of most normal adult samples, and relatively high self-acceptance.

It appears that adults with optimal self-concepts use their intellectual abilities more effectively than those with poor self-concepts. In addition, self-concept is a partial predictor of occupational performance and is also affected by the quality of occupational performance. In general, self-concept is associated with self-actualization (Fitts, 1972; Duncan, 1966; Fitts, Stewart, and Wagner, 1969; Garvey, 1970; McClain, 1969; Seeman, 1966).

There is some indication that among mothers in single parent families, the self-concepts of those who were working were normal, but the self-concepts of those who were not working were much lower and more negative (Fitts, 1972). Vocational rehabilitation clients who achieved stable employment were compared with work-inhibited clients whose subsequent occupational performance was characterized by work-adjustment difficulties, frequent short-term job placements, and long periods of unemployment. Those with stable employment records had clearly differentiated self-concepts, higher self-esteem, less evidence of maladjustment, and fewer deviant features (Tiffany and others, 1970).

Most people reach a peak in their uncertainty about their self-concepts during the high school years. TSCS profiles that would indicate maladjustment for the adult population are fairly typical of adolescents. The profiles do discriminate between well-adjusted and maladjusted young people but in a lower range. For example, when Neighborhood Youth Corps dropouts were compared with those who persisted, the dropouts were characterized by low self-esteem, difficulty with self-definition, defensiveness, and conflict in self-concept (Fitts, 1972).

The TSCS profiles for older adults beyond age sixty are substantially more variable than the norm group. The typical pattern is of above-average self-esteem, a less adequate view of physical self, but relatively high views of social self, moral-ethical self, self-satisfaction, and certainty of self-description. However, these profiles also reflect low self-criticism and high defensiveness in self-report. It appears that part of the increase in self-esteem for older adults reflects the trend toward an increasingly rigid, sharply differentiated, and decisive self-description (W. Thompson, 1972).

In one study, the TSCS was administered to a sample of five hundred adults between twenty-one and sixty-nine years of age. There were some variations between blue collar and white collar adults in feelings about self. Age trends in self-concept differed somewhat between men and women, which partly reflected differential role relationships. For all age groups, men placed more emphasis than women on denial and preservation of positive self-images. Older adults reflected greater concern about physical limitations and problems. However, the most general finding was that from the twenties through the sixties self-concept becomes more positive (Grant, 1969). Beyond the sixties self-concept tends to become more negative. Studies with other measures show that the increase in self confidence from age twenty until age forty or fifty is substantial, even though there are fluctuations and variations for men and women from blue and white collar families (E. L. Kelly, 1955; Brozek, 1952). There is some indication that the increase in self confidence is greater for men than for women (Block and Haan, 1971; Haan, 1972).

The shifts in self confidence, particularly any turning points at which a trend toward more positive views of self is reversed and a negative trend begins, are likely to reflect age norms and interactions with significant others and members of the individual's reference groups. This seems likely in light of the TSCS evidence of an increase in self-esteem for older adults.

For example, although there are variations among white and blue collar women and men, within each category there is great similarity in the age norms and expectations that regulate how individuals view themselves regarding their prime in occupational and family life cycles. The white collar worker's shifting self-perception is reflected in the way in which adulthood is divided into stages, each with its own themes. Early young adulthood until age thirty is a time of exploration. Age forty is seen as the prime of life and the time of greatest self-confidence. Middle age begins about age fifty and old age about seventy. By contrast, early young adulthood for the blue collar worker is seen as a period of increasing responsibilities and restrictions that ends about age twenty-five; a person is middle aged by forty, and old by sixty. This differential perception of age norms for oneself and others is reinforced by the earlier ages at which blue collar adults typically leave school, get married, and become parents and grandparents. Age norms also exist regarding the best age for people to marry (Neugarten and Paterson, 1957). Social stratification is also associated with incidence of psychological disorders (Dohrenwend and Dohrenwend, 1969). For women who raise a family and then return to school or go to work, there are emerging social norms that affect

self-concept in roles as "a student again" or as someone beginning a "second career," that have an impact on self-concept in
general and self-confidence in particular. As these generalizations indicate, societal expectations and norms affect self-concept.

There is a general trend for self-concept to become more
negative from the fifties on through the seventies and eighties
(Kogan and Wallach, 1961). This trend is sometimes masked
by increased defensiveness. Associated characteristics include
submissiveness and self-belittling comments (Sward, 1945). Some
of the decline reflects lower levels of health, social interaction,
and economic condition by older adults (Mason, 1954). The
trends are usually gradual, however, with little appreciable
change occurring during a six-year period (Britton, 1963). In
a study based on Erikson's concepts of ego development for
older adults, age trends did not emerge. The emphasis was on
adaptive qualities of personality (Gruen, 1964). Some of the
shifts in self-concept for older men and women are in contrasting directions. Older men's self-concepts become more tolerant
of affiliative and nurturant tendencies and older women's self-
concepts become more tolerant of egocentric and aggressive
tendencies (Neugarten and Gutmann, 1958).

Developmental Sequences. In recent years there has
been a surge of scholarly attention to adulthood, following
earlier eras during which research on human development focused on childhood and then adolescence. Many aspects of adulthood have been analyzed, but particular attention has been
given to the evolving sense of self. A generation ago, this developmental process was being analyzed psychologically as ego
stage development during adulthood and sociologically as developmental tasks of adulthood (Erikson, 1950; Havighurst,
1957b). Gerontological research has steadily expanded tested
knowledge about older adults during the past generation. Recent efforts have concentrated on young adulthood and middle
age and have included perspectives from the humanities as well
as the social and behavioral sciences (Levinson and others, 1974;
Lowenthal, Thurnher, and others, 1975; Gould, 1975; Daedalus,
1976). Most of the recent analyses of the evolving sense of self

have been transactional in nature and have included attention to thinking and feeling, to acting, and to the societal setting.

Between adolescence and old age the sense of self can and often does change greatly. Although these changes are produced by some similar processes, adults become increasingly diverse in their outlooks and sense of who they are. Some young adults, as illustrated by the case study of Joseph Kidd, become more competent, confident, and fulfilled. Others with an inadequate sense of self and direction crumble under the stress of living and become institutionalized or commit suicide. Adults vary greatly in the specific tasks they assume and in the social structures they construct in the forms of family, work, and recreational groups. However, there is emerging evidence of developmental sequences that occur for many people during young adulthood and middle age. There is a tendency for many adults to become more tolerant of themselves, more understanding of personal and situational complexity, and more self-directed (Gould, 1975; Levinson and others, 1974, 1976). The following summary of such developmental sequences can serve two purposes for practitioners who work with adults: (1) to portray for some types of adults how an evolving sense of self is interconnected with personality, learning, performance, and context and how personal and situational blocks affect development; and (2) to illustrate the developmental process so that practitioners can use the related concepts to help other types of adults better understand their own developmental sequences, which may be quite different. The following summary is based mainly on studies of white collar men or working women between their late teens and sixties.

During the late teens, many young people are concerned about escape from parental domination and the emergence of an adult sense of identity. Their sense of themselves as trusting of others, industrious in school and work, and hopeful for the future reflects their earlier experiences in family and community. Such aspects of the functioning self can occur subconsciously and be reflected implicitly in choices that are made, as well as in conscious decisions. During early adolescence the family typically serves as a home base, psychologically as well as socially. Other institutions, such as college or the military, may replace the family during late adolescence as the main home base. Even so, for most late adolescents, leaving the family and shifting the balance toward institutional settings that have adult role expectations and reinforce an adult sense of self characterizes the developmental transition from adolescence to early young adulthood (Levinson and others, 1974; Gould, 1972, 1975; Erikson, 1976).

For some people, early young adulthood parallels the typical college years whether or not they attend college. During this period of growing independence and sense of adult identity, friends tend to be substituted for family. In addition to a transfer of functions formerly performed by the family to friends, the new friends who know the individual only as an adult help reinforce the individual's sense of adult self. The emerging sense of identity depends on the person's ability to make commitments freely and to honor them in spite of inevitable conflicts of loyalties. Confirming value systems and affirming friends facilitate this process. Many adolescents feel isolated, and mature love provides the basis for intimacy as the individual broadens the concern for self to include concern for others. As the young adult experiences mutual love and devotion, ethical concern is typically deepened. During this stage, many young adults establish an initial structure of participation composed mainly of family and work commitments. For half the young people in this age group, this structure of participation or set of societal commitments entails marriage. For most, it entails the exploratory and establishment phases of occupational choice, which may include educational preparation. Participation in religious, community, and recreational groups is also part of this structure. Occupational development and a sense of adult identity evolve and interact in a great variety of ways. For the young adult who has no stable occupation or major adult role, crossing the boundary between the family of adolescence and the fully adult world is a major developmental task, one that has psychological as well as economic consequences (Levinson and others, 1974; Gould, 1972, 1975; Erikson, 1976).

During the mid-twenties many white collar young

adults focus on building for a personal and professional future and on purposefully developing competence and specialized strengths. Some young people create adolescent dreams that give a sense of direction and aspiration to their lives. The decision to pursue valued goals entails the setting aside of other goals that cannot be pursued at the same time. This focusing and restricting tends to reduce time devoted to less-valued activities but also to deemphasize the playful and spontaneous. During the twenties, people tend to use friends less as substitutes for their adolescent family as their sense of identity and self-reliance enables them to enter into more mutual interpersonal relationships (Gould, 1972, 1975; Erikson, 1976).

The period of the late twenties and most of the thirties tends to be characterized by settling down, order, and striving. The complexity of both personality and structure of participation typically expands. Adolescent dreams, or other goals and aspirations, are influential regarding the culmination that is hoped for in the forties and the parts of oneself that are left out in order to focus one's efforts. This period also tends to be accompanied by increasing marital disillusionment as the young adult yearns for greater acceptance as a person. For many white collar young adults it is a period of current denial to achieve future benefits (Levinson and others, 1974; Gould, 1975; Erikson, 1976).

The late thirties and early forties is a period of quiet urgency for many adults, and a time for reorientation of outlook and activity. There is a growing awareness of problems associated with physical condition and health for oneself and others and a general decline in personal comfort. Some of the abstract commitments and aspirations that were formed in adolescence and young adulthood begin to wane. During this period most adults become more eager to share the joys and sorrows of human experience, and the quality of friendships becomes more important. The earlier sense of adult self that largely reflected role relationships as worker, spouse, and parent seems inadequate. The reexamination of the fit between the current sense of self and the structure of participation that evolved leads to the mid-life transition that is becoming increasingly widespread. This transition is reflected in an increase in work reentry by mothers whose children are older, by the second peak in the divorce rate during this period, and by major mid-career shifts for many white collar workers. Being one's own person seems to be especially salient to one's sense of self during this period. Personal recognition for one's accomplishments is typically quite important, and realization or frustration regarding specific desired forms of recognition tends to have broad symbolic significance for some people that greatly affects their sense of self-worth. Earlier caring for the young tends to be widened to encompass societal caring.

The transition that tends to occur around age forty is well illustrated by the relationship between the mentor and mentee or apprentice. Some young men in white collar occupations encounter somewhat more established members of the occupational field who provide orientation, advice, criticism, assistance, and sponsorship. The mentor tends to be about ten years older than the mentee, and in a role such as teacher, supervisor, or more experienced coworker establishes a big brother relationship. Many young men never have a mentor relationship, and few have more than three or four. They mostly last a few years, seldom more than ten; and few mentees or apprentices are over forty. Outgrowing the mentee relationship and becoming one's own person seems to be a normal but often difficult developmental process. Although a mentor relationship can end gradually and become a more modest friendship, more often it is terminated by forced separation or increasing conflict that leaves an aftermath of ill will. However, the separation can enhance the process of internalization of the valued qualities of the mentor by the mentee. In some instances, major values of the relationship occur for the mentee after it ends, but only if the relationship was fruitful. The likelihood of becoming a mentor appears to be small unless one was a mentee. After age forty, the likelihood of being in the mentee role decreases sharply, and the likelihood of being in the mentor role continues to increase at least through the forties. This in part reflects a shift in the sense of self (Levinson and others, 1974). For young women, a similar mentor relationship may develop in relation to work settings, but a dimension of heterosexual relationships is added. For many working women, there are few female role models who can serve as mentors. Most of the people who are in a position in the occupational field to serve as mentors are men. As a result, fewer women benefit from mentor relationships, and when they do, mentor and affectional relationships tend to become intertwined (Sheehy, 1976).

Between the mid-forties and the early sixties the variability in the sense of self continues to increase. In instances in which the period around age forty was characterized by quiet urgency, many people have accomplished some form of mid-life transition regarding family, work, or community; and there has been a restabilization. Many experience a sense of "arrival" characterized by stability, maturity, competence, and responsibility (Neugarten, 1968). This sense of personal control begins to decline gradually about age fifty or fifty-five. A shift in time orientation tends to occur during this period, in which the individual thinks of him or herself as someone who has used up much of their time allotment. For some, time remaining until death becomes more salient than time spent since birth (Jaques, 1965; Neugarten, 1968). Many experience a shift in interests and activities that are in the direction of the stereotype for the opposite sex. Increasing awareness of decline in physical condition and health increases the salience of mortality. The quest for the adolescent dream has been replaced by protection of gains. Under favorable personal and societal conditions, the older adult is able to extract wisdom from the mental struggle between a sense of integrity and a sense of despair about the meaning and worth of one's life. Such wisdom reflects a detached yet active concern with life in the face of physical decline and death (Back, 1971; Levinson and others, 1974; Gould, 1975; Erikson, 1976). During the first two thirds of life the sense of self tends to develop outwardly, incorporating expectations of others and reactions to accomplishment in external settings. During the final third the focus tends to shift inward to more personal concerns and intrapsychic relationships.

Adult life cycle variability related to self-concept also occurs among lower-middle-class adults in which most of the women are full-time or part-time homemakers (Lowenthal, Thurnher, and others, 1975). The self-images of men and women tend to differ both in their substantive content and in the course of their development during adulthood. Women tend to value the ideal traits of assertiveness and competitiveness less than men do. Even women who desire to possess more of these attributes usually desire them as a supplement rather than a replacement of traditional roles and relationships. Self-criticism tends to be relatively stable during most of adulthood, but lower-middle-class women are typically more critical of themselves than men. This greater intensity of self-criticism among women seems to reflect their greater dependence on the assessment of significant others, in contrast with men's greater reliance on instrumental performance for their self-image. There is also some indication that women more readily acknowledge their shortcomings, whereas men tend to deny them.

Between late adolescence and the onset of old age there are some distinct shifts related to the self-concept of lower-middle-class men. From late adolescence to the early young adult period, men tend to experience a change from a discontented and insecure self-image and concern about inadequate perseverance to a self-image characterized by greater confidence and by diffuse and at times uncontrolled energy to be expended in diverse pursuits. The self-concept of middle-aged men reflects orderliness and control, industry but caution. Men during the preretirement period tend to perceive themselves as less driving and hostile but more reasonable and mellow than younger men.

Newlywed young women perceive their personal qualities in ways that are similar to the self-perceptions of older women. Two exceptions that probably reflect the expectations and insecurities of their recent marriage are greater warmth and jealousy. For middle-aged women greater situational distress seems to be reflected in greater reference to unhappiness and absentmindedness in their self-descriptions. During the preretirement period, women perceive themselves as more assertive and less dependent and helpless. Although for much of adulthood the self-image of men becomes increasingly crystallized while many women continue to have uncertainties, during the preretirement period many women appear to have resolved concerns about independence, competence, and interpersonal relations (Lowenthal, Thurnher, and others, 1975).

For adults generally, transitions in self-concept can occur throughout life as a stable sense of self supported by habit and external expectations changes in response to internal or external pressures. When an identity crisis occurs during late adolescence when many peers are also establishing a sense of adult identity, the experience can be exhilarating. Societal acceptance of this stage of life as a moratorium period during which many young people examine inherited values, pursue dreams, and develop personal convictions aided by peer support helps many people to confront feelings of uncertainty and aloneness. For those who draw back, the identity issues are likely to erupt at a later time. Those who resolve the transition in self-concept tend to be better able to do so at subsequent stages of adulthood.

The sense of self and direction formed in young adulthood tends to be single minded. The inner uncertainties of adolescence combined with the outer multiplicity of alternatives encourage young people to suppress aspirations and dimensions of self that seem to conflict with the chosen path through adulthood. Commitment to the role or the goal seems to require that the individual accentuate the positive and eliminate the negative. The negative can include both the strictures of conscience and the unwelcome dimensions of self such as fear and weakness that are so unsettling when we want to feel confident.

The gap between actual and ideal self is often a source of concern. Too little discrepancy between performance and expectations for oneself can lead to stagnation for lack of aspiration. Too great concern about the perceived discrepancy can lead to inadequate disclosure, which contributes to a personal self-concept that differs from the image of the individual held by others, and this interferes with both being and becoming. Especially during middle age, a moderate gap between actual and ideal self provides impetus and direction for continuing personal growth (Beiser, 1971; Lowenthal, Thurnher, and others, 1975).

During late adolescence and early young adulthood, the shoulds and should nots of conscience have a major impact on self-concept. Many parental and societal admonitions and prohibitions are incorporated in the sense of self, and because they are mostly unexamined, they are not easily modified. In childhood and adolescence, parent figures typically reinforce the conscience. Circumstances and conscience encourage a young person to suppress some aspects of self in the process of forming an adult identity. When a spouse or mentor becomes a replacement parent figure, the young adult is discouraged from developing a more autonomous adult sense of self.

Major issues of conscience and identity that individuals have not resolved by their mid-twenties are likely to erupt during the late thirties or early forties. Maturity, defined as stability and integration of self-concept, tends to be consistently predictive of subsequent occupational adaptation (Heath, 1976). Even among college men selected for psychological good health, there is much fluctuation in psychological adjustment, and major mid-life reassessments and transitions are widespread (Vaillant, 1971; Vaillant and McArthur, 1972). At any stage of adulthood, the fragments of the sense of self that result from an identity crisis or transition become the building blocks for a reintegration that should enable an individual to become a more fully functioning person.

Application by Practitioners. Practitioners can use generalizations about typical adult life cycle shifts in self-concept to help adult clients understand their experience and plan programs and services that are responsive to needs related to personality development. There is evidence that shifts in the sense of self are reflected in the reasons adults participate in educational programs (Boyd, 1961; Boyd and Koskela, 1970).

A critical aspect of one's general outlook and personality, and one that combines elements of self-concept and decision making, is the balance that the individual achieves between action and contemplation. There is a long history of tension between these two poles of human endeavor, and of efforts to combine them. The action pole includes attention to initiative, work, assertiveness, and defense of beliefs worth fighting for. The contemplation pole includes attention to reflection, knowledge, passivity, receptivity, enjoyment, humility, and loving surrender. Sometimes individuals and entire societies have concluded that they must select one of these poles, and they typically reflect this conviction in their sense of self. However, there have been some prominent leaders of the past who have combined major elements of action and contemplation. In their efforts to realize ethical action in the world, they have questioned the status quo and helped create a new one. Confucius, Gandhi, and Jefferson are well-known examples of people who have combined contemplation and action (Bellah, 1976; Erikson, 1976).

Thomas Jefferson was a singularly inspiring and American exemplar of a person who combined action and contemplation (Erikson, 1974). He was protean in the excellence he achieved as he alternated among roles as farmer, architect, statesman, and scholar. However, his sense of self was evident as he made firm commitments that he pursued competently.

Some of Jefferson's sense of self was inherited. Aspects of his inheritance were evident, such as his tall, lanky stature and sensitive features and his family wealth. Other aspects were less immediately evident, such as a fierce independence of spirit, a belief in self-improvement through work and study, and a passion to analyze the details of the immediate and to survey the prospects of the distant. As with each new generation, Jefferson's conscience was implanted in the helplessness of childhood and contained elements of guilt as well as compliance with the values of generations past. A shaping influence on his sense of self and of political functioning was his idea that the ideal size of a communal group (township or neighborhood) was one that enabled each person to be part of a network of direct personal and communal communication with the power to persuade others in matters that influenced their daily lives.

However, Jefferson's sense of the importance of the active present was reflected in his belief that the earth belongs always to the living. This concern for the sovereignty of the living generation included a concern for the influence of the present on the future. He urged that adults consider their actions in part as examples that influence the values and practices of the young. Inhumane actions were seen as damaging the self and witnesses as well as the victim. He believed that an informed love of humanity was necessary to help a person to overcome his or her worst self.

Jefferson was aware of his higher self and his lower self. His higher self reflected the historical and contemporary figures whom he admired and whose wisdom and power he tried to emulate. This included the parent figures whose admonishing and punishing became incorporated into his conscience. His lower self reflected those qualities that were small and weak and sick and that were sometimes pursued with conspiratorial pleasure until checked by the higher self. In the self and in others, the qualities of the lower self provide something to be against in contrast with something to be for in striving to achieve the higher self.

For Jefferson, as for other people, the sense of adult self helps to balance more than the higher and lower self. Other balances include past and future, inner and outer, joining and opposing, symbolic and passionate, work and play. Especially for someone like Jefferson, who not only was engaged in the formation of a personal sense of self but also was instrumental in the formulation of a collective sense of political and social selfhood during a time of transition, it was important to be able to validate events in the societal context, the evolving sense of self, and their interaction. Erikson suggests three sources of validation: (1) verifiable observations and facts that are logically arranged; (2) a sense of reality in which old and new experiences are emotionally confirmed; and (3) active participation in personal, family, occupational, political, and social activities that are affirmed by consensual validation. In short, people can validate their sense of self by knowing, by feeling, and by doing.

Although Jefferson and similarly gifted people seem to thrive on protean possibilities, there is a more modest parallel with the developmental process of many young people as they experience a variety of roles and ways of thinking as vehicles for personal growth and an adult sense of self. Jefferson's example seems to suggest an approach to personality development that fits the current era of rapid social change: adjusting to overwhelming change by adopting a stance of deliberate changeability. Those who have the courage of their convictions and are able to deal with complexity but are open to their subconscious resources may learn to take the initiative in dealing with change and find a new sense of centrality and originality in the flux of our time. Jefferson illustrates how competent adult role models can help a person balance a conscience shared with past generations, with ideal images of a new reality. As the adult of any age alternates between action and contemplation, both understanding and productivity are affected and the human personality continues to evolve (Erikson, 1974).

For the practitioner who works with adults, there is ample evidence that the sense of self evolves throughout adulthood. It is influenced by experiences that occurred during childhood and by experiences that occur during each period of adulthood. Generalizations regarding the evolving sense of self provide the practitioner with optimism about the modifiability of adult personality, with indications of the powerful influence that role changes can have on the sense of self, and with understanding of the developmental process that can enable the practitioner to help adults learn, adapt, and grow. Such understanding is especially important when adults seek assistance to achieve learning objectives that entail modification of feelings.

Practitioners who understand shifting concerns about self can better help adult clients understand them and use external resources and assistance to cope with them (Bugental, 1967; Jourard, 1974; Patterson, 1973). For example, the preoccupation with self during childhood and adolescence is widely recognized. From adolescence through young adulthood there is a trend for people to transcend their preoccupation with self and increasingly relate to others in their own right, to deepen interests, to humanize values, and to expand caring (Erikson, 1976). For young adults who experience difficulty because they have not successfully made such transitions, practitioners can help them to reflect on their aspirations, behavior, and satisfactions related to interpersonal relations, can identify educational activities on interpersonal relations in which they might participate, and can encourage them to engage in relationships in which effective concern for others is likely to be reinforced (Boyd, 1961; Arieti, 1967; Felker, 1974).

The relation between concern for self and concern for others can be highlighted in the process of making life decisions such as a job change, a return to school, a move to a new community, early retirement, or assumption of a major public responsibility. Adults vary greatly in the relative priority they give their own preferences in relation to the preferences of others. Many people know their own preferences, but some ignore the preferences of others, some seek the approval of others in preference to their own concerns, and some take the preferences of others into account along with their own. Still other people are uncertain about their own preferences and take their leads from others.

Practitioners sometimes try to help adults, especially those who are greatly influenced by the expectations of others, to increase their sense of self, values, feelings, and preferences. Many procedures for making contact with one's true self have been advanced over the years. The following were selected because they require a minimum of external assistance (Gendlin, 1964; Stevens, 1971).

Be willing to devote time to unstructured solitude. Our inner feelings that we should be doing something constructive, when combined with external demands, make it difficult to set aside periods of solitude in which to discover our thoughts and feelings, to know ourselves.

Be willing to daydream and speculate. By allowing our minds to wander on the edge of fantasy, we can discover much about ourselves and our desires that we usually censor. Daydreams are not reality, but they can encourage innovation and flexible problem solving. By guiding our dreams of what might be, we can help clarify priorities, explore plans to achieve some of our dreams, and sustain our motivation to persevere.

Be willing to be reflective, to consider strengths and

weaknesses, along with problems and opportunities and a sense of direction. One way to focus on important questions is to freely list the phrases that come to mind to complete sentences that begin with phrases such as "I'd like to," "I choose to," "I have to," "I won't," "I'm afraid to," or "I can't." Then examine the types of responses in each list. Could any of the phrases in the "I choose to" list be interchanged with phrases in the "I have to" list? What does this suggest about the extent to which personal priorities are influential? Or consider instances in which you said "yes" or "no" when you really wanted to say the opposite. Reflect on why you did so, what you gained and lost by doing so, and what the consequences were for yourself and others. Knowing why we say yes and no helps us to be our own persons.

Be willing to express your feelings to help discover them. Many feelings become more defined and susceptible to change as we disclose them to others who are caring and accepting. In the process, implicit meanings are revealed and we can sometimes attain even greater understanding.

Other instances in which practitioners help adults gain a greater sense of self are efforts to assist older adults to achieve greater life satisfaction. Individual or group psychotherapy can be beneficial (Truax and Carkhuff, 1967; Wolff, 1959, 1966; Oberleder, 1966; Isaacs, 1967; Yalom and Terrazas, 1968). Usually, however, assistance is provided by family, friends, and practitioners from many of the helping professions. Some conditions for high morale for the elderly, which with slight modifications would apply to most adults (Clark and Anderson, 1967), are some activity that provides for an intense involvement with life, in part to avoid preoccupation with death; sufficient autonomy to sustain a sense of personal integrity; sufficient personal comfort related to mind, body, and physical environment; satisfactory relationships with others, some of whom can provide assistance without losing respect; stimulation of the imagination in ways that do not overburden stamina; and sufficient mobility to permit variety.

Practitioners who use a transactional model of personality functioning take into account ways in which adult experience influences personality and ways in which personality influences the selection and perception of experience. In some instances practitioners may want to help clients recognize how other people and external events contribute to their development and to persuade them to be open to new experiences. In other instances, practitioners may want to help clients be themselves and avoid overdependence on others. Deepening one's understanding of oneself and broadening one's experience through friendship are both valuable processes of growth. So is deciding on whether to shift the balance toward self or others. Practitioners can assist by encouraging clients to use an increased understanding of their past to deal more effectively with the present and plan for the future. Practitioners can also help clients understand and cope with their emotional needs, some of which entail interpersonal relations. For example, for many adults a sense of well-being depends in part on having at least one person as a confidant. Over the years, the individual's pattern of friendships changes as family and friends move and die and drift away, and as children grow up. As this occurs, important confidant relationships may be lost but, like "the pea in the old shell game," the individual may not notice. In such circumstances, a practitioner can help a client recognize that this important relationship is missing and explore ways to replace or establish it.

Decision Making

The executive function of personality consists of making decisions and choices. The decision-making process is both explicit and implicit, and it is critical when there is conflict among the alternatives. It is reflected in self-awareness, selectivity, mastery, assertiveness, self-directedness, influence on the environment, and goal setting.

Part of the executive function of personality is intentional and is reflected in deliberate goal setting, in which pursuit of an objective or goal provides a meaning and purpose to life and can contribute to personality integration (Frankl, 1963; Lowenthal, 1971; Land, 1973). Human striving is varied in extent, direction, and satisfaction. For some people, striving seems to be unrealistic, contradictory, fragmenting, and unsatisfying. For other people, striving seems to be effective, fulfilling, and integrating. Some goals are specific, and it is apparent when they are achieved. Some goals reflect a more generalized achievement motive that is manifested in various forms of productivity (McClelland, Atkinson, and others, 1953). Early in life, goals tend to reflect basic needs and awareness of limited resources and opportunities in the societal context. Some adults pursue complex and long-term goals. Adults who effectively pursue goals and achieve fulfillment tend to learn from the past to decide in the present what will benefit the future.

Buhler developed a rationale and a life goal inventory to explain the following four tendencies or dimensions around which she believes life goals cluster (Buhler and Massarik, 1968): (1) need satisfaction (love, family, sex, self-gratification); (2) self-limiting adaptation (caution, adaptiveness, submissiveness, avoidance of hardships); (3) creative expansion (self-development, power, fame); and (4) upholding of internal order (moral values, political or religious commitments). In contrast with less well-adjusted and integrated adults, adults who function well tend to have goal patterns characterized by love, concern for the welfare of others, awareness of reality, acceptance of reasonable limitations and hardships, and belief in their own self-realization. Buhler views personality as undergoing an expansion and contraction throughout life in which need satisfaction goals occur early and provide the conditions for creative expansion goals. She also believes that emphasis on upholding the internal order occurs later in life and that attention to self-limiting adaptation occurs more during adolescence and old age. However, fulfillment at any age requires favorable goal patterns, and it is the emphasis that changes developmentally.

Many of those people who have studied adult personality have concluded that most adults lack life goals that enable their striving and deciding to be effective, fulfilling, and integrating. For most adults, choosing and deciding tends to be implicit (Kohn, 1969; Lowenthal, 1971). It appears that from late adolescence through middle age, and for some adults through old age, people become more aware of and likely to use their experience. This use of experience occurs in relation to the shifting sense of self that often accompanies major role changes, such as marriage, career changes, death of spouse, and retirement. It also occurs in relation to the ways in which the individual structures and restructures his or her social world and deals with major themes, such as time, love, work, and death. During young adulthood and into middle age, self-concept as it relates to impulses, coping, and competence typically assumes that the environment rewards boldness and risk taking and that the self has the energy and mastery needed to deal with any opportunities. Around the forties, there is often an increase in reflection, stock taking, introspection, and restructuring of experience and time orientation as the adult realizes that the future toward which adolescent dreams were aimed is now. Beyond sixty many adults perceive their environment as complex and dangerous and of themselves as increasingly passive, as people who conform to and accommodate external demands. These changes are mainly reflected in the adult's inner world orientation as there are shifts from active to passive mastery and to greater interiority. For relatively healthy adults through their seventies, actual coping, adaptation, and social behavior generally depend mainly on the selection and application of well-established habit patterns that change little with age.

An example of a gradual change in the self-awareness and choice-making and mastery process occurs in the area of interpersonal relationships. Between adolescence and young adulthood, many people overcome some of the anxiety and defenses that interfere with interpersonal relationships. As a result, there is a shift away from some of the impulsive inconsiderateness that often reflects an extreme concern with personal feelings and behavior that interferes with a clear perception of the behavior or feelings of others. As the individual's identity stabilizes and as experience with adult interaction accumulates, the individual often becomes more friendly and respectful and less burdened by inappropriate reactions from the past. The results are more varied and flexible responses, greater attention to subtle behavior and feelings in others, and more readiness to make allowances. At this stage the individual relates to others as persons in their own right. It becomes possible to view parents and peers more objectively and to express warm and emphatic appreciation as well as dispassionate criticisms and assertiveness (R. W. White, 1961).

Another aspect of personality change during adulthood that is related to decision making is autonomy, in contrast with an other-directed locus of control. Some behavior is reactive in that the individual responds to the initiatives of others and to circumstances in the societal context. Reactive behavior tends to be responsive or at least to be influenced by the expectations and goals of others. Some behavior is proactive in that individuals initiate and seek to implement their goals. Proactive behavior tends to be action oriented and goal directed, as in various forms of leadership. Every adult engages in some proactive and in some reactive behaviors, and the balance and tension between the two is strongly related to general personality patterns, especially in relation to decision making. Prevailing stereotypes portray some categories of people as more reactive in orientation, such as children, women, and the elderly. The stereotype of men and the middle aged is mainly proactive. In reality there are typically substantial variations in the extent of proactive and reactive behavior across types of activities. A young child may be proactive in demanding food and attention but reactive in strange social situations. A blue collar worker may be reactive in a work situation in which he or she feels powerless but proactive in a favorite recreational activity. A homemaker may be reactive in a family setting but proactive in a community organization. A business executive may be proactive on the job before retirement but reactive in the family afterwards. Perhaps wisdom consists of knowing when and how to be effectively proactive and reactive from situation to situation.

One of the main transitions from adolescence to young adulthood is the shift from dependence on parental or other influences to greater personal autonomy. Aspects of increasing autonomy include personal locus of control, assumption of responsibility, and ability to take risks. The main influences on a child's decision making are external, in the form of personal admonitions, institutional expectations, and societal norms. Because many of the circumstances and alternatives are considered by these other people, the individual tends to deal with decision making absolutely in terms of right or wrong. The shift to more autonomous adult responsibility for decision making typically entails relativistic consideration of alternatives and criteria for selection of the course of action that is consistent with the individual's own values.

Shifts in autonomy, relativism, commitment, and proactive behavior occur during adolescence and adulthood in family, occupation, and community. The late adolescent college student assumes greater responsibility for considering alternative courses, deciding on personal priorities, and dealing with the uncertainty and risk that is entailed. A woman in her late thirties who had been proactive and focused in relation to the upbringing of her young children feels increasingly reactive and directionless as they grow up and leave home. A few years later the same woman may attain the greatest sense of commitment and autonomy in her life as she becomes actively engaged in career or community activities. Retirement can contribute to greater dependence and reactive behavior and feelings of loss of control.

This type of shift in the locus of control and the contribution that can be made by a practitioner are illustrated by career development and career counseling. Many formulations that are used for diagnosis and assistance regarding occupational choice and adjustment entail the stages of exploration, choice, and implementation. At the exploration stage, the practitioner assists an adult who is interested in occupational entry, reentry, or change to consider a range of alternatives so that the selected course of action is as desirable as possible. This typically entails consideration of personal preferences and abilities as well as available career opportunities. Especially for adults who have internalized societal stereotypes, an important contribution of the practitioner can be to encourage the client to dream a bit and find out about and entertain a broader range of alternatives than might otherwise be considered. As the client considers several courses of action, the practitioner can help the client foresee the likely consequences of each choice. Sometimes a practitioner can be especially helpful and supportive as a client deals with the uncertainty, risk, and adjustments entailed in the implementation of a selected course of action. This may be especially so for the client whose past orientation to decision making has been directionless, dependent, absolute, and reactive (*Counseling Psychologist*, 1976).

There has been some study of self-directed personal change, mainly with young adults. When college undergraduate and graduate students between the ages of twenty and thirty-five participated in a project in which they engaged in diagnosis of a personal problem, goal setting, and personal efforts to change themselves, some were successful and some were unsuccessful in that a low amount of personal change was achieved. When the low-change young adults were asked to identify personal goals, they dealt mainly with the current self and seemed to be closed to other possibilities. In addition to their limited recognition of alternative possibilities, the low-change young adults were more tentative about themselves, more closed-minded generally, and gave more evidence of identity diffusion, such as indecisiveness, vagueness about how they were perceived by others, and the sense of playing an artificial role. Because there was little recognition of discrepancies between present behavior and desired changed behavior as reflected in an ideal or future goal, there was little dissonance or gap between current and changed circumstances and thus little motivation to change. More of the high-change young adults stated goals with implicit recognition that they had not been attained. More of them indicated a desire to attain a goal, and phrased goal statements conditionally by expressing simultaneous awareness of two dissonant elements, the current self and the goal. One way in which the person can reduce the dissonance is to change present behavior so that the gap is narrowed between the current and the ideal (Winter and others, 1968; Kolb and others, 1968). There is some evidence that adults can become more self-directed in the achievement of personal change.

During the past generation there has been a rapidly increasing number of practitioners who have sought to assist adults to become more self-directed, especially regarding interpersonal relations. Such programs have focused on human relations, communications, sensitivity, and assertiveness. Many programs have included encouragement for the adult client to recognize discrepancies between present and changed circumstances and to gain commitment and procedures to close the gap. Practitioners can acquire competence to facilitate this process or can refer clients to others who can.

Adults vary greatly in the deliberateness of their goal setting and in the extent to which they want to become more self-directed. Only a small portion of this variability is associated with age, such as the shift from active to passive mastery. However, many adults reach a point in their life when they conclude that they would like to become more self-directed in their priority setting and decision making. Fortunately, there is evidence that adults can become more decisive and assertive if they want to. Also, practitioners have available some procedures to help adults become more self-directed (Arieti, 1972; Biggs, 1973; Branden, 1972; Browne, 1973; Lakein, 1973; O'Neill and O'Neill, 1974).

Effective decision making is the result of many factors, including clear specification of the issue to be decided, accurate diagnosis of major facilitators and barriers in the situation, fit between personal values and those of others affected by the decision, the extent to which the decision maker is self-directed, and the effectiveness of the process used for priority setting and decision making. Self-directed decision making takes other people and their preferences into account, but these external influences and expectations are balanced with the values and priorities of the individual. An assertive adult is willing to assume some responsibility for helping to shape and implement decisions that affect his or her life. Otherwise major decisions are made by others or by default and the individual mainly reacts. An active and self-directed approach to life entails the addition of aspiration and commitment to status and ability, which enables the individual to transcend limitations. Active efforts to grow and develop are aided greatly by the individual's sense of values and priorities. At a fork in the road, it is difficult to know which direction is preferable if you do not know where you are going. This sense of direction is especially important because priorities shift during adulthood.

Practitioners can help adults become more self-directed by encouraging them to become more proficient in such activities as values clarification and priority setting (Miller, 1974). Some techniques for doing so can be easily understood from reading and readily developed by discussion, ranking priorities, and adjusting time and effort to fit shifting priorities. For example, a client can list ten to twenty top priorities related to self, others, and creative activities. By transferring to a middle priority list those items that are important but not essential, an adult can produce a high-priority list of commitments and aspirations. Each of these priorities deserves time and effort, even if this conflicts with other high-priority items or even the elimination of lower priority activities. Shifts of time and effort toward emerging high priorities at the expense of activities of declining priority usually reflect development.

With a clearer understanding of their values and priorities, clients can reflect on the utility of the decision-making process they typically use for life decisions. Although most adults have developed a distinctive approach to decision making, many of the lists of steps for successful decision making suggest modifications that can increase self-directedness. Following are some typical suggestions:

1. If possible, select a time for decision making when you feel most optimistic and prepared to deal with the decision.
2. Obtain information that is relevant to the decision so that you understand what the problem really is.
3. Explore the problem when it is of active concern,

but, if possible, delay the decision until it can be put in perspective. Especially avoid major decisions in the heat of anger or the depths of despair.

4. Consider both the evident alternatives and the novel ones that may be the most satisfactory.
5. Analyze the consequences of the major alternatives for you and for others to identify the most promising solutions.
6. Select the most desirable and feasible alternative by taking into account your priorities as well as other factors.
7. Make a commitment of time, effort, and willingness to deal with risk to implement the decision.
8. Realize that a decision may have to be changed after a fair trial, so have a contingency plan in case it does not work out.

The growing sense by many middle-aged adults that the future is now reflects a change in time orientation regarding the past as well as the future. The global reassessment that many experience around age forty is similar to the reconsideration of priorities and options that occur for many major change events. However, adults sometimes react to prospects of change not with optimism and action but with alarm and inertia. Practitioners can assist by helping adults overcome barriers to action. Following are four suggestions that practitioners can make to help clients deal with change in a way that encourages growth:

1. Recognize that the general approach to the new or the different can become a self-fulfilling prophecy. A positive attitude and self-confidence can turn an uncertain situation into success. A defeatist attitude contains the seeds of defeat. Selective perception enables us to easily confirm the preconceived idea, as illustrated by the person who says, "I expect the worst from people and am seldom disappointed."
2. Try to overcome the fear associated with the new, the

difficult, or the unknown by putting the apprehension in perspective. Ask yourself, "What is the worst thing that can happen?" Consider also how likely that is and what can be done to minimize its occurrence. There are usually enough real and likely problems in a major change without disabling ourselves by worrying about unlikely ones.

3. Focus on past successes. Self-confidence can be increased by reviewing similar instances that have been successful and by considering what seemed to contribute to that success.

4. When making a major change, try to retain stability in other parts of your life. Continuity and predictability in domains not necessarily affected by a change provide the basis for a sense of security that contributes to the strength and perspective to deal with adjustments related to the change. If clients recognize this, they can make an effort to stabilize other domains during a period of change.

Attitudes

People have attitudes or feelings about themselves, about what they attempt to accomplish, and about the people, things, and circumstances in their societal context. Attitudes are the residue of past experience in the form of inclinations or feelings that predispose a person in the choice of activities, companions, and locations. Attitudes reflect internal and external influences, and they shift over time as the individual interacts with the environment. Internal influences on attitudes include biological drives such as hunger and subconscious motives related to affiliation. The internal energy and drives aroused or stimulated by experience and opportunities for experience might be termed motivation or needs. A need is a gap perceived by an individual or others between a present and a changed set of circumstances. External influences on attitudes include societal norms that become internalized as values; the press of images and expectations of significant others, reference groups, institutions, and community; and the opportunity system as perceived by the individual.

Values tend to be generalized, are usually internalized without conscious effort early in life, and are implicit in people's more apparent attitudes and choices. Values are one influence on interests that develop. Interests are demonstrated preferences for activity in which personal tendencies and competencies are absorbed in an interaction with ideas, people, or objects. People invest themselves in activities because of the attractiveness of the process and the anticipated outcomes or goals, but the relative emphasis between process and outcomes varies greatly. Interests tend to move forward and to wax and wane. If the sequence is experience, dissatisfaction, disinclination, and avoidance, the likely result is a decline in interest. If the sequence is participation, satisfaction, mastery, predisposition, involvement, and accomplishment, the likely result is an increase in interest. As interests deepen, increased competence and understanding tend to extend the goals that are seen as attractive. During adulthood, interests and attitudes tend to be stable over the months but to change and evolve over the years.

Biological drives and physiologically related needs are relatively influential on the performance of those who are very young, very old, or in ill health. However, most of the needs, motives, and interests that influence adult performance result from interaction with the physical and social environment and reflect the adult's feelings about that context. The movement from childhood and adolescence to young adulthood typically entails an expansion of caring. In this process the person extends his or her sense of self to incorporate a deep concern for the welfare of others (R. W. White, 1961). In doing so, the individual transcends a preoccupation with self and becomes an organic part of something greater, which in the instance of concern for the next generation is a sense of generativity.

Some needs and motives are especially important aspects of personality and are major influences on performance during adulthood, vary substantially among adults, are relatively stable within individuals over the years, but tend to follow some predictable adult life cycle shifts. Examples of such needs and motives include affiliation, achievement, expansion, and defense.

Affiliation. The need for affiliation with other people is widespread. It is reflected in informal interaction with friends and neighbors as well as in formal participation in organizations. The strength of the need for affiliation during adulthood is somewhat associated with life cycle shifts but even more so with individual differences among people and contrasts between accustomed level of interaction and current opportunities.

Needs for affiliation and expectations regarding extent of social interaction evolve during childhood and adolescence and are greatly affected by the socialization process. Some family and neighborhood settings which provide satisfying opportunities for interpersonal activity can interact with strong personal needs for reassurance and variety with the result that the individual enters adulthood with a high level of need for affiliation. As a result, the individual's feelings of well-being depend greatly on being around other people who provide social-emotional support and a sense of security. Deprivation of social interaction or an inadequate sense of autonomy and identity can also contribute to a high compensatory need for affiliation. Some settings that provide moderate opportunities for interpersonal activity, such as can occur in some rural areas, can interact with a strong sense of identity that reflects autonomy and industry, which together contribute to a low need for affiliation. However, the individual's level of self-esteem may be so low due to feelings of mistrust and inferiority that gratification of the need for affiliation may be blocked by a fear of rejection.

As a result of energy level, self-concept, and accustomed level of social interaction, people enter adulthood with widely varying levels of need for affiliation. During most of adulthood, variability in need for affiliation mainly reflects these individual differences, and age is not a major factor. During the period of late adolescence and early young adulthood, the need for affiliation tends to be somewhat higher, mainly reflecting the active search for identity, intimacy, and career during that period, which often entails interaction with other people. During old age, the need for affiliation tends to be somewhat lower, mainly reflecting a drop in energy level and an increasing proportion of energy required for personal functioning.

There are times and circumstances during adulthood when people experience a sharp change in their opportunities for social interaction. For example, young women with young children tend to have greatly reduced opportunities to interact with other adults, and the same thing happens to many older men at the time of retirement. The typical response to the deprivation in social interaction is an increase in need for affiliation. If the lower level of social interaction is extended for years, the lowered level of accustomed interaction that typically results is reflected in a reduction in expectations and need for affiliation.

Achievement.   The need for achievement is also widespread and has been extensively studied in the United States and in other national settings. As with affiliation, need for achievement reflects both personal characteristics, such as levels of energy and ability, and societal characteristics, such as national values regarding productivity and community opportunities for productive effort. The individual's need for achievement is influenced by past experience and optimism about the future. Workers who are optimistic about their chances for promotion are far more likely to invest time and effort to increase their competence. Adults vary in level of need for achievement, but there is also a general gradual decline past middle age. Part of the decline reflects somewhat higher levels of need for achievement by white collar adults who constitute a higher proportion of young adults than by blue collar adults who constitute a higher proportion of older adults (McClelland, Atkinson, and others, 1953; Veroff, Atkinson, and others, 1960). College-bound young adults tend to have higher levels of need for achievement than non-college-bound young adults, but the distribution of need for achievement for non-college-bound young adults is comparable to the distribution for the total adult population (Knox, 1970). The association with age is stronger than the association with educational level, but in cross-sectional studies the age comparisons also include differences in level of formal education. Part of the lower level of need for achievement by older adults reflects their lower average educational level.

The need for achievement by college-educated women tends to follow a cyclical pattern related to the family life cycle. A high need for achievement before the childbearing and rearing period declines while the children are young but then increases to the previous high level when the children are grown (Baruch, 1967). In addition to relationships between family and occupational roles, motives related to achievement of college-educated women reflect societal expectations and stereotypes of success and femininity (Horner, 1972; Hoffman, 1974).

Expansion. During young adulthood there are several related trends regarding achievement, expansion, values, and interests. During four years of college, many students develop a more intellectual orientation involving originality, confidence, and independence of thought (Feldman and Newcomb, 1969). This trend reflects partly the press of the college environment and partly the developmental trends for non-college-bound young adults as well (Trent and Medsker, 1968; Knox, 1970). There is also evidence of a trend toward more liberal attitudes on social issues between young adulthood and middle age (Nelson, 1954, 1956). This longitudinal trend that occurs for typical students after graduation runs contrary to the trend for many of the more radical college students whose attitudes tend to become more conservative during the following decade.

During young adulthood, especially for college graduates there is evidence of a deepening of interests, a humanizing of values, and an expansion of caring. As an interest develops, it tends to encourage activities and to facilitate increased competence related to the interest. Especially for interests related to science or the arts, the interests begin early and often develop into vocational or major avocational pursuits. The deepening of an interest is reflected not only in amount of time spent but also in the quality of attention, in persistence of effort, and in extent of intrinsic satisfaction. Many interests and values are acquired wholesale during childhood by identification, and some of them are abandoned during adolescent rebellion. During late adolescence and early young adulthood, values become more relativistic as the individual develops a broader base of experience and empathy for other people. As a result, in young adulthood, values and interests increasingly become a personalized reflection of one's purposes and experiences. When an adult of any age is greatly threatened, personal anxiety and defensiveness consumes energy, and often little remains for creative tasks and interests. So also, preoccupation with self, rivalry, and anxiety interfere with an expansion of caring and concern for the welfare of others. Through family life, work, and community activities, many young adults come to realize that their welfare is closely associated with the welfare of others, that they are part of a larger human community (A. Kahn, 1972; Piliavin, Rodin, and Piliavin, 1969). Genuine love of a spouse, a child, or a friend entails spontaneous efforts to contribute to the welfare of the loved one and empathy when the loved one rejoices or suffers. Although caring depends on feeling, its development requires action and interaction. As the individual comes to understand the self and others, the resulting more discriminating awareness of reality provides a basis for deciding what is worth caring about (Arieti, 1966; Friedman, 1972; Mayeroff, 1971; Moustakas, 1972; Otto and Mann, 1968).

The relationship between feeling and interaction is illustrated by the adult life cycle shifts in the expression of feelings by lower middle class men and women. Young women tend to be most open and expressive of feelings and emotional intimacy, far more so than young men. By middle age, there appears to be a reversal as men become more expressive of feelings and women less so. In contrast with preretirement men, who typically express feelings to a moderate or limited extent, older women tend toward one of two extremes, either high emotional content or avoidance of feelings.

The experiences of late adolescence and young adulthood do not automatically produce a deepening and humanizing of interests and values and an expansion of caring. Conflict and frustration in family, work, and community can block these growth trends. Instead of growth and development, inter-dependent arrangements can lead to domination and stagnation. However, under congenial circumstances young adult-hood can be a period of great growth and change in attitudes and interests (R. W. White, 1961). In spite of adolescent rebellion from family influences, the values of young people are typically more similar to their parents' values than to those of other people in their own generation (R. Hill and others, 1970).

Time Orientation. In middle age there tends to be a shift in some attitudes and interests. Part of this shift is associated with a change in time orientation (Bortner and Hultsch, 1972; Goldrich, 1967; Soddy, 1967; Lowenthal, Thurnher, and others, 1975). Many people, especially adolescents, fantasize about what they will do or become in the future. Some adolescent fantasies materialize as plans or accomplishments. Many fantasies, however, are set aside until sometime in the future. Then sometime between the mid-thirties and the mid-forties, many people realize that the future is now. The number of years remaining begins to take on more significance than the number of years lived, and, especially for white collar adults, there is a reconsideration of goals.

Those who recognize that they are not going to achieve their adolescent dream but refuse to accept this conclusion and set more realistic goals are likely to become frustrated and depressed. Those who adjust may use their more mature perspective to embrace very fulfilling goals. Those who realize their dream may confront an even more difficult transition than those who do not. If they fail to set new goals, they will not look forward to a future that holds challenge and promise, and often they will attempt to wring satisfactions out of past accomplishments. Those "early successes" who set new goals and develop neglected talents are often able to avoid stagnation and instead open up a challenging and satisfying new career.

Vocational and avocational interests remain relatively stable during young adulthood, except for a decline in activities that involve great physical activity and danger (Campbell,

1971). In middle age there is a rearrangement of interests and attitudes that reflects personal and situational changes. Interest in the job or other current major activity tends to decline, but so does the expectation of a change to a different type of work. After age forty, goals related to retirement are more frequently mentioned (Kuhlen and Johnson, 1952).

Changing time orientations contribute to adult life cycle shifts in interests and attitudes. For example, among lower-middle-class adults before retirement, past or future orientations tend to reflect engagement, change little over the years, and influence adaptation. Compared with older adults, younger adults report more recent change events in their recent past and anticipate more in the near future. Also, more younger adults report becoming so engrossed in activities that they lose track of time and place. Attitudes toward young adulthood reflect both the density of role performance during that period and preferences for life-style. Adults of all ages who value the younger years most typically express preferences for excitement, challenge, and active involvement; those who value the middle years most typically express preferences for ease and contentment.

Future time orientations tend to have contrasting meanings for young and older adults. Young adults who are most future oriented are lower on perceived health and ratings of competence, when compared with young adults who are more present oriented. By contrast, older adults who are in poor health tend to be more past oriented, and future-oriented older respondents have higher ratings of competence when compared with other older adults. It appears that for some younger adults a heavy future orientation may be a form of escape from present problems, whereas among older adults a future orientation tends to reflect engagement in life, along with physical and psychological adjustment. For older adults a lack of futurity and a preoccupation with stress is associated with unhappy feelings about the past and present, pessimism about the future, and interference with adaptive processes.

Between young adulthood and old age there tend to be changes in values and attitudes that reflect some of the changes that typically occur in their lives. Older adults' attitudes become slightly more favorable toward minority groups, such as blacks, and especially the subculture of retired older adults with which they identify. This developmental trend runs contrary to the historical trend in which older adults were socialized in an earlier era in which there was less acceptance of minority groups, and they have lower levels of formal education. By contrast, young adults hold more favorable attitudes toward such idealistic concepts as life, the future, and the ideal person. Older men hold more favorable attitudes toward imagination, not because there is a difference compared with older women but because the attitude toward imagination by younger men is less favorable than that for younger women. Older women hold more favorable attitudes toward death than younger women, but less favorable attitudes toward love. The general age trend is toward more accepting attitudes about perceived realities (Kogan and Wallach, 1961).

In old age there tends to be an increase of interest in topics that emphasize connections between the individual and the rest of mankind through time and space. Examples of such topics include history, genealogy, philosophy, religion, and societal issues. During a period of life when many connections with old friends and activities are being severed and social life space is contracting, such broad interests provide a compensatory expansion of interests and concerns. For instance, Lowell Thomas personified present-oriented, high adventure for two generations. In his recent autobiography, Thomas reports that while in the Himalayas when he was fifty-seven, he was thrown from a horse and suffered a broken hip. As a result, his drive for adventure and movement, which has been his entire life, was tempered by the first subtle stirrings of reflective memory. When Thomas got around to writing his autobiography, twenty-five years later, he reported that he reviewed his life with nostalgia, humor, and occasionally surprise. (As barriers to participation by older adults in educational and recreational programs are being reduced, participation rates by older adults in programs on these topics appear to be increasing.)

Popular stereotypes of older adults characterize them in at least two ways that seem to be contradictory: (1) as rigid and lacking in mental or emotional flexibility and (2) as overly conforming, acquiescent, and easily persuaded. However, tested knowledge does not support these stereotypes. It does appear that older adults do dislike disruptions of their established habits. However, this preference provides a defense mechanism that protects the older adult against the problems of having to deal with the unexpected and the unmanageable during later life when it is necessary to compensate for physical losses. It also appears that many older adults hold to their views more firmly than middle-aged adults (Schaie, 1958; Riegel and Riegel, 1960). Conservatism tends to increase (Glenn, 1974; Gaertner, 1973). However, variability in rigidity and conformity is great at all ages. The current evidence indicates that older adults are about as rigid and as conforming as younger adults (Chown, 1961; Peck, 1960). It may even be that a degree of rigidity and obsessiveness, which may interfere with adaptation in young adulthood, may be adaptive in old age and provide for continuity of self-concept and facilitate stability during a period when many older adults must face difficult changes.

Changes in interests and attitudes tend to reflect the complex personality shifts that occur during adulthood. Attitude surveys and interest inventories provide convenient and inexpensive means to estimate adult needs for programs and services. When information about preferences is combined with information about response to programs by similar adults and information from practitioners about client needs, the result is a needs assessment that can enable practitioners to provide programs and services which are responsive and relevant.

Practitioners' Applications. The application by practitioners of generalizations about attitudes is illustrated by the assessment of absolutist versus relativistic personality characteristics and the use of the conclusions in planning educational activities for adults. This type of personality development toward more relativistic thinking and personal commitment is most widespread and rapid during late adolescence and young adulthood, but it occurs through middle age and beyond (Heath, 1965; Marcia, 1966). Adults with an absolutist outlook tend to view the world categorically, to be reactive, conforming, authoritarian, externally directed, and low in conceptual level. As learners, such adults are typically less skilled in complex learning tasks and tend to prefer a highly structured educational experience. Adults with a relativistic outlook tend to be proactive, independent, rational, self-directed, and high in conceptual level and to view the world in conditional, complex, and integrated ways. As learners, such adults tend to prefer more flexible educational experiences that emphasize personal autonomy, discovery, and relevance (Stern and Cope, 1956; R. J. Hill, 1960). In addition to helping the absolutist learners become more relativistic and the relativistic learners more committed, continuing education programs can be designed with alternative sections that allow adult learners to select the instructional emphasis which fits their outlook and preferred learning style. For example, a section for more absolutist learners might emphasize high structure, limited freedom, direct experience, moderate relativism, and assistance with analytic skills and dealing with conflicting content. A section for more relativistic learners might emphasize low structure, extensive freedom, indirect experience, implicit relativism, and assistance with personal intellectual commitment (Perry, 1970).

In addition to planning educational programs that deal directly with personality development, practitioners sometimes assist adults with tasks which are mainly mental or physical but have an affective dimension. An instructor may conduct review sessions to help young adults prepare for an examination; a health professional may help older adults recover from a physical disability. In these and many other situations, feelings play an important part in the success of the activity. It takes a while for most people to adjust to new activities, people, and surroundings. Practitioners can assist by helping provide familiar ingredients and by accelerating the process of making the new familiar. By recognizing that major changes are likely to produce anxiety and disorientation, practitioners can schedule activities which contribute to orientation and calm during periods of disruption and can schedule more demanding activities when people feel more secure. For instance, a supervisor might delay an explanation of complex procedures until after a new employee felt at home with basic job requirements. Even after an adult is familiar with an activity or setting, any type of temporary social or emotional maladjustment is likely to interfere with comprehension and skill. Practitioners can take this into account when they supervise the activity and can help clients recognize this for themselves when in other settings so that they can prepare or compensate for the disruption in their typical performance.

Moral Development

One aspect of personality that has been studied longitudinally during adolescence and young adulthood is moral development. The focus was on irreversible and qualitative changes in the ways in which people deal with value judgments, moral choices, and concepts of right action. To date six or perhaps seven stages of moral development have been suggested (Kohlberg and Kramer, 1969; Kohlberg, 1973). It should be noted that moral choices have been studied in hypothetical situations, and the correspondence with choices in daily life has not been demonstrated. The early stages are achieved by most children and adolescents. They tend to reflect biological and cognitive development, and most people move through them before adulthood. Only a small proportion of people achieve the highest stages of moral development, and many remain at the middle stages. Thus, in a representative sample of young adults there would typically be some people at each of five or six stages of moral development. However, so little research has been done on people beyond their twenties that it is unclear if more than a very few ever reach the highest levels of moral development.

Very young children who have not achieved a discernible stage of moral development assume that the good is what they want and like. Children soon enter a preconventional level at which they become responsive to reward, punishment, exchange of favors, and the power of those who enforce the rules. The orientation of stage one moral development is toward punishment and obedience. For example, at this stage the person sees no difference between the moral value of life and its status as a physical value. The physical consequences of action determine its goodness. The orientation of stage two moral development is toward instrumental hedonism and concrete reciprocity. For example, at this stage the person sees the value of a human life as based on satisfaction of the needs of its possessor or of others. Fairness and equal sharing occur on the basis of reciprocal exchange instead of gratitude, justice, or loyalty. This is the typical basis for the moral judgments of a small percentage of young adults.

There are several moral stages within a conventional level in which response to the expectations of others is perceived as valuable regardless of consequences. This attitude entails conforming to, maintaining, and justifying the social order, and identification with and loyalty to the individuals or group involved. The orientation of stage three moral development is toward interpersonal relations of mutuality. For example, at this stage the person sees the value of a human life as based on the sharing and love of others toward its possessor. Good behavior is behavior that meets the expectations of significant others, helps or pleases them, and is approved by them. Approval depends on being nice or good, and intentions are important bases for judgments.

Stage four moral development is oriented toward the maintenance of social order through fixed rules and authority. For example, at this stage the person sees the value of a human life as sacred in terms of its place in a moral order of rights and duties. Right behavior includes doing one's duty, maintaining the social order, and showing respect for authority.

During childhood, the surrounding moral world remains relatively constant, and the child's movement through moral stages reflects his or her changing perception of it. Moral stage development largely involves symbolic thinking and does not require great amounts of personal experience. Some of the adolescents at the lower three stages continued to develop toward stage four between sixteen and twenty-four. However, the trend is not the same for boys and girls. During high school about the same proportions of boys and girls are at stage four. All but 6 percent of stage three boys moved on to stage four in young adulthood. However, by young adulthood there are three or four times as many stage three women as stage three men. As young women leave school or college to become homemakers, many remain at stage three, and young men are replacing stage three with stage four. It appears that stage three personal concordance morality is functional for wives and mothers but not for businessmen and professionals who have moved to social concordance on a national scale.

Beyond the conventional level, there are two moral stages that reflect efforts to use moral principles which have validity apart from the individuals and groups who hold them. Stage five moral development is oriented toward a social contract that is intended to serve participating citizens, and it may be reflected in a utilitarian, law-making perspective or a higher law and conscience perspective. For example, at this stage the person sees life as valued in relation to community welfare and as a universal human right. Right action is judged in relation to socially accepted standards. This is illustrated by a democratic emphasis on a government of laws. The relativism of personal values is balanced by procedural rules for reaching consensus and changing laws. However, in stage five moral development, the law serves people.

Stage six moral development is oriented toward universal and abstract ethical principles. For example, at this stage the person sees the sacredness of a human life as a universal human value of respect for the individual as an object of moral principle. Right is derived from ethical principles based on logical comprehensiveness, consistency, and universality. Universal principles, such as the Golden Rule, include concern for equality, reciprocity, justice, human rights, and respect for the dignity of individual persons.

The foregoing six moral stages have evolved from studies

with a longitudinal sample through young adulthood. It is possible that beyond young adulthood, some adults may achieve a seventh stage of moral development, such as cosmic perspective on the meaningfulness of human lives in the face of death. Because there has been so little study of moral development in middle and old age, the proportions of adults who attain various stages of moral development and the dynamics of stage progression are currently largely speculation.

In contrast to the maturational quality of moral development, which tends to be influential during childhood and into adolescence, moral development during adulthood seems to result from transactional effects of experience on development (Kohlberg, 1969). This is especially so for stage five and six principled thinking. People appear to prefer solutions that are at the highest moral stage available to the individual. Therefore, as a person achieves stage four, five, or six, lower stage orientations tend to be dropped.

The stage progression process varies for about one-fifth of high school students who go on to college, most of whom have been from white collar families. They tend to be among the most able students who reached the more advanced levels of moral stage development for adolescents. At around college sophomore age, they regress to a stage two hedonism and reciprocity orientation and do not use the highest moral stages of which they are capable. This form of regression, which is often embellished with philosophical and sociopolitical jargon, is part of the process in which they reject the conventional morality they internalized earlier and proceed more consciously to the stage five principled morality that is stabilized as part of their own identity.

Principled thinking at the fifth and sixth stages of moral development has not been found before the mid-twenties. An ideological awareness of moral principles sometimes emerges during adolescence, but ethical thinking and a commitment to the use of moral principles seem to require experiences of personal moral choice and responsibility based on commitment to an adult identity and a sense of fidelity of the self and of others. Principled moral judgment requires going beyond an adequate perception of what the social system is. It is necessary to recognize principles to which the self and society ought to be committed, along with a commitment to an actual society in which one's performance is consistent with these ideals.

The movement to stage five and six principled thinking seems to entail several ingredients. One is a sustained responsibility for the welfare of others and the experience of irreversible moral choice that is associated with a sense of generativity in adulthood. This transaction with the societal context provides a second ingredient—the experience with conflicting values, identity questioning, and recognition of the need for commitment—such as can be encouraged in the college environment. A third ingredient is a degree of personal choice and conscious effort not apparent in the earlier stages. This helps explain why relatively few young adults achieve stabilized principled thought. Those who have achieved stage five moral development have been older than twenty-three, and those who have achieved stage six moral development have been older than thirty. An educational experience, such as a moral discussion program, has been a major factor in helping young adults acquire principled thought (Kohlberg, 1973, 1974).

Kohlberg's speculation about a seventh stage of moral development that may emerge during middle age or beyond is parallel to Erikson's eighth stage of ego development in which a sense of integrity prevails over despair and results in wisdom (Erikson, 1976). Erikson defines wisdom as the detached and yet active concern with life itself in the face of death itself. A sense of integrity provides vital strength for the life cycle as well as the cycle of generations.

The conclusion by Kohlberg that the highest levels of moral development occur during adulthood, when combined with increasing adult interest beyond middle age in moral and social issues, leads to several implications for practitioners. Movement to stage five and six principled thought tends to depend on the accumulation of experiences that typically occur during adulthood when the individual confronts conflicts of loyalties. This occurs, for example, when a man or a woman with teen-aged children confronts a move to a new community that seems very desirable to the employer but very undesirable to the family. Many of the significant experiences of adulthood thus contribute to periodic reconsideration of the ways in which adults think and feel about issues.

An aspect of personality development that is related to moral development is changing value orientations during the adult life cycle. A cross-sectional study of lower-middle-class adults included an analysis of continuities and discontinuities in value orientations (Lowenthal, Thurnher, and others, 1975). The analysis of value orientation in relation to personal adaptation included consideration of dominant beliefs, value hierarchies, perceptions of how values had changed and were likely to change, and characteristics associated with reported value change.

Content analysis of recurrent themes regarding social and religious values and beliefs yielded such categories as achievement, family, humanitarianism, coping, happiness, legacy, and religious life. Young adults tended to emphasize values that reflect expansiveness and high expectations in contrast with older adults who tended to emphasize self-limitation and reduction of frustrations. During late adolescence and young adulthood, such values as personal achievement and happiness tend to predominate, except for newlywed women who place far less emphasis on achievement than on nurturance of family and others. In contrast with the emphasis on reaching out for life's satisfactions by those in late adolescence and young adulthood, those in middle age and beyond tend to be more concerned with coping and reduction of frustrations. The values emphasized by older adults in the preretirement stage transcend the self and family to include people generally. Older women stress personal caring and religious life. Older men stress leaving a tangible legacy or contribution to society.

Another approach to the identification of life course variations in value hierarchy used such categories as instrumental, expressive, religious, service, ease, pleasure, and growth. Adolescents and young adult men, in their concern for establishing themselves through educational and occupational achievement, emphasize instrumental values and material accomplishments. Young adult women and middle-aged adults, with their family orientation, emphasize expressive values and interpersonal relationships. Older adults at the pre-retirement stage seem to anticipate a withdrawal from striving and emphasize ease and contentment. For men, growth values are much lower for the middle aged than for the young adults. By comparison, the largest differences occur between middle-aged and preretirement men because there is a decline in both instrumental and expressive values and an increase in values related to ease and pleasure. The largest differences for women occur between late adolescence and young adulthood because newlywed young women place less emphasis on instrumental values and pleasure and more on expressive values and inter-personal relations. Middle-aged women place less emphasis on instrumental values and more on ease and contentment.

It also appears that openness to future change as reflected in receptivity to value change and desire to grow requires at least moderate levels of self-acceptance and self-assurance. For example, during late adolescence, girls tend to assess accurately their extent of physical and social maturation, and those who are late maturers anticipate more change than those who are on pace in their developmental cycle. Among middle-aged women, the most future and change oriented tended to be those who feel most confident that they can influence their environment or have the strongest desire to compensate for past frustrations. In middle age, the most resourceful women focus on past changes, whereas the most resourceful men focus on future changes. The middle-aged men who are most concerned about value change reflect their distress about present circumstances in their expression of low life satisfaction. The more change-oriented older men tend to be high on hope and family values, which probably reflects the importance of supportive interpersonal relationships for those who venture change in later life (Lowenthal, Thurnher, and others, 1975).

Sometimes adults will seek out a practitioner, such as a

psychiatrist, clergyman, or personnel department counselor, to explore an issue of great concern. However, many adults seem interested in discussing personal and social issues in ways that help them understand not only the issues but also how they and others think and feel about the issues. This testing of one's own values against external standards occurs in such diverse educational settings as great books discussion groups, assertiveness training, values clarification discussion groups, world affairs conferences, and encounter groups. Similar reflection can be stimulated by reading, sermons, films, plays, and encounters with other people in work and social settings. Practitioners can help adults recognize the process of moral development during adulthood and the types of experience likely to facilitate it. In addition, practitioners can help increase the variety and accessibility of opportunities for adults to explore moral issues in active ways likely to lead to growth and development. Practitioners can use older adults' increasing ability and interest in dealing with moral and ethical issues as a springboard for the development of materials and programs that will facilitate the process. It seems likely that materials and procedures, such as discussion groups, which are most effective for older adults, may differ somewhat from those for young adults.

Adaptation

Adults vary greatly in the ways in which they adapt to shifts in aspirations, circumstances, problems, and opportunities. Their adjustments to interpersonal relations, work, or life changes affect morale and even health. Some of the variability in adjustment is associated with age and changing circumstances. An indication of the success of adaptation and adjustment during adulthood is reflected in trends in the level of happiness during the adult life cycle. The environmental circumstances that confront the individual and often call for adaptation differ somewhat from young adulthood to middle and old age. For example, in youth major adaptations are associated with the establishment of an adult identity and entry into adult roles in work, family, and community. In old age, life review and anticipation of death reflect widespread adjustments (Bradburn, 1969; Goffman, 1960).

Happiness and morale depend on more than an individual's objective circumstances; they reflect personal adjustment and acceptance of circumstances. For example, number of material possessions is less associated with happiness than how the person feels about them. Satisfaction is a function of aspiration and expectation as well as accomplishment (Burr, 1970). When adults are unhappy because of the great discrepancy between their expectations and achievement, practitioners can help raise their satisfaction level by helping them increase their performance, reduce their aspirations, or both. Adolescent dreams and fantasies have much to do with the way in which middle-aged adults evaluate their success and their level of happiness and adjustment (Chinoy, 1955). Even the perceived rate of the passage of time depends how the person feels about the current or anticipated activity. Throughout life the level of morale and happiness is related to the extent to which individuals (1) feel emotionally secure, are accepting of self in general and when comparing aspirations with accomplishments, and lack cynicism; (2) receive acceptance and affection from others; (3) feel that they can influence desirable outcomes and lack a strong sense of powerlessness; and (4) believe that life has meaning and that their values are sound.

During late adolescence and young adulthood, in addition to identity concerns, the happiness and unhappiness of young men and women is closely associated with interpersonal relations and emerging adult role relationships (Bortner and Hultsch, 1970; Lieberman, 1970). One of the dominant worries of late adolescence is about heterosexual relations. In addition, in recent generations adolescent boys have tended to be less happy than girls, partly because of the greater pressure they have felt toward independence and accomplishments. Retrospective reports on periods of greatest happiness tend to include childhood as a period of greatest happiness, but this reflects more selective recollection and fantasy than fact (Rosenzweig and Rosenzweig, 1952). The period of greatest feelings of freedom

reported by middle-aged men tends to be before family responsibilities began; for middle-aged women it tends to be after
major family responsibilities are finished.

Middle age tends to bring a more deliberate and judi-
cious approach to aspirations, adjustment, and happiness. Many
people at mid-life come to understand that life has both problems and rewards. Many people seek compensations for losses
and disappointments (Billig and Adams, 1965). Reports of
worrying reach a peak in the forties (Pressey and Jones, 1955).
Reported life satisfaction tends to decline during child-rearing
years and then tends to rise (Campbell and Converse, 1975).
Some of the maladjustment that appears during middle age
reflects long-standing unresolved emotional problems that are
revealed more clearly as a result of major role changes, such as
a move to a new community, a major job change, divorce or
death of a spouse, or the youngest child's leaving home (Rose,
1965; Deutscher, 1964; Bradburn and Caplovitz, 1965). Worries during middle age tend to focus on problems of health and
frustrated ambitions (Lowenthal and Chiriboga, 1973; Kornhauser and Reid, 1965).

Adult life cycle fluctuations in happiness and perceived
well-being are relatively stable when compared with correlates of
happiness other than age (Wessman and Ricks, 1966; Bradburn,
1969; Campbell and Converse, 1975). From late adolescence
to old age there are some minor fluctuations in life satisfaction and happiness that are relatively low in late adolescence,
become much higher in young adulthood, drop in early middle
age, rise in late middle age before retirement, and then decline
in old age (Cantril, 1965; Campbell and Converse, 1975;
Lowenthal, Thurnher, and others, 1975; Bradburn, 1969;
Gurin, Veroff, and Feld, 1960). However, the characteristics
most highly associated with happiness include higher socioeconomic status, greater self-esteem, better physical health, and
more varied social participation (Bradburn, 1969; Wessman
and Ricks, 1966; Havighurst, Neugarten, and Tobin, 1968;
Cantril, 1965; Maddox, 1963).

There are some indications of developmental relationships between happiness and performance for lower-middle-

class adults (Lowenthal, Thurnher, and others, 1975). Among young adults, life satisfaction is higher for those who are more active in family and community. Among older adults there is little association between extent of participation and life satisfaction. It appears that with age the quality rather than the scope of interpersonal relationships becomes increasingly important. For those who remain married, there is a widespread perception throughout adulthood that the individual's marital relationship improved over the years.

Happiness and adaptability seem to be associated with the individual's psychological resources, such as accommodation, growth, hope, mutuality, and intelligence. Accommodation reflects the individual's balance between proactive and reactive behavior. There tends to be a decline in reactive behavior from late adolescence through middle age, followed by an increase in old age. Growth and self-realization are reflected in characteristics such as curiosity and willingness to change. Men tend to be more growth oriented than women, and young adults more open to new experiences than older adults. Lack of growth orientation does not interfere with life satisfaction, however, except during periods in which the individual confronts a major change event, such as losing a spouse, retirement, or disability. It appears that adults who are more defense oriented experience more difficulty with adaptation than those who are more growth oriented (Beiser, 1971). Hopefulness, as a precondition to action, is similarly distributed for men and women but tends to decline gradually during adulthood. Mutuality, which reflects relationships characterized by empathy, trust, respect, support, and responsibility, along with the capacity to both give and receive, tends to be very stable during adulthood, although there is substantial variability within age groups. Mental ability also tends to be fairly stable during most of adulthood.

In addition to resources, adults vary in their psychological deficits, which include symptoms of emotional problems and malfunctioning likely to interfere with performance, such as extreme depression, phobias, and feelings of inferiority. In general, happiness is associated with high resources and low deficits. Those who are high on both resources and deficits tend to have a more complex psychological outlook. In general, the happiest adults tend to be those who have high resources and deficits, those who have low resources and deficits, or those who have moderate resources and low deficits. The importance of psychological complexity tends to decrease during adulthood. The happiest newlyweds have high resources and low deficits. The happiest middle-aged adults have moderate resources and low deficits. The happiest preretirees have relatively low resources and deficits. It appears that because of societal restrictions during old age, psychological complexity becomes maladaptive. Indeed, among preretirees, those with high resources and deficits were even unhappier than those with high deficits and low resources. Throughout adulthood, those with low psychological complexity experience few change events, scope of activity increases gradually with age, and future orientation and goal complexity tend to be low (Lowenthal, Thurnher, and others, 1975).

Even desirable changes produce stress that can affect physical and emotional health (Levine and Scotch, 1970; Dohrenwend, 1973; Korchin, 1965; Lazarus, 1966; Jaco, 1970; J. Henry, 1973; Carai, 1970; Selye, 1974; Gurin, Veroff, and Feld, 1960). An instrument such as Rahe's life-change units scale can be used to estimate how much change an individual has experienced during a given time period. The changes may be seen by the individual as desirable or undesirable and may or may not be under the individual's control. Events vary in their impact, and there is high agreement on the relative importance of various life changes and the adaptation they entail. For example, the death of a spouse is rated as five times as impactful as a move to a new home and ten times as impactful as a vacation. There is clear evidence of the association between life change and physical health. Those in the top 10 percent of change tend to have about twice as much illness in the following months as those in the bottom 10 percent of change. It appears that an abrupt increase in change can reduce the body's defenses and make the individual more susceptible to the ever-present viruses within or outside the body. High death rates for widows and widowers during the year after the death of a spouse reflect a similar impact of change on emotional as well as physical health (Rahe, McKean, and Arthur, 1967; Holmes and Rahe, 1967).

Perception of, response to, and preoccupation with stress varies across the adult life cycle (Lowenthal, 1964b; Thompson, 1965; U.S. Census, 1970; Lowenthal, Thurnher, and others, 1975). The incidence of change events that can contribute to stress tends to decline markedly from young adulthood to middle age and then gradually until retirement. White collar adults tend to experience more change events and thus more potential exposure to stress. Among adults with high exposure to change and stress, some are challenged and some are overwhelmed. Among those with low exposure to stress, some feel fortunate but others appear to be self-defeating in their preoccupation with a presumed stress level that is relatively low compared with other adults.

Newlyweds report more stress during the previous decade than do preretirees. Among the highly stressed young, more men feel overwhelmed than women. Among the highly stressed middle-aged and older adults, more women feel overwhelmed than men. It appears that older women are less prepared than men to deal with relatively high stress levels. Also, those older adults who have experienced life-threatening illnesses in earlier years perceive chronic illnesses as less stressful than those without such experiences.

Although characteristics such as self-image and preoccupation with death distinguish between the fortunate and self-defeating lightly stressed groups, they do not differentiate between the challenged and overwhelmed highly stressed groups. Mutuality and the existence of close interpersonal and confidant relationships is characteristic of those who are challenged in response to stress but not of those who are overwhelmed. The challenged tend to have robust outlooks in contrast with the low-stressed fortunates who tend toward detachment and inflated self-concepts that may provide protection from emotional attachments. The low-stressed self-defeating tend toward characteristics such as low self-esteem, restricted social horizons, and preoccupation with the past and death. It appears that the way in which an adult deals with stress affects adaptation (Lowenthal, Thurnher, and others, 1975).

Some changes, such as mandatory retirement, can be anticipated and planned for during middle age. However, when only half the middle-aged working adults have positive attitudes toward retirement, there are strong tendencies to deny and close out thoughts and information about such a disturbing topic (Anderson, 1962). Some adjustment problems have their roots in earlier experiences and feelings. For example, when recent mothers report on their satisfaction with pregnancy and delivery, there are strong associations with related attitudes. Far more of those who reported a difficult pregnancy, including nausea, also reported long-standing negative attitudes toward intercourse. Far more of those who bottle fed their babies expressed the feeling that childbirth was difficult. Both young men and old women tend to feel that their spouses are overdependent (Lowenthal, Thurnher, and others, 1975). Adjustment and satisfaction reflect both the experience and the feelings and expectations about it.

Life satisfaction and morale in old age is little related to age trends as such but highly related to conditions that tend to be associated with old age (Neugarten, Havighurst, and Tobin, 1968; Birren and others, 1963; Reichard, Livson, and Peterson, 1962). If the individual has a long-standing pattern of poor adjustment, marginal engagement, and unhappiness, then maladjustment in old age is almost certain. In general, however, the older individual tends to use the former self more than current reference groups as the main yardstick for arriving at a sense of relative deprivation in old age (Lowenthal, 1965).

The main conditions associated with life satisfaction and morale in old age are (Lowenthal and Haven, 1968; P. Cameron, 1969a, b): health, financial resources, work status, marital status, living arrangements, and social contacts.

Personality patterns are associated with adjustment in old age (Reichard, Livson, and Peterson, 1962; Williams and Wirths, 1965). Some of the intrapsychic personality functioning that appears to change as early as the fifties seems to have little relation to social interaction, which in turn has little relation to age through the sixties and into the seventies.

Beyond the sixties most adults must deal in some way with the imminent prospect of death. There is evidence that distance from death becomes more salient than chronological age and that there are systematic cognitive and affective changes that occur (Lieberman, 1965; Lieberman and Coplan, 1960). Many older adults engage in an active, purposeful form of reminiscence termed *life review*. They recall facts and unresolved conflicts of the past but also weave them into an acceptable perspective (Butler, 1963).

Practitioners can help adults recognize the types of adjustments they are likely to confront and understand how they can facilitate adaptation and growth (Gunther, 1968a, 1968b; Zimbardo and Ebbsen, 1969; Coulding, 1972; Mosher and Sprinthall, 1972; Fagan and Shepherd, 1973; Marmor, 1974). Stress and morale are some of the ingredients associated with adaptation that practitioners can help clarify. Programs and services related to adaptation can be preventive as well as remedial.

Throughout adulthood people confront major change events such as shifts in family composition, job changes, and physical disabilities. Practitioners can help adults make these adjustments by understanding the personal changes that are likely, developing realistic and constructive attitudes toward the resultant problems and opportunities, acquiring the needed understanding and competence, and arranging for supportive services. An especially important form of assistance during a period of adjustment when there are major physical or societal changes is to help an adult maintain and enhance the sense of self. Often during a transition period a person experiences strong feelings of panic, vulnerability, powerlessness, apathy, or may even have difficulty getting in touch with feelings. This makes it difficult to maintain continuity and a sense of identity and worth.

The most desirable course of action for all concerned is for a person to meet a crisis head on, solve problems in self-directed ways, obtain assistance when needed, and grow in the process. However, there are times when the individuals need some short-term ways to get by and buy time until they are prepared to deal with the stressful situation (Menninger, 1963). Some methods entail venting emotions by laughing, crying, cursing, contracting a psychosomatic illness, or even blaming others. Other methods entail obtaining physical reassurance by eating, sleeping, taking tranquilizers, working or exercising. Still other methods provide substitutes for action, such as discussing the problem, going shopping, or escaping through television, movies, or books. Practitioners can help clients understand the functions these methods serve, but such methods do not usually solve the problem.

Successful adaptation in relation to major change events typically requires planful and growthful action (Arieti, 1966). One component of successful adaptation is educative activity. Participation in an educational program can enable an adult to increase understanding and competence to deal with a change that has already occurred; such is the case with a recent widow who takes a refresher course in preparation for a return to work. Educational programs can also increase understanding of likely future changes; one example is a television series on preparation for retirement that encourages and facilitates planning for middle-aged workers (Knox, 1968).

Case Examples: Miss Chips and Mrs. Hirt

Generalizations about personality development during adulthood tend to be especially useful when practitioners can apply them to understand or facilitate role performance. Although some mental health practitioners, such as counselors and psychotherapists, seek to help emotionally disturbed adults deal with emotional problems, most practitioners in the helping professions seek to help adults perform more effectively in family, work, or community or cope with a physical health problem. The following case descriptions illustrate the influence of contrasting personality patterns on the interpersonal relationships of two older women.

Williams and Wirths prepared a detailed analysis of styles

of life and successful aging as part of a Kansas City study of
adult life (1965). They interviewed a panel of adults between
forty-nine and ninety years of age on successive occasions during a period of about five years and collected data on both the
structural characteristics of their social systems (such as social
position and types of social interaction) and the functional
characteristics (such as amount of energy and level of performance as reflected in alienation and coping). The ratings of
success in aging reflect two aspects: (1) autonomy versus dependency regarding the balance of exchange of energy and feelings between the individual and others, and (2) persistence
versus precariousness regarding actual or probable continuity
in external relations with others. Six major life-styles were included, and varying degrees of success in aging were identified
within each. The six life-styles were work oriented, family
oriented, living alone, couplehood, minimal involvement, and
living fully in multiple settings. The case descriptions of Miss
Chips and Mrs. Hirt are based on the more detailed case descriptions that were reported, both of which were classified in
the couplehood life-style. Each illustrates interactions between
context, condition, personality, and performance of a woman
around the retirement period and indicates developmental
processes that reflect both stability and change.

Miss Chips was fifty-five when first interviewed. She was
described as a pleasant and kind single woman who had been a
school teacher since age seventeen, when both her parents died,
and she left school to go to work to help support her sisters.
Over the years she continued her education until she completed
her master's degree. She was a dedicated teacher who was beloved in both the school and the community.

Miss Chips' closest friend was another teacher from whom
she rented a room. They traveled together during their summer
vacations. The house they lived in was also shared with her
housemate's retired brother, who died of cancer during the
second year of the interviewing for the study. Religion was important to Miss Chips as a source of solace and security. She had
not changed much between age forty-five and fifty-five, except
that she took it easy and watched television more because her

health was worse. She disliked the prospect of retirement, and, other than typical financial arrangements, made no plans for it. About the time her housemate's brother died, her housemate retired, and Miss Chips was operated on for cancer. These changes had a major impact on her life. Although Miss Chips had four or five other close friends and maintained close and warm relationships with her two sisters, even though one lived far away, her special friendship and confidant relationship with her housemate was of great significance, and during this period they spent far more time together.

Miss Chips continued to gain much satisfaction from her teaching and liked to do it well, spending much time evenings and weekends in preparation of special materials. However, her attitude toward retirement changed greatly. Following her operation and her housemate's retirement, she began to look forward to it because there were so many activities that they enjoyed sharing. It was clear that in her relations with many friends, she extended and received affection.

She returned to teaching after her operation. However, she found the work getting harder, looked forward with special anticipation to the summer vacation, and began talking frankly of retirement. In May of the school year she did so. The sudden decision reflected the pressures of ill health and age, along with the attractiveness of shared activities with her housemate.

A difficult adjustment to retirement reflected the great importance of teaching in her life and the feeling of lost contact with the children. She especially missed being needed by them. During the following year she gained greater acceptance of and contentment with retirement. There was no pressure in her quiet days spent shopping, visiting, doing chores, taking care of an ancient dog, and going to church regularly. She assumed fewer new responsibilities, made fewer new friends, and was less concerned with new clothes and good impressions. Her autonomous and persistent functioning in a couple-oriented life-style was most successful.

Mrs. Hirt was sixty-four when first interviewed. She had grown up in a large family with the feeling that if she had not been unloved and inept in interpersonal relations, she could have been "the best." Her father died when she was in her teens, and she went to work to help support the family. She was outwardly willing but inwardly resentful. During adolescence, her peers enjoyed and accepted her fully, which contributed to her feelings during adulthood that she possessed great strength and could do no wrong. She looked back on adolescence as the happiest time of her life.

As an adult, Mrs. Hirt extended herself to others, but her omniscient and condescending attitudes were so annoying to others that she received little in exchange. The harder she tried, the more she alienated those she most wanted to be close to. Her feelings of rejection and frustration and hurt became more and more intense. Her problems in functioning were increasingly aggravated by major physical ailments. The Hirts never had children, but spent much time caring for near relatives. She also tried to maintain a close relationship with her nearest sister, but by her mid-sixties all these relationships had broken down. Repeated personal conflicts in church and community groups had resulted in alienation and rejection. Her husband was understanding and tried to help her understand herself, but she made little progress.

Toward the end of the five-year period of interviewing, Mrs. Hirt was deteriorating physically, mentally, and socially. Her only close relationship was with her husband, on whom she was very dependent. Her dependent and precarious functioning in a couple-oriented life-style reflected unsuccessful aging that resulted from a long history of personality problems and inadequate performance.

Both Miss Chips and Mrs. Hirt experienced health problems around the retirement period, and each had a couplehood life-style in which another played a very important role as a confidant and source of interaction. The relationship with this significant other person, along with each woman's sense of self-esteem, was well established during middle age and continued as a form of stability and continuity during the retirement period. However, Mrs. Hirt's omniscient attitudes alienated her from other people, which resulted in her feelings of rejection. Her unsuccessful aging reflected long-standing personality problems and inadequate interpersonal relationships, along with great dependence on her husband. This precarious and dependent pattern of functioning was directly opposed to the persistent and autonomous functioning of Miss Chips with her long-standing high self-esteem and effective interpersonal relationships. Although health problems precipitated her retirement, she did not feel rejected by others. Her friendship relationships were satisfying, and her relationship with her housemate was interdependent, in contrast with Mrs. Hirt's dependent relationship with her husband. Miss Chips' positive self-concept and effective interpersonal relationships enabled her to deal with health problems and retirement far more successfully than Mrs. Hirt.

Many of the influences on success in aging displayed by Miss Chips and Mrs. Hirt apply for most older adults. Practitioners can help clients understand such influences on successful aging. In recent years there has been growing attention to aging and social gerontology, and more and more writers are taking a transactional and developmental approach that includes consideration of the interplay among context, performance, condition, learning, and personality. Some have emphasized interaction between the older adult and his or her societal context (Clark and Anderson, 1967; Busse, 1969; Atchley, 1972; Kastenbaum, and others, 1972; Bengston, 1973; Kimmel, 1974), and the literature provides a useful overview of transactional relationships that can be used by practitioners who work with older adults. The impact of physical condition and health on performance is increasingly widespread with advancing age (Botwinick, 1973). Family relationships and living arrangements are closely associated with successful aging for older adults whether they live in their own households or in institutional settings (Field, 1972; Eisner, 1975). As the worker role declines in centrality, use of leisure can be a major factor in adjustment by older adults (Havighurst and Feigenbaum, 1959; Nystrom, 1974).

The foundations of successful aging are typically established at least by middle age. Two major ingredients are interpersonal relations and personality. A satisfactory pattern of interpersonal relations in middle age provides the external basis for both stability and growth in old age (Lowenthal, Thurnher, and others, 1975; Riley and others, 1969). Satisfactory personality functioning by middle age provides the internal basis for both stability and growth in old age (Lidz, 1968). The range of individual differences in personality functioning in later life is great (Maddox and Douglas, 1974). Case histories, such as the one about Mark Twain's last decade, can help practitioners understand the types of deterioration that can occur as a result of loneliness and grief (H. Hill, 1973).

Aspects of personality such as needs, values, attitudes, aspirations, and self-concept often help mediate between aspects of condition and contexts and give direction to performance and learning. Satisfactory or outstanding performance is more likely when abilities and opportunities are well matched. But there are various abilities and numerous opportunities, and satisfactory matching depends in part on personality. Difficulty with close interpersonal relationships and low self-esteem can be barriers not only to satisfactory performance but also to growth that would otherwise lead to improved performance in the future. For clients whose personality problems are barriers to satisfactory performance, practitioners can help to arrange for assistance so that the individual becomes better able to deal effectively with feelings, aspirations, and decisions. In dealing with most adults, however, practitioners can help them realize how much personality can develop throughout adulthood. There are many ways in which adults can review their uses of time and resources to identify implicit priorities and explore values and satisfactions. If unmet needs are clarified, practitioners can help adults recognize ways in which at least some of the needs can be better met. For example, many older adults recognize their need for security but may be less aware of their needs for relatedness or creativity. Exposure to other older adults who are meeting these needs and to recreational and educational programs can open up new and attractive horizons for many older adults.

It appears that, at any age, performance is more satisfactory and life more satisfying for people whose personality patterns are more mature, integrated, and self-actualized. Adults whose personality patterns approach the optimal tend to function more fully. Some aspects of personality, such as dependability and productivity, tend to be prized by adults of all ages. The happiest and best-adjusted adults of all ages tend to be mentally alert and socially engaged. Although personality patterns are relatively stable during adulthood, there are some widespread shifts. Young adults tend to value activity and objectivity, while older adults place relatively greater value on interpersonal relations. All adults confront problems and opportunities. Personality patterns influence how they are dealt with, and the results in turn influence personality development (Coan, 1974; Alpaugh, Renner, and Birren, 1976). Practitioners can help middle aged and older adults to age successfully in many ways including counseling, educational programs, and group work (Havighurst and Orr, 1956; Hendrickson and Barnes, 1967; K. Wolff, 1963; Yalom and Terrazas, 1968; Burnside, 1970).

Summary

Personality characteristics and tendencies provide continuity across specific times and situations that enables us to predict likely thoughts, feelings, and actions. However, in addition to stability and continuity from year to year, there is evidence of substantial change and modification in aspects of adult personality from decade to decade. An understanding of general personality constructs and trends during adulthood can enable practitioners to help adults gain a broader perspective on variability within each phase of adulthood and typical trends from phase to phase. In addition, there are adult life cycle shifts in self-concept, decision making, attitudes, moral development, and adaptation.

Personality stability and change is influenced by characteristics that are universal, characteristics that are widespread, and characteristics that are unique. Throughout life as these characteristics interact, there is some tension between differentiation and integration of personality. As adults interact with their environment, interrelations among biological, experiential, societal, and historical systems influence personality development. Some adults are able to transcend societal goals that conflict with personal goals. This reflects striving toward fulfillment through actualization of personal potential and through improvement of the quality of life in the society. The main impetus for personality change may come from either the individual or society, change is more likely when facilitated by both personal striving and societal encouragement, and great consistency in personal characteristics and societal circumstances helps maintain personality stability.

The extent and type of personality change that occurs during various phases of adulthood vary with age and other characteristics. Between late adolescence and middle age, the typical rate of personality change is great enough to facilitate growth. The extent of change is greater for persons with higher levels of intellectual ability. The extent of change varies across aspects of personality and among people with differing personality characteristics. Some early personality shifts are later reversed. Both personality differentiation and integration increase during young adulthood. From middle to old age there is often a gradual shift from active to passive mastery. In old age, extent of personality change and adaptation is associated with a variety of contrasting personality patterns.

Practitioners can help adult clients resist false stereotypes about age-related personality characteristics, recognize the great variability in adult personality patterns, and understand the extent to which personality change occurs during adulthood. In some instances, practitioners help clients recognize how other people contribute to their development, and in other instances they help clients avoid overdependence. Shifts occur between deepening self-understanding and broadening experience through friendship. Practitioners can help clients use an increased understanding of their past to deal more effectively with the present and plan for the future.

A central aspect of adult personality development is the shifting manner in which the person strives to maintain and enhance his or her sense of self during adulthood. The evolving sense of self is reflected in both personality differentiation and integration, in both planning and accommodating of contending forces. The sense of self tends to become more positive until middle age and then to stabilize or gradually become less positive. Generalizations about the evolving sense of self provide the practitioner with optimism about the modifiability of adult personality, with indications of the influence of role changes on self-concept, and with understanding of the developmental process that can enhance the practitioner's efforts to help adults learn, adapt, and modify feelings. The evolving sense of self reflects many influences including significant others and major activities such as work and parenthood.

The sense of self during adulthood is affected by the individual's resolution of childhood and adolescent ego crises related to trust, autonomy, initiative, industry, and identity. If the transition from adolescence to young adulthood is successful, the individual achieves a fit between past potential and experience, current sense of identity and aspirations, and societal expectations and opportunities for the future. Similar transitions occur at various stages of adulthood. A mature sense of adult self may be achieved by age twenty or may not develop until the thirties. During adulthood, additional ego crises relate to intimacy, generativity, and integrity. The evolving self-concept of those who do not attend college tends to be similar to those who do, except that non-college-bound youths tend to have a less positive view of their performance than of their acceptance of self, and they typically view themselves as having less influence in interpersonal relations than their peers who attend college.

A positive self-concept reflects high self-esteem and self-confidence, and both self-differentiation and personality integration. Positive self-concept is associated with self-actualization and effective occupational performance. There are few age-related trends in self-concept between twenty and sixty. Many people are most uncertain about their self-concepts during late adolescence. Variability is great. The shift from parental family to adult responsibilities is part of this transition. From the twenties through the fifties or sixties there tends to be an increase in positive self-concept, self-esteem, and self-confidence. The perceived age norms by white collar adults include the prime of life and time of greatest self-confidence around age forty and the onset of old age around age seventy. By contrast, blue collar adults perceive these transitions as occurring about ten years younger. For many older adults, self-concept becomes more variable, defensive, and negative. However, the trends are usually gradual with little appreciable change in a six-year period.

Self-concept and performance interact during adulthood. Some young people create adolescent dreams that give a sense of direction and aspiration to their lives. As friends are substituted for family and adult commitments are made, the young adult's personality structure and pattern of participation becomes more complex. In mid-life, some of the abstract commitments and aspirations that were formed in adolescence begin to wane. Being one's own person seems to be especially salient. This may be reflected in the transition from having a mentor to being a mentor. The increasingly widespread mid-life transition entails a reexamination between the current sense of self and the structure of participation and commitments that evolved. Around the forties there is often an increase in stock taking as the adult realizes that the future is now. Although the stability and integration of self-concept tends to be predictive of subsequent adaptation, there is much variability in mid-life adjustments. At any stage, the fragments of the sense of self that result from an identity transition become the building blocks for a reintegration that can allow the individual to become a more fully functioning person. For older adults, the adolescent dream is replaced by protection of gains and an inward shift toward more personal concerns. For many, a shift in time orientation occurs in which time remaining until death becomes more salient than time spent since birth.

An aspect of personality, in addition to self-concept, is the process of making choices or decisions. This executive function of the self entails assertiveness, goal setting, accommodation, and self-directedness. It also includes the mix of proactive and reactive behavior. Adults can become more assertive and decisive in the achievement of personal change. An active and self-directed approach to life entails the addition of commitment to ability to transcend limitations. Practitioners can assist adults to become more self-directed through activities such as values clarification and priority setting. In addition, people can be helped to deal with change in a growthful way by recognizing that a positive attitude can turn an uncertain situation into success, by putting apprehension about an unknown situation in perspective, by focusing on past successes, and by retaining stability in other aspects of one's life when making a major change.

Most of adults' needs, motives, interests, and attitudes were formed by interaction with others and continue to be modified by such interaction. As the residue of such interaction, attitudes predispose a person in the choice of activities, companions, and locations. For example, either abundance or deprivation of social interaction can contribute to a high need for affiliation in which feelings of well-being depend on interaction with others who provide social-emotional support and a sense of security. The need for achievement is associated with both educational level and age. For college-educated women, a high need for achievement before childbearing declines while the children are young but then increases to the previous high level when the children are grown.

Other adult life cycle shifts in attitudes reflect developmental transactions between individual and context. Part of the increased intellectual orientation during the college years also occurs for non-college-bound youths. Some of the gains during the college years are reversed unless the subsequent setting encourages originality. Many attitudes are acquired wholesale during childhood by identification. Adolescent rebellion includes wholesale rejection of some of these values. As young adults gain experience and commitments, they realize that they are part of a larger human community.

Vocational and avocational interests remain relatively stable during young adulthood. Change events are more frequent than for older adults. Those who recognize that they are not going to achieve their adolescent dreams but refuse to accept this conclusion and set more realistic goals are likely to experience frustration and depression. Those who achieve their dreams are often able to avoid stagnation by starting a challenging new career. Adults who value the younger years most typically prefer challenge and excitement, in contrast with those who value the middle years most and typically prefer ease and contentment. Similar attitudes have different meanings at various phases of the adult life cycle. For example, for some younger adults, a heavy future orientation provides escape from present problems, whereas a future orientation for older adults may reflect engagement in life. Older adults tend to develop more accepting attitudes about perceived realities. There is an increase in interest in topics such as history and philosophy that emphasize connections between the individual and the rest of mankind. When many associations are being severed, such broad interests provide a compensatory expansion of concern. Even a degree of rigidity that might interfere with adaptation in young adulthood may be adaptive and provide continuity and stability in old age.

Practitioners can use an understanding of developmental shifts in adult attitudes to help adults achieve transitions that entail attitude change. For example, especially during late adolescence and young adulthood, many people shift from absolute to more relative thinking and personal commitment. Those who plan educational programs can provide alternative sections. A section for more absolute learners might emphasize high structure, direct experience, and assistance with analytic skills and dealing with conflicting content. A section for more relative learners might emphasize low structure, indirect experience, and assistance with personal intellectual commitment.

Recent studies of moral development which have extended into adulthood suggest the effect that experience has on moral development. People tend to express a preference for moral solutions that are at the highest stage of moral development to which they have advanced. One exception occurs during late adolescence when some people reject the conventional morality that they had earlier internalized, regress to a lower stage of moral development, and then proceed more consciously to a higher stage of morality that is stabilized as a part of their own identity. Movement to the higher levels of moral development seems to require adult experience, such as sustained responsibility for the welfare of others, experience with conflicting values, and conscious choice and commitment. Significant adult experiences can contribute to reconsideration of thoughts and feelings about issues that can lead to wisdom. Erikson concluded that wisdom results from the detached yet active concern with life itself in the face of death itself.

Adult life cycle shifts in value orientations also occur. Young adults emphasize expansiveness and high expectations, middle-aged adults emphasize self-limitation and reduction of frustrations, and older adults emphasize transcendence of self and family to include people generally. Older women stress personal caring and religious life, and older men stress leaving a tangible legacy or contribution to society. Women tend to experience large value shifts with marriage and men with retirement. Practitioners can help adults recognize the process of value shifts and moral development during adulthood and can increase the availability and accessibility of opportunities for adults to explore moral and value issues in active ways likely to lead to growth and development.

Happiness, morale, and life satisfaction also fluctuate during adulthood and reflect both objective circumstances and approach to life. Satisfaction is a function of expectation as well as performance. Happiness is related to feelings of personal security, acceptance by others, personal efficacy, and a belief that life has meaning. Some maladjustments that appear during middle age reflect long-standing unresolved emotional problems that are revealed more clearly as a result of major role changes. Even desirable changes produce stress that can affect physical and mental health. Prior experience can provide perspective on problems. For example, older adults who experienced life-threatening illnesses in earlier years perceive chronic illnesses as less stressful than those without such prior experience. Life satisfaction in old age is little related to age as such but is much related to conditions, such as illness and poverty, that are associated with old age. If the individual has a long-standing pattern of poor adjustment, then maladjustment in old age is almost certain.

Adult life cycle fluctuations in happiness are relatively stable when compared with other characteristics, such as socioeconomic status, self-esteem, physical health, and social participation. Perceived well-being typically rises from late adolescence to young adulthood, drops in early middle age, rises in late middle age before retirement, and then declines in old age. Happiness tends to be associated with the individual's psychological resources. Reactive behavior tends to decline from late adolescence through middle age, followed by an increase in old age. Men tend to be more growth oriented than women and young adults more open to new experiences than older adults. Many older adults reminisce and weave recollected facts and unresolved conflicts of the past into an acceptable perspective. Often during a transition, a person experiences strong feelings of vulnerability and panic that make it difficult to maintain continuity and a sense of worth. Practitioners can assist adults to recognize the types of adjustments they are likely to confront, to develop realistic and constructive attitudes toward the resultant problems and opportunities, to acquire the needed understanding and competence, and to acquire supportive services.

In general, practitioners can help adults gain a broad perspective on stability and change in adult personality development. That perspective includes a recognition of the wide range of personality patterns that men and women have as a result of intelligence, sense of self, openness, role relationships, and emotional adjustment from childhood. Because it is affected by both personal and contextual influences, adult personality is malleable and responds to shifts in the fit between personal characteristics and societal circumstances. Getting established in young adulthood, a mid-life transition, and retirement can be major factors in personality development. Although relative activity level is quite stable, there is a trend for most adults during adulthood from active to passive mastery. Practitioners can assist adults of any age to become more proactive and self-directed through combining action and contemplation.

7

Adult
Learning

☙☙ ☙☙ ☙☙ ☙☙ ☙☙ ☙☙ ☙☙ ☙☙

Throughout life people remember, and think, and solve problems. During adulthood the process by which people modify their performance in family, occupation, and community roles partly reflects such cognitive activities. Many of the developmental changes in the ways in which adults think about themselves and their social and physical surroundings occur gradually and incidentally as a result of their transactions with their environment. For most adults, the typical monthly round of activities and thoughts tends to reinforce stability and minimize change. Major influences that encourage stability include societal values, role expectations, personality, interests, activities, habit, and inertia. It is typically easier to think and do things the same way unless boredom, frustration, or external circumstances precipitate a change.

Sometimes adults experience substantial changes in behavior as a result of personal effort or external circumstances that may precipitate, facilitate, force, or frustrate learning. The learning that occurs varies greatly in the mix of skill, attitude, and knowledge change that is entailed. The acquisition and modification of neuromuscular skills entailed in such activities as bowling, silver work, playing the organ, embroidery, operating a wood lathe, or playing darts, are related to adult life cycle trends in physical condition. Efforts to learn such skills are more likely to be successful if the efforts take into account the adult's condition and experience with similar skills. Changes in attitudes and feelings are sometimes the focus of deliberate learning efforts, as in individual and group therapy sessions. Attitude change is typically part of learning activities that deal mainly with changes in skill or knowledge. Efforts to change attitudes and modify the affective domain are more likely to be successful if they take into account the adult's personality dynamics and history of dealing with feeling. This chapter deals mainly with the cognitive domain and changes in knowledge and understanding.

In most instances in which adults purposefully engage in systematic and sustained learning activities, their intent is to modify performance. Their reasons for engaging in the learning activity and their anticipated uses of the new learnings typically relate to a coherent area of activity or performance. For example, during late adolescence and early young adulthood, most people in the United States learn to drive a car and obtain a driver's license. If passing the written driver's test was the only criterion of learning, comprehending and recalling the information in the state driver's manual would be the main learning activity, and answering a sufficient number of items on the written test would indicate successful performance. Actually, the main criterion in learning to drive a car is competent and safe operation of the car. In addition to the written test, a vision test and a road test are required as a basis for an examiner to estimate whether competent and safe performance is likely. Actually, performance is unsatisfactory if during the first year or two after obtaining a license it is revoked because of traffic. violations. Learning that results in competent and satisfactory performance entails the integration of new and changed knowledge, skills, and attitudes. Of particular importance is the development of judgment and responsible attitudes.

Some middle-aged workers with experience in specialized jobs become supervisors. This occurs, for example, when a secretary becomes an office supervisor, a loading dock worker becomes a foreman, an engineer becomes a manager, or a dancer becomes a choreographer. Learning to supervise others effectively typically entails many types of learning activities, such as closely observing others, on-the-job training, supervisory coaching by one's manager, supervisory training sessions, reading about supervision, and receiving feedback about the adequacy of supervisory performance. The supervisory position may include keeping track of time, materials, and money, which may require the acquisition of skill in the use of a calculator or other office machines. Often the new supervisor must acquire large amounts of new information about procedures and related operations that extend beyond his or her former specialized job. Supervisory training or management development sessions typically focus on helping the new supervisor to understand concepts about planning and interpersonal relations and to apply these concepts to improve supervisory performance. This may entail role playing and sensitivity training to develop greater empathy, as well as practice in conducting meetings or preparing reports. These learning activities are successful to the extent that the new supervisor integrates relevant experience and recent changes in knowledge, skills, and attitudes to produce improved performance.

A few older adults take up gardening for the first time as a leisure time activity about the time of retirement. Although they may take an evening course in home gardening and do some reading on the subject, much of their learning about gardening is likely to come from more-experienced gardeners and trial and error. In addition to information about germination periods, planting dates, and optimum amounts of sunlight, water, and soil acidity, the recent gardener typically applies already acquired skills in the process of planting, watering, and pruning. The attitudes that are acquired are likely to influence the attention to detail that contributes to success and the outlook on helping things grow that aids the inexperienced gardener in dealing with unsatisfactory results. In gardening, as in many other new tasks that adults attempt to master, it is not information but competence and performance that counts.

Because adults typically want to use what they learn soon after they learn it, it is usually easy to establish the connection between specific learning activities and the area of performance to which the new knowledge is to be applied. Although this sometimes creates some tension between the generalities of an educational program and the specifics of the individual's life to which new learning is applied, it does facilitate the less formal and deliberate learning activities in which adults typically engage as they attempt to increase understanding and mastery in a new area. Substantial adult learning occurs informally as adults seek to understand and deal with changes in their roles as family members, workers, citizens, and users of leisure, as well as in more formalized educational and therapeutic settings.

The purpose of this chapter is to review generalizations about adult learning with an emphasis on the personal and situational circumstances under which adults with various characteristics, including age level, learn most effectively. Some of these generalizations are about age trends in learning abilities, including some indices that increase during much of adulthood while others decline. Others are about how the adult approaches the learning task in terms of prior experience, motivation, and expectancy; how the adult processes information, including acquisition, memory, and forgetting in relation to exposure and pacing; and thinking and problem solving including attention to cognitive style and complexity of learning tasks.

Although much of adult learning is global and diffuse, almost all adults engage in some systematic and sustained learning episodes each year with the intention of increasing competence (Tough, 1967, 1971). These learning episodes may focus on a specific problem area or field of subject matter, such as practical politics, adolescent behavior, or accounting. However, they also provide a vehicle for the adult to test and modify understandings of self, others, and society. They may enable adults to explore and modify what they know about how they feel, or how they feel about what they know. When practitioners who work with adults are concerned about learning, the emphasis is often on cognition and verbal learning. Much of the tested knowledge on adult learning pertains to meaningful verbal learning. Therefore, this chapter deals mainly with the cognitive domain and age trends in the process by which adults modify their knowledge, understanding, thinking, and problem solving.

There are various types of cognitive learning. Gagné has listed eight that seem to be hierarchical, in that lower order types of learning are prerequisite to higher order types as the individual attempts to master any area of content (Gagné, 1972). Listed in ascending order are his eight types of learning:

1. Signal. The person learns to make a generalized response to a signal, as in classical conditioning.
2. Stimulus-Response. The person acquires an instrumental response to a discriminated stimulus.
3. Chaining. The person acquires a chain of two or more stimulus-response connections.
4. Verbal Association. The person learns and assembles verbal chains that are assembled from a previously learned repertoire of language.
5. Multiple Discrimination. The person learns to make differentiated responses to varied stimuli.
6. Concept. The person learns to identify and make a common response to an entire class of events or objects that serve as stimuli.
7. Principle. The person learns and is able to apply a principle that consists of a chain of two or more concepts.
8. Problem Solving. The person internally thinks through the combination of two or more previously acquired principles to produce a new capability that depends on a higher order principle.

In most instances in which adults deliberately set out to learn something, much of the prerequisite learning of the four or five lower order types has already been acquired, and the learner concentrates on concepts, principles, and problem solving. Where prerequisite learning has not occurred, a practitioner can diagnose the type of learning that is needed. For example, someone who experienced difficulty applying the principle of ecological balance in natural areas, such as a woodlot, might use field trip observations and reading to form concepts on relations between terrain, soil type, average rainfall, extent of groundwater, type of foliage, type of animal life, and erosion. The types of learning vary in the circumstances under which learning occurs most effectively.

Learning and intellectual performance is modified by various characteristics of the individual and of his or her context. Some of the main modifiers are:

1. Condition. Physiological condition and physical health can affect learning and cognition in various ways. Sensory impairment, such as poor vision or hearing loss, can restrict sensory input. Inadequate cerebral circulation or stress can impair memory. Ill health can restrict attention given to external events. In efforts to assess learning ability accurately and to facilitate learning performance, the adult learner should be in an environment that minimizes the extent to which physical condition and health interfere with learning. Examples include provision of good illumination without glare, sound amplification with good acoustics, and conditions that minimize fatigue and anxiety.

2. Adjustment. The effective assessment or facilitation of learning is less likely when there is substantial personal or social maladjustment in the learning situation. Such maladjustment is usually associated with learner defensiveness and anxiety and should not be confused with moderate levels of arousal and motivation. If a person believes that he or she can deal with a situation, it may be a challenge; if not, it may be perceived as a threat. People deal best with a failure when they have experienced many successes. Support and

assistance is especially important for adults with few recent educational experiences.

3. Relevance. The adult's motivation and cooperation in the learning activity is more likely when the tasks are meaningful and of interest to the learner. Active interest and participation are more likely when the learner helps identify objectives, selects learning tasks, and understands procedures.

4. Speed. Especially for older adults, time limits and pressures tend to reduce learning performance. Optimal learning performance is more likely when learners can proceed at their own pace.

5. Status. Socioeconomic circumstances are associated with values, demands, constraints, and resources that can affect learning ability. Level of formal education tends to be the status index most highly associated with adult learning. The influence of status on learning depends on the type of learning activity. For example, for learning the metric system, oral communications might be more effective for blue collar adults, and white collar adults might learn abstract concepts through written communication more effectively.

6. Change. Social change can create substantial differences between older and younger age cohorts (such as two generations) regarding the experience and values internalized during childhood and adolescence. This makes it difficult to compare two age cohorts regarding learning performance and conclude that the differences are the result of age.

7. Outlook. Personal outlook and personality characteristics, such as openmindedness or defensiveness, can affect the way in which an adult deals with specific types of learning situations.

As practitioners seek to understand and apply generalizations about adult learning and age, it is helpful to consider the areas of performance to which the learning is related, the

types of learning that seem needed, and the characteristics of
the learner and the context that are likely to affect learning
effectiveness.

Ability

There are times when adults of any age want to test or
estimate or predict their ability to learn or perform well in
educative activities. This occurs when a young man who
dropped out of school considers returning full time, when a
middle-aged woman with grown children considers taking some
courses to help launch a second career, and when an older adult
confronts the prospect of adopting a modified diet and medication for recently diagnosed diabetes. Their estimates of their
own learning ability are usually based on their composite recollection of how well they have performed in learning situations
in the past. There is a tendency for adults to overemphasize
their early formal schooling experience and to underemphasize
their recent experience with gradual and informal learning
and, in most instances, their learning ability.

Practitioners who work with adults sometimes want to
help adults improve their own estimates of their learning ability. One way in which supervisors, teachers, counselors, and
health professionals do so is to suggest that the adult engage in
a relevant educative activity on a modest scale and see how it
goes. For the adult with sufficient self-confidence to try, this
approach has the great advantage of the direct correspondence
between the modest educative activity from which the prediction is made and the more major educative activity that the
adult is considering. This approach also encourages the adult
to think developmentally about the series of educative activities
that have occurred over the years, about his or her typical learning style, and about the relation between learning interests and
learning abilities. There are several disadvantages with this
approach. One is that when the adult lacks confidence and does
not engage in a modest learning activity, there is no basis for
an estimate. A second disadvantage is that it is difficult to in-

terpret results as they might apply to other adults with varying characteristics, such as age and educational level.

At present there is no instrument or efficient procedure to estimate adult learning ability. The concepts and procedures for assessing intelligence were developed to estimate some combination of potential and actual ability to learn, reason, and solve problems. Early intelligence tests emphasized the potential ability of children and adolescents to master school subjects. The tests were predicated on the assumption that all young people had access to a common fund of information and experience and that when presented with intelligence test items the brighter ones would have accumulated a greater amount of competence so that more of the items would be familiar and would master the unfamiliar items more readily and rapidly. However, few intelligence test items correspond with the types of competencies that adults actually try to acquire. The most rigorous, widely used, and well-researched test of adult intelligence is the Wechsler Adult Intelligence Scale (Wechsler, 1958). Its eleven subtests are grouped into verbal and performance scales that vary with age. Scores from the Wechsler Adult Intelligence Scale (WAIS) are designed to provide a general estimate of ceiling performance on mental tasks. Adults who score high on the WAIS typically learn more effectively when they make a maximum effort than do adults who score low on the WAIS and make a maximum effort. Such scores usually provide a helpful estimate of adult ability to perform verbal learning tasks in educational settings (Knox, Grotelueschen, and Sjogren, 1968). It is less clear that they provide an accurate estimate of adult learning ability related to social effectiveness, such as modification of occupational performance or mastery of gourmet cooking.

Generalizations about adult learning ability and age are based on three types of indices. Almost all the tested knowledge about stability and change in learning ability during adulthood has been based on scores on intelligence tests, such as the WAIS. A few studies have been conducted in which comparable samples of adults at various ages have engaged in actual learning activities and their learning gains were compared (Sjogren and Knox, 1965; Knox and Sjogren, 1965). It is also possible to interpret tested knowledge about achievement and age as an indication of trends in learning ability. Adult learning performance reflects both innate ability and accumulated experience that the individual combines in performance. The adult who learns or creates or discovers something that neither he nor anyone else had accomplished before is evidencing new learning (Lehman, 1953). The adult who adopts a new practice or applies concepts in a new way is also evidencing new learning (Rogers and Shoemaker, 1971). In each of these instances, the accomplishments are complex, and factors other than learning ability, such as motivation and opportunity, are entailed. However, age trends in accomplishment and achievement at least indicate that advanced new learning by able adults continues to occur throughout life.

Estimates of learning ability are estimates of ceiling capacity. In practice people perform substantially below their capacities. Even for indices of learning ability that may decline gradually during adulthood, if the person functions throughout adulthood at no more than two thirds of young adult capacity, a decline in ceiling capacity of less than one third by old age would have no practical effect on performance. A general portrayal of this relation between capacity and performance is presented in Figure 19.

One of the best ways to discover age trends in learning

Figure 19. Capacity, Performance, and Age

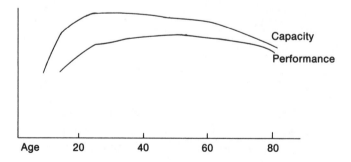

ability during adulthood would be to have the same representative panel of adults complete comparable relevant sets of learning tasks periodically throughout adulthood and compare their performance. These longitudinal findings would be misleading to the extent that social change or life cycle change altered the types of learning activities which are relevant at various stages of adulthood and that fewer of the least able survived (Riegel, Riegel, and Meyer, 1967; Baltes, Schaie, and Nardi, 1971).

However, if the purpose was to discover current age-related individual differences in learning ability, the preferred way would be to conduct a cross-sectional study at one time composed of a representative sample of adults of various ages. These findings would indicate the learning abilities that would be likely to occur among a representative sample of adults with whom a practitioner might work at one time, regardless of how their learning ability might have changed in the past or might change in the future. However, because older adults differ so much from young adults in extent and type of formal education, values internalized in youth, health condition, and interest in learning activities, cross-sectional findings provide an inadequate indication of age trends in learning ability. In practice, a combination of cross-sectional and longitudinal findings obtained for successive generations will provide the most comprehensive understanding of adult learning ability in relation to age, cohort (generation), and time of measurement (period of time in history).

Longitudinal studies of learning ability, mainly based on readministrations of intelligence tests, indicate a high degree of stability between twenty and fifty years of age and even beyond (Glanzer and Glaser, 1959; Anderson, 1960a; Kagan and Moss, 1962; Jarvik, Kallman, and Falek, 1962; Tuddenham, Blumenkrantz, and Wilkin, 1968; Schaie and Strother, 1968a, b, c; Green, 1969; Blum, Jarvik, and Clark, 1970; Piaget, 1972; Jarvik, Blum, and Varma, 1972; Furry and Baltes, 1973; Jarvik, Eisdorfer, and Blum, 1973; Blum, Clark and Jarvik, 1973; Cunningham, Clayton, and Overton, 1975; Cunningham and

Birren, 1976). The relation between learning ability and age, based on longitudinal studies, is represented by the upper trend line in Figure 20.

Most of the longitudinal studies of mental abilities during adulthood have been based on samples of those who attended college or who were intellectually gifted. People with the greatest learning ability tend to learn more rapidly and to learn complex tasks more readily. There was evidence of a somewhat greater increase or stability in learning ability for the more able adults, in contrast with the general adult population, although increases and decreases with age occurred at all ability levels (Owens, 1953, 1959, 1966; Bayley and Oden, 1955; Terman and Oden, 1959; Bradway and Thompson, 1962; Kagan, 1964; D. P. Campbell, 1965a, b; Burns, 1966; Schaie and Strother, 1968a, b, c; Blum, Fosshage, and Jarvik, 1972; Blum and Jarvik, 1974).

Some longitudinal studies have been based on samples of people who were diagnosed mentally retarded. The general trend from adolescence to young adulthood and into middle age reflected an increase in learning ability with age (Baller, Charles, and Miller, 1967; Skeels, 1966). The increase tends to be smaller, and to level off and decline sooner. The relationship between learning ability, learning performance, and age is presented in Figure 21.

Cross-sectional studies of learning ability typically report a decline with age in test performance (Willoughby, 1927;

Figure 20. Learning Ability and Age Based on Longitudinal and Cross-Sectional Studies

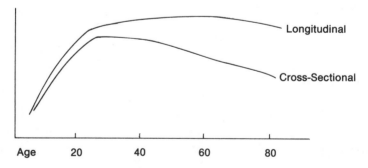

Source: Owens (1966), Jones and Conrad (1933).

Figure 21. Learning Performance and Age by High- and Low-Ability Adults

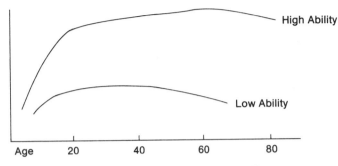

Source: Bayley and Oden (1955), Baller, Charles, and Miller (1967).

Thorndike, 1928; Miles and Miles, 1932; Jones and Conrad, 1933; Miles, 1934; Fox, 1947; Doppelt and Wallace, 1955; Ghiselli, 1957; Wechsler, 1958; Birren and Morrison, 1961; Horn and Cattell, 1966a, b; Fozard and Nuttall, 1971; Fozard, 1972; Fozard, Nuttall and Waugh, 1972). The relation between learning ability and age based on cross-sectional studies is represented by the lower trend line in Figure 20.

Based mainly on cross-sectional studies, there is evidence of an increasing range of individual differences in learning abilities, at least through the fifties. It appears that the most intellectually able people increase their learning ability more rapidly during childhood and adolescence, reach a higher plateau later in young adulthood, and then either continue to increase gradually or maintain learning ability during adulthood. By contrast the least intellectually able people increase learning ability more slowly, reach a lower plateau earlier, and decline more rapidly. This decline seems to be more rapid when based on cross-sectional studies on which Figure 22 is based than in longitudinal studies on which Figure 21 is based. As a result of these differential trends, a representative sample of fifty-year-olds is more varied in learning ability than a representative sample of twenty-year-olds (Foulds and Raven, 1948; Foulds, 1949; Roberts, 1968).

Especially for older adults, ill health can substantially reduce learning ability. When the healthy aged, whose learning ability is little different than it was a decade earlier, are com-

418   Adult Development and Learning

Figure 22. Increased Variability in Learning Ability with Age

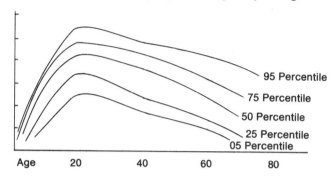

Source: Foulds and Raven (1948).

bined with the ill aged, some of whom experienced an abrupt
deterioration in learning ability, the average test performance
tends to be unrepresentative of either subpopulation (Birren
and others, 1963; Granick and Patterson, 1971). The relation
between health and mental performance is presented in Figure 23.

During the past thirty-five years there have been a fairly
large number of cross-sectional studies of intellectual functioning during a major portion of the life span. When these studies
are reviewed in chronological order, there is a trend toward a
rising age when peak performance occurred. In the studies conducted in the early thirties, peak performance occurred about
age twenty.. In the studies conducted in the fifties, peak per-

Figure 23. Very Healthy, Average, and Ill Aged:
Comparison of Mental and Social Performance Age Trends

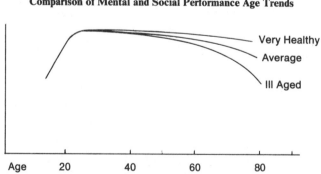

Source: Birren and others (1963), Granick and Patterson (1971).

formance occurred in the late twenties and early thirties (Schaie, 1974; Schaie and Gribben, 1975). This trend seems to reflect higher average levels of formal education and the impact of mass media during the past generation, and it illustrates both transactional influences on change in learning ability during adulthood and the importance of taking social change into account when interpreting cross-sectional findings as a basis for estimating aging trends.

When the global concept of potential learning ability or intelligence is operationalized through factor analysis of the thousands of available ability tests, between two and four dozen primary mental abilities or factors emerge (Horn, 1970). Some of the cross-sectional studies have included adults (Balinsky, 1941; Cohen, 1956, 1957; Maxwell, 1961; Green and Berkowitz, 1964; Weiner, 1964). Before adulthood there is a general factor that emerged from factor analytic studies of intelligence, and a similar general factor seems to emerge in later life. A general factor indicates that a substantial number of the ability variables are highly associated. During childhood and adolescence the factorial structure of intelligence becomes more differentiated. There is a high degree of stability during most of adulthood and perhaps less differentiation in old age.

When the primary mental abilities are further analyzed, the four second-order factors that emerge are speed, visualization, fluid intelligence, and crystallized intelligence (Horn and Cattell, 1967; Horn, 1968, 1970; Cattell, 1971). The latter two follow very different age trends during adulthood, and together they provide a useful basis for better understanding shifts in the ability to learn various types of tasks during adulthood. The theory of fluid and crystallized intelligence was developed by Cattell (1963) and has been further tested and refined by Cattell and by Horn (Horn and Cattell, 1966a, b; Horn, 1967; Cattell, 1968). The basic premise is that cohesion in intelligence is produced by two contrasting but interacting influences: neurophysiology and acculturation.

Fluid intelligence consists of the ability to perceive complex relations, engage in short-term memory, form concepts, and engage in abstract reasoning. Underlying fluid intelligence

420 Adult Development and Learning

is the neurophysiological base, referred to by Horn as the main ingredient in the anlage function, which consists of the unlearned reactivities and capacities that serve as a limit on the ability to process time-based information. Physiology depends on both heredity and the accumulation of injury to neural structures caused by disease, severe shocks, poisons, drugs, and injuries. Fluid intelligence is relatively formless and independent of experience and education. It can "flow into" various intellectual activities. Examples of subtests classified as fluid include rote memory, common word analogies, matrices, and verbal reasoning with common materials. An example of memory span is remembering a telephone number long enough to dial it, especially with direct distance dialing. An example of inductive reasoning is to discover the underlying rule that enables one to figure out the next number in a series, such as 1, 3, 6, 10, 15, ___.

Crystallized intelligence consists of the ability to perceive relations and to engage in formal reasoning and abstraction based on a familiarity with knowledge of the intellectual and cultural heritage of society. Crystallized intelligence is based on acculturation, including formal education and active information seeking, in which the individual mixes fluid intelligence with cultural knowledge. Examples of subtests classified as crystallized include general information, vocabulary, social situations, and arithmetic reasoning. Vocabulary tests, such as synonyms, along with reading comprehension and current events tests, assess how much knowledge the individual extracts from the social and physical environment.

Together these two kinds of intelligence cover many of the learning tasks that adults confront and constitute the global capacity to learn, reason, and solve problems that most people refer to as intelligence. Fluid and crystallized intelligence are complementary in that some learning tasks can be mastered mainly by exercising either fluid or crystallized intelligence. Examples include general reasoning and semantic relations. One person may solve a problem through brilliance that another solves through the application of accumulated wisdom (Horn, 1967, 1970).

Fluid intelligence, along with crystallized intelligence, increases during childhood and into adolescence. However, with the slowing of the maturation process and the lifelong accumulation of injury to neural structures, fluid intelligence tends to peak during adolescence and decline gradually during adulthood (Tuddenham, Blumenkrantz, and Wilkin, 1968; Fozard and Nuttall, 1971). This general decline in fluid intelligence during adulthood is reflected in the progressively lower performance with age on performance subtests than on verbal subtests of omnibus intelligence tests. However, it should be noted that the decline by the end of middle age is to a point comparable to the middle of adolescence.

By contrast, crystallized intelligence continues to increase gradually throughout adulthood. When untimed tests were used, especially in longitudinal studies, the scores related to crystallized intelligence were the same or higher in the fifties as in the twenties (Owens, 1953; Doppelt and Wallace, 1955; Droege, Crambert, and Henkin, 1963; Horn and Cattell, 1966a, b; Schaie and Strother, 1968a, b, c; Blum, Jarvik, and Clark, 1970; Cunningham, Clayton, and Overton, 1975). In the National Assessment of Educational Progress, achievement test scores were higher for adults than for seventeen-year-olds (U.S. DHEW, 1976). Beyond age sixty, as well as before, continued growth of crystallized intelligence depends on the continuing acculturation through information seeking and educative activity (Sward, 1945; Bayley and Oden, 1955; D. P. Campbell, 1965a, b). The relationships among these related variables and age are presented in Figure 24.

During adulthood, as fluid intelligence decreases and as crystallized intelligence increases, general learning ability remains relatively stable, but the older person tends to increasingly compensate for the loss of fluid intelligence by greater reliance on crystallized intelligence, to substitute wisdom for brilliance.

Although a wide variety of mental abilities have been analyzed and age trends indicated, some, such as listening and incidental learning from experience, have received little attention. When a wide range of learning abilities is included, the

Figure 24. Fluid and Crystallized Intelligence: Related Variables and Age Trends

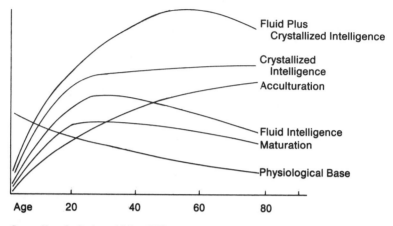

Source: Horn (in Goulet and Baltes, 1970).

general conclusion is that most adults in their forties and fifties have about the same ability to learn as they had in their twenties and thirties, when they can control the pace. There is evidence of some decline in learning ability during the sixties and beyond. The characteristics of learning tasks that are most associated with a decline in learning ability with age (even in middle age) are tasks that are fast paced, unusual, and complex.

Age trends in learning ability are associated with such factors as physical condition, social class, and personality. Care should be taken not to attribute to aging learning trends that actually reflect these other factors. For example, physiological functioning has some association with learning ability. This is reflected in the decline in later life in performance on learning tasks that are fast paced, involve physical skill, and are grouped in the category of fluid intelligence. The biological influence on learning ability and age is further corroborated by the greater similarity in learning ability among pairs of aged identical twins than among aged fraternal (or two-egg) twins and much greater similarity than among siblings. In addition, deterioration in learning ability by older adults sometimes reflects pathological conditions such as cerebral atherosclerosis and Pick's or Alzheimer's diseases. Deterioration can also result from mental and physical inactivity (Jarvik, 1975). At each age level, the learning abilities of some adults are greatly affected by such physiological conditions, but many adults are not. Although average trends in learning ability are thus lowered by affected older adults, the abilities of those unaffected remains high.

Another factor associated with learning ability and age is social class level and especially extent of education. As each recent generation has attained higher levels of formal and informal education, performance on tests of learning ability has been higher in young adulthood and has maintained the relative advantage at successive ages (Schaie, 1974). In addition, when initial abilities were controlled for a sample of older adults, there was a positive association between educational level and intellectual functioning (Blum and Jarvik, 1974). Social class level and extent of education are consistently far more associated with learning ability than is age (Fozard and Nuttall, 1971; Birren and Morrison, 1961). Educational and social activities in later life appear to be very valuable in this regard, along with those that occur earlier (Jarvik, 1975).

A third factor associated with learning ability is personality (Schaie and Strother, 1968c; Honzik and McFarlane, 1973). An individual's outlook can greatly affect the approach taken to a learning task, including a test of learning ability. Feelings of alienation, hopelessness, and defensiveness can discourage an individual from trying something new. Lack of engagement can also reflect depression that may result from emotional concerns as well as malnutrition and inactivity (Jarvik, 1975). Rigidity and inflexibility can also affect learning performance, especially for tasks that require novel solutions or divergent approaches. For example, adaptability to changed work conditions is associated more with flexibility than with age (Chown, 1972). The range of individual differences in personality as well as learning increases with age at least until the sixties.

Practitioners can help adults understand age trends in learning abilities and recognize the other factors that are also associated with learning ability. Such understanding is also useful to practitioners themselves as they plan educational activities for various categories of adults.

In helping people gain a more accurate understanding of adult learning ability, practitioners can emphasize several basic points. Almost all adults can learn almost anything they want to. The main exception to this generalization is that some older adults experience a terminal decline or severe health condition that greatly reduces the ability to remember, learn, and modify behavior deliberately. Otherwise, the maintenance of learning ability during adulthood is well substantiated by both longitudinal studies and anecdotal experience of adults of all ages who learn effectively in family, occupational, and community settings. With each decade there are more and more instances in which adult learning achievement is clearly demonstrated as men and women of all ages and walks of life increase their competence. This occurs as grandmothers earn high school diplomas, middle-aged men successfully complete occupational retraining programs, middle-aged women return to college, and retirees master new vocational or avocational fields. Human interest stories and other local examples of adults learning can help supplement generalizations from tested knowledge, and they are more convincing to many people.

Between the twenties and the sixties the range of individual differences in learning ability increases. Although there is some decline in more abstract learning abilities that are grouped in the category of fluid intelligence, crystallized learning abilities, which relate more directly to daily experience, are either stable or gradually increase during most of adulthood. Regarding both ability to learn and related background, a representative sample of adults in their fifties is more varied than a representative sample of adults in their twenties. Many of the educational programs for adults sponsored by employers, associations, religious institutions, community agencies, or educational institutions attract specific groups of people who are somewhat similar to each other. However, those who help adults learn typically confront a wider range of interest, background, and ability when the average age is older.

Adults sometimes want an estimate of their learning ability. When the intended learning activity consists mainly of verbal content, a brief vocabulary test provides a satisfactory estimate. However, available tests provide inadequate estimates of learning ability for many of the competencies that adults want to acquire. For many adults the most useful estimate is provided by their trying to learn a small aspect of the topic or activity, usually with competent assistance and frequent feedback about learning achievement. This approach to estimating learning ability also helps assess related considerations, such as interest and methods of learning.

Approach

The effectiveness of adult learning varies with learning ability, but it is also affected by the approach the adult takes to the learning activity. An adult's approach to a learning activity reflects previous experience, including extent and type of formal education, recent use of learning procedures, and current circumstances that give rise to the need for increased competence. Most adults approach learning activities with specific expectations about what they will gain from the experience. Other people associated with the learning activity, such as other participants and practitioners who help adults learn, also have specific expectations and, in some instances, educational objectives. Both persistence in a learning activity and actual learning achievement can be greatly affected by the educational climate and procedures that enable the identification of congruent expectations and objectives. For example, in some educational programs for adults time is spent on exploring and agreeing on learning topics and activities that are very relevant to the participants. This involvement contributes to interest, achievement, and application.

One aspect of previous experience that affects adult learning is formal preparatory education during childhood and adolescence. The preparatory education experience can both facilitate and inhibit adult learning. If the early school experience is characterized by low achievement and feelings of failure, the likely results are reduced accumulated knowledge, learning skills, persistence in school, self-confidence as a learner, and participation and interest in educative activity. However, the person who obtains more formal education typically has acquired greater educational interest and skills, is active in occupational and social settings that encourage and support educative activity, and brings to the activity a heightened level of learning ability (Campbell, 1965a, b). The average older adult has less formal education than the average younger adult, and that which was learned is typically more remote in time and relevance. For the person in late adolescence or young adulthood whose school experience was very negative, it may take several years for negative attitudes to fade and be replaced by the perception of benefits and voluntary participation in educational activities as an adult.

Because about one out of five United States adults participates in a major educational activity during the course of a year, recency of educational activity is not solely a function of age. Recent participation in educative activity results in increased knowledge and content competence. Such participation also results in increased competence in the process of learning. For adults with comparable ability, those who recently participated in educational activities learned more effectively than those who did not (Sorenson, 1930, 1938; Sjogren and Knox, 1965).

Recent experience and current circumstances influence an adult's interest in educative activity. Recent role changes that call for adaptation, urging by significant others to obtain more education, and optimism regarding a future job promotion help increase awareness of needs for increased competence and encourage educative activity. The typical result is greater motivation to engage and persist in learning activities (Havighurst and Orr, 1956; Knox, 1970). For most people, the first half of adulthood has more role changes, encouragement regarding further education, and optimism for the future than the last half of adulthood. There are, however, developmental concerns, tasks, and role changes during the latter half of adulthood that provide a stimulus to educative activity and a focus for the acquisition and application of new learnings. Examples include job changes, widowhood, and grandparenthood. The age trend for number of role changes, based on scattered findings from many studies, is presented in Figure 25.

Figure 25. Typical Number of Role Changes at Each State of the Adult Life Cycle

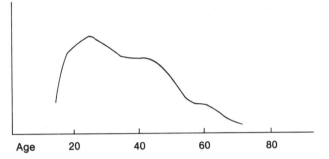

Age   20   40   60   80

An adult typically approaches a learning activity with expectations and understandings that influence learning effectiveness. One type of expectation has to do with the relative emphasis given to the mix of anticipated benefits, such as use of increased competence to achieve an external goal, interest in the subject matter content, and enjoyment of the activity. Although most adults engage in educative activity for multiple reasons, often one predominates. Young adults tend to be goal oriented. Older adults are more likely to emphasize reasons related to content and activity. Another type of expectation concerns the learning process. Many adults have a preference for some learning procedures, such as reading, observation, or group discussion. This preference is more likely to be clear and accurate if there were recent similar learning activities. Because rates of participation in educative activity decline with age, those older adults who lack recent educational activity but participate in an educational program may be especially unfamiliar with the process. Practitioners who are alert to this can provide orientation and assistance to facilitate their getting started.

When adults engage in a learning activity on a self-directed basis, their own expectations provide the primary guide to activity, and other people serve mainly as sources of encouragement and learning resources (Tough, 1967, 1971). However, when other people, such as teachers, counselors, supervisors, and other participants, also take part in planning and conducting the educational activity, their expectations influence the learning activity. These other expectations can enrich and deepen the learning activity through the raising of productive questions and the sharing of useful insights and information. The combining of expectations can also cause severe compromises with an adult's learning objectives and reduce achievement and satisfaction. It is usually helpful to have some way of exploring the expectations of the adults who participate in an educational activity and of arriving at congruent shared expectations and objectives.

One way in which adult learners can clarify their expectations about a learning activity is to have an example or model of what they should know or be able to do as a result of a successful educational experience. Especially in some work, athletic, and health settings, it is helpful if this mode is personified by someone who is already competent. Seeing someone like yourself who recently learned to do a stem turn in skiing or to walk for the first time with crutches provides both a role model and a source of encouragement. A model of criterion performance can also be conveyed by a diagram or by written or oral descriptions. Practitioners can arrange for such exemplars for both educational groups and self-directed learners.

Usually, when an adult sets out to learn about something, it is related to a large amount of experience and information that the adult already possesses. The person's current understanding of the topic or problem is typically organized around his or her previous encounters with it. This results in a cognitive structure. For example, an adult's understanding of and ability to get around in a strange city is affected by first impressions when approaching the city and by related information from maps and directions provided by others. From this the individual forms a cognitive map of the parts of town to which he or she wants to travel. If this initial mental map is relatively accurate, it becomes easier for the adult to add new information and get around effectively. A trip to an unfamiliar part of town is then relatively straightforward to the extent that the individual is able to use accurate and relevant information from the mental map or from external aids, such as a printed map or assistance from others.

Adults acquire relevant cognitive structures from many

sources. More extensive and accurate cognitive structures facilitate mastery of related concepts. An adult with a master's degree that included political science and economics courses is likely to have acquired some general concepts about our political and economic system that can undergird new ideas confronted in a management development program on current social issues. An adult with a tenth grade education who has extensive experience with school and tenant groups is likely to have formed a cognitive structure about institutional and intergroup behavior into which new information from a neighborhood discussion group is fitted. Older adults are more likely to have formed detailed cognitive structures around most of the topics about which they learn, not because they are older but because there has been more time to accumulate relevant experience. When these cognitive structures are inadequate, they can interfere with effective learning. It appears that young people may use the structure of content to facilitate retention more than older adults (Craik, 1968; Rabbitt, 1968).

When prior learning and experience has not produced an adequate mind set or expectancy regarding a learning task, questions and instructions can be used to help the learner organize in advance some of the main ideas into which to fit the subsequent learning. When practitioners who seek to help adults learn are uncertain about their existing cognitive structure, it is usually worth the effort to help them diagnose their current view of the topic or problem, and then, if needed, use questions and basic ideas to establish a more adequate cognitive structure on which to build further understanding.

In facilitating the approach that adults make to learning activities, it is perhaps most important to establish a rapport and climate that encourages and allows learners to consider their own expectations and those of others and to select learning objectives which are attractive and realistic. Self-directed adult learners usually perform this function for themselves. When others participate in the learning activity, up to one quarter of the available time can be devoted to this process of diagnosis, need appraisal, and objective setting; if it is well done, the learning achievement can be greater than if the entire time were

430 Adult Development and Learning

devoted to the learning activities. This type of involvement of participants in goal setting can be especially effective when potential goals are diffuse and interpersonal needs are high.

Adults develop a positive approach to the use of educative activity as a result of successful experiences in the use of intentional learning to achieve their purposes. Learning from one's experience contributes to judgment and effective priority setting. For some adults, early life experience in educative activities in and out of formal education brought satisfaction and recognition, with the result that the adult has a high sense of educational efficacy. Such adults believe that educative activity is an effective means to increase competence, and they enter educational activities with optimism and confidence. Adults are also encouraged to have a positive image of educative activity when they are aware of a varied range of relevant educational programs, especially if some of the people they know report satisfaction from participation. However, it is difficult for practitioners to alter an adult's sense of educational efficacy or the available opportunity system as a basis for encouraging more educative activity. One way would be to provide successful experiences in which educative activities help achieve personal purposes.

There are several ways in which practitioners can assist adults to develop a more positive approach to education. One is to help them use intentional learning activities to cope with changes and adjustments in their life. Examples of such adjustments include changes in major life roles, patient education, and organization development activities. In each of these instances, a change in performance heightens readiness to learn and focuses the adult's attention on needed changes in competence. A second way in which practitioners can provide encouragement is to help adults become more aware of role models who have already acquired the competence they desire. A third way is to create settings in which adults have the freedom to explore within democratic limits both the achievement of their current educational objectives and the discovery of additional desirable objectives. Adults with a positive approach to learning are more likely to engage in an educational activity and to persist until their objectives are achieved. For adults who do not already have a positive approach to learning, practitioners can use procedures to help develop more positive attitudes.

A more positive approach to learning can result when a person better understands connections between organized knowledge and personal experience. Those who help adults learn in ways that closely relate knowledge resources to action concerns of the learners typically give serious attention to cognitive and affective development of the participants before, during, and after the educational activity. A practitioner, such as a teacher or counselor, who obtains an estimate of a learner's extent of cognitive complexity and flexibility can more readily use appropriate approaches to instruction or guidance. Learners can then be helped to confront pluralistic viewpoints in terms they can handle (D. E. Hunt, 1970). Participants with a high need for structure can be helped to deal with relative concepts. Those who are becoming more able to deal with relative concepts can be helped to make personal commitments that reflect such concepts (Perry, 1970; Stern and Cope, 1956; R. J. Hill, 1960).

An example of an instructional approach that emphasizes connections between organized knowledge and personal experience is the laboratory for student development, which combines some features of an encounter group with the content of a college psychology course on personality (Madison, 1969). In this approach, the instructor works with about a dozen students. The course syllabus lists the readings on personality theory and provides detailed instructions for students to prepare related materials on their own experience. These materials include autobiographical reports and a weekly journal that emphasizes emotionally charged experiences. The student-prepared materials include both descriptions and interpretations of the personal meanings of the experiences. Copies of these materials are shared with the instructor and with all other group members as a basis of class discussion and illustration of concepts from the course readings. In this way basic concepts are discussed in relation to both organized knowledge and personal understanding. As a way of helping students understand interrelationships among personality concepts as they occur holistically for an individual, the entire set of materials for individual course members are used as case examples that are discussed by the entire group in an effort to understand and explain personality dynamics as an aspect of personal performance. In some instances, students can further apply concepts from the course in "contracts for changing." Such agreements reflect an individual student's commitment to try to achieve a specific growth goal with assistance from the instructor and other course members. An example might be to shift the emphasis from unwanted "shoulds" acquired from others to "shoulds" that the student accepts as desirable.

Educational programs that explicitly deal with alternation between knowledge and action can occur in many fields. In the humanities, social sciences, and occupational fields such as education and social work, there are many opportunities to use discussion, field experiences, and simulation to bring together organized knowledge and personal understanding. This concern for application is even more straightforward for many adult groups in which the participants can apply what they learn in their daily lives.

Processing

In addition to ability and approach, there are age-related individual differences in some aspects of the information processing entailed in adult learning. The process of learning includes many aspects, only some of which have been studied in relation to age, including adulthood. Most studies of adult learning have been of knowledge acquisition, in contrast with modification of skills and attitudes. Aspects of adult learning for which available tested knowledge provides the basis for developmental generalizations include: (1) attention to information (perception, meaning, persistence, set, association); (2) memory (registration, retention, and recall; short- and long-term memory; forgetting); (3) practice and reinforcement (rehearsal, reward, conditioning); (4) interference (relearning, retroaction, unlearning); (5) pacing (speediness); (6) transfer (application); and (7) incidental learning. For many of these aspects, the effectiveness of the learning process partly depends on whether the adult is able to interact with appropriate learning resources.

Attention. Most purposeful learning by adults occurs as a result of attention by the learner to information in some form. The learner attends to information in many ways, such as looking at a display, reading a book, discerning attitudes, and listening to a presentation or discussion. In most learning situations there is far more information available than the learner can assimilate. In some instances the degree of complexity and detail can be overwhelming unless the adult engages in selective perception. If the new material to be learned is related to a relatively large amount of detailed and accurate information that the person already possesses, this accumulated familiarity can enable the learner to be selective in his or her perception in a useful and accurate way. Many older learners have acquired a broad understanding that they lacked when they were younger. Effective adult learning typically entails an active search for meaning and discovery of relationships between current competence and new learnings. Unfamiliar and complex learning tasks are especially confusing for elderly adults. Under these circumstances the learner may attempt to extract meaning from the meaningless by misperception. The effort to inappropriately apply familiar concepts in an unfamiliar situation leads to perceptual distortion.

When an adult who is voluntarily engaged in an educational activity discovers a lack of fit between his or her current understanding and new information, there are a variety of alternative responses. Included are acceptance of a challenge with increased or focused effort, distortion of information to minimize the discrepancy, and withdrawal from the learning situation. The alternative an adult selects in a specific instance is a function more of personality, experience, and situational constraints than of age. In some instances, the individual's reasons for wanting the understanding or competence are so weak that persistence in the learning activity will occur only with a minimum of obstacles. In other instances, the reasons may be too strong. Overly intense motivation becomes anxiety, which interferes with learning (M. D. Vernon, 1969; Heim, 1970; Cofer, 1972).

One way to encourage adults of any age and background to persist and learn is to help them set educational objectives that lie between apathy and disabling anxiety and constitute realistic objectives and a satisfying challenge. This can be done in some instances by providing questions, prompts, organizers, or directions that guide the learner's attention and help establish the connection between current and new information. In contrast with younger adults, older adults learning new verbal associations more readily learn connections that build on well-established linguistic habits and less readily learn connections that are in competition with such habits (Kausler and Lair, 1966; Canestrari, 1966; Lair, Moon, and Kausler, 1969).

There is a tendency during adulthood for a greater task orientation and for a set or expectancy that emphasizes accuracy in learning tasks (Arnhoff, 1959). In some basic learning tasks which entail instrumental conditioning with an emphasis on stimulus generalization, some older adults are so task oriented that they reduce speed to maintain a high degree of accuracy and in some instances achieve errorless performance. The remainder of older adults have about the same level and variability of performance as young adults. This intense concern for accuracy can contribute to persistence, success, and satisfaction in learning activities, but it can also block flexibility and innovation. Useful exploration can be hindered by adults' feeling that they must be "right" to avoid "making fools" of themselves.

Memory. Especially for older adults, memory ability has a major influence on learning. Memory includes three phases: registration, retention, and recall. Registration includes exposure to the stimulus or information, the acquisition of the information, and the electrochemical process by which the information is encoded in the brain. Retention includes the persistence or decay of the neural traces that are encoded. Recall includes the searching and retrieval process by which the individual recovers or remembers the information. There appears to be a clear physiological distinction between primary storage for immediate and short-term memory and for intermediate and long-term memory. Most of the tested knowledge on adult memory and age is about immediate and short-term memory.

With advancing age, there is an increasing registration deficit. This occurs for information acquired by both visual and auditory means, but especially for visual memory, perhaps because of a breakdown in the conversion of visual information into auditory memory storage (Arenberg, 1967b).

The ability to retain information in immediate access and short-term memory tends to be relatively stable during most of adulthood if the material is meaningful, if the criterion for learning is errorless acquisition of all material, and if the amount of information to be stored is not too large for immediate access memory (Moenster, 1972; Clark and Knowles, 1973; Schonfield, 1969). However, when the material was not meaningful and the criterion for acquisition was a fixed number of trials, there was a marked decline in retention with age (Wimer and Wigdor, 1958; Wimer, 1960; Hulicka and Rust, 1964; Hulicka, 1965; Hulicka and Weiss, 1965; Laurence, 1967a, b; A. Smith, 1975). There is clear evidence that meaningful memory is distinct from memory of nonsensical material (Kelley, 1964).

The recall or retrieval of information is greatest when the material is meaningful and when the recall conditions are very similar to those under which the original registration occurred. This is especially so for older adults. When individuals try to respond to and store new information at the same time that they are trying to recall stored information, there is a memory deficit, especially for older adults. This occurs, for example, when someone's comment triggers a flood of old memories and the next few sentences are missed. Over the years, as adults acquire more information related to a topic, they can make more cross references and potential connections between new and stored information. As a result older adults tend to expand the scope of search when trying to recall information, which takes more time and may result in greater interference with the new material to be learned. There is also an age trend toward greater caution. The errors in recall by older adults tend to be errors of omission (forgetting items) rather than errors of commission (mistakes) (J. Rees and Botwinick, 1971). In general there is a gradual decline in recall ability during adulthood. Part of this decline reflects greater memory decay for older adults. However, interference from other information previously stored and from simultaneously engaging in the search process accounts for a greater portion of the decline (Shakow, Dolkart, and Goldman, 1941; M. A. Speakman, 1954; Clay, 1956; Welford, 1958; Kay, 1959; Talland, 1965; Laurence, 1967a, 1967b; Craik, 1968; Anders, Fozard and Lillyquist, 1972; Brinley, Jovick, and McLaughlin, 1974).

Some portion of remembering, especially for older adults, reflects the effectiveness with which the individual groups and relates stored information. Individuals who cluster information on the basis of categorical or associative relationships have greater recall for information that is amenable to organization, but older adults tend to make less use of organizational processes and thus experience a decrement in recall performance. However, under conditions that maximize the possibility for meaningful organization, older adults have less of a recall deficit. There are little or no age differences in recall for adults with high verbal ability, but there are significant declines in recall from young adulthood onward for adults with low ability. It is likely that older low ability adults are less able or less willing than younger low ability adults to organize information for retrieval. Although there is some decline in registration with age, it appears that the decline in memory with age mainly reflects a decreased ability to recall or retrieve information mainly because of inadequate organization at the time of input (Hultsch, 1971a, b; Hultsch, 1969; Bower, 1970; Hultsch and Craig, 1976). Noncognitive and perceptual difficulties can also depress learning by older adults, even when there is little or no deterioration in short-term memory (Moenster, 1972; Clark and Knowles, 1973).

For material that is once learned, the decline with age in extent of immediate recall from short-term memory is much greater than the decline in recall of old material from long-term memory (Bromley, 1958; Caird, 1966; Craik, 1968; Inglis and others, 1968). Decades after material has been learned during which there has been little or no practice, only a small amount is forgotten, and it can usually be regained by practice (Botwinick, 1967).

Forgetting depends on the strength of the original registration of information and on factors, such as disuse and interference, that erase the registration. The strength of registration results from frequency, intensity, and importance of exposure and tends to require more time for older adults. Because immediate memory tends to decay more rapidly for older adults, they require an optimum spacing schedule that contains adequate time to attend to the information without distraction and relatively short intervals between information. If the rate is too fast or too slow, there is increasingly more forgetting, is too fast or too slow, there is increasingly more forgetting Hultsch, 1971).

Practitioners can help adults compensate for inadequate memory in several ways. The presentation of new information can include aids to help the learner organize it for more complete recall. Summary materials can facilitate review. The pacing of each learning session can allow the learner to proceed at a rate that allows both mastery and continuity. If an educational program consists of a series of weekly sessions, crucial prerequisite ideas from earlier sessions can be reviewed at the outset of a session. If older adults experience difficulty recalling and expressing in words what they learned, the selection of posters or other displays that illustrate a concept can be used to evaluate learning.

Practice. Most learning requires more than a single trial or exposure. Practice or rehearsal occurs in many forms. In some instances it is apparent, as in learning to play a musical instrument or speak a foreign language. In other instances, practice occurs in a less evident form, such as working accounting problems or reviewing text materials. A degree of rehearsal even occurs through discussion as participants acquire and refine concepts and are conditioned to associate terms with definitions. Part of the conditioning process in any of these practice situations is the reinforcement, recognition, or reward that the learner receives. The type of reinforcement varies greatly in adult learning situations. Examples include having the engine run after learning how to repair it properly, completing a self-scoring proficiency examination after having read some home study materials, or having the ceramics instructor point out some sound and some questionable procedures to a person beginning to use the potter's wheel. In verbal learning tasks that entail successive trials until the learner reaches a criterion, older adults typically require more practice or trials (Levinson and Reese, 1967; Taub and Long, 1972; Taub, 1973). Some of the forms of reinforcement, such as occupational achievement, prospects for future success, or recognition by peers, become less salient rewards for many older adults.

Practitioners have little tested knowledge about what kind and how much reinforcement is most effective for adults of various ages and characteristics. However, the most effective practitioners acquire competencies in planning and conducting educational programs that include attention to practice reinforcement. Included are matching program objectives to learner needs so that the prospect of major and multiple benefits encourages the learner to attend to the learning tasks; providing a variety of learning tasks so that practice and review are encouraged; having feedback and recognition for educational achievement; encouraging learning group support; and connecting educational activities with activities in family, work, or community to which new competencies are to be applied (Knox, 1974, 1976; Gagné, 1972). For older adults, or for persons with low learning ability, practitioners can simplify learning tasks and use more tangible forms of reinforcement (Belbin, 1972; Botwinick, 1967; Zimmerman and others, 1969). Adults who have not engaged in educational activities for many years become less effective learners for various reasons, one of which is a more restricted range of incentives and rewards to reinforce learning activity (Sjogren, Knox, and Grotelueschen, 1968). Practitioners can give special attention to such learners and can partially offset their disuse of learning procedures by orientation, assistance with study skills, and support from resource persons and other learners.

Interference. In most adult learning tasks, the person acquires some related information before or after the learning activity that can interfere with an accurate recall of the material which was learned. The interfering information inhibits the recall or retrieval efforts of the learner. Proactive inhibition occurs when the interfering information was acquired before the learning activity, and retroactive inhibition occurs when it was acquired afterward. When an adult studies a topic over an extended period, some prior learning facilitates new learning, some interferes, and some is unrelated. When an adult already has some broad and accurate understanding of a topic being studied, it is likely that this prior learning will facilitate the new learning. However, when prior learning is similar but different in some important respects, it often interferes with the new learning. Examples include a new telephone number that is very similar to one which was familiar years before, the similarity between a word or pronunciation in a familiar language and a similar instance in a new language, or learning slightly different lyrics to a long familiar song. The old habit is so strong that it is difficult to establish and follow the similar but different new one (Monge, 1969). It is as though the new association is a bicycle rider who attempts to take the left fork in a deeply rutted country lane where the auto tracks follow the right fork. Unless the rider is very attentive, the bicycle will take the right fork automatically.

When there is troublesome interference, the adult learner may take longer to master a learning task because it is necessary to unlearn the interfering material as well as to learn the new material. Reviewing information while recalling other information from memory causes more interference in middle age than in young adulthood (Talland, 1965; Taub, 1968; Hultsch, 1974). Although there is evidence that interference is a greater detriment to learning for older adults, this seems to be a result more of the strength of the habit that develops over the years in relation to a familiar topic area than of age itself (Hulicka, 1967). Therefore, less interference would be expected for an older adult who is learning in an entirely new topic area than for a young adult who attempts to learn new material for which major interference conditions exist.

Pacing. The speed or pace at which learning occurs is one of the major age-related influences on adult learning effectiveness. Adults of any age, but especially older adults, learn most effectively when they set their own pace, take a break periodically, and fit the distribution of learning episodes to the content. Adults vary greatly in the speed at which they learn most effectively. Older adults tend to reduce speed of learning and to give greater attention to accuracy. If adults are forced to proceed much faster or slower than their preferred pace, their learning effectiveness typically declines (Eisdorfer, 1963; Sjogren and Knox, 1965; Botwinick and Thompson, 1967). For older adults much of the decline in educational performance reflects a deficit due to speed instead of a decline in learning power. Slowing down is one of the most characteristic features of old age (Botwinick, 1973; Gaylor, 1975). This reduction in speed is mainly due to physiological changes. Greater available time and adequate pacing can help reduce age differences in learning performance. When there is a longer time or delay or anticipation interval preceding the presentation of serial information, however, there is a greater deficit for older learners (Brinley and Botwinick, 1959; Canestrari, 1963, 1968; Arenberg, 1965, 1967a).

Transfer. Adults usually engage in purposeful learning because they want to apply or transfer what they learn to a variety of conditions beyond the one in which the learning occurred. On simple memory association tasks there tends to be greater learning transfer by young adults than for adults in middle and old age (Gladis and Braun, 1958). It is not clear to what extent transfer is related to age for more complex and familiar learning tasks. Older adults tend to persist with nonproductive problem-solving task strategies, but more young adults learn from experience and modify their strategy. It appears that the range of individual differences in learning transfer increases during adulthood at least until the sixties.

Incidental. In addition to the learning that results from intentionally attending to a learning task, the adult incidentally acquires from the general learning situation other information that is also remembered. Most of the studies of adult learning have dealt with intentional learning; only a few have dealt with incidental learning. Extent of incidental learning tends to parallel the adult life cycle trend in intentional learning of either stability or gradual decline. When the intentional learning task is simple and when the learner proceeds at a slower rate, greater incidental learning typically occurs. There are several interpretations of any decline in incidental learning by older adults. One is that it represents a loss of valuable related information which could enrich understanding and establish connections with related knowledge. Another is that it is adaptive for older adults to concentrate on relevant cues and ignore irrelevant ones (Wimer, 1960; Hulicka, 1965; Kausler and Lair, 1965).

Resources. For each foregoing aspect of the learning process, the individual interacts with some external source of information or subject matter content. These sources of information and content come in many forms, such as radio lectures, small group discussion, reading articles, field trip observations, and supervisory coaching. The people and materials with which the learner interacts constitute resources for learning. Some of these learning resources, such as a textbook or a study group session, are typically designed by someone else to facilitate learning. Other resources, such as a radio program or a period of intensive observation, may be used by the learner to increase understanding. The effectiveness of adult learning depends in part on the availability, appropriateness, and effectiveness of such resources for learning.

Effective learning resources help adults: (1) become more interested in the topic, (2) understand major aspects of the topic around which details can be organized, (3) relate new information to current understanding, (4) persist in the learning activity, (5) register information so that it is retained as long as needed and can be recalled when needed, (6) obtain sufficient practice and reinforcement, (7) minimize interference, (8) proceed at an optimum pace, (9) make the transfer of information learned to the situations to which it is likely to be applied, and (10) maintain a balance between intentional and incidental learning.

The learning resources that are likely to meet the foregoing criteria will vary substantially with some characteristics of the learner, such as interest in the topic, opportunity for application, level of education, and age. The process of adaptation and change during adulthood tends to produce heightened readiness to learn. Learning resources can contribute to interest and application by relating to these developmental concerns. The level of experience, education, and specific understanding that the individual has in relation to a topic influences the type of learning resources which are likely to be challenging instead of boring or overwhelming. In addition there are some adult life cycle shifts in the types of learning resources that are most effective. These developmental trends reflect changes in interests, memory, and pacing. Practitioners can select and prepare learning resources that are appropriate for each clientele group and can assist adult clients to do so for themselves (Knox, 1976).

To summarize major generalizations about adult learning, some ways practitioners can help adults with various characteristics, including age, learn effectively include:

1. Emphasize Abilities. Adults vary in their abilities and disabilities related to learning. For example, there is great variability at any age in abstract conceptualization or in mechanical aptitudes, and although fluid intelligence may decline with age, crystallized intelligence is very stable or increases. Educational activities for adults can be designed to minimize features related to disabilities and to emphasize features that build on abilities and experience.

2. Clarify Structure. If adults understand major aspects of a topic, they are more able to relate it to what they already know and to accumulate additional knowledge. Advance organizers facilitate the process of building a useful cognitive structure. So does the provision of clear instructions and explanation of concepts and a gradual progression from easy and basic concepts and procedures to more difficult ones.

3. Memorable Encounters. What adults remember and can recall of what they learn depends partly on how

they feel about what they learn. The words and concepts that have great salience in the lives of adults are
more likely to have the affective intensity and importance which will result in a strong registration in
memory. Memorable encounters and materials are also
more likely to result in rehearsal and reinforcement.

4. Personal Pacing. Adults learn more effectively when
   they proceed at their own pace.

5. Varied Resources. Adults learn from many resources
   including books, tape recordings, films, experts, and
   peers. They tend to persist and to learn better when
   they are able to use preferred resources.

6. Feedback. Learning persistence and effectiveness is
   enhanced if the adult can obtain feedback about the
   extent and type of change in competence that results
   from educative activity. This feedback can result from
   test situations, comparisons with external standards,
   and reactions by peers (Belasco and Trice, 1969).

Thinking

Most of the tested knowledge about adult learning is
concerned with either general indices of learning ability or
specialized aspects of learning process. However, there have
been efforts to understand developmental changes in thinking
during adulthood as reflected in creativity, problem solving,
and critical thinking. For practitioners who work with adults,
it is especially useful to understand interrelationships between
modification of thinking and changes in competence and performance. In general, it is in relation to competence and performance in naturalistic settings that adults obtain their most
useful feedback regarding extent of attainment of learning objectives. Three themes around which generalizations about
thinking and age are clustered are content, cognitive style, and
achievement.

   Content. The competencies that adults attempt to acquire vary greatly. Most include the acquisition of some new
organized knowledge, such as learning a set of interrelated gen-

eralizations about rates of population growth, industrialization, production of food and industrial products, and currency exchange in relation to international trade and tariff policies in an educational program on world affairs. Some efforts to acquire a new competence also include skill acquisition, such as learning how to embroider, repair engines, bowl, or sail a boat. Many efforts to acquire greater competence also include some modification of attitudes toward other people, the natural environment, or oneself. For some learning activities, such as an encounter group, attitude change may be the main purpose. However, for many learning activities on such topics as music appreciation, ecology, and family relations, the feelings and attitudes of people associated with the learning activity are part of the content, and their modification is part of the purpose for participation. Some of the developmental changes in learning and thinking that typically occur during adulthood interact with various types of educational objectives and content. A better understanding of these typical interactions among thinking, content, and age can help practitioners create circumstances under which adults with various characteristics including age will learn most effectively.

Problem solving is a way of thinking in relation to many adult life roles, especially occupational roles. In some occupations, such as engineering, medicine, and equipment repair, an accurate diagnosis or formulation of the problem and the development and implementation of a plan to remedy the situation or solve the problem is at the core of what the effective practitioner does. In most fields there is much anecdotal evidence that older, more-experienced practitioners tend to be more effective in the solution of complex and subtle problems than younger, less-experienced practitioners. The physicians who are reputed to be the most effective diagnosticians tend to be those who have been in practice for many years, not those who are a few years out of medical school. However, the conclusion based on this anecdotal evidence fails to distinguish between experience and age. Studies designed to discover age trends in problem-solving performance have been based on samples of adults of various ages who have dealt with problem-solving tasks that minimize transfer from accumulated experience. However, such artificial problem-solving tasks may reduce the interest and effort of older learners.

There is evidence from various problem-solving experiments based on cross-sectional samples of adults that effectiveness of problem-solving performance declines with age. Some portion of the decline may reflect the greater emphasis on scientific problem solving in the preparatory education and early life experience of today's young adults, in contrast with that which occurred one or two generations ago when today's older adults were in their youth. Even so, there are several characteristics of the less effective problem-solving strategies of the older learners. Among these are: (1) the greater tendency to repeat nonproductive efforts to solve a problem and to repeat noninformative inquiries; (2) the memory requirement that adversely affects problem-solving performance of older adults, a deficit which partly persists even when note-taking techniques are used to decrease memory demands; and (3) a tendency of older adults to rely on concepts and strategies that have been effective in the past, even though they are not effective in a specific current instance. Under circumstances such as the latter, some older adults misinterpret feedback on errors as though it confirmed their responses. The unfounded conclusion that they were proceeding successfully toward a solution avoided feelings of discomfort but delayed the solution. Even when a successful solution strategy was presented, a small number of the older adults experienced great difficulty in applying it (Jerome, 1962; Wetherick, 1964, 1965, 1966; Glixman, 1965; Young, 1966; Arenberg, 1968a, b, 1973; Eisdorfer, 1969). However, in a six-year longitudinal study, an important age decrement occurred only for adults beyond age seventy (Arenberg, 1974).

Regardless of the generalizability of conclusions from artificial problem-solving tasks, it appears that adults tend to enlarge their repertoire of prepared solutions over the years. The solution process for older adults then consists mainly of searching the repertoire instead of generating novel solutions. This is likely to result in more effective problem solving with age through most of adulthood, even though on problem-solving tasks that require novel solutions there may be a decline in effectiveness with age (Birren, 1964a).

For some purposes and content areas, critical thinking is crucial. Critical thinking includes the ability to interpret data, weigh evidence, and engage in deductive thinking. There is evidence of a decline in critical thinking beyond the thirties, based on cross-sectional data. The older adults exhibited somewhat less objectivity and flexibility, which reduced their critical-thinking performance (Friend and Zubek, 1958; Brinley, Jovick, and McLaughlin, 1974). However, when cross-sectional and ten-year longitudinal follow-up data for a sample of young and middle-aged men were compared, although there was a small decline with age in critical thinking subtests based on the cross-sectional data, the longitudinal data showed a significant increase (Glanzer and Glaser, 1959).

Creativity is another aspect of thinking. Most of the studies of scientific and artistic creativity and age have used the creative output as the index. The conclusions are that peak ages for men vary with types of creative fields, the peaks typically occur in the first half of adulthood, and the decline is sharper and earlier for the works of highest quality. When performance on a measure of creative intellectual output was studied, the test performance of men and women was parallel to the trends from the productivity studies (Bromley, 1956). In one study on the use of brainstorming in courses on applied imagination, it was concluded by Parnes and Meadow that the adults in their thirties and forties gained as much as did younger students (Taylor and Barron, 1963). There is some evidence regarding creativity during adulthood which indicates that it is both feasible and desirable and that educational activity can facilitate it (MacKinnon, 1960; Barron, 1963; Foster, 1973; Alpaugh, Renner, and Birren, 1976). There is some physiological evidence that highly creative adults approach tasks in a distinctive way. The brain wave patterns of creative adults reflect their greater sensitivity to external stimuli and receptivity to internal impulses, combined with less mental control and censoring during the exploratory and innovative stage of creative effort. Less creative adults concentrate too earnestly, stifle novelty, and often concentrate on the defects of an approach instead of exploring its potential. It appears that creativity mainly reflects physiology and personality and is little related to age.

Another aspect of learning and thinking in naturalistic situations is task complexity. Adults tend to learn most effectively when learning tasks are complex enough not to be boring but not so complex that they are overwhelming. An optimum degree of complexity tends to minimize mistakes that sometimes have to be unlearned. As task complexity increases, age differences also increase. Many older adults learn more complex tasks less well and are more readily distracted by irrelevant information (Clay, 1954; Young, 1966, 1971).

Cognitive Style. Most of the study of cognitive style has occurred with preadults in artificial rather than naturalistic settings. However, because of the potential for better understanding adult learning, some of the major dimensions are presented.

The term *cognitive style* refers to the individual's typical modes of information processing as he or she engages in perceiving, remembering, thinking, and problem solving. Cognitive style reflects consistencies in the form of cognition in contrast with the content of cognition or the competence displayed. Individual differences have been demonstrated on many aspects of cognitive style, most of which can be subsumed within the following nine dimensions:

1. Tolerance versus Intolerance for Incongruity. The extent of acceptance of perceptions that differ from conventional experience (Klein, Gardner, and Schlesinger, 1962; Rokeach, 1960; Gardner and others, 1959).
2. Reflectiveness versus Impulsiveness. The extent to which various possibilities are considered before deciding (Kagan, Rosman, and others, 1964).
3. Constricted versus Flexible Control. The extent of susceptibility to distraction and cognitive interference (Klein, 1954; Gardner and others, 1959; Gardner, 1962).

4. Focusing versus Scanning. The extent and intensity of attention deployment and span of awareness (Holtzman, 1966; Schlesinger, 1954; Gardner and others, 1959; Gardner and Long, 1962).

5. Leveling versus Sharpening. The extent to which memory blurs and merges similar objects or events (Holtzman, 1954; Holtzman and Klein, 1954; Holtzman and Gardner, 1960; Gardner and others, 1959).

6. Complexity versus Simplicity. The extent to which the world, especially social behavior, is construed in a multidimensional and discriminating way (G. A. Kelly, 1955; Bieri, 1955, 1961; Bieri and others, 1966; H. Leventhal, 1957; W. A. Scott, 1963).

7. Conceptual Differentiation versus Description. The extent to which categorization uses many differentiated concepts, such as thematic, functional, descriptive, and class membership (Gardner and Schoen, 1962; Messick and Kogan, 1963; Kagan, Moss, and Sigel, 1960, 1963; Hess and Shipman, 1965).

8. Analytic versus Global. The extent to which items are perceived as discrete from their backgrounds and embedding context (Witkin and others, 1962; Davis, 1967; Kagan, 1965; Gardner, 1964; Gardner and others, 1959; Gardner, Jackson, and Messick, 1960; Gardner and Schoen, 1962).

9. Breadth versus Narrowness of Categorizing. The extent of preference for an acceptable category range that is broad and inclusive rather than narrow and exclusive (Pettigrew, 1958; Bruner and Tajfel, 1961; Kagan, Rosman, and others, 1964).

Presently there are only hints of associations between cognitive style and learning effectiveness for adults. For example, analytic learners seem to be more effective than global learners, although global learners may be more effective on some nonanalytic tasks. The more cognitively complex learners tend to stress differences, and the more cognitively simple learners tend to stress similarities. Cognitively complex learners tend to achieve better under conditions of independence, and cognitively simple learners achieve better under conditions of conformity. Persons with a high degree of "set" may be more effective in problem solving, except when unexpected and novel solutions are required. There seems to be a shift toward a more analytic style between childhood and adolescence, which tends to stabilize during early adulthood. There appear to be cognitive style changes during adulthood that may be substantial between middle and old age (Witkin and others, 1954, 1962; Heglin, 1956; Kagan, Rosman, and others, 1964; Santostefano, 1964; Young, 1966; Hulicka and Grossman, 1967; Frederick, 1968; Hultsch, 1969, 1971a, b, 1974; Gruber, 1973; Arlin, 1975; Botwinick, 1975; Kahana, 1975).

Achievement. Adults who engage in intentional learning, whether they do so on a self-directed basis or through participation in an educational program, usually do so with an orientation toward an application of the increased competence. The application is typically in the form of changed performance in family, work, or community, including roles as citizen and user of leisure. Examples of changed performance as a result of new learnings include caring for a young baby, establishing a farm record system, playing poker, performing open heart surgery, bird watching, and conducting meetings. An adult might do some reading, attend a lecture, participate in a study group, or receive assistance from a more experienced person in an effort to increase competence in relation to any of these areas of performance. In doing so, the adult typically has some model or example in mind of other adults who are already able to perform well. The example may be one person or a composite, and it may actually reflect either excellent or inadequate performance, but for the potential learner, it serves as a reference point of desired performance against which to compare the adult's current performance. The gap between the two constitutes the educational need as perceived by the adult that often activates educative activity. In some instances, the discrepancies between current and desired competencies are clearly delineated, as with the self-assessment inventories that are used in some professional fields. An example is the comparison of a physician's diagnostic procedure on a simulated patient management problem with that of a panel of outstanding diagnosticians, followed by a listing of selected readings at points where major discrepancies occur. Usually, however, the adult has only a dim feeling of discrepancy between aspiration and actuality. Once the adult is engaged in a learning activity, the reference point of desired performance serves as an objective against which to assess progress.

For almost all adults and almost all learning tasks adults are likely to undertake, successful achievement is a function of perseverance (Sjogren, 1967). Persistence in a learning activity is encouraged by a sense of progress in closing the gap between current and desired competence and in redefining and sometimes extending the reference point of desired competence. As is the case for learners at any age, adults learn more effectively when they receive feedback about how well they are progressing. Information about excellent performance helps clarify goals for learning efforts. Feedback about current performance helps learners locate themselves on a scale of progress in the educational activity. This is especially important, because objectives are often broad and progress gradual. Immediate feedback, recognition, and reward help shape and reinforce new learning. Positive reinforcement (reward) is far more effective than negative reinforcement (punishment).

In one major study with a representative sample of adults who studied brief topics typical of educational programs for adults, all participants learned satisfactorily. More than 98 percent persisted throughout the series of weekly or biweekly learning activities that lasted about half a year. For each topic, the learner completed a pretest, a posttest, and a retest several weeks later and a follow-up test a half year later. The content that was studied consisted of unfamiliar verbal subject matter on familiar topics, such as insurance, art, stocks, and government. Those who learned more effectively were those with higher scores on the Wechsler Adult Intelligence Scale (WAIS), higher levels of formal education, and recent experience in educational programs. There was no significant association with age (Sjogren and Knox, 1965).

The learning materials were highly programmed, and the participants received frequent and detailed feedback. There was high association between learning gain and WAIS scores, thus confirming a strong relationship between adult intelligence and ability to learn verbal materials (Knox, Grotelueschen, and Sjogren, 1968). Even a score based on less than twenty items from a separate vocabulary test had a high correlation with the WAIS, which indicates its potential for diagnostic use with adult learners (Grotelueschen and Knox, 1967).

Adults vary in the outcomes they emphasize as desired achievement and in the methods they prefer for attaining even the same outcome. Some adults with open and flexible personality characteristics and learning styles achieve better with such methods as discussion, while some adults with more rigid and structured personality characteristics and learning styles achieve better with such methods as the lecture (R. J. Hill, 1960). Feedback about learning achievement should reflect variability in both the emphasis on various areas of competence that adults seek to acquire and the methods they prefer for acquiring the competence.

Generalizations about thinking and age can be used by practitioners in various ways. As with other aspects of learning and cognition, the range of individual differences in reasoning, problem solving, and cognitive style tends to increase throughout most of adulthood. For example, although there is some evidence of a decline in deductive reasoning beginning in the fifties, many people who have achieved outstanding creative accomplishments based on deductive reasoning have done so in their fifties and sixties. As practitioners provide programs and services for various groups of adults, their background, experience, and learning style can be taken into account. Particular attention can be given to helping adults learn how to learn more effectively (Argyris and Schön, 1967; Belbin and Belbin, 1972; Bradford and others, 1964; Chisholm, 1958; Gold, 1972; Jamieson, 1966; Rogers, 1973; Zimmerman and others, 1969). As practitioners plan and conduct educational activities for adults, generalizations about thinking and age can be used to facilitate the learning process for the specific adults who will participate. Some adults are very able learners, are highly self-directed, and have ample educational resources available. Others will benefit from assistance (Crovitz, 1966; Fisher and Pierce, 1967; Cautela, 1969).

As adults engage in intentional learning activities, they do more than acquire knowledge, skill, and attitudes. They also modify the strategies they use for learning. Learning strategies partly reflect the individual's cognitive style, based on intelligence, personality, and past experience. They also reflect the characteristics of the content, including complexity, and the emphasis on problem solving, critical thinking, or creativity. With age, adults tend to acquire a larger repertoire of strategies. However, older adults may concentrate on selection from their available repertoire and may not recognize when novel solutions or approaches are needed. An important contribution of practitioners is to help adults acquire a more satisfactory repertoire of learning strategies.

There is very little tested knowledge available about adult learning strategies, but it does appear that many adults typically use some relatively stable and predictable strategies in attempting to master a variety of problems and learning tasks. Many intentional learning activities for adults consist of one or a series of learning episodes that last an hour or so. Examples of the types of learning tasks that might be the focus of a learning episode include location of the solution to a problem, memorization of meaningful verbal material, and identification of generalizations within specific concrete information. There are various ways in which the effectiveness of learning strategies might be judged, such as short completion time, accurate mastery of task, few errors before completion, elegance of solution, retention of content that is mastered, and extent of transfer to similar tasks. Some learning strategies seem to be more effective than others. Of special use are the strategies that adults use to alternate between the action problems they confront and relevant knowledge resources.

It may be some years until research on adult learning strategies has identified the strategies that are typically most effective for adults with various characteristics. In the meantime, practitioners who help adults learn can be alert to the strategies that adults use when they learn, can note features that seem to be associated with learning effectiveness, and can suggest modifications where warranted. For example, a practitioner may note that an adult who already knows something about a topic being studied starts at the beginning of the materials, reads at an even rate until the end, and then goes on to other activities. The practitioner might discuss with the adult learner the value of fitting new ideas with what the learner already knows. If the learner understands and is interested in pursuing this concept, the practitioner might suggest that next time the learner should skim the reading materials, looking at headings and topic sentences to decide how familiar he or she already is with each section. If a self-scoring quiz on the material is available, the learner might take the quiz first as another way to identify familiarity with the several sections. As a result of some type of preliminary review, the learner can consider both familiarity and importance and then quickly skim the sections of high familiarity and low importance and carefully read and analyze the sections of low familiarity and high importance. After reading the material, the learner might think about how the contents of the readings are likely to be used in the future and pose questions to guide a review of the major points that were noted when the material was being read.

Another illustration of an attempt to modify a learning strategy also starts with a description of the sequence of activities in which an adult learner typically engages but focuses on the method by which the information is obtained. Some adults have difficulty with reading as a method of acquiring new ideas but are able to acquire substantially the same ideas from conversation or demonstration. If this seems to be the case in a specific instance, a practitioner such as a work supervisor might suggest to a worker that the worker might observe someone performing the new task, ask questions, and then use the manual and the training sessions to consolidate comprehension of a procedure which the worker basically understands.

Some new tasks that an adult confronts entail elements of a problem-solving strategy for mastery. When this is the case, most of the suggestions about decision making that were included in Chapter Six on personality could be presented by a practitioner. In addition, the client might be helped to understand that many life problems are global and interconnected with many related problems. If the individual tries to grapple with all aspects of such a global problem, the result tends to be overwhelming and self-defeating. A more effective approach is to recognize the larger context but select an aspect of the global problem on which to focus and proceed to clarify that specific problem in the search for the most desirable and feasible solutions. In discussion related to problem solving, specific questions thus tend to be more useful than broad topics.

Although the evidence is somewhat mixed, there are clear indications of some deterioration of problem-solving performance in old age (Canestrari, 1967). For practitioners who work with older adults, such generalizations are most useful when combined with suggestions about how to compensate for the deterioration. Following are some of the factors that seem to contribute to a deterioration of problem-solving performance, along with ways in which practitioners can help older adults compensate:

1. Decline in Short-term Memory Capacity—Provide for memory aids, such as paper and pencil for notes and lists of needed information for ready reference.
2. Increased Difficulty Organizing Complex Material—Provide advance organizers, sets of categories, and generalized structures to assist in the grouping of information in a form useful for problem solving.
3. Greater Interference from Previous Learning—Help learners identify old and interfering ideas or practices that need to be unlearned and engage in activities to extinguish the old and unwanted association as well as to acquire the new learning.
4. More Difficulty Disregarding Irrelevant Aspects in Learning Situation—Minimize distracting and irrelevant information and activities, both in instructional materials and in the setting in which learning occurs.

5. Reduced Ability to Discriminate between Stimuli—
Increase the contrast between similar stimuli, for example, by providing reading materials with large, clear
print and large diagrams that emphasize distinguishing
characteristics.

The success of learning and problem-solving strategies
depends partly on the adult's belief that reading and discussion
and other educative activities can actually contribute to the
achievement of any important personal goals. Adults with a low
sense of educational efficacy believe that they are unable to
increase their understanding and competence, or even if they
could, it would not help them much. The first belief is reflected
in the saying, "You can't teach an old dog new tricks," and the
second by the saying, "It's not what you know but who you
know." Over a period of time, a series of success experiences in
which systematic efforts to increase competence have led to
greater effectiveness and satisfaction can lead to an increase in
a sense of educational efficacy. Practitioners might encourage
adults with a low sense of educational efficacy to acquire these
types of success experiences.

Practitioners sometimes complain about the diversity of
backgrounds and interests in a group of adults with whom they
work. The expressed concern is that it is difficult to be clear
and relevant with such a diverse group. This variability in part
reflects the varied experiences that each member has accumulated. However, many effective practitioners have discovered
that this wealth of varied experience also constitutes a valuable
resource which can be used by other group members. In addition, practitioners can help adults recognize that their own
experience is a valuable resource. Especially during transition
periods, prior experience can be deliberately used to provide
organization and direction. Almost forgotten information and
a recollection of successful previous growth experiences can be
reviewed, selected, and consolidated. By learning from one's
experience, the conclusions from the past can become the raw
materials with which to build the future.

The conclusion from many research studies that almost

all adults can learn is generally heartening and contributes to optimism, but practitioners usually need something more specific. The importance of intellectual activities in daily life has been rapidly increasing during the past three generations. To merely maintain one's knowledge level and ability to understand during a knowledge explosion is to fall behind in relative terms and to experience some degree of obsolescence. This puts a premium on ways to increase competence. Some methods are helpful for all adults. For instance, practice and review increase memory for adults of all ages but are not more helpful for older adults than younger adults. However, some methods are generally more important for older adults. When information is presented rapidly and with brief exposure, older adults have greater difficulty storing and recalling the information. Practitioners can therefore slow down presentations and allow more exposure time. Many older adults also feel increased fear of failure in educational settings, which calls for greater reassurance and support in educational programs for many older adults.

Some of the changes with age in learning effectiveness reflect the interaction of experience and intelligence. As adults accumulate experience and information, an increasingly complex structure of related information is stored in memory. Depending on the fit between the new learning and the accumulation from prior learning, the learning of a specific topic or task may be either facilitated or inhibited. Changes in an individual's cognitive structure are partly produced by significant life experiences that entail the use of intelligence. Practitioners can help adults increase their learning effectiveness by diagnosing their current understanding of a new topic and then building on relevant areas of understanding and competence as well as modifying and adding understanding where needed.

Intelligence tests and other estimates of learning ability are useful as modest predictors of achievement by adults in formal educational activities. However, such test scores are less predictive of performance in life tasks where motivation and circumstances are even more influential on results. For example, there is some indication that being dissatisfied with one's

life and thus trying harder is one of the personality characteristics that is most highly associated with an increase in intelligence between young adulthood and middle age (Honzik and
McFarlane, 1973).

Practitioners can help adults learn in almost any setting
by assisting them with activities and approach. Generalizations
about adult learning can be used to design educational activities
and materials so that they are optimal to facilitate learning.
This entails attention to such matters as structure, pacing, and
feedback. Assistance with learning approach entails helping
individual adults understand their own characteristic learning
strategy and sense of educational efficacy and recognize ways
in which their approach might be improved. This often includes an expansion and refinement of the adult's repertoire of
strategies for alternating between action problems and knowledge resources.

Case Examples: Jack, Carl, Evelyn, and Pearl

Personality development during adolescence and young
adulthood tends to be more extensive and to continue longer
at a rapid pace for high ability people than for those with low
mental ability. However, there is evidence of personality development and improved performance by low ability adults as
well.

The report of a longitudinal study of people who in
childhood were diagnosed as mentally retarded contained biographical sketches of some of the people who were interviewed
through their fifties (Baller, Charles, and Miller, 1967). This
section contains highlights from the sketches of four low ability
adults, a relatively successful and a relatively unsuccessful
male, and a relatively successful and a relatively unsuccessful
female. The section concludes with an identification of factors
asssociated with effective performance by low ability adults
generally.

When compared to people with average ability, a much
higher proportion of those with low ability came from blue
collar families in which their father had an occupation of very

low prestige, such as unskilled labor. For some, a language other than English was typically spoken in the home. As youngsters, their repeated IQ scores below 70 and their inability to do acceptable work in regular classes resulted in their assignment to special education "Opportunity Rooms" until they left school. Their school performance and life-styles as adults in part reflected their generally low social class backgrounds as well as low mental ability. Compared with average adults, the group with low ability generally held very low status occupations, participated in much less social activity, experienced much more marital instability, had slightly more problems with the law, had a higher death rate, and lacked optimism for the future. Although they typically got off to a slow start, however, between young adulthood and middle age there was a steady trend toward greater self-support. Many of the people with low ability improved their intelligence test performance from adolescence to young adulthood and maintained or further improved their intellectual performance into middle age. Many fared far better than expected.

Jack's performance was relatively effective in work, family, and community. His first work was in a large manufacturing company, and after seven years of reliable performance in unskilled tasks, he obtained a steady job with the railroad that he retained for more than twenty years. Jack's self-acceptance was reflected in his willingness to do his best, even if it was not much. At age twenty-nine, he married a woman who was three years younger, had completed two years of high school, was well trained in housekeeping by her mother, and was interested in music and church. She worked after their marriage as an ironing woman at a laundry. They owned a modest but well-kept house in which they lived for most of their married life. Their health was good. Family life with their one son was stable and congenial, and included regular church attendance, some organizational participation, and fishing.

Carl's success in life was minimal. He rejected both parents and school when, as an adolescent still at the third-grade level, he quit and "hopped a freight." A series of unskilled jobs in farming, mining, and construction took him all over the

country—he lived in four different cities during his forties—
although he always returned to his childhood home. In his early
fifties Carl was living with his second wife and five children in
a rented home. Since he had sustained a back accident two
years earlier, he was totally on welfare.

Although Evelyn grew up as one of eight children in
the poverty-stricken family of an unskilled truck driver, she
acquired hope for a better life. She left school at the seventh
grade level and at age sixteen got a job as a chocolate dipper
in a candy factory where she worked for seven years until she
was married. She enjoyed working and also family life as she
later raised three children, cared for the house, and engaged in
some organizational participation, such as the PTA. Her husband was a successful masonry contractor, and their attractive
stone home, motorboat for fishing, and camping unit reflected
their above-average income.

Pearl left school, her parents, and her five siblings at age
sixteen and began a series of housecleaning or dishwashing
jobs for a month or two at a time until she was married at age
twenty to a man who also had low mental ability. When she
had been married eight years, she and her husband and five
children lived in two exceedingly filthy rooms. Her husband
was able to obtain only part-time and low-paying jobs, and the
family was on relief. Her first husband died of lung cancer
when she was forty-six, and her second husband died of a heart
attack six years later. A pattern of sexual promiscuity began
during her teens and continued much of her life. In her mid-
fifties, she lived with a mentally retarded son, on welfare and
meager earnings from her sewing.

These brief biographical sketches illustrate factors associated with effective performance in work and family by low
ability adults that emerged from the total study. The more
successful males acquired occupational competence early and
worked at it regularly, usually with a large organization, instead of trying a variety of jobs. They typically stayed in one
community or neighborhood instead of drifting around. They
married better educated, well-adjusted women who brought
planning and stability to the family. The more successful fe-

males learned grooming and health care early, worked steadily, and married well. Unlike Pearl, most of the less successful females were more dependent on their mother and home, perhaps reflecting an overprotection of low ability daughters that results in lifelong inadequacy. The sense of being somebody and a positive outlook by low ability adults was fostered by early experiences, positively reinforcing work experiences, and the influence of significant persons. Older relatives, neighbors, employers, and sometimes teachers provided guidance and encouragement for low ability adults to "do the right thing" and "become somebody." More of the less successful low ability adults, especially the males, did not live with their parents, received little advice and encouragement, and had parents who expressed little interest in the lifework of their offspring. The contribution of stability in work and family is related to the problem of newness for those of low ability. Lack of ways to cope with unfamiliar situations can lead to dysfunctional behavior.

Practitioners can help low ability adolescents and young adults reduce problems of newness by reducing the attractiveness of some goals, increasing frustration tolerance, avoiding some new situations, acquiring competencies to reduce newness, and obtaining specific social skills to facilitate acceptance (Meyerson, 1963; Tobias and Gorelick, 1960; Farber, 1968). In addition to direct assistance to low ability clients, practitioners can help their significant others to recognize how much they can contribute to stability and how much they can assist people with low ability to cope with newness. During the past two decades there has been substantial progress in the development of settings, such as sheltered workshops and simplified training procedures, that enable retarded adults from sixteen to sixty-five years of age who have IQ scores between 50 and 75 to achieve at least partial self-support and a real sense of accomplishment (Bailey, 1958; Hunt and Zimmerman, 1969). In one Chicago agency, about five hundred retarded adults produce pillow covers, candles, and wooden games. Each new worker starts at a task geared to his or her ability. Procedures for testing, training, and assistance from counselors and supervisors assist workers to progress to more difficult jobs. Special patterns simplify choices by workers and help increase productivity. Wages are based on regular industrial rates, but if workers operate at two-thirds capacity, they are paid at that ratio. As individuals' productivity improves, so do their wages. Workers whose performance warrants are placed in similar jobs in industrial firms.

The four case examples of low ability young adults illustrated several ways in which the societal context can interact with the other major aspects of adult development. Many of the low ability people who were studied grew up in blue collar families in which very limited income and understanding of sound nutritional and sanitation practices adversely affected physical condition and health. In contrast, performance of physically active chores and work in some instances helped members of blue collar families to increase physical condition and decrease tension. The work and home settings of blue collar adults are more often hazardous, as reflected in higher accident rates in unskilled jobs in fields such as construction and mining and in the incidence of fires related to space heaters in homes during very cold weather. In contrast, the stability and predictability of life-styles for some blue collar adults in rural areas and small towns can contribute to higher levels of health, safety, and physical well being than that associated with larger urban areas or white collar neighborhoods.

In some families, friends and relatives helped low ability people to develop a concept of themselves as worthwhile human beings. Others did not. During adulthood, spouses or close friends can help increase or decrease confidence and self-esteem. Especially for the low ability adult, a stable context over the years helps reduce problems of newness. The slow rate at which learning occurs allows the person to accumulate competence gradually, adapt slowly to new tasks, and not have to adjust rapidly, which places the low ability adult at a great disadvantage.

Some portion of low mental ability is inherited, but some part of low intelligence reflects typically lesser stimulation and opportunities in the setting. Especially for the low ability person, the acquisition of some areas of competence, and recognition for it, contributes to a more positive self-concept. This in turn can contribute to persistence in learning activities and performance in various life roles.

In most types of performance there are alternative patterns that an adult might consider. Many occupational tasks can be satisfactorily achieved in various ways. This is taken into account in management by objectives. In recent generations, young adults have been increasingly aware of a variety of lifestyles and patterns of family life. Great variability exists in patterns of leisure and community participation. Practitioners can help adults who confront choices regarding family, work, and community activities to recognize some of the relevant alternatives, along with some of the conditions and processes typically associated with successful performance. Examples include the young adult who decides on a combination of work and educational experiences to pursue career goals and the older adult who reduces some role relationships and augments others as part of the adjustment to retirement.

In earlier times, when social change occurred more slowly, many adult life roles had relatively standardized scenarios that were apparent from observation of people at successive stages of adulthood as they engaged in role performance. Because adults today are less certain about what lies ahead for them, practitioners can help by indicating typical ways in which adult role relationships evolve over the months and years. Examples include the several career changes that most adults experience during their work life, the shifts in family life that occur as the children grow up, and the use of part-time educational activities to facilitate adaptation to major change events.

Practitioners can also help adults recognize the ways in which they can assume major responsibility for systematic adaptation and learning in relation to health, skills, attitudes, knowledge, and all types of performance. In an era and society with widespread change and complexity, the process of lifelong learning seems essential if adult life is to be purposeful, full of growth, productive, and satisfying. Practitioners can facilitate this process by helping adults discover the processes and resources needed for their continual development.

Some of the main implications related to role performance pertain to newness, encouragement, personality, and abilities. In each instance practitioners can help the adults with whom they work better understand and guide their own unfolding lives. Most people enjoy new experiences. However, some adults experience great difficulty with the unfamiliar. This is especially so for some adults who have very low mental ability, become very anxious under conditions of uncertainty, or are elderly. Especially for adults who have great difficulty coping with unfamiliar tasks and situations, practitioners can help in several ways. One way is to assist the adult to understand that unfamiliar situations generally are difficult for the individual to cope with and to recognize the main unfamiliar tasks which are especially troublesome. A second form of assistance is to explore the individual's sources of stability and security that enable him or her to deal most effectively with new tasks and situations that the individual confronts. A third contribution by the practitioner is to help the adult develop habits that minimize the unexpected. Examples include defensive driving and accident-prevention precautions in home, work, and community. A fourth way in which a practitioner can be helpful is to suggest more modest new experiences that the individual can handle and that can provide variety and interest. When persons confront any major adjustment, if it is possible to help them master some of the main new elements beforehand, the period of major transition is likely to be more satisfactory. Examples include some training and orientation before a major job change and development of some leisure activities before retirement.

Summary

Adults continually learn informally as they adjust to role changes and in various ways achieve adaptation and growth. Many engage in at least one systematic self-directed learning activity each year, and some adults engage in more formal part-time educational programs. Practitioners who work with adults in relation to occupational, family, and community roles are often in a position to facilitate adult learning. Generalizations about developmental trends in condition and personality are useful to practitioners, especially in relation to modification of skills and attitudes. The generalizations in this chapter relate mainly to acquisition of knowledge.

Learning achievement is modified by various characteristics of the individual and the learning context. Included are physical condition, social adjustment, content relevance, pacing, socioeconomic status, social change, and personal outlook.

Both practitioners and their adult clients are sometimes concerned about trends in learning ability during adulthood. Adults tend to underestimate their learning ability by overemphasizing their early school experience and underemphasizing their recent informal learning experiences. Tests and other estimates of learning ability indicate the individual's ceiling capacity. In practice, people perform substantially below their capacity. Although cross-sectional studies of learning ability indicate a gradual decline during adulthood, longitudinal studies of the same people over the years indicate great stability during much of adulthood and even increases for the more able adults and for familiar topics. Almost any adult is able to learn almost any subject given sufficient time and attention. However, there is an increasing range of individual differences in learning abilities, at least through the fifties.

Performance on tests of fluid intelligence, such as short-term memory and abstract reasoning, tends to peak after adolescence and to decline gradually during adulthood. Performance on tests of crystallized intelligence, such as general information and formal reasoning, continues to increase gradually throughout most of adulthood. As fluid intelligence decreases and crystallized intelligence increases, general learning ability remains fairly stable. As a result, when they can control the pace, most adults in their forties and fifties have about the same ability to learn as they had in their twenties and thirties. Older adults experience the greatest difficulty with learning tasks that are fast paced, unusual, and complex. Level of formal education is far more associated with learning ability than is age.

Learning effectiveness is also affected by the adult's approach to the learning activity. This approach partly reflects personality characteristics such as self-directedness and preference for structure. It also reflects recency of educational experience. For adults with comparable ability, recent participants in educational activities typically learn more effectively than those who had not. Role models and other ways of portraying criterion performance help adults focus their learning efforts.

Adults acquire cognitive structures from many sources that are relevant to the topics they seek to learn about. The cognitive structures of older adults tend to be more detailed because they have had more time to accumulate relevant experience. When practitioners are uncertain about their clients' cognitive structures, it is usually worth the effort to help diagnose their current view of the topic, and if needed, to help build a more adequate cognitive structure to facilitate further understanding.

Practitioners can assist adults to develop a more positive approach to education in several ways. One way is to help them successfully use intentional learning activities to cope with adjustments. Major role changes can produce heightened readiness to learn and focus attention on needed competence. A second way is to help adults become aware of role models who have already acquired the competence to which they aspire. A third is to create settings in which adults have the freedom to explore within democratic limits both the achievement of their current educational objectives and the discovery of additional desirable objectives.

There are also age-related individual differences in information processing. Related generalizations apply mainly to knowledge acquisition and include attention, memory, reinforcement, interference, pacing, transfer, and incidental learning.

Effective adult learning typically entails an active search for meaning in which new learnings build on current competence. Broad familiarity with a topic provides the basis for selectivity. Practitioners encourage adults to attend to learning tasks when assistance is provided in the setting of realistic educational objectives that provide a satisfying challenge.

Short-term memory of moderate amounts of meaningful material with adequate opportunity for acquisition tends to be relatively stable during most of adulthood. For older adults, there is an increasing registration deficit. This is especially so when older adults try to store new information and recall stored information at the same time. Older adults become more cautious and errors tend to entail forgetting instead of mistakes. The greater accumulation of related information causes older adults to expand the scope of their search in efforts to recall that may result in greater interference. Conditions that aid meaningful organization facilitate recall, especially for older adults with high verbal ability. Long-term memory is retained even better with age and the small amount that is forgotten can usually be regained by practice. Practitioners can use advance organizers, summary materials, personal pacing, and reviews of previous material to compensate for inadequate memory.

One form of reinforcement is practice. Older adults typically require more practice to master new verbal material. Other forms of reinforcement include advancement and recognition. Practitioners can increase reinforcement by matching program objectives to learner needs, by varying learning tasks to encourage practice, by recognizing educational achievement, by encouraging group support, and by connecting learning activities with opportunities for application.

When an adult studies a topic, some prior learning facilitates new learning, some interferes, and some is unrelated. When prior learning interferes, it may take longer to master a learning task because it is necessary to unlearn the interfering materials as well as to learn the new material. Older adults tend to experience more interference from conflicting prior learning, but they also obtain more assistance from facilitative prior learning, which largely reflects extent of experience with the topic instead of age itself.

Older adults especially learn most effectively when they set their own pace, when they take a break periodically, and when the distribution of learning episodes is fitted to the content. The speed at which learning occurs is a major age-related influence on learning effectiveness. Much of the decline in educational performance by older adults reflects a speed deficit instead of a decline in learning power. Older adults tend to reduce speed and emphasize accuracy. Sufficient time and personal pacing can help reduce age differences in learning performance.

Learning transfer tends to decline with age. A larger proportion of older adults persist with nonproductive problem-solving strategies. The range of individual differences in learning transfer increases until the sixties. The extent of incidental learning tends to be stable or to decline during adulthood. When intentional learning tasks are simple and slow paced, greater incidental learning occurs.

Practitioners can help create circumstances under which adults with various characteristics, including age, learn effectively. Because adults vary in their abilities and disabilities related to learning, educational activities can be designed to minimize features related to disabilities and to emphasize features that build on abilities and experience. Because an understanding of major aspects of a topic enables adults to relate prior knowledge and accumulate additional knowledge, advance organizers composed of those major aspects facilitate the building of a useful cognitive structure and progress from basic concepts to more difficult ones. Because affective intensity contributes to strong registration in memory, memorable encounters encourage rehearsal and reinforcement. Because adults learn more effectively when they proceed at their own pace and are able to use preferred resources, effective educational programs provide for individualization. Because feedback enhances learning effectiveness and persistence, program evaluation procedures are very desirable.

Developmental changes in thinking during adulthood are reflected in problem solving, critical thinking, and creativity. Adults obtain useful feedback regarding attainment of learning objectives through their efforts to apply what is learned. An understanding of age trends and thinking entails consideration of the content that is thought about and the relative emphasis on knowledge, skills, and attitudes.

Regarding problem solving, there appears to be a decline with age based on cross-sectional studies, no change with age until seventy based on longitudinal studies, and an improvement with age based on anecdotal evidence that older, more experienced practitioners tend to be more effective in the solution of complex and subtle problems than younger, less experienced practitioners. For some older adults, memory deficits and reliance on formerly effective concepts and strategies that are not currently effective contribute to a solution process that entails searching the repertoire instead of generating novel solutions.

Regarding critical thinking, cross-sectional studies show small declines with age, but longitudinal studies show significant increases. Regarding task complexity, individual differences increase with age, and many older adults are distracted by irrelevant information and learn complex tasks less well than younger adults. Creativity mainly reflects physiology and personality and is little related to age, although test results on creative intellectual output parallel findings from productivity studies. The more creative adults at any age are more sensitive to external stimuli and more receptive to internal impulses. They are less censoring during the exploratory stage of creative effort. Less creative adults concentrate too earnestly, stifle novelty, and often concentrate on the defects of an approach instead of exploring its potential.

Practitioners can help older adults compensate for declines in problem-solving ability by using advance organizers and memory aids, and by minimizing distracting and irrelevant information. Practitioners can help adults of any age in learning activities by clarifying the discrepancy between current understandings and desired increased competence, by providing reassurance to offset the fear of failure, by assisting adults to use their own experience and that of associates as a valuable resource for growth, and by encouraging clients to use the conclusions from the past as raw materials with which to build the future.

Most of all, practitioners can help all adults realize that

although there are substantial individual differences in learning ability, little of the variability is related to age. Almost any adults can learn almost anything they want to, given time, persistence, and assistance. Practitioners can help adults take optimistic, proactive and effective approaches to learning tasks and use reflection and learning episodes as ways to modify and direct their performance in action settings.

8

Women's Roles

Women's multiple roles in family, occupation, education, and community illustrate interrelationships among role performance, context, condition, personality, and learning. Women's role performance in home and work was selected for analysis because of current interest and recent studies on the topic. Comparable developmental analyses could be prepared for other categories of adults and roles, such as relationships between personality and leisure activity by blue collar young men, assumption of major leadership roles in community organizations by middle-aged women, and relationships between activity and health in retirement. This chapter on women's roles thus explores only one of many potential instances of developmental interrelationships in role performance.

Public awareness and support of changing roles and expectations for women has increased dramatically since the early 1960s. In the short span of a dozen years, the proportion of shaped by historical trends. Consider the contrasting prospects women respondents to Gallup public opinion polls who believed that greater equality for women was a major issue went from a small minority, to about half, to two thirds. This shift in public opinion has been associated with changes in role performance by women as reflected in rising age at first marriage, declining birth rates, increasing rates of employment by mothers of young children, rising divorce rates, and increased public leadership. Increased economic equality for women is also affecting values related to family and community life. The following analysis of women's roles in family, work, and education emphasizes developmental interrelationships based on tested knowledge. However, major value issues are also involved (Kreps, 1976; M. B. Smith, 1969).

The dual roles in family and work that many United States women experience provide a distinctive example of developmental interrelationships. Each role has a long history of typical performance and varied expectations. The family roles as wife and mother tend to emphasize solidarity, affection, and cooperation among family members and diffuse forms of contribution and recognition related to these roles. The worker role tends to emphasize contractual relationships, individual accomplishment, and more explicit forms of recognition, such as monetary incentives and rewards.

In recent generations, many of the women who perform both worker and homemaker roles concurrently experience some role conflict, which reflects in part male-oriented societal expectations regarding roles as worker, wife, and mother. Sex-role stereotypes that are part of the societal context of the adult woman also influenced her outlook during childhood and adolescence. These stereotypes are based partly on beliefs about similarities and differences between males and females, including the extent to which differences are the result of inheritance or socialization. Such interactions between condition and context are currently the focus of much discussion and a growing amount of research.

Performance in education interacts with all the other components of adult development. In addition to the contribution of formal education to career development for adults generally, the amount and type of education that a young woman has influences her approach to work and family roles. In addition, educational participation is sometimes part of the reentry process for married women who go to work full time after their children are somewhat grown.

Personality variables interact with performance, context, condition, and learning variables in many ways. The sense of self as a person somewhat independent of role expectations, as a woman generally, and as an incumbent in major life roles can contribute to flexibility and adaptation. In turn, successful and compatible performance in work and family roles can contribute to a strong and growing sense of self.

This chapter on women's roles provides a more detailed analysis of ways in which personality variables such as self-concept interact with biological differences and societal stereotypes of women's roles, in the performance of women in family, work, and educational settings. This is reflected in the types of tasks women typically perform in family and in work, along with the process by which adjustments are sometimes made.

Sex Differences

There are many widespread and persistent beliefs about inherent differences between males and females. A small but growing amount of tested knowledge has verified a few sex differences and has demonstrated that many beliefs about inherent and acquired sex differences are unfounded myths. However, such research has left most such beliefs untested, especially with regard to the relative influence of nature and nurture (Maccoby and Jacklin, 1974; Bardwick, 1971; J. A. Sherman, 1971).

Because inherent sex differences would most likely appear in early childhood before being greatly affected by socialization practices, most of the relevant research has concentrated on the early years of life. The tested knowledge shows that contrary to popular myths, girls are equivalent to boys regarding environmental influences; suggestibility; achievement motivation; and cognitive style and processing, such as analytic or auditory emphases. Also, boys and girls are equally sociable, although girls tend to prefer somewhat smaller peer groups. Levels of self-esteem are equivalent, although girls tend to express greater self-confidence in the area of social competence, and boys tend to see themselves as more powerful. By college age, young women have a lower sense of efficacy and of confidence to perform well in new tasks (Maccoby and Jacklin, 1974; Stein and Bailey, 1973; Parelius, 1975; Turner, 1964).

The few sex differences that have been demonstrated cluster around intellectual abilities and assertiveness. These differences mainly reflect differential rates of development at various ages. The differences between the averages for the two sexes are seldom greater than a quarter to a half of a standard deviation. This means that even when there are significant differences between the averages for males and females, at least a quarter of the lower group typically score above the average of the higher group.

During childhood and especially early adolescence, the average verbal ability of girls is somewhat greater than that of boys. This encompasses reading and writing tasks, including verbal fluency, comprehension, analogies, and creative writing. During much of adulthood, average intellectual ability of men and women is comparable, but among gifted adults, men tend to score higher on intelligence tests (Bayley and Oden, 1955; Kangas and Bradway, 1971). Among adults over sixty, women tend to score slightly higher, but the rate of decline is the same for men and women (Blum, Fosshage, and Jarvik, 1972). The average visual-spatial ability of males is greater than for females during adolescence and most of adulthood, but this difference is not evident during childhood. High spatial ability reflects the biological contribution of a recessive sex-linked gene that benefits about half of the males and about one quarter of the females. The biological contribution is only potential, however, and when socialization practices are supportive, members of both sexes develop satisfactory visual-spatial skills. Although male superiority on visual-spatial tasks occurs during most of adulthood (Maccoby and Jacklin, 1974), there is typically no difference between visual-spatial performance of men and women over sixty (Davies, 1965; Schwartz and Karp, 1967). Although average quantitative abilities of boys and girls are equivalent during childhood, during adolescence boys' mathematical abilities increase faster. There is also evidence of average male superiority on mathematical tasks during college and adulthood (Very, 1967; Grotelueschen, 1967; Grotelueschen and Sjogren, 1968).

The greater average assertiveness of males is reflected in aggressiveness, competitiveness, and dominance. The greater verbal and physical aggressiveness of males is apparent in early social play and extends through the college years into adulthood. The relative decline in aggressiveness during later life tends to be greater for men, so that men and women become more similar in this regard. The biological component of greater male aggressiveness is supported by its similar occurrence in subhuman primates, its consistent occurrence in all human cultures studied, and its relation to sex hormones. (It appears that testosterone level is affected by emotional state.) These findings, when combined with the evidence that adults do not reinforce boys' aggression more than girls' aggression and perhaps even less, support some biological basis for greater average male aggressiveness. Aggressive behavior is learned, but males are biologically more predisposed to learn it. Usually the recipients of aggressive behavior are other males.

Competitiveness is usually similar for both sexes, but when differences do emerge from studies, boys tend to be more competitive. Competitive behavior is affected by circumstances, such as the hesitancy of young women to compete against their boyfriends. Although no overall pattern of dominance and submission between males and females has been demonstrated, the issue of dominance tends to be more of an issue with males, and they typically make more dominance attempts. Formal leadership tends to go to men in initial phases of interaction. With time, influence on decisions typically becomes more shared and divided, and the relative female influence increases. In marital settings, when both partners want a mutually rewarding relationship, there are typically deliberate efforts to restrict aggression and dominance. Because maintaining a marriage tends to be more important to the wife in many instances, there can be strong pressures for some wives to accept an unsatisfactory submissive relationship.

There are only fragmentary research findings about individual differences and age changes in cognitive and social measures by men and women during adulthood. For example, men and women have similar pain thresholds, but men have much greater tolerance for pain. No sex differences were found regarding personal time perspective (Bortner and Hultsch, 1972; Goldrich, 1967); self-derogation; and happiness by older college graduates (Schaie and Strother, 1968a, b, c). In response to an adjective checklist, men tend to be more personally oriented and women more socially oriented (Carlson and Levy, 1968). When people were in need of assistance, more men than women responded (Piliavin, Rodin, and Piliavin, 1969; Gaertner, 1973; Gaertner and Bickerman, 1971), but when college students distributed group resources, men were less generous than women (A. Kahn, 1972; Leventhal and Lane, 1970). Some women experience fluctuations in affect related to the menstrual cycle (Ivey and Bardwick, 1968). The evidence of substantial differences, let alone superiority of men or women is fragmentary. Aside from physical strength and complementary roles in the reproductive process, the actual differences that do occur mainly reflect role expectations and previous socialization. Aggressiveness and visualization are among the few differences that have been substantiated.

Sex-role Stereotypes

If men and women are in most respects so similar, then what accounts for their contrasting performance in family and work? Part of the explanation might be that the limited areas of difference between men and women actually make a big difference. The small differences in verbal, mathematical, and visual-spatial abilities hardly account for the contrasting role performance of men and women. However, the greater average size, strength, and aggressiveness of men may partly explain the widespread patterns of male dominance in home and work. The only other major aspect of physical condition that contributes to differential role performance by women is child-bearing. In earlier times, carrying, bearing, and nursing children consumed a major portion of the typical number of years between puberty and death. By contrast, in recent generations, the number of years between the birth of the first child and the time the youngest child starts school is a very small portion of a woman's adulthood.

Societal values probably have a greater influence on performance than either male dominance or female childbearing. These values take the forms of generalized sex-role stereotypes and specific role expectations. Stereotypes of feminine and masculine characteristics and roles evolved during thousands of years. The stereotypes regarding girls and women incorporated context-related features such as economic, family, educational, and religious roles for women from preindustrial societies in which men were typically in the most visible and influential positions. During the past century United States society has changed greatly in ways that affect women's roles. The changes include increased education, reduced period of childbearing, increased average life expectancy, increased standard of living and home mechanization, transfer of functions from family to other institutions, women's suffrage, increased separation of work settings from home, and increased participation of women in the labor force. There is a cultural lag, however, in which sex-role stereotypes from an earlier age persist.

Sex-role stereotypes are reflected in children's books, in the mass media generally, in available role models, and in the attitudes of parents and work supervisors. Such stereotypes are widespread and convey a traditional sense of rightness. Even fathers, husbands, and male employers who otherwise have very equalitarian values seem to accept quite limited stereotypes of women's roles in family and work.

In addition to generalized stereotypes of women's roles, performance is influenced by specific expectations of people in reciprocal role relationships. The wife and mother who seeks to alter her family role will be likely to affect the performance of her husband and children who reside in the household. Their expectations about her role typically influence her performance and even contribute to conflict or satisfaction. Likewise, her expectations influence their performance. If a woman changes her family roles in ways that the other family members perceive as generally beneficial to them, they are likely to be supportive of the change, without much attention to the woman's rationale for the change. However, if the other family members perceive the change as disadvantageous to them, then their support for the change is likely to depend mainly on an explicit acceptance of the benefits of the change for the wife and mother. Similar adjustments in work role expectations occur slowly as demands for equity challenge stereotypes, and as male workers accommodate emerging moral and legal values with their traditional values of male dominance in most work settings.

Family Role

In recent generations, women's options regarding family roles have increased. Today's young woman has more latitude to select from several acceptable family life options than her mother or grandmother had. A young woman may confront this wider range of choice with pleasure or dismay. Her mother may have mixed feelings, however.

Despite much publicized concerns about family and work opportunities for women, most girls and young women want to and do get married. Only 4 or 5 percent never marry or have children. Another 5 percent marry but do not have children. The percent who have children but never marry is small, but there are more than six and a half million female family heads, due to desertion, divorce, and widowhood. During the 1973–1974 period, more than half a million were under age twenty-five and more than two and a half million were between twenty-five and forty-five years of age. For married women under age thirty-five with husband present, more than 70 percent of those with no children under age eighteen are employed, as were almost 40 percent of married women under age thirty-five with husband present and children under eighteen. Before examining occupational trends and prospects for married and single women, it seems desirable to summarize some of the family life cycle trends that influence role performance and happiness for women.

Greater societal acceptance of alternative life-styles has contributed to the wider range of family options that a young woman may consider. Although unusual styles, such as those of communal groups and unmarried mothers, are sometimes widely publicized, for most women family life is a variation on a familiar theme of marriage and children. The children's ages greatly influence the mother's role. Outside employment due to choice or necessity interacts with family finances, marital adjustment, and the woman's preferences. At any time, 10 percent of United States women are divorced. In their later years, an increasing proportion are widowed. During the past generation, employment rates for married women have peaked in the early twenties, declined until the early thirties (during the childbearing years), risen to a second peak in the early fifties, and then dropped sharply. During the decade before 1973, the percentage of working wives increased from about 33 to about 43 percent (Hayghe, 1973). Recent increases in the age at first marriage and decreases in the birth rate also affect the woman's family life cycle.

There are many variations on the marriage and children theme for women. Included are the female head of household (both employed and on welfare) and the minority of women who never work outside the home. Also included are the women who work before the first child is born and resume work only after the youngest child is grown and the women who continue to work full time with only brief maternity leaves when each child is born. The accommodation between the two roles in work and family depends in part on how attractive working is, how necessary it seems, and how satisfactory family life is. The patterns of relationship among family, work, and aspiration are exceedingly complex, and their impact on satisfactory performance by women of dual roles in work and family is little understood. For the married couple with young children, a woman's performance and satisfaction in family roles is influenced by the expectations of other family members, as well as by their performance of reciprocal roles and general societal expectations about the roles of wife and mother (Kaley, 1971; Lopata, 1971; Alper, 1973; Oliver, 1972).

The tasks of the wife and mother of young children are many and well known. Cooking, laundering, chauffeuring, nursing, consoling, managing, buying, loving, planning, encouraging, cleaning—the list seems endless. During the past two generations, the slight increase in time devoted to family-related tasks by homemakers who are not employed outside the home reflects both time savings due to mechanization and food preparation and increased time devoted to child care, shopping, and home management. A woman's family-related tasks tend to cluster around wife and mother roles, taking care of the house, and relations with other groups, such as extended family, friends, church, and youth groups. Women vary greatly in the amount of satisfaction they gain from these individual tasks, but one widespread feature of their great fragmentation is that most of the tasks tend to be taken for granted and few women receive much appreciation or recognition for their family roles. Some tasks, such as cooking a special and delicious meal or attractively redecorating a room, may receive praise, but such tasks as cleaning, laundering, and shopping are taken for granted except when they are not done satisfactorily. The family expresses appreciation on a few days, such as a woman's birthday or Mother's Day, but most weeks a homemaker has to depend on her own personal sense of accomplishment. In a society in which contractual exchanges, pursuit of self-interest, and monetary rewards are widespread, the diffuse and giving tasks of the homemaker with intangible rewards may be relatively unattractive to many women.

To further compound the situation, some of the former family functions related to children's education, health, and recreation have in recent generations shifted toward community institutions, such as schools, hospitals, and youth-serving agencies. Although tasks related to these functions sometimes carried heavy responsibilities in years past, when women performed them well they could obtain a deep sense of accomplishment. Such peak experiences are now more likely to be ex-

perienced by the teacher, nurse, or recreation supervisor. Even
many of the volunteer activities in the community (from which
some white collar women derived satisfaction a generation or
two ago as a quasi-extension of the family role) are now paid
jobs in an expanding range of service occupations. When the
scattered, mundane, familiar, and unappreciated tasks of homemaking are compared with outside employment, it is understandable that labor force participation for married women
has been increasing steadily. Smaller families in which the
youngest child is in school while the mother is relatively young,
combined with increased average life expectancy and an interest in a higher standard of living from a two-income family,
also contribute to the rising proportion of working wives.

During late adolescence and early young adulthood, today's young women are probably more aware of more work and
family options than were previous generations. However, it is
unclear to what extent most young women realistically assess
the attractive and unattractive features of married life before
they are married. In addition to unfamiliarity, there is variability in personal preference. Tasks such as laundry and gardening are illustrative.

Doing the laundry with an automatic washer and dryer
is relatively routine. It is less disagreeable and takes less time
than doing the washing by hand and hanging it out on the
line, especially in cold weather. Sorting the dirty clothes for
separate loads by color and fabric and folding or hanging the
clean clothes on hangers constitute much of the task. Modern
fabrics are easier to care for, but there tends to be more
laundry each week for each family member than was the case
a generation or two ago. Although some of the drudgery has
been lost, so has some of the social quality of the past, when
other family members helped with the laundry and visited
while doing so. Today, it is more difficult to make doing the
laundry a shared activity. In some instances, an increase in
efficiency and a reduction in drudgery have been accompanied
by an increase in loneliness. Especially for homemakers who are
restricted by young children and whose husbands are away
much of the time, the lack of adult conversation can contribute

to dissatisfaction. Doing the laundry and similar tasks around a coffee break with a neighbor or supervision of young children can help increase the attractiveness of the task.

The specific tasks entailed in gardening are relatively standard. Caring for house plants or having a flower or vegetable garden entails providing the conditions and care for plants to grow. Satisfactory gardening requires some basic understandings and practices. However, the satisfaction from (and part of the success of) gardening depends on the individual's attitudes toward the activity. Positive associations with working the earth and helping plants grow, past success in doing so, and learning about new varieties and procedures help make gardening an attractive activity. Some people grudgingly do gardening chores, but others approach the same activities as a special treat and source of satisfaction. For some people, gardening tasks are to be shared whenever possible, whereas others welcome the solitary periods of gardening as opportunities to be reflective and dream a little. People also vary in the relative satisfaction they gain from the process in contrast with the enjoyment that they and others derive from the fruits of their labors. These interrelationships between attitudes, activities, and satisfaction apply to other household tasks, such as cooking and sewing. Most people experience a mix of activities that includes some that are interesting and satisfying and many that just need to be done. On balance, a homemaker's tasks can become very unsatisfying. For each individual woman, happiness hinges in part on maintaining a satisfactory balance that includes some activities she perceives as worthwhile and satisfying.

For the woman who worked before her first child arrived, the perceived attractiveness of the family roles of wife, mother, and homemaker depends in part on her attitudes toward her work. Resigning from a dreary and unrewarding job to start a family can be accompanied by feelings of relief and anticipation. Resigning from a stimulating and rewarding job can be accompanied by feelings of regret and concern that it may be difficult to resume one's career later on. Under such circumstances, arrangements to maintain contact with career interests during childbearing years may contribute to both career development and satisfaction in family roles.

During the child-rearing years, a woman's family role performance tends to reflect the ages of her children. When the children are young, the mother's tasks typically focus on their care and supervision, mothering consumes a relatively high proportion of her family time, and community activities with other adults are often restricted. When the children are between nine and thirteen, the mother's tasks shift to guidance, mothering consumes a smaller portion of her family time, and more time is likely to be spent working with youth groups and other community activities. As the children move into the later teens they develop interests and activities of their own that relate less and less to their mother and home.

These family life cycle shifts related to the ages of the children influence both the tasks to be performed and the assistance available to help perform the tasks. When the children are young, the burdens of mother and homemaker are heavy; the children are too young to help much; family finances are typically low, which restricts hiring outside help; the household has usually not acquired older relatives who might assist; and the husband usually feels the pressure to invest much of his time and energy in the early stages of his career. This tends to redouble the homemaker's burden. Chronic fatigue and the unending list of unfinished tasks also contribute to the trapped housewife feeling, especially for many women who are particularly conscientious. When the children are old enough to assume responsibilities for chores and household tasks, much depends on how the parents go about including them in family work. On a farm or in some family businesses there is important work to be done that children can help with, and some tasks are even attractive, at least to the younger children. In many urban and suburban homes, it may be more difficult to match children's interests and abilities to work that actually needs doing. An irony of parenthood is that when growing children attain the age when they could really be helpful around the house, their interests are moving outside the family, and it is often difficult to maintain their participation.

Another aspect of the division of labor within the household is division between husband and wife. The distinction between man's work and woman's work has occurred in all types of societies throughout history. Under some circumstances, sharp distinctions between masculine and feminine tasks seem to be understandable. Hunting and protecting seem to go together, as do child rearing and cooking. A task analysis of homemaking activities today would not reveal many that must be performed by the wife or the husband. The division of tasks between husband and wife mainly reflects traditional sex-role stereotypes and negotiation by each couple. When the husband had a full-time job outside the home and the wife was a full-time homemaker, she had a weak bargaining position to convince her husband that he should do part of the laundry, dusting, and cooking. When husbands have been unemployed for extended periods or retired, their reasons for not helping with the housework have related to competence and sex-role stereotypes regarding men doing women's work. During the past generation more women have pursued careers and have tried to minimize their time off for child rearing, and the challenge to traditional sex roles has become most intense. With the benefit of raised consciousness and renewed assertiveness, some women have pointed out to their husbands that in addition to personal benefits regarding time to devote to her career, equitable division of homemaking tasks will teach the children more equalitarian attitudes and less rigid sex-role stereotypes. There seems to be a shift toward more equalitarian marital relationships, especially in some younger white collar families and some marriages of professional couples in middle age.

During recent decades, relationships between husbands and wives regarding home and family decisions have become more varied. Especially for blue collar families, when the wife works there are shifts toward a greater share for the wife in economic decision making and fewer decisions about household tasks, but there is little change in the influence husband and wife have over each other. Husbands of working wives tend to help a little more with household tasks, but not much

(Blood and Wolfe, 1960; Propper, 1972). For middle-aged, lower-middle-class couples, the desire of wives for major activities beyond the family, along with the desire of husbands for more attention from their wives, can result in a collision course (Lowenthal, Thurnher, and others, 1975). The existence of employment opportunities for wives and the wife's paycheck increase the bargaining position of some wives. It also enables some to terminate "empty shell" marriages that would have continued in past generations. For some white collar families, when the children are all in school, and the wife launches into a full-time career in her late thirties or early forties, both the children and the husband typically devote more time to running the household. Husbands who are dynamic and successful in their own careers tend to encourage their wives to develop their own identities, activities, and careers in work and community. Job changes that entail a move to a new community affect marital relationships in several ways. When a husband or a career wife receives an attractive job opportunity elsewhere, but the other spouse has little or no prospects for one, severe conflict can develop. Affirmative action procedures pose some unique barriers to an organization's hiring both a husband and a wife at the same time. For full-time homemakers, there appears to be some increase in resistance to job-related moves that disrupt family life. In the 1980s, as the number of people in the young adult age cohort begins to decline, it is possible that there will be even more emphasis on family life (Kreps, 1976).

The central issue regarding the division of labor between husband and wife in family roles is the extent and type of complementarity in sex roles that is desirable. Few people seriously advocate either of the two extreme positions: (1) that each partner emphasize stereotyped sex-role attitudes (dominant, nurturant) and activities (carpentry, laundry) and minimize overlap or (2) that both partners strive to achieve the same range of attitudes and activities in their similar performance of spouse, parent, and homemaker roles, with the possible exception of bearing and nursing children. Many people, especially younger white collar couples, seem to take a middle position

between these two extremes. Unfortunately, little tested knowledge is available regarding marital role complementarity. It is
likely that the issue hinges mainly on value judgments about
desirable characteristics of people and society.

Parenting provides an example. The concepts of fathering and mothering tend to emphasize the distinctive emphases
of the male and female adults in a family. The concept of
parenting emphasizes the shared contributions of both parents
in an effort to encourage role flexibility. But are there any
attitudes or activities that should be distinctive regarding men
or women? Are there any qualities that are important in the
development of sons and daughters which require distinctive
emphasis by fathers or mothers? If we conclude that empathy
and nurturance are desirable qualities, are they any more important for girls than for boys? Is there any reason why women
are more able or more likely to develop and display these
qualities? Is there any problem of compatibility between these
qualities and other qualities and activities that are associated
with traditional masculine and feminine roles, such as care of
young children, relations with opposite sex teenagers, competitive work relationships, and physical combat? Even if incompatibility is demonstrated, does this raise questions about
the desirability of nurturance or belligerence? If we conclude
that men are more assertive than women, should tasks be divided so that those requiring more assertiveness are performed
by men, or should women be encouraged to be more assertive
and men less so? Is complementarity desirable for marriages
that are interesting and always growing and for parenting that
provides children with contrasting outlooks and talents? Or is
it more desirable for each person to develop a wide range of
attitudes and abilities to be applied flexibly to fit the circumstances? Is it not feasible and desirable for any man or woman
to be tough minded or tender hearted when appropriate? These
same questions seem to apply to many role relationships other
than parenting and to other qualities such as physical activity,
competitiveness, loyalty, and love (Hetherington, 1965; Goldstein, 1972).

In spite of ambiguity about the desirability of complementarity in the family roles of men and women, and lack of adequate tangible recognition for women's family role performance, there are some positive features of being an effective wife, mother, and homemaker. The process of conceiving, carrying, delivering, nursing, and rearing a child can be an exceedingly creative process. It is of the utmost importance to society that this function be performed well, and the process can nurture the mother as well as the child. The responsibility can be great, but so can the satisfaction. Effective performance as mother, wife, and homemaker can immerse a woman in holistic, developmental, and humanistic activities that are at the core of our highest values. There are many societal pressures toward fragmentation and dehumanization. Satisfactory family life can contribute much to personal coherence and social cohesion. The "fostering of becoming" that is sometimes associated with the helping professions and many service occupations appears to be central to satisfactory family life. All family members can accept responsibility to foster growth and basic human values. A woman who devotes much of her effort to family roles for a period of years can be a moving force and a major beneficiary. Such benefits of women's family roles are not automatic. Unsatisfactory performance, accidents, and lack of cooperation by other family members can nullify many of the potentially positive features. However, for many women, family roles are potentially growthful and satisfying.

A recent major study provides an analysis of relationships between extent of life satisfaction and stage of family life cycle for United States men and women (Campbell and Converse, 1975). A large representative sample of adults was asked about their general life satisfaction, their feelings about their lives, their moods, and their feelings of stress. Their responses were global and included their lives in family, work, and community. Men and women expressed about the same levels of satisfaction with their lives, although there were differences associated with family life cycle stage. About 80 percent expressed high life satisfaction, characterizing their lives as worthwhile, full, hopeful, and interesting. Less than 10 percent characterized their lives as boring, empty, miserable, lonely, and useless, and only

1 percent indicated that they were extremely dissatisfied with
their lives.

However, when men and women at various stages of the
family life cycle were compared regarding level of life satisfaction, some striking contrasts were apparent (see Figure 26).
Married people were happier than singles, and childless couples
were happier than couples with young children. The level of
life satisfaction was relatively low for unmarried young adults.
It was much higher for young married couples without children,
especially the wives who expressed the highest average levels of
life satisfaction of any subgroup. When there were children
under age six in the home, satisfaction declined and feelings of
stress rose to their highest level for any subgroup other than
divorced women. The mothers of young children especially
expressed feelings of being tied down, had doubts about their
marriages, and sometimes wished to be free of the responsibilities of parenthood. Level of life satisfaction increased and feelings of stress decreased for couples with children between six

**Figure 26. Life Satisfaction in Relation to Age,
Marital Status, Children, and Divorce**

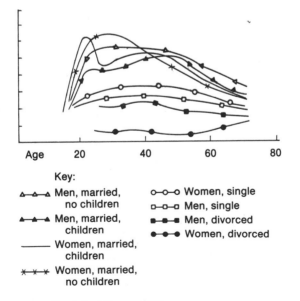

Source: Campbell and Converse (1975).

and seventeen and for those with children over seventeen years of age. Couples with grown children reported feelings of companionship and mutual understanding to a greater extent than newlyweds.

Married people who were over thirty and childless expressed relatively high life satisfaction, and those who were widowed expressed relatively low satisfaction. Although some studies have indicated that single women are psychologically and physically healthier than married women, on the average they report less happiness than any category of married women. When comparing all single adults, men tend to be more anxious and women more carefree, contrary to the popular stereotype. The satisfaction levels were lowest for adults who were separated or divorced, especially the women. The stress level expressed by divorced women was the highest of any subgroup, but the stress level for divorced men was very low, and only the feelings of stress reported by widowers were lower.

The foregoing findings about satisfaction and family life cycle do not prove that family roles alone create or destroy happiness. Unhappy adults may be more likely to divorce. Some adults may derive satisfaction from other roles to compensate for unsatisfying family roles and thus raise the general level of life satisfaction. However, the findings related to the presence and age of children in the family, especially for women, do suggest some general developmental shifts regarding family role performance and satisfaction.

Some of the interrelationships between family role performance and personality are illustrated by the experience of some middle-aged lower-middle-class women. Between twenty and sixty years of age, women whose youngest children are about to leave home for adult roles tend to have more adaptation problems than other categories of married men and women. Women vary greatly in the stability and change in role relationships in family, work, and community during this transition when their grown children are leaving home, including expansion, shift, stability, and constriction. However, expressed feelings of life satisfaction and well-being are generally higher during this postparental period than before (Campbell and

Converse, 1975; *Counseling Psychologist*, 1976). For women in the preretirement period, those who still had children at home reported more self-pity, dissatisfaction, and difficulty in interpersonal relations than those whose children were launched. In addition to dissatisfaction toward the end of the child-rearing period, there is some indication that motherhood responsibilities tend to limit the personal development of some women, even when time is available for the increase of competence and the acquisition of roles. The greatest differences occur between the life-styles of men and women during the thirties and early forties (Lowenthal, Thurnher, and others, 1975).

Work Role

Women's performance in the worker role reflects both personal and societal influences. Personal influences include a woman's needs, interests, and aspirations that result from both abilities and earlier socialization. Another type of personal influence on a woman's work role performance is the extent to which her other current roles encourage or discourage working. Societal influences include the actual facilitators and barriers to women's doing the type of work they want to do, along with their own perceptions of occupational opportunities available to women. These influences interact over the years to produce the profile of labor force participation of women generally and to shape the career development of individual women.

In 1974 women constituted two fifths of the total labor force. Working women, who numbered more than thirty-five million, included about 45 percent of all women sixteen years of age and over. This compares with about 20 percent of all women of working age who were in the labor force in 1900, and only 25 percent in 1940 (U.S. Department of Labor, 1973). In recent decades, working rates for single and no longer married women have been quite constant, but there has been a sharp increase for married women with husband present. The number of married women in the labor force has more than doubled since 1950. During the early part of this period, the major increases in working rates occurred mainly for women beyond the usual childbearing years. During the past decade there has also been a major increase in labor force participation by younger married women (Kievit, 1972; U.S. BLS, 1975). The increase in working rates during the past generation for most categories of women tends to obscure the life cycle shifts for individual women. Many married women leave the labor force temporarily while their children are very young, but the recent rapid increases in working rates for mothers with husband present and with children under three years of age indicates that many are returning to work sooner after childbirth than had been the case in earlier years. After a dip in working rates for married women from a first peak in their early twenties, there is a second peak around age fifty (Hayghe, 1973, 1974, 1975). The general increases in labor force participation by married women during the past decade reflect influences including desire for higher family income as a result of the wife's earnings; needs for actualization, independence, and social contact; increased interest by women in occupational achievement, status, and recognition; more tolerant societal attitudes toward working wives; later age at first marriage; decline in birth rate; increased availability of child care services; and reduced sex discrimination (Hoffman and Nye, 1974; Kreps, 1976). The rates of working by age category for single, married, and other women are presented in Figure 27.

In recent decades the employment rate for white collar women has increased. The rates are now highest in the middle range of family income. Over the years employment of black women has increased black family income and narrowed the gap between black and white family incomes. However, there has been a more rapid increase in employment rates for white wives, which tends to maintain or increase the disparity between black and white family incomes. There has been little change in the relative distribution of family income in recent decades, however. The top one fifth of United States families receive two fifths of the income, and the bottom one fifth receive one twentieth of the income.

The female-headed family is a special instance of women

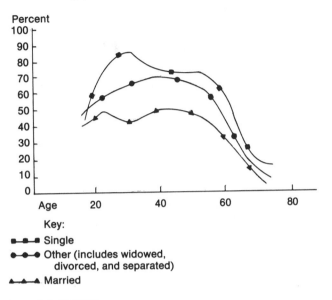

**Figure 27. Percent of Working Women in Each Age Category
for Single, Married with Husband Present, and Other**

Key:
■—■—■ Single
●—●—● Other (includes widowed,
        divorced, and separated)
▲—▲—▲ Married

Source: U.S. BLS (1975).

working. In recent years more than 10 percent of all families
were headed by women. These female family heads, who numbered more than six and a half million, were widowed, divorced, separated, or single, and about two thirds have children
under eighteen years of age. More than seven out of ten divorced women work, compared with almost six out of ten
women who never married, more than half of married women
with husband absent, more than four out of ten married
women with husband present, and one quarter of widows.
Half the female family heads were over forty-four years of age,
but one tenth were under twenty-five. During the past decade
or two the number of female-headed families has increased far
more rapidly than the number of families generally. The median income for female-headed families was less than half that
for male-headed families. This was partly because only about
one third of the females who headed families worked full time
all year. About one quarter of female family heads were black,

and their median family income was about one third that of
male-headed families. Female-headed families constituted more
than one third of all low-income families, and almost half of
all poor children under eighteen years of age were in female-
headed families. About 30 percent of all female-headed families
received public assistance payments (Kreps, 1971; U.S. Department of Labor, 1973). About two thirds of the female family
heads under age sixty-five worked or looked for work, and the
percentage increased from almost 60 percent for those under
age twenty-five to almost 70 percent for those between forty-five
and sixty-four. About one out of six female family heads over
age sixty-four worked or looked for work. For female family
heads under age sixty-five who were in the labor force, the
unemployment rate was three times as high as for women
workers generally, which was somewhat higher than for men.
One out of three female family heads under age twenty-five
were unemployed, compared with one out of five of those between age twenty-five and forty-four, and one out of ten of
those between forty-five and sixty-four. A similar pattern
emerged for year-round work. For female family heads who
were under age twenty-five, more than one third worked all
year, compared with almost one half who worked less than
twenty-seven weeks. From age forty-five to sixty-four eight out
of ten worked all year compared with one out of ten who
worked less than twenty-seven weeks (Hayghe, 1974). In general, unemployment rates for female family heads declined
with age.

For working women generally, the unemployment rates
are somewhat higher than for men, especially from twenty-five
to fifty-four, and the differential has increased slightly in recent
years. Movement in and out of the labor force tends to be the
greatest influence on unemployment for women. Those women
who remain continuously in the labor force typically have
lower unemployment rates than those whose working was interrupted. Pregnancy, home responsibilities, and husband's relocation are major reasons for leaving the labor force. Reentry
unemployment is also more widespread for women, affecting
two out of five unemployed women in contrast with one out of

five unemployed men. About one third of unemployed women lost their previous job compared with more than half of unemployed men. Because of high turnover, women typically have less seniority and are more vulnerable to layoffs. Some women become discouraged about lack of job opportunities and discontinue active search. The greater representation of women in lower status occupations, which have higher unemployment rates for both sexes, also contributes to greater unemployment for women. Married women are also less able to move to increase job prospects. Because women's employment has been heavily concentrated in "women's" occupations, the relatively large increases in the female labor force have overcrowded some occupations and increased unemployment for women who seek those jobs. Teaching is a recent example; it is also affected by reductions in enrollment. A small contribution to differential female unemployment rates occurs because homemakers who seek employment are listed as unemployed, whereas men with a job who seek another one are not. As for men, unemployment rates are higher for the young and nonwhite (U.S. Department of Labor, 1973; U.S. BLS, 1975).

The types of occupations in which most women are employed differ markedly from the types of occupations in which most men are employed, and the distributions have not changed greatly during the past generation. Although working women are included in all categories, they are concentrated mainly in clerical, service, operative, professional, and sales occupations, in contrast with men who are concentrated mainly in crafts, operative, management, professional, and service occupations. In 1974 women constituted 98 percent of private household workers, 78 percent of clerical workers, and 59 percent of service workers, but only 4 percent of crafts workers, 5 percent of transport operatives, 8 percent of laborers, 16 percent of farm workers, and 18 percent of managers (see Figure 28). When analyzed separately by educational level, the differential occupational distributions of men and women were even more striking. For high school graduates, women were concentrated mainly in clerical (50 percent), service (15 percent), and operative (11 percent) occupations, in contrast with men who were

**Figure 28. Occupational Distribution of Employed Persons
by Education and Sex, 1970 (in Percent)**

Occupational Groups	High School				College Graduates	
	1–3 Years		4 Years		Men	Women
	Men	Women	Men	Women		
Total employed	100.0	100.0	100.0	100.0	100.0	100.0
Professional, Technical, and Kindred Workers	2.8	3.6	7.6	7.1	58.9	77.4
Managers and Proprietors	6.9	2.9	11.4	3.8	20.1	4.8
Salesworkers	5.6	10.2	7.5	8.1	8.6	2.3
Clerical and Kindred Workers	6.8	25.3	10.0	50.4	4.9	12.1
Craftsmen	25.6	2.4	26.4	1.8	3.3	.4
Operatives	27.3	22.5	20.6	11.4	1.4	.6
Nonfarm Laborers	9.9	1.6	5.3	.8	.5	.1
Farm Laborers and Foremen	1.9	.6	.9	.3	.2	.1
Farmers and Farm Managers	2.2	.2	2.9	.2	.8	.1
Service Workers Excluding Private Household	10.8	25.4	7.5	14.5	1.4	1.9
Private Household Service Workers	.2	5.2	1	1.7	1	.3

[1]Less than one tenth of 1 percent.
Note: Detail may not add to totals because of rounding.
Source: U.S. Census (1973b).

concentrated mainly in crafts (26 percent), operative (21 percent), and management (11 percent) occupations. For college graduates, women were concentrated mainly in professional (77 percent), clerical (12 percent), and management (5 percent) occupations, in contrast with men who were concentrated mainly in professional (59 percent), management (20 percent), and sales (9 percent) occupations. The higher proportion of college-educated women in professional occupations reflects the preponderance of women in elementary and secondary school teaching and in nursing, occupations which include small numbers of college-educated men. More women workers than men graduated from high school, but fewer completed four or more years of college. Young women workers have more formal education than their older counterparts.

The differential occupational distributions for men and women reflect several major influences. Because women have been discouraged from entering occupations other than the typical "female" fields, there have been few role models to encourage girls and young women to consider entering male-oriented fields. A primary interest in marriage and family roles has also discouraged many females from pursuing some of the more demanding occupations because they believe those occupations would be incompatible with their family roles. Women college students have traditionally enrolled in the more cultural fields and in a few occupational fields such as education, nursing, and library science. Differential achievement motivation has had some influence (Baruch, 1967). Recent percentage increases of women graduates in such fields as medicine, law, and engineering have been substantial, but the base a few years ago was very small. Another influence has been discrimination against working women in most fields in hiring, promotion, and salary. In professional and managerial occupations, the proportions of women have increased in some and have been stable or declined in others. For example, in recent decades the proportion of physicians, journalists, and lawyers who were women has increased, whereas the proportion of higher education faculty members who were women has decreased. In general, however, the occupational distributions of men and women have become more similar during the past decade or two (U.S. Department of Labor, 1973).

A contrasting pattern of career development is provided by the few exceptional women who defer or avoid marriage and become top executives of large financial and business corporations. In one study of twenty-five women executives, the career pattern was surprisingly consistent (Hennig and Jardim, 1976). They were typically firstborn children, whose mothers were full-time homemakers and whose fathers were dynamic and successful men who encouraged their daughters to use their abilities and not restrict themselves to sex-role stereotypes. They excelled academically in college, typically in business and economics, and many received help from their fathers in their early careers. They remained within the same company until they achieved the top management position. An older executive provided assistance and encouragement as their fathers had done before. During their mid-thirties, when they had achieved middle management positions, many of the women executives experienced a discontinuation of the mentor-mentee relationship, became concerned about the family life that they had deferred in their twenties, and married. Many experienced a transition during this period in which they renewed a romantic side of themselves that they had denied early in their careers.

When women enter management positions, many experience difficulty due to lack of understanding of informal interpersonal relationships among male managers that greatly affect organizational functioning. Beginning in youthful team play, males are encouraged to subordinate their personal concerns to the achievement of organizational goals, to interact satisfactorily with individuals they dislike, and to develop flexibility in interpersonal relations. Male managers also tend to respond to risk in relation to future goals and to consider opportunity and gain as well as danger and loss. By contrast, many inexperienced female managers tend to emphasize interpersonal relationships as ends in themselves without reference to organizational goals. Many respond to risk as entirely negative and a threat to current achievement, without consideration of future gain (Hennig and Jardim, 1976). Assertiveness and risk taking are qualities that many effective women administrators have or acquire.

Women's annual median earnings are lower than men's earnings, partially because more women are concentrated in the lower paid occupations, work fewer hours a week and weeks a year, have fewer years of work service, have less job-related education and training, and are concentrated in fields characterized by oversupply and depressed earnings levels (Sommers, 1974). Women's earnings are most comparable to men's in professional, clerical, and laborer occupations, and the disparity is greatest in sales work (U.S. BLS, 1975). The income of working women is highly associated with level of formal education. When men and women in the same occupations and who have comparable qualifications and years of service are compared, women's median earnings are only 75 or 80 percent of men's earnings. When comparisons are made within detailed job classifications and within the same establishment, the differential is reduced. Much of the remaining differential in women's earnings no doubt reflects discrimination, in that women with equal qualifications and responsibilities are paid less or are less often hired by establishments with higher pay rates. Interestingly, single women who worked continuously since leaving school earned slightly more than single men. In general, the disparity has been reduced only a small amount during the past two decades. Although the rate of improvement of earnings of women in professional occupations has been high relative to all workers and more recently relative to male professionals, the rate of improvement of earnings of women in clerical and operative occupations has been relatively low (U.S. Department of Labor, 1973; Sommers, 1974; Fuch, 1974; U.S. BLS, 1975).

The issue of discontinuity in women's work life appears to help depress earnings for women workers and reflects the main connection between women's two roles in home and work. Stopping work when the first child is expected and starting work when the youngest child is in school are transition points in a woman's career, but they are also transition points in the family role for many women. Actual occupational opportunities for women, along with their perceptions of the attractive and unattractive features of outside employment, have combined with women's aspirations to influence the extent to which women engage in the two roles concurrently and consecutively. The segmentation of occupations so that there are "women's" jobs such as clerical and nursing has served to pull some women into the labor market during periods when such service fields have been expanding rapidly and qualified applicants have been in short supply. There has also been a push from the home for many women that reflects urbanization, household technology, family relationships, and fewer children.

The cultural contradictions of women's two roles in home and work create major conflicts for some women who combine them concurrently and even for some of those who in turn make the transition from one to the other. The motive of avoiding success, which may help explain some of women's occupational performance until recent years, appears to be decreasing (Myrdal and Klein, 1956; Ginzberg and Yohalem, 1966; Horner, 1972). Given the traditional expectations for women's worker and family roles, the woman who combines them is likely to confront some difficult choices. Faced with employers' resistance to "flex-time" and part-time work arrangements, and the resistance of other family members to major realignments of homemaking and parenting tasks, some women choose to pursue only one of the roles seriously, but some women try to perform both. Many married women who work simply add this new role to their other tasks (Wilensky, 1968). Some adjustments are of course necessary. In the Kansas City Study of Adult Life the minority of older women who worked felt their attention to the spouse role was not reduced, but their time and attention to parent and homemaker roles was negatively associated with their performance in the worker role. In general, employed women spend about half as many hours on housework as do nonemployed women (Kreps, 1976). However it is handled, some accommodation between the dual roles in family and work is required, and this produces distinctive patterns of career development for women (Holmstrom, 1971). The contribution of supportive husbands to satisfactory career development by working wives is also clearly indicated (Rapoport and Rapoport, 1971a, b). Two-career marriages tend to be happier when the husband moderates his career involvement. However, in most two-career families, it appears that men still expect their own career to be primary (Orden and Bradburn, 1969; Rapoport and Rapoport, 1969; Rosen, Jerdee, and Prestwich, 1975).

Another issue is the effect of maternal employment on their children. An understanding of this relationship also entails consideration of social class differences, maternal dissatisfaction, and provision for child care. Early studies that found higher levels of family friction, child neglect and maladjustment, and delinquent behavior when the mother worked outside the home failed to take these related variables into account. More recent studies that have taken these variables into account have shown that maternal employment in itself does not adversely affect children (Wallston, 1973; Hoffman and Nye, 1974). School achievement is associated with the social status of the student's family. If more blue collar mothers are employed, it might appear that maternal employment causes lower school achievement. When data were analyzed separately by the mother's educational level, the only negative associations between mothers' employment and their children's school achievement was for mothers who had only completed high school (Hunter, 1972). In other words, lower school achievement when the mother worked occurred mainly for families where the mother had only completed high school.

The mothers' role satisfaction was also associated with their children's adjustment and school achievement. Both working and nonworking mothers who were satisfied with and did not reject their roles appeared to be "better mothers" than their dissatisfied counterparts. Furthermore, school-aged children of working mothers who liked work, liked the child, used mild discipline, and avoided inconveniencing the child with many household tasks were less hostile than were children of working mothers who disliked working, were less involved with the child, and obtained the child's help with homemaking tasks under duress (Hoffman, 1963).

With adequate substitute child care, a mother's working need not be detrimental to the child. For preschool children, the warmth, friendliness, continuity, and stability of substitute care are important. Some of the ill effects of maternal employment that have emerged include psychosomatic complaints by daughters, lower school achievement by sons in white collar families, and more frequent parent-child disagreements. Daughters of working mothers tend to perceive women as more competent and to give more credit to women's accomplishments than the daughters of nonworking women (Kreps, 1976). Current tested knowledge related to this topic suggests ways to help make family life more satisfactory for all members when the mother is employed. Under these circumstances, the issue probably hinges on value judgments regarding the relative priority that should be given to satisfaction and development of the mother in relation to satisfaction and development of the children (Hoffman and Nye, 1974).

Some women must make a critical adjustment when they enter or reenter the male-oriented world of work after an extended period in the female-oriented world of home. This transition is especially difficult for women who never worked outside the home before or did so only briefly many years before and have few work-related skills, attitudes, and experiences that can be adapted and applied to the work setting. If the woman is forced to work because of widowhood or divorce, the adjustment may be especially difficult due to negative attitudes and lack of financial and emotional support. Some groups and educational institutions have sponsored informal groups and counseling services to assist women who are entering school or work. Such arrangements can help them marshal resources, plan time, assess interests and abilities, recognize opportunities, increase self-confidence, and prepare resumés.

Student Role

During their thirties and forties, some women resume a student role, often as part of the transition from family to work. In recent generations, many millions of United States women have facilitated this transition through part-time participation in many types of informal educational programs. Continuing education programs allow purposeful women to pursue college without the usual obstacles (*Counseling Psychologist*, 1976). More recently, a small but growing number of mature women have enrolled full time in graduate school to pursue master's degrees or doctorates. Two studies have analyzed their reasons for doing so and the developmental process by which roles and attitudes change (Hiestand, 1971; LeFevre, 1972).

The reasons women resume the student role are generally positive and very diverse. Unlike men in the same age group who are more likely to return to graduate school to facilitate a change within a broad field or between closely related fields, a larger proportion of mature women graduate students are there to enter a profession, often after being a full-time homemaker for some years. Many women who enter graduate school are experiencing a major occupational shift or entering a profession and do so because of their great interest in the field or because such a change seems to be necessary or very desirable.

They are less likely than men to report that they are doing so because increased financial ability now makes such a move possible (Hiestand, 1971; Ginzberg and others, 1966).

Married women with children typically enter graduate school by choice to implement their sense of themselves as they are and would like to become, rather than because of role expectations or economic necessity. In contrast with similar women who remain full-time homemakers, the returning students give higher priority to personal development. Those who continue full-time as homemakers typically find satisfaction and security in individual and social activities in the home and community as their family responsibilities decline. Their interests and outlook emphasize femininity, cheerfulness, and neatness and play down self-confidence, expansiveness, and reading. They feel that they have become somewhat more autonomous and assertive since their early homemaking days, and they are relatively satisfied with themselves and their lives. The returning students feel that they have been very competent in and continue to value their family roles but that their family responsibilities are declining and that prospects are low for further self-development in their family roles. For them, a return to school holds the prospect of personal development, interesting productive work, and stimulating associates. They express low interest in domestic activities and reject typical women's groups and volunteer activities as superficial and unsatisfying. Their husbands generally share their values and support their decisions to return to school. Some of the returning students have been working or going to school part time as homemakers before becoming full-time graduate students.

Mature women graduate students typically complete their degree programs in about the same time as other graduate students, and they then become full-time professionals. However, during the process there are usually some shifts in their attitudes toward themselves and their roles in family, work, and school. As they enter graduate study, they tend to be unusually capable and energetic women who are confident and excited but slightly apprehensive as their dreams are about to confront reality. They express positive attitudes toward their homemaker roles and look forward to new experience and greater individuality.

During their first year of graduate study, the women students report that it is strenuous but satisfying. Many substantially reduce their family roles. About half feel that the effects on their children have been mixed. Husbands are supportive, which helps in role adjustments, and only a few express guilt about the adjustments. Some make adjustments in course load or family responsibilities so that they can carry the combined load. There is already evidence of socialization into the professional role and identity and out of the traditional feminine role.

As the women complete their course work and proceed to examinations and research proposals, some shifts occur. They are now aware of how much perseverance is required, are concerned that they have not made as much progress as they had hoped, are apprehensive about the major hurdles yet to be overcome, are less certain about the remaining and more independent academic stage after the relative security of course work, and are becoming concerned about their husbands' and children's increasingly negative attitudes toward their graduate study. Their loss of self-confidence is somewhat compensated for by their growing sense of progress and accomplishment. In contrast with the sense of self as a homemaker returning to school as they began graduate study, toward the end of the process most of the women increasingly reject their former homemaking role and see themselves as graduate students with homemaking responsibilities. As the women complete their degrees and assume professional responsibilities, there is an increase in confidence, self-esteem, and assertiveness. They express satisfaction with their accomplishment at having progressed toward their ideal self. Most report improvements in their family life although some express guilt feelings in relation to their family (LeFevre, 1972). Not only do mature women achieve well in college, but they tend to achieve as well as or better than women students who attend right after high school (Halfter, 1962).

Greater understanding of the developmental process that

typically occurs when mature women reenter formal education has several benefits. Women whose children are growing up and who consider resumption of the student role can gain a more realistic idea of the process and plan accordingly. Many people concerned with career education and development can better appreciate the distinctive features of career development for women. Occupational choice occurs for some women, and men also, well into middle age and beyond. In addition to the implications for mature women who consider a transition from family to study and work, these conclusions have implications for orientation of young people regarding the uncertainty and variability of career development and for personnel in higher education admissions offices.

Self

The foregoing consideration of women's family, work, and student roles gives rise to a concern about the sense of self that permeates these several roles. Adults typically have a sense of "me" in each of their life roles that is affected by the tasks and expectations associated with each role. The attitudes and activities typical of the individual's performance in the work role may contrast in some ways with the attitudes and activities typical of the mother role. However, most people have a sense of "I" that is stable across time and settings. This sense of self begins to develop early in life, but for many people it continues to develop throughout life. Self-concept affects the way in which an individual considers a role change as well as role performance and satisfaction.

For many women, a sense of "femaleness" is a major aspect of self-concept. This reflects sex differences, but it reflects sex-role stereotypes even more. Women seem to vary greatly in the importance of femaleness in their self-concept and in the positiveness or negativeness of their feelings toward femaleness. The role performance of a woman who considers herself a person who happens to be female and whose aspirations and activities have been little restricted by being a woman is likely to be guided by the major values inherent in her self-concept with little influence from feelings about femaleness. However, the role performance of a woman whose sense of self is dominated by traditional sex-role stereotypes is likely to be influenced accordingly. Deep resentment about constraints caused by sex discrimination would also be expected to affect role performance.

Wives' satisfaction and happiness with their roles in family, work, and community tend to be associated heavily with their preferences. Life satisfaction of middle-aged women tends to be higher for those who are home and community oriented than for those who are work oriented. Unemployed wives who want to work tend to be lonely and dissatisfied, to have low self-esteem, and to feel trapped and powerless. Many are married to husbands in blue collar occupations, and they are not working because of a poor job market, illness, and family responsibilities. Employed wives are able to spend the least time on housework or themselves because of their dual roles. They tend to be less happily married but have higher feelings of competence and self-esteem than full-time homemakers. The full-time homemakers who do not want to work tend to have higher family incomes, happy marriages, and high physical and mental health and to feel satisfied and in control. The interaction between role performance and preferences helps explain the very different attitudes toward family roles of full-time homemakers.

Self-concept and aspirations are also affected by experience in various life roles. The woman whose early educational and work experience is very satisfying and growthful is less likely to perceive herself as only a wife and mother and to seek complete fulfillment from family roles. The woman whose roles as wife, mother, and homemaker are very satisfying and growthful is less likely to reject them in favor of a career. The woman who is satisfied in both work and family role experiences and who enjoys flexibility in each is likely to evolve a satisfactory but distinctive pattern of role performance.

Some of the main implications related to women's roles pertain to minimizing stereotypes, recognizing alternatives, understanding stages, and facilitating transitions. Practitioners have a unique responsibility with regard to women's roles because of the fundamental value judgments implicit in societal practices and individual decisions related to women's roles in family, work, and community. Examples include differentiation of family responsibilities between husbands and wives, community organization dependence on volunteer effort by women, and sex discrimination in employment.

Sex-role stereotypes are mostly based on assumptions and myths. Practitioners can help women and men recognize such stereotypes, take them into account, and reduce them (Friedan, 1962; Le Shan, 1973; Janeway, 1971, 1975). Women have various alternatives regarding combinations of education, work, and family life. Practitioners can help young women recognize and explore the alternatives, can encourage young couples to strive for mutually satisfactory role relationships, and can assist women with their role adjustments. During the family life cycle, as children arrive, grow up, and leave to start their own families, there are great changes in mothers' tasks and satisfactions. Practitioners can assist mothers and fathers to understand the series of family life stages so that each stage can be accepted and appreciated as a part of the larger process. Many of women's transitions, such as those from work to family to school to work, require understanding and persistence. Practitioners can facilitate these transitions by the provision of educational programs, counseling services, and mutual support groups that facilitate career and educational development and personal growth.

During the past decade there has been a rapid expansion of career and personal counseling services for women. This expansion of programs and services reflects both the great increase in the number of women in transition and the unique problems that women confront. The reasons for working are very similar for men and women, but the reasons for not working are quite different. Such arrangements as day care for dependent children loom larger in career plans for mothers of young children than for fathers. Less than 10 percent of day care is provided in organized facilities; more than 90 percent depends on informal arrangements with family and friends. Decisions that working women make about home and work tend to be highly interdependent (Schlossberg and Pietrofesa, 1973; Harmon, 1975; U.S. BLS, 1975; Kreps, 1976). Some important issues for practitioners with women clients are associated with such client characteristics as age, marital status, skin color, and native language. For example, unemployment and advancement problems are quite different for women under twenty-five and women over fifty-five. As another example, for many years a black female confronted two negatives that in recent years have often combined to produce a positive asset (C. Epstein, 1973; Gump and Rivers, 1975). Practitioners must take changing social and economic conditions into account. The downturn in economic conditions during the mid-seventies has contributed to family stress, as reflected in increased incidence of divorce and child abuse. It is even possible that an extended period of high unemployment for men will precipitate a backlash that could worsen employment conditions for women (Kreps, 1976).

The foregoing implications are based on generalizations about women's roles. However, practitioners could derive comparable implications from developmental generalizations about young adults from minority groups, career development by blue collar men, retirees, or women who assume major community leadership responsibilities.

Summary

Women's dual roles in family and work illustrate developmental interrelationships. Family roles as wife and mother emphasize solidarity and have diffuse forms of recognition. The worker role emphasizes contractual relationships and has more explicit forms of recognition. As a woman moves from one role to the other or performs both concurrently, conflicts can occur in role expectations and the sense of self. In the developmental process, variables related to personality, learning, condition, and context interact as well.

Sex differences reflect context as well as condition. Many of the widespread and persistent beliefs about inherent and acquired sex differences are unfounded myths. To be sure, men and women are different and complementary in their physiology related to reproduction. However, contrary to popular myths, girls are equivalent to boys regarding environmental effects, suggestibility, achievement motivation, cognitive style, sociability, and self-esteem.

The few sex differences that have been demonstrated cluster around intellectual abilities and assertiveness. During adolescence the average verbal ability of girls is somewhat greater than for boys, but during much of adulthood average intellectual ability of men and women is comparable. Beyond sixty, women tend to score slightly higher on verbal ability tests, but the rate of decline is the same for men and women. The higher average visual-spatial ability of males reflects the biological contribution of a recessive sex-linked gene that benefits more males. During adolescence and young adulthood there is evidence of male superiority on mathematical tasks. Hormonal differences help account for the greater average assertiveness of males. Practitioners can help people separate the substantiated similarities and differences between men and women from the unfounded myths and distinguish between what is and what ought to be.

Many of the differences in performance by men and women in family and work are part of a widespread pattern of male dominance. This pattern partly reflects the historical biological function of women in childbearing and the greater average size, strength, and aggressiveness of men. However, societal values, in the forms of generalized sex-role stereotypes and specific role expectations, have an even greater influence than physiology on women's performance. Over the centuries, roles for women in economic, family, educational, religious, and political institutions have tended to be complementary to those of men, who have typically been in the most visible and influential positions. Even though recent social change has greatly affected women's roles, sex-role stereotypes from an earlier age persist. In addition, when a wife and mother seeks to alter her family role performance, the expectations of other family members typically influence her performance and contribute to conflict or satisfaction.

Recently women's family role options have increased.

Furthermore, there are many influences that together make the
full-time homemaker role as wife and mother relatively unattractive to many women. Included are the heavy societal
emphasis on self-interest, contractual exchanges, and monetary
rewards in the larger society; the giving tasks and intangible
rewards of the homemaker role; the shift of former family functions to other institutions; shrinking purchasing power of family
income; and an extended postparental period.

Mothering tasks shift as the children grow up. When
they are young, mothering and direct supervision consumes a
high proportion of the woman's family time. As the children
become adolescents, they develop interests and activities of their
own and relate less to their mother and home. When the
children are young, an unending list of unfinished tasks and
chronic fatigue contribute to the trapped housewife feeling.
The homemaker's burden is usually redoubled because this
period is when her husband feels the most pressure to invest
heavily in the early stages of his career. When the children are
old enough to be able to really help with household chores, their
interest in doing so typically declines. Much depends on how
parents include them in family work.

The division of family tasks between husband and wife
mainly reflects traditional sex-role stereotypes, along with some
negotiation by each couple. Although traditional sex-role
stereotypes persist, there is some shift toward more equalitarian
marital relationships, especially for young white collar couples
and where husbands are very successful in their own careers. In
spite of the problems associated with women's family role performance, the satisfaction can also be great. Effective performance can immerse a woman in holistic, developmental, and
humanistic activities that contribute to personal coherence,
social cohesion, and movement toward our highest values.

There are substantial variations during the family life
cycle in level of life satisfaction for various categories of adults,
part of which reflects family role performance. Married people
are typically happier than singles and childless couples are
happier than couples with young children. For parents with
young children, satisfaction is low and feelings of stress are

higher than for any category except divorced women. The trend is for satisfaction to increase and stress to decrease as the children grow up and leave. Childless married people over thirty express high satisfaction, and widowed adults express low satisfaction. Single women express less happiness than any category of married women. Satisfaction levels are lowest for adults who are separated or divorced, especially for women. Other aspects of life besides family role performance also affect happiness. However, practitioners can help adults understand shifts in role performance and satisfaction that relate to the presence and age of children in the family.

During the past generation, employment rates for married women were highest in the early twenties and in the early fifties, with low rates during the child-rearing years in between. However, during the decade before 1973, the percentage of working wives increased from about 33 percent to about 43 percent. In recent decades, working rates for single and divorced or widowed women have been quite constant, but there has been a sharp increase for married women with husband present. Earlier increases were for women who no longer had young children, but more recent increases have been for women with young children. In recent years, more than one out of ten families are headed by women, and about two thirds of them have dependent children. More than seven out of ten divorced women work, compared with almost six out of ten women who never married, more than half of married women with husband absent, more than four out of ten married women with husband present, and one quarter of widows. About two-thirds of female family heads under age sixty-five work or seek work.

For working women generally, the unemployment rates are somewhat higher than for men. Women who remain continuously in the labor force typically have lower unemployment rates than those whose working was interrupted. The greater representation of women in lower status occupations also contributes to greater unemployment for women.

Although women are included in all occupational categories, they are concentrated mainly in clerical, service, operative, professional, and sales occupations. A primary interest in marriage and family roles has discouraged many women from pursuing more demanding occupations. The lack of female role models in most fields has also been a hindrance. In recent decades, the proportions of women in professional and managerial occupations have increased in such occupations as law, and have been stable or declined in others, such as college teaching.

Women's annual earnings are lower than men's earnings. This reflects the concentration of women in lower paid occupations, fewer years of service, and fewer hours worked each year. Single women who work continuously after leaving school earn slightly more than single men. When men and women in the same occupations, with comparable qualifications and service, and within the same establishment are compared, the women's median earnings are only a little more than 80 percent of men's earnings. Much of the differential no doubt reflects discrimination.

Regarding the effects of maternal employment on young children, with adequate substitute care, along with constructive attitudes and practices, maternal employment need not have any major adverse effects on the children. School-aged children of working mothers who liked work, liked the child, used mild discipline, and avoided inconveniencing the child with many household tasks were less hostile than were children of working mothers who disliked working, were less involved with the child, and obtained the child's help with homemaking tasks under duress. Daughters of working mothers tend to perceive women as more competent and to give more credit to women's accomplishments than daughters of nonworking women.

In general, the career development patterns of working women are distinctive because of the accommodation that is required between their dual roles in family and work. In most two-career families, it appears that men still expect their own careers to be primary. Some organizations and educational institutions have sponsored informal groups and counseling services to assist women who are entering school or work.

During their thirties and forties some women resume a student role, often as a part of the transition from family to work. For example, unlike men in the same age group, who usually return to graduate school for further specialization, a larger proportion of mature women graduate students are there to enter a profession, often after being full-time homemakers for some years. Married women with children typically enter graduate school by choice to implement their sense of themselves as they are and would like to become, rather than because of role expectations or economic necessity. During the first year of graduate study, there is evidence of socialization into the professional role and identity and out of the traditional feminine role. Many substantially reduce their family roles. As they complete course work and proceed to dissertations, some further shifts in viewpoint typically occur. Loss of self-confidence is compensated for by a growing sense of accomplishment. They become concerned about more negative attitudes toward their graduate study by their husbands and children. In contrast with the sense of self as a homemaker returning to school when they began graduate study, toward the end of the process most women see themselves as graduate students with homemaking responsibilities. They typically complete their degree programs in about the same time as other graduate students and then become full-time professionals. Completion is associated with increased confidence, self-esteem, and assertiveness.

For most women a sense of self permeates their roles in family, work, and school. Self-concept affects role change, performance, and satisfaction. For example, unemployed wives who want to work tend to be lonely and dissatisfied, to have low self-esteem, and to feel trapped and powerless. Employed wives tend to be less happily married, but have higher feelings of competence and self-esteem than full-time homemakers. The full-time homemakers who do not want to work tend to have higher family incomes, happy marriages, and high physical and mental health and to feel satisfied and in control. The interaction between role performance and preferences helps explain the very different attitudes toward family roles of homemakers.

Consideration of women's dual roles illustrates developmental interrelationships among context, performance, condition, personality, and learning. Social change has created a lag between past expectations and current realities and a wider range of alternative women's roles. Practitioners can help women understand such aspects of the societal context along with implications for their own performance. Practitioners can also help clients distinguish between what is and what ought to be. This is especially important during a period of rapid change.

Relations with family members illustrate both interaction at one point in time and developmental trends over time. This is especially so for shifting relationships with growing children. Practitioners can help women gain greater perspective regarding these interrelationships and trends. As was illustrated by mothers who return to graduate school, such an experience tends to affect the individual's view of self. Practitioners can assist women with such transitions by providing relevant educational programs and counseling services and referring them to mutual support groups, so that the process contributes to career and educational development and personal growth.

❦ 9 ❧

Adjusting to Change Events

The relative stability of adult life is periodically punctuated by change events, such as marriage, a job change, or the death of a close friend, that alter significantly the individual's relationships with other people and disturb the routine of social participation. Such change events may influence a person's self-concept, morale, and aspiration and are often turning points that entail increased vulnerability and heightened potential (Erikson, 1976). An individual's adjustment to these events is influenced by the interaction of both personal characteristics (such as openness of personality and physical condition) and contextual characteristics (such as encouragement from others and access to opportunities). As the person moves from relatively stable social relationships, through the disruption of the change event, to a reorganized structure of participation, the developmental processes by which an individual adapts become most apparent. Also, the changes in activity and outlook that result from such events help explain why adults change so much over the years in spite of great stability during many months

513

and years (Clausen, 1972; R. W. White, 1972; Gerlach and Hine, 1973).

This chapter analyzes the process by which adults adapt when a major and abrupt role gain or loss requires them to modify their structure of participation. It gives particular attention to alternative ways for dealing with role changes and to the heightened readiness to learn that sometimes results from them.

Stability and Change

Although adults change gradually in many ways over the years, change events require them to adapt to inescapable additions and losses in major role relationships with others. These events may occur in any relationship—family, occupational, or community. They may entail a gain, a loss, or a combination of gains and losses in role relationships. For example, role gains include entering college, beginning the first full-time job, getting married, having a child, and assuming a major leadership responsibility in a community organization. Role losses include the youngest child's leaving home, retirement, and death of loved ones. Role changes that involve both gains and losses include changing jobs, changing churches, and moving to a new neighborhood or community.

Change events may also vary in extent of option or compulsion. In some events, such as accepting an attractive job offer, the individual has some latitude in deciding whether or not to make the change and in selecting those aspects of life that are altered. With such optional changes, individuals in effect volunteer to undergo adaptation and growth. Other events, such as the death of someone close, mandatory retirement from a job or children growing up and leaving home, are inescapable and may be forced on the individual. Some change events, such as retirement, can be anticipated months or years in advance, whereas others may occur without warning. Some are common to everyone; others affect only some adults, such as those with children. They can vary in their emotional intensity and in the duration of their impact, as witness the contrast between the birth of quadruplets versus that of a fourth child, or a move to a different type of job in a different country versus a change of status in the same office. And they vary regarding their most likely occurrence during the adult life cycle.

Except for times of major change events, adult activities are characterized by a high degree of stability. This predictability regarding what a person does, where, when, and with whom results from personality, habit, and the relatively constant expectations of others. Each adult has a characteristic structure of participation in family, occupational, political, organizational, church, educational, and leisure activities. These activities, such as preparing dinner or watching television, tend to occur at predictable times and places and with certain people because of stable circumstances. Indeed, life consists largely of a patterned set of recurring activities—some occurring during the early mornings, evenings, and weekends in the home with family members; others during working hours at the place of employment with fellow workers; still other organizational, church, and political activities at other times and places with still other persons. The stability or equilibrium in the structure of these activities is distinctive for each individual and provides the baseline against which to discern the disruption of a change event and subsequent reorganization of activities. The punctual time-bound clerk and the free-wheeling bohemian artist provide striking contrasts in predictability of daily and weekly rounds of activities, but both most likely have their own stable structure of participation.

The structure of participation has both objective and subjective dimensions. The objective dimension is basically the patterned flow of activities as viewed by others in terms of time, place, and participants, almost like a report of a private investigator as a result of continual surveillance. People vary in the extent to which an activity can be reconstructed from a knowledge of just one element. Some adults are so rigidly ordered that knowing a day and time period or a group of associates is sufficient to predict accurately the remaining elements.

At the other extreme, there are adults whose activities and associates appear to be randomly related, and they seem to be independent of time and place. For those whose activities are more predictable, the dominant recurrent feature of participation varies. Some adults will engage in favorite activities with almost anybody, while other adults will engage in almost any activity with particular individuals. The structure of participation also varies among people regarding the extent to which activities and interpersonal relations are regulated by formal norms, such as occurs in some work settings and voluntary associations. Aside from the number of separate activities engaged in during a time period, adults vary regarding the number of different activities and/or persons. At one extreme is the frontier family in which a few people participate in most activities. At the other extreme is the joiner who participates in many specialized activities, with little repetition of associates. The subjective dimension includes goals and values, as well as feelings about past and present experience. Included is the extent to which the individual feels that he or she engages in an activity because of preference or obligation, as well as the extent to which the individual can classify activities as to personal importance or similarity.

The interaction of the objective and subjective dimensions of participation is illustrated by the interplay between activities and preoccupations during the transition from adolescence to young adulthood. Activities such as work, school, dancing, cycling, parties, crafts, and attending events can be described as the objective dimension of participation. However, the meanings that these activities have for the young people who engage in them reflect their preoccupations and interests. An overriding preoccupation is their quest for an adult identity. This quest is reflected in preoccupations with autonomy, work, physical maturation, mental development, and moral sensitivity. Related concerns include stimulation, sociability, and balance. Especially in their leisure activities, young people tend to pursue interests that enable them to explore and satisfy their main preoccupations (Rapoport and Rapoport, 1975).

An adult's structure of participation evolves over time and is shaped by both personal and situational influences. There are many personal influences, although only a few may impinge on a specific change event. Social class background is highly associated with many types of activities. Men and women have engaged in somewhat different types of activities in past generations, although for young white collar couples this seems to be changing. Marital and employment status are related to family and work activities, and there are adult life cycle shifts in activity patterns. Poor health can restrict activity. Openness or rigidity of personality can influence the ease and effectiveness with which a person enters new activities, and learning ability is related to the rapidity of adjustment as well as the complexity of the structure of participation (W. G. Smith, 1971; Lowenthal, Thurnher, and others, 1975).

There are several types of situational influences on an individual's structure of participation. A broad feature of the societal context is the opportunity system. This includes not only the general opportunities in the individual's community, such as employers and job openings, health care services, recreational facilities, potential marriage partners, and educational programs, but also the actual accessibility of these opportunities to the individual. Although such resources and services may exist in a community, they are not part of the opportunity system if the adult lacks the awareness, money, or background to take advantage of them. Discrimination on the basis of age, sex, religion, race, or ethnic background can restrict the opportunity system and thus influence an individual's structure of participation.

A more specific situational influence on participation is the diversity and flexibility of an individual's role relationships. Role relationships in family, work, or community settings are reciprocal and reflect the expectations of the individual and of other people in the role set. For example, young draftsmen may prefer to devote their time to more creative and managerial tasks than those expected of them by their supervisors and even the client. In some situations, adults may have relatively little flexibility in the ways in which they can achieve satisfactory role performance, due to strong role stereotypes and rigid expectations by those in related roles. The availability of role models who demonstrate alternative modes of role performance or even life-styles, can help people alter their own structure of participation in similar directions. The contribution of other people to the formation or modification of an individual's structure of participation can be even more personal. Sometimes, someone who is already experienced in an unfamiliar type of activity provides encouragement and assistance. This mentor-mentee relationship occurs, for example, in the big sister or brother relationship for college freshmen, in the host family relationship for new church members, and in the on-the-job training that some supervisors provide new workers.

These types of personal and situational influences help establish and maintain an adult's structure of participation, and they also affect the process by which a person deals with a change event. Often those in related roles are affected by a change event. Examples include members of a work group when one is appointed supervisor and the wife and children when a middle-aged husband is unemployed. If they have convictions regarding directions in which they would like the person who experiences the change event to develop, they have both the motive and the opportunity to be influential. Because their expectations and reciprocal role relationships are likely to have helped maintain the individual's structure of participation before the change event, a change in their own performance and attitudes can be quite influential. Even during periods when no major change events occur, changes in the performance and attitudes of significant others help bring about gradual adult development. However, there is a tendency for personality, habit, and the expectations of others to maintain stability in an adult's life, until a change event disrupts the pattern. Such an event may be catalytic and open an individual to new external opportunities and new personal potential, or it may result in withdrawal and the erection of further defenses. Over the years, the result may be a constant, differing, expanding, or contracting structure of participation. Various writers concerned with adult development and learning recognized the potential of change events for explaining some of the dynamics of adult development (Harris, 1957; Brim, 1966; B. Fried, 1967; Neugarten, 1968, 1973; Ahammer, 1973; Looft, 1973; Lowenthal, Thurnher, and others, 1975; *Counseling Psychologist*, 1976; Brim, 1976; Levinson and others, 1976). To do so will require an analysis of some specific types of change events.

Change or Gain

All major role change events, by definition, entail modifications of the structure of participation. When a major activity or role relationship is added, changed, or lost, there must be some alteration of the individual's time use, usually to make way for the new relationship or to fill in the time released because a relationship is lost. Often the compensation for a major role change takes the form of many minor contractions or expansions of other activities. For example, if a woman is elected president of a community group, she may make small reductions in the time she spends on bowling, bridge, and church, instead of dropping any one altogether. However, when the activity is major, important, and lost, it is more likely that an adult will try to replace it. Role relationships and activities mean more than time allocation; they have meanings for the individual regarding status, satisfaction, and a sense of belonging. When a confidant moves away, just increasing the time devoted to many other activities and relationships is not likely to take his or her place. Most adults will seek to enter into a closer confidant relationship with someone else during the subsequent year or two, so that the important confidant relationship is served.

Because the loss of a major role relationship has some unique characteristics, it is covered separately in the next section; this section deals with change events that entail a gain or change of role relationships. When all types of change events are distributed along the adult life cycle in terms of the age at which they typically occur, a high proportion are concentrated in early young adulthood. Furthermore, most of the change events during young adulthood entail gains of role relationships, most of those during middle age entail changes, and most of those during old age entail losses. For example, during the transition from adolescence to young adulthood, most Americans begin driving a car, voting, and working; get married; and become parents. Some go to college, which for some may be a substitution of one student role in high school for another student role in college, but which for many people constitutes a new and more independent educational and social experience.

During young adulthood and middle age, some white collar adults assume responsibilities for organizational leadership. A change of job or even career is a widespread occurrence. Familiar examples are men or women who receive promotions or are laid off from work for a while and women who return to work as their children get older. However, a large and increasing proportion of United States workers experience two, three, and four major career changes. The stock clerk who becomes a supervisor, the secretary who becomes a bookkeeper, and the engineer who becomes a manager are relatively familiar, and we are becoming more aware of the retired military officer who becomes a real estate broker, the clergyman who becomes a college professor, and the businessman who becomes a clergyman. Another change event that occurs for an increasing proportion of adults is divorce and remarriage. A move to a new dwelling in the same community or in another one is a change event that declines in frequency and alters in character during adulthood. Young adult moves are more frequent, and although in some instances there may be difficulty breaking parental home ties, the moves tend to be upward and outward to seize new opportunities. Mixed feelings are more likely to characterize moves during middle age. Possessions tend to accumulate, so that there is more to discard and more to move. Adolescent children are more likely to resent leaving their friends when a move means leaving their school system. Relocation for older adults often entails a reluctant move that seems to be necessary but not desirable. For older convalescent patients with a serious physical or mental impairment, relocation to another facility is associated with higher death rates (Lieberman, 1961; Kasteler, Gray, and Carruth, 1968; Goldfarb, Shahinian, and Burr, 1972;

Kastenbaum and Candy, 1973). A change event that is associated with middle age, the so-called "empty nest" period when the youngest children leave home, is often referred to as a major role loss but typically entails far less stress and upset than is generally assumed (Lowenthal and Chiriboga, 1972).

For many people, the idea of going to college means packing up during the late summer after high school graduation and moving to a dormitory on a college campus. It means somewhat different types of courses and expectations from faculty members and peers, but perhaps even more it means relatively independent living and social arrangements away from parents. However, urbanization, transportation arrangements, higher proportions of young people attending college, an increase in community colleges, and an increasing proportion of adults of all ages who attend college part time have varied the reasons and circumstances surrounding the decision to participate in higher education, and the former stereotype applies to far less than half of those who go to college.

Although the student role is familiar to everyone who attends college, being a college student is a new role relationship for several reasons. One is because of the deliberate choice involved. Few children think of deciding to attend elementary or secondary school. This decision was made for them by compulsory education laws and by parents and truant officers. The high school student's deliberate choice regarding attendance is most likely to occur, if at all, in regard to dropping out after age sixteen or continuing to graduation. By contrast, almost all college students decide to attend, or at least acquiesce in a decision they are willing to accept. This even occurs for local community colleges with an "open door" policy, where the recent high school graduate may experience a minimum of adjustment.

For many of those who decide to attend college, on a full-time or part-time basis, in late adolescence or in middle age, the decision reflects the interplay of personal and situational influences. Personal influences include learning ability, self-concept, and aspirations. Situational influences include encouragement by significant others, ability to pay costs, and accessibility of courses that match interests. The types, strength, and interaction of these influences vary somewhat between the person who considers college attendance at the end of high school and one who considers it twenty years later.

A young man from a blue collar family in the bottom third of his class in a high school where more than half of the graduates go to college is likely to be ambivalent about college. Influences in favor of college include good friends who urge him to attend with them, parents who encourage him to attend and are able to help him financially, an enjoyment of reading, and the lack of available jobs. Influences against it include a dislike of school experiences, a lack of career goals, the prospect of an attractive job right out of high school, and an interest in early marriage. Sometimes financial assistance, local college courses with an attractive image, or a strong related interest and talent, such as sports or the arts, can be sufficient to tip the balance. If a young man with above average learning ability decides not to go to college because of a dislike of school activities and a lack of career goals, sometimes the experience of being out of school working for a few years can result in far more positive attitudes toward further education and far greater success in college. Attending part time while holding a job can provide a useful transition.

A woman in her thirties with family background and high school experience comparable to the man described above, but who worked briefly as a waitress or sales clerk and then was married and raised children, may also consider college. The attitudes of parents and school mates will have little influence, but her husband's attitudes are likely to be crucial. If she reads and is at least somewhat active in voluntary associations, she is more likely to consider college seriously and to have acquired competencies that can be adapted to facilitate successful study. Perhaps most important is her own sense of self and becoming. If she thinks of herself mainly as a homemaker, is unaware of any major discrepancy between her current competence and what she would like to become, and lacks confidence in her ability to learn and develop, she is not likely to enroll in a college course. However, if she aspires to increased competence and a new stage of life and has confidence in her ability to grow and change, she is more likely to enter college. Under such circumstances, participation in a short-term, noncredit educational program on a topic of high interest provides a transitional opportunity to explore interest, test ability, and consolidate competence. Some continuing education programs for women are designed for this purpose.

Men in their thirties and forties are changing professions more often and are including a return to college as a part of the transition to their second careers. One study compared men who made such a mid-life career shift with similar men who persisted in their original career field (Clopton, 1973). The main differences between the shifters and the persisters related to adult life circumstances and personality. The two groups were very similar regarding family background and childhood experiences, including birth order and family changes. They were also similar in their extent of success in their original career, their geographic mobility as adults, and their family responsibilities. However, more of the shifters had experienced divorce or separation, had received personal counseling, and had access to financial resources sufficient to support themselves and their families during the transition. Also, shifters had higher self-esteem and had thought more seriously about their personal mortality than was the case for persisters. Shifters and persisters were similar regarding personal adjustment and stability, sense of direction, need for achievement, pattern of vocational interests, and flexibility.

Within the shifters, there were three main types of reasons for their mid-life career shift. One was a gradual disenchantment with the first career that led to a search for a new profession which would allow the individual to realize his potential more fully. The second reason was discovery of a new career that promised more satisfaction even though the individual continued to enjoy his first career. In such instances, the second career typically evolved from a strong avocational interest. The third reason was a reformulation of the individual's goals and meaning precipitated by a major change event. Examples of such change events include religious conversion, a crucial insight from psychotherapy, and sudden unemployment. In such instances, the change event, such as when an aerospace engineer experiences technological unemployment, causes a mid-career shift that entails another change event—returning to school—that leads to another change event—entering the second career.

A move to a new residence is a change event that may be viewed by any family member as a gain, a change, or a loss. Objectively, when a family moves from one dwelling to another, they leave one set of friends and activities behind to be replaced by another set in the new location. Subjectively, the individual seldom feels that the exchange has been equal, and members of the same family are likely to have different opinions about whether they gained or lost in the process. Some factors that contribute to positive feelings about a change of residence include: a voluntary move, increased income and prestige after the move, lack of close friends and relations left behind with the move, and interesting new friends and activities after the move. The distance of the move and the contrast in the two community settings also influence the extent of adjustment required. For example, a move within the same neighborhood might affect the structure of participation very little, with the exception of relations with immediate neighbors. Informal contacts with the family that lives in the adjoining house or apartment often change substantially as a result of a move of just a mile. By contrast a move from a small town to a large city hundreds of miles away brings many adjustments regarding friends and neighbors, schools, jobs, church, and even general life-style. The activities, commitments, friends, and expectations in the former community help maintain stability in an individual's life. For people who depend greatly on these external relationships, a change can bring about major and upsetting feelings of insecurity. For adults who have a sense of who they are and want to become, a move can facilitate major modifications of life style and outlook.

Loss

Some change events are usually associated with strong feelings of loss and grief. Examples include temporary unemployment; some divorces; a major property loss; retirement; loss of a function, such as vision or movement of arms or legs; death of a spouse or loved one. Especially for the loss entailed in death and dying, our literature over the centuries refers to the grieving process. However, most of the research on how people react to death has occurred during the past decade or so (Feifel, 1959; Jeffers and others, 1961; Glaser and Strauss, 1965, 1968; Hinton, 1967; Ross, 1969; Kutscher, 1969; Schoenberg, 1974; G. Vernon, 1970; Kastenbaum and Aisenberg, 1972; Parkes, 1972; Shneidman, 1960, 1966, 1972; Silverman, 1972; Lopata, 1973; Shibles, 1974; Butler, 1975). Although there are individual differences in the ways in which people react to loss and variations related to the type of loss they sustain, there appears to be a general developmental process through which adults go from the initial shock of finding out that the loss has occurred or will soon occur to some personal resolution in the form of acceptance or at least stable attitude toward the loss. Any major loss experience is a form of personal crisis in that the individual is faced with a very undesirable situation in which a retreat to what used to be becomes a very desirable but impossible goal (Bowlby, 1969). Thus, a better understanding of the developmental process by which adults typically modify their thoughts and feelings regarding a major loss can assist the person who experiences a loss, and those who try to help, to use that understanding as the basis for constructive action (*Counseling Psychologist*, 1976).

The stages that often occur when someone reacts to and tries to accommodate a major loss do not necessarily occur in sequence, some stages may not occur at all, and several may occur together. Such stages include the shifts in thoughts and feelings that occur regarding the loss and do not include the actions taken in a specific instance, such as calling the insurance adjuster, or arranging for an artificial limb, or buying a new car. The five general and widespread stages are denial, anger, depression, bargaining, and acceptance (Ross, 1969).

Denial. Sudden bad news is shocking. Some confusion often occurs as well. The implications of the loss are sometimes so awful that many people try to "soften the blow" by refusing to accept that the loss is likely. When the car or truck is missing, it is underinsured, and the problems of doing without it or trying to replace it are enormous, it is understandable that many people try to postpone as long as possible the conclusion that it has been stolen and will not be recovered. Many people who approach mandatory retirement and strongly want to continue to work make few realistic plans to prepare for retirement but instead try not to think about it. When many people find out that they are terminally ill, the initial reaction is denial. The prospect of death is often so awful that they want to believe that the diagnosis is incorrect and that the lab tests or the X rays should be checked again because some mistake has probably been made. As Scarlett O'Hara said, "I'll think about it to-morrow."

Anger. Few people like to lose. Even small losses are likely to elicit negative feelings. It should not be surprising then that major losses, such as having one's house destroyed by a tornado, being unable to walk as a result of a freak accident, or being informed that one has terminal cancer, produce for most people at some stage strong negative feelings, such as regret, resentment, or anger. If a worker whose productivity and work habits have been uneven is fired, the reaction may range from remorse and a commitment to do better next time to indignation at the unfairness of the system. However, the competent and conscientious worker who is technologically unemployed due to a downturn in the industry will probably react with resentment or anger. The person who through no fault of his own loses an arm in an accident is likely to cry out in anguish at some point, "Why me?" The mother or father whose school-aged child becomes progressively worse during several weeks following an accident or illness and then dies is likely to experience anger or similar feelings at some points in the process. If the individual feels some responsibility for the loss, guilt feelings are also likely. Angry feelings can be difficult to deal with, but to repress them can lead to even greater difficulties in recovering from grief.

Depression. There is an old saying that it is always darkest just before the dawn. As individuals increasingly realize more and more of the unhappy implications of a loss, such as destruction of a home, they typically become depressed (M.

Fried, 1963). At that point it is difficult to look on the bright side. The young man who recently lost his sight may well become despondent. The loss seems so great, but many of the things that will partially compensate for the loss have not become apparent. The blindness separates him from much of his world, and his depression separates him even further. A few people who experience a major loss remain depressed for exceedingly long periods, sometimes until they die. This is reflected in periods of extended mourning. More often, they realize that life must go on, that there are ways to accept the loss and to compensate for lost relationships at least partly. Sometimes extreme emphasis on remaining values and abilities or on the virtue of persevering against adversity helps end the depression and enable the individual to move toward acceptance and growth.

Bargaining. For some types of losses, even though the loss seems irrevocable, some people will try to bargain for a new lease on life. The desire for a second chance is understandable and if it is obtainable is probably the most desirable course of action. This occurs when a young couple's first child is stillborn, and after a while they have another child. It also occurs when a prisoner vows to go straight. Sometimes, however, bargaining seems to be a last desperate effort to stay the inevitable. One party to an especially bitter divorce proceeding may at a late stage suggest conditions for a reconciliation. A worker faced with the final weeks before mandatory retirement from an organization with a strict policy of no extensions may plead for an exception. The terminally ill patient may entreat the physician or pray to God for a reprieve.

Acceptance. Some people never come to accept a major loss. Perhaps for some types of losses, such as a child who disappears, this is fitting. However, for an irrevocable loss, a continuation of denial, anger, and depression can block satisfactory functioning and progress in the remainder of one's life. After the car has been missing for several months, and the insurance company is ready to pay the claim, it seems to be time to accept that it is not likely to be recovered and to make plans accordingly. For many people who are angry about having to retire, during the subsequent year or two there is increased acceptance and life satisfaction, which partly reflects a modification of expectations. When a deeply loved spouse dies, the losses are so great and the compensations are so small that it sometimes seems impossible to accept the loss. The remarriages that sometimes occur under such circumstances indicate that a degree of acceptance can occur. It is not that the first spouse is forgotten or that the second spouse is a direct replacement. Often the surviving spouse is able to place the loss in perspective and to make the best of options that are realistically available.

A time of crisis can become a time of growth (Gardner, 1961). For an adult who is confronting his or her own imminent death, acceptance is facilitated by reminiscence or life review. This occurs especially for older adults who actively recall details from their life and weave them into an acceptable perspective. This sometimes includes consideration of unresolved conflicts from the past. Active and purposeful reminiscence can contribute to increased candor, wisdom, and serenity. A terminal decline in physical and mental condition can interfere with this process. However, some older adults in particular are able to achieve a remarkable acceptance of impending death.

One of the most studied forms of loss is retirement, including the more general aspects of activity and disengagement that often surround it. From year to year, most of adult life is characterized by continuity. However, older adults tend to lose roles related to work, family, and community. The level and type of activity and social participation in which an older adult engages reflect influences beyond the environmental press from role expectations, opportunity system, and general values and attitudes regarding aging in family, neighborhood, and community. These other influences include health, income, and personality. A general physical slowing down produces some reduction in activity for many older adults. A gradual psychological and social disengagement occurs for some older adults, but this is only one of several alternative participatory responses to aging (Videbeck and Knox, 1965). Some ways of dealing with old age are more satisfactory to the older adults themselves, although there are major variations associated with personality.

Social and psychological disengagement often occurs during old age, although for many people it is not associated with higher life satisfaction and successful aging. Disengagement is characterized by decreased social interaction that reflects mutual withdrawal by society and the aging person. The individual's withdrawal is accompanied by decreased emotional involvement in the activities and social relationships of middle age (Cumming and Henry, 1961). Social disengagement takes many forms. It even includes separation from possessions, such as when an older adult moves from a house to an apartment and then into an institution. The marginal roles in which some older adults find themselves within many community organizations can be accompanied by losses of authority, prestige, and dignity and by feelings of estrangement. As family members and friends of an older adult die or move away, there may be fewer people with whom to interact and less social engagement.

Perhaps the most significant form of social disengagement is occupational retirement because of its impact on income, contact with work associates, satisfaction from the work itself, and sense of identity, self-worth, and productivity. Compulsory retirement rules reflect societal values regarding the relative worth of older people, beliefs about the relative productivity of older workers, and pressures to make way for younger workers. With the variability in the health and productivity of older people, set age limits for compulsory retirement provide an impartial basis for separation from employment. Although compulsory retirement may have some benefits, an economic advantage to the employer does not seem to be one of them (Schulz, 1974). Compulsory retirement forces some very productive workers to terminate their employment, which results in both personal hardships and societal loss. Some of the healthiest and most able retired workers who want to do so are able to find postretirement jobs, although the demand far exceeds the opportunities (Fillenbaum, 1971).

Some workers retire before their mid-sixties. Aside from military personnel, policemen, and firemen, who typically retire much earlier and often enter a second career, an increasing proportion of workers are voluntarily retiring early. Some of those who appear to do so actually retire because of health problems or employer pressure. Although about one third of those who retire early do so because of health problems, this proportion is declining in part because of an increase in the numbers of workers who retire to enjoy their leisure (Pollman, 1971). Some executives retire early to pursue other interests (Morgenthaler, 1971). However, some skilled workers retire early because of work demands, and actual or anticipated job changes (Barfield and Morgan, 1969; Pollman and Johnson, 1974). In contrast with those who worked until the compulsory retirement age, those who retired early were in a better financial position and spent more time discussing retirement with others (Walker, 1975). More than half of those who retire as planned report general contentment with retirement compared with less than one quarter of those whose retirement was unexpected (Barfield and Morgan, 1969).

Retirement at any age and under any conditions can be upsetting and result in increased insecurity, dependency, tension, apprehension, depression, and anger. However, after a period of transition, most retirees do achieve satisfactory adjustment and morale. The highest satisfaction in retirement is associated with high income before retirement and high standard of living during it, high level of education, good health, and evidence of preretirement preparation and planning (Friedmann and Havighurst, 1954; Streib and Schneider, 1971; Belbin, 1972; Carp, 1972; Eisdorfer, 1972; Keahey and Seaman, 1974; Atchley, 1975; Beverley, 1975).

Early statements of disengagement theory and research findings indicated that when both the individual and society wanted withdrawal, the individual's adjustment would be satisfactory. However, when society forces the individual to disengage against his or her will (as sometimes occurs from compulsory retirement) or when the individual withdraws when others want continued engagement (as sometimes occurs in cases of abandonment by a parent), then maladjustment occurs. The conclusion that many older adults prefer disengagement was based on findings that intrapsychic withdrawal tends to precede reduction of social behavior. Older adults tend to have less ego energy, respond increasingly to their own thoughts and feelings instead of external challenges and opportunities for assertiveness and action, withdraw emotional investment, and use passive instead of active forms of coping. The statements drew an analogy with the person approaching death who puts his or her estate in order and withdraws emotional investments to make it easier to depart. However, the early disengagement studies gave insufficient attention to psychological disengagement as a defense mechanism that older adults develop to facilitate adjustment to unwanted and forced social disengagement; to the independence between reductions in ego energy and emotional investment and preferred level of social engagement; and to multiple patterns of successful aging that entail varying types and degrees of engagement (Cumming and Henry, 1961; Cumming, 1963; W. E. Henry, 1964; Rose, 1964; Palmore, 1968; Videbeck and Knox, 1965; Lowenthal and Bowler, 1965; Maddox, 1966; Carp, 1968; Havighurst and others, 1968; Neugarten, 1968; Tallmer and Kutner, 1969).

Although psychological disengagement tends to precede social disengagement and to have developmental properties, disengagement theory provides an inadequate description of successful aging. There is much evidence of a positive relationship between life satisfaction and engagement (Maddox, 1963; Havighurst and others, 1968; Lipman and Smith, 1968). For more than a generation, much of the literature on social gerontology has reflected an implicit "activity theory" that implies that except for physical condition and health, older adults have substantially the same social and psychological characteristics and needs as they did when they were middle aged. The conclusion is that social disengagement is forced by society and undesirable for the older person, and that optimal aging occurs when an older adult remains active. However, there is evidence that some older adults welcome the reduction of social constraints because of the freedom they gain to select activities which fit their preferences. Because of the social withdrawal of some activities, such as work and community leadership, and because of social change, such as generational trends in educational level and life-style, cross-sectional studies have suggested that with increasing old age activities and attitudes decline. However, longitudinal studies show that until a terminal decline occurs, most older adults maintain a relatively constant level of activity and attitudes related to social participation, and the individual's position relative to peers is fairly constant (Palmore, 1968; Maddox and Douglas, 1974). Some shifts in values and goals tend to occur during the later years, and disengagement may vary among such domains of life as family, work, and social groups. For example, disengagement from other people generally, activities, mental stimulation and possessions that tend to be interrelated for some aged adults over several years, tended to be quite independent of their interest in performing an influential role in the family (Carp, 1968). The emphasis in "activity theory" is on replacement of lost roles (Atchley, 1972). In more recent formulations a "continuity theory," including attention to both activity theory and disengagement theory as partial explanations, has been presented as a broader view of aging as a complex developmental process in which continuing modifications of activities and preferences reflect past adjustments (Havighurst and others, 1968; Atchley, 1972). At the same time, many older adults want to withdraw somewhat to enjoy their leisure, but they also want to remain active to retain their sense of self-worth. Furthermore, disengagement from certain role relationships does not produce major shifts in values internalized over a lifetime. In addition to general developmental trends, there are some varying patterns of aging that can be satisfying to many of the older adults who follow them.

Three characteristics of older adults are associated with their patterns of aging: health, status, and personality. The general societal stereotype of old age includes physical deterioration and ill health. However, most older adults experience few health constraints on desired activities. In contrast with the atypical instances in which retirement seems to be followed by decline and death, research on the health of recent retirees found many more reports of improved health than of failing health (Eisdorfer, 1972). This partly reflects some retirees' relief that they no longer have the burden of strenuous physical or mental work.

However, within most samples of older adults, and especially in health care facilities, there are some people whose formerly stable history of mental functioning was interrupted by a sharp decline referred to as terminal decline. The death rates during the subsequent year or two for older adults who experience this type of abrupt decline in mental functioning, are much higher than for the majority of older adults who do not experience such a discontinuity (Goldfarb, 1969; Jarvik and Blum, 1971; Granick and Patterson, 1971; Reimanis and Green, 1971; Riegel and Riegel, 1972). This type of terminal decline is understandably associated with extensive psychological and social disengagement. Other forms of ill health, especially chronic illness, can force the individual to withdraw from life to some extent. In fact, ill health seems to be more highly associated with disengagement than any other factor studied, including age (Tallmer and Kutner, 1969, 1970; Shanas, 1970; Shanas and others, 1968a, 1968b).

The status-related characteristics associated with patterns of aging include levels of income and formal education, along with prestige level of the individual's or spouse's occupation during working years. These status-related characteristics reflect associated values, resources, expectations, and opportunities. They are also part of the press of the larger environment that includes interaction with family, neighborhood, and community. Some of these contextual characteristics, such as prestige level of education or former occupation, do not change with retirement, but some, such as income level or interaction with work associates or former neighbors if the retiree moves, do change and sometimes greatly. Furthermore, the meanings of work or of possessions may be altered for the older adult.

White collar workers tend to be more attached to and interested in the work that they do than most blue collar workers, so that retirement removes a more important area of activity for most white collar workers, and they experience more disengagement as a result (Lipman and Smith, 1968; Heidbreder, 1972; Barresi, 1974). However, white collar workers typically have more resources in retirement and thus react to it more favorably (Simpson and McKinney, 1966). In contrast with

534   Adult Development and Learning

blue collar couples who tend to be passive in their anticipation
of retirement, white collar families from clerical and skilled
occupations tend to welcome retirement, and white collar
families from professional and managerial occupations tend
not to resent it. In the short run, blue collar workers tend to
adapt better to retirement, but in the long run the greater
resources of white collar workers facilitate a more satisfactory
adjustment (Stokes and Maddox, 1967).

The retirees' relationships with family, neighbors, and
community activities also relate to their patterns of aging. For
example, in one study, the husband's participation in household
tasks was associated with higher levels of morale for both husbands and wives (Simpson and McKinney, 1966). Social interaction with neighbors tends to have meanings for older blue
collar workers that are similar to the meanings felt by older
white collar workers for interactions with work associates. For
most older people, satisfying social participation and warm human relationships can moderate many aspects of aging. Even
community settings and cultural values and traditions affect the
life-styles and aging patterns of older adults. Morale of older
adults tends to be higher when there is congruence between the
individuals' readiness to disengage and the press from their
societal context than when readiness to withdraw and life space
are unmatched (Tissue, 1971).

Although variables related to condition, such as health,
are associated with disengagement, and variables related to
context, such as status, are associated with adjustment, variables
related to personality are most predictive of successful aging.
An older adult with a dependent and passive personality may
enjoy disengagement. Another with an achieving and striving
personality may dislike disengagement and strive to replace lost
roles. Understanding of the feelings of older adults about retirement is increased by familiarity with their previous life
patterns, current activities, and current perceptions and expectations. Not only do the self-perceptions, expectations, and
other aspects of personality have substantial consistency from
year to year, but older adults become more like themselves as
central features of personality become more prominent and

cherished values become more salient. As older adults with varied life-styles and personality patterns select activities that reflect their self-concepts, ego involvement, and values, a variety of patterns of successful aging emerge. In each pattern some older adults achieve moderate or high levels of life satisfaction that reflect a match between personality type and level of role activity (Reichard, Livson, and Petersen, 1962; Williams and Wirths, 1965; I. Rosow, 1967; Neugarten, Havighurst, and Tobin, 1968; Lipsitt, 1969; Kalish, 1971; Streib and Schneider, 1971; Palmore, 1964, 1970, 1974).

For example, in one study of men and women in their seventies who had somewhat better than average income, health, and well-being, eight patterns emerged that reflected relationships between personality, role activity, and life satisfaction (Neugarten, Havighurst, and Tobin, 1968). The pattern for people with well-integrated personalities and high levels of role activity and life satisfaction was labeled "reorganizers." These older adults were competent and functioned well. Their mental abilities and sense of self were intact. They maintained comfortable control over their impulses and were open to new ideas and activities. They tried to stay young by staying active, and when they lost roles or activities such as work, they reorganized their structure of participation by adding new activities or by expanding time devoted to community or church groups.

By contrast, a pattern labeled "disengaged" included people with integrated personalities and high life satisfaction but low role activity. These older adults had withdrawn from role commitments from preference and not in response to physical or external losses. They tended to be self-directed people with high self-esteem and strong interests in the world that were not dependent on extensive social interaction. They were socially withdrawn but personally contented.

A third pattern labeled "holding on" consisted of people with great needs to maintain defenses against anxiety and impulses, along with high levels of role activity and life satisfaction. Their response to the threatening prospect of aging was to rigidly maintain middle-aged activities and attitudes as much as possible. Activity level tended to be important in itself, but they were typically successful in maintaining relatively high levels of activity and satisfaction.

A fourth pattern labeled "constructed" consisted of people whose personalities were characterized by maintenance of defenses against anxiety, but they defended themselves against aging by restricting social interaction and insulating themselves from experience. They structured their lives to minimize newness, change, and difficult demands in order to guard against situations with which they felt unable to cope, but in the process they maintained moderate or high levels of life satisfaction.

Other patterns related to people with passive or un-integrated personalities also emerged. Some had been disengaged most of their lives. In most instances, unless there were major health or social disruptions, patterns of aging were consistent with longstanding life-styles.

Even for the "reorganizers," a high level of activity and satisfaction depended on adaptation, such as addition of replacement activities. An individual's adaptation level reflected both personal competence and environmental press. When situational pressures were either very weak or very strong, many people were less likely to engage in adaptive behavior and more likely to have negative feelings and engage in maladaptive behavior. This may be especially so for persons with low levels of competence whose ability to deal flexibly with societal demands, constraints, and expectations is more limited (Wohlwill, 1966).

Adaptation

Most change events can be described as a sequence of time periods during which there are changes in the individual's structure of participation, especially as it relates to the specific type of change event. Five time periods typically occur. The first period is the prestructure, which consists of the period of relative stability before the introduction of the change event. Examples include the period during which there is a stable pattern of work and family life before the first pregnancy or the period during which there is a stable pattern of work activity before the decision on a definite date for retirement. The second period is the anticipation period between when the individual becomes aware that the change event will occur and its occurrence. The change event may be precipitated by a personal decision, by uncontrolled events, or by a combination of both. Examples include the period between making the decision to move to another community and packing to be ready for the movers or the period between conception and delivery. The third period is the actual change event. This period is usually quite brief and serves as a point of demarcation. Examples include very abrupt changes, such as a stolen car, the transition from work to unemployed status, or the sudden death of a friend from a fatal accident, and more gradual changes, such as divorce proceedings or the lingering death of a parent. The fourth period is the disorganization period between the change event and the reestablishment of a stable structure of participation. This homeostatic process is related to both the individual's adaptation strategy and the resources available. Examples include getting the new house settled and becoming active in some new groups after the move or developing some interests after retirement. The fifth period is the poststructure period of relative stability that reflects the reorganization of the structure of participation following the change event. Examples include the period during which there is a changed but stable pattern of work and family life after the new baby arrives or the period during which there is a stable pattern of postretirement activity.

During the sequence of time periods surrounding a change event, an adult must adapt to a changed structure of participation. The adaptation strategy begins when the individual first initiates some efforts to accommodate to the changed circumstances associated with the change event and ends when a stable structure of participation has been reestablished. Elements of the adaptation strategy may be deliberate or reactive, and they may be passive or active. Examples of active forms of adaptive behavior include seeking advice and obtaining instruction. Adaptive behaviors may vary in extent of activity, self-direction, and effectiveness. Some of the ways in which adults try to adapt to change events are:

1. Frantic Activity. Characterized at the extreme by racing wildly from one alternative to another with little contemplation or plan, in a way that resembles trial and error behavior at a high level of activity.
2. Action. Characterized at its most effective level by deliberately placing in operation a considered or habitual plan.
3. Educative Activity. Characterized by purposeful efforts to alter one's own competence by means of systematic and sustained learning activities.
4. Seeking Assistance. Characterized by requesting another person or an agency to give advice or arrange for, or at least plan the necessary adaptation.
5. Contemplation. Characterized by thinking about the circumstances that surround the change event and various ways to adapt. This type of effort does not include the follow-through of action as part of the response, but action may ensue.
6. Withdrawal. Characterized by distorted thinking, flight behavior, and autism.

Although there has been little systematic study of the adaptation strategies that adults use to adjust to change events, it is likely that situational, biographical, and attitudinal characteristics will influence the process, as well as the characteristics of the structure of participation. Examples of situational influences include voluntariness and desirability of the change, whether the change event constitutes a gain or a loss, and availability of opportunities and resources. Examples of biographical influences include age and verbal ability. Examples of attitudinal influences include level of aspiration, dogmatism, and sense of educational efficacy.

One feature of the structure of participation is diversity and variety. It would be expected that the greater the diversity of the structure of participation, the easier the substitution and expansion to compensate for a lost role. For example, a person with numerous avocational interests before retirement should more readily adapt to the loss of a job at retirement than one with few interests other than the job. When the change event entails the addition of a major role relationship, the process is facilitated if the new role fits into an established and important domain of participation. For example, the birth of a second child can be a modest change event for parents with strong commitments to raising two or three children. Similarly, the individual's reaction to unemployment or widowhood depends in part on how positively or negatively the person felt about the last job or the departed spouse.

When a change event occurs, the need for some adaptation produces, for some adults at least, a heightened readiness to engage in educative activity. The resulting educative activity may be directly or indirectly related to the change event, and the relation may or may not be recognized by the individual. This period of heightened readiness has been referred to as a teachable moment. The educative activity may include all types of informal information seeking such as reading and talking with others, as well as more formal participation in part-time, externally sponsored educational programs. Familiar instances of increased educative activity related to change events occur in relation to the birth of the first child, the purchase of a new car, or a major job change. There is no tested knowledge, however, about when readiness to engage in educative activity is highest, when educational participation is most likely to occur, or when learning effectiveness is likely to be greatest.

A recent cross-sectional study suggests the ways in which lower-middle-class men and women at four stages of adulthood approach major change events. As their experience actually doing so during the coming years is studied in the longitudinal phase of the study, additional insights into the process of adaptation seem likely (Lowenthal, Thurnher, and others, 1975). The four change events that most of the men and women in the study are likely to encounter in the subsequent few years are leaving home, starting a family, having their youngest children leave home, and retirement. As in findings from other studies of adult development, lower-middle-class men and women have somewhat similar structures of participation at some stages of the adult life cycle and quite different ones at other stages.

The newlyweds have not started to have children. More than four out of five of the wives are working, but very few have serious occupational commitments. They express less concern about the transition to parenthood than their husbands. By contrast, the middle-aged women are the most negative of any subgroup toward their impending "empty nest" when they no longer have any children living at home. Those with a greater sense of control are doing more planning, mainly in relation to their children's lives. The "planners" are characterized by greater cognitive complexity and a greater sense of futurity. Their goal orientations are flexible, but they anticipate future goals that differ from their current ones. The more intellectually able middle-aged women tend to view their impending transition as either positive or negative. The less able tend to view it with ambivalence. Those with the richest network of family roles expect the fewest problems. However, as a total subgroup, the middle-aged women are less sure of themselves and report more unhappiness and stress than any other subgroup.

Although more of the women express concern about mid-life transitions, more of them have confidants to whom they can turn for advice and emotional support during a time of crisis. During stressful periods in college, mid-life transitions, retirement, and impending death, more adults turn to close friends than to professionals. However, fewer men than women have confidant relationships, and more men than women mention their spouses as confidants. The inability of many men to disclose themselves intimately and draw support from interpersonal resources has been suggested as an influence on the higher stress-related problems of middle-aged and older men (Jourard, 1974; Lowenthal and Haven, 1968).

The unpredictability of major change events contributes

to apprehension and fear. This applies to starting college, the empty nest, retirement, and the prospect of dying in nonnormal, unexpected circumstances (*Counseling Psychologist,* 1976, Thurnher, 1974). Major and abrupt change events not only alter the structure of participation, which requires adaptation, but also have an impact on the individual's sense of self. Formerly stable interpersonal relationships and values are reexamined. During that reexamination process, most adults seem to benefit from a confidant relationship or some group or professional relationship to help restructure their inner and outer lives (Lowenthal, Thurnher, and others, 1975; Coulding, 1972).

Practitioners can help adults deal with major change events by helping them understand the process they are experiencing and recognize that priority setting, problem solving, and coping with stress are major features of dealing successfully with change events (Burr, 1972). Effectively dealing with change events (including those the individual feels are desirable or undesirable and those that entail losses, changes, and gains of role relationships) depends on how the individual comprehends and reacts to the change. People vary in their ability to deal with change. Practitioners can be especially helpful by encouraging adults not to panic or assume that there is a quick and easy solution but to use the change event as an opportunity for growth. This positive approach is facilitated if the individual analyzes the nature of the change and how it relates to personal priorities. Some changes mainly reflect personal shifts, while others result from external changes. The sense of crisis often results from the combination of major external and internal changes. When several changes occur together, it is usually helpful to separate them for consideration. Change events sometimes constitute major turning points, but they also entail problems to be solved. In the problem-solving process, practitioners can encourage adults to explore alternative solutions and evaluate them against the change and their values and priorities. Practitioners can also indicate how important it is for most people to have a confidant with whom to discuss reactions, feelings, goals, and plans during a period of major change (Lowenthal,

Thurnher, and others, 1975). Such a period can entail much loneliness, but this can also be approached creatively as a time to reflect on values and set new and desirable directions.

As illustrated by the generalizations regarding retirement and disengagement, there are alternative patterns for successfully dealing with change events. The pattern that is most satisfactory for an individual reflects condition-related variables, such as ability and health, and context-related variables, such as opportunities and resources. Adjustment and growth also reflect personality-related variables, such as values and interpersonal relations, and learning-related variables, such as learning effectiveness and use of educative activities (Havighurst and deVries, 1969). Practitioners can help adults who confront major change events to recognize some of the pertinent ways to deal with them and to reflect this understanding in their own strategies (Stonecypher, 1974).

Major change events can be very influential, and part of effective coping is attending to such influences. However, these events tend to overwhelm the individual. Practitioners can help adults move toward a more satisfactory level of self-directedness. Part of self-directedness entails problem solving and decision making about the nature of the change, its relation to personal priorities, and the use of effective strategies to deal with the change. Another part of self-directedness entails dealing with feelings, which includes interpretation of the meaning of events and expression of aspirations. Sometimes self-directedness also entails altering established ways of thinking and acting by creating a personal sense of challenge. An openness to growth and a commitment to development depend on a sense of selfhood and responsibility for one's life and future (Logan, 1970).

Practitioners have a critical responsibility to help adults concerned with change, adaptation, and growth gain access to opportunities and resources that can facilitate their efforts to adapt. A useful matching of needs and opportunities is often difficult to achieve. Even when change events increase an individual's readiness to learn and adapt, it takes further effort to specify needs and interests to the extent that the person will engage in activity to meet the needs. Practitioners can provide counseling and advisement (*Counseling Psychologist,* 1976; J. E. Rosow, 1974; Bolles, 1972). Examples include the agency and community-based offices where an adult can find out about educational, recreational, occupational, family, or health programs and services that are relevant to the individual's background and interests. To be effective, such offices require accurate and current information about programs and services and efficient procedures to select those that are relevant to the individual. Otherwise the many programs and details tend to be confusing, especially to less educated adults. In addition to increasing adult access to community opportunities, such arrangements help identify the match between available programs and expressed needs so that unmet needs can be identified as one basis for planning additional programs and services.

When practitioners help adults adapt to change, the specific instances are unique but the process is generalizable. Adult clients vary in their characteristics and in the particularities of the developmental tasks they confront, but each developmental task tends to have a broad outline that is similar for many adults. As a couple decides to marry, makes preparations for the wedding, experiences the ceremony and related events on the day of the wedding, and experiences marital adjustments during their first year of marriage, there are some characteristic activities and feelings that cluster together in some widespread patterns. When someone starts a new job or moves to a new community, there are typical patterns of transition, each of which is reflected in the specific sequence of choices and adjustments that some adults experience as they progress through the change event. Practitioners can help adults choose wisely and act effectively by broadening their perspective on the general process of change, the range of ways to deal with change, and procedures for making the process more satisfactory (Bolles, 1972; O'Neill and O'Neill, 1974). In those instances in which a change becomes a crisis, practitioners with an understanding of the developmental process a client is going through and of facilitators and barriers to resolution of the crisis, can more effectively help the individual adapt and grow in the process (*Counseling Psychologist,* 1976; Simon, Lowenthal, and Epstein,

1970). In some instances this will entail referral to another practitioner with specialized expertise.

During the early part of adulthood, some major change events are part of the worker role or are greatly affected by it. Examples of the former include starting the first major job and changing jobs. Examples of the latter include a job-related move to a new community and family adjustments during a period of unemployment. Practitioners can be more helpful to clients if they understand typical patterns of career development, including ways in which occupational performance, maturity, values, and attitudes interact (Super and others, 1967; Distefano, 1969; Astin and Myint, 1971; Miller, 1974; Kreps, 1976).

During middle adulthood, change events related to family roles tend to assume greater salience. For parents this entails launching grown children into college, work, or marriage. For some men it also entails a shift of attention toward the family after a decade or two of predominant attention to occupational concerns. For some women it also entails a major confrontation between the dual roles in family and work. The period around age forty is also a peak for divorce and remarriage. Practitioners can assist adults by helping clarify the family transitions of middle adulthood and by referring clients to individuals, groups, and other resources that can facilitate these role change events (Fried, 1967; Cutright, 1971; Spence and Lonner, 1971).

During later adulthood, retirement is a major change event for many adults. Family life takes on increased importance for many adults, but it does not compensate for many of the work-related benefits that are lost (Rapoport and Rapoport, 1975). Practitioners have available an increasing amount of literature on retirement that can be used for planning and for adaptation at the time (Hepner, 1969; Margolius, 1969; Collins, 1970). Widowhood is another major loss experience in old age. Practitioners can assist clients with this change event both directly and by referrals to other resources such as a widow-to-widow self-help group (Silverman, 1972; Lopata, 1973). Practitioners can also contribute to satisfactory adjustment by older adults by assisting with the planning of neighborhood and community facilities and services that enable the elderly to function in satisfying circumstances as long as possible. In urban neighborhoods, modest provisions for housing, shopping, security, and health services oriented toward the elderly can greatly benefit older residents (Regnier, 1975). Services such as meals-on-wheels and daily phone calls can delay institutionalization for many years. Practitioners can also help older adults work together for social policies that are beneficial to them (Schmidhauser, 1968).

Perhaps the central contribution that can be made by practitioners to adaptation and growth by their adult clients is to help them understand and influence the transactional relationships within which adult development occurs. The societal context reflected in the community opportunity system of family, work, civic, and leisure activities can either encourage or discourage growth and fulfillment. The individual's outlook and general personality characteristics can either be outgoing and responsive or closed and defensive (Coan, 1974; DiCaprio, 1974). The challenge to practitioners is to help clients match needs and opportunities. Developmental tasks and major change events during adulthood provide useful foci for planning responsive programs and services (Burkett, 1960). Adults who are self-directed can locate resources to facilitate their self-actualization and service to others (Knox, 1974). To facilitate this interaction, practitioners can help adults expand their repertoire of effective strategies for alternating between their action problems and relevant knowledge resources.

Early Career Change

The process by which a young adult might deal with a change event is illustrated by the following example. At age twenty-six, married with two young children, and partway through a master's degree in philosophy, Dave began to confront a major career shift. He had always been a fairly good student as a result of both ability and hard work. He completed a bachelor's degree in liberal arts at twenty-one with the benefit of a scholarship and much encouragement but modest financial support from his father, who operated a small business. He then married a nurse who continued to work except for a few months surrounding the birth of their two children. Dave had worked at a variety of short-term and part-time jobs, mostly graduate assistantships. The major one entailed working for a professor of philosophy for almost three years on a research project he was conducting, but then the grant ran out. Dave was a teaching assistant for several courses and taught a non-credit course for adults at a nearby community college on several occasions, which he enjoyed very much.

After several years of pursuing his master's degree on a part-time basis, Dave decided that he wanted to continue through the Ph.D. and become a college professor. The more he thought about this career decision, and discussed it with his wife and other graduate students, the more committed he became to it. He had been associated with educational institutions most of his life, understood and enjoyed the setting, and liked reading and discussing philosophy. Because he had not really entered a full-time job for any extended period, his occupational and related social life had not solidified, and becoming a professor was an attractive prospect. At the start of the semester when he was scheduled to complete his master's degree in philosophy, Dave reviewed his hopes and plans with his faculty adviser and received a rude awakening.

His adviser indicated that the leveling out of higher education enrollments, the large number of Ph.D.'s in philosophy who were unable to obtain teaching positions, and reductions in the number of doctoral students in the department made it quite unlikely that Dave would be admitted to the doctoral program. During the following few weeks, Dave talked with several faculty members and graduate students in the department and concluded that his prospects for doctoral study and a career as a professor of philosophy were similar at other comparable universities. He was surprised at how much he had begun thinking of himself as an aspirant philosopher during the past year or two and how keenly disappointed he was.

During the next month Dave's initial disbelief gave way to periods of anger because of the unfairness that circumstances largely beyond his control were preventing him from doing what he wanted, and to periods of depression because he did not know what to do instead. However, he was proceeding satisfactorily with the completion of his master's degree, and his wife commented that it was good that he was able to work out some of his tension and frustration in his studies.

Russ, a boyhood friend who was a few years older and now worked as a conference coordinator in the university's continuing education division, had talked with Dave about career plans several times during the previous year. When it appeared that prospects for doctoral study in philosophy were not very promising, Russ mentioned that Dave might consider something in the field of continuing education and that it was likely that there would be an opening for a conference coordinator within the year. During the first month or so after it began to look as though doctoral study in philosophy was unlikely, Dave felt very much alone. After several years of planning and talking about becoming a professor of philosophy, he had difficulty discussing the impending change of direction with his wife or his parents. He and Russ, however, discussed it frequently. Russ urged him not to panic but to explore the most attractive alternatives.

In his conversations with Russ, Dave reflected on some of his personal characteristics that seemed relevant to a shift in career direction. He concluded that his learning ability and self-esteem were high and that he enjoyed working with people and with educational programs. Furthermore, he prided himself on his mental flexibility and receptivity to new ideas, and he felt that he was developing an increasing sense of futurity. As he discussed situational factors with Russ, he concluded that he was interested in exploring something in continuing education of adults. Dave and his wife concluded that between her job and his part-time work, they could swing another year or so of graduate study for him. Dave had been active in leadership positions in student and community organizations and had enjoyed planning and conducting his courses for adults. Russ indicated that the field of continuing education was expanding rapidly and that there were attractive opportunities. Dave decided to complete his master's degree in philosophy that semester and seriously pursue a career shift into continuing education.

During the semester he applied for and was accepted into the master's degree program in continuing education in the college of education, and during the summer he received an appointment as a conference coordinator in the continuing education division. During the subsequent two years he worked as a coordinator and completed his master's degree in continuing education on a part-time basis. He found that his work and his study complemented each other. When he completed the second master's degree, he accepted a position as assistant director of continuing education in a nearby community college, his wife stopped work to have their third child, and Dave had established a new structure of participation around his career as a continuing education administrator.

Summary

Adult life is periodically punctuated by such change events as the birth of a child, a move to a new community, or retirement. An adult's approach to a change event is influenced by both personal and situational characteristics. The resulting changes help explain how adults experience so much change over the years in spite of great stability over the months. Because change events entail alterations in role relationships, some adaptation is inescapable. Change events vary regarding whether role relationships are gained, lost, or changed and regarding extent of voluntariness, predictability, intensity, and stage of adulthood when they are most likely to occur. They tend to be concentrated in young adulthood.

In between change events, each adult has a stable structure of participation that consists of a patterned set of recurring episodes. The subjective and objective dimensions of participation evolve over time and are shaped by both personal and situational influences. Personal influences include learning ability and openness of personality. Situational influences include social class background and diversity of role relationships. There is a tendency for personality, habit, and the expectations of others to maintain stability in an adult's life until a change event disrupts the pattern.

The subjective dimension of participation includes status, satisfaction, and a sense of belonging. This was illustrated by the findings from a study that compared men who made a mid-career shift with similar men who persisted in their original career field. More of the shifters experienced divorce, received personal counseling, had access to financial resources during the transition, had high self-esteem, and thought seriously about their personal mortality than was the case for persisters. Three main reasons for the mid-career shift were gradual disenchantment with the first career, discovery of a more attractive second career, and a change event that precipitated a reformation of goals.

Change events such as temporary unemployment or the death of a loved one are associated with feelings of loss. There is a general developmental process that often occurs when adults find out that a loss has or will soon occur. The stages are denial, anger, depression, bargaining, and acceptance. They do not necessarily occur in sequence; several may occur together, and some may not occur at all.

Occupational retirement is one form of loss that is part of the social and psychological disengagement process that occurs during old age. Influences on the structure of participation and retirement process include the environmental press from role expectations, opportunity system, general values and attitudes about aging, health, income, and personality. Some of the workers who retire early do so because of health problems or pressure from the employer. An increasing proportion are doing so voluntarily to enjoy their leisure, and a higher proportion enjoy their leisure than when retirement was unexpected.

It appears that aging is a complex developmental process in which continuing modifications of activities and preferences reflect past adjustments. Personality characteristics are most predictive of successful aging. In addition, satisfying social participation and warm human relationships can moderate many aspects of aging. In the short run blue collar workers tend to adapt better to retirement, but in the long run white collar workers tend to do so. In general life satisfaction results from the match between personality type and structure of participation.

Most change events consist of five time periods in the modification of the structure of participation. They are the prestructure, anticipation period, change event, disorganization period, and poststructure. There are various ways in which adults try to adapt to change events. They include frantic activity, action, educative activity, seeking assistance, contemplation, and withdrawal. When a change event occurs, the need for adaptation tends to produce a heightened readiness to engage in educative activity. Some adults are more planful than most in their approach to such transitions. The more planful tend to have a more cognitive complexity and sense of futurity.

Practitioners can help adults in many ways to deal better with change. They can encourage them not to panic or assume that there is a quick and easy solution but instead to use the change event as an opportunity for growth. They can indicate that a change period can entail much loneliness, but that it can provide time to reflect on values and set new and desirable directions. Practitioners can help clients gain access to opportunities and resources that facilitate adaptation and become more self-directed. Adults can be helped to broaden their perspective on alternatives and the process of change. As adults match needs and opportunities, they tend also to expand their ability to relate knowledge resources to action problems.

❧ 10 ☙

Perspective
on Adulthood

The intent of this handbook has been to provide practitioners in the helping professions and their adult clients with a more comprehensive and developmental perspective on adulthood. A detailed understanding of developmental transactions between adults and others in their societal context is especially important for clients as well as practitioners in fields such as education, religion, counseling, social work, recreation, occupational supervision, and the health professions. Clients' understanding and participation are important because their values and efforts are so influential on the progress they achieve.

There are many interweaving trends of stability and change in the life of an adult. These trends include performance in family, work, and community. They also include shifts in condition, personality, and learning that influence performance. Developmental trends for an individual adult are subtly shaped by historical trends. Consider the contrasting prospects of those entering young adulthood in 1895, 1915, 1935, 1955, or 1975. A young adult in the affluent 1950s took for granted opportunities that Fred (see Chapter One) never dreamed of two generations before.

Adults vary in the mix of problems and opportunities they perceive in comparable situations. The individual's goals and aspirations affect striving and satisfaction in specific ways that may vary from work to family to community activities. With the increasing variability in education and life-style, adults confront difficult choices in which they have greater freedom than in past generations but for which they bear heavier personal responsibility. A weakened sense of community contributes the added burden of loneliness.

Major change events, such as the onset of parenthood, a move to a new community, and occupational retirement, tend to influence not only performance but also condition, personality, and learning activities. The substantial changes that can occur in relation to such events help punctuate the relative stability during much of adulthood. Practitioners from many fields can help adults discover relevant resources within themselves as well as in the community. Some practitioners also help set policy regarding the types of services to be provided for adults, along with needed research related to adult development and learning. This chapter contains highlights from current tested knowledge about adult life and emphasizes implications for professional practice, research, and social policy.

Interrelated Trends

Practitioners in the helping professions want to help. Those who work with adults can use generalizations about adult development and learning as a comprehensive and developmental perspective for themselves and their clients. The generalizations can be used to help prevent problems, solve problems, or pursue opportunities. Not only are the adult clients developing over time, but their networks of interpersonal relationships evolve and their settings change. The major decisions that adults make reflect the shifting mix of stability and change within themselves and their societal context. The resulting complexity of individual adults and of the situation within which they make decisions contributes to the uniqueness of the decision and web of relationships surrounding it.

Perspective. The utility of generalizations about adult development and learning lies not in the provision of generalized solutions and conclusions, but in the enrichment of the perspective that adults (and the practitioners who seek to assist them) bring to the making of specific and unique decisions and choices. Such decisions will be made, whether by careful thought and action, or by default through inaction. Decisions reflect the individual's assumptions, values, and aspirations. In the face of the actual complexity of the web of relationships that surround most major decisions, there is a great tendency toward oversimplification. Although the body of tested knowledge about adult development and learning is fragmentary, it can suggest useful questions to ask and promising alternatives to explore when considering a specific decision, with the uncertainty that typically surrounds it (Eisdorfer and Lawton, 1973; Troll, 1975; Kalish, 1975). Such a holistic and developmental perspective can reduce the tendency toward either mindless oversimplification or inaction. Research would be especially helpful on the process by which adults make decisions and on the ways in which practitioners can best assist in the process.

In best practice, practitioners in the helping professions help adults help themselves. In almost all instances, forms of assistance that encourage initiative and self-sufficiency are desirable, and forms of assistance that foster dependency on professionals or others are undesirable. Effective practitioners sometimes serve as knowledge brokers and change agents. The comprehensive review of research on knowledge utilization by Havelock (1969) provides a promising foundation for future research on the role of the knowledge broker. An understanding of adult development and learning can enable practitioners to link client needs with relevant resources, and to facilitate client self-directedness. Competent professionals assist adult clients to obtain understanding of adult development and learning for themselves. The main distinction is that the practitioners may apply concepts more deliberately and effectively than do most clients. Competent and responsive professionals help adults realize their potential and use relevant resources, and they avoid imposing values and practices. A holistic and developmental understanding of adulthood can enable a practitioner to be more responsive to adult clients, both as an individual professional and as one of several specialists with whom a client deals.

A developmental perspective on adulthood can be useful to practitioners in several ways. Those in leadership positions within each of the helping professions can use such a perspective to plan preparatory education, supervised internships, and continuing professional education activities for practitioners that emphasize interrelated trends during adulthood. The clients themselves can be helped to acquire a developmental perspective on their own lives and those around them. If practitioners from various helping professions gained a more holistic and developmental sense of adulthood, perhaps they could better articulate their services to a client whom they jointly seek to serve and avoid an overemphasis on specialization and exclusion of clients from active participation in the helping process in the name of professionalism. A transactional view of adult development can alert practitioners to ways in which they can relate generalized knowledge to specific local circumstances. Practitioners can be encouraged to perform as knowledge brokers. They can also encourage researchers to study the process.

Trends. A developmental and holistic perspective on adulthood includes an appreciation of the shifting mix of stability and change during the adult life cycle. Some aspects of adult functioning, such as activities, values, interests, physical condition, and generalized learning ability, vary widely among all adults of a given age but are quite stable over the decades for each adult. Some of the changes that typically occur, such as increased confidence during early adulthood or decreased speed during late adulthood, take place very gradually. Other changes, such as marriage or retirement, typically occur more abruptly. This continual reordering of emphasis is reflected in the changing structure of participation during adulthood. The interaction of stability and change over time that occurs among activities also occurs within an activity or interest. Learning is often characterized by bursts of new ideas and insights followed by periods of consolidation. Progress in many fields entails periods concerned with improvement, practice, reflection, and change followed by periods of stable performance (such as in music or athletics), which can lead to still further improvement.

For a practitioner or a client to gain a more holistic and developmental perspective, it is important to understand how various trends are interrelated. One interrelationship is between historical and personal trends. For example, since World War II, there has been a rapid increase not only in the number of college-aged youth but also in the proportion that seeks college entrance. If no significant increase in college opportunities had occurred, the proportion would have declined. In actuality, there was a rapid expansion of higher education and college entrance rates rose to an unprecedented level. During the 1960s, with the military draft for an unpopular war abroad and a secure sense of economic affluence at home, student activism on behalf of social causes increased on college campuses, but it declined sharply by the mid-1970s. This decline was due partly to the lack of a dramatic cause, such as the war in Southeast Asia, and partly to an increase in more personal career concerns related to a depressed job market for college graduates in many fields.

Similar interrelations between personal and historical trends also occur during the later part of adulthood. Since the turn of the century, the number and proportion of older adults has increased greatly. During the past generation or two, there has also been an increase in services, legislation, and public awareness related to aging. From middle to old age there tends to be an increase in sensory impairments, especially for hearing and vision. During the past generation the increases in hearing aids, corrective lenses, and cataract surgery have favorably influenced the problems and adjustments that individual older adults face, which in turn has had some impact on the extent of reading and television viewing by older adults.

Practitioners and clients alike can feel overwhelmed by the complexity of varied trends for the many specific aspects of adult functioning. Social participation provides an example. During most of adulthood religious participation tends to be stable, attendance at athletic events declines, social activities with family and close friends increase through middle age, number of organizational memberships expands and then contracts during adulthood, and frequency of attendance at meetings fluctuates during adulthood as responsibilities shift. The aggregate result is a stable plateau of social participation during most of adulthood. However, there is a gradual developmental shift in the character of social participation during the adult life cycle. During late adolescence and young adulthood, activities tend to be physically vigorous and action oriented. During middle age, activities tend to be understanding oriented and concerned with interpersonal relations. Beyond middle age, activities tend to be cultural and privately oriented. In addition to this general developmental shift, it is important to keep in mind that there is a much higher association of social participation with social class level than with age.

Some developmental trends are more short term and reflect changing role relationships and personality development more than physical condition. For example, during childhood many attitudes are acquired wholesale by identification and assimilation. Adolescent rebellion often includes wholesale rejection of some of these attitudes, as the individual strives for a sense of personal identity and adult maturity. Most people tend to acquire a more intellectual orientation during late adolescence and young adulthood, especially those who attend college. However, some of the gains during the college years are reversed unless the subsequent setting encourages originality. As young adults gain experience and community. Similarity, for many women the onset of mother-community. Similarly, for many women the inset of motherhood shifts their attention toward child-oriented activities, but it shifts back toward adult-oriented activities as the children grow up. The need of college-educated mothers for achievement follows a similar pattern of decline during child-rearing years and increase to the former level when the children are grown. Practitioners can help adults recognize such likely trends and adjustments.

Practitioners can also be alert to subtle shifts in the character of an activity from one stage of adulthood to another. For example, on complex problem-solving tasks, such as diagnosis in the health professions, young adults more often generate novel solutions, whereas older adults more often rely on formerly effective strategies and search their repertoire for a solution. There are also instances in which similar attitudes have different meanings at various phases of the adult life cycle. For example, for some younger adults, a heavy future orientation provides escape from present problems, whereas a future orientation for some older adults may reflect engagement in life. General learning ability remains fairly stable during much of adulthood, as fluid intelligence decreases and crystallized intelligence increases.

A perspective on such interrelated long-term and short-term trends regarding stability and change can enable practitioners to approach the specific and immediate concerns of adult clients in holistic and developmental ways. Clients can also be helped to understand how earlier characteristics and circumstances shape subsequent characteristics and attitudes. Other developmental concepts may also be useful. For example, developmental changes occur over time but few occur as a result of time. Developmental changes vary in desirability; some are perceived as progress and others as aspects of deterioration. However, each stage of life tends to have its own values for judging the desirability of behavior. A venturesome approach to learning may be most desirable for the youngster, but the reverse may be most desirable for the oldster. An understanding of orderly and sequential development provides a basis for understanding and predicting subsequent behavior. Adults who understand and anticipate developmental changes as normal can approach many changes not as isolated problems but as part of the total life cycle, affected by changes that preceded them and affecting changes yet to come. A developmental perspective also recognizes the important interweaving of stability and change. Such a perspective helps the individual recognize more options in the process of coping with adjustments. It would be useful for future research to identify features of changes that are generally perceived as desirable or undesirable.

Adaptation and learning occur constantly during adulthood. Proactive approaches to life and an intentional approach to learning contribute to a dynamic, evolving adulthood in contrast to one that is static and unfulfilled. Self-actualization and realization of adult potential depend on personal assertiveness and growthful relationships with others. Current tested knowledge about self-directed approaches to adult life and learning is fragmentary. Additional research on this topic would be useful to both practitioners and their adult clients. Increased public understanding of the desirability and accessibility of lifelong learning for individuals and of the importance of an educative community that encourages growth and development throughout life has enriched the learning opportunities available to adults in recent decades. Practitioners in many fields help adults systematically learn, and they typically do so as a lesser part of a wide variety of life roles and responsibilities. The work supervisor engaged in on-the-job training and the physician engaged in patient education facilitate adult learning, along with teachers, clergymen, counselors, recreation specialists, and social workers.

Generalizations regarding trends in adult development and learning enable practitioners both to assist individual adults and to shape social policy. A developmental perspective can help individual adults gain a better sense of likely trends and focus on the important issues amidst all the complex and often confusing detail of life. Practitioners with a commitment to human growth and development can assist clients to become more proactive in dealing with the shifting fabric of social participation, major role changes, shifting priorities, and increasing options. Practitioners can also work to achieve greater public acceptance of shifting values from one stage of adulthood to another. A tangible result would be availability and access to programs and services that are responsive to the needs and interests of adults of every age. Additional research is needed on age trends and adjustment mechanisms during adulthood, especially regarding the impact of such changes on learning and growth.

Interrelationships. In addition to typical trends, a developmental perspective includes a holistic concern about interrelationships among context, performance, condition, personality, and learning for the functioning adult. Most people realize that such interrelationships exist, but a developmental perspective can clarify them and can suggest implications for using them to enhance productivity and satisfaction during adulthood. Because most practitioners assist adults in relation to specific types of performance, such as work, recreation, or family life, the following examples of interrelationships focus on types of performance.

Career development often occurs throughout the work life. Social change, as reflected in a rapidly changing occupational structure, contributes to more widespread shifts from one type of job to another during the occupational life cycle. Self-concept affects career selection, which in turn helps establish one's self-concept as well as one's level of living and prestige. Career development is also influenced by such attitudes as assertiveness and willingness to accept new responsibilities. The age at which outstanding occupational achievement is most likely to occur varies with the type of work. Although adults who are very creative typically maintain their achievement well into middle age and beyond, the few most outstanding achievements tend to occur during the twenties in fields that depend heavily on physical capacities, during the thirties in fields that depend heavily on intellectual capacities, and even later in fields that depend heavily on social capacities.

Interrelationships between a husband and wife evolve during the family life cycle. Early marital adjustment is associated with the personal characteristics that each partner brings to the marriage, such as personal adjustment and similarity of background, and with evolving interrelationships among them, such as love, finances, and sexual adjustment. With the addition of children, more of women's social participation is associated with family and community, and more of men's social participation is related to work. In recent decades the alternatives for women's roles have increased even though expectations from the past tend to persist. Wives' satisfaction depends in part on their expectations. For example, full-time homemakers who do not want to work tend to feel satisfied, while unemployed wives who want to work tend to feel dissatisfied. Full-time homemakers who return to graduate school typically experience socialization into the professional role and out of the traditional feminine role. An initial reduction in self-confidence tends to be replaced by an increased sense of accomplishment, confidence, self-esteem, and assertiveness.

Physical condition is influenced by heredity, living conditions, emotional stress, nutrition, and the accumulation of impairments from disease, accidents, and practices such as drinking and smoking. Regular exercise enhances strength, endurance, and vitality. The decline in maximum physical capacity for older adults tends to be less for the physically active than for the sedentary. Many older adults pace themselves in work and recreation so that they maintain a high level of performance. Prior experience can provide perspective on health problems. For example, older adults who experienced life-threatening illnesses in earlier years perceive chronic illnesses as less stressful than those without such experience. Physical functioning thus reflects the interplay of many factors.

Most practitioners recognize that the interactions among context, performance, condition, personality, and learning are complex. However, most of the tested knowledge about adulthood consists of research findings on interrelationships among only a few variables. Such findings are more useful if practitioners can fit them into a broad perspective on developmental trends and holistic interrelationships (Birren, 1964; Carlson and Price, 1966; McCammon, 1970; Schwartz and Proppe, 1970; Thomae, 1970; Kastenbaum and others, 1972; Wohlwill, 1973). For example, all adults confront problems and weaknesses. Practitioners can help them use individual and community strengths to help combat weaknesses. Such an out-

come is more likely if practitioner and client alike understand
the network of community opportunities, constraints, and ways
to acquire relevant resources. Likewise, individual performance reflects personal attributes and interpersonal relations
along with expectations (Cronbach, 1975; Sarason, 1976).
Many strands in this web of influences are beyond the individual's control. A developmental perspective can help adults
identify relevant relationships and become more proactive in
guiding their own lives. Research is needed regarding complex
developmental relationships between personal attributes and
interpersonal relations. In addition to helping adult clients
interrelate various parts of their life, practitioners can strive
to deal with each client as a whole person. This includes an
appreciation of ways in which the practitioner's specialized
assistance in relation to work, family, health, or recreation
interacts with many other aspects of the client's life. It also
includes an effort to take into account the influences of other
specialized practitioners. Adults are frequently caught in a
cross fire of conflicting recommendations from various practitioners who are unaware of each other's efforts to assist the
same client with related problems. Some of the ways in which
such discrepancies can be reduced include comprehensive
career and educational counseling, clinics that maintain a common health and medical record for each patient that all specialists may consult, and comprehensive multipurpose senior
citizens' centers. However, in any instance a practitioner can
alert each adult client to the importance of trying to accommodate varied sources of assistance, obtain information about
other practitioners who currently or recently worked with the
client, and strive to use referrals to and consultants with other
practitioners in ways that treat each client as a whole person.
Evaluation studies of efforts to provide coordinated services
would help to identify effective approaches.

Adult Assertiveness

As adults interact with people and things throughout
most of adulthood, they establish an increasingly complex network of interpersonal relationships and become more different

from one another. One way in which adults at any age vary is in their relative emphasis on problems or opportunities in a similar set of circumstances. Whether an adult has an optimistic or a pessimistic approach to life is related to assertiveness. Adults who are effectively assertive have some goals that provide a sense of direction and are somewhat proactive in their efforts to plan and achieve goals, in comparison with just being reactive and trying only to accommodate to the expectations of others.

Much of adult life is devoted to performance and participation in family, occupation, and community. In each of these settings there are tasks and expectations. However, the individual's performance reflects personal aspirations and limitations as well as the demands and constraints of the societal context. Aspirations, stereotypes, and other attitudes and values are formed and modified as a result of the individual's transactions with his or her societal context. For example, many middle-aged adults tend to misperceive adolescents as more autonomy oriented than they are and older adults as less autonomy oriented than they are. Middle-aged adults who have fairly accurate and positive attitudes toward older adults have typically experienced interaction with the elderly but have avoided major burdens or conflicts.

Learning occurs throughout adulthood as a result of deliberate efforts to modify knowledge, skills, and attitudes. It also occurs incidentally as a result of experience and is reflected in changes in performance and outlook. For example, some young people create adolescent dreams that give a sense of direction and aspiration to their lives. This often entails a fit between past potential and experience, current sense of identity and aspirations, and societal expectations and opportunities for the future. Similar transactions occur at various stages of adulthood. Around the forties, many adults realize that the future in their adolescent dream is now. They compare their aspirations with their current sense of self and pattern of participation. When the discrepancy is great, the adult can make major mid-life adjustments if sufficiently self-directed. For many older adults the adolescent dream is replaced by protection of gains and an inward shift toward more personal concerns. Practitioners can help adults place such transitions in perspective as a desirable aspect of a proactive approach to life. The creation and modification of adolescent dreams and their impact on adult performance and satisfaction is a provocative research topic.

Learning effectiveness is modified by individual characteristics such as intelligence, physical condition, and personal outlook, and learning context factors, such as social change, content relevance, and pacing. This interaction between personal and contextual characteristics is illustrated by the full-time college experience for young people. Colleges that are most influential on personality development have images that attract students who are open to the types of changes that the colleges want them to acquire and then accentuate those distinctive characteristics. Further research is needed regarding the use of public information about distinctive characteristics of institutions of higher education in relation to benefits for both students and institutions. In general, the college experience has an impact on intellectual and personality change, although those who attend college are most likely to change anyway and personality changes tend to revert unless supported by the postcollege environment. Similar young adults who do not attend college also show increasing openness to new experience and growing tolerance but perhaps not to the same extent.

Societal trends also have an impact on learning activity. For example, beginning in 1970 the job market for college graduates began to deteriorate as the long-term growth in job demand for college graduates slowed and supply increased, reflecting earlier increases in birth rates and more recent increases in rates of college attendance. The impact on attendance rates and job prospects has varied with student characteristics. The rates have been stable for young women, have increased for black males, and have decreased for white males from lower-middle-class families. The tighter job market has also been reflected in selection of major and in attention to studies rather than the widespread participation in social activism of the nineteen sixties.

The relative availability and attractiveness of alternative

courses of action also influences choices regarding family life. In recent decades women have had a wider range of family role options. Influences on attitudes toward being a full-time wife and mother include the heavy societal emphasis on self-interest, contractual exchanges, and monetary rewards in the larger society; the giving tasks and intangible rewards of the home-maker role; the shift of former family functions to other institutions; shrinking purchasing power of family income; and an extended postparental period. As a result of such changes and a wider range of options, many women are considering and making choices that formerly seemed unavailable. This is reflected in trends regarding age at marriage, size of family, working mothers, and divorce. Greater self-direction and assertiveness is apparent in work and community as well as in family settings.

For older adults, living arrangements tend to interact with personal characteristics and preferences in ways that are similar to family patterns for the middle-aged and the college settings for some young adults. Alternative living arrangements for older adults include maintaining one's own home, moving in with family, public housing for the elderly, and retirement communities. The accessibility and satisfactoriness of these alternative living arrangements vary substantially with the health and wealth of the older adult. Each alternative living arrangement has its costs and benefits. Residents of retirement communities report less interaction with family but more with friends. Further research about alternative living arrangements for older adults would enable practitioners to be more helpful to adults who seek to make the most satisfactory choice.

Practitioners can help adults in any setting to recognize some of the major forces that affect their lives, capitalize on those that are desirable, and try to deflect those that are undesirable. An understanding of distinctive features of alternative settings can be used by adults to guide their own activities and aspirations and select settings that encourage what they want to become.

There is great variability among adults in performance and outlook. This variability is far more associated with characteristics such as intelligence, socioeconomic status, or physical condition than it is with age. However, adults become more different from each other as a result of their transactions in family, work, and community, and thus the range of variability increases for most of adulthood (Butler, 1975; Botwinick, 1970; Bromley, 1966). This variability makes it difficult for individual adults to grasp the essential current and unfolding features of their own lives and to recognize similarities and differences between their lives and those of others.

Some types of variability, such as in performance, are fairly evident. For example, in family life there are some experiences and outlooks that tend to be associated with such patterns as being married with children, married but childless, single, divorced, or widowed. Each of these role relationships yields some distinctive experiences, such as raising children as a parent without a partner, and distinctive shared attitudes are fostered by interaction with people in similar role relationships.

Other types of increased variability with age, such as aspects of learning and personality, are less evident. Some age-related trends are associated with assertiveness. For example, reactive behavior tends to decline from late adolescence through middle age and then to increase in extreme old age in the form of dependency. The peak of self-confidence during middle age is reflected in perceived age norms. Many older adults experience an increasing registration deficit in short-term memory. They become more cautious in learning tasks, and their errors tend to entail forgetting instead of mistakes. For some older adults, problem solving consists mainly of searching the repertoire of formerly effective solutions instead of generating novel solutions. However, the most able and creative people tend to retain their ability and creativity throughout most of adulthood. They tend to be more sensitive to external stimuli, more receptive to internal impulses, and less censoring during the exploratory stage of creative effort. By contrast, less creative adults of any age concentrate too earnestly, stifle novelty, and often focus on the defects of an approach instead of exploring its potential. Too little research has been conducted on ways to help people become more creative. Health problems during later life also affect general functioning. The composite result of these age-related trends is that the range of individual differences in a group of seventy-five-year-olds is greater than was the case when they were all thirty (Maas and Kuypers, 1974).

There are various ways in which practitioners can help adults maintain and enhance their self-directedness in life roles generally and in specific learning activities. Adults can be encouraged to revise old dreams and aspirations and to create or adopt new ones to provide a sense of direction. The likelihood that a person will approach adulthood as a period of continued growth and change is enhanced by contact with similar people whose approach to life is growthful. Practitioners can encourage adults to associate with such role models and to be alert to societal expectations and opportunities that foster continued growth. The mentor-mentee relationship has recently received some systematic study, and much more is warranted.

A self-directed approach to adulthood entails making choices and decisions. Practitioners can facilitate self-directedness by increasing client awareness of likely transitions and available options. Rapid rates of social change and great variability among adults make it difficult for the individual to have a sense of likely developmental trends in his or her own unfolding life. Practitioners can help clarify general developmental trends and identify important similarities and differences with others.

Practitioners can also help adult clients recognize some of the major influences on their lives, capitalize on those that are desirable to the client, and deflect those that are undesirable. Examples include the selection of college, family, or housing arrangements to provide the associates and settings that influence individuals in directions in which they want to develop. Self-directedness and self-confidence are also fostered by encouraging adults to emphasize abilities and lead from strength rather than dwelling on liabilities and limitations.

Adult Aspiration

Practitioners who understand and facilitate adult development need to appreciate the outlook of the individual client as well as the networks of interpersonal relations in family, work, and community through which interaction occurs and altered performance is evident. A practitioner typically understands only a few of the important connections in the client's network of interactions. When a health professional, clergyman, or social worker obtains biographical information about a client, one purpose is to understand major contextual influences that might be useful in helping the client. For practitioners in the helping professions, information about contextual influences must typically be combined with information about the individual's outlook and aspirations. For example, the life-style and social space of blue collar and white collar adults differs in both prior experience and current problems and opportunities. Generalizations about contrasting patterns of participation and information seeking in relation to social class level become more useful to the practitioner when they are combined with insights about the outlook of the individual client. An adult who strongly prefers informal social groups and personalized information sources will probably adjust more successfully to a major role change if a family- or neighborhood-based self-help group rather than a formal organization is available. Likewise an adult whose typical learning strategy is characterized by openness and challenge seeking is likely to respond to a provocative educational program, whereas an adult whose typical learning strategy is characterized by rigidity and defensiveness is likely to respond to a more structured educational program. Effective practitioners are able to match personal preferences of clients with facilitative people, resources, and settings.

However, the same set of circumstances can be perceived quite differently by two adults with contrasting outlooks. The individual's outlook affects whether a problem is perceived as a threatening obstacle that produces frustration and disillusionment or as a challenging opportunity that produces growth and renewal (Gardner, 1961). For example, mid-career occupational changes can reach crisis proportions and adversely affect family life, but they can also present new opportunities and directions. Much depends on the individual's aspirations and goals. Practitioners would benefit from additional research findings on the modifiability of outlook during adulthood.

The interweaving of goals and developmental processes can be illustrated by several family life transitions. Around the time that the youngest child enters school, many full-time home-makers rethink their interest and activity patterns. Those who want to work outside the home but are unable to do so typically become unhappy, whereas those who prefer to remain full-time homemakers tend to be satisfied with the role. The husband's goals and attitudes can also be a major influence on the satis-factoriness of the wife's working outside the home. The impact of maternal employment on young children depends mainly on parental attitudes and satisfactory child-care arrangements. Un-der favorable conditions, maternal employment need not have any major adverse effects on the children. Adolescents typically assert their independence, which can be stressful for parents, especially if they interpret it as a rejection of themselves and their values. However, if parents have a broader developmental perspective, it may help them realize that growing independence is crucial to the establishment of an adult identity for the son or daughter, and that the questioning of each new generation contributes to the ongoing renewal of societal values. When the children grow up and leave home, most homemakers face an adjustment. This often entails mixed feelings about lost satisfactions from active parenthood and gained freedom to pursue personal interests. Much depends on the parent's goals and outlook. There are indications that research findings from a generation ago regarding the impact of the "empty nest" on homemakers apply less well today and that further research is needed.

Practitioners can be more effective if they understand that the goals and values of their clients are important ingredi-ents in the successful living of an adult life. In addition to tested knowledge about adult development and learning from the social and behavioral sciences, there are valuable insights to be gained from the humanities. Drama, biographies, novels, and poetry deal with many of the same issues of adulthood and tend to do so with an emphasis on conflicts of values and dilemmas that confront functioning adults. The recent and unprecedented practice of devoting issues of scholarly and professional journals to adulthood reflects a growing commitment to the provision of a more comprehensive perspective on adulthood for practitioners who work with adults (*Daedalus*, 1976; *Counseling Psychologist*, 1976; *The Personnel and Guidance Journal*, 1976).

Aspects of adult aspiration, direction, and assertiveness are reflected in a proactive approach to life. A proactive approach seems to be desirable for the individual and for the other people with whom the individual interacts in family, work, and community settings. An effective proactive approach to life seems to contribute to the individual's sense of self and accomplishment. Further research on the dynamics of this phenomenon is much needed. Individual initiative and creativity also contributes to the vitality and renewal of groups, organizations, and society. Differences will occur between individuals and societal groups with which they are associated, but these differences can be approached as sources of creative tension leading to individual growth and societal renewal as well as sources of destructive conflict.

An effective proactive approach to life and society can evolve. It is enhanced by a sense of security, self-esteem, and direction as the basis for responsible involvement. Reactive adults can strive to increase their sense of security, esteem, and direction, as well as their assertiveness. This often entails planning. For example, a middle-aged married woman can prepare to be more proactive in her probable future adjustment to widowhood through consideration of both financial planning and recognition of the contribution of friends to help deal with feelings of loss. In most transitions there is an interaction between personal preferences and societal opportunities. Practitioners can help adults of any age become more proactive and self-directed through combining action and contemplation. In most instances, some balance is required between assertiveness and accommodation. In some instances practitioners can help clients recognize how other people contribute to their development, and in other instances they can help clients avoid overdependence. Broadening of experience and deepening of self-understanding are both important. Personality differentiation and integration can both be enhanced by assertiveness and by accommodation of contending forces. Practitioners can assist adults to become more self-directed in their use of educative activity both for contemplation and for consideration of alternative courses of action. Research on typical learning strategies and on their modification if they are not effective constitutes one of the most promising directions regarding adult learning.

Developmental Processes

Whether an adult is mainly proactive or mainly reactive is likely to have some influence on broad developmental trends over the decades. Extent of assertiveness is likely to be even more influential on the way in which an adult deals with major change events and with the related developmental processes. Many of the change events that are major entail some alteration of role relationships. Role changes related to the family life cycle are familiar to most people and include leaving one's parents' home, marriage, birth of children, grown children leaving home, and the loss of a spouse through death or divorce. Role changes related to the occupational life cycle are somewhat less familiar and include job entry, job changes and promotions, mid-career shifts, and retirement. Even less familiar are role changes related to the community life cycle and to education. Such changes include joining a voluntary association or religious organization, becoming active in political activities, assuming a community leadership position, making a major change in recreational activities, leaving a community organization, and becoming a participant in an educational program. When an adult goes through such a change event the experience is unique in its detailed characteristics. Each type of change event, however, has some distinctive features that are shared by other experiences of that type and that distinguish it from most other types of change events. For example, the feelings and experiences associated with the birth of the first child are readily separable from those associated with losing one's job or a move to another community.

There are some basic developmental processes that are common to most change events. There is a tendency for per-

sonality, habit, and the expectations of others to maintain
stability in an adult's life until a change event disrupts the
pattern. For most change events an anticipation period occurs
between the time the individual realizes a change event will
occur and the time the change event actually occurs. A disorganization period tends to follow most change events until a
poststructure of participation is established. The need for adaptation associated with most change events tends to produce a
heightened readiness to engage in educative activity. Other
ways in which adults try to adapt to change events include
frantic activity, action, search for assistance, contemplation,
and withdrawal. Some change events, such as sudden unemployment or the loss of a loved one, are associated with feelings of
loss. When confronted with a major loss, many adults experience a general developmental process that typically includes
reactions such as denial, anger, depression, bargaining, and
acceptance.

Even for desirable change events, adults vary greatly in
their outlooks regarding change. Many people fear and resist
changes, reacting to them with regret about what might have
been and using their regret as an excuse for inaction. They
become more vulnerable and less open, and their restriction
of experience leads to narrowness. However, change events can
also heighten an individual's potential, increase susceptibility to
influence, and provide an impetus and an opportunity to grow.
Adults who are more open, but have a sense of direction, are
able to reconcile contradictions between the old and the new
and achieve growth through action and contemplation. Research findings on how adults can be helped to approach change
events in positive ways and ways that would encourage growth
would be very useful to practitioners.

In addition to a modified structure of participation as a
result of a transition to changed role relationships, there is
typically some shift in attitudes and outlook. After marriage,
the purchase of a car, divorce, a move to another community,
or retirement, most people rationalize the decision to emphasize
the soundness of the decision and deemphasize alternative
courses of action. The socialization process in the new role
relationships also facilitates the transition. Married women who

enter graduate school after their children are grown typically do so by choice to implement their sense of who they are and who they would like to become. They typically do so with a sense of self as a homemaker returning to school, but toward the end of the process, most women see themselves as graduate students with homemaking responsibilities. Another example occurs for many people around the time of retirement. When a husband retires from his job, he usually shifts from the role of family provider to a subordinate role in his wife's domain. In general a mutually satisfactory relationship over the years contributes to a satisfactory relationship in retirement with the great increase in time together. However, longstanding friction is likely to contribute to increased friction and unhappiness with the onset of retirement. The anger that some workers experience around the time of retirement typically subsides as the individual engages in activities that fill some of the time formerly occupied by work, perhaps discovers some unanticipated satisfactions in retirement, and tends to rationalize about retirement. The nature and satisfactoriness of the adjustment to retirement is sometimes highly associated with the marital relationship. The relation between change events and attitude change constitutes a useful research topic.

Adults usually cope with change events. Some manage to acquire considerable insight and wisdom in the process. With an understanding of adult development and learning, practitioners can help their clients deal more effectively with change. They can encourage them not to panic or assume that there is a quick and easy solution but to use the change event as an opportunity for growth. Practitioners can help clients become more self-directed and gain access to opportunities and resources that can facilitate adaptation. Adults can be encouraged to realize their potential more fully and to broaden their perspective on alternatives and on the process of change.

The most fundamental way in which practitioners can assist clients is through broadening their perspective on adult development and learning. As adults better understand the orderly and sequential developmental changes in characteristics and attitudes that have occurred to them and to others in the past, they will become more able to predict and understand their subsequent behavior. A developmental perspective can enable adults to grasp essential current and unfolding features of their own lives and to recognize similarities and differences between their own lives and those of others. This can be difficult because of the great variability among adults and the differences from generation to generation due to rapid social change. A developmental perspective also helps minimize the imposition of value judgments on the changes. Each stage of life tends to have its own values, which are used to judge which combinations of changes are most desirable and constitute progress. The shift from leadership of youth groups in middle age to discussion of social issues in old age can be viewed as an expansion of engagement with mankind as well as a contraction of life space. Age-related stereotypes exist. Tested knowledge regarding adult development can be combined with personal values to counteract false stereotypes and to foster self-realization.

Practitioners in many of the helping professions deal with issues related to stability and change in personality during adulthood. A central aspect of adult personality development is the shifting manner in which the person strives to maintain and enhance his or her sense of self. Generalizations about the evolving sense of self provide the practitioner with optimism about the modifiability of adult personality, with indications of the influence of role changes on self-concept, and with understanding of the developmental process that can enhance the practitioner's efforts to help adults learn and modify feelings. Generalizations about adult attitudes and happiness can be used to help adults recognize the types of adjustments they are likely to confront; develop realistic and constructive attitudes toward the resultant problems and opportunities; and acquire the needed understanding, competence, and supportive services. Adults can also be helped to become more self-directed through activities such as assertiveness training, values clarification, and priority setting.

Developmental generalizations regarding physical condition and health enable practitioners to assist adults in various ways. Generalizations about nutrition can be used to encourage balanced meals and mealtime sociability. Generalizations about social isolation can be used to increase awareness of and access to social and physical activities. Generalizations about sensory impairment can encourage use of adequate levels of illumination and sound transmission and combined visual and auditory communication. Generalizations about physical condition and age indicate the importance of exercise to increase vitality. Practitioners have a related responsibility regarding the availability of health and recreation services to adults of all ages.

The resources related to adult learning exist in many settings related to family, work, and community. Practitioners in many fields can help create circumstances under which adults with various characteristics including age learn effectively. For example, educational activities can be designed to minimize disabilities and emphasize abilities and experience. Advance organizers can help establish a useful cognitive structure to enable adults to progress from basic concepts to more difficult ones. Memorable encounters encourage the rehearsal and reinforcement that aid memory. Effective learning activities tend to provide for self-pacing, feedback, and individualization.

During the past generation, a long-term trend toward lifelong learning has been accelerating. Almost every type of organization and institution in our society provides some educational programs for adults. Schools, community colleges, and universities are not the only ones to do so. Continuing education programs for adults are also provided by professional associations, religious institutions, employers, labor unions, libraries, hospitals, and a wide variety of voluntary associations. Increasing priority is being given to public support of educational programs for adults. Practitioners throughout the helping professions are recognizing that part of their professional role entails helping adult clients use educational resources to facilitate individual growth and competence.

Social Policy

In addition to the foregoing implications for individual practitioners, generalizations about adult development and learning have implications for social policy. This includes public understanding of adult development, access by all adults to various opportunity systems, preparation of practitioners in the helping professions to work effectively with adults, and future research priorities. Following are suggestions about leadership that practitioners in the helping professions can exert regarding social policy related to adult development.

Many generalizations about adult development and learning can be used to increase general public understanding of the dynamic and varied character of adulthood. The mass media and educational programs for youth and adults can all contribute. Rapid social change with resulting future shock makes it difficult for individual adults to develop a comprehensive and developmental perspective on the adult life cycle. Instead, many adults are overwhelmed by details and have difficulty identifying important issues. Journalists, educators, and practitioners can highlight the crucial generalizations. Recent popular articles on mid-career shifts and adult discussion groups on interpersonal relations indicate that a start has already been made.

Preparatory education of children and youth can also include attention to adulthood and aging. Some change events affect young people directly, such as moving to another community, entering college, starting a job, getting married, and having grandparents retire and move away. This personal connection with the change event can serve to alert them to the likely impact of various changes during adulthood on themselves and on other people. However, materials and programs aimed at adults who usually have the main responsibility for decisions related to change events will typically be more specific regarding processes of change and alternative courses of action.

Self-directedness is another important issue. Many adults would like to become more proactive and assertive, and also more reflective and responsive. The stereotype is to be one or the other, but the challenge is to be each when appropriate. Shifting values from one phase of adulthood to another should also be better understood as a way of counteracting the false stereotype of one set of expectations for all of adult life. Perhaps the most neglected aspect of adult development is family life education. Few roles are more important to the individual and society but receive less preparation than marriage and parenthood. Practitioners who deal with family conflict—such as marriage counselors, divorce lawyers, and health professionals who treat child abuse victims—can testify about how unprepared many adults are in their roles as spouse and parent. Such practitioners also indicate that some adults acquire valuable insights into these roles as a result of bitter experience. Surely we can more effectively orient young people to their adult responsibilities and opportunities in family life. *Practitioners should work with journalists and educators to increase public understanding of adult development.*

Along with increased public understanding of adult development and learning, it is important that all adults have access to various opportunity systems related to recreation, health, education, work, and community life. For example, in the past, recreation facilities and activities were oriented toward young adults. In recent years, there has been increased attention to the types, times, and locations of recreational activities that are appropriate for older adults. Similarly, until recently the images and policies of higher education institutions were oriented mainly toward preparatory education for full-time students in their late teens and early twenties. However, now that adults who attend part-time constitute more than half of enrollments, on-campus resident instruction programs are becoming more accessible to adults of all ages, in addition to the continuing education programs for adults that have been offered off-campus or in the evenings over the years.

The tendency for personality changes that occur during college to revert unless the post-college setting is supportive has implications for work supervisors. Procedures for management by objectives, developmental staffing, and organizational development can contribute to both manpower development and organizational renewal. Flexible policies by employers can also contribute increased employee productivity and satisfaction in relation to work related change events such as job entry, mid-career shifts, and retirement. Especially the large employers have extensive education and training departments that conduct educational programs to help employees become more competent. Occupationally related educational programs for current employees are also conducted by schools, universities, labor unions, and professional associations. Especially for those who work for small employers collaborative efforts with these other providers of continuing education can increase access to opportunities for continued growth.

All adults should also have access to opportunities for growth in roles other than the worker role. For example, extensive geographic mobility has undermined a sense of community for many people. Religious and community organizations can do much to assist lonely adults to establish interpersonal relationships. This includes helping adults to understand the value of extended family members, friends, and confidants as well as introducing adults to community groups such as newcomers and foster grandparents. Organizations that bring together young and old can be especially useful. An example is a public issues discussion group that includes young adults with their sense of alternative futures and older adults with their sense of history. Many practitioners in the helping professions can serve as knowledge brokers to help adults become aware of opportunities related to recreation, health, education, work, and community life. *Practitioners should work with others to increase adult access to such opportunity systems.*

A comprehensive and developmental perspective on adulthood can help practitioners offset an overemphasis on professionalism including specialization and inadequate inclusion of the client in decision making. For example, patient education programs reflect the efforts of health professionals to approach people holistically and developmentally. Such a perspective can be fostered by preparatory education programs before practitioners enter the field, by continuing professional education programs reflect the efforts of health professionals to approach sociations. Particular attention should be given to programs for practitioners in related fields. Such joint programs can enable practitioners from related specialties to learn from each other and to find ways to minimize discrepancies between the recommendations of several practitioners. *Practitioners should en-*

hance their developmental perspective on adulthood through preparatory and continuing education, professional associations, and collaborative efforts.

In recent years there has been a steady increase in scholarly attention to adulthood. Scholars from many fields with developmental interests will find many intriguing topics and practitioners who welcome findings. Examples of promising research directions include: variability in developmental trends for white collar and blue collar adults, comparative analyses of adult development in various national settings, circumstances under which adults with various characteristics learn most effectively, procedures for dealing effectively with change events, and evaluation of the relative effectiveness of ways in which practitioners assist adults. *Practitioners should encourage and support research on adult development.*

The results of greater public attention to adult development should enable practitioners in education and the other helping professions to more effectively assist adults. Practitioners can provide leadership to achieve such policy changes.

❧ Appendix ❧

Conducting Research on Adult Development and Learning

❧❧❧❧❧❧❧❧❧❧❧❧❧❧

This appendix briefly describes the major tasks in planning and conducting research on aspects of adult development and learning and identifies the main references related to each task.

Early tasks in the research process include formulating a general researchable question and reviewing the available literature; planning the general research approach or mode of inquiry; deciding on the specific research design; deciding on data collection and analysis; and, if necessary, drafting the project proposal.

Formulating the Question and Reviewing Literature

Most research projects begin with an idea that the researcher would like to pursue further or with a question that cannot be answered by current knowledge. Researchable questions related to adult development and learning are varied, and the researcher can select from among many specific questions that are interesting, important, and feasible to investigate. Assistance in the formulation of a researchable question can be gained from the advice of interested researchers, from descriptive information about historical trends and current conditions, and from suggestions by practitioners in the helping professions. A question or topic that is particularly important to the researcher helps to sustain interest through the completion of the project. For an applied study, a topic that is attractive to practitioners or others associated with the project helps to sustain their cooperation. In addition to the desirability of the topic, the researcher must consider its feasibility, which typically depends on the availability of necessary resources such as time, money, data-collection instruments, and related research personnel.

An expanding literature of research on adult development and learning is available and indispensable to those who plan studies, and research topics typically evolve during the course of reviewing this literature. Overviews of developmental research can guide and enrich the efforts of those who study aspects of adult development and learning. For example, historical overviews of developmental psychology are provided in chapters by Charles (Goulet and Baltes, 1970) and by Havighurst (Baltes and Schaie, 1973). Foundations of gerontology are described in chapters by Zubin and by Riegel (Eisdorfer and Lawton, 1973). Theoretical constructs for life-span developmental psychology are presented in the chapters by Baltes and Goulet and by Reese and Overton (Goulet and Baltes, 1970). Reviews of theory and research on cognitive and affective development for older adults are contained in the section on the "Developmental Psychology and Aging" in Eisdorfer and Lawton (1973). Once a specific topic is identified, a more focused review of relevant research reports and journal articles can contribute to the preparation of the study rationale and objectives.

A general idea for a research topic can be refined and sharpened by reading overviews of the topic. Some overviews of literature on adult development and learning are prepared mainly for practitioners (Birren, 1964a; Butler, 1975; Hurlock, 1968; Kalish, 1975; Neugarten, 1968; Troll, 1975). Others are directed mainly at researchers (Baltes and Schaie, 1973; Eisdorfer and Lawton, 1973; Goulet and Baltes, 1970). Overviews, major sources, and indexes can help the researcher locate specific studies on context, performance, condition, personality, and learning related to adulthood.

Context: In addition to the interweaving of stability and change over time, research on human development includes attention to the comprehensive functioning of the individual as he or she interacts with the social and physical environment. A small but growing research literature exists on the societal context of adult development. Part of the societal context reflects the historical moment (Erikson, 1975). For purposes of understanding adult functioning, it is necessary to study the transaction between the individual and the societal context (Schwartz and Proppe, 1970). Much of Baltes and Schaie (1973) concerns interactions between socialization and personality development during adulthood. Similar attention to such transactions is provided in the chapters by Riegel and by Willems in Nesselroade and Reese (1973) and by the section on the "Social Environment of the Aging" in Eisdorfer and Lawton (1973). Research and theory on community and on social networks are increasingly providing procedures for assessment of the societal context (Barker, 1968; Proshansky, 1970; Barker and Schoggen, 1973; Sarason, 1974). The study of adults in naturalistic settings, with attention to both individual and context, facilitates the application of findings by practitioners who work with adults (Cronbach, 1975; Glaser and Strauss, 1967; Schaie, 1974). A compilation of findings on the societal context for older adults was prepared by Riley, Foner, and others (1968). McTavish (1971) describes findings and methods regarding societal perceptions of older adults. Feldman and Newcomb (1969) synthesize the findings of many studies of the impact of college on students, and Freeman (1971) analyzes the labor market for college graduates. Kreps (1976) summarizes the work environment for women. A review of literature on societal context allows the researcher to identify likely facilitators and barriers to adult performance, along with existing instruments for data collection regarding context. For most studies of adult development, however, it is necessary to relate societal characteristics to personal characteristics such as performance, condition, personality, and learning.

Performance: Conceptualizations of the process of diffusion and adoption of practices (Rogers and Shoemaker, 1971), and of influences on the decision to adopt innovations (Katz and Lazarsfeld, 1955; Havelock, 1969), provide a useful basis for relating context and performance. There are many helpful compilations of theory and research regarding marriage and family life (Anthony and Benedek, 1970; Bernard, 1973; Carter and Glick, 1970; Eshleman, 1974; Hill, 1970; Hoffman and Nye, 1974). A comprehensive overview of student performance in college is provided by Feldman and Newcomb (1969) and of part-time educational participation by adults by Johnstone and Rivera (1965). More focused studies have been conducted on college students (Trent and Medsker, 1968; Perry, 1970), on educational activities by adults (Tough, 1971; Knox, 1970, 1974), and on adult information seeking (Parker and Paisley, 1966). A major treatment of leisure performance is provided by Rapoport and Rapoport (1975) and of sexual performance by Masters and Johnson (1965). There are many books and articles on work (Crites, 1969; Holland, 1973; Super and others, 1967; Tiedeman and O'Hara, 1963; Tiedeman and Miller-Tiedeman, 1976), and an increasing number on working women (Kreps, 1976; U.S. BLS, 1975). Findings from the first round of a longitudinal study by Lowenthal, Thurnher, and others (1975) focus on transitions in work and family at four stages of adulthood.

Condition: Timiras (1972) has prepared the most recent and comprehensive volume on developmental trends in physical condition and health during adulthood. Welford's (1958) compilation of studies on physical skills and age is still useful. Recent statistical summaries on nutrition, health, and accidents help to place descriptive information about physical condition of specific adults in a national perspective (HRA, 1974; NSC, 1975). Analyses of age-related physical performance and the contribution of exercise are provided by Astrand (1968) and by deVries (1974). A review of research on psychology of sex differences was prepared by Maccoby and Jacklin (1974).

Personality: Overviews of personality theory that give some attention to adulthood have been prepared by Hall and Lindzey (1970), Maddi (1972), and Sanford (1970). Baltes and Schaie (1973) emphasize empirical research on adult personality development. Findings from specific studies on aspects of adult personality are reported in Neugarten and others (1964) on ego development, Fitts (1965) and Thompson (1972) on self concept, Campbell and Converse (1975) on happiness, Kastenbaum and Aisenberg (1972) and Jaques (1965) on attitudes toward death.

Learning: Adult learning is given more attention in Gagné (1972) than in most educational psychology texts. Research on cognitive processes during adulthood is synthesized by Botwinick (1967, 1973); by Jarvik, Eisdorfer, and Blum (1973); by Arenberg (Eisdorfer and Lawton, 1973); by Kagan (Baltes and Schaie, 1973); and by Flavell, Botwinick, Horn, and Schaie (Goulet and Baltes, 1970). Longitudinal studies have been especially useful in demonstrating the growth in intellectual abilities that occurs during much of adulthood, growth that tends to be obscured by cross-sectional findings that also reflect social change (Owens, 1966; Baller, Charles, and Miller, 1967). A major experimental study of adult performance in actual learning experiences, in contrast with intelligence test performance, showed no age-related trend between the twenties and the sixties (Sjogren and Knox, 1965). However, recent participation in part-time educational activity was associated with greater learning effectiveness (Sjogren, Knox, and Grotelue-

schen, 1968). Belbin and Belbin (1972) report on efforts to re-
train older adults.

Planning the General Research Approach

Research projects on an aspect of adult development and
learning typically share a general research approach with other
studies in the social and behavioral sciences (Kerlinger, 1973;
Fox, 1969; Hymen, 1955; Cattell, 1966; Edwards, 1971; Cole,
1972; Wood, 1974). General research approaches may focus on
theory building, theory testing, intervention, and comparative
analysis; and the general research approach that is selected depends on the research topic and on the available findings and
methods related to the topic. When few, if any, research findings related to a research question are found, the literature
review can suggest the types of qualitative data that might be
collected for the purpose of theory building. Where an accumulation of related research is identified, it can be used to
construct a rationale and predictions or hypotheses to be tested
by the data to be collected and analyzed in the proposed research project.

Theory Building: Some research approaches are designed
mainly to generate theory instead of to test theory. A general
approach that draws from anthropological and sociological field
research is presented by Glaser and Strauss (1967). The chapter
by Bromley (Goulet and Baltes, 1970) explores theory construction regarding adult development.

Theory Testing: Most research approaches in studies of
adult development and learning are concerned mainly with
theory testing and use either correlational or experimental
methods. Most of the experimental studies have dealt with cognition, as indicated in the chapters by Botwinick, by Horn,
and by Reinert (Goulet and Baltes, 1970), by Kogan (Baltes and
Schaie, 1973), and by Arenberg (Eisdorfer and Lawton, 1973).

Intervention: An increasingly widespread activity related
to research on adult development and learning is social intervention. In addition to the social psychological literature on
social intervention, as illustrated by Hornstein and others

(1971), intervention has been considered in relation to research on adult development and learning, as illustrated by the chapters by Baer (Nesselroade and Reese, 1973), by Birren and Woodruff, and by Harshbarger (Baltes and Schaie, 1973), and by the section on "Clinical Psychology" in Eisdorfer and Lawton (1973). Procedures to plan for and to evaluate innovation are suggested by Havelock (1969), Rogers and Shoemaker (1971), by Belbin and Belbin (1972), and by Knox (1974, 1976).

Comparative Analysis: Some research approaches are comparative, including comparative analysis of patterns of adult development by subcultures within the United States, as well as by cross-national comparisons. Shanas and others (1968b) report on a major cross-national study of aging, and Eckensberger (Nesselroade and Reese, 1973) reviews methodological issues of cross-cultural research in developmental psychology.

Although most of the research on adult development and learning has been conducted within the broad discipline of psychology (including physiological and educational psychology), other disciplines in the social and behavioral sciences are well represented. Included are social psychology (Bengston, 1973), sociology (Glaser and Strauss, 1968; Atchley, 1975), and anthropology (Clark and Anderson, 1967). Havighurst (Baltes and Schaie, 1973) has indicated the utility of biography and autobiography as a source of insight regarding adult development.

Deciding on the Specific Research Design

Developmental research designs may be either descriptive or experimental, with the major descriptive designs including cross-sectional, longitudinal, time lag, and sequential. Although most studies on aspects of adult development and learning use cross-sectional samples and collect data by means of interviews and tests, other research approaches are available and are described by Schaie and Wohlwill (Goulet and Baltes, 1970), Baltes and Schaie (Baltes and Schaie, 1973), and Cattell (Nesselroade and Reese, 1973). In addition to this general methodological literature on data collection and analysis procedures, illustrative studies show how these several procedures are used in practice.

Descriptive Designs: During most of this century, research relevant to adulthood has been mostly descriptive and cross-sectional, with more concern with individual differences than with change trends and processes. Samples of adults have been unrepresentative, and data collection instruments have been child-oriented. For example, during the decades before and after World War II, some cross-sectional studies were made of gross age trends for adults regarding such variables as learning ability or interests. But only during the past two decades, and with the completion of longitudinal studies following particular individuals through adulthood, have almost all of the important theory building and research on adult development and learning occurred. Follow-up of earlier study samples composed of children or young adults has yielded longitudinal data spanning most of adulthood (Nelson, 1954; Bayley and Oden, 1955; Terman and Oden, 1959; Owens, 1966; Baller, Charles, and Miller, 1967; Maas and Kuypers, 1974). More recently, cross-sequential studies or recursive "block" studies involving overlapping cohorts of individuals have been designed to follow up periodically on fairly representative cross-sectional samples so that data analysis can indicate trends attributable to personal change and to social change (Knox and Videbeck, 1963; Schaie and Strother, 1968a; Lowenthal, Thurnher, and others, 1975). Data collection procedures are beginning to include depth interviews, tests designed for adults, and use of existing records. Studies of older twins, such as the longitudinal study lasting more than two decades by Jarvik, Blum, and Varma (1972), allow the separation of the influences of nature and nurture.

The advantages and disadvantages of major descriptive research designs related to adult development require careful consideration in light of the researcher's purposes and resources. The cross-sectional study can be completed in a few months, is relatively inexpensive, has much precedent, and accurately reflects the current range of individual differences related to age. This is why most studies on adult development and learning are cross-sectional. However, most such cross-sectional studies are limited in relation to developmental conclusions because of the impact of social change and the problem of comparability of research instruments across age groups. For instance, conclusions based on occupational performance data and expectations collected by questionnaire administered to three samples of adults at ages 15, 45, and 75 would provide an unsatisfactory estimate of developmental changes that individuals experience over the years. The reasons are attributable to selective survival, social change, and the tendency for averages to mask major contrasting trends. The longitudinal study provides a relatively accurate description of developmental trends for individuals. However, it requires much cooperation, resources, and time. Few researchers are able to make such an investment. Additional problems include sample attrition over the years and the continued use of obsolete data-collection instruments to maintain comparability.

The time-lag study describes changes in the societal, institutional, and group setting over time. It is designed to assess situational changes that influence adult development more than personal changes themselves. Although observations and records help to document descriptions of the societal context, it is difficult to deal with the complexity of situational influences and the differing perceptions that individuals have of the same occurrence. The sequential study allows comparison between age-related trends that emerge from analysis of cross-sectional data and trends that emerge from follow-up data collection from individuals over time. This reduces the time and expense but increases the complexity of data analysis.

Most of the major long-term longitudinal studies of adult development and learning benefited from earlier data collection usually designed for other purposes, which could be followed up in subsequent years (Birren and others, 1963, followed up by Granick and Patterson, 1971; Block and Haan, 1971; Maas and Kuypers, 1974; Owens, 1966; White, 1961, 1972). It is less usual that researchers design a longitudinal study of adult development from the outset (Neugarten and others, 1964; Williams and Wirths, 1965; Palmore, 1974; Lowenthal, Thurnher and others, 1975). Procedures for longitudinal studies of proactive and changing adults are suggested by Goulet and by Hopper (Nesselroade and Reese, 1973).

In sum, for most research projects on adult development and learning, decisions about sample selection and data collection and analysis are interconnected in reflecting the main purpose of the study. The assessment of short-term or long-term stability and change is characteristic of most developmental studies. A general model for descriptive studies on adult development consists of three dimensions: the individual's age, the cohort of people of a similar age, and the point in time when the data are collected. A cross-sectional study is typically used to analyze age differences among individuals at one point in time, but it is difficult to separate age and cohort differences. A longitudinal study is typically used to analyze age-related changes in an individual, but it is difficult to separate the influences of age and of experience between the times of data collection.

A time-lag study is typically used to analyze changes in the societal context between the times of data collection. Short-term changes often consist of modifications of facilitators and barriers to performance. Long-term changes often consist of historical trends. In time-lag studies, it is difficult to separate the influences of cohort differences and experiences between the times of data collection. A variety of sequential research designs enable the developmental researcher to study multiple age cohorts concurrently. For example, a series of follow-up rounds of data collection from a representative cross-section of adults would help to separate personal change from social change and to identify the likely influence of life experiences. Procedures for the initial selection of a panel of adults for a longitudinal study are described in the appendix of Neugarten and others (1964). Problems of selective attrition during a longitudinal study are described by Schaie, Labouvie, and Barrett (1973). Procedures for minimizing attrition are described by Eckland (1968).

Experimental Design: For some research questions related to adult development and learning, experimental research designs are most appropriate. This is especially so for processes of adult learning and for the relative effectiveness of intervention procedures. Experimental studies are being conducted with representative samples of adults to allow age comparisons (Sjogren and Knox, 1965). Research findings relevant to adult learning result from many studies that focus on context, performance, condition, and personality. An example is the influence of change events, openness of outlook, and encouragement of significant others on the decision by adults to participate in educational activity. In earlier decades, most of the developmental research on adult learning focused on age trends regarding learning ability. Currently, the main thrust of research on adult learning is on the process of learning during adulthood.

In the typical experimental study of learning, learners are randomly assigned to two or more parallel experimental treatments and sometimes a control treatment. For example, in a study of optimum pacing, learners in one treatment would study at their preferred pace; in another treatment, they would study at a rate faster than their preferred pace; and, in a third treatment, they would study at a rate slower than their preferred pace. For each treatment there would be periodic evaluation or assessment of learning achievement or gain, such as a pretest, midway test, posttest, and retest. The analysis of test results allows conclusions on the relative effectiveness of treatments regarding learning achievement. Especially in developmental research on adult learning, achievement data are analyzed in relation to age, ability, and prior learning. A series of experimental studies can be conducted with the same learners or with parallel samples to assess modification of learning performance related to changes in personal outlook or in instructional procedures. Experimental studies of adult learning might focus on such dynamics as readiness, expectancy, memory aids, pacing, complexity, or application (Fox, 1969; Kerlinger, 1973).

Perhaps the most promising emerging research topic regarding adult learning is learning strategies or styles. There are very few studies on this topic. In research on learning strategy, the learner has many options regarding types of learning activities (such as reading, listening, problem solving, and test taking) and the sequence and amount of time devoted to each. The researcher describes the individual's characteristic learning strategy and compares strategies with achievement and personal characteristics including age. Experimental studies can then be used to explore the modifiability of learning strategies and the extent to which adults who have relatively ineffective learning strategies can be helped to adopt strategies that, for other similar adults, are more effective.

Deciding on Data Collection and Analysis

Some descriptive developmental studies include use of existing data such as U.S. Census reports or institutional records. *Statistical Abstracts* provides convenient summaries of historical trends (U.S. Census, 1960, 1975). The decennial census reports provide detailed information related to adult development, which can be further analyzed in relation to selected geographic areas or population characteristics relevant to a specific study (U.S. Census, 1973a). Compilations sometimes assemble information related to a topic from many sources (U.S., DHEW, 1976). In addition to existing records, there are many sources of research data that entail a minimum of intrusion on the lives of the adults who are studied (Webb and others, 1966). Descriptive information about social networks in a community or organization is sometimes pertinent (Barker, 1968). Surveys that use questionnaires or structured or focused interviews often include items on such biographical characteristics as past experience and current status, as well as on current activities and interests.

Research on adult development and learning can include both existing instruments or items and the construction of new ones. Sound procedures for survey design and analysis can contribute much to the validity of the resulting data (Hymen, 1955; Kerlinger, 1973; Fox, 1969). Clear and precise wording of questions is especially important (Payne, 1951). Issues in measurement and data collection regarding adult development and learning are discussed by Nunnally and by Risley and Wolf (Nesselroade and Reese, 1973).

The social readjustment rating scale is an instrument designed to assess extent of recent change (Holmes and Rahe, 1967). A wide variety of instruments related to personality are available (Shaw and Wright, 1967; Cattell, 1973). Widely used instruments include the Tennessee Self Concept Scale (Fitts, 1965) and the Campbell-Strong Interest Inventory (Campbell, 1971). Some use has been made of projective tests, such as the Thematic Apperception Test (Neugarten and Guttmann, 1958). Many tests have been used as estimates of adult mental ability (Wechsler, 1958; Knox, Grotelueschen, and Sjogren, 1968; Fozard and Nuttall, 1971).

Analysis of quantitative data for many developmental studies tends to be complex because of the desirable focus on multivariate analysis over time. Such methodological issues are discussed by Nesselroade (Goulet and Baltes, 1970), by Willems, and by Risley and Wolf (Nesselroade and Reese, 1973). Qualitative data can also be analyzed to describe developmental change and to contribute to theory construction (Glaser and Strauss, 1967). Biographical information provides a useful source of holistic insight into unfolding lives.

For almost any research approach, the methodological issues discussed by Jones in his chapter on "Intelligence and Problem Solving" (Birren, 1959) provide useful cautions. Such cautions relate to subject motivation, sensory restrictions, educational level, instrument availability, cognitive structure, test practice, speed bias, instrument composition, task difficulty, and emphasis on accuracy. These methodological cautions are useful to researchers because the problems they note can be minimized if they are recognized prior to data collection; otherwise, they could vitiate the collected data.

Drafting the Project Proposal

Some developmental research projects are conducted by a researcher without external resources and are reported in journal articles. However, many studies are sufficiently large and complex to require written plans to coordinate the efforts of the project director and other personnel associated with the project. In addition, they often take the form of a proposal to acquire external resources and support or cooperation to conduct the project and prepare research monographs or books. A successful proposal culminates the planning process and constitutes a plan that can be implemented. It typically describes how both available and additional resources will be used to answer the research question.

A research proposal typically contains the following six broad categories of information:

1. *Purpose.* What are the proposed outcomes? Why is the purpose important and relevant?
2. *Rationale.* What is the theoretical framework for the study, including reference to the major related studies? What are the specific objectives, hypotheses, or predictions?
3. *Procedures.* What is the general research design for the study? What specific procedures are planned for sampling, data collection, and analysis?
4. *Resources.* What resources are available to conduct the study, such as people, equipment, materials, and money? What additional resources are required? Who will conduct the study, and what indication is there that they are competent to do so? What evidence is there of the feasibility of the project?
5. *Budget.* What is the time schedule for the project? What is the expenditure budget, and what are the sources of internal and external funds?
6. *Reporting.* How will the findings be reported? How will the success of the project be evaluated and against what criteria and standards?

The literature referred to in this appendix can contribute to the preparation of the first three categories. The fourth category on resources typically describes the qualifications and experience of the project director and the main members of the research team, with an emphasis on why they are likely to successfully achieve the research objectives. In addition to personnel, other available resources for the project are usually described—such as materials, equipment, and working relationships—and additional resources needed to conduct the study are identified.

The fifth category on the project budget usually identifies the planned expenditures from both internal and external funds, along with a time schedule indicating the major tasks to be accomplished during each stage of the project. Proposal reviewers examine the timetable, budget, staff qualifications, and local resources, along with objectives and procedures for evidence of feasibility.

The sixth category, reporting, may entail more than plans for a technical report or a journal article. Especially in relation to applied research projects and evaluations of demonstration projects of adult development, practitioners are included in advisory and dissemination activities to encourage the application of findings. It is helpful to include a statement of criteria by which to judge the success of the project and a description of evaluation procedures to provide evidence of success.

A sound research proposal should reflect the creative planning process that preceded it, should help to acquire needed resources and cooperation, and should provide the basic guide to the implementation and conduct of the entire project.

References

AARONSON, B. S. "Personality Stereotypes of Aging." *Journal of Gerontology*, 1966, *21*, 458–462.

ADAMS, B. N. "Isolation, Function, and Beyond: American Kinship in the 1960's." In C. B. Broderick (Ed.), *A Decade of Family Research and Action*. Minneapolis: National Council on Family Relations, 1971.

AHAMMER, I. M. "Social-Learning Theory as a Framework for the Study of Adult Personality Development." In P. Baltes, and W. Schaie (Eds.), *Life-Span Developmental Psychology: Personality and Socialization*. New York: Academic Press, 1973.

AHAMMER, I. M., and BALTES, P. B. "Objective Versus Perceived Age Differences in Personality: How Do Adolescents, Adults and Older People View Themselves and Each Other?" *Journal of Gerontology*, 1972, *27*, 46–51.

ALPAUGH, P. K., RENNER, V. J., and BIRREN, J. E. "Age and Creativity: Implications for Education and Teachers." *Educational Gerontology*, 1976, *1*, 17–37.

ALPENFELS, E. J. *Families of the Future*. Ames: The Iowa State University Press, 1971.

ALPER, T. G. "The Relationship Between Role-Orientation and Achievement Motivation in College Women." *Journal of Personality*, 1973, *41*, 9–31.

ANDERS, T. R., FOZARD, J. L., and LILLYQUIST, T. D. "The Effects of Age

594

Upon Retrieval from Short-Term Memory." *Developmental Psychology*, 1972, *6*, 214–217.

ANDERSON, J. E. "The Relation Between Adult Adjustment and Early Experience Over a Twenty-Eight-Year Interval." *American Psychologist*, 1960a, *15*, 385–386 (abstract).

ANDERSON, J. E. "Prediction of Adjustment Over Time." In I. Iscoe, and H. A. Stevenson (Eds.), *Personality Development in Children*. Austin: University of Texas Press, 1960b.

ANDERSON, J. E. "Aging and Educational Television: A Preliminary Survey." *Journal of Gerontology*, 1962, *17*, 447–449.

ANGYAL, A. *Foundations for a Science of Personality*. Cambridge, Mass.: Harvard University Press, 1941.

ANTHONY, E., and BENEDEK, T. (Eds.) *Parenthood, Its Psychology and Psychopathology*. Boston: Little, Brown, 1970.

ARENBERG, D. "Anticipation Interval and Age Differences in Verbal Learning." *Journal of Abnormal Psychology*, 1965, *70*, 419–425.

ARENBERG, D. "Regression Analysis of Verbal Learning on Adult Age at Two Anticipation Intervals." *Journal of Gerontology*, 1967a, *22*, 411–415.

ARENBERG, D. "Age Differences in Retroaction." *Journal of Gerontology*, 1967b, *22*, 88–91.

ARENBERG, D. "Concept Problem Solving in Young and Old Adults." *Journal of Gerontology*, 1968a, *23*, 279–282.

ARENBERG, D. "Input Modality in Short-Term Retention of Old and Young Adults." *Journal of Gerontology*, 1968b, *23*, 462–465.

ARENBERG, D. "Cognition and Aging: Verbal Learning, Memory, Problem Solving, and Aging." In C. Eisdorfer and M. P. Lawton (Eds.), *The Psychology of Adult Development and Aging*. Washington, D.C.: American Psychological Association, 1973.

ARENBERG, D. "A Longitudinal Study of Problem Solving in Adults." *Journal of Gerontology*, 1974, *29*, 650–658.

ARGYRIS, C. *Integrating the Individual and the Organization*. New York: Wiley, 1964.

ARGYRIS, C., and SCHÖN, D. A. *Theory in Practice: Increasing Professional Effectiveness*. San Francisco: Jossey-Bass, 1967.

ARIETI, S. "Creativity and Its Cultivation." In S. Arieti (Ed.), *Handbook of Psychiatry*. Vol. 3. New York: Basic Books, 1966.

ARIETI, S. *The Intrapsychic Self*. New York: Basic Books, 1967.

ARIETI, S. *The Will To Be Human*. New York: Quadrangle Books, 1972.

ARLIN, P. K. "Cognitive Development in Adulthood: A Fifth Stage?" *Developmental Psychology*, 1975, *11*, 602–606.

ARNHOFF, F. N. "Adult Age Differences in Performances on a Visual-

Spatial Task of Stimulus Generalization." *Journal of Educational Psychology*, 1959, *50*, 259–265.

ARNOTT, C. "Husbands' Attitudes and Wives' Commitment to Employment." *Journal of Marriage and Family*, 1972, *34* (4), 673–684.

ARONOFF, C. "Old Age in Prime Time." *Journal of Communication*, 1974, *24* (4), 86–87.

ASTIN, H. S., and MYINT, T. "Career Development of Young Women During Post-High School Years." *Journal of Counseling Psychology*, 1971, *18*, 369–393.

ASTRAND, P. O. "Human Physical Fitness with Special Reference to Sex and Age." *Physiological Reviews*, 1956, *36*, 307–329.

ASTRAND, P. O. "Physical Performance as a Function of Age." *Journal of the American Medical Association*, 1968, *205*, 105–109.

ATCHLEY, R. C. *The Social Forces in Later Life: An Introduction to Social Gerontology*. Belmont, Calif.: Wadsworth, 1972.

ATCHLEY, R. C. *The Sociology of Retirement*. Cambridge, Mass.: Schenkman, 1975.

AXELROD, M. "Urban Structure and Social Participation." *American Sociological Review*, 1956, *21*, 13–15.

AXELROD, S., and EISDORFER, C. "Attitudes Toward Old People: An Empirical Analysis of the Stimulus Group Validity of the Tuckman-Lorge Questionnaire." *Journal of Gerontology*, 1961, *16*, 75–80.

BABCHUCK, N. "Primary Friends and Kin: A Study of the Associations of Middle-Class Couples." *Social Forces*, 1965, *43*, 483–493.

BABCHUCK, N., and BATES, A. P. "The Primary Relations of Middle-Class Couples: A Study in Male Dominance." *American Sociological Review*, 1963, *28*, 377–384.

BACK, K. W. "Transition to Aging and the Self-Image." *Aging and Human Development*, 1971, *2*, 296–304.

BAILEY, J. O. "The Work Trial Method of Vocational Evaluation." *Journal of Rehabilitation*, 1958, *24* (1), 12–14.

BAILYN, L. "Psychology of Professional Women." In R. J. Lifton (Ed.), *The Woman in America*. Boston: Beacon Press, 1964.

BAILYN, L. "Career and Family Orientation of Husbands and Wives in Relation to Mental Happiness." *Human Relations*, 1970, *23*, 97–113.

BALINSKY, B. "An Analysis of the Mental Factors of Various Age Groups From Nine to Sixty." *Genetic Psychology Monographs*, 1941, *23*, 191–234.

BALLER, W. R., CHARLES, D. C., and MILLER, E. L. "Mid-Life Attainment of the Mentally Retarded: A Longitudinal Study." *Genetic Psychology Monographs*, 1967, *75*, 235–329.

BALTES, P. B. "Longitudinal and Cross-Sectional Sequences in the

Study of Age and Generation Effects." *Human Development,* 1968, *11,* 145–171.

BALTES, P. B., and GOULET, L. R. "Status and Issues of a Life-Span Developmental Psychology." In L. R. Goulet and P. B. Baltes (Eds.), *Life-Span Developmental Psychology: Research and Theory.* New York: Academic Press, 1970.

BALTES, P. B., and SCHAIE, K. W. (Eds.) *Life-Span Developmental Psychology: Personality and Socialization.* New York: Academic Press, 1973.

BALTES, P. B., SCHAIE, K. W., and NARDI, A. H. "Age and Experimental Mortality in a Seven-Year Longitudinal Study of Cognitive Behavior." *Developmental Psychology,* 1971, *5,* 18–26.

BARDWICK, J. M. *Psychology of Women.* New York: Harper & Row, 1971.

BARDWICK, J. M. "The Dynamics of Successful People." *New Research on Women.* Ann Arbor: University of Michigan, 1974.

BARFIELD, R., and MORGAN, J. *Early Retirement: The Decision and the Experience.* Ann Arbor: Institute for Social Research, University of Michigan, 1969.

BARKER, R. G. *Ecological Psychology.* Stanford, Calif.: Stanford University Press, 1968.

BARKER, R. G., and SCHOGGEN, P. *Qualities of Community Life.* San Francisco: Jossey-Bass, 1973.

BARRESI, C. "The Meaning of Work: A Case Study of the Elderly Poor." *Industrial Gerontology,* 1974, *1,* 25–34.

BARRON, F. *Creativity and Psychological Health.* Princeton: Van Nostrand, 1963.

BARROWS, C. H., JR. "The Challenge—Mechanisms of Biological Aging." *The Gerontologist,* 1971, *11* (1), 5–11.

BARUCH, R. "The Achievement Motive in Women: Implications for Career Development." *Journal of Personality and Social Psychology,* 1967, *5,* 260–267.

BATH, J. A., and LEWIS, E. C. "Attitudes of Young Females Toward Some Areas of Parent-Adolescent Conflict." *Journal of Genetic Psychology,* 1962, *100,* 241–253.

BAYLEY, N., and ODEN, M. H. "The Maintenance of Intellectual Ability in Gifted Adults." *Journal of Gerontology,* 1955, *10,* 91–107.

BEAL, G. M., and ROGERS, E. M. "Informational Sources in the Adoption Process of New Fabrics." *Journal of Home Economics,* 1960, *49,* 630–634.

BECKER, H. S., GEER, B., HUGHES, E., and STRAUSS, A. *Boys in White: Student Culture in Medical School.* Chicago: University of Chicago Press, 1961.

BECKER, H. S., and STRAUSS, A. L. "Careers, Personality, and Adult

Socialization." *American Journal of Sociology,* 1956, *62,* 253–256.

BEISER, M. "A Study of Personality Assets in a Rural Community." *Archives of General Psychiatry,* 1971, *24,* 244–254.

BEKKER, L. D., and TAYLOR, C. "Attitudes Toward the Aged in a Multi-generational Sample." *Journal of Gerontology,* 1966, *21,* 115–118.

BELASCO, J. A., and TRICE, H. M. *The Assessment of Change in Training and Therapy.* New York: McGraw-Hill, 1969.

BELBIN, E., and BELBIN, R. M. "New Careers in Middle Age." In B. Neugarten (Ed.), *Middle Age and Aging.* Chicago: University of Chicago Press, 1968.

BELBIN, E., and BELBIN, R. M. *Problems in Adult Retraining.* London: Heinemann, 1972.

BELBIN, R. M. "Retirement Strategy in an Evolving Society." In F. Carp (Ed.), *Retirement.* New York: Behavioral Publications, 1972.

BELL, A. B. "Role Models of Young Adulthood: Their Relationship to Occupational Behaviors." *Vocational Guidance Quarterly,* 1970, *18,* 280–284.

BELL, B., WOLF, E., and BERNHOLZ, C. D. "Depth Perception as a Function of Age." *Aging and Human Development,* 1972, *3,* 77–82.

BELL, H. M. "Ego-Involvement in Occupational Decisions." *Personnel and Guidance Journal,* 1960, *38,* 732–736.

BELL, R. R., and BLUMBERG, L. "Courtship Stages and Intimacy Attitudes." *Family Life Coordinator,* 1960, *8,* 61–63.

BELL, R. R., and CHASKES, J. B. "Premarital Sexual Experience Among Coeds, 1958 and 1968." *Journal of Marriage and the Family,* 1970, *32,* 81–84.

BELL, W., and FORCE, M. T. "Urban Neighborhood Types and Participation in Formal Associations." *American Sociological Review,* 1956, *21,* 25–34.

BELLAH, R. N. "To Kill and Survive or To Die and Become: The Active Life and the Contemplative Life As Ways of Being Adult." *Daedalus,* 1976, *105* (Spring).

BENAIM, S., and ALLEN, I. (Eds.) *The Middle Years.* London: T. V. Publications, 1967.

BENGSTON, V. L. "The Generation Gap: A Review and Typology of Social-Psychological Perspectives." *Youth and Society,* 1970, *2,* 7–32.

BENGSTON, V. L. *The Social Psychology of Aging.* Indianapolis: Bobbs-Merrill, 1973.

BENNETT, R. "Distinguishing Characteristics of the Aging from a

Sociological Viewpoint." *Journal of American Geriatric Society,* 1968, *16,* 127–135.

BERARDO, F. M. "Survivorship and Social Isolation: The Case of the Aged Widower." *The Family Coordinator,* 1970, *19,* 11–25.

BERESFORD, J. C., and RIVLIN, A. M. *The Multigeneration Family. Occasional Papers in Gerontology,* vol. 3. Ann Arbor and Detroit: Institute of Gerontology, University of Michigan and Wayne State University, 1969.

BERGER, B. M. "The Myth of Suburbia." *Journal of Social Forces,* 1961, *17* (1), 38–49.

BERGMAN, M. "Changes in Hearing with Age." *The Gerontologist,* 1971, *11* (2), 148–151.

BERNARD, J. *Remarriage: A Study of Marriage.* New York: Holt, Rinehart and Winston, 1956.

BERNARD, J. *Marriage and Family Among Negroes.* Englewood Cliffs, N.J.: Prentice-Hall, 1966.

BERNARD, J. *The Future of Marriage.* New York: World, 1973.

BEVERLEY, E. V. "Turning the Realities of Retirement Into Fulfillment." *Geriatrics,* 1975, *30* (1), 126–139.

BIERI, J. "Cognitive Complexity-Simplicity and Predictive Behavior." *Journal of Abnormal and Social Psychology,* 1955, *51,* 263–268.

BIERI, J. "Complexity-Simplicity as a Personality Variable in Cognitive and Preferential Behavior." In D. W. Fiske and S. Maddi (Eds.), *Functions of Varied Experience.* Homewood, Ill.: Dorsey, 1961.

BIERI, J., ATKINS, A. L., SCOTT, B., LEAMAN, R. L., MILLER, H., and TRIPODI, T. *Clinical and Social Judgment: The Discrimination of Behavioral Information.* New York: Wiley, 1966.

BIGGS, D. *Breaking Out.* New York: McKay, 1973.

BILLIG, O., and ADAMS, R. W. "Emotional Conflicts of the Middle-Aged Man." In C. B. Vedder (Ed.), *Problems of the Middle-Aged.* Springfield, Ill.: Thomas, 1965.

BIRREN, J. E. *The Psychology of Aging.* Englewood Cliffs, N.J.: Prentice-Hall, 1964a.

BIRREN, J. E. (Ed.) *Relations of Development and Aging.* Springfield, Ill.: Thomas, 1964b.

BIRREN, J. E., BICK, M. W., and FOX, C. "Age Changes in the Light Threshold of the Dark Adapted Eye." *Journal of Gerontology,* 1948, *3,* 267–271.

BIRREN, J. E., BUTLER, R. W., GREENHOUSE, S. W., SOKOLOFF, L., and YARROW, M. R. (Eds.) *Human Aging: A Biological and Behavioral Study.* Washington, D.C.: U. S. Government Printing Office, 1963.

BIRREN, J. E., CASPERSON, R. C., and BOTWINICK, J. "Age Changes in Pupil Size." *Journal of Gerontology*, 1950, *5*, 216–221.

BIRREN, J. E., and MORRISON, D. F. "Analysis of the WAIS Subtests in Relation to Age and Education." *Journal of Gerontology*, 1961, *16*, 363–369.

BLANCK, G., and BLANCK, R. *Ego Psychology: Theory and Practice.* New York: Columbia University Press, 1974.

BLANCK, R., and BLANCK, G. *Marriage and Personal Development.* New York: Columbia University Press, 1968.

BLENKER, M., BLOOM, M., and NIELSON, M. "A Research and Demonstration Project of Protective Services." *Social Casework*, 1971, *52*, 483–499.

BLOCK, J., and HAAN, N. *Lives Through Time.* Berkeley, Calif.: Bancroft Books, 1971.

BLOOD, M. R., and HULIN, C. L. "Alienation, Environmental Charteristics, and Worker Responses." *Journal of Applied Psychology*, 1967, *51* (3), 284–290.

BLOOD, R. O., and HAMBLIN, R. L. "The Effect of the Wife's Employment on the Family Power Structure." *Social Forces*, 1958, *36*, 347–352.

BLOOD, R. O., and WOLFE, D. M. *Husbands and Wives.* New York: Free Press, 1960.

BLOOM, B. S. *Stability and Change in Human Characteristics.* New York: Wiley, 1964.

BLUM, J. E., CLARK, E. T., and JARVIK, L. F. "The New York State Psychiatric Institute Study of Aging Twins." In L. F. Jarvik, C. Eisdorfer, and J. Blum (Eds.), *Intellectual Functioning in Adults.* New York: Springer, 1973.

BLUM, J. E., FOSSHAGE, J. L., and JARVIK, L. F. "Intellectual Changes and Sex Differences in Octogenarians: A Twenty-Year Longitudinal Study of Aging." *Developmental Psychology*, 1972, *7*, 178–187.

BLUM, J. E., and JARVIK, L. F. "Intellectual Performance of Octogenarians as a Function of Educational and Initial Ability." *Human Development*, 1974, *17*, 364–375.

BLUM, J. E., JARVIK, L. F., and CLARK, E. T. "Rate of Change on Selective Tests of Intelligence: A Twenty-Year Longitudinal Study of Aging." *Journal of Gerontology*, 1970, *25*, 171–176.

BLUMENTHAL, H. T. *The Regulatory Role of the Nervous System in Aging. Interdisciplinary Topics in Gerontology*, vol. 7. New York: Karger, 1970.

BOLLES, R. N. *What Color Is Your Parachute? A Practical Manual for Job-Hunters and Career Changers.* Rev. ed. Berkeley, Calif.: Ten Speed Press, 1972.

BORTNER, R. W., and HULTSCH, D. F. "A Multivariate Analysis of

Correlates of Life Satisfaction in Adulthood." *Journal of Gerontology,* 1970, *25* (1) , 41–47.

BORTNER, R. W., and HULTSCH, D. F. "Personal Time Perspective in Adulthood." *Developmental Psychology,* 1972, *7,* 98–103.

BOSHIER, R. "Conservatism Within Families: A Study of the Generation Gap." In G. D. Wilson (Ed.) , *The Psychology of Conservatism.* London: Academic Press, 1973.

BOSHIER, R., and THOM, E. "Do Conservative Parents Nurture Conservative Children?" *Social Behavior and Personality,* 1973, *1,* 108–110.

BOSSARD, J. H. "Marrying Late in Life." *Social Forces,* 1951, *29,* 405–408.

BOSSARD, J. H., and BOLL, E. S. "Marital Unhappiness in the Life Cycle." *Marriage and Family Living,* 1955, *17,* 10–14.

BOSSARD, J. H., and BOLL, E. S. *The Sociology of Child Development.* 4th ed. New York: Harper & Row, 1966.

BOTWINICK, J. "Theories of Antecedent Conditions of Speed of Response." In A. T. Welford and J. E. Birren (Eds.) , *Behavior, Aging and the Nervous System.* Springfield, Ill.: Thomas, 1965.

BOTWINICK, J. *Cognitive Processes in Maturity and Old Age.* New York: Springer, 1967.

BOTWINICK, J. "Geropsychology." In P. H. Mussen, and M. R. Rosenzweig (Eds.) , *Annual Review of Psychology.* Palo Alto, Calif.: Annual Reviews, 1970.

BOTWINICK, J. *Aging and Behavior.* New York: Springer, 1973.

BOTWINICK, J. "Qualitative Vocabulary Response and Age." *Journal of Gerontology,* 1975, *30,* 574–577.

BOTWINICK, J., and THOMPSON, L. W. "Practice of Speeded Response in Relationship to Age, Sex, and Set." *Journal of Gerontology,* 1967, *22,* 72–77.

BOTWINICK, J., and THOMPSON, L. W. "Individual Differences in Reaction Time in Relation to Age." *Journal of Genetic Psychology,* 1968, *112,* 73–75.

BOWER, G. H. "Organizational Factors in Memory." *Cognitive Psychology,* 1970, *1,* 18–46.

BOWLBY, J. *Attachment and Loss.* Vol. 1. New York: Basic Books, 1969.

BOWMAN, H. A. *Marriage for Moderns.* 7th ed. New York: McGraw-Hill, 1974.

BOYD, R. D. "Basic Motivation of Adults in Non-Credit Programs." *Adult Education,* 1961, *11,* 92–98.

BOYD, R. D., and KOSKELA, R. "A Test of Erikson's Theory of Ego-Stage Development by Means of a Self-Report Instrument." *Journal of Experimental Education,* 1970, *38,* 1–14.

BRADBURN, N. M. *The Structure of Psychological Well-Being.* Chicago: Aldine, 1969.

BRADBURN, N. M., and CAPLOVITZ, D. *Reports on Happiness: A Pilot Study of Behavior Related to Mental Health.* Chicago: Aldine, 1965.

BRADFORD, L. P., GIBB, J. R., and BENNE, K. D. (Eds.) *T-Group Theory and Laboratory Method: Innovation in Re-Education.* New York: Wiley, 1964.

BRADWAY, K. P., and THOMPSON, C. W. "Intelligence at Adulthood: A 25-Year Follow-Up." *Journal of Educational Psychology,* 1962, *53,* 1–14.

BRANDEN, N. *Breaking Free.* New York: Bantam Books, 1972.

BREEN, L. Z., and SPAETH, J. L. "Age and Productivity Among Workers in Four Chicago Companies." *Journal of Gerontology,* 1960, *15,* 68–70.

BRIM, O. G. "Socialization through the Life Cycle." In O. B. Brim and S. Wheeler (Eds.), *Socialization After Childhood.* New York: Wiley, 1966.

BRIM, O. G. "Theories of the Male Mid-Life Crisis." *Counseling Psychologist,* 1976, *6,* 2–9.

BRINLEY, J. F., and BOTWINICK, J. "Preparation Time and Choice in Relation to Age Differences in Response Speed." *Journal of Gerontology,* 1959, *14,* 226–228.

BRINLEY, J. F., JOVICK, T. J., and MCLAUGHLIN, L. M. "Age, Reasoning, and Memory in Adults." *Journal of Gerontology,* 1974, *29,* 182–189.

BRITTON, J. H. "Dimensions of Adjustment of Older Adults." *Journal of Gerontology,* 1963, *18,* 60–65.

BRITTON, J. H., and BRITTON, J. O. *Personality Changes in Aging.* New York: Springer, 1972.

BROMLEY, D. B. "Some Experimental Tests of the Effect of Age on Creative Intellectual Output." *Journal of Gerontology,* 1956, *11,* 74–82.

BROMLEY, D. B. "Some Effects of Age on Short-Term Learning and Remembering." *Journal of Gerontology,* 1958, *13,* 398–406.

BROMLEY, D. B. *The Psychology of Human Aging.* Baltimore: Penguin, 1966.

BROTMAN, H. B. *Facts and Figures on Older Americans.* Washington, D.C.: Department of Health, Education, and Welfare, 1972.

BROWN, M., KNOX, A. B., and GROTELUESCHEN, A. "Persistence in University Adult Education Classes." *Adult Education,* 1966, *16,* 101–114.

BROWNE, H. *How I Found Freedom in an Unfree World.* New York: Macmillan, 1973.

BROZEK, J. "Personality of Young and Middle Age Normal Men: Item Analysis of a Psychosomatic Inventory." *Journal of Gerontology,* 1952, *7,* 410–418.

BRUNER, J. S., and TAJFEL, H. "Cognitive Risk and Environmental Change." *Journal of Abnormal and Social Psychology,* 1961, *62,* 231–241.

BUGENTAL, J. F. T. (Ed.) *Challenges of Humanistic Psychology.* New York: McGraw-Hill, 1967.

BUHLER, C., and MASSARIK, F. (Ed.) *The Course of Human Life.* New York: Springer, 1968.

BULTENA, G. L., and WOOD, V. "The American Retirement Community: Bane or Blessing?" *Journal of Gerontology,* 1969, *24,* 209–217.

BURCHINAL, L. M. "Some Social Status Criteria and Church Membership and Church Attendance." *Journal of Social Psychology,* 1959, *49,* 53–64.

BURCHINAL, L. G. "Trends and Prospects for Young Marriages in the United States." *Journal of Marriage and the Family,* 1965, *27,* 243–254.

BURGESS, E. W. (Ed.) *Aging in Western Societies.* Chicago: University of Chicago Press, 1960.

BURKETT, J. "Comprehensive Programming for Life-Long Learning." *Adult Education,* 1960, *10,* 116–121.

BURNS, R. B. "Age and Mental Ability: Re-Testing with Thirty-Three Years Interval." *British Journal of Educational Psychology,* 1966, *36,* 116.

BURNSIDE, I. M. "Group Work with the Aged: Selected Literature." *Gerontologist,* 1970, *10,* 241–246.

BURR, W. R. "Satisfaction with Various Aspects of Marriage over the Life Cycle: A Random Middle Class Sample." *Journal of Marriage and the Family,* 1970, *32,* 29–37.

BURR, W. R. "Role Transitions: A Reformulation of Theory." *Journal of Marriage and the Family,* 1972, *34,* 407–416.

BUSSE, E. W. "The Treatment of Hypochondriasis." *Tri-State Medical Journal,* 1954, *2,* 7–12.

BUSSE, E. W. "Theories of Aging." In E. W. Busse and E. Pfeiffer (Eds.), *Behavior and Adaptation in Late Life.* Boston: Little, Brown, 1969.

BUTLER, R. N. "The Life Review: An Interpretation of Reminiscence in the Aged." *Psychiatry,* 1963, *26,* 65–76.

BUTLER, R. N. *Why Survive? Being Old in America.* New York: Harper & Row, 1975.

CAIRD, W. K. "Aging and Short Term Memory." *Journal of Gerontology,* 1966, *21,* 295–300.

CAMERON, N. "Acute and Chronic Brain Disorders." In N. Cameron, *Personality Development and Psychopathology*. Boston: Houghton Mifflin, 1963.

CAMERON, P. "The Life Force and Age." *Journal of Gerontology*, 1969a, *24*, 199–200.

CAMERON, P. "Age Parameters of Young Adult, Middle-Aged, Old, and Aged." *Journal of Gerontology*, 1969b, *24*, 201–202.

CAMERON, P. "The Generation Gap: Beliefs about Adult Stability of Life." *Journal of Gerontology*, 1971, *26*, 81.

CAMPBELL, A., and CONVERSE, P. *Monitoring the Perceived Quality of Life*. New York: Russell Sage Foundation, 1975.

CAMPBELL, D. P. "A Cross-Sectional and Longitudinal Study of Scholastic Abilities over Twenty-Five Years." *Journal of Counseling Psychology*, 1965a, *12*, 55–61.

CAMPBELL, D. P. *The Results of Counseling: Twenty-Five Years Later*. Philadelphia: Saunders, 1965b.

CAMPBELL, D. P. *Handbook for the Strong Vocational Interest Blank*. Stanford, Calif.: Stanford University Press, 1971.

CANESTRARI, R. E. "Paced and Self-Paced Learning in Young and Elderly Adults." *Journal of Gerontology*, 1963, *18*, 165–168.

CANESTRARI, R. E. "The Effects of Commonality on Paired-Associate Learning in Two Age Groups." *Journal of Genetic Psychology*, 1966, *108*, 3–7.

CANESTRARI, R. E. "Research in Learning." *Gerontologist*, 1967, *7*, 61–66.

CANESTRARI, R. E. "Age Differences in Verbal Learning and Verbal Behavior." In S. Chown and K. F. Riegel (Eds.), *Interdisciplinary Topics in Gerontology*. Vol. 1. Basel, Switzerland: Karger, 1968.

CANTRIL, H. *The Pattern of Human Concerns*. New Brunswick, N.J.: Rutgers University Press, 1965.

CARAI, J. E. "Sex Differences in Mental Health." *Genetic Psychology Monographs*, 1970, *81*, 123–143.

CARLSON, R., and LEVY, N. "Brief Method for Assessing Social-Personal Orientation." *Psychological Reports*, 1968, *23*, 911–914.

CARLSON, R., and PRICE, M. A. "Generality of Social Schemas." *Journal of Personality and Social Psychology*, 1966, *3*, 589–592.

CARP, F. M. "Some Components of Disengagement." *Journal of Gerontology*, 1968, *23*, 382–386.

CARP, F. M. *The Retirement Process*. Washington, D.C.: U.S. Government Printing Office, 1969.

CARP, F. M. (Ed.) *Retirement*. New York: Behavioral Publications, 1972.

CARTER, H., and GLICK, P. C. *Marriage and Divorce: A Social and Eco-*

nomic Study. Cambridge, Mass.: Harvard University Press, 1970.

CASE, H. W., HULBERT, S., and BEERS, J. *Driving Ability As Affected by Age* (Report 70–18). Los Angeles: Institute of Transportation and Traffic Engineering, UCLA, 1970.

CATTELL, R. B. "Theory of Fluid and Crystallized Intelligence: A Critical Experiment." *Journal of Educational Psychology,* 1963, *54,* 1–22.

CATTELL, R. B. (Ed.) *Handbook of Multivariate Experimental Psychology.* Chicago: Rand McNally, 1966.

CATTELL, R. B. "Fluid and Crystallized Intelligence." *Psychology Today,* 1968, *3,* 56–62.

CATTELL, R. B. *Abilities: Their Structure, Growth, and Action.* Boston: Houghton Mifflin, 1971.

CATTELL, R. B. *Personality and Mood by Questionnaire.* San Francisco: Jossey-Bass, 1973.

CAUTELA, J. "A Classical Conditioning Approach to the Development and Modification of Behavior in the Aged." *The Gerontologist,* 1969, *9,* 109–113.

CAVAN, R. S. *The American Family.* 3rd ed. New York: Crowell, 1963.

CAVAN, R. S. "Family Tensions between the Old and the Middle-Aged." In C. B. Vedder (Ed.), *Problems of the Middle-Aged.* Springfield, Ill.: Thomas, 1965.

CAVAN, R. S., BURGESS, E. W., HAVIGHURST, R. J., and GOLDHAMER, H. *Personal Adjustment in Old Age.* Chicago: Science Research Associates, 1949.

CHARNEY, I. *Marital Love and Hate.* New York: Macmillan, 1972.

CHICKERING, A. W. *Education and Identity.* San Francisco: Jossey-Bass, 1969.

CHILMAN, C. S., and MEYER, D. L. "Single and Married Undergraduates' Measured Personality Needs and Self-Rated Happiness." *Journal of Marriage and the Family,* 1966, *28,* 67–76.

CHINOY, E. *Automobile Workers and the American Dream.* New York: Doubleday, 1955.

CHISHOLM, B. *Can People Learn to Learn?* New York: Harper & Row, 1958.

CHOWN, S. M. "Age and the Rigidities." *Journal of Gerontology,* 1961, *16,* 353–362.

CHOWN, S. M. "The Effect of Flexibility-Rigidity and Age on Adaptability in Job Performance." *Industrial Gerontology,* 1972, *13,* 105–121.

CHOWN, S. M., and HERON, A. "Psychological Aspects of Aging in Man." In P. R. Farnsworth, O. McNemar and Q. McNemar (Eds.), *Annual Review of Psychology.* Palo Alto, Calif.: Annual Reviews, 1965.

CHRISTENSEN, H. T. "Timing of First Pregnancy as a Factor in Divorce: A Cross-Cultural Analysis." *Eugenics Quarterly*, 1963, *10*, 119–130.

CHRISTENSEN, H. T., and SWIHART, M. M. "Postgraduate Role Preferences of Senior Women in College." *Marriage and Family Living*, 1956, *18*, 52–57.

CHRISTENSON, C. V., and GAGNON, J. H. "Sexual Behavior in a Group of Older Women." *Journal of Gerontology*, 1965, *20*, 351–356.

CLARK, A. L., and WALLIN, P. "Women's Sexual Responsiveness and the Duration and Quality of Their Marriages." *American Journal of Sociology*, 1965, *71*, 187–196.

CLARK, L. E., and KNOWLES, J. B. "Age Differences in Dichotic Listening Performance." *Journal of Gerontology*, 1973, *28*, 173–178.

CLARK, M., and ANDERSON, B. G. *Culture and Aging: An Anthropological Study of Older Americans.* Springfield, Ill.: Thomas, 1967.

CLAUSEN, J. A. "The Life-Course of Individuals." In M. W. Riley, M. Johnson and others (Eds.), *A Sociology of Age Stratification.* New York: Russell Sage Foundation, 1972.

CLAY, H. M. "Changes in Performance with Age in Similar Tasks of Varying Complexity." *British Journal of Psychology*, 1954, *45*, 7–13.

CLAY, H. M. "An Age Difficulty in Separating Spatially Contiguous Data." *Journal of Gerontology*, 1956, *11*, 318–322.

CLIFFORD, E. "Expressed Attitudes on Pregnancy of Unwed Women and Married Primigravida and Multigravida." *Child Development*, 1962, *33*, 945–951.

CLINE, V. B., and RICHARDS, J. M. "A Factor-Analytic Study of Religious Belief and Behavior." *Journal of Personality and Social Psychology*, 1965, *1*, 569–578.

CLINEBELL, H. J., and CLINEBELL, C. H. *The Intimate Marriage.* New York: Harper & Row, 1970.

CLOPTON, W. "Personality and Career Change." *Industrial Gerontology*, 1973, *17*, 9–17.

COAN, R. W. *The Optimal Personality: An Empirical and Theoretical Analysis.* New York: Columbia University Press, 1974.

COFER, C. N. *Motivation and Emotion.* Glenview, Ill.: Scott, Foresman, 1972.

COHEN, J. "A Comparative Factor Analysis of WAIS Performance for Four Age Groups Between Eighteen and Eighty." *American Psychologist*, 1956, *11*, 449.

COHEN, J. "The Factorial Structure of the WAIS Between Early Adulthood and Old Age." *Journal of Consulting Psychology*, 1957, *21*, 283–290.

COLE, S. *The Sociological Method.* Chicago: Markham, 1972.

COLEMAN, J. S. *The Adolescent Society.* New York: Free Press, 1961.

COLEMAN, J. S., KATZ, E., and MENZEL, H. "The Diffusion of an Innovation Among Physicians." *Sociometry,* 1957, *20,* 253–269.

COLLINS, T. *The Complete Guide to Retirement.* New Jersey: Prentice-Hall, 1970.

COOMBS, R. H. "Value Consensus and Partner Satisfaction Among Dating Couples." *Journal of Marriage and the Family,* 1966, *28,* 166–173.

COOPER, D. G. *The Death of the Family.* New York: Vintage, 1970.

CORAH, N. L. "Differentiation in Children and Their Parents." *Journal of Personality,* 1965, *33,* 300–308.

CORSO, J. F. "Age and Sex Differences in Pure Tone Thresholds." *Journal of the Acoustical Society of America,* 1958, *31,* 498–507.

CORSO, J. F. "Sensory Processes and Age Effects in Normal Adults." *Journal of Gerontology,* 1971, *26,* 90–105.

COULDING, R. "New Directions in Transactional Analysis: Creating an Environment for Redecision and Change." In C. J. Sager and H. S. Kaplan (Eds.), *Progress in Group and Family Therapy.* New York: Bruner-Mazel, 1972.

COUNSELING PSYCHOLOGIST, 1976, *6* (1), Special Issue on Counseling Adults.

CRAIK, F. I. M. "Short-Term Memory and the Aging Process." In G. A. Talland (Ed.), *Human Aging and Behavior.* New York: Academic Press, 1968.

CRITES, J. O. *Vocational Psychology.* New York: McGraw-Hill, 1969.

CRONBACH, L. J. "Beyond the Two Disciplines of Scientific Psychology." *American Psychologist,* 1975, *30* (2), 116–127.

CROSBY, J. F. *Illusion and Disillusion: The Self in Love and Marriage.* Belmont, Calif.: Wadsworth, 1973.

CROVITZ, E. "Reversing a Learning Deficit in the Aged." *Journal of Gerontology,* 1966, *21,* 236–239.

CRYNS, A. G., and MONK, A. "Attitudes of the Aged Toward the Young: A Multivariate Study in Intergenerational Perception." *Journal of Gerontology,* 1972, *27,* 107–112.

CUBER, J. F., and HARROFF, P. B. *The Significant Americans.* New York: Appleton-Century-Crofts, 1965.

CUMMING, E. "Further Thoughts on the Theory of Disengagement." *International Social Science Journal,* 1963, *15,* 337–393.

CUMMING, E., and HENRY, W. E. *Growing Old: The Process of Disengagement.* New York: Basic Books, 1961.

CUNNINGHAM, W. R., and JOHANNIS, T. B. "Research on the Family and Leisure: A Review and Critique of Selected Studies." *Family Life Coordinator,* 1960, *9,* 25–32.

CUNNINGHAM, W. R., and BIRREN, J. E. "Age Changes in Human

Abilities: A 28-Year Longitudinal Study." *Developmental Psychology*, 1976, *12* (1), 81–82.

CUNNINGHAM, W. R., CLAYTON, V., and OVERTON, W. "Fluid and Crystallized Intelligence in Young Adulthood and Old Age." *Journal of Gerontology*, 1975, *30* (1), 53–55.

CURTIS, H. J. *Biological Mechanisms of Aging*. Springfield, Ill.: Thomas, 1962.

CUTRIGHT, P. "Income and Family Events: Marital Stability." *Journal of Marriage and the Family*, 1971, *33* (2), 291–305.

DAEDALUS, 1976, *105*. Special Issue on Adulthood.

DALTON, G. W., and THOMPSON, P. H. "Accelerating Obsolescence of Older Engineers." *Harvard Business Review*, 1971, *49* (5), 57–67.

DAME, N. G., and others. "The Effect on the Marital Relationship of the Wife's Search for Identity." *Family Life Coordinator*, 1965, *14*, 133–136.

DANSEREAU, H. K. "Work and the Teenager." *Annals of the American Academy of Political and Social Science*, 1961, *338*, 44–52.

DAVIES, A. D. "The Perceptual Maze Test in a Normal Population." *Perceptual and Motor Skills*, 1965, *20*, 287–293.

DAVIS, J. K. *Concept Identification as a Function of Cognitive Style, Complexity, and Training Procedures*. Technical Report No. 32. Madison: Wisconsin Research and Development Center for Cognitive Learning, University of Wisconsin, 1967.

DEAUX, K. K. "Honking at the Intersection: A Replication and Extension." *Journal of Social Psychology*, 1971, *84*, 159–160.

DE LA MARE, G., and SERGEAN, R. "Two Methods of Studying Changes in Absence with Age." *Occupational Psychology*, 1961, *35*, 245–252.

DE LISSOVOY, V. "High School Marriages: A Longitudinal Study." *Journal of Marriage and the Family*, 1973, *35*, 245–255.

DEMOTT, B. *Surviving the 70's*. New York: Dutton, 1971.

DENNIS, W. "Creative Productivity between the Ages of 20 and 80 Years." *Journal of Gerontology*, 1966, *21*, 1–8.

DESPERT, J. L. *Children of Divorce*. Garden City, N.Y.: Doubleday, 1953.

DEUTSCHER, I. "The Quality of Postparental Life: Definitions of the Situation." *Journal of Marriage and the Family*, 1964, *26*, 52–59.

DEVRIES, H. A. *Physiology of Exercise*. 2nd ed. Dubuque, Iowa: Wm. C. Brown, 1974.

DICAPRIO, N. S. *Personality Theories: Guides to Living*. Philadelphia: Saunders, 1974.

DISTEFANO, M. K. "Changes in Work Related Attitudes with Age." *The Journal of Genetic Psychology*, 1969, *114*, 127–144.

DOHRENWEND, B. S. "Life Events as Stressors: A Methodological Inquiry." *Journal of Health and Social Behavior*, 1973, *14*, 167–175.

DOHRENWEND, B. P., and CHIN-SHONG, E. "Social Status and Attitudes toward Psychological Disorder: The Problem of Tolerance of Deviance." *American Sociological Review*, 1967, *32*, 417–433.

DOHRENWEND, B. P., and DOHRENWEND, B. S. *Social Status and Psychological Disorder: A Causal Inquiry.* New York: Wiley, 1969.

DONALD, M. N., and HAVIGHURST, R. J. "The Meaning of Leisure." *Social Forces*, 1959, *37*, 355–360.

DOPPELT, J. E., and WALLACE, W. L. "Standardization of the Wechsler Adult Intelligence Scale for Older Persons." *Journal of Abnormal and Social Psychology*, 1955, *51*, 312–330.

DOTY, C. N., and HOEFLIN, R. M. "A Descriptive Study of Thirty-Five Unmarried Graduate Women." *Journal of Marriage and the Family*, 1964, *26*, 91–94.

DROEGE, R. C. "Effects of Aptitude-Score Adjustments by Age Curves on Prediction of Job Performance." *Journal of Applied Psychology*, 1967, *51* (2), 181–186.

DROEGE, R. C., CRAMBERT, A. C., and HENKIN, J. B. "Relationship between GATB Aptitude Scores and Age for Adults." *Personnel and Guidance Journal*, 1963, *41*, 502–508.

DUBIN, S. S. "Obsolescence or Life-Long Education: A Choice for the Professional." *American Psychologist*, 1972, *27*, 486–498.

DUBLIN, L. I. *Suicide.* New York: Ronald Press, 1963.

DUNCAN, C. B. "A Reputation Test of Personality Integration." *Journal of Personality and Social Psychology*, 1966, *3*, 516–524.

DUVALL, E. M. *Family Development.* 4th ed. Philadelphia: Lippincott, 1971.

ECKLAND, B. K. "Social Class and College Graduation: Some Misconceptions Corrected." *American Journal of Sociology*, 1964a, *70*, 36–50.

ECKLAND, B. K. "A Source of Error in College Attrition Studies." *Sociology of Education*, 1964b, *38*, 60–72.

ECKLAND, B. K. "Retrieving Mobile Cases in Longitudinal Surveys." *Public Opinion Quarterly*, 1968, *32*, 51–64.

EDWARDS, A. E. *Experimental Design in Psychological Research* (4th ed.). New York: Holt, Rinehart and Winston, 1971.

EDWARDS, A. E., and WINE, D. B. "Personality Changes with Age: Their Dependency on Concomitant Intellectual Decline." *Journal of Gerontology*, 1963, *18*, 182–189.

EHRLE, R. "Vocational Maturity, Vocational Evaluation, and Occupational Information." *The Vocational Guidance Quarterly,* 1970, *19,* 41–45.

EHRMANN, W. W. *Premarital Dating Behavior.* New York: Holt, Rinehart and Winston, 1959.

EISDORFER, C. "The WAIS Performance of the Aged: A Retest Evaluation." *Journal of Gerontology,* 1963, *18,* 169–172.

EISDORFER, C. "Intellectual and Cognitive Changes in the Aged." In E. W. Busse and E. Pfeiffer (Eds.), *Behavior and Adaptation in Late Life.* Boston: Little, Brown, 1969.

EISDORFER, C. "Adaptation to Loss of Work." In F. Carp (Ed.), *Retirement.* New York: Behavioral Publications, 1972.

EISDORFER, C., and LAWTON, M. P. *The Psychology of Adult Development and Aging.* Washington, D.C.: American Psychological Association, 1973.

EISNER, D. A. "Conservation Ability of Elderly Men Living in the Community and an Institution." *Psychological Reports,* 1975, *37,* 333–334.

ELDER, G. H. *Adolescent Socialization and Personality Development.* Chicago: Rand McNally, 1971.

ELDER, G. H. *Children of the Great Depression.* Chicago: University of Chicago Press, 1974.

ENNIS, P. M. *Adult Book Reading in the United States: A Preliminary Report.* National Opinion Research Center Report No. 105. Chicago: University of Chicago, 1965.

EPSTEIN, C. "Positive Effects of the Multiple Negative: Explaining the Success of Black Professional Women." *American Journal of Sociology,* 1973, *78* (4), 912–935.

EPSTEIN, J. *Divorced in America.* New York: E. P. Dutton, 1974.

ERIKSON, E. H. *Childhood and Society.* New York: Norton, 1950.

ERIKSON, E. H. "The Problem of Ego Identity." *Journal of the American Psychoanalytic Association,* 1956, *4,* 51–121.

ERIKSON, E. H. "Inner and Outer Space: Reflections in Womanhood." In N. W. Bell and E. F. Vogel (Eds.), *A Modern Introduction to the Family.* New York: Free Press, 1968.

ERIKSON, E. H. *Dimensions of a New Identity.* New York: Norton, 1974.

ERIKSON, E. H. *Life History and the Historical Moment.* New York: Norton, 1975.

ERIKSON, E. H. "Reflections on Dr. Borg's Life Cycle." *Daedalus,* Spring, 1976.

ESHLEMAN, J. R. *The Family.* Boston: Allyn and Bacon, 1974.

ESPENSCHADE, A., and MELENEY, H. E. "Motor Performances of Adolescent Boys and Girls of Today in Comparison with Those of 24 Years Ago." *Research Quarterly of the American Association for Health, Physical Education, and Recreation,* 1961, *32,* 186–189.

FAGAN, J., and SHEPHERD, I. L. (Eds.) *What Is Gestalt Therapy?* New York: Harper & Row, 1973.

FALK, L. L. "Occupational Satisfaction of Female College Graduates." *Journal of Marriage and the Family,* 1966, *28,* 177–185.

FARBER, B. *Mental Retardation: Its Social Concept and Social Consequences.* New York: Houghton Mifflin, 1968.

FARLEY, R., and HERMALIN, A. I. "Family Stability: A Comparison of Trends between Blacks and Whites." *American Sociological Review,* 1971, *36,* 1–17.

FARMER, H. "Helping Women to Resolve the Home-Career Conflict." *Personnel and Guidance Journal,* 1971, *49* (10), 795–801.

FARMER, H., and BOHN, M. "Home-Career Conflict Reduction and the Level of Career Interest in Women." *Journal of Counseling Psychology,* 1970, *17* (3), 228–232.

FARMER, M. L. *Counseling Services for Adults in Higher Education.* Metuchen, N.J.: Scarecrow Press, 1971.

FEATHERSTONE, M. S., and CUNNINGHAM, C. M. "Age of Manual Workers in Relation to Conditions and Demands of Work." *Occupational Psychology,* 1963, *37,* 197–208.

FEIFEL, H. "Attitudes Toward Death in Some Normal and Mentally Ill Populations." In H. Feifel (Ed.), *The Meaning of Death.* New York: McGraw-Hill, 1959.

FEINBERG, I. "Effects of Age on Human Sleep Patterns." In A. Kales (Ed.), *Sleep Physiology and Pathology.* Philadelphia: Lippincott, 1969.

FELDMAN, K. A., and NEWCOMB, T. M. *The Impact of College on Students.* San Francisco: Jossey-Bass, 1969.

FELKER, D. W. *Building Positive Self-Concepts.* Minneapolis, Minn.: Burgess, 1974.

FICHTER, J. H. "The Profile of Catholic Religious Life." *American Journal of Sociology,* 1952, *58,* 145–150.

FIELD, M. *The Aged, The Family, and The Community.* New York: Columbia University Press, 1972.

FILLENBAUM, G. G. "On the Relation Between Attitude to Work and Attitude to Retirement." *Journal of Gerontology,* 1971, *26* (2), 244–248.

FISHER, J., and PIERCE, R. C. "Dimensions of Intellectual Functioning of the Aged." *Journal of Gerontology,* 1967, *22,* 166–173.

FITTS, W. H. *Manual for the Tennessee Self Concept Scale.* Nashville, Tenn.: Counselor Recordings and Tests, 1965.

FITTS, W. H., STEWART, O. C., and WAGNER, M. K. *Three Studies of Self-*

Concept Change. Nashville: Nashville Mental Health Center Research Bulletin, No. 6, 1969.

FITTS, W. H. *The Self Concept and Performance*. Nashville, Tenn.: Dede Wallace Center, 1972.

FOSKETT, J. M. "Social Structure and Social Participation." *American Sociological Review*, 1955, *20*, 431–438.

FOSTER, J. "Creativity." *Educational Research*, 1973, *15*, 217–220.

FOULDS, G. A. "Mill Hill Vocabulary and Matrices." *American Journal of Psychology*, 1949, *62*, 238–246.

FOULDS, G. A., and RAVEN, J. C. "Neural Changes in Mental Abilities of Adults as Age Advances." *Journal of Mental Science*, 1948, *94*, 133–142.

FOX, C. "Vocabulary Abilities in Later Maturity." *Journal of Educational Psychology*, 1947, *38*, 484–492.

FOX, D. J. *The Research Process in Education*. New York: Holt, Rinehart and Winston, 1969.

FOZARD, J. L. "Predicting Age in the Adult Years from Psychological Assessments of Abilities and Personality." *Aging and Human Development*, 1972, *3* (2), 175–182.

FOZARD, J. L., and NUTTALL, R. L. "GATB Scores for Men Differing in Age and Socio-economic Status." *Journal of Applied Psychology*, 1971, *55* (4), 372–379.

FOZARD, J. L., NUTTALL, R. L., and WAUGH, N. C. "Age-Related Differences in Mental Performance." *Aging and Human Development*, 1972, *3*, 19–43.

FRANKL, V. E. *Man's Search for Meaning* (rev. ed.). Boston: Beacon Press, 1963.

FRANZBLAU, R. N. *The Middle Generation*. New York: Holt, Rinehart and Winston, 1971.

FREDERICK, W. C. *Information Processing and Concept Learning at Grades 6, 8, and 10 As a Function of Cognitive Style*. Madison: Wisconsin Research and Development Center for Cognitive Learning, University of Wisconsin, 1968.

FREEDMAN, M. B., and BEREITER, C. "A Longitudinal Study of Personality Development in College Alumnae." *Merrill-Palmer Quarterly*, 1963, *9*, 295–302.

FREEDMAN, R., and AXELROD, M. "Who Belongs to What in a Great Metropolis." *Adult Leadership*, 1952, *1*, 6–9.

FREEDMAN, R., and COMBS, L. "Child Spacing and Family Economic Position." *American Sociological Review*, 1966, *31*, 631–648.

FREEMAN, J. T. "Sexual Capacities in the Aging Male." *Geriatrics*, 1961, *16*, 37–43.

FREEMAN, R. *The Labor Market for College Trained Manpower*. Cambridge, Mass.: Harvard University Press, 1971.

FREEMAN, R. "Overinvestment in College Training." *Journal of Human Resources*, 1975, *10*, 287–311.

FREEMAN, R., and HOLLOMON, J. H. "The Declining Value of College Going." *Change*, September 1975, *7*, 24–31, 62.

FRIED, B. *The Middle-Age Crisis*. New York: Harper & Row, 1967.

FRIED, M. "Grieving for a Lost Home." In L. J. Duhl (Ed.), *The Urban Condition*. New York: Basic Books, 1963.

FRIED, M. *The World of the Urban Working Class*. Cambridge, Mass.: Harvard University Press, 1973.

FRIEDAN, B. *The Feminine Mystique*. New York: Dell, 1962.

FRIEDLANDER, F. "Relationships between the Importance and the Satisfaction of Various Environmental Factors." *Journal of Applied Psychology*, 1965, *49*, 160–164.

FRIEDMAN, M. *Touchstones of Reality*. New York: Dutton, 1972.

FRIEDMAN, M., and ROSENMAN, R. H. *Type A Behavior and Your Heart*. New York: Knopf, 1974.

FRIEDMANN, E., and HAVIGHURST, R. J. *The Meaning of Work and Retirement*. Chicago: University of Chicago Press, 1954.

FRIEND, C. M., and ZUBEK, J. P. "The Effects of Age on Critical Thinking." *Journal of Gerontology*, 1958, *13*, 407–413.

FUCH, V. "Women's Earnings: Recent Trends and Long-Run Prospects." *Monthly Labor Review*, 1974, *97*, 23–25.

FURRY, C. A., and BALTES, P. B. "The Effect of Age Differences in Ability: Extraneous Performance Variables in the Assessment of Intelligence in Children, Adults, and the Elderly." *Journal of Gerontology*, 1973, *28*, 73–80.

GAERTNER, S. L. "Helping Behavior and Racial Discrimination Among Liberals and Conservatives." *Journal of Personality and Social Psychology*, 1973, *25*, 335–341.

GAERTNER, S. L., and BICKERMAN, L. "Effects of Race on the Elicitation of Helping Behavior: The Wrong Number Technique." *Journal of Personality and Social Psychology*, 1971, *20*, 218–222.

GAGNÉ, R. M. "Contributions of Learning to Human Development." *Psychological Review*, 1968, *65*, 177–191.

GAGNÉ, R. M. *The Conditions of Learning*. Rev. ed. New York: Holt, Rinehart and Winston, 1972.

GARAI, J. E. "Sex Differences in Mental Health." *Genetic Psychology Monographs*, 1970, *81*, 123–143.

GARDNER, J. W. *Excellence*. New York: Harper & Row, 1961.

GARDNER, R. W. "Cognitive Control in Adaptation: Research and Measurement." In S. Messick and J. Ross (Eds.), *Measurement in Personality and Cognition*. New York: Wiley, 1962.

GARDNER, R. W. "The Development of Cognitive Structures." In

C. Scheerer (Ed.), *Cognition: Theory, Research, Promise.* New York: Harper & Row, 1964.

GARDNER, R. W., HOLZMANN, R. S., KLEIN, G. G., LINTON, H. B., and SPENCE, D. P. "Cognitive Control: A Study of Individual Consistencies in Cognitive Behavior." *Psychological Issues,* 1959, *1* (4).

GARDNER, R. W., JACKSON, D. N., and MESSICK, S. J. "Personality Organization in Cognitive Controls and Intellectual Abilities." *Psychological Issues,* 1960, *2* (4), 1–148.

GARDNER, R. W., and LONG, R. L. "Control, Defense, and Centration Effect: A Study of Scanning Behaviour." *British Journal of Psychology,* 1962, *53,* 129–140.

GARDNER, R. W., and SCHOEN, R. A. "Differentiation and Abstraction in Concept Formation." *Psychological Monographs,* 1962, *76* (41), 1–21.

GARVEY, R. "Self Concept and Success in Student Teaching." *Journal of Teacher Education,* 1970, *21* (3), 357–361.

GAYLOR, S. "Age Difference in the Speed of a Spatial Cognitive Process." *Journal of Gerontology,* 1975, *30,* 674–678.

GEBHARD, P. H. "Factors in Marital Orgasm." *Journal of Social Issues,* 1966, *22* (2), 88–95.

GELWICKS, L. E. "Home Range and Use of Space by an Aging Population." In L. A. Pastalan and D. H. Carson (Eds.), *Spatial Behavior of Older People.* Ann Arbor and Detroit: Institute of Gerontology, University of Michigan and Wayne State University, 1970.

GENDLIN, E. T. "A Theory of Personality Change." In P. Worchel and D. Byrne, *Personality Change.* New York: Wiley, 1964.

GERLACH, L. P., and HINE, V. H. *Lifeway Leap: The Dynamics of Change in America.* Minneapolis: University of Minnesota Press, 1973.

GHISELLI, E. E. "The Relationship between Intelligence and Age among Superior Adults." *Journal of Genetic Psychology,* 1957, *90,* 131–142.

GILBERT, J. C. "Age Changes in Color Matching." *Journal of Gerontology,* 1957, *12,* 210–215.

GINOTT, H. G. *Between Parent and Teenager.* New York: Macmillan, 1969.

GINZBERG, E., with BERG, I. E. *Life Styles of Educated Women.* New York: Columbia University Press, 1966.

GINZBERG, E., and YOHALEM, A. M. *Educated American Women: Life Styles and Self Portraits.* New York: Columbia University Press, 1966.

GLADIS, M., and BRAUN, H. W. "Age Differences in Transfer and Retroaction as a Function of Intertask Response Similarity." *Journal of Experimental Psychology*, 1958, *55*, 25–30.

GLANZER, M., and GLASER, R. "Cross-Sectional and Longitudinal Results in a Study of Age-Related Changes." *Educational and Psychological Measurement*, 1959, *19*, 89–101.

GLASER, B. G., and STRAUSS, A. L. *Awareness of Dying*. Chicago: Aldine, 1965. Entire issue.

GLASER, B. G., and STRAUSS, A. L. *The Discovery of Grounded Theory: Strategies for Qualitative Research*. Chicago: Aldine, 1967.

GLASER, B. G., and STRAUSS, A. L. *Time for Dying*. Chicago: Aldine, 1968.

GLENN, N. D. "Aging and Conservatism." *Political Consequences of Aging: The Annals of the American Academy of Political and Social Science*, 1974, *415*, 176–186.

GLICK, P. C. "The Life Cycle of the Family." *Journal of Marriage and Family Living*, 1955, *17*, 3–9.

GLIXMAN, A. F. "Categorizing Behavior as a Function of Meaning Domain." *Journal of Personality and Social Psychology*, 1965, *2*, 370–377.

GLOCK, C. Y., and STARK, R. *Religion and Society in Tension*. Chicago: Rand McNally, 1965.

GLOREIG, A., and DAVIS, H. "Age, Noise, and Hearing Loss." *Annals of Otology, Rhinology, and Laryngology*, 1961, *70*, 556–571.

GOFFMAN, E. *The Presentation of Self in Everyday Life*. Garden City, N.Y.: Doubleday, 1960.

GOLD, M. W. "Stimulus Factors in Skill Training of Retarded Adolescents on a Complex Assembly Task: Acquisition, Transfer, and Retention." *American Journal of Mental Deficiency*, 1972, *76*, 517–526.

GOLDBERG, S. *The Inevitability of Patriarchy*. New York: Morrow, 1973.

GOLDE, P., and KOGAN, N. "A Sentence Completion Procedure for Assessing Attitudes toward Old People." *Journal of Gerontology*, 1959, *14*, 355–363.

GOLDFARB, A. I. "Predicting Mortality in the Institutionalized Aged." *Archives of General Psychiatry*, 1969, *21*, 172–176.

GOLDFARB, A. I., SHAHINIAN, S. P., and BURR, H. T. "Death Rate of Relocated Nursing Home Residents." In D. P. Kent, R. Kastenbaum and S. Sherwood (Eds.), *Research Planning and Action for the Elderly*. New York: Behavioral Publications, 1972.

GOLDRICH, J. M. "A Study in Time Orientation: The Relation between Memory for Past Experience and Orientation to the Future." *Journal of Personality and Social Psychology*, 1967, *6*, 216–221.

GOLDSTEIN, H. S. "Internal Controls in Aggressive Children from Father-Present and Father-Absent Families." *Journal of Consulting and Clinical Psychology,* 1972, *39* (3), 512.

GOLDSTEIN, S., and MAYER, K. B. "Illegitimacy, Residence, and Status." *Social Problems,* 1965, *12,* 428–436.

GOODCHILDS, J. D., and SMITH, E. E. "The Effects of Unemployment as Mediated by Social Status." *Sociometry,* 1963, *26,* 287–293.

GOODE, W. J. *After Divorce.* New York: Free Press, 1956.

GOODE, W. J. *The Family.* Englewood Cliffs, N. J.: Prentice-Hall, 1964.

GOODMAN, M., BLEY, N., and DYE, D. "Adjustment of Aged Users of Leisure Programs." *American Journal of Orthopsychiatry,* 1974, *44,* 142–149.

GOULD, R. "The Phases of Adult Life: A Study in Developmental Psychology." *American Journal of Psychiatry,* 1972, *129,* 521–531.

GOULD, R. "Adult Life Stages: Growth toward Self-Tolerance." *Psychology Today,* 1975, *8* (9), 74–78.

GOULET, L. R., and BALTES, P. B. (Eds.) *Life-Span Developmental Psychology: Research and Theory.* New York: Academic Press, 1970.

GRANICK, S., and PATTERSON, R. (Eds.) *Human Aging II: An Eleven-Year Followup Biomedical and Behavior Study.* DHEW Publication No. [ADM] 74-123. Rockville, Md.: National Institute of Mental Health, 1971.

GRANT, C. H. "Age Differences in Self Concept from Early Adulthood through Old Age." *Proceedings of the 77th Annual Convention of the American Psychological Association,* 1969, *4* (2), 717–718.

GREEN, R. F. "Age-Intelligence Relationships between Ages Sixteen and Sixty-Four: A Rising Trend." *Developmental Psychology,* 1969, *1,* 618–627.

GREEN, R. F., and BERKOWITZ, B. "Changes in Intellect with Age: II. Factorial Analysis of Wechsler-Bellevue Scores." *Journal of Genetic Psychology,* 1964, *104,* 3–18.

GROTELUESCHEN, A. D. *Differentially Structured Introductory Learning Materials and Learning Tasks.* Washington, D.C.: U.S. Office of Education, 1967.

GROTELUESCHEN, A. D., and KNOX, A. B. "Analysis of the Quick Word Test as an Estimate of Adult Mental Ability." *Journal of Educational Measurement,* 1967, *4,* 169–177.

GROTELUESCHEN, A. D., and SJOGREN, D. D. "Effects of Differentially Structured Introductory Materials and Learning Tasks of Learning and Transfer." *American Educational Research Journal,* 1968, *5,* 191–202.

GRUBER, H. E. "Courage and Cognitive Growth in Children and Scientists." In M. Schwebel and J. Raph (Eds.), *Piaget in the Classroom*. New York: Basic Books, 1973.

GRUEN, W. "Adult Personality: An Empirical Study of Erikson's Theory of Ego Development." In B. Neugarten (Ed.), *Personality in Middle and Late Life: Empirical Studies*. New York: Atherton, 1964.

GUMP, J., and RIVERS, L. "The Consideration of Race in Efforts to End Sex Bias." In E. Diamond (Ed.), *Issues of Sex Bias in Interest Measurement*. Washington, D.C.: U.S. Government Printing Office, 1975.

GUNTHER, B. *Sense Awakening*. New York: Macmillan, 1968a.

GUNTHER, B. *Sense Relaxation Below Your Mind*. New York: Macmillan, 1968b.

GURIN, G., VEROFF, J., and FELD, S. *Americans View Their Mental Health: A Nationwide Interview Study*. New York: Basic Books, 1960.

GUTH, S. K., EASTMAN, A. A., and MCNELIS, J. F. "Lighting Requirements for Older Workers." *Illuminating Engineering*, 1956, *51*, 656–660.

HRA. *First Health and Nutrition Examination Survey, United States, 1971–72: Dietary Intake and Biochemical Findings*. Washington, D.C.: Health Resources Administration, 1974.

HAAN, N. "Personality Development from Adolescence to Adulthood in the Oakland Growth and Guidance Studies." *Seminars in Psychiatry*, 1972, *4* (4).

HAAN, N., and DAY, D. "A Longitudinal Study of Change and Sameness in Personality Development, Adolescence to Later Adulthood." *Aging and Human Development*, 1974, *5* (1), 11–39.

HALFTER, I. T. "The Comparative Academic Achievement of Women." *Adult Education*, 1962, *12* (2), 106–115.

HALL, C. S., and LINDZEY, G. *Theories of Personality*. 2nd ed. New York: Wiley, 1970.

HALL, E. "Ordinal Position and Success in Engagement and Marriage." *Journal of Industrial Psychology*, 1965, *21*, 154–158.

HARMON, I. "Career Counseling for Women." In D. Carter and E. Rawlings (Eds.), *Psychotherapy for Women: Treatment Toward Equality*. Springfield, Ill.: Thomas, 1975.

HARRIS, D. (Ed.) *The Concept of Development*. Minneapolis: University of Minnesota Press, 1957.

HARRIS, D. "Work and the Adolescent: Transition to Maturity." *Teachers College Record*, 1961, *63*, 146–153.

HARRIS, L., and ASSOCIATES. *Myth and Reality of Aging in America*. Washington, D.C.: National Council on Aging, 1975.

HARRISON, L. *Career Guidance for Adults: Focus on Women and Ethnic Minorities.* Palo Alto, Calif.: American Institutes of Research, 1976.

HAUSER, S., and HOBART, C. W. "Premarital Pregnancy and Anxiety." *Journal of Social Psychology,* 1964, *63,* 255–263.

HAVELOCK, R. G. *Planning for Innovation.* Ann Arbor: CRUSK, ISR, University of Michigan, 1969.

HAVIGHURST, R. J. "The Leisure Activities of the Middle-Aged." *American Journal of Sociology,* 1957a, *63,* 152–162.

HAVIGHURST, R. J. "The Social Competence of Middle-Aged People." *Genetic Psychology Monographs,* 1957b, *56,* 297–375.

HAVIGHURST, R. J. "Body, Self and Society." *Sociology and Social Research,* 1965, *49,* 261–267.

HAVIGHURST, R. J., and ALBRECHT, R. *Older People.* New York: Mc-Kay, 1953.

HAVIGHURST, R. J., and DE VRIES, A. "Life Styles and Free-Time Activities of Retired Men." *Human Development,* 1969, *12,* 34–54.

HAVIGHURST, R. J., and FEIGENBAUM, K. "Leisure and Life Style." *American Journal of Sociology,* 1959, *64,* 396–404.

HAVIGHURST, R. J., NEUGARTEN, B. L., and TOBIN, S. S. "Disengagement and Patterns of Aging." In B. Neugarten (Ed.), *Middle Age and Aging.* Chicago: University of Chicago Press, 1968.

HAVIGHURST, R. J., and ORR, B. *Adult Education and Adult Needs.* Chicago: Center for the Study of Liberal Education for Adults, 1956. (Available from Syracuse University, Publications in Continuing Education.)

HAYGHE, H. *Labor Force Activity of Married Women.* Special Labor Force Report No. 153. Washington, D.C.: Bureau of Labor Statistics, 1973.

HAYGHE, H. *Marital and Family Characteristics of the Labor Force in March 1973.* Special Labor Force Report No. 164. Washington, D.C.: Bureau of Labor Statistics, 1974.

HAYGHE, H. "Marital and Family Characteristics of Workers, March 1974." *Monthly Labor Review,* 1975, *98* (1), 60–63.

HEALY, C. C. "The Relation of Esteem and Social Class to Self-Occupational Congruence." *Journal of Vocational Behavior,* 1973, *3,* 43–51.

HEARN, H. L. "Career and Leisure Patterns of Middle-Aged Urban Blacks." *The Gerontologist,* 1971, *11* (2), 21–26.

HEATH, D. H. *Explorations of Maturity.* New York: Appleton-Century-Crofts, 1965.

HEATH, D. H. *Growing Up in College: Maturity and Liberal Education.* San Francisco: Jossey-Bass, 1968.

HEATH, D. H. "Adolescent and Adult Predictors of Vocational Adaptation." *Journal of Vocational Behavior,* 1976, *9,* 1–19.

HEGLIN, H. J. "Problem Solving Set in Different Age Groups." *Journal of Gerontology,* 1956, *11,* 310–317.

HEIDBREDER, E. "Factors in Retirement Adjustment: White Collar/Blue Collar Experience." *Industrial Gerontology,* 1972, *12,* 69–79.

HEIM, A. *Intelligence and Personality.* Middlesex: Penguin, 1970.

HENDRICKSON, A., and BARNES, R. F. "Educational Needs of Older People." *Adult Leadership,* 1967, *16* (1), 2ff.

HENDRICKSON, A., and FOSTER, E. *Educational Needs of Out of School Youth in Columbus, Ohio.* Columbus: Ohio State University, 1960.

HENNIG, M., and JARDIM, A. *The Managerial Woman.* New York: Doubleday, 1976.

HENRY, J. *Pathways to Madness.* New York: Vintage Books, 1973.

HENRY, J. P., and CASSEL, J. C. "Psychosocial Factors in Essential Hypertension: Recent Epidemiologic and Animal Experimental Evidence." *American Journal of Epidemiology,* 1969, *90,* 171–200.

HENRY, W. E. "The Theory of Intrinsic Disengagement." In P. F. Hansen (Ed.), *Age with a Future* (Proceedings of the 6th International Congress of Gerontology, 1963). Copenhagen: Munksgaard, 1964.

HENRY, W. E. "The Role of Work in Structuring the Life Cycle." *Human Development,* 1971, *14,* 125–131.

HENRY, W. E., SIMS, J., and SPRAY, L. *The Fifth Profession: Becoming a Psychotherapist.* San Francisco: Jossey-Bass, 1971.

HEPNER, H. W. *Retirement—A Time to Live Anew.* New York: McGraw-Hill, 1969.

HERZBERG, F. *Work and the Nature of Man.* Cleveland, Ohio: World, 1966.

HERZBERG, F., MAUSNER, B., and SNYDERMAN, B. *The Motivation to Work.* New York: Wiley, 1959.

HESS, R. D., and SHIPMAN, V. C. "Early Experience and the Socialization of Cognitive Modes in Children." *Child Development,* 1965, *36,* 869–886.

HETHERINGTON, E. M. "A Developmental Study of the Effects of Sex of the Dominant Parent on Sex-Role Preference, Identification, and Imitation in Children." *Journal of Personality and Social Psychology,* 1965, *2,* 188–194.

HICKEY, T., and KALISH, R. A. "Young People's Perceptions of Adults." *Journal of Gerontology,* 1968, *23,* 216–219.

HIESTAND, D. L. *Changing Careers after Thirty-Five.* New York: Columbia University Press, 1971.

HILL, H. *Mark Twain: God's Fool.* New York: Harper & Row, 1973.

HILL, R. J. *A Comparative Study of Lecture and Discussion Methods.* New York: Fund for Adult Education, 1960.

HILL, R. "Decision Making and the Family Life Cycle." In E. Shanas and G. Streib (Eds.), *Social Structure and the Family: Generational Relations.* Englewood Cliffs, N.J.: Prentice-Hall, 1965.

HILL, R., FOOTE, N., ALDOUS, J., CARLSON, R., MACDONALD, R. *Family Development in Three Generations.* Cambridge, Mass.: Schenkman, 1970.

HIMWICH, W. A., and HIMWICH, H. E. "Neurochemistry of Aging." In J. E. Birren (Ed.), *Handbook of Aging and the Individual.* Chicago: University of Chicago Press, 1959.

HINTON, J. *Dying.* Baltimore: Penguin, 1967.

HOBBS, D. F. "Parenthood as a Crisis: A Third Study." *Journal of Marriage and the Family,* 1965, *27,* 367–372.

HOFFMAN, L. W. "Mother's Enjoyment of Work and Effects on the Child." In F. I. Nye and L. W. Hoffman (Eds.), *The Employed Mother in America.* Chicago: Rand McNally, 1963.

HOFFMAN, L. W. "Fear of Success in Males and Females: 1965 and 1972." *Journal of Consulting and Clinical Psychology,* 1974, *42,* 353–358.

HOFFMAN, L. W., and NYE, F. I. *Working Mothers.* San Francisco: Jossey-Bass, 1974.

HOLLAND, J. L. *Making Vocational Choices.* Englewood Cliffs, N.J.: Prentice-Hall, 1973.

HOLMES, T. H., and RAHE, R. H. "The Social Readjustment Rating Scale." *Journal of Psychosomatic Research,* 1967, *11,* 213–218.

HOLMSTROM, L. "Career Patterns of Married Couples." In A. Theodore (Ed.), *The Professional Woman.* Cambridge, Mass.: Schenkman, 1971.

HOLTZMAN, P. S. "The Relation of Assimilation Tendencies in Visual, Auditory, and Kinesthetic Time-Error to Cognitive Attitudes of Leveling and Sharpening." *Journal of Personality,* 1954, *22,* 375–394.

HOLTZMAN, P. S. "Scanning: A Principle of Reality Contact." *Perceptual and Motor Skills,* 1966, *23,* 835–844.

HOLTZMAN, P. S., and GARDNER, R. W. "Leveling-Sharpening and Memory Organization." *Journal of Abnormal Social Psychology,* 1960, *61,* 176–180.

HOLTZMAN, P. S., and KLEIN, G. S. "Cognitive System-Principles of Leveling and Sharpening: Individual Differences in Assimilation Effects in Visual Time-Error." *Journal of Psychology,* 1954, *37,* 105–122.

HONZIK, M. P., and MCFARLANE, J. W. "Personality Development and

Intellectual Functioning." In *Intellectual Functioning of Adults.* New York: Springer, 1973.

HORN, J. L. "Intelligence—Why It Grows, Why It Declines." *Transaction,* 1967, *4,* 23–31.

HORN, J. L. "Organization of Abilities and the Development of Intelligence." *Psychological Review,* 1968, *75,* 242–259.

HORN, J. L. "Organization of Data on Life-Span Development of Human Abilities." In L. R. Goulet and P. B. Baltes (Eds.), *Life-Span Developmental Psychology: Research and Theory.* New York: Academic Press, 1970.

HORN, J. L., and CATTELL, R. B. "Age Differences in Primary Mental Ability Factors." *Journal of Gerontology,* 1966a, *21,* 210–220.

HORN, J. L., and CATTELL, R. B. "Refinement and Test of the Theory of Fluid and Crystallized Intelligence." *Journal of Educational Psychology,* 1966b, *57,* 253–270.

HORN, J. L., and CATTELL, R. B. "Age Differences in Fluid and Crystallized Intelligence." *Acta Psychologica,* 1967, *26,* 107–129.

HORNER, M. S. "The Motive to Avoid Success and Changing Aspirations of Women." In J. M. Bardwick (Ed.), *Readings on the Psychology of Women.* New York: Harper & Row, 1972.

HORNSTEIN, H. A., BUNKER, B. B., BURKE, W. W., GINDES, M., and LEWICKI, R. J. (Eds.) *Social Intervention: A Behavioral Science Approach.* New York: Free Press, 1971.

HOWELL, S. C., and LOEB, M. B. "Nutrition and Aging: Monograph for Practitioners." *The Gerontologist,* 1969, *9* (3), entire issue.

HULICKA, I. M. "Age Differences for Intentional and Incidental Learning and Recall Scores." *Journal of the American Geriatrics Society,* 1965, 13, 639–649.

HULICKA, I. M. "Age Differences in Retention as a Function of Interference." *Journal of Gerontology,* 1967, *22,* 180–185.

HULICKA, I. M., and GROSSMAN, J. L. "Age Group Comparisons for the Use of Mediators in Paired-Associate Learning." *Journal of Gerontology,* 1967, *22,* 46–51.

HULICKA, I. M., and RUST, L. D. "Age-Related Retention Deficit as a Function of Learning." *Journal of the American Geriatrics Society,* 1964, *12,* 1061–1065.

HULICKA, I. M. and WEISS, R. L. "Age Differences in Retention as a Function of Learning." *Journal of Consulting Psychology,* 1965, *29,* 125–129.

HULTSCH, D. F. "Adult Age Differences in the Organization of Free Recall." *Developmental Psychology,* 1969, *1,* 673–678.

HULTSCH, D. F. "Organization and Memory in Adulthood." *Human Development,* 1971a, *14,* 16–29.

HULTSCH, D. F. "Adult Age Differences in Free-Classification and Free Recall." *Developmental Psychology*, 1971b, *4*, 338–342.

HULTSCH, D. F. "Learning to Learn in Adulthood." *Journal of Gerontology*, 1974, *29*, 308–309.

HULTSCH, D. F., and CRAIG, E. R. "Adult Age Differences in the Inhibition of Recall as a Function of Retrieval Cues." *Developmental Psychology*, 1976, *12*, 83–84.

HUNT, D. E. "A Conceptual Level Matching Model for Coordinating Learner Characteristics with Educational Approaches." *Interchange*, 1970, *1*, 68–72.

HUNT, J. G., and ZIMMERMAN, J. "Stimulating Productivity in a Simulated Sheltered Workshop Setting." *American Journal of Mental Deficiency*, 1969, *74*, 43–49.

HUNT, M. M. *The World of the Formerly Married*. New York: McGraw-Hill, 1966.

HUNTER, F. C. "Mother's Education and Working: Effect on the School Child." *Journal of Psychology*, 1972, *82*, 27–37.

HURLOCK, E. B. *Developmental Psychology*. 3rd ed. New York: McGraw-Hill, 1968.

HYMAN, H. H. *Survey Design and Analysis*. New York: Free Press, 1955.

INGLIS, J., ANKUS, M. N., and SYKES, D. H. "Age-Related Differences in Learning and Short-Term Memory from Childhood to the Senium." *Human Development*, 1968, *11*, 42–52.

ISAACS, B. "Group Therapy in the Geriatric Unit." *Gerontologia Clinica*, 1967, *9*, 21–26.

IVEY, M., and BARDWICK, J. "Patterns of Affective Fluctuation in the Menstrual Cycle." *Psychosomatic Medicine*, 1968, *30*, 336–345.

JACO, E. G. "Mental Illness in Response to Stress." In S. Levine, and N. A. Scotch (Eds.) *Social Stress*. Chicago: Aldine, 1970.

JACOBSON, P. H. *American Marriage and Divorce*. New York: Holt, 1959.

JACOBZINER, H. "Attempted Suicide in Adolescence." *Journal of the American Medical Association*, 1965, *191*, 7–11.

JAMES, B. J., and MONTROSS, H. W. "Focusing Group Goals." *Adult Education*, 1956, *6*, 95–100.

JAMIESON, G. H. "Age, Speed, and Accuracy: A Study in Industrial Training." *Occupational Psychology*, 1966, *40*, 237–242.

JANEWAY, E. *Man's World, Woman's Place*. New York: Delta, 1971.

JANEWAY, E. *Between Myth and Morning: Women Awakening*. New York: Morrow, 1975.

JAQUES, E. "Death and the Mid-Life Crisis." *International Journal of Psychoanalysis*, 1965, *46*, 502–514.

JARVIK, L. F. "Thoughts on the Psychobiology of Aging." *American Psychologist,* 1975, *30* (5) , 576–583.

JARVIK, L. F., and BLUM, J. E. "Cognitive Declines as Predictors of Mortality in Twin Pairs: A Twenty-Year Longitudinal Study of Aging." In E. Palmore, and F. C. Jeffers (Eds.) , *Prediction of Life Span.* Lexington, Mass.: Heath, 1971.

JARVIK, L. F., BLUM, J. E., and VARMA, A. O. "Genetic Components and Intellectual Functioning During Senescence: A 20-Year Study of Aging Twins." *Behavior Genetics,* 1972, *2,* 159–171.

JARVIK, L. F., and COHEN, D. "A Biobehavioral Approach to Intellectual Changes with Aging." In C. Eisdorfer, and M. P. Lawton (Eds.) , *The Psychology of Adult Development and Aging.* Washington, D.C.: American Psychological Association, 1973.

JARVIK, L. F., EISDORFER, C., and BLUM, J. (Eds.) *Intellectual Functioning in Adults.* New York: Springer, 1973.

JARVIK, L. F., KALLMAN, F. J., and FALEK, A. "Intellectual Changes in Aged Twins." *Journal of Gerontology,* 1962, *14,* 289–294.

JEFFERS, F., NICHOLS, C. R., and EISDORFER, C. "Attitudes of Older Persons toward Death." *Journal of Gerontology,* 1961, *16,* 53–56.

JEROME, E. A. "Decay of Heuristic Processes in the Aged." In C. Tibbitts, and W. Donahue (Eds.) , *Social and Psychological Aspects of Aging.* New York: Columbia University Press, 1962.

JOHNSTONE, J. W. C., and RIVERA, R. J. *Volunteers for Learning.* Chicago: Aldine, 1965.

JONES, H. B. "A Special Consideration of the Aging Process, Disease, and Life Expectancy." In J. H. Lawrence, and C. A. Tobias (Eds.) , *Advances in Biological and Medical Physics,* 1956, *4,* 281–337.

JONES, H. E. "Consistency and Change in Early Maturity." *Vita Humana,* 1960, *3,* 17–31.

JONES, H. E., and CONRAD, H. S. "The Growth and Decline of Intelligence: A Study of a Homogenous Group between the Ages of Ten and Sixty." *Genetic Psychology Monographs,* 1933, *13,* 223–298.

JOURARD, S. M. *Healthy Personality.* New York: Macmillan, 1974.

JUNG, C. G. *The Undiscovered Self.* New York: Mentor Books, 1957.

KAGAN, J. "American Longitudinal Research on Psychological Development." *Child Development,* 1964, *35,* 1–32.

KAGAN, J. "Reflection-Impulsivity and Reading Ability in Primary Grade Children." *Child Development,* 1965, *36,* 609–628.

KAGAN, J., and MOSS, H. A. *Birth to Maturity: A Study in Psychological Development.* New York: Wiley, 1962.

624 Adult Development and Learning

KAGAN, J., MOSS, H. A., and SIGEL, I. E. "Conceptual Style and the Use of Affect Labels." *Merrill-Palmer Quarterly*, 1960, *6*, 261–278.

KAGAN, J., MOSS, H. A., and SIGEL, I. E. "Psychological Significance of Styles of Conceptualization." *Monographs of the Society for Research in Child Development*, 1963, *28* (2, Whole No. 86), 73–112.

KAGAN, J., ROSMAN, B. L., DAY, D., ALBERT, J., and PHILLIPS, W. "Information Processing in the Child: Significance of Analytic and Reflective Attitudes." *Psychological Monographs*, 1964, *78* (Whole No. 58).

KAHANA, B. "The Relationship of Impulse Control to Cognition and Adjustment among Institutionalized Aged Women." *Journal of Gerontology*, 1975, *30*, 679–687.

KAHN, A. "Reactions to Generosity or Stinginess from an Intelligent or Stupid Work Partner: A Test of Equity Theory in a Direct Exchange Relationship." *Journal of Personality and Social Psychology*, 1972, *21*, 116–123.

KAHN, E. "The Effects of Age on Sleep." In E. Hartmann (Ed.), *Sleep and Dreaming*. Boston: Little, Brown, 1970.

KAHN, H., and WIENER, A. *The Year 2000*. New York: Macmillan, 1967.

KALEY, M. "Attitudes toward the Dual Role of the Married Professional Woman." *American Psychologist*, 1971, *26* (3), 301–306.

KALISH, R. A. "Sex and Marital Role Differences in Anticipation of Age-Produced Dependency." *Journal of Genetic Psychology*, 1971, *119*, 53–62.

KALISH, R. A. *Late Adulthood: Perspectives on Human Development*. Monterey, Calif.: Brooks/Cole, 1975.

KALISH, R. A., and JOHNSON, A. I. "Value Similarities and Differences in Three Generations of Women." *Journal of Marriage and the Family*, 1972, *34*, 49–55.

KALLMAN, F. J., and SANDER, G. "Studies in Senescence." *American Journal of Psychiatry*, 1949, *106*, 29–36.

KANGAS, J., and BRADWAY, K. "Intelligence at Middle Age: A Thirty-Eight Year Followup." *Developmental Psychology*, 1971, *5*, 333–337.

KAPLAN, H. B., and POKORNY, A. D. "Aging and Self-Attitude: A Conditional Relationship." *Aging and Human Development*, 1970, *1*, 241–250.

KASTELER, J. M., GRAY, R. M., and CARRUTH, M. L. "Involuntary Relocation of the Elderly." *Gerontologist*, 1968, *8*, 276–279.

KASTENBAUM, R. (Ed.) *Contributions to the Psycho-Biology of Aging*. New York: Springer, 1965.

KASTENBAUM, R., and AISENBERG, R. *The Psychology of Death.* New York: Springer, 1972.

KASTENBAUM, R., and CANDY, S. E. "The 4% Fallacy: A Methodological and Empirical Critique of Extended Care Facility Population Statistics." *Aging and Human Development,* 1973, *4,* 15–22.

KASTENBAUM, R., DERBIN, V., SABATINI, P., and ARTT, S. "The Ages of Me: Toward Personal and Interpersonal Definitions of Functional Aging." *Aging and Human Development,* 1972, *3* (2), 197–211.

KASTENBAUM, R., and DURKEE, N. "Young People View Old Age." In R. Kastenbaum (Ed.), *New Thoughts on Old Age.* New York: Springer, 1964.

KATCHADOURIAN, H., and KATCHADOURIAN, L. *Fundamentals of Human Sexuality.* New York: Holt, Rinehart and Winston, 1972.

KATZ, E. "The Two-Step Flow of Communication." *Public Opinion Survey,* 1957, *21,* 61–78.

KATZ, E., and LAZARSFELD, P. F. *Personal Influence.* Glencoe, Ill.: Free Press, 1955.

KAUFMAN, H. G. *Obsolescence and Professional Career Development.* New York: American Management Association, 1974.

KAUSLER, D. H., and LAIR, C. V. "R-S ('Backward') Paired-Associate Learning in Elderly Subjects." *Journal of Gerontology,* 1965, *20,* 29–31.

KAUSLER, D. H., and LAIR, C. V. "Associative Strength and Paired-Associate Learning in Elderly Subjects." *Journal of Gerontology,* 1966, *21,* 278–280.

KAY, H. "Theories of Learning and Aging." In J. E. Birren (Ed.), *Handbook of Aging and the Individual.* Chicago: University of Chicago Press, 1959.

KEAHEY, S. P., and SEAMAN, D. F. "Self-Actualization and Adjustment in Retirement." *Adult Education,* 1974, *24,* 220–226.

KELLER, O. J., and VEDDER, C. B. "The Crimes that Old Persons Commit." *The Gerontologist,* 1968, *8* (1), 43–50.

KELLEY, H. P. "Memory Abilities: A Factor Analysis." *Psychometric Monographs,* 1964 (11).

KELLY, E. L. "Consistency of the Adult Personality." *American Psychologist,* 1955, *10,* 659–681.

KELLY, G. A. *The Psychology of Personal Constructs.* New York: Norton, 1955.

KENISTON, K. *The Uncommitted: Alienated Youth in American Society.* New York: Harcourt Brace Jovanovich, 1965.

KENT, D. P. "Social and Cultural Factors Affecting the Mental Health of the Aged." *American Journal of Orthopsychiatry,* 1966, *36,* 680–685.

KERCKHOFF, A. C. "Husband-Wife Expectations and Reactions to Retirement." *Journal of Gerontology,* 1964, *19,* 510–516.

KERLINGER, F. N. *Foundations of Behavioral Research.* New York: Holt, Rinehart and Winston, 1965.

KERLINGER, F. N. *Foundations of Behavioral Research* (2nd ed.). New York: Holt, Rinehart and Winston, 1973.

KIEVIT, M. *Review and Synthesis of Research on Women in the World of Work.* Washington, D.C.: U.S. Government Printing Office, 1972.

KIMMEL, D. *Adulthood and Aging.* New York: Wiley, 1974.

KINANE, J. F., and PABLE, M. W. "Family Background and Work Value Orientation." *Journal of Counseling Psychology,* 1962, *9,* 320–325.

KING, H. F. "The Response of the Older Rural Craftsman to Individual Training." *Journal of Gerontology,* 1955, *10,* 207–211.

KINSEY, A. C., POMEROY, W. B., and MARTIN, C. E. *Sexual Behavior in the Human Male.* Philadelphia: Saunders, 1948.

KINSEY, A. C., and others. *Sexual Behavior in the Human Female.* Philadelphia: Saunders, 1953.

KIRKENDALL, L. A. "Toward a Clarification of the Concept of Male Sex Drive." *Journal of Marriage and Family Living,* 1958, *20,* 367–372.

KIRKENDALL, L. A. "Evaded Problem: Sex on the Campus." *Family Life Coordinator,* 1965, *14,* 20–24.

KLAUSNER, S. Z. *On Man in His Environment.* San Francisco: Jossey-Bass, 1971.

KLEIN, G. S. "Need and Regulation." In M. R. Jones (Ed.), *Nebraska Symposium on Motivation.* Lincoln: University of Nebraska Press, 1954.

KLEIN, G. S., GARDNER, R. W., and SCHLESINGER, H. J. "Tolerance for Unrealistic Experiences: A Study of the Generality of a Cognitive Control." *British Journal of Psychology,* 1962, *53,* 41–55.

KLEMER, R. H. "Factors of Personality and Experience which Differentiate Single from Married Women." *Journal of Marriage and Family Living,* 1954, *16,* 41–44.

KLUCKHOHN, C., and MURRAY, H. A. (Eds.) *Personality in Nature, Society, and Culture.* New York: Knopf, 1949.

KNOX, A. B. "Interests and Adult Education." *Journal of Learning Disabilities,* 1968, *1,* 220–229.

KNOX, A. B. *Factors Related to Educative Activity by Non-College Bound Young Adults.* Final Report, USOE Project 6–1826. New York: Teachers College, Columbia University, Center for Adult Education, 1970.

KNOX, A. B. "Life Long Self-Directed Education." In R. J. Blakely

(Ed.), *Fostering the Growing Need to Learn*. Rockville, Md.: Division of Regional Medical Programs, Bureau of Health Resources Development, U.S. Department of HEW, 1974.

KNOX, A. B. *Helping Adults to Learn*. Washington, D.C.: Continuing Library Education Network and Exchange (CLENE Concept Paper #4), 1976.

KNOX, A. B., and ANDERSON, A. H. *Living in Nebraska*. Lincoln: Adult Education Research, University of Nebraska, 1964.

KNOX, A. B., GROTELUESCHEN, A. D., and SJOGREN, D. D. "Adult Intelligence and Learning Ability." *Adult Education*, 1968, *18* (3), 188–196.

KNOX, A. B., and SJOGREN, D. D. "Achievement and Withdrawal in University Adult Education Classes." *Adult Education*, 1964, *15* (2), 74–88.

KNOX, A. B., and SJOGREN, D. D. "Research on Adult Learning." *Adult Education*, 1965, *15* (3), 133–137.

KNOX, A. B., and VIDEBECK, R. "Adult Education and Adult Life Cycle." *Adult Education*, 1963, *13,* 102–121.

KNOX, A. B., and VIDEBECK, R. *The Changing Fabric of Participation* (an analysis of adult life cycle changes in fifty-two non-sustenance participation variables), unpublished report. Lincoln: Office of Adult Education Research, University of Nebraska, 1964.

KNUPFER, G., CLARK, W., and ROOM, R. "The Mental Health of the Unmarried." *American Journal of Psychiatry*, 1966, *122,* 841–851.

KOGAN, N. "Attitudes toward Old People in an Older Sample." *Journal of Abnormal and Social Psychology*, 1961, *62,* 616–622.

KOGAN, N., and SHELTON, F. "Images of 'Old People' and 'People in General' in an Older Sample." *Journal of Genetic Psychology*, 1962a, *100,* 3–21.

KOGAN, N., and SHELTON, F. "Beliefs About 'Old People': A Comparative Study of Older and Younger Samples." *Journal of Genetic Psychology*, 1962b, *100,* 93–111.

KOGAN, N., and WALLACH, M. A. "Age Changes in Values and Attitudes." *Journal of Gerontology*, 1961, *16,* 272–280.

KOHLBERG, L. "Stage and Sequence: The Cognitive-Developmental Approach to Socialization." In D. A. Goslin (Ed.), *Handbook of Socialization Theory and Research*. Chicago: Rand McNally, 1969.

KOHLBERG, L. "Continuities in Childhood and Adult Moral Development Revisited." In P. B. Baltes, and K. W. Schaie (Eds.), *Life Span Developmental Psychology*. New York: Academic Press, 1973.

628 Adult Development and Learning

KOHLBERG, L. "Continuities in Childhood and Adult Moral Development Revisited." In L. Kohlberg and E. Turiel (Eds.), *Moralization, The Cognitive Developmental Approach.* New York: Holt, Rinehart and Winston, 1974.

KOHLBERG, L., and KRAMER, R. "Continuities and Discontinuities in Childhood and Adult Moral Development." *Human Development,* 1969, *12,* 93–120.

KOHN, M. L. *Class and Conformity: A Study in Values.* Homewood, Ill.: Dorsey Press, 1969.

KOLB, D. A., WINTER, S. K., and BERLEW, D. E. "Self-Directed Change: Two Studies." *Journal of Applied Behavioral Science,* 1968, *4* (4), 453–471.

KORCHIN, S. J. "Some Psychological Determinants of Stress Behavior." In S. Z. Klausner (Ed.), *The Quest for Self-Control.* New York: Free Press, 1965.

KORNHAUSER, A., and REID, O. M. *Mental Health of the Industrial Worker: A Detroit Study.* New York: Wiley, 1965.

KREPS, J. M. *Sex in the Marketplace: American Women at Work.* Baltimore: Johns Hopkins Press, 1971.

KREPS, J. M. (Ed.) *Women and the American Economy.* New York: Prentice-Hall, 1976.

KRONUS, C. L. "Patterns of Adult Library Use." *Adult Education,* 1973, *23* (2), 115–131.

KUHLEN, R. G. "Age Differences in Personality during Adult Years." *Psychological Bulletin,* 1945, *42,* 333–358.

KUHLEN, R. G., and JOHNSON, C. H. "Changes in Goals with Increasing Adult Age." *Journal of Consulting Psychology,* 1952, *16,* 1–4.

KUTSCHER, A. *Death and Bereavement.* Springfield, Ill.: Thomas, 1969.

LABOUVIE-VIEF, F., and BALTES, P. B. "Creating a Healthy Institutional Environment for Elderly Via Behavior Management—Nurse As a Change Agent." *International Journal of Nursing,* 1975, *12,* 5–12.

LAING, R. D. *The Politics of the Family.* New York: Random House, 1971.

LAIR, C., MOON, W., and KAUSLER, D. "Associative Interference in the Paired-Associate Learning of Middle-Aged and Old Subjects." *Developmental Psychology,* 1969, *1,* 548–552.

LAKEIN, A. *How to Get Control of Your Time and Your Life.* New York: Wyden, 1973.

LAND, G. T. L. *Grow or Die.* New York: Random House, 1973.

LANDIS, J. T. "Social Correlates of Divorce or Nondivorce among the Unhappy Married." *Journal of Marriage and Family Living,* 1963, *25,* 178–180.

LANDIS, P. H. "Sequential Marriage." *Journal of Home Economics,* 1950, *42,* 625–627.

LANSING, J. B., and KISH, L. "Family Life Cycle as an Independent Variable." *American Sociological Review,* 1957, *22,* 512–519.

LAURENCE, M. W. "Memory Loss with Age: A Test of Two Strategies for Its Retardation." *Psychonomic Science,* 1967a, *9,* 209–210.

LAURENCE, M. W. "A Developmental Look at the Usefulness of List Categorization as an Aid to Free Recall." *Canadian Journal of Psychology,* 1967b, *21,* 153–165.

LAWTON, M. P., and BADER, J. "The Wish for Privacy among Young and Old." *Journal of Gerontology,* 1970, *25,* 48–54.

LAWTON, M. P., and NAHEMOW, L. "Ecology and the Aging Process." In C. Eisdorfer and M. P. Lawton (Eds.), *The Psychology of Adult Development and Aging.* Washington, D.C.: American Psychological Association, 1972.

LAZARSFELD, P., and MERTON, R. "Friendship as a Social Process: A Substantive and Methodological Analysis." In M. Berger, T. Abel, and C. Page (Eds.), *Freedom and Control in Modern Society.* New York: Octagon Books, 1964. (Originally published 1954.)

LAZARUS, R. S. *Psychological Stress and the Coping Process.* New York: McGraw-Hill, 1966.

LEAF, A. "Getting Old." *Scientific American,* 1973, *229,* 45–52.

LEDERER, F. L. "Hearing Loss from the Womb to the Tomb." *Archives of Otolaryngology,* 1961, *74,* 391–398.

LEDERER, W. J., and JACKSON, D. D. *The Mirages of Marriage.* New York: Norton, 1968.

LEFEVRE, C. "The Mature Woman as Graduate Student." *School Review,* 1972, *80* (2), 281–297.

LEHMAN, H. *Age and Achievement.* Princeton, N.J.: Princeton University Press, 1953.

LEHNER, G. F. J., and GUNDERSON, E. K. "Height Relationships on the Draw-A-Person Test." *Journal of Personality,* 1953, *21,* 392–399.

LEHR, U., and RUDINGER, G. "Consistency and Change of Social Participation in Old Age." *Human Development,* 1969, *12,* 255–267.

LEMASTERS, E. E. "Parenthood as a Crisis." *Journal of Marriage and Family Living,* 1957, *19,* 352–355.

LE SHAN, E. *The Wonderful Crisis of Middle Age.* New York: McKay, 1973.

LEVENTHAL, G. S., and LANE, D. W. "Sex, Age, and Equity Behavior." *Journal of Personality and Social Psychology,* 1970, *15,* 312–316.

LEVENTHAL, H. "Cognitive Processes and Interpersonal Predictions." *Journal of Abnormal and Social Psychology,* 1957, *55,* 176–180.

LEVINE, S., and SCOTCH, N. A. (Eds.) *Social Stress.* Chicago: Aldine, 1970.

LEVINGER, G. "Sources of Marital Dissatisfaction among Applicants for Divorce." *American Journal of Orthopsychiatry,* 1966, *36,* 803–807.

LEVINSON, B., and REESE, H. W. "Patterns of Discrimination Learning Set in Preschool Children, Fifth-Graders, College Freshmen, and the Aged." *Monographs of Society for Research in Child Development,* 1967, *32* (Whole No. 7).

LEVINSON, D. J., DARROW, C. M., KLEIN, E. B., LEVINSON, M. H., and MCKEE, B. "The Psychosocial Development of Men in Early Adulthood and the Mid-Life Transition." In D. E. Ricks, A. Thomas, and M. Roff (Eds.), *Life History Research in Psychopathology.* Vol. 3. Minneapolis: University of Minnesota Press, 1974.

LEVINSON, D. J., DARROW, C. M., KLEIN, E. B., LEVINSON, M. H., and MCKEE, B. "Periods in the Adult Development of Men: Ages 18 to 45." *Counseling Psychologist,* 1976, *6,* 21–25.

LEWIN, K. *Dynamic Theory of Personality.* New York: McGraw-Hill, 1935.

LEWIN, K. *Resolving Social Conflicts.* New York: Harper, 1948.

LEWIN, K. "Group Decision and Social Change." In Maccoby, Newcomb, and Hartley (Eds.), *Readings in Social Psychology.* 3rd ed. New York: Holt, 1958.

LIDZ, T. *The Person: His Development Throughout the Life Cycle.* New York: Basic Books, 1968.

LIEBERMAN, L. R. "Life Satisfaction in the Young and the Old." *Psychological Reports,* 1970, *27,* 75–79.

LIEBERMAN, M. A. "The Relationship of Mortality Rates to Entrance to a Home for the Aged." *Geriatrics,* 1961, *16,* 515–519.

LIEBERMAN, M. A. "Psychological Correlates of Impending Death: Some Preliminary Observations." *Journal of Gerontology,* 1965, *20,* 181–190.

LIEBERMAN, M. A., and COPLAN, A. S. "Distance from Death as a Variable in the Study of Aging." *Developmental Psychology,* 1960, *2,* 71–84.

LIEBERMAN, M. A., YALOM, I. D., and MILES, M. B. *Encounter Groups: First Facts.* New York: Basic Books, 1972.

LINK, H. C., and HOPF, H. A. *People and Books.* New York: New York Book Industry Committee, Book Manufacturers Institute, 1946.

LIPMAN, A., and SMITH, K. J. "Functionality of Disengagement in Old Age." *Journal of Gerontology*, 1968, *23*, 517–521.

LIPSITT, D. "A Medical-Psychological Approach to Dependency in the Aged." In R. A. Kalish (Ed.), *Dependencies of Old People, Occasional Papers in Gerontology*. Vol. 6. Ann Arbor and Detroit: Institute of Gerontology, University of Michigan and Wayne State University, 1969.

LOESCH, J. C., and GREENBERG, N. H. "Some Specific Areas of Conflict Observed during Pregnancy: A Comparative Study of Married and Unmarried Pregnant Women." *American Journal of Orthopsychiatry*, 1962, *32*, 624–636.

LOGAN, F. A. *Fundamentals of Learning and Motivation*. Dubuque, Iowa: Brown, 1970.

LONDON, J., WENKERT, R., and HAGSTROM, W. O. *Adult Education and Social Class*. Berkeley: University of California Survey Research Center, 1963.

LONG, H. B. *The Physiology of Aging: How It Affects Learning*. Englewood Cliffs, N.J.: Prentice-Hall, 1972.

LOOFT, W. "Socialization and Personality Throughout the Life Span: An Examination of Contemporary Psychological Approaches." In P. Baltes, and W. Schaie (Eds.), *Life-Span Developmental Psychology: Personality and Socialization*. New York: Academic, 1973.

LOPATA, H. Z. "The Life Cycle of the Social Role of Housewife." *Sociological and Social Research*, 1966, *51*, 5–22.

LOPATA, H. Z. *Occupation: Housewife*. London: Oxford University Press, 1971.

LOPATA, H. Z. *Widowhood in an American City*. Cambridge: Schenkman, 1973.

LOWENTHAL, M. F. "Social Isolation and Mental Illness in Old Age." *American Sociological Review*, 1964a, *29*, 54–70.

LOWENTHAL, M. F. *Lives in Distress*. New York: Basic Books, 1964b.

LOWENTHAL, M. F. "Antecedents of Isolation and Mental Illness in Old Age." *Archives of General Psychiatry*, 1965, *12*, 245–254.

LOWENTHAL, M. F. "Intentionality: Toward a Framework for the Study of Adaptation in Adulthood." *Aging and Human Development*, 1971, *2*, 79–95.

LOWENTHAL, M. F., and BOWLER, D. "Voluntary Versus Involuntary Social Withdrawal." *Journal of Gerontology*, 1965, *20*, 363–375.

LOWENTHAL, M. F., and CHIRIBOGA, D. "Transition to the Empty Nest." *Archives of General Psychiatry*, 1972, *26*, 8–14.

LOWENTHAL, M. F., and CHIRIBOGA, D. "Social Stress and Adaptation: Toward a Life-Course Perspective." In C. Eisdorfer and M. P. Lawton (Eds.), *The Psychology of Adult Develop-*

ment and Aging. Washington, D.C.: American Psychological Association, 1973.

LOWENTHAL, M. F., and HAVEN, C. "Interaction and Adaptation: Intimacy as a Critical Variable." *American Sociological Review,* 1968, *33,* 20–30.

LOWENTHAL, M. F., THURNHER, M., CHIRIBOGA, D., BEESON, D., GIAY, L., LURIE, E., PIERCE, R., SPENCER, D., and WEISS, L. *Four Stages of Life: A Comparative Study of Women and Men Facing Transitions.* San Francisco: Jossey-Bass, 1975.

LOWRIE, S. H. "Early Marriage, Premarital Pregnancy and Associated Factors." *Journal of Marriage and the Family,* 1965, *27,* 48–56.

MAAS, H. S., and KUYPERS, J. A. *From Thirty to Seventy.* San Francisco: Jossey-Bass, 1974.

MACCOBY, E. E., and JACKLIN, C. N. *The Psychology of Sex Differences.* Stanford, Calif.: Stanford University Press, 1974.

MACE, D., and MACE, V. *We Can Have Better Marriages If We Really Want Them.* New York: Abingdon Press, 1974.

MACFARLANE, J. W. "Perspectives on Personality Consistency and Change from the Guidance Study." *Vita Humana,* 1964, *7,* 115–126.

MACKINNON, D. W. "The Highly Effective Individual." *Teachers College Record,* 1960, *61,* 367–378.

MADDI, S. R. *Personality Theories: A Comparative Analysis.* Rev. ed. Homewood, Ill.: Dorsey Press, 1972.

MADDOX, G. L. "Activity and Morale: A Longitudinal Study of Selected Subjects." *Social Forces,* 1963, *42,* 195–204.

MADDOX, G. L. "Persistence of Life Style Among the Elderly: A Longitudinal Study of Patterns of Social Activity in Relation to Life Satisfaction." *Proceedings of the 7th International Congress of Gerontology* (Vienna), 1966, *6,* 309–311.

MADDOX, G. L., and DOUGLAS, E. B. "Aging and Individual Differences." *Journal of Gerontology,* 1974, *29* (5), 555–563.

MADISON, P. *Personality Development in College.* Reading, Mass.: Addison-Wesley, 1969.

MARCIA, J. E. "Development and Validations of Ego-Identity Status." *Journal of Personality and Social Psychology,* 1966, *3* (5), 551–558.

MARGOLIUS, S. *Your Personal Guide to Successful Retirement.* New York: Random House, 1969.

MARMOR, J. *Psychiatry in Transition.* New York: Brunner/Mazel, 1974.

MARTIN, W. T. "The Structuring of Social Relationships Engendered by Suburban Residence." *American Sociological Review,* 1956, *21,* 446–464.

MASON, E. P. "Some Correlates of Self-Judgments of the Aged." *Journal of Gerontology*, 1954, *9*, 324–337.

MASTERS, W. H., and JOHNSON, V. E. *Human Sexual Response*. Boston: Little, Brown, 1965.

MASTERS, W. H., and JOHNSON, V. E. *Human Sexual Inadequacy*. Boston: Little, Brown, 1970.

MAXWELL, A. E. "Trends in Cognitive Ability in the Older Age Ranges." *Journal of Abnormal and Social Psychology*, 1961, *61*, 449–452.

MAYEROFF, M. *On Caring*. New York: Harper & Row, 1971.

MCCAMMON, R. W. *Human Growth and Development*. Springfield, Ill.: Thomas, 1970.

MCCLAIN, E. W. "A Program for Increasing Self Understanding for Counselors." *Counselor Education and Supervision*, 1969, *8* (4), 296.

MCCLELLAND, D. C., ATKINSON, J. W., CLARK, R. A., and LOWELL, E. L. *The Achievement Motive*. New York: Appleton-Century-Crofts, 1953.

MCCLURE, L., and BUAN, C. (Eds.) *Essays on Career Education*. Washington, D.C.: U.S. Government Printing Office, 1973.

MCCLUSKY, H. Y. *Background Report on Education*. Washington, D.C.: White House Conference on Aging, February, 1971.

MCCORD, J., MCCORD, W., and THURBER, E. "Effects of Maternal Employment on Lower-Class Boys." *Journal of Abnormal Social Psychology*, 1963, *67*, 177–182.

MCFARLAND, R. A. "Psycho-Physiological Problems of Aging in Air Transport Pilots." *Journal of Aviation Medicine*, 1954, *25*, 210–220.

MCFARLAND, R. A., and FISHER, M. P. "Alterations in Dark Adaption as a Function of Age." *Journal of Gerontology*, 1955, *10*, 424–428.

MCGLONE, R. E., and HOLLIEN, H. "Vocal Pitch Characteristics of Aged Women." *Journal of Speech and Hearing Research*, 1963, *6*, 164–170.

MCKAIN, W. *Retirement Marriage*. Storrs: University of Connecticut Press, 1968.

MCMAHON, W. W., HOANG, N., and WAGNER, A. "Returns to Investment in Higher Education: Expected and Realized Rates of Return by Occupational Objective, Degree Level, Type of Institution, Race, and Sex." Faculty Working Paper No. 301. College of Commerce and Business Administration, University of Illinois at Urbana-Champaign, February 24, 1976.

MCTAVISH, D. G. "Perceptions of Old People: A Review of Research Methodologies and Findings." *The Gerontologist*, 1971, *11* (4), 90–102.

MEAD, G. H. *Mind, Self, and Society.* Chicago: University of Chicago Press, 1934.

MEAD, M. "The Pattern of Leisure in Contemporary American Culture." *Annals of the American Academy of Political and Social Science,* 1957, *313,* 11–15.

MEAD, M. *Culture and Commitment.* New York: Natural History Press, 1970.

MELTZER, H. "Age Differences in Happiness and Life Adjustments of Workers." *Journal of Gerontology,* 1963, *18,* 66–70.

MELTZER, H. "Attitudes of Workers Before and After Age 40." *Geriatrics,* 1965, *20,* 425–432.

MENNINGER, K. *The Vital Balance.* New York: Viking Press, 1963.

MENZEL, H., and KATZ, E. "Social Relations and Innovation in the Medical Profession: The Epidemiology of a New Drug." *Public Opinion Quarterly,* 1955, *19,* 337–352.

MESSICK, S., and KOGAN, N. "Differentiation and Compartmentalization in Object-Sorting Measures of Categorizing Style." *Perceptual and Motor Skills,* 1963, *16,* 47–51.

MEYER, H. D. "The Adult Cycle." *Annals of the American Academy of Political and Social Science,* 1957, *313,* 58–67.

MEYERSON, L. "Somatopsychology of Physical Disability." In W. Cruickshank, *Psychology of Exceptional Children and Youth.* Englewood Cliffs, N.J.: Prentice-Hall, 1963.

MILES, C. C. "Influence of Speed and Age on Intelligence Scores of Adults." *Journal of General Psychology,* 1934, *10,* 208–210.

MILES, C. C., and MILES, W. R. "The Correlation of Intelligence Scores and Chronological Age from Early to Late Maturity." *American Journal of Psychology,* 1932, *44,* 44–78.

MILLER, D. "Leisure and the Adolescent." *New Society,* 1966, 7 (193).

MILLER, M. "Relationship of Vocational Maturity to Work Values." *Journal of Vocational Behavior,* 1974, *5,* 367–371.

MILLS, E. W. *Career Change Among Ministers: A Socio-Psychological Study.* Cambridge: Harvard Studies in Career Development No. 46, Center for Research in Career, 1966.

MILNE, L. J., and MILNE, M. *The Ages of Life.* New York: Harcourt Brace Jovanovich, 1968.

MISCHEL, W. "Continuity and Change in Personality." *American Psychologist,* 1969, *24,* 1012–1018.

MITCHELL, J. H., and BLOMQUIST, G. "The Effects of Physical Training on Sedentary American Men." *Cardiac Rehabilitation,* 1972, *2* (4), 33–36.

MOBERG, D. O. "Religiosity in Old Age." In B. L. Neugarten (Ed.), *Middle Age and Aging.* Chicago: University of Chicago Press, 1968.

MOENSTER, P. A. "Learning and Memory in Relation to Age." *Journal of Gerontology*, 1972, *27*, 361–363.

MONGE, R. H. "Learning in the Adult Years—Set or Rigidity." *Human Development*, 1969, *12*, 131–140.

MONGE, R. H., and HULTSCH, D. "Paired-Associate Learning As a Function of Adult Age and the Length of the Anticipation and Inspection Intervals." *Journal of Gerontology*, 1971, *26*, 157–162.

MORGAN, M. W. "Changes in Refraction over a Period of Twenty Years in a Non-Visually Selected Sample." *American Journal of Optometry*, 1958, *35*, 281–299.

MORGENTHALER, E. "More Executives Elect to Retire Early, Tackle Something Different." *The Wall Street Journal*, Oct. 19, 1971, p. 1.

MORRIS, D. *Intimate Behavior*. New York: Random House, 1971.

MOSHER, R., and SPRINTHALL, N. "Deliberate Psychological Education." *The Counseling Psychologist*, 1972, *2*, 3–82.

MOSS, J. J. "Teen-Age Marriage: Cross-National Trends and Sociological Factors in the Decision of When to Marry." *Journal of Marriage and the Family*, 1965, *27*, 230–242.

MOSS, J. J., APOLONIO, F., and JENSEN, M. "The Premarital Dyad during the Sixties." In C. B. Broderick (Ed.), *A Decade of Family Research and Action*. Minneapolis: National Council on Family Relations, 1971.

MOUSTAKAS, C. E. *Loneliness and Love*. Englewood Cliffs: Prentice-Hall, 1972.

MULVEY, M. C. "Psychological and Sociological Factors in Prediction of Career Patterns of Women." *Genetic Psychology Monographs*, 1963, *68*, 309–386.

MURRAY, J., POWERS, E., and HAVIGHURST, R. J. "Flexible Careers." *Gerontologist*, 1971, *11* (4), 4–12.

MURSTEIN, B. I. "The Relationship of Mental Health to Marital Choice and Courtship Progress." *Journal of Marriage and the Family*, 1967, *29*, 447–451.

MURSTEIN, B. I. "Person Perception and Courtship Progress among Premarital Couples." *Journal of Marriage and the Family*, 1972, *34*, 621–626.

MYRDAL, A., and KLEIN, V. *Women's Two Roles: Home and Work*. London: Routledge & Kegan Paul, 1956.

MYSAK, E. "Pitch and Duration Characteristics of Older Males." *Journal of Speech and Hearing Research*, 1959, *2*, 46–54.

MYSAK, E., and HANLEY, T. D. "Aging Processes in Speech: Pitch and Duration Characteristics." *Journal of Gerontology*, 1958, *13*, 309–313.

NIAAA. *Alcohol and Health: New Knowledge*. Washington, D.C.:

HEW, National Institute on Alcohol Abuse and Alcoholism, 1975.

NSC. *Accident Facts.* Chicago, Ill.: National Safety Council, 1975.

NEALE, D., SONSTROEM, R. J., and METZ, K. F. "Physical Fitness, Self Esteem and Attitudes toward Physical Activity." *Research Quarterly,* 1969, *40,* 743–749.

NELSON, E. "Persistence of Attitudes of College Students Fourteen Years Later." *Psychological Monographs,* 1954, *68* (2), 1–13.

NELSON, E. "Patterns of Religious Attitudes: Shifts from College to Fourteen Years Later." *Psychological Monographs,* 1956, *70* (17), 1–15.

NESSELROADE, J. R., and REESE, H. W. *Life-Span Developmental Psychology: Methodological Issues.* New York: Academic Press, 1973.

NEUGARTEN, B. L. (Ed.) *Middle Age and Aging.* Chicago: University of Chicago Press, 1968.

NEUGARTEN, B. L. "Personality and the Aging Process." *The Gerontologist,* 1972, *12,* 9–15.

NEUGARTEN, B. L. "Personality Change in Late Life: A Developmental Perspective." In C. Eisdorfer and P. M. Lawton (Eds.), *The Psychology of Adult Development and Aging.* Washington, D.C.: American Psychological Association, 1973.

NEUGARTEN, B. L., and ASSOCIATES (Eds.) *Personality in Middle and Late Life.* New York: Atherton, 1964.

NEUGARTEN, B. L., and DATAN, N. "Sociological Perspectives on the Life Cycle." In P. B. Baltes and K. W. Schaie (Eds.), *Life-Span Developmental Psychology.* New York: Academic Press, 1973.

NEUGARTEN, B. L., and GUTMANN, L. "Age-Sex Roles and Personality in Middle Age: A Thematic Apperception Study." *Psychological Monographs,* 1958, *72* (17), 1–33.

NEUGARTEN, B. L., HAVIGHURST, R. J., and TOBIN, S. S. "Personality and Patterns of Aging." In B. L. Neugarten (Ed.), *Middle Age and Aging: A Reader in Social Psychology.* Chicago: University of Chicago Press, 1968.

NEUGARTEN, B. L., and KRAINES, R. J. "Menopausal Symptoms in Women of Various Ages." *Psychosomatic Medicine,* 1965, *27,* 266–273.

NEUGARTEN, B. L., MOORE, J. W., and LOWE, J. C. "Age Norms, Age Constraints, and Adult Socialization." *American Journal of Sociology,* 1965, *70,* 710–717.

NEUGARTEN, B. L., and PATERSON, W. A. "A Study of the American Age Grade System." In *Proceedings of the Fourth Congress of the International Association of Gerontology,* Vol. 3.

Florence, Italy: International Association of Gerontology, 1957.

NEUGARTEN, B. L., and WEINSTEIN, K. K. "The Changing American Grandparent." *Journal of Marriage and the Family*, 1964, *26*, 199–204.

NIE, N. H., POWELL, G. B., JR., and PREWITT, K. "Social Structure and Political Participation: Developmental Relationships, Part I." *American Political Science Review*, 1969a, *63*, 361–378.

NIE, N. H., POWELL, G. B., JR., and PREWITT, K. "Social Structure and Political Participation: Developmental Relationships, Part II." *American Political Science Review*, 1969b, *63*, 808–832.

NORTON, A. "The Family Life Cycle Updated." In R. F. Winch and G. B. Spanier (Eds.), *Selected Studies in Marriage and the Family*. 9th ed. New York: Holt, Rinehart and Winston, 1974.

NYE, F. I., and HOFFMAN, L. W. *The Employed Mother in America*. Chicago: Rand McNally, 1963.

NYE, F. I., and BERARDO, F. *The Family: Its Structure and Interaction*. New York: Macmillan, 1973.

NYSTROM, E. P. "Activity Patterns and Leisure Concepts among the Elderly." *American Journal of Occupational Therapy*, 1974, *28*, 337–345.

OBERLEDER, M. "Psychotherapy with the Aging: An Art of the Possible?" *Psychotherapy: Theory, Research, and Practice*, 1966, *3*, 139–142.

OLIVER, L. W. "Achievement and Affiliation Motivation in Career-Oriented and Homemaking-Oriented College Women." *Journal of Vocational Behavior*, 1972, *2*, 317–331.

OLSEN, I. A. "Discrimination of Auditory Information as Related to Age." *Journal of Gerontology*, 1965, *20*, 394–397.

O'NEILL, N., and O'NEILL, G. *Shifting Gears*. New York: Avon, 1974.

ORDEN, S. R., and BRADBURN, N. M. "Working Wives and Marriage Happiness." *American Journal of Sociology*, 1969, *74* (4), 392–407.

ORGAN, D. W. "Locus of Control and Clarity of Self-Concept." *Perceptual and Motor Skills*, 1973, *37*, 100–102.

O'TOOLE, J. "The Reserve Army of the Underemployed. I. The World of Work." *Change 6*, 1975 (May), 26.

OTTO, H. A. (Ed.) *The Family in Search of a Future*. New York: Appleton-Century-Crofts, 1970.

OTTO, H. A., and MANN, J. (Eds.) *Ways of Growth*. New York: Viking Press, 1968.

OWENS, W. A. "Age and Mental Abilities: A Longitudinal Study." *Genetic Psychology Monographs*, 1953, *48*, 3–54.

OWENS, W. A. "Is Age Kinder to the Initially More Able?" *Journal of Gerontology,* 1959, *14,* 334–337.

OWENS, W. A. "Age and Mental Ability: A Second Adult Follow-Up." *Journal of Educational Psychology,* 1966, *57,* 311–325.

PALMORE, E. "Retirement Patterns among Aged Men: Findings of the 1963 Survey of the Aged." *Social Security Bulletin,* 1964, *27* (Aug.) , 3–10.

PALMORE, E. "The Effects of Aging on Activities and Attitudes." *Gerontologist,* 1968, *8,* 250–263.

PALMORE, E. *Normal Aging: Reports from the Duke Longitudinal Study (1955–1969).* Durham, N.C.: Duke University Press, 1970.

PALMORE, E. (Ed.) *Normal Aging II.* Durham, N.C.: Duke University Press, 1974.

PAPANEK, H. "Men, Women and Work: Reflections on the Two-Person Career." *American Journal of Sociology,* 1973, *78,* 852–870.

PARELIUS, A. P. "Emerging Sex-Role Attitudes, Expectations, and Strains among College Women." *Journal of Marriage and the Family,* 1975, *37,* 146–153.

PARIS, B. L., and LUCKEY, E. B. "A Longitudinal Study in Marital Satisfaction." *Sociological and Social Research,* 1966, *50,* 212–222.

PARKER, E. *The Seven Ages of Woman.* Baltimore: Johns Hopkins, 1960.

PARKER, E. B., and PAISLEY, W. J. *Patterns of Adult Information Seeking.* Final report on USOE Project No. 2583. Stanford, Calif.: Stanford University, 1966.

PARKER, S. *The Future of Work and Leisure.* New York: Praeger, 1971.

PARKER, S., and KEINER, R. J. "Characteristics of Negro Mothers in Single-Headed Households." *Journal of Marriage and the Family,* 1966, *28,* 507–513.

PARKES, C. M. *Bereavement: Studies of Grief in Adult Life.* New York: International Universities Press, 1972.

PARNES, H. S., NESTEL, G., and ANDRISANI, P. *The Pre-Retirement Years: A Longitudinal Study of the Labor Market Experience of Men.* Vol. 3. Columbus, Ohio: Center for Human Resource Research, 1972.

PASCAL, A., and others. *An Evaluation of Policy Related Research on Programs for Mid-Life Career Redirection.* Santa Monica: Rand Corp., 1975.

PATTERSON, C. H. *Humanistic Education.* Englewood Cliffs, N.J.: Prentice-Hall, 1973.

PAYNE, S. *The Art of Asking Questions.* Princeton: Princeton University Press, 1951.

PECK, R. F. "Personality Factors in Adjustment to Aging." *Geriatrics,* 1960, *15*, 124–130.

PERRY, J. B., and PFUHL, E. H. "Adjustment of Children in 'Solo' and Remarriage Homes." *Marriage and Family Living,* 1963, *25*, 221–223.

PERRY, W., JR. *Intellectual and Ethical Development in the College Years.* New York: Holt, Rinehart and Winston, 1970.

Personnel and Guidance Journal, 1976, *55* (3), November.

PETERSON, J. A., and PAYNE, B. *Love in the Later Years.* New York: Association Press, 1975.

PETTIGREW, T. F. "The Measurement and Correlates of Category Width as a Cognitive Variable." *Journal of Personality,* 1958, *26*, 532–544.

PFEIFFER, E. "Sexual Behavior in Old Age." In E. W. Busse and E. Pfeiffer (Eds.), *Behavior and Adaptation in Late Life.* Boston: Little, Brown, 1969.

PFEIFFER, E. "Survival in Old Age: Physical, Psychological, and Social Correlates of Longevity." *Journal of the American Geriatrics Society,* 1970, *18*, 273–285.

PFEIFFER, E., VERWOERDT, A., and DAVIS, G. G. "Sexual Behavior in Middle Life." *American Journal of Psychiatry,* 1972, *128*, 1262–1267.

PHILLIPS, D. L. "Social Participation and Happiness." *American Journal of Sociology,* 1967, *72*, 479–488.

PHILLIPS, W. S., and GREENE, J. E. "A Preliminary Study of the Relationship of Age, Hobbies, and Civil Status to Neuroticism among Women Teachers." *Journal of Educational Psychology,* 1939, *30*, 440–444.

PIAGET, J. "Intellectual Evolution from Adolescence to Adulthood." *Human Development,* 1972, *15*, 1–12.

PILIAVIN, I. M., RODIN, J., and PILIAVIN, J. A. "Good Samaritanism." *Journal of Personality and Social Psychology,* 1969, *13*, 289–299.

PINARD, M. "Marriage and Divorce Decisions and the Larger Social System: A Case Study in Social Change." *Social Forces,* 1966, *44*, 341–355.

PINEO, P. C. "Disenchantment in the Later Years of Marriage." *Journal of Marriage and Family Living,* 1961, *23*, 3–11.

PLANEK, T. W., CONDON, M. E., and FOWLER, R. C. *An Investigation of the Problems and Opinions of Aged Drivers.* Chicago: National Safety Council, 1968.

PLANT, W. T., and MINIUM, E. W. "Differential Personality Development in Young Adults of Markedly Different Aptitude Levels." *Journal of Educational Psychology,* 1967, *58,* 141–152.

PLUTCHIK, R., WEINER, M., and CONTE, H. "Studies of Body Image, Body Worries, and Body Discomforts." *Journal of Gerontology,* 1971, *26,* 244–350.

POLLIS, C. A. "Dating Involvement and Patterns of Idealization: A Test of Waller's Hypothesis." *Journal of Marriage and the Family,* 1969, *31,* 765–771.

POLLMAN, A. W. "Early Retirement: A Comparison of Poor Health to Other Retirement Factors." *Journal of Gerontology,* 1971, *26,* 41–45.

POLLMAN, A. W., and JOHNSON, A. C. "Resistance to Change, Early Retirement, and Managerial Decisions." *Industrial Gerontology,* 1974, *1* (1), 33–41.

POWELL, M. "Age and Sex Differences in the Degree of Conflict Within Certain Areas of Psychological Adjustment." *Psychology Monographs,* 1955, *69* (2), 1–14.

POWELL, M., and BLOOM, V. "Development of and Reasons for Vocational Choices of Adolescents through the High School Years." *Journal of Educational Research,* 1962, *56,* 126–133.

PRESSEY, S. L., and JONES, A. W. "1923–1953 and 20–60 Age Changes in Moral Codes, Anxieties, and Interests, as Shown by the 'X-O Tests'." *Journal of Psychology,* 1955, *39,* 485–502.

PRINCE, A. J. "A Study of 194 Cross-Religious Marriages." *Family Life Coordinator,* 1962, *11,* 3–7.

PROPPER, A. M. "The Relationship of Maternal Employment to Adolescent Roles, Activities, and Parental Relationships." *Journal of Marriage and the Family,* 1972, *34,* 417–421.

PROSHANSKY, H. M., ITTELSON, W. H., and RIVLIN, L. G. (Eds.) *Environmental Psychology: Man and His Physical Setting.* New York: Holt, Rinehart and Winston, 1970.

QUINN, R., STAINES, G., and MCCULLOUGH, M. *Job Satisfaction: Is There a Trend?* U.S. Department of Labor, Manpower Research Monograph No. 30. Washington, D.C.: Government Printing Office, 1974.

RABBITT, P. "Age and The Use of Structure in Transmitted Information." In G. A. Talland (Ed.), *Human Aging and Behavior.* New York: Academic Press, 1968.

RAHE, R., MCKEAN, J. D., JR., and ARTHUR, R. J. "A Longitudinal Study of Life-Change and Illness Patterns." *Journal of Psychosomatic Research,* 1967, *10,* 355–366.

RAINWATER, L. "Some Aspects of Lower Class Sexual Behavior." *Journal of Social Issues,* 1966, *22* (2), 96–108.

RALLINGS, E. M. "Family Situations of Married and Never-Married Males." *Journal of Marriage and the Family,* 1966, *28,* 485–490.

RALSTON, N. C., and THOMAS, G. P. *The Adolescent: Case Studies for Analysis.* New York: Chandler, 1974.

RAMSDELL, D. A. "The Psychology of the Hard of Hearing and Deafened Adult." In H. Davis and R. Silverman (Eds.), *Hearing and Deafness.* New York: Holt, Rinehart and Winston, 1965.

RAPOPORT, R., and RAPOPORT, R. N. "New Light on the Honeymoon." *Human Relations,* 1964, *17,* 33–56.

RAPOPORT, R., and RAPOPORT, R. N. "Work and Family in Contemporary Society." *American Sociological Review,* 1965, *30,* 381–394.

RAPOPORT, R., and RAPOPORT, R. N. "The Dual-Career Family." *Human Relations,* 1969, *22,* 3–30.

RAPOPORT, R., and RAPOPORT, R. N. *Dual-Career Families.* Harmondsworth, England: Penguin, 1971a.

RAPOPORT, R., and RAPOPORT, R. N. "Early and Later Experiences as Determinants of Adult Behavior: Married Women's Family and Career Patterns." *British Journal of Sociology,* 1971b, *22,* 16–30.

RAPOPORT, R., and RAPOPORT, R. N. *Leisure and the Family Life Cycle.* London: Routledge & Kegan Paul, 1975.

RAPPOPORT, L. *Personality Development: The Chronology of Experience.* Glenview, Ill.: Scott, Foresman, 1972.

RAUNER, I. M. "Occupational Information and Occupational Choice." *Personnel and Guidance Journal,* 1962, *41,* 311–317.

REES, J., and BOTWINICK, J. "Detection and Decision Factors in Auditory Behavior of the Elderly." *Journal of Gerontology,* 1971, *26,* 133–136.

REES, M. B., and PAISLEY, W. J. *Social and Psychological Predictors of Information Seeking and Media Use.* Stanford, Calif.: Institute for Communication Research, Stanford University, 1967.

REES, M. B., and PAISLEY, W. J. "Social and Psychological Predictors of Adult Information Seeking and Media Use." *Adult Education,* 1968, *19* (1), 11–29.

REGNIER, V. "Neighborhood Planning for the Urban Elderly." In D. Woodruff and J. Birren (Eds.), *Aging: Scientific Perspectives and Social Issues.* New York: D. Van Nostrand, 1975.

REICHARD, S., LIVSON, F., and PETERSEN, P. *Aging and Personality.* New York: Wiley, 1962.

REIMANIS, G., and GREEN, R. F. "Imminence of Death and Intellectual Decrement in the Aging." *Developmental Psychology,* 1971, *5,* 270–272.

REISS, I. L. "The Sexual Renaissance: A Summary and Analysis." *Journal of Social Issues,* 1966, *22,* 123–137.

REISSMAN, L. "Class, Leisure, and Social Participation." *American Sociological Review,* 1954, *19,* 76–84.

REVIS, J. S. *Transportation* (White House Conference on Aging background papers). Washington, D.C.: U.S. Government Printing Office, 1971.

RIEGEL, K. F., and RIEGEL, R. M. "A Study on Changes of Attitudes and Interests during Later Years of Life." *Vita Humana,* 1960, *3,* 177–206.

RIEGEL, K. F., and RIEGEL, R. M. "Development, Drop and Death." *Developmental Psychology,* 1972, *6,* 306–319.

RIEGEL, K. F., RIEGEL, R. M., and MEYER, G. "A Study of the Dropout Rates in Longitudinal Research on Aging and the Prediction of Death." *Journal of Personality and Social Psychology,* 1967, *5,* 342–348.

RILEY, M. W., FONER, A., and others. *Aging and Society: Volume I. An Inventory of Research Findings.* New York: Russell Sage, 1968.

RILEY, M. W., FONER, A., HESS, B., and TOBY, M. L. "Socialization for the Middle and Later Years." In D. A. Goslin (Ed.), *Handbook of Socialization Theory and Research.* Chicago: Rand McNally, 1969.

ROBERTS, D. M. "Abilities and Learning: A Brief Review and Discussion of Empirical Studies." *Journal of School Psychology,* 1968, *7,* 12–21.

RODSTEIN, M. "Accidents among the Aged: Incidence, Causes, and Prevention." *Journal of Chronic Diseases,* 1964, *17,* 515–526.

ROGERS, E. M. "Personality Correlates of the Adoption of Technical Practices." *Rural Sociology,* 1957, *22,* 267–268.

ROGERS, E. M., and BEAL, G. M. "The Importance of Personal Influence in the Adoption of Technological Changes." *Social Forces,* 1957, *36,* 329–334.

ROGERS, E. M., and SHOEMAKER, F. F. *Communication of Innovations.* New York: Free Press, 1971.

ROGERS, J. *Adults Learning.* Baltimore: Penguin Books, 1973.

ROHER, J. H., and EDMONSON, M. S. (Eds.) *The Eighth Generation.* New York: Harper, 1960.

ROLLINS, B. C., and FELDMAN, H. "Marital Satisfaction over the Family Life Cycle." *Journal of Marriage and the Family,* 1970, *32,* 20–28.

ROKEACH, M. *The Open and Closed Mind*. New York: Basic Books, 1960.

ROSE, A. M. "A Current Theoretical Issue in Social Gerontology." *Gerontologist,* 1964, *4* (1), 46–50.

ROSE, A. M. "Factors Associated with the Life Satisfaction of Middle-Class, Middle-Aged Persons." In C. B. Vedder (Ed.), *Problems of the Middle-Aged*. Springfield, Ill.: Thomas, 1965.

ROSE, A. M. "Class Differences among the Elderly: A Research Report." *Sociological and Social Research,* 1966, *50,* 356–360.

ROSEN, B., JERDEE, T. H., and PRESTWICH, T. L. "Dual-Career Marital Adjustment: Potential Effects of Discriminatory Managerial Attitudes." *Journal of Marriage and the Family,* 1975, *37,* 565–572.

ROSENBERG, B. G., and SUTTON-SMITH, B. "Family Interaction Effects on Masculinity-Feminity." *Journal of Personality and Social Psychology,* 1968, *8,* 117.

ROSENBERG, G. S. *The Worker Grows Old*. San Francisco: Jossey-Bass, 1970.

ROSENGREN, W. R. "Social Sources of Pregnancy as Illness or Normality." *Social Forces,* 1961, *39,* 260–267.

ROSENZWEIG, S., and ROSENZWEIG, L. "Aggression in Problem Children and Normals as Evaluated by the Rosenzweig Picture Frustration Study." *Journal of Abnormal Social Psychology,* 1952, *47,* 683–688.

ROSOW, I. *Social Integration of the Aged*. New York: Free Press, 1967.

ROSOW, J. E. (Ed.) *The Worker and the Job: Coping with Change*. Englewood Cliffs, N.J.: Prentice-Hall, 1974.

ROSS, E. K. *On Death and Dying*. New York: Macmillan, 1969.

ROSSI, A. "Transition to Parenthood." *Journal of Marriage and the Family,* 1968, *30,* 26–39.

RUBIN, T. "Transition in Sex Values—Implications for the Education of Adolescents." *Journal of Marriage and the Family,* 1965, *27,* 185–192.

RUEBSAAT, H. J., and HULL, R. *The Male Climacteric*. New York: Hawthorn Books, 1975.

SALTZ, R. "Aging Persons as Child-Care Workers in a Foster Grandparent Program: Psychosocial Effects and Work Performance." *Aging and Human Development,* 1971, *2,* 314–340.

SAMIS, H. V. "Aging: The Loss of Temporal Organization." *Perspectives in Biology and Medicine,* 1968, *12,* 95–102.

SANFORD, N. *Issues in Personality Theory*. San Francisco: Jossey-Bass, 1970.

SANTOSTEFANO, S. "Cognitive Controls and Exceptional States in Children." *Journal of Clinical Psychology,* 1964, *20,* 213–218.

SARASON, S. B. *The Creation of Settings and the Future Societies.* San Francisco: Jossey-Bass, 1972.

SARASON, S. B. *The Psychological Sense of Community: Prospects for a Community Psychology.* San Francisco: Jossey-Bass, 1974.

SARASON, S. B. "Community Psychology, Networks, and Mr. Everyman." *American Psychologist,* 1976, *31* (5), 317–328.

SATURDAY REVIEW, September 20, 1975. Special Issue on Life Long Learning.

SCHAIE, K. W. "Rigidity-Flexibility and Intelligence: A Cross-Sectional Study of the Adult Life Span from 20 to 70 Years." *Psychological Monographs,* 1958, *72* (9), 1–26.

SCHAIE, K. W. "Translations in Gerontology—From Lab to Life. Intellectual Functioning." *American Psychologist,* 1974, *29,* 802–807.

SCHAIE, K. W., and GRIBBEN, K. "Adult Development and Aging." *Annual Review of Psychology,* 1975, *26,* 65–96.

SCHAIE, K. W., LABOUVIE, G. V., and BARRETT, T. J. "Selective Attrition Effects in a Fourteen-Year Study of Adult Intelligence." *Journal of Gerontology,* 1973, *28,* 328–334.

SCHAIE, K. W., and STROTHER, C. R. "Cognitive and Personality Variables in College Graduates of Advanced Age." In G. A. Talland (Ed.), *Human Aging and Behavior.* New York: Academic Press, 1968a.

SCHAIE, K. W., and STROTHER, C. R. "A Cross-Sequential Study of Age Changes in Cognitive Behavior." *Psychological Bulletin,* 1968b, *70,* 671–680.

SCHAIE, K. W., and STROTHER, C. R. "The Effects of Time and Cohort Differences on the Interpretation of Age Changes in Cognitive Behavior." *Multivariate Behavioral Research,* 1968c, *3,* 259–294.

SCHEIN, E. H. "How 'Career Anchors' Hold Executives to Their Career Paths." *Personnel,* 1975, *52* (3), 11–24.

SCHLESINGER, H. J. "Cognitive Attitudes in Relation to Susceptibility to Interference." *Journal of Personality,* 1954, *22,* 354–374.

SCHLOSSBERG, N. K. "Adult Men: Education or Re-Education?" *Vocational Guidance Quarterly,* 1970, *19,* 36–40.

SCHLOSSBERG, N. K., and PIETROFESA, D. "Career Counseling for Women." *The Counseling Psychologist,* 1973, *4* (1), 44–53.

SCHLOSSBERG, N. K., and TROLL, L. *Perspectives on Counseling Adults.* College Park: University of Maryland, 1976.

SCHMIDHAUSER, J. "The Political Influence of the Aged." *Gerontologist,* 1968, *8,* 44–49.

SCHOENBERG, B. (Ed.). *Anticipatory Grief.* New York: Columbia University Press, 1974.

SCHONFIELD, D. "Learning and Retention." In J. E. Birren (Ed.), *Contemporary Gerontology: Concepts and Issues.* Los Angeles: Andrus Gerontology Center, 1969.

SCHRAMM, W., and WHITE, D. M. "Age, Education, and Economic Status: Factors in Newspaper Reading." *Journalism Quarterly,* 1949, *26,* 149–159.

SCHULZ, J. H. "The Economics of Retirement." *Industrial Gerontology,* 1974, *1* (1), 1–10.

SCHUPACK, M. B. "Research on Employment Problems of Older Workers." *Gerontologist,* 1962, *2,* 157–163.

SCHUTZ, W. C. *FIRO—A Three-Dimensional Theory of Interpersonal Behavior.* New York: Holt, Rinehart and Winston, 1958.

SCHWARTZ, A. N., and PROPPE, H. G. "Toward Person-Environment Transactional Research in Aging." *Gerontologist,* 1970, *10,* 228–232.

SCHWARTZ, D. W., and KARP, S. A. "Field Dependence in a Geriatric Population." *Perceptual and Motor Skills,* 1967, *24,* 495–504.

SCOTT, J. C. "Membership and Participation in Voluntary Organizations." *American Sociological Review,* 1957, *22,* 315–326.

SCOTT, W. A. "Conceptualizing and Measuring Structural Properties of Cognition." In O. J. Harvey (Ed.), *Motivation and Social Interaction.* New York: Ronald Press, 1963.

SEARLS, L. G. "Leisure Role Emphasis of College Graduate Homemakers." *Journal of Marriage and the Family,* 1966, *28,* 77–82.

SEEMAN, J. "Personality Integration in College Women." *Journal of Personality and Social Psychology,* 1966, *4* (1), 91–93.

SELTZER, M. M., and ATCHLEY, R. C. "The Concept of Old: Changing Attitudes and Stereotypes." *Gerontologist,* 1971, *11* (1), 226–230.

SELYE, H. *Stress Without Distress.* Philadelphia: Lippincott, 1974.

SESSOMS, A. D. "An Analysis of Selected Variables Affecting Outdoor Recreation Patterns." *Social Forces,* 1963, *42,* 112–115.

SHAKOW, D., DOLKART, M. B., and GOLDMAN, R. "The Memory Function in Psychosis of the Aged." *Diseases of the Nervous System,* 1941, *2,* 43–48.

SHANAS, E. *The Health of Older People: A Social Survey.* Cambridge, Mass.: Harvard University Press, 1962.

SHANAS, E. "Health and Adjustment in Retirement." *Gerontologist,* 1970, *10* (1), 19–21.

SHANAS, E., TOWNSEND, P., WEDDERBURN, D., FRIIS, H., MILHOJ, P., and STEHOUWER, J. "The Psychology of Health." In B. Neugarten (Ed.), *Middle Age and Aging.* Chicago: University of Chicago Press, 1968a.

SHANAS, E., TOWNSEND, P., WEDDERBURN, D., FRIIS, H., MILHOJ, P., and STEHOUWER, J. (Eds.). *Old People in Three Industrial Societies.* New York: Atherton, 1968b.

SHAW, M. E., and WRIGHT, J. M. *Scales for the Measurement of Attitudes.* New York: McGraw-Hill, 1967.

SHEEHY, G. *Passages: Predictable Crises of Adult Life.* New York: Dutton, 1976.

SHEPPARD, H. L. (Ed.) *Toward an Industrial Gerontology.* Cambridge, Mass.: Schenkman, 1970.

SHEPPARD, H. L. *New Perspectives on Older Workers.* Washington, D.C.: W. E. Upjohn Institute for Employment Research, 1971.

SHERMAN, J. A. *On the Psychology of Women.* Springfield, Ill.: Thomas, 1971.

SHERMAN, S. R. "Leisure Time Activities in Retirement Housing." *Journal of Gerontology,* 1974, *29,* 325–335.

SHIBLES, W. A. *Death: An Interdisciplinary Analysis.* Whitewater, Wis.: Language Press, 1974.

SHNEIDMAN, E. "Orientations Toward Death: A Vital Aspect of the Study of Lives." *International Journal of Psychiatry,* 1966, *2,* 167.

SHNEIDMAN, E. *Death and the College Student.* New York: Behavioral Publications, 1972.

SHUTTLEWORTH, F. K. "A Biosocial and Developmental Theory of Male and Female Sexuality." *Journal of Marriage and Family Living,* 1959, *21,* 163–170.

SIEGELMAN, M. "College Student Personality Correlates of Early Parent-Child Relationships." *Journal of Consulting Psychology,* 1965, *29,* 558–564.

SILVERMAN, P. R. "Widowhood and Preventive Intervention." *The Family Coordinator,* 1972, *21,* 95–102.

SILVERMAN, P. R. *Widow-to-Widow Program.* New York: Health Sciences, 1973.

SIMON, A. "Mental Health." In *Physical and Mental Health.* White House Conference on Aging background papers. Washington, D.C.: U.S. Government Printing Office, 1971.

SIMON, A., LOWENTHAL, M., and EPSTEIN, L. *Crisis and Intervention.* San Francisco: Jossey-Bass, 1970.

SIMPSON, I. H., and MCKINNEY, J. C. (Eds.). *Social Aspects of Aging.* Durham, N.C.: Duke University Press, 1966.

SIMPSON, R. L. "Parental Influence, Anticipatory Socialization, and Social Mobility." *American Sociological Review,* 1962, *27,* 517–522.

SJOGREN, D. D. "Achievement as a Function of Study Time." *American Educational Research Journal,* 1967, *4,* 337–343.

SJOGREN, D. D., and KNOX, A. B. *The Influence of Speed, Set and Prior Knowledge on Adult Learning.* Final Report on Cooperative Research Project No. 2233. Lincoln: Adult Education Research, University of Nebraska, 1965.

SJOGREN, D. D., KNOX, A. B., and GROTELUESCHEN, A. D. "Adult Learning in Relation to Prior Adult Education Participation." *Adult Education,* 1968, *19* (1), 3–10.

SKEELS, H. M. "Adult Status of Children with Contrasting Early Life Experience." *Monographs of the Society for Research in Child Development,* 1966, *31,* 1–65.

SKERLJ, B. "Further Evidence of Age Changes in Body Form Based on Material of D. A. W. Edwards." *Human Biology,* 1954, *26,* 330–336.

SLATAPER, F. J. "Age Norms of Refraction and Vision." *Archives of Ophthalmology,* 1950, *43,* 446–481.

SLATER, C. "Class Differences in Definition of Role and Membership in Voluntary Associations among Urban Married Women." *American Journal of Sociology,* 1960, *65,* 616–619.

SMITH, A. "Aging and Interference with Memory." *Journal of Gerontology,* 1975, *30,* 319–325.

SMITH, D. W., and BIERMAN, E. L. *The Biologic Ages of Man.* Philadelphia: Saunders, 1973.

SMITH, M. B. *Social Psychology and Human Values.* Chicago: Aldine, 1969.

SMITH, W. G. "Critical Life-Events and Prevention Strategies in Mental Health." *Archives of General Psychiatry,* 1971, *25,* 103–109.

SNYDER, E. C. "Attitudes: A Study of Homogamy and Marital Selectivity." *Journal of Marriage and the Family,* 1964, *26,* 332–336.

SODDY, K. *Men in Middle Life.* New York: Lippincott, 1967.

SOMMERS, D. "Occupational Rankings for Men and Women by Earnings." *Monthly Labor Review,* 1974, *97* (8), 34–51.

SONSTROEM, R. "Attitude Testing Examining Certain Psychologic Correlates of Physical Activity." *Research Quarterly,* 1974, *45,* 93.

SORENSON, H. "Adult Ages as a Factor in Learning." *Journal of Educational Psychology,* 1930, *21,* 451–457.

SORENSON, H. *Adult Abilities*. Minneapolis: University of Minnesota Press, 1938.

SPEAKMAN, D. *Bibliography of Research on Changes in Working Capacity with Age*. London: Ministry of Labour and National Service, National Advisory Committee on the Employment of Older Men and Women, 1956.

SPEAKMAN, M. A. "The Effect of Age on the Incidental Relearning of Stamp Values: The Use of Deduction in a Subsidiary Test." *Journal of Gerontology*, 1954, *9*, 162–167.

SPEALMAN, C. R., and BRUYERE, P. T. "The Changing Age Distribution of Pilots Holding First Class Medical Certificates." *Journal of Gerontology*, 1955, *10*, 341–344.

SPENCE, D. L., and LONNER, T. D. "The 'Empty Nest': A Transition within Motherhood." *Family Coordinator*, 1971, 369–375.

SPIETH, W. "Cardiovascular Health Status, Age, and Psychological Performance." *Journal of Gerontology*, 1964, *19*, 277–284.

STEIN, A. H., and BAILEY, M. M. "The Socialization of Achievement Orientation in Females." *Psychological Bulletin*, 1973, *80* (5), 345–366.

STEINER, G. *The People Look at Television*. New York: Knopf, 1963.

STERN, G., and COPE, A. "Differences in Educability between Stereopaths, Non-Stereopaths and Rationals." *American Psychologist*, 1956, *11* (8), 362.

STEVENS, J. O. *Awareness: Exploring, Experimenting, Experiencing*. Moab, Utah: Real People Press, 1971.

STOKES, R. G., and MADDOX, G. L. "Some Social Factors on Retirement Adaptation." *American Journal of Gerontology*, 1967, *22*, 329–333.

STONE, C. L. "Three-Generation Influences on Teenagers' Conceptions of Family Culture Patterns and the Parent-Child Relationships." *Journal of Marriage and Family Living*, 1962, *12*, 85–87.

STONECYPHER, D. D. *Getting Older and Staying Young*. New York: Norton, 1974.

STREIB, G. F. "Intergenerational Relations: Perspectives of the Two Generations on the Older Parent." *Journal of Marriage and the Family*, 1965, *27*, 469–476.

STREIB, G. F., and SCHNEIDER, C. J. *Retirement in American Society: Impact and Process*. Ithaca, N.Y.: Cornell University Press, 1971.

STRONG, E. K. *Vocational Interests of Men and Women*. Stanford, Calif.: Stanford University Press, 1943.

STRONG, E. K. "Permanence of Interest Scores of 22 Years." *Journal of Applied Psychology*, 1951, *35*, 89–91.

STRONG, E. K. "Satisfactions and Interests." *American Psychologist*, 1958, *13*, 449–456.

SUPER, D. C., KOWALSKI, R. S., and GOTKIN, E. H. *Floundering and Trial after High School.* Final Report, Cooperative Research Project No. 1393. New York: Teachers College, Columbia University, 1967.

SUSSMAN, M. B. "Intergenerational Family Relationships and Social Role Changes in Middle Age." *Journal of Gerontology*, 1960, *15*, 71–75.

SUSSMAN, M. B. "Relationships of Adult Children with Their Parents in the United States." In E. Shanas and G. Streib (Eds.), *Social Structure and the Family: Generational Relations.* Englewood Cliffs, N.J.: Prentice-Hall, 1965.

SUSSMAN, M. B., and COGSWELL, B. "Family Influences on Job Movement." *Human Relations*, 1971, *24*, 447–487.

SUTTON-SMITH, B., ROBERTS, J. M., and KOZELKA, R. M. "Game Involvement in Adults." *Journal of Social Psychology*, 1963, *60*, 15–30.

SWARD, K. "Age and Mental Ability in Superior Men." *American Journal of Psychology*, 1945, *58*, 443–479.

SWENSON, W. M. "The Many Faces of Aging." *Geriatrics*, 1962, *17*, 659–663.

SYMONDS, P. M. *From Adolescent to Adult.* New York: Columbia University Press, 1961.

SZAFRAN, J., and BIRREN, J. E. "Perception." In J. E. Birren (Ed.), *Contemporary Gerontology: Concepts and Issues.* Los Angeles: Andrus Gerontology Center, 1969.

TALLAND, G. A. *Deranged Memory.* New York: Academic Press, 1965.

TALLMER, M., and KUTNER, B. "Disengagement and the Stresses of Aging." *Journal of Gerontology*, 1969, *24*, 70–75.

TALLMER, M., and KUTNER, B. "Disengagement and Morale." *The Gerontologist*, 1970, *10* (4), 317–320.

TAUB, H. A. "Visual and Short-Term Memory as a Function of Age, Rate of Presentation, and Schedule of Presentation." *Journal of Gerontology*, 1966, *21*, 388–392.

TAUB, H. A. "Age Differences in Memory as a Function of Rate of Presentation, Order of Report, and Stimulus Organization." *Journal of Gerontology*, 1968, *23*, 159–164.

TAUB, H. A. "Memory Span, Practice, and Aging." *Journal of Gerontology*, 1973, *28*, 335–338.

TAUB, H. A., and LONG, M. K. "The Effects of Practice on Short-Term Memory of Young and Old Subjects." *Journal of Gerontology*, 1972, *27*, 494–499.

TAUBMAN, P. J., and WALES, T. *Higher Education and Earnings: College as an Investment and a Screening Device.* New York: McGraw-Hill, 1974.

TAYLOR, C. W., and BARRON, F. *Scientific Creativity.* New York: Wiley, 1963.

TERKEL, S. *Working: People Talk About What They Do All Day and How They Feel About What They Do.* New York: Pantheon Books, 1972.

TERMAN, L. M., and MILES, G. C. *Sex and Personality.* New York: McGraw-Hill, 1936.

TERMAN, L. M., and ODEN, M. H. *The Gifted Group at Mid-Life.* Stanford, Calif.: Stanford University Press, 1959.

THOMAE, H. "Theory of Aging and Cognitive Theory of Personality." *Human Development,* 1970, *13,* 1–16.

THOMPSON, L. J. "Stresses in Middle Life from the Psychiatrist's Viewpoint." In C. B. Vedder (Ed.), *Problems of the Middle-Aged.* Springfield, Ill.: Thomas, 1965.

THOMPSON, L. W., and MARSH, G. "Psychological Studies of Aging." In C. Eisdorfer and M. P. Lawton (Eds.), *The Psychology of Adult Development and Aging.* Washington, D.C.: American Psychological Association, 1973.

THOMPSON, W. *Correlates of the Self Concept.* Nashville, Tenn.: Dede Wallace Center, June, 1972.

THORNDIKE, E. L. *Adult Learning.* New York: Macmillan, 1928.

THORSON, J. A. "Attitudes Toward Aging as a Function of Race and Social Class." *Gerontologist,* 1975, *15,* 343–344.

THORSON, J. A., HANCOCK, K., and WHATLEY, L. "Attitudes Toward Aged as a Function of Age and Education." *Gerontologist,* 1973, *13,* 82–94.

THORSON, J. A., HANCOCK, K., and WHATLEY, L. "Attitudes Toward the Aged as a Function of Age and Education." *Gerontologist,* 1974, *14,* 316–318.

THURNHER, M. "Goals, Values, and the Life Evaluations at the Pre-Retirement Stage." *Journal of Gerontology,* 1974, *29,* 85–96.

TIEDEMAN, D. V., and MILLER-TIEDEMAN, A. "A Model for Structuring Personal Perception into Career Decision Making." *Texas Tech Journal of Education,* 1976, *3* (1), 7–31.

TIEDEMAN, D. V., and O'HARA, R. P. *Career Development: Choice and Adjustment.* New York: College Entrance Examination Board, 1963.

TIFFANY, D. W., COWAN, J. R., and TIFFANY, P. *The Unemployed: A Social-Psychological Portrait.* Englewood Cliffs, N.J.: Prentice-Hall, 1970.

TIMIRAS, P. S. *Developmental Physiology and Aging.* New York: Macmillan, 1972.

TISSUE, T. "Disengagement Potential: Replication and Use as an Explanatory Variable." *Journal of Gerontology,* 1971, *26* (1), 76–80.

TOBIAS, J., and GORELICK, J. "An Investigation of 'Orderliness' as a Characteristic of Mentally Retarded Adults." *American Journal of Mental Deficiency,* 1960, *64,* 761–764.

TOFFLER, A. *Future Shock.* New York: Random House, 1970.

TOFFLER, A. (Ed.) *The Futurists.* New York: Random House, 1972.

TOFFLER, A. (Ed.) *Learning for Tomorrow, the Role of the Future in Education.* New York: Random House, 1974.

TOUGH, A. *Learning Without a Teacher.* Toronto: Ontario Institute for Studies in Education, 1967.

TOUGH, A. *Why Adults Learn.* Toronto: Ontario Institute for Studies in Education, 1968a.

TOUGH, A. *A Study of the Major Reasons for Beginning and Continuing a Learning Project.* Toronto: Ontario Institute for Studies in Education, 1968b.

TOUGH, A. *The Adult's Learning Projects.* Research in Education Series No. 1. Toronto: Ontario Institute for Studies in Education, 1971.

TRENT, J. W., and MEDSKER, L. B. *Beyond High School.* San Francisco: Jossey-Bass, 1968.

TROLDAHL, V. C., and VAN DAM, R. "Face-to-Face Communication about Major Topics in the News." Reported in Troldahl, V. C., "Studies of Consumption of Mass Media Content." *Journalism Quarterly,* 1965, *42,* 596–603.

TROLDAHL, V. C., VAN DAM, R., and ROBECK, G. B. "Public Affairs Information-Seeking from Expert Institutionalized Sources." *Journalism Quarterly,* 1965, *42,* 403–412.

TROLL, L. E. "The Family of Later Life: A Decade Review." *Journal of Marriage and the Family,* 1971, *33,* 263–290.

TROLL, L. E. *Early and Middle Adulthood.* Monterey, Calif.: Brooks/Cole, 1975.

TROLL, L. E., NEUGARTEN, B. L., and KRAINES, R. J. "Similarities in Values and Other Personality Characteristics in College Students and their Parents." *Merrill-Palmer Quarterly,* 1969, *15,* 323–357.

TRUAX, C. B., and CARKHUFF, R. P. *Toward Effective Counseling and Psychotherapy: Training and Practice.* Chicago: Aldine, 1967.

TRUMBULL, R., PACE, C. R., and KUHLEN, R. G. "Expansion and Constriction of Life Activities during the Adult Life Span as Reflected in Civic and Political Participation." *American Psychologist*, 1950, *5*, 367.

TUCKMAN, J., and LORGE, I. "The Best Years of Life: A Study in Ranking." *Journal of Psychology*, 1952, *34*, 137–149.

TUCKMAN, J., and LORGE, I. "Attitudes toward Old People." *Journal of Social Psychology*, 1953, *37*, 249–260.

TUCKMAN, J., and LORGE, I. "Old People's Appraisal of Adjustment over the Life Span." *Journal of Personality*, 1954, *22*, 417–422.

TUCKMAN, J., and LORGE, I. "Perceptual Stereotypes about Life and Adjustments." *Journal of Social Psychology*, 1956, *43*, 239–245.

TUDDENHAM, R. D. "The Constancy of Personality Ratings over Two Decades." *Genetic Psychology Monographs*, 1959, *60*, 3–29.

TUDDENHAM, R. D., BLUMENKRANTZ, J., and WILKIN, W. R. "Age Changes on AGCT: A Longitudinal Study of Average Adults." *Journal of Consulting and Clinical Psychology*, 1968, *32* (6), 659–663.

TURNER, F. B. "Common Characteristics among Persons Seeking Professional Marriage Counseling." *Journal of Marriage and Family Living*, 1954, *16*, 143–144.

TURNER, R. H. "Some Aspects of Women's Ambition." *American Journal of Sociology*, 1964, *70*, 271–284.

TURNEY-HIGH, H. H. *Man and System*. New York: Appleton-Century-Crofts, 1968.

UDRY, J. R. "Marital Instability by Race, Sex, Education, and Occupation, Using 1960 Census Data." *American Journal of Sociology*, 1966, *72*, 203–209.

U.S. BLS. *U.S. Working Women: A Chartbook*. Bureau of Labor Statistics Bulletin 1880. Washington, D.C.: U.S. Department of Labor, 1975.

U.S. CENSUS, Department of Commerce. *Statistical Abstract of the United States: Colonial Times to 1957*. Washington, D.C.: U.S. Government Printing Office, 1960.

U.S. CENSUS, Department of Commerce. *Selected Symptoms of Psychological Distress*. Rockville, Md.: National Center for Health Statistics, 1970.

U.S. CENSUS, Department of Commerce. *Age at First Marriage and Children Ever Born, for the United States: 1970*. Washington, D.C.: U.S. Government Printing Office, 1973a.

U.S. CENSUS, Department of Commerce. *1970 Census of Population: Characteristics of the Population*. Washington, D.C.: U.S. Government Printing Office, 1973b.

U.S. CENSUS, Department of Commerce. *Teenagers: Marriages, Divorces, Parenthood, and Mortality.* DHEW Publication No. (HRA) 74-1901. Rockville, Md., 1973c.

U.S. CENSUS, Department of Commerce. *Statistical Abstract of the United States.* Washington, D.C.: U.S. Government Printing Office, 1975.

U.S. DHEW, Department of Health, Education, and Welfare (NCES). *Condition of Education.* Washington, D.C.: U.S. Government Printing Office, 1975.

U.S. DHEW (NCES). *The Condition of Education: A Statistical Report on the Condition of Education in the United States.* Washington, D.C.: U.S. Government Printing Office, 1976.

U.S. DEPARTMENT OF LABOR, Women's Bureau, Employment Standards Administration. *The Economic Role of Women* (reprinted from Economic Report of the President, 1973). Washington, D.C.: U.S. Department of Labor, 1973.

U.S. NCHS, Public Health Service, Department of Health, Education, and Welfare, Reports of the National Center for Health Statistics. *Vital and Health Statistics.* Data from the National Health Survey, United States, July 1962–June 1963. No. 1000, Series 10, No. 1, 5, 9, 1963.

VAILLANT, G. E. "Theoretical Hierarchy of Adaptive Ego Mechanisms: A Thirty-Year Followup of Thirty Men Selected for Psychological Health." *Archives of General Psychiatry,* 1971, *24,* 107–118.

VAILLANT, G. E., and MCARTHUR, C. C. "Natural History of Male Psychologic Health. I. The Adult Life Cycle from 18–50." *Seminars in Psychiatry,* 1972, *4* (4), 415–427.

VAN GENNEP, A. *The Rites of Passage.* Chicago: University of Chicago Press, 1960.

VEDDER, C. B. *Problems of the Middle-Aged.* Springfield, Ill.: Thomas, 1965.

VEDDER, C. B., and LEFKOWITZ, A. S. (Eds.) *Problems of the Aged.* Springfield, Ill.: Thomas, 1965.

VEEVERS, J. E. "Voluntary Childlessness: A Neglected Area of Family Study." *The Family Coordinator,* 1973, *22,* 199–205.

VERNON, G. *Sociology of Death.* New York: Ronald Press, 1970.

VERNON, M. D. *Human Motivation.* Cambridge: University Press, 1969.

VERNON, P. E. *Intelligence and Cultural Environment.* London: Methuen, 1969.

VEROFF, J., ATKINSON, J. W., FELD, S. C., and GURIN, G. "The Use of Thematic Apperception to Assess Motivation in a Nationwide Interview Study." *Psychological Monographs,* 1960, *74* (12), 1–32.

VEROFF, J., and FELD, S. C. *Marriage and Work in America: A Study of Motives and Roles.* New York: Van Nostrand Reinhold, 1970.

VEROFF, J., FELD, S. C., and GURIN, G. "Dimensions of Subjective Adjustment." *Journal of Abnormal and Social Psychology,* 1962, *64,* 192–205.

VERY, P. S. "Differential Factor Structures in Mathematical Ability." *Genetic Psychology Monographs,* 1967, *75,* 169–207.

VIDEBECK, R. E., and KNOX, A. B. "Alternative Participatory Responses to Aging." In A. M. Rose and W. A. Peterson (Eds.), *Older People and Their Social World.* Philadelphia: F. A. Davis, 1965.

VINCENT, C. E. "Social and Interpersonal Sources of Symptomatic Frigidity." *Journal of Marriage and Family Living,* 1956, *18,* 355–360.

VINCENT, C. E. *Unmarried Mothers.* New York: Free Press, 1961.

VINCENT, C. E. "Sexual Interest in Someone Older or Younger." *Medical Aspects of Human Sexuality,* 1968, *11,* 6–11.

VINCENT, E. L., and MARTIN, P. C. *Human Psychological Development.* New York: Ronald, 1961.

WALKER, J. W. "The New Appeal of Early Retirement." *Business Horizons,* 1975, June, 43–48.

WALLIN, P., and CLARK, A. L. "Religiosity, Sexual Gratification and Marital Satisfaction in the Middle Years of Marriage." *Social Forces,* 1964, *42,* 303–309.

WALLSTON, B. "The Effects of Maternal Employment on Children." *Journal of Child Psychology and Psychiatry,* 1973, *14,* 81–95.

WANG, H. S. "Organic Brain Syndromes." In E. Busse and E. Pfeiffer (Eds.), *Behavior and Adaptation in Late Life.* Boston: Little, Brown, 1969.

WEBB, E. J., CAMPBELL, D., SCHWARTS, R., and SECHREST, L. *Unobtrusive Measures: Non-Reactive Research in the Social Sciences.* Chicago: Rand McNally, 1966.

WECHSLER, D. *The Measurement and Appraisal of Adult Intelligence.* 3rd ed. Baltimore: Williams and Wilkins, 1958.

WEINER, M. "Organization of Mental Abilities from Ages 14 to 54." *Educational and Psychological Measurement,* 1964, *24,* 573–587.

WELFORD, A. T. *Aging and Human Skill.* London: Oxford University Press, 1958.

WELFORD, A. T. "Psychomotor Performance." In J. E. Birren (Ed.), *Handbook of Aging and the Individual.* Chicago: University of Chicago Press, 1959.

WESSMAN, A. E., and RICKS, D. F. *Mood and Personality.* New York: Holt, Rinehart and Winston, 1966.

WESTLEY, B., and SEVERIN, W. J. "A Profile of Daily Newspaper Non-Reader." *Journalism Quarterly,* 1964, *41,* 45–50.

WETHERICK, N. E. "A Comparison of the Problem-Solving Ability of Young, Middle-Aged, and Old Subjects." *Gerontologia,* 1964, *9,* 164–178.

WETHERICK, N. E. "Changing an Established Concept: A Comparison of the Ability of Young, Middle-Aged, and Old Subjects." *Gerontologia,* 1965, *11,* 82–95.

WETHERICK, N. E. "The Inferential Basis of Concept Attainment." *British Journal of Psychology,* 1966, *57,* 61–69.

WHALEN, R. E. "Sexual Motivation." *Psychology Review,* 1966, *73,* 151–163.

WHITE, R. C. "Social Class Differences in the Uses of Leisure." *American Journal of Sociology,* 1955, *61,* 145–150.

WHITE, R. W. *Lives in Progress.* New York: Holt, Rinehart and Winston, 1961.

WHITE, R. W. (Ed.) *The Study of Lives.* New York: Atherton Press, 1963.

WHITE, R. W. *The Enterprise of Living.* New York: Holt, Rinehart and Winston, 1972.

WHITMARCH, R. E. "Adjustment Problems of Adolescent Daughters of Employed Mothers." *Journal of Home Economics,* 1965, *57,* 201–204.

WILENSKY, H. L. "Orderly Careers and Social Participation: The Impact of Work History on Social Integration in the Middle Class." *American Sociological Review,* 1961, *26* (4), 521–539.

WILENSKY, H. L. *Women's Work: Economic Growth, Ideology and Structure.* Institute of Industrial Relations, Reprint Series No. 7. Berkeley: Institute of Industrial Relations, University of California, 1968.

WILKIE, F. L., and EISDORFER, C. "Intelligence and Blood Pressure in the Aged." *Science,* 1971, *172,* 959–962.

WILKIE, F. L., and EISDORFER, C. "Systemic Disease and Behavioral Correlates." In L. F. Jarvik, C. Eisdorfer, and J. Blum (Eds.), *Intellectual Functioning in Adults.* New York: Springer, 1973.

WILLIAMS, R. H., and WIRTHS, C. G. *Lives Through the Years.* New York: Atherton Press, 1965.

WILLIE, C. V. *The Family Life of Black People.* Columbus, Ohio: Merrill, 1970.

WILLOUGHBY, R. R. "Family Similarities in Mental-Test Abilities." *Genetic Psychology Monographs,* 1927, *2,* 235–277.

WIMER, R. E. "Age Differences in Incidental and Intentional Learning." *Journal of Gerontology,* 1960, *15,* 79–82.

WIMER, R. E., and WIGDOR, B. T. "Age Difference in Retention of Learning." *Journal of Gerontology,* 1958, *13,* 291–295.

WINCH, R. F. "Another Look at the Theory of Complementary Needs in Mate Selection." *Journal of Marriage and the Family,* 1967, *29* (4), 756–762.

WINCH, R. F. *The Modern Family.* 3rd ed. New York: Holt, Rinehart and Winston, 1971.

WINDHAM, G. O. "Formal Participation of Migrant Housewives in an Urban Community." *Sociology and Social Research,* 1963, *47,* 201–209.

WINTER, S. K., GRIFFITH, J. C., and KOLB, D. A. "Capacity for Self-Direction." *Journal of Consulting and Clinical Psychology,* 1968, *32* (1), 35–41.

WIRTZ, W. *The Boundless Resource: A Prospectus for an Education-Work Policy.* Washington, D.C.: New Republic, 1975.

WITKIN, H. A., and others. *Psychological Differentiation: Studies of Development.* New York: Wiley, 1962.

WITKIN, H. A., LEWIS, H. B., HERTZMAN, M., MEISSNER, P. B., and WOPNER, S. *Personality through Perception.* New York: Harper & Row, 1954.

WOHLWILL, J. F. "The Physical Environment: A Problem for a Psychology of Stimulation." *Journal of Social Issues,* 1966, *22,* 29–38.

WOHLWILL, J. F. *The Study of Behavioral Development.* New York: Academic Press, 1973.

WOLFE, L. *Playing Around.* New York: William Morrow, 1975.

WOLFF, K. "Group Psychotherapy with Geriatric Patients in a State Hospital Setting: Results of a Three-Year Study." *Group Psychotherapy,* 1959, *12,* 218–222.

WOLFF, K. *Geriatric Psychiatry.* Springfield, Ill.: Thomas, 1963.

WOLFF, K. "Group Psychotherapy of Geriatric Patients." In J. H. Masserman (Ed.), *Current Psychiatric Therapies.* Vol. 6. New York: Grune and Stratton, 1966.

WOOD, G. *Fundamentals of Psychological Research.* Boston: Little, Brown, 1974.

WOODRUFF, D. S., and BIRREN, J. E. "Age Changes and Cohort Differences in Personality." *Developmental Psychology,* 1972, *6,* 252–259.

WOODRUFF, R. M., FRIEDMAN, C. D., SIEGELAUB, A. B., and COLLON, M. F. "Pain Tolerance: Differences According to Age, Sex, and Race." *Psychosomatic Medicine,* 1972, *34,* 548–556.

WRIGHT, C., and HYMEN, H. "Voluntary Association Memberships of American Adults—Evidence from National Sample Surveys." *American Sociological Review,* 1958, *23,* 284–294.

YALOM, I., and TERRAZAS, F. "Group Therapy for Psychotic Elderly

Patients." *American Journal of Nursing*, 1968, *68*, 1690–1694.

YOESTRING, D., and BURKHEAD, D. "Significance of Childhood Recreational Experience on Adult Leisure Behavior: An Exploratory Analysis." *Journal of Leisure Research*, 1973, *5*, 25–36.

YOUNG, M. L. "Problem Solving Performance in Two Age Groups." *Journal of Gerontology*, 1966, *21*, 505–509.

YOUNG, M. L. "Age and Sex Differences in Problem Solving." *Journal of Gerontology*, 1971, *26*, 330–336.

ZBOROWSKI, M. "Aging and Recreation." *Journal of Gerontology*, 1962, *17*, 302–309.

ZIMBARDO, P. G., and EBBSEN, E. B. *Influencing Attitudes and Changing Behavior*. Reading, Mass.: Addison-Wesley, 1969.

ZIMMER, B. G., and HAWLEY, A. H. "The Significance of Membership in Associations." *American Journal of Sociology*, 1959a, *65*, 196–201.

ZIMMER, B. G., and HAWLEY, A. H. "Suburbanization and Church Participation." *Social Forces*, 1959b, *37*, 348–354.

ZIMMERMAN, J., STUCKEY, T., GARLICK, B., and MILLER, M. "Effects of Token Reinforcement on Productivity in Multiple Handicapped Clients in a Sheltered Workshop." *Rehabilitation Literature*, 1969, *30*, 34–41.

ZUCKERMAN, H. "Nobel Laureates in Science: Patterns of Productivity, Collaboration, and Authorship." *American Sociological Review*, 1957, *32*, 391–403.

Name Index

A

Subject Index

A

Ability, 412–425; learning, 17, 28; verbal, 473; visual-spatial, 473

Abortion, 98, 151

Absolutist/relativist orientation, 374–376

Accident: prevention, 297, 298; work-related, 189

Achievement, 368–369, 449, 472; desire for, 51–52

Action, and contemplation, 351–355, 571

Activity theory, 532

Adaptation, 389–391, 536–545

Adolescent: assertiveness, 104, 105, 141–142; and conflict with parents, 103–107; dreams, 345; rebellion, 556; and relocation, 118

Adoption, 119, 121, 140, 142

Adulthood: attitude toward, 49–53; paths through, 72–74; perspective on, 551–578; single, 135–139

Affiliation, 367–368; desire for, 51

Aging: biological, 246, 247, 249; patterns of, 532–533

Aggressiveness, 474

Alcoholism, 268–270

Alzheimer's disease, 304, 422

American Heart Association, 294

Aspiration, 566–570

Assertiveness, 362, 474, 496, 561–566, 570; adolescent, 104, 105, 141–142; training, 30

Attention, 433–434

Attitude, 365–376; toward adulthood, 49–53; toward sex, 149

Autonomic nervous system, 261

B

Bargaining, and loss, 527

Biofeedback, 300

Biological aging, 246, 247, 249

Black adult: and depression, 305; family, 91, 97–98; and hypertension, 294; participation in educational activity by, 185; and

673